Contemporary Theatre, Film and Television

ISSN 0749-064X

Contemporary Theatre, Film and Television

A Biographical Guide Featuring Performers, Directors, Writers, Producers, Designers, Managers, Choreographers, Technicians, Composers, Executives, Dancers, and Critics in the United States, Canada, Great Britain and the World

Thomas Riggs, Editor

Volume 83

GALE
CENGAGE Learning

Detroit • New York • San Francisco • New Haven, Conn • Waterville, Maine • London

GALE
CENGAGE Learning

Contemporary Theatre, Film & Television, Vol. 83

Editor: Thomas Riggs

CTFT Staff: Erika Fredrickson, Mariko Fujinaka, Annette Petrusso, Susan Risland, Lisa Sherwin, Arlene True, Andrea Votava, Pam Zuber

Project Editor: Michael J. Tyrkus

Editorial Support Services: Ryan Cartmill

Composition and Electronic Capture: Gary Oudersluys

Manufacturing: Drew Kalasky

For product information and technology assistance, contact us at
Gale Customer Support, 1-800-877-4253.
For permission to use material from this text or product,
submit all requests online at **www.cengage.com/permissions.**
Further permissions questions can be emailed to
permissionrequest@cengage.com

While every effort has been made to ensure the reliability of the information presented in this publication, Gale, a part of Cengage Learning, does not guarantee the accuracy of the data contained herein. Gale accepts no payment for listing; and inclusion in the publication of any organization, agency, institution, publication, service, or individual does not imply endorsement of the editors or publisher. Errors brought to the attention of the publisher and verified to the satisfaction of the publisher will be corrected in future editions.

EDITORIAL DATA PRIVACY POLICY. Does this publication contain information about you as an individual? If so, for more information about our editorial data privacy policies, please see our Privacy Statement at www.gale.cengage.com.

Gale
27500 Drake Rd.
Farmington Hills, MI, 48331-3535

LIBRARY OF CONGRESS CATALOG CARD NUMBER 84-649371

ISBN-13: 978-1-4144-0023-5
ISBN-10: 1-4144-0023-3

ISSN: 0749-064X

This title is also available as an e-book.
ISBN 13: 978-1-4144-3796-5
ISBN-10: 1-4144-3796-X
Contact your Gale sales representative for ordering information.

Printed in the United States of America
1 2 3 4 5 6 7 12 11 10 09 08

Contents

Preface

Provides Broad, Single-Source Coverage in the Entertainment Field

Contemporary Theatre, Film and Television (*CTFT*) is a biographical reference series designed to provide students, educators, researchers, librarians, and general readers with information on a wide range of entertainment figures. Unlike single-volume reference works that focus on a limited number of artists or on a specific segment of the entertainment field, *CTFT* is an ongoing publication that includes entries on individuals active in the theatre, film, and television industries. Before the publication of *CTFT*, information-seekers had no choice but to consult several different sources in order to locate the in-depth biographical and credit data that makes *CTFT*'s one-stop coverage the most comprehensive available about the lives and work of performing arts professionals.

Scope

CTFT covers not only performers, directors, writers, and producers, but also behind-the-scenes specialists such as designers, managers, choreographers, technicians, composers, executives, dancers, and critics from the United States, Canada, Great Britain, and the world. With 183 entries in *CTFT 83*, the series now provides biographies on approximately 23,441 people involved in all aspects of theatre, film, and television.

CTFT gives primary emphasis to people who are currently active. New entries are prepared on major stars as well as those who are just beginning to win acclaim for their work. *CTFT* also includes entries on personalities who have died but whose work commands lasting interest.

Compilation Methods

CTFT editors identify candidates for inclusion in the series by consulting biographical dictionaries, industry directories, entertainment annuals, trade and general interest periodicals, newspapers, and online databases. Additionally, the editors of *CTFT* maintain regular contact with industry advisors and professionals who routinely suggest new candidates for inclusion in the series. Entries are compiled from published biographical sources which are believed to be reliable, but have not been verified for this edition by the listee or their agents.

Revised Entries

To ensure *CTFT*'s timeliness and comprehensiveness, entries from previous volumes, as well as from Gale's *Who's Who in the Theatre*, are updated for individuals who have been active enough to require revision of their earlier biographies. Such individuals will merit revised entries as often as there is substantial new information to provide. Obituary notices for deceased entertainment personalities already listed in *CTFT* are also published.

Accessible Format Makes Data Easy to Locate

CTFT entries, modeled after those in Gale's highly regarded *Contemporary Authors* series, are written in a clear, readable style designed to help users focus quickly on specific facts. The following is a summary of the information found in *CTFT* sketches:

- *ENTRY HEADING:* the form of the name by which the listee is best known.

- *PERSONAL:* full or original name; dates and places of birth and death; family data; colleges attended, degrees earned, and professional training; political and religious affiliations when known; avocational interests.

- *ADDRESSES:* home, office, agent, publicist and/or manager addresses.

- *CAREER:* tagline indicating principal areas of entertainment work; resume of career positions and other vocational achievements; military service.

- *MEMBER:* memberships and offices held in professional, union, civic, and social organizations.

- *AWARDS, HONORS:* theatre, film, and television awards and nominations; literary and civic awards; honorary degrees.

- *CREDITS:* comprehensive title-by-title listings of theatre, film, and television appearance and work credits, including roles and production data as well as debut and genre information.

- *RECORDINGS:* album, single song, video, and taped reading releases; recording labels and dates when available.

- *WRITINGS:* title-by-title listing of plays, screenplays, scripts, and musical compositions along with production information; books, including autobiographies, and other publications.

- *ADAPTATIONS:* a list of films, plays, and other media which have been adapted from the listee's work.

- *SIDELIGHTS:* favorite roles; portions of agent-prepared biographies or personal statements from the listee when available.

- *OTHER SOURCES:* books, periodicals, and internet sites where interviews or feature stories can be found.

Access Thousands of Entries Using *CTFT*'s Cumulative Index

Each volume of *CTFT* contains a cumulative index to the entire series. As an added feature, this index also includes references to all seventeen editions of *Who's Who in the Theatre* and to the four-volume compilation *Who Was Who in the Theatre.*

Available in Electronic Format

Online. Recent volumes of *CTFT* are available online as part of the Gale Biographies (GALBIO) database accessible through LEXIS-NEXIS. For more information, contact LEXIS-NEXIS, P.O. Box 933, Dayton, OH 45401-0933; phone (937) 865-6800, toll-free: 800-543-6862.

Suggestions Are Welcome

Contemporary Theatre, Film and Television is intended to serve as a useful reference tool for a wide audience, so comments about any aspect of this work are encouraged. Suggestions of entertainment professionals to include in future volumes are also welcome. Send comments and suggestions to: The Editor, *Contemporary Theatre, Film and Television,* Gale, 27500 Drake Rd., Farmington Hills, MI 48331-3535; or feel free to call toll-free at 1-800-877-GALE.

Contemporary Theatre, Film and Television

BILLINGTON, Stephen 1969–

PERSONAL

Born December 10, 1969, in Bolton, Lancashire, England. *Education:* Studied acting at the Drama Centre London.

Addresses: *Contact*—Markham and Froggatt, Ltd., Julian House, 4 Windmall St., London W1P 1HF, England.

Career: Actor. Appeared with the Royal Shakespeare Company.

Awards, Honors: British Soap Award, villain of the year, 1999, for *Coronation Street.*

CREDITS

Film Appearances:
Phillip, *Braveheart,* Paramount, 1995.
Mr. White, *Resident Evil,* Columbia TriStar Home Entertainment, 2002.
Brendan, *Callas Forever,* Regent Releasing, 2002.
Tulse Luper as adult, *The Tulse Luper Suitcases, Part 3: From Sark to the Finish,* 2003.
Dracula II, *Dracula II: Ascension* (also known as *Wes Craven Presents "Dracula II: Ascension"*), Buena Vista Home Video, 2003.
Ion, *The Prophecy: Uprising,* Dimension Films, 2005.
Dracula (flashback), *Dracula III: Legacy,* Dimension Films, 2005.
Julian Salinger, *The Un–Gone* (short), 2006.
David, *Oh Happy Day,* 2007.
Theo, *Exitz,* Conquistador Entertainment, 2007.

Television Appearances; Series:
Alex Holder, *Out of the Blue,* BBC, 1995.
Greg Kelly, *Coronation Street,* ITV and CBC, 1998–99, 2003.

Television Appearances; Miniseries:
Lieutenant James, *The Buccaneers,* BBC and PBS, 1995.
Lysander Hawkley, *The Man Who Made Husbands Jealous,* ITV, 1997.

Television Appearances; Movies:
Lord Vortigen, *Young Arthur,* NBC, 2002.
The healer, *Inquisition,* 2002.

Television Appearances; Specials:
A Nightmare on Coronation Street, ITV, 2004.
"Coronation Street": The Battersby Family Album, ITV, 2005.

Television Appearances; Pilots:
Gary, *Rules of Engagement,* 1997.

Television Appearances; Episodic:
Ross, "Time to Kill," *Space Precinct,* syndicated, 1994.
"Mmm ... Men of the Moment," *Light Lunch,* Channel 4, 1997.
Neville Bruce, "The Problem at Gallows Gate: Parts 1 & 2," *Jonathan Creek,* 1998.
Derrick Markham, "Love and Death," *Highlander: The Raven* (also known as *L'Immortelle*), 1999.
Bernardo, "Kidnapped," *Queen of Swords* (also known as *Reina de espadas* and *Tessa, a la pointe de l'epee*), 2001.
Palmer, "The Royal Ring," *Relic Hunter* (also known as *Relic Hunter—Die Schatzjagerin* and *Sydney Fox l'aventuriere*), syndicated, 2001.
Colin Tierney, "Greener Grass," *Doctor,* BBC, 2006.

Stage Appearances:
Giovanni, *'Tis Pity She's a Whore,* Drama Centre, London, 1994.

Antonelli, *The White Devil,* Swan Theatre, Stratford–upon–Avon, England, 1996.

Margarelon, *Troilus and Cressida,* Royal Shakespeare Theatre, Stratford–upon–Avon, 1996.

The bloody captain, *Macbeth,* Royal Shakespeare Theatre, Stratford–Upon–Avon, 1996.

Title role, *Gabriel,* Soho Theatre, London, 1997.

Tony Paxton, *Our Betters,* Chichester Festival Theatre, Chichester, England, 1997.

Judas Iscariot, *Corpus Christi,* Edinburgh Festival, Scotland, then Pleasance Theatre, London, 1999.

Guy Haines, *Strangers on a Train,* Poole Arts Centre, Dorset, Poole, England, then Yvonne Arnaud Theatre, Surrey, England, 2000.

A medical student, *Pains of Youth,* Finborough, England, 2000.

BOGERT, William 1936–
(Bill Bogert)

PERSONAL

Born January 25, 1936, in New York, NY.

Career: Actor.

CREDITS

Film Appearances:
Television anchorman, *Dog Day Afternoon,* Warner Bros., 1975.

Parks, *The Front,* Columbia, 1976.

(As Bill Bogert) Insurance doctor, *Fire Sale,* 1977.

Lawson, *Heaven Can Wait,* Metro–Goldwyn–Mayer, 1978.

Dancing man, *The Last Married Couple in America,* Universal, 1980.

Television moderator, *Hero at Large,* Metro–Goldwyn–Mayer, 1980.

Mr. Lightman, *WarGames,* Metro–Goldwyn–Mayer/United Artists, 1983.

(As Bill Bogert) Timmy Shaughnessy, *Whatever It Takes,* 1986.

Roger Weidermeyer, *Stewardess School,* Columbia, 1986.

A. J. (Al) Brown, *Walk Like a Man,* Metro–Goldwyn–Mayer, 1987.

Harrington, *A Perfect Murder,* Warner Bros., 1998.

Dad, *Backseat,* 2005.

The Flying Scissors, 2007.

Television Appearances; Series:
Les Carlisle, *The Greatest American Hero,* ABC, 1981–83.

Brandon Brindle, *Small Wonder,* syndicated, 1986–89.

(As Bill Bogert) Kent Wallace, himself, and wrap–up announcer, *Chappelle's Show,* Comedy Central, 2003–2004.

Television Appearances; Miniseries:
William Bellamy (chapter 11), *Centennial,* NBC, 1978.

Favorite Son (also known as *Target: Favorite Son*), NBC, 1988.

Television Appearances; Movies:
Ernie, *The Death of Ritchie* (also known as *Richie*), NBC, 1977.

Silvers, *Kill Me If You Can* (also known as *The Caryl Chessman Story*), NBC, 1977.

Parson, *Ziegfield: The Man and His Women,* NBC, 1978.

Major Holloway, *Sergeant Matlovich vs. the U.S. Air Force,* NBC, 1978.

Lustus, *A Fire in the Sky,* NBC, 1978.

Friendly Fire, ABC, 1979.

Rapist, *Better Late Than Never,* NBC, 1979.

Russell Birdwell, *The Scarlett O'Hara War* (also known as *Moviola: The Scarlett O'Hara War*), NBC, 1980.

Alfred Lawson, *Charlie and the Great Balloon Chase* (also known as *Charlie's Balloon*), 1981.

Prosecution judge, *I Want to Live,* ABC, 1983.

Stevens, *Carpool,* CBS, 1983.

Dr. Oscar Reback, *Take My Daughters, Please,* NBC, 1988.

Roger Leopold, *Ask Me Again,* PBS, 1989.

Randall Thurston, *Columbo: Strange Bedfellows,* ABC, 1995.

Television Appearances; Pilots:
Lawson, *This Is Kate Bennett ...* (movie), ABC, 1982.

Cashmam, *Work With Me,* CBS, 1999.

Television Appearances; Specials:
Mr. Small, "The Contest Kid and the Big Prize," *ABC Weekend Specials,* ABC, 1978.

Mr. Small, "The Contest Kid Strikes Again," *ABC Weekend Specials,* ABC, 1979.

Television Appearances; Episodic:
Doctor, "My Son, the Genius," *Mary Tyler Moore* (also known as *The Mary Tyler Moore Show*), CBS, 1976.

"Banker's Hours," *Police Woman,* NBC, 1977.

Samuel Garner, "The Committee," *Starsky and Hutch,* ABC, 1977.

Steven Sherwin, "Affair of the Heart," *McMillan & Wife* (also known as *McMillan*), NBC, 1977.

(As Bill Bogert) Becker, "The Runaways," *Baretta,* ABC, 1977.

Baxter, "The Sky Is Falling," *Baretta,* ABC, 1977.

Stevenson, *Mulligan's Stew,* 1977.

"I Quit," *Eight Is Enough,* ABC, 1977.

Colin, "Takeover," *Lou Grant,* 1977.

Dr. Elliot, *Forever Fernwood,* syndicated, 1977.

Korchak, "Rape," *Barney Miller,* ABC, 1978.

Bank teller, "Take the Money," *One Day at a Time,* CBS, 1978.

James Broderick, "Come As You Aren't," *Taxi,* ABC, 1978.

Timothy Hooper, "Sighting 4021: The Superstition Mountain Incident," *Project U.F.O.* (also known as *Project Blue Book*), NBC, 1978.

Frank Miller, "Florence's Union," *The Jeffersons,* CBS, 1978.

K. Ross, "Mode of Death," *Quincy M.E.* (also known as *Quincy*), NBC, 1979.

Roger Prescott, "Yessir, That's Our Baby," *M*A*S*H,* CBS, 1979.

Jeff Parker, *The Facts of Life,* NBC, 1979.

Joseph Callahan, Susan's employer, *Miss Winslow and Son,* CBS, 1979.

Frank Miller, "Louise Takes a Stand," *Quincy M.E.* (also known as *Quincy*), CBS, 1980.

Mr. Parker, "Molly's Holiday," *The Facts of Life,* NBC, 1980.

Captain Maurice Allen, "Depressing News," *M*A*S*H,* CBS, 1980.

Fox, "Raid," *Hart to Hart,* ABC, 1980.

Langston Birch, "Bye Bye Birdie," *Alice,* CBS, 1981.

"Bye, Bye American Spy," *House Calls,* CBS, 1981.

Mr. Melton, "The Harder They Fall," *The Incredible Hulk,* CBS, 1981.

Minister, "Marcy's Wedding," *Benson,* ABC, 1981.

Salesman, "The Magic Camera/Mata Hari/Valerie," *Fantasy Island,* ABC, 1982.

Osgood Hotchkiss, "Soldiers of Misfortune," *The Fall Guy,* ABC, 1982.

Carillo, "Some Like It Hot–Wired," *Hill Street Blues,* NBC, 1982.

Alan Tepperman, "Muffy's Bat Mitzvah," *Square Pegs,* CBS, 1982.

"South Side Story," *Trapper John M.D.,* CBS, 1983.

Hunt, "Supernurse," *Trapper John M.D.,* CBS, 1983.

"Bones of Contention," *Bring 'Em Back Alive,* CBS, 1983.

Wendell Kanter, "Too Close to Hart," *Hart to Hart,* ABC, 1983.

"The Affair," *Condo,* ABC, 1983.

Phillip Barbanell, "Reconcilable Differences," *Knots Landing,* CBS, 1984.

Mr. Buncan, "The Little Hotel That Could," *Benson,* ABC, 1984.

"The Geronimo Machine," *Crazy Like a Fox,* CBS, 1985.

"It's Only a Show," *The Paper Chase,* Showtime, 1985.

Brandon Bendl, *Small Wonder,* syndicated, 1985.

Harold Jessup, "My Father's House," *The Colbys* (also known as *Dynasty II: The Colbys*), ABC, 1986.

Harold Jessup, "The Outcast," *The Colbys* (also known as *Dynasty II: The Colbys*), ABC, 1986.

Dean Derensky, "Research and Destroy," *Trapper John M.D.,* CBS, 1986.

Mr. Wallingford, "The Rat Pack," *Matlock,* NBC, 1987.

Klopf, "All This and a Gold Card Too," *Leg Work,* CBS, 1987.

Preacher, "Swingers," *The Wonder Years,* ABC, 1988.

Prosecutor Evans, "A Slight Case of Murder (1)," *Amen,* NBC, 1988.

Mr. Merkin, "Ben's First Kiss," *Growing Pains,* ABC, 1988.

Mr. Wiggins, "The Debate," *Mr. Belvedere,* 1989.

Doctor number one, "Man of the Year," *Empty Nest,* NBC, 1989.

Jules Simon, "The Wages of Love," *Law & Order,* NBC, 1991.

Rearden, "Sweeps," *Law & Order,* NBC, 1993.

Doctor, "Otherwise Engaged," *Melrose Place,* Fox, 1994.

Dean Sumner, "Body & Soul & Dick," *3rd Rock from the Sun* (also known as *3rd Rock* and *Life As We Know It*), NBC, 1996.

The priest, "Grand Illusion," *Spin City,* ABC, 1996.

"Crisis," *Profiler,* NBC, 1997.

Man, "What I Really Want to Do Is Direct," *Fired Up,* NBC, 1998.

Professor Alren Howard, "Haven," *Law & Order,* NBC, 1999.

Jerry MacAllister, "Second Chances," *Ed,* NBC, 2003.

Alvin Hartmann, "Floater," *Law & Order,* NBC, 2003.

Mr. Simmons, "Queer as Hope," *Hope & Faith,* ABC, 2004.

College dean, "Unto the Breach," *Gilmore Girls,* The WB, 2007.

Also appeared as Deputy District Attorney Caster, "Throwaway," *The Blue Knight,* CBS; Karl Miller, "Diamond Volcano," *Salvage 1,* ABC.

Television Director; Episodic:

Directed episodes of *Alice,* CBS.

Stage Appearances:

A boy, *The Country Wife,* Renata Theatre, New York City, 1957.

Haberdasher, *The Taming of the Shrew,* Belvedere Theatre, New York City, 1960.

Nuns, citizens, attendants, gentlemen, soldiers, *Measure for Measure,* Belvedere Theatre, 1960.

Earl of Warwick, *King Henry V,* Belvedere Theatre, 1960.

Richard Rich, *A Man for All Seasons,* American National Theatre and Academy (ANTA), New York City, 1963.

Understudy Horatio, then Horatio, *Hamlet,* Lunt–Fontanne Theatre, New York City, 1964.

Dumaine and understudy King Ferdinand, *Love's Labor's Lost,* Delacorte Theatre, New York City, 1965.

Harvey, *Cactus Flower,* Royale Theatre, New York City, 1965–68, then Longacre Theatre, New York City, 1968.

Understudy Andy Hobart and Norman Cornell, *The Star–Spangled Girl,* Plymouth Theatre, New York City, 1966–67.

Linden, *A Gun Play,* Cherry Lane Theatre, New York City, 1971.

Charlie Revere, *The Kildeer,* Joseph Papp Public Theatre, 1974.

The Freedom of the City, Alvin Theatre, New York City, 1974.

Brick Brock, "Yanks," and Mr. Bapp, "Rubbers," *Rubbers/ Yanks 3 Detroit 0 Top of the Seventh,* American Place Theatre, New York City, 1975.

Neil's Garden, Rattlestick Theatre, New York City, 2001.

BOLLEA, Terry
   See HOGAN, Hulk

BRINKMAN, Melissa Gilbert
   See GILBERT, Melissa

C

CATHERINE
See OXENBERG, Catherine

CLAUSEN, Alf 1941–
(Alf Clauson)

PERSONAL

Full name, Alf Heiberg Clausen; born March 28, 1941, in Minneapolis, MN; son of Alf and Magdalene (maiden name, Heiberg) Clausen; married Judy Kaye Landstrom, June 5, 1965 (marriage ended); married Sally Maureen Taron, January 9, 1993; children: (first marriage) Karen Leigh, Scott Owen, Kyle Evan. *Education:* North Dakota State University, B.A., 1963; attended University of Wisconsin, 1963; diploma in music composition and arranging from Berklee College of Music, 1966; studied with John Bavicchi, William Maloof, Herb Pomeroy, and Earle Hagen. *Politics:* Republican. *Religion:* Lutheran. *Avocational Interests:* Record collecting, carpentry, sports, computers.

Addresses: *Agent*—Soundtrack Music Associates, 2229 Cloverfield Blvd., Santa Monica, CA 90405.

Career: Composer and orchestrator. Karleigh Music Co., president; Dick Grove Music Workshops, instructor; University of California, Los Angeles, instructor in music arranging and composition. Composer for Los Angeles Neophonic Orchestra Concert Series, 1968; adjudicator for Playboy All–Star Intercollegiate Jazz Festival Competition and Western Division Intercollegiate Jazz Festival Competition.

Member: National Academy of Recording Arts and Sciences (member of jazz crafts committee), Academy of Television Arts and Sciences, American Society of Composers, Authors, and Publishers (ASCAP), American Society of Music Arrangers, National Association of Jazz Educators, Dramatists Guild, Songwriters Guild, Society of Composers and Lyricists (member of board of directors), American Federation of Musicians, Screen Actors Guild, Blue Key, Phi Kappa Phi, Kappa Kappa Psi.

Awards, Honors: One O'Clock Awards, North Texas State University, 1978, 1979, 1980; Clio nomination, 1979; Emmy Award nomination (with Jack Elliot and Bill Goldstein), outstanding achievement in music direction, 1981, for *Omnibus;* Alumnus Recognition Award, Berklee College of Music, 1984; Emmy Award nominations, outstanding achievement in music composition for a series—dramatic underscore, 1986, 1987, 1988, 1989, and outstanding achievement in music direction (with others), 1988, 1989, American Society of Composers, Authors and Publishers Award, top television series, 1988, all for *Moonlighting;* Alumni Achievement Award, North Dakota State University, 1986; Emmy Award (with others), outstanding music and lyrics, 1997, 1998, Emmy Award nominations, outstanding individual achievement in music composition for a series—dramatic underscore, 1992, 1993, 1994, 1995, 1998, 1999, 2000, 2004, 2005, outstanding music direction, 1997, 1998, and outstanding individual achievement in music and lyrics (with others), 1994, 1995, 1996, 2002, 2003, 2004, 2005, American Society of Composers, Authors, and Publishers Awards, top television series, 1995, 1996, 2001, 2002, 2003, 2004, Annie Award, best individual achievement—music in a television production, 1997, Annie Award (with others), outstanding individual achievement for music in an animated television production, International Animated Film Society, 1998, 2000, 2004, all for *The Simpsons;* University of Wisconsin scholar; National Endowment of the Arts fellow; Berklee College of Music fellow.

CREDITS

Film Orchestrator:
The Beastmaster (also known as *Beastmaster—Der Befreier*), United Artists, 1982.
(Uncredited) *Mr. Mom* (also known as *Mr. Mum* and *Perfect Daddy*), Twentieth Century–Fox, 1983.
(Uncredited) *The Last Starfighter*, 1984.
Weird Science, Universal, 1985.
Into the Night, Universal, 1985.
My Science Project, Buena Vista, 1985.
Wise Guys, United Artists, 1986.
Ferris Bueller's Day Off, Paramount, 1986.
Number One with a Bullet, Cannon, 1987.
(As Alf Clausen) *Dragnet*, Universal, 1987.
The Naked Gun—From the Files of Police Squad!, Paramount, 1988.

Also worked as orchestrator for *Buddy, Buddy; Jinxed; Table for Five; Up the Creek; Miracles.*

Film Additional Orchestrator:
Splash, Buena Vista, 1984.
Micki + Maude, Columbia, 1984.

Film Appearances:
Himself, *Memories of "Moonlighting,"* Lions Gate Films Home Entertainment, 2006.

Television Work; Series:
Orchestra leader, *Mary*, CBS, 1978.
Musical director, *The Mary Tyler Moore Show*, 1979.
Music arranger, *Face the Music*, 1980.
Music arranger (with Bill Goldstein), *Omnibus*, ABC, 1980.
Music director and music arranger, *Moonlighting*, ABC, 1985–87.

Television Orchestrator; Movies:
Lots of Luck, 1985.
Mirrors, 1985.

Also worked as orchestrator for *Happy Endings; Remembrance of Love; Miss All–American Beauty; This Is Kate Bennett; For Ladies Only; The Other Lover; Letting Go; The Long Way Home; Sparkling Cyanide; Princess Daisy; Quarterback Princess; Caribbean Mystery; I Want to Live; Legs; Six Months with an Older Woman; Two of a Kind; Listen to Your Heart.*

Television Appearances; Specials:
"The Simpsons": America's First Family, 2000.

Stage Orchestrations:
Mother Earth, Belasco Theatre, New York City, 1972.

WRITINGS

Film Music:
Number One with a Bullet, Cannon, 1987.
Half Baked, 1998.
Memories of "Moonlighting" (documentary short), Lions Gate Films Home Entertainment, 2006.
Level Seven, Power Point Films, 2008.

Also wrote music for (uncredited) *Force: Five; An Eye for an Eye; Fast Walking; Forced Vengeance; Airplane II: The Sequel;* and *The Journey of Natty Gann.*

Film Additional Music:
Weird Science, Universal, 1985.
(As Alf Clausen) *Dragnet*, Universal, 1987.

Television Music; Series:
Mary, 1978.
The Mary Tyler Moore Hour, CBS, 1979.
Moonlighting, ABC, 1985–87.
Lime Street, ABC, 1985.
Alf, NBC, 1986–89.
Harry, ABC, 1987.
The Simpsons, Fox, 1990—.
My Life and Times, 1991.
The Critic (animated), 1993–95.
Bette, CBS, 2000.

Television Theme Songs:
Alf, NBC, 1986.
Spacecats, NBC, 1991.

Television Music; Movies:
Stranded, NBC, 1986.
Agatha Christie's "Murder in Three Acts" (also known as *Murder in Three Acts*), CBS, 1986.
Double Agent, ABC, 1987.
The Watch Commander (also known as *Police Story* and *Police Story: The Watch Commander*), ABC, 1988.
My First Love (also known as *Second Chance* and *One More Time*), ABC, 1988.
Mutts, 1988.
She Knows Too Much (also known as *Lady Be Good*), NBC, 1989.
Easy Come, Easy Go (also known as *Christine Cromwell*), ABC, 1989.
The Wickedest Witch, 1989.
Only the Good Die Young, ABC, 1990.
In Vino Veritas, ABC, 1990.

Also composer for *Happy Endings; Remembrance of Love; Miss All–American Beauty; This Is Kate Bennett; For Ladies Only; The Other Lover; Letting Go; The Long Way Home.*

Television Music; Specials:
The Paul Lynde Comedy Hour, ABC, 1978.
A Very Retail Christmas, NBC, 1990.

Television Music; Pilots:
Mutts (also known as *Conversations with My Dog*), ABC, 1988.
Channel 99, NBC, 1988.

Television Music; Episodic:
"Easy Come, Easy Go," *Christine Cromwell,* 1989.

Wrote music for episodes of *Father Murphy; Little House on the Prairie; Shell Game; The Mississippi; Fame; Wizards and Warriors; Partners in Crime; Dads; Bronk; Jigsaw; The FBI; Ripley's Believe It or Not; Scene of the Crime;* and *Trauma Center.*

Video Game Music:
The Simpsons: Cartoon Studio, 1996.

OTHER SOURCES

Periodicals:
Variety, August 2, 1989, p. 32.

CLEGHORNE, Ellen 1965–
　　(Ellen Cleghorn, Ellen L. Cleghorne, G. Ellen Cleghorne)

PERSONAL

Born November 29, 1965, in Brooklyn, New York, NY; divorced; children: Akeyla. *Education:* Hunter College, City University of New York, B.A., theatre, 1989.

Addresses: *Agent*—Frederick Levy, Management 101, 5527 1/2 Cahuenga Blvd., North Hollywood, CA 91601.

Career: Actress and comedienne. Performed stand–up comedy at clubs in New York City. Member of the acting group The Family, Inc. and performed at various venues.

CREDITS

Television Appearances; Series:
Regular performer, *Saturday Night Live* (also known as *NBC's "Saturday Night," Saturday Night, Saturday Night Live '80, SNL,* and *SNL 25*), NBC, 1991–95.

(As G. Ellen Cleghorne) Ellen Carlson, *Cleghorne!,* The WB, 1995.

Television Appearances; Miniseries:
Herself, *I Love the '70s,* VH1, 2003.
Herself, *I Love the '80s Strikes Back,* VH1, 2003.
Host, *The National Body Challenge,* 2005.

Television Appearances; Movies:
Lauren Amber, *Midnight Blue,* Black Entertainment Television (BET), 2000.

Television Appearances; Specials:
Herself, *1989 Johnnie Walker National Comedy Search,* 1989.
Retaining Laughter, 1991.
Why Bother Voting?, 1992.
The Second Annual Saturday Night Live Mother's Day Special, NBC, 1993.
Whoopi Goldberg, *Saturday Night Live Presents President Bill Clinton's All–Time Favorites,* NBC, 1994.
But ... Seriously, Showtime, 1994.
Def Comedy Jam Primetime, HBO, 1994.
The Ms. Foundation's Women of Comedy at Caroline's, 1998.
Audience member, *Saturday Night Live: 25th Anniversary* (also known as *Saturday Night Live: 25th Anniversary Primetime Special*), NBC, 1999.
Comedy Central Presents Behind–the–Scenes at the American Comedy Awards, Comedy Central, 1999.
My Funny Valentine, American Movie Classics and Romance Classics, 2000.

Television Appearances; Uncredited Appearances in Archive Footage; Specials:
Anita Hill, *Saturday Night Live: Presidential Bash,* NBC, 1992.
Herself and various characters, *Saturday Night Live: Bad Boys* (also known as *The Bad Boys of Saturday Night Live*), NBC, 1998.
Shakira's mother, *Saturday Night Live: The Best of Phil Hartman,* NBC, 1998.
Various characters, *Saturday Night Live: The Best of Chris Farley,* NBC, 1998.
Serena Williams and other characters, *Saturday Night Live: Game Show Parodies,* NBC, 1998 and 2000.
Chocolate Pudding, *Saturday Night Live: The Best of Adam Sandler,* NBC, 1999.
Herself, *Saturday Night Live: The Best of Steve Martin,* NBC, 1999.
Herself and various characters, *Saturday Night Live: The Best of Chris Rock,* NBC, 1999.
Airline passenger, *Saturday Night Live: The Best of David Spade,* NBC, 2005.
Herself and various characters, *Saturday Night Live in the 90s: Pop Culture Nation,* NBC, 2007.

Television Appearances; Episodic:

(As Ellen Cleghorn) Woman in courtroom, *In Living Color,* Fox, 1991.

Woman in restaurant, *In Living Color,* Fox, 1991.

Performer, *Def Comedy Jam* (also known as *Russell Simmons' "Def Comedy Jam"*), HBO, various episodes, beginning c. 1992.

Bus driver Sally Knorp, "Day of the Dot," *The Adventures of Pete & Pete* (also known as *Pete and Pete*), Nickelodeon, 1993.

Bus driver Sally Knorp, "Yellow Fever," *The Adventures of Pete & Pete* (also known as *Pete and Pete*), Nickelodeon, 1994.

Herself, *Late Show with David Letterman* (also known as *The Late Show* and *Late Show Backstage*), CBS, 1995 (multiple episodes).

Tamara, "Radio FBI," *C–16: FBI* (also known as *C–16*), ABC, 1997.

Tamara, "The Sandman," *C–16: FBI* (also known as *C–16*), ABC, 1997.

Jackie, "An Affair to Forget," *The Parent 'Hood,* The WB, 1998.

Herself, Uta Sven, and various characters, *The Roseanne Show,* syndicated, multiple episodes, 1998–2000.

Herself, "Her Ego's Got Its Own Zip Code," *Rendez-View,* syndicated, 2001.

Herself, *The Test,* FX Network, 2001.

Herself, "Saturday Night Live," *TV Tales,* E! Entertainment Television, 2002.

Esperanza, "Hell Mall," *The Chronicle* (also known as *News from the Edge*), Sci–Fi Channel, 2002.

Esperanza, "The Mists of Avalon Parkway," *The Chronicle* (also known as *News from the Edge*), Sci–Fi Channel, 2002.

Herself, *Tough Crowd with Colin Quinn* (also known as *Tough Crowd*), Comedy Central, 2002.

Commentator, *101 Most Unforgettable SNL Moments* (also known as *E's "101"*), E! Entertainment Television, 2004 (multiple episodes).

Television Appearances; Pilots:

Marsha, *What's Alan Watching?,* CBS, 1989.

Tamara, *C–16: FBI* (also known as *C–16*), ABC, 1997.

Neurotic Tendencies, NBC, 2001.

Film Appearances:

Turk 182! (also known as *Turk 182*), Twentieth Century–Fox, 1985.

Cocktail waitress, *Strictly Business* (also known as *Go Natalie!*), Warner Bros., 1991.

Television talk show host, *This Is My Life,* Twentieth Century–Fox, 1992.

Officer Rhoades, *The Perez Family,* Samuel Goldwyn Company, 1995.

Doris, *Rescuing Desire,* 1996.

Jane, *Mr. Wrong,* Buena Vista, 1996.

Marguerite, *Dear God* (also known as *Cher bon Dieu, Deus nos Acuda!, Hej gud, Hilfe, ich Komm' in den Himmel, Querido Deus, Suoraan sydaemestae,* and *Un timador con alas*), Paramount, 1996.

Helga (a nurse), *Armageddon* (also known as *Armageddon—Das juengste Gericht, Armageddon—giudizio finale,* and *Armagedon*), Buena Vista, 1998.

Marlene, *The Million Dollar Hotel* (also known as *The Billion Dollar Hotel*), Lions Gate Films, 2000.

Mother, *Little Nicky,* New Line Cinema, 2000.

Music publishing representative, *Coyote Ugly* (also known as *Coyote Bar, Coyote Girls, Show Bar, El Bar Coyote, Le ragazze del Coyote Ugly, Sakaltanya,* and *Wygrane marzenia*), Buena Vista, 2000.

Hoover Blue, *MacArthur Park,* Northshire Entertainment Group/Wirthwhile, 2001.

(As Ellen L. Cleghorne) Lady number one, *Kingdom Come* (also known as *El reino que se viene, Mejor en el cielo, Tjocka slaekten, Um ritual do barulho, Um ritual muito louco,* and *Venga il tuo regno*), Fox Searchlight Pictures, 2001.

(Uncredited) Trustee, *Old School,* DreamWorks, 2003.

Ma Dukes, *Full Clip* (also known as *Blood Money*), Lions Gate Films, 2004.

Al Lewis, *Mattie Fresno and the Holoflux Universe,* Marvista Entertainment, 2007.

Stage Appearances:

Gertha, clerk, wife, and mistress, *Insurrection: Holding History,* New York Shakespeare Festival, Joseph Papp Public Theater, LuEsther Hall, New York City, 1996.

Behind the Funny (solo show), HBO Workspace, Los Angeles, 1999, and Joseph Papp Public Theater, New York City, beginning 2002.

The Vagina Monologues, Coronet Theatre, Los Angeles, c. 2001.

Appeared in *Looking for Tomorrow* and *Marriage Proposal,* both New York Shakespeare Festival.

RECORDINGS

Videos:

Voice of Sabrina, *The Best of the Blues Brothers* (documentary), Broadway Video, 1993.

Appeared in other videos.

WRITINGS

Teleplays; with Others; Episodic:

The Roseanne Show, syndicated, episodes from 1998–2000.

Writings for the Stage:
Behind the Funny (solo show), HBO Workspace, Los Angeles, 1999, and Joseph Papp Public Theater, New York City, beginning 2002.

OTHER SOURCES

Periodicals:
People Weekly, September 25, 1995, p. 18.

COHEN, Bobby 1970–

PERSONAL

Born January 8, 1970, in NY; father, an attorney; mother, an attorney; married Katie; children: Jack, Molly.

Addresses: *Office*—Cohen Pictures, 11835 West Olympic Blvd., Suite 1135, Los Angeles, CA 90064.

Career: Producer. Writers & Artists Agency, New York City, assistant; Miramax Films, various positions including senior vice president of production, through 2003; Cohen Productions, Los Angeles, CA, founder and principal, 1999; Red Wagon Entertainment, president.

CREDITS

Film Executive Producer:
54 (also known as *Fifty–Four*), Miramax, 1998.
Rounders, Miramax, 1998.
The Cider House Rules, Miramax, 1999.
Down to You, Miramax, 2000.
Bewitched, Columbia, 2005.
Jarhead (also known as *Jarhead—Willkommen im dreck*), Universal, 2005.
Memoirs of a Geisha, Columbia, 2005.
RV (also known as *RV: Runaway Vacation* and *Die Chaoscamper RV*), Columbia, 2006.
Definitely, Maybe, Universal, 2008.

Film Coproducer:
Bounce, Miramax, 2000.
Happy Endings, Lions Gate Films, 2005.

Film Producer:
View from the Top, Miramax, 2003.
Revolutionary Road, DreamWorks, 2008.

Television Work; Movies:
Executive in charge of production, *Since You've Been Gone,* ABC, 1998.

COLLINS, Clifton, Jr. 1970–
(Clifton Gonzalez Collins, Clifton Gonzalez Gonzalez, Clifton Gonzalez–Gonzalez)

PERSONAL

Full name, Clifton Craig Collins, Jr.; born June 16, 1970, in Los Angeles, CA; son of Clifton Collins (an actor); grandson of Pedro Gonzalez–Gonzalez (an actor and comedian). *Avocational Interests:* Snowboarding.

Addresses: *Agent*—William Morris Agency, One William Morris Place, Beverly Hills, CA 90212; (voice work) Special Artists Agency, 9465 Wilshire Blvd., Suite 890, Beverly Hills, CA 90212. *Manager*—ROAR, 9701 Wilshire Blvd., Eighth Floor, Beverly Hills, CA 90212.

Career: Actor and producer. Appeared in advertisements. Stone Free Productions, founder.

Awards, Honors: Margo Albert Award, most promising actor, Nosotros Golden Eagle awards, 1998; Screen Actors Guild Award (with others), outstanding performance by the cast of a theatrical motion picture, 2001, for *Traffic;* ALMA Award nomination, outstanding supporting actor in a motion picture, American Latin Media Arts awards, 2002, for *The Last Castle;* ALMA Award nomination, outstanding actor in a motion picture, and Screen Actors Guild Award nomination (with others), outstanding performance by the cast of a motion picture, both 2006, for *Capote;* Emmy Award nomination, outstanding supporting actor in a miniseries or movie, 2006, for the pilot of *Thief;* Copper Wing Award (with others), best ensemble acting, Phoenix Film Festival, 2007, for *Little Chenier.*

CREDITS

Film Appearances; as Clifton Gonzalez Gonzalez:
Carlos's second friend, *Grand Canyon,* Twentieth Century–Fox, 1991.
Mail room supervisor, *Poetic Justice* (also known as *Fugir do bairro, Justicia poetica,* and *Murhan jaelkeen*), Columbia, 1993.
Nino Gomez, *Fortress,* Dimension Films, 1993.
Vato, *Menace II Society* (also known as *Die Strassenkaempfer, Nella giungla di cemento, Perigo para a sociedade, Uehiskonna nuhtlus, Vakivallan kierre,* and *Veszelyes elemek*), New Line Cinema, 1993.

Tack, *The Stoned Age* (also known as *The Stoened Age* and *Tack's Chicks*), Trimark Pictures, 1994.

Betancourt, *Dead Presidents,* Buena Vista, 1995.

Clif, *Milestone* (short film), Barracano Pictures, 1995.

Second jarhead, *One Tough Bastard* (also known as *North's War* and *One Man's Justice*), LIVE Entertainment, 1995.

Second soldier, *Sgt. Bilko* (also known as *Sergeant Bilko*), Universal, 1996.

Cesar Sanchez, *One Eight Seven* (also known as *187*), Warner Bros., 1997.

Loco, *The Replacement Killers,* Columbia, 1998.

Martinez, *The Wonderful Ice Cream Suit,* Buena Vista/Walt Disney Pictures, 1998.

First townsperson, *The Bad Pack,* Lions Gate Films Home Video/Avalanche Home Entertainment/Showcase Entertainment/Ascot Video, 1998.

Kyle, *Mascara,* Phaedra Cinema, 1999.

Robert "Rivers" Tremont, *Light It Up* (also known as *High School Jack*), Twentieth Century–Fox, 1999.

Francisco Flores, *Traffic* (also known as *Traffic—Die Macht des Kartells*), USA Films, 2000.

Jimmy Ortega, *Price of Glory,* New Line Cinema, 2000.

Private Miter, *Tigerland,* Twentieth Century–Fox, 2000.

Corporal Ramon Aguilar, *The Last Castle* (also known as *The Castle* and *Untitled Rod Lurie Project*), DreamWorks, 2001.

Horton, *My Sweet Killer* (also known as *The Seventh Sense*), Method Fest Releasing, 2001.

Rupert Guest, *The Rules of Attraction* (also known as *Animal College, Fuck the Rules,* and *Die Regeln des Spiels*), Lions Gate Films, 2002.

Hip, Edgy, Sexy, Cool, 2002.

Buddy, *American Girl* (also known as *Confessions of an American Girl* and *Lifers' Picnic*), 2002, Metro–Goldwyn–Mayer Home Entertainment, 2005.

Claudio Castillo, *I Witness* (also known as *Nur tote Zeugen schweigen—I Witness*), Promark Entertainment Group, 2003.

Officer Armando Sancho, *Dirty,* Silver Nitrate Releasing, 2005.

Perry Smith, *Capote* (also known as *Truman Capote*), United Artists, 2005.

Tom Picasso, *Tom 51,* Assembly Line Studios/MEB Entertainment/August Heart Entertainment, 2005.

Vince Sherman, *Mindhunters,* Dimension Films, 2005.

Kenneth Bianchi, *Rampage: The Hillside Strangler Murders* (also known as *The Hillside Strangler*), Silver Nitrate Releasing, 2006.

Officer at border crossing, *Babel,* Paramount Vantage, 2006.

TV: The Movie (also known as *National Lampoon's "TV the Movie"*), Xenon Pictures, 2006.

Jacob, *Still Waters,* Perfect Weekend, 2007.

Stingray, *The Horsemen,* Lionsgate, 2007.

T–Boy Trahan, *Little Chenier,* Radio London Films, 2007.

Ayel, *Star Trek* (also known as *Star Trek XI*), Paramount, 2008.

Cesar, *The Perfect Game,* Prelude Pictures, 2008.

Sunshine Cleaning, Back Lot Pictures/Big Beach Films, 2008.

Some sources cite an appearance in *The Third Miracle,* Sony Pictures Classics, 1999.

Film Producer; with Others:

Co–executive producer, *Mindhunters,* Dimension Films, 2005.

Tom 51, Assembly Line Studios/MEB Entertainment/August Heart Entertainment, 2005.

Rampage: The Hillside Strangler Murders (also known as *The Hillside Strangler*), Silver Nitrate Releasing, 2006.

TV: The Movie (also known as *National Lampoon's "TV the Movie"*), Xenon Pictures, 2006.

Little Chenier, Radio London Films, 2007.

Television Appearances; Series:

Nando Taylor, *Crisis Center,* NBC, 1997.

Jack "Bump" Hill, *Thief,* fX Channel, 2006.

Television Appearances; Movies:

(As Clifton Gonzalez Gonzalez) Coworker, *For Richer, for Poorer* (also known as *Father, Son and the Mistress*), HBO, 1992.

Jesus Martinez, *Sworn to Vengeance,* CBS, 1993.

(As Clifton Gonzalez Gonzalez) Tyrone, *Witch Hunt,* HBO, 1994.

(As Clifton Gonzalez Gonzalez) Nelson Rodriguez, *The Defenders: Taking the First,* Showtime, 1998.

Raymo Serrano, *Road Dogz,* Cinemax, 2001.

Loco, *Undefeated,* HBO, 2003.

Kipp, *Life of the Party* (also known as *Glory Days*), Lifetime, c. 2005.

Television Appearances; Specials:

(In archive footage) *Cannes 2006: Cronica de Carlos Boyero,* 2006.

Television Appearances; Awards Presentations:

(In archive footage from *Babel*) Officer at border crossing, *51 premis Sant Jordi de cinematografia,* 2007.

Television Appearances; Episodic:

(As Clifton Gonzalez Collins) Mickey, "Interior Loft," *Freddy's Nightmares* (also known as *Freddy's Nightmares: A Nightmare on Elm Street: The Series, Freddy, le cauchemar de vos nuits, Freddyn painajaiset, Las pesadillas de Freddy,* and *Les cauchemars de Freddy*), syndicated, 1990.

Manager, "Slow Violence," *Veronica Clare,* Lifetime, 1991.

Roberto, "Street of Dreams," *Jake and the Fatman,* CBS, 1991.

(As Clifton Gonzalez Gonzalez) David Kern, "Code Name: Desert Dragon," *Acapulco H.E.A.T.,* syndicated, 1993.

Carlos Sandoval, "For Whom the Stinkin' Bell Tolls," *Live Shot,* UPN, 1995.

(As Clifton Gonzalez–Gonzalez) Fito, "El Coyote: Parts 1 & 2," *Walker, Texas Ranger* (also known as *Walker*), CBS, 1996.

"Red Cadillac," *Land's End,* syndicated, 1996.

(As Clifton Gonzalez Gonzalez) Jimmy Cortez, "I Love Lucy," *NYPD Blue,* ABC, 1997.

(As Clifton Gonzalez Gonzalez) Mr. Brown (jaywalker), "Tribes," *ER* (also known as *Emergency Room*), NBC, 1997.

(As Clifton Gonzalez Gonzalez) Boyd Harcourt, "Rear Windows '98," *Diagnosis Murder,* CBS, 1998.

Burns, "The Friendly Skies," *Martial Law* (also known as *Le flic de Shanghai, Ley marcial,* and *Piu forte ragazzi*), CBS, 1999.

James Garcia, "Comenzando de Nuevo," *Resurrection Blvd.,* Showtime, 2000.

James Garcia, "No Te Muevas," *Resurrection Blvd.,* Showtime, 2000.

James Garcia, "Lagrimas en el Cielo," *Resurrection Blvd.,* Showtime, 2001.

Himself, "Inside the Walls of 'The Last Castle,'" *HBO First Look,* HBO, 2001.

Andy Perez, "Last Lap," *The Twilight Zone,* UPN, 2002.

Javier Perez, "A Missing Link," *Alias,* ABC, 2003.

Javier Perez, "Prelude," *Alias,* ABC, 2003.

Javier Perez, "Repercussions," *Alias,* ABC, 2003.

(Uncredited) Himself, *Corazon de …,* Television Espanola (TVE, Spain), 2006.

Hernan, "Exiled," *The Shield* (also known as *The Barn* and *Rampart*), fX Channel, 2007.

Hernan, "Haunts," *The Shield* (also known as *The Barn* and *Rampart*), fX Channel, 2007.

Appeared as Jorge, *Madman of the People,* NBC. Appeared in "Little Brother," an unaired episode of *Masters of Science Fiction,* ABC.

Television Appearances; Pilots:

Lessons Learned, HBO, 2000.

Mouse, *Bounty Hunters,* CBS, 2005.

Jack "Bump" Hill, *Thief,* fX Channel, 2006.

Internet Appearances; Episodic:

Sam's friend, "Sam's New Friend," *Roommates* (also known as *Roommates the Series*), 2007.

RECORDINGS

Videos:

Himself, *Gettin' Dirty* (short), Sony Pictures Entertainment, 2006.

Music Videos:

Blow–Up, "Fly with Me," 2003.

Video Games:

Voice of Cesar Vialpando, *Grand Theft Auto: San Andreas* (also known as *GTA: San Andreas* and *San Andreas*), Rockstar Games, 2004.

OTHER SOURCES

Periodicals:

Beacon Journal, February 28, 1997.

Cinema, issue 10, pp. 88–92.

Smoke, spring, 1998.

Venice, February, 1998.

CRUZ, Alexis 1974–

PERSONAL

Born September 29, 1974, in the Bronx, New York, NY; son of Edwin and Julie (a songwriter) Cruz. *Education:* Attended the Fiorello H. LaGuardia High School of Music & Art and Performing Arts, New York City; Boston University, College of Fine Arts, theatre degree; also earned a certificate to teach creative dramatics. *Religion:* Christian. *Avocational Interests:* Various academic disciplines, writing short stories, martial arts, video games, other games, singing, football, basketball.

Addresses: *Agent*—Ann Geddes, The Geddes Agency, 8430 Santa Monica Blvd., Suite 200, West Hollywood, CA 90069. *Manager*—Steve Rodriguez, McGowan–Rodriguez Management, 8733 West Sunset Blvd., Suite 103, West Hollywood, CA 90069.

Career: Actor. Appeared in advertisements. East Los Angeles Classic Theatre/LAUSD Teacher's Program, creative dramatics instructor for middle school students; East Los Angeles College, instructor in art. National Council of La Raza, spokesperson; National Hispanic Foundation for the Arts, member. According to some sources, Cruz is an ordained minister and certified emergency medical technician.

Awards, Honors: ALMA Award nomination, outstanding actor in a made–for–television movie or miniseries, American Latin Media Arts awards, 1998, for *Detention: The Siege at Johnson High;* ALMA Award nomination, outstanding supporting actor in a supporting in a feature film, 1999, for *Why Do Fools Fall in Love?;*

ALMA Award nomination, outstanding supporting actor in a television series, 2002, for *The District;* award from Hispanic Unity USA.

CREDITS

Television Appearances; Series:
Alex, *Sesame Street* (also known as *The New Sesame Street, Open Sesame, Sesame Park, Sesame Street Unpaved, Canadian Sesame Street,* and *Les amis de Sesame*), PBS, 1990–91.
Rafael, *Touched by an Angel,* CBS, 1997–2003.
Skaara and Klorel, *Stargate SG–1* (also known as *La porte des etoiles* and *Stargaate SG–1*), Showtime and syndicated, 1997–2002, Sci–Fi Channel and syndicated, 2002–2003.
Sergeant Joaquin Garcia, *American Family* (also known as *American Family: Journey of Dreams*), PBS, 2004.
Martin Allende, *Shark,* CBS, beginning 2006.

Television Appearances; Miniseries:
Joey Garza, *Streets of Laredo* (also known as *Larry McMurtry's "Streets of Laredo"*), CBS, 1995.
Raymond, *Grand Avenue,* HBO, 1996.

Television Appearances; Movies:
Alberto (some sources cite Edilberto), *The Price of Love,* Fox, 1995.
Carlos, "Caught in the Fever," *Riot* (also known as *Riot in the Streets*), Showtime, 1997.
Frankie Rodriguez, *Detention: The Siege at Johnson High* (also known as *Hostage High* and *Target for Rage*), ABC, 1997.
Nestor, *Almost a Woman* (also known as *Casi una mujer* and *Prawie kobieta*), broadcast as part of *The American Collection* on *Masterpiece Theatre* (also known as *ExxonMobil Masterpiece Theatre* and *Mobil Masterpiece Theatre*), PBS, 2002.
Alex, *Slayer,* Sci–Fi Channel, 2006.

Television Appearances; Specials:
Manolo, "The Old Man and the Sea" (also known as "Ernest Hemingway's 'The Old Man and the Sea'"), *Hallmark Hall of Fame,* CBS, 1990.
Alex, *Big Bird's Birthday or Let Me Eat Cake,* PBS, 1991.

Television Appearances; Awards Presentations:
The 1999 ALMA Awards, ABC, 1999.

Television Appearances; Episodic:
Enrique Tarron, "Mr. Quiet," *The Cosby Show,* NBC, 1985.
Ricky, "Gryphon," *WonderWorks,* PBS, 1990.

Eddie Matos, "POWER: The Eddie Matos Story," *Lifestories: Families in Crisis,* HBO, 1994.
Terry, "Long Day's Journey," *ER* (also known as *Emergency Room*), NBC, 1995.
Art Gonzalez, "Moonstruck," *Dangerous Minds,* ABC, 1996.
Art Gonzalez, "Trust Me," *Dangerous Minds,* ABC, 1996.
Roberto Santos, "Sleep Over," *NYPD Blue,* ABC, 2000.
Victor Ortiz, "You Can Count on Me," *Providence,* NBC, 2001.
Eduardo Castillo, "Foreign Affair," *The District* (also known as *Washington Police, The District—Einsatz in Washington, Mannions distrikt,* and *Poliisipaeaellikkkoe Mannion*), CBS, 2001.
Eduardo Castillo, "Convictions," *The District* (also known as *Washington Police, The District—Einsatz in Washington, Mannions distrikt,* and *Poliisipaeaellikkkoe Mannion*), CBS, 2002.
Private first class Phillip Riley, "No Humans Involved," *CSI: Crime Scene Investigation* (also known as *C.S.I., CSI: Las Vegas, CSI: Weekends,* and *Les experts*), CBS, 2004.
Oliver Sanchez, "Whereabouts," *Eyes,* ABC, 2005.
(In archive footage) Skaara, "Citizen Joe," *Stargate SG–1* (also known as *La porte des etoiles* and *Stargaate SG–1*), Sci–Fi Channel and syndicated, 2005.
Himself, "David Bisbal," *Vivo,* 2006.
Himself, "Leachman Passes a Milestone/Golf/Stuff Style & Jules Verne Gets the Star Treatment," *In the Mix* (also known as *In the Cutz*), Urban America Channel, 2006.

Appeared in other programs, including *Arli$$* (also known as *Arliss*), HBO.

Television Appearances; Pilots:
Bobby Castillo, *Time Well Spent,* 1995.
Skaara and Klorel, "Children of the Gods," *Stargate SG–1* (also known as *La porte des etoiles* and *Stargaate SG–1*), Showtime and syndicated, 1997.
Martin Allende, *Shark,* CBS, 2006.

Film Appearances:
Charlie, *The Pick–Up Artist,* Twentieth Century–Fox, 1987.
Squeak, *Rooftops,* New Visions Entertainment Corporation, 1989.
Skaara, *Stargate* (also known as *Stargate, la porte des etoiles*), Metro–Goldwyn–Mayer/United Artists, 1994.
Weyman, *The Brave,* Acappella Pictures/Brave Pictures/Majestic Films International, 1997.
Herman Santiago, *Why Do Fools Fall in Love?,* Warner Bros., 1998.
Guillermo, *Learning to Swim* (short film), 1999.
Smiley, *That Summer in L.A.,* 2000.
Sung, *Bug,* Curb Entertainment, 2002.

Miguel, *Dark Wolf* (also known as *Darkwolf*), Twentieth Century–Fox, 2003.

Ralph Lazo, *Stand Up for Justice* (short film), Visual Communications, 2004.

Sean, *Spectres* (also known as *Soul Survivor*), Xenon Pictures, 2004.

Young Dominic, *Last Call* (short film), 2005.

Alvarez, *The Last Time,* Sony Pictures Entertainment, 2007.

Marco, *Tortilla Heaven,* Archangel Entertainment, 2007.

Stage Appearances:

Appeared in various productions, including productions at Carnegie Hall and Lincoln Center, both New York City.

Stage Work:

Directed various productions at the Fiorello H. La-Guardia High School of Music & Art and Performing Arts, New York City.

Major Tours:

Latinologues, U.S. cities, c. 2005.

OTHER SOURCES

Periodicals:

Cyberex, January, 2003.

TV Zone, March, 2001, pp. 32–36.

CULLEN, Peter 1956–

PERSONAL

Born in 1956 in Montreal, Quebec, Canada; son of Clay Cullen (a stuntman); children: Clay, Claire, and Pilar E. *Education:* Studied acting at the National Theatre. *Avocational Interests:* Raising cattle and horses.

Career: Actor and voice artist. Also provides voice work for commercials and movie previews.

CREDITS

Film Appearances:

Allen, *Prologue,* Vaudeo Films, 1970.

Voice of Gruffle, *Heidi's Song* (animated), Paramount, 1982.

(Uncredited) Voice of Murky Dismal, *Rainbow Brite: San Diego Zoo Adventures* (animated), 1983.

Voice, *Robotix* (animated), 1985.

Voice of Murky, Cassie Monster, Glitterbot, Guard, Skydancer, and Slurthic, *Rainbow Brite and the Star Stealer* (animated), Warner Bros., 1985.

Voice of Arthur Ravenscroft, *Bigfoot and the Muscle Machines,* 1985.

Voice of Optimus Prime and Ironhide, *The Transformers: The Movie* (animated; also known as *Matrix Forever* and *Transformers: Matrix yo eien ni*), DEG, 1986.

Voice of Grundle and Ahgg, *My Little Pony: The Movie* (animated), DEG, 1986.

Heathcliff: The Movie (animated), Clubhouse Pictures, 1986.

Voice, *Noah's Ark,* 1986.

Voice of King Alfor, Commander Hawkins, Coran, and narrator, *Voltron: Fleet of Doom* (animated), 1986.

Voice of Pincher, Tombstone, and Stones, *GoBots: War of the Rock Lords* (animated; also known as *GoBots: Battle of the Rock Lords*), Clubhouse Pictures, 1986.

Voice of Zander and Nemesis enforcer, *G.I. Joe: The Movie* (animated; also known as *Action Force: The Movie*), 1987.

Voice of 1359, *Voyage of Rock Aliens* (animated), 1988.

Voice of Eeyore, *Winnie the Pooh and Christmas Too* (animated), 1991.

Voice of Pete, *The Little Engine That Could* (animated), 1991.

Narrator, *Making "Hamlet,"* 1996.

Voice of Eeyore, *Pooh's Grand Adventure: The Search for Christopher Robin* (animated; also known as *Winnie the Pooh's Most Grand Adventure*), Buena Vista Home Video, 1997.

Voice of Eeyore, *A Winnie the Pooh Thanksgiving* (animated), 1998.

Voice of Eeyore, *Winnie the Pooh Friendship: Pooh Wishes* (animated), 1999.

Speaking voice of Eeyore, *Winnie the Pooh: Seasons for Giving* (animated; also known as *Disney's "Winnie the Pooh: Seasons for Giving"*), Buena Vista Home Video, 1999.

Voice of Eeyore, *The Tigger Movie* (animated; also known as *Tigger: The Movie*), Buena Vista, 2000.

Narrator, *Sleepy Hollow: Behind the Legend,* 2000.

Voice of Eeyore, *Mickey's Magical Christmas: Snowed in at the House of Mouse* (animated), Buena Vista Home Video, 2001.

Narrator, *Enemy at the Gates: Through the Crosshairs* (documentary short), 2001.

Narrator, *Making "The Score"* (documentary short), Paramount Home Video, 2001.

Voice of Eeyore, *Piglet's Big Movie* (animated), Buena Vista, 2003.

Voice of Eeyore, *Winnie the Pooh: Springtime with Roo* (animated short), Buena Vista Home Video, 2004.

Voice of Eeyore, *Pooh's Heffalump Movie* (animated), Buena Vista, 2005.

Voice of Eeyore, *Winnie the Pooh: Wonderful Word Adventures* (animated short), Buena Vista Home Entertainment, 2006.

Voice of Optimus Prime, *Transformers,* DreamWorks, 2007.

Film Work:

Special vocal effects, *Gremlins,* Warner Bros., 1984.

Vocalizations, *Predator,* 1987.

Television Appearances; Series:

Additional voices, *The Jetsons* (animated), 1962.

Commander Bi Bi Latuque, *The Buddies,* 1967.

Announcer, *The Smothers Brothers Comedy Hour,* CBS, 1967–70.

Comedy Cafe, 1970.

Zut!, 1970.

Regular performer, *The Sonny and Cher Comedy Hour,* CBS, 1971–74.

Puppeteer (Calvin Calaveris and Jonathan Rebel), *The Bobby Goldsboro Show,* 1973.

Regular, *The Hudson Brothers Razzle Dazzle Show,* CBS, 1974.

(Uncredited) Announcer, *The Bobbie Gentry Show* (also known as *Bobbie Gentry's Happiness*), 1974.

Luke Warm, *Down Home Country,* 1975.

The Wolfman Jack Show, 1976.

Additional voices, *Scooby and Scrappy–Doo* (animated), ABC, 1979.

Voice of Mighty Man, *The Plastic Man Comedy/ Adventure Show* (animated), ABC, 1979.

(English version) Voice of Commander Hawkins, Coran, King Alfor, narrator, and Stride the Tiger, *Hyakuju o Go–Lion* (animated; also known as *King of Beasts Go–lion*), 1981.

Additional voices, *The Smurfs* (animated; also known as *Smurfs Adventures*), NBC, 1981.

Voice of Sour Puss, *Pac–Man* (animated), ABC, 1981.

Voice, *The Kwicky Koala Show,* 1981.

Voice of Lucky, *The Scooby and Scrappy–Do Puppy Hour* (animated; also known as *The Scooby–Doo Puppy Hour*), 1982.

Voice of Commander Hawk and narrator, *Kiko Kantai dairugger XV* (animated; also known as *Armored Squadron Dairugger XV*), 1982.

Voice, *Meatballs and Spaghetti,* 1982.

Voice of Sour Puss, *Pac–Man* (animated), 1982.

Officer Ed, *The Little Rascals,* 1982.

Voice of Shreeker, Snitchitt, and Gonker, *Monchichis* (animated), ABC, 1983.

Voice of Venger, *Dungeons and Dragons* (animated), CBS, 1983–85.

Voice of Mario, *Donkey Kong* (animated), CBS, 1983.

Voice of Scratch, Fang, and Dog Foot, *The Biskitts* (animated), 1983.

Voice of King Alfor, Commander Hawkins, Coran, and narrator, *Voltron: Defender of the Universe* (animated; also known as *The New Adventure of Voltron* and *Voltron*), syndicated, 1984.

Voice of Optimus Prime, Ironhide, Streetwise, and Skids, *Transformers* (animated; also known as *Transformers: 2010* and *The Transformers*), syndicated, 1984.

Voice of Airborne and Zander, *G.I. Joe* (animated), syndicated, 1984.

Voice of Bertram, *Dragon's Lair* (animated), ABC, 1984.

Voice of Spoiler, Tank, and Pincher, *Challenge of the GoBots,* syndicated, 1984.

Additional voices, *Heathcliff & the Catillac Cats* (animated), 1984.

Additional voices, *Snorks* (animated), 1984.

Voice, *The 13 Ghosts of Scooby–Doo* (animated), ABC, 1985.

Voice of Murky, Monstromurk, and narrator, *Rainbow Brite* (animated; also known as *Blondine au pays e l'arc–en–ciel* and *Maho shojo rainbow brite*), 1985.

Voice of Airborne, Nemesis enforcer, and Zandar, *G.I. Joe* (animated; also known as *Action Force* and *Chijo saikyo no Expert Team G.I. Joe*), 1985.

Voice of Boltar, Nemesis, and Spiro, *Robotix* (animated), 1985.

Voice, *Goltar and the Golden Lance* (animated), 1985.

Additional voices, *Rambo,* syndicated, 1986.

Saber Rider and the Star Sheriffs (also known as *Bismarck the Star Musketeers*), syndicated, 1986.

Murky, Monstromurk, and narrator, *Rainbow Brite* (animated), syndicated, 1986.

Voice of Captain Crabnasty, *My Little Pony 'n' Friends* (animated), syndicated, 1986.

Voice, *Jonny Quest* (animated), syndicated, 1986.

Voice of Eddie, *Ghostbusters* (animated; also known as *The Original Ghostbusters*), syndicated, 1986.

Felix Faust, *The Super Powers Team: Galactic Guardians* (also known as *SuperFriends VI*), 1986.

Voice, *The Flintstone Kids* (animated), 1986.

Voice, *Sectaurs—Warriors of Symbion* (animated), 1986.

Voice of Cindarr, *Visionaries: Knights of the Magical Lamp* (animated; also known as *Visionaries*), syndicated, 1987.

Voice, *Little Wizards,* 1987.

Voice, *BraveStarr,* 1987.

Saber Rider and the Star Sheriffs (also known as *Bismarck the Star Musketeers*), 1987.

Admiral Grimmace, *DuckTales* (animated; also known as *Disney's "DuckTales"*), ABC, 1987–88.

Voice of Eeyore, *The New Adventures of Winnie the Pooh* (animated), ABC, 1988–90.

Voice of Gunner, Antor, and Bomba, *Dino–Riders* (animated), syndicated, 1988.

Voice of Meps, Muldoon, and Kirby, *Chip 'n Dale Rescue Rangers* (animated), syndicated, 1989.

Voice of Eeyore, "Winnie the Pooh," *Disney's "Gummi Bears/Winnie the Pooh" Hour* (animated), 1989.

Additional voices, *Widget, the World Watcher* (animated; also known as *Widget*), syndicated, 1990.

Voice, *Tom and Jerry Kids Show*, 1990.

Voice, *The Adventures of Don Coyote and Sancho Panda* (animated), 1990.

Additional voices, *Tale Spin* (animated), syndicated, 1990.

Voice of Mantis, *Pirates of Darkwater* (animated; also known as *Dark Water*), Fox, 1991–93.

Voice of Abominable Snowman and Mackey McSlime, *Bonkers* (animated; also known as *Disney's "Bonkers"*), syndicated, 1993.

Fox announcer, *Hardball*, 1994.

Voice, *The New Adventures of Voltron* (animated), 1997.

Narrator, *Places of Mystery*, 2000.

Voice of Eeyore and additional characters, *House of Mouse* (animated), ABC, 2001–2002.

Voice of Eeyore, *The Book of Pooh* (animated), 2001.

Announcer, *Who Wants to Marry My Dad?*, NBC, 2002–2003.

Voice of Eeyore, *My Friends Tigger & Pooh* (animated), 2007.

Also provided voice of narrating announcer, *Toonami*, Cartoon Network.

Television Appearances; Miniseries:

Voice of Airborne and Ramar, *G.I. Joe: A Real American Hero,* syndicated, 1983.

Mantor, Skito, and Toxid, *Sectaurs,* syndicated, 1986.

Voice of Myzor and Chief Eldor, *Vytor: The Starfire Champion* (animated; pilot), syndicated, 1989.

Television Appearances; Movies:

Voice of Gruff, Commander Comsat, and Bouncer, *Rockin' with Judy Jetson* (animated), 1988.

Television Appearances; Specials:

Announcer, *Joey and Dad,* CBS, 1975.

Lola, ABC, 1975, 1976.

The Richard Pryor Special?, 1977.

Voice of Sour Puss and Santa Claus, *Christmas Comes to PacLand* (animated), 1982.

Voice of Yukon 'Ukie Pete—familydog, Earless—Pollywog's cat, and Long John Silver, "The Secret World of Og," *ABC Weekend Specials,* ABC, 1983.

Voice of Lucky, "The Puppy's Further Adventures," *ABC Weekend Specials,* ABC, 1983.

Voice, "The Return of the Bunjee," *ABC Weekend Specials,* ABC, 1985.

Voice of Robert's father, "The Velveteen Rabbit," *ABC Weekend Specials,* ABC, 1985.

Voice of Zandar, *G.I. Joe: Arise, Serpentor, Arise!* (also known as *Action Force: Arise, Serpentor, Arise!*), 1986.

Voice of Wizard, *Mickey's 60th Birthday* (animated; also known as *Mickey's 60th Birthday Anniversary Shorts Programme*), 1988.

Voice of title character, *Hagar the Horrible* (animated), CBS, 1989.

Voice of Kirby and Muldoon, *Chip 'n Dale, Rescue Rangers to the Rescue* (animated), 1989.

Voice, *The Monster Bed,* ABC, 1989.

Voice of Eeyore, *Winnie the Pooh & Christmas Too* (animated), 1991.

Voice of Eeyore, *Boo to You, Too, Winnie the Pooh* (animated), 1996.

Voice of Eeyore, *A Winnie the Pooh Thanksgiving* (animated), 1998.

Voice of Eeyore, *Winnie the Pooh: A Valentine for You* (animated), 1999.

Television Appearances; Pilots:

Voice of The Evil One and Murkey, *Rainbow Brite* (animated), syndicated, 1985.

Television Appearances; Episodic:

Himself and various characters, *The Sonny Comedy Revue,* ABC, 1974.

Voice of Red Skull, "The Capture of Captain America," *Spider-Man* (animated; also known as *Spiderman* and *Spiderman 2000*), 1981.

Voice of K.A.R.R., "Crust Doesn't Rust," *Knight Rider,* NBC, 1982.

Voice of Mario ("Donkey Kong"), "Donkey Kong in Gorilla My Dreams," *Saturday Supercade,* 1983.

Voice of K.A.R.R., "K.I.T.T. vs. K.A.R.R.," *Knight Rider,* NBC, 1984.

Sports announcer and television actor, "Vacation from Sex, *Three's a Crowd* (also known as *Three's a Crowd Too*), ABC, 1984.

Airline captain, "The Honeymooners," *Three's a Crowd* (also known as *Three's a Crowd Too*), ABC, 1984.

Voice of Optimus Prime, "The Return of Optimus," *Transformers* (animated; also known as *Transformers: 2010* and *The Transformers*), syndicated, 1986.

Voice of Baby, "Nothing to Sneeze At," *Foofur* (animated), 1986.

Voice of Baby, "A Royal Pain," *Foofur* (animated), 1986.

Voice of Baby, "This Little Piggy's on TV," *Foofur* (animated), 1986.

Voice of Baby, "Russian Through New York," *Foofur* (animated), 1986.

Voice of Doctor Destructo, "Captain Steel Saves the Day," *The Real Ghost Busters* (animated), 1987.

Kerwin the conqueror, "Good Neighbor Gummi," *The Gummi Bears* (animated; also known as *Disney's "Adventures of the Gummi Bears"*), 1988.

Fox announcer, "Lee's Bad, Bad Day," *Hardball,* Fox, 1994.

Voice of Eeyore, "Unplugged Club," *House of Mouse* (animated), ABC, 2001.

"I Love 1984," *I Love 1980's,* BBC2, 2001.

Voice of Klaar, "A Clockwork Megas," *Megas XLR* (animated), 2004.

Voice of Zanzoar, "Coop D'Etat," *Megas XLR* (animated), 2005.

(English version) Voice of narrator, "Time to Shine," *IGPX: Immortal Grand Prix* (animated), Cartoon Network, 2005.

Also appeared as Bristletooth, *Crazy Claws* (animated); additional voices, *Muppet Babies* (animated); *Pound Puppies* (animated).

RECORDINGS

Video Games:
Voice of Optimus Prime, *Transformers: The Game*, Activision, 2007.

CULP, Robert 1930–
(Robert M. Culp)

PERSONAL

Full name, Robert Martin Culp; born August 16, 1930, in Berkeley (some sources cite Oakland), CA; some sources cite parents' names as Crozie Culp and Bethel Collins; married Elayne Wilner (some sources cite name as Elayne Carroll), September 23, 1951 (divorced); married Nancy Ashe (divorced, c. 1967; some sources cite 1966); married France Nuyen (an actress), December 9, 1967 (divorced, c. 1969; some sources cite 1970); married Sheila Sullivan (an actress), December 25, 1971 (divorced, 1981); married Candace Faulkner, December 31, 1981 (some sources cite 1991); children: (with Ashe) Joshua, Jason (an actor), Joseph (an actor), Rachel; (with Faulkner) Samantha Hallie. *Education:* Attended College of the Pacific, Washington University, St. Louis, MO, and San Francisco State College (now San Francisco State University); studied at Herbert Berghof Studios (now HB Studio).

Addresses: *Manager*—Hillard Elkins, Elkins Entertainment, 8306 Wilshire Blvd., PMB 3643, Beverly Hills, CA 90211.

Career: Actor, director, and writer. Involved with various causes.

Awards, Honors: Obie Award, best actor, *Village Voice*, c. 1956, for *He Who Gets Slapped;* Emmy Award nominations, outstanding continued performance by an actor in a leading role in a dramatic series, 1965, 1966,

1967, and 1968, and outstanding writing achievement in drama, 1967, and Golden Globe Award nomination, best male television star, 1967, all for *I Spy;* Physicians Committee for Responsible Medicine (PCRM), member of honorary committee.

CREDITS

Television Appearances; Series:
Hoby Gilman, *Trackdown*, CBS, 1957–59.

Kelly Robinson, *I Spy* (also known as *Danny Doyle*), NBC, 1965–68.

William "Bill" Maxwell, *The Greatest American Hero*, ABC, 1981–83.

Host, *Could It Be a Miracle?*, syndicated, beginning c. 1996.

Warren, *Everybody Loves Raymond* (also known as *Raymond, Alla aelskar Raymond, Alle elsker Raymond, Alle lieben Raymond, Kaikki rakastavat Raymondia, Svi vole Raymonda, Todo el mundo quiere a Raymond, Tothom estima en Raymond, Tout le monde aime Raymond,* and *Tutti amano Raymond*), CBS, between 1996 and 2004.

Television Appearances; Miniseries:
Chester "Chet" Loomis, "Sammy, the Way–Out Seal" (also known as "Sammy"), *Walt Disney's Wonderful World of Color* (also known as *Disneyland, Disneylandia, Disney's Wonderful World, The Disney Sunday Movie, The Magical World of Disney, Walt Disney, Walt Disney Presents, The Wonderful World of Disney,* and *The World of Disney*), NBC, 1962.

From Sea to Shining Sea, syndicated, 1974–75.

Anthony Broadhurst, *Women in White*, NBC, 1979.

Lyle Pettijohn, *Roots: The Next Generations* (also known as *Racines 2, Raices: Las siguientes generaciones,* and *Roots—Die naechsten Generationen*), ABC, 1979.

General Erwin Rommel, *The Key to Rebecca* (also known as *Ken Follett's "The Key to Rebecca"*), Operation Prime Time, 1985.

General Walter Davies, *Voyage of Terror: The Achille Lauro Affair* (also known as *Voyage of Terror* and *Die Entfuehrung der Achille Lauro*), syndicated, 1990.

Television Appearances; Movies:
Harry Pace, *The Hanged Man*, NBC, 1964.

Ben Taylor, *See the Man Run* (also known as *The Second Face*), ABC, 1971.

Investigator Brimmer, *Columbo: Death Lends a Hand*, NBC, 1971.

Paul Hanlon, *Columbo: The Most Crucial Game*, NBC, 1972.

Dr. Bart Keppel, *Columbo: Double Exposure*, NBC, 1973.

Dr. Jim Kiler, *Outrage!* (also known as *One Angry Man*), ABC, 1973.

Dr. Robert Jones, *A Cold Night's Death* (also known as *The Chill Factor*), ABC, 1973.

Jack Halsey, *Strange Homecoming,* NBC, 1974.

Steve Bell, *Houston, We've Got a Problem,* ABC, 1974.

Harry Freeman, *A Cry for Help* (also known as *End of the Line*), ABC, 1975.

Steve Brannigan (some sources cite Steve Banning), *Flood!,* NBC, 1976.

William Sebastian, *Spectre,* NBC, 1977.

Sergeant Nichols, *Last of the Good Guys,* CBS, 1978.

Charles Huston, "Word Games," *Mrs. Columbo* (also known as *Kate Columbo, Kate Loves a Mystery,* and *Kate the Detective*), NBC, 1979.

T. L. Munn, *Hot Rod* (also known as *Rebel of the Road*), ABC, 1979.

Frank McGuire, *The Night the City Screamed,* ABC, 1980.

Henry Farnum, *The Dream Merchants,* syndicated, 1980.

Lou Corbin, *Killjoy* (also known as *Who Murdered Joy Morgan?*), CBS, 1981.

Steve Nevins, *Thou Shalt Not Kill,* NBC, 1982.

Dave Fleming, *Her Life as a Man,* NBC, 1984.

Richard Trainor, *The Calendar Girl Murders* (also known as *Insatiable, Victimised,* and *Victimized*), ABC, 1984.

General Edward "Ed" Woods, *Combat High* (also known as *Combat Academy*), NBC, 1986.

Lester McInally, *The Blue Lightning,* CBS, 1986.

Lieutenant Frank Mason, *The Gladiator,* ABC, 1986.

Billy Bob Claiborne, *What Price Victory* (also known as *Hail Alma Mater* and *The Price of Victory*), ABC, 1988.

Jordan Rowe, "Columbo Goes to College" (also known as "Columbo"), *The ABC Sunday Night Movie,* ABC, 1990.

Richard Stuart, *Perry Mason: The Case of the Defiant Daughter* (also known as *Perry Mason: The Case of the Deadly Deal*), NBC, 1990.

Dr. Bordinay, *Murderous Vision,* USA Network, 1991.

Kelly Robinson, *I Spy Returns* (also known as *The Return of I Spy*), CBS, 1994.

Actor playing Noble Hart, "Greed," *Favorite Deadly Sins* (also known as *National Lampoon's "Favorite Deadly Sins"*), Showtime, 1995.

McClean, *Mercenary,* HBO and Cinemax, 1997.

Father Patrick, *Wanted,* Cinemax, 2000.

Senator William Parker "Gabe" Gable, *Running Mates* (also known as *Washington Slept Here*), TNT, 2000.

Television Appearances; Specials:

The Wonderful World of Burlesque II, NBC, 1966.

Narrator, *Operation Breadbasket* (documentary), ABC, c. 1969.

Give Me Liberty, syndicated, 1975.

Himself, *The Making of "Goldengirl,"* 1979.

Himself, *Circus of the Stars VII* (also known as *Circus of the Stars 7*), CBS, 1982.

Himself, *NBC's 60th Anniversary Celebration* (also known as *NBC 60th Anniversary Celebration*), NBC, 1986.

The Golden Globes 50th Anniversary Celebration, NBC, 1994.

Voice, *In Search of the Oregon Trail,* PBS, 1996.

Host, *Canned Ham: Spyography–Austin Powers: International Man of Mystery,* Comedy Central, 1997.

Himself, *Big Guns Talk: The Story of the Western,* TNT, 1997.

Host, *Canned Ham: The Spy Who Shagged Me,* Comedy Central, 1999.

Host, *Comedy Central's "Canned Ham": The Dr. Evil Story* (also known as *Canned Ham: The Dr. Evil Story, The Dr. Evil Story,* and *Spyography: The Dr. Evil Story*), Comedy Central, 1999.

Narrator, *Hollywood Screen Tests: Take 1,* American Movie Classics, 1999.

Host, *Hollywood Screen Tests: Take 2,* American Movie Classics, 1999.

Himself, *Outer Limits Farewell Tribute,* 2000.

National Memorial Day Concert, PBS, 2000.

Narrator, *Cleopatra: The Film That Changed Hollywood,* American Movie Classics, 2001.

Host, *Reel Comedy: Austin Powers in Goldmember,* Comedy Central, 2002.

Himself, *NBC 75th Anniversary Special* (also known as *NBC 75th Anniversary Celebration*), NBC, 2002.

Himself, *Playboy: Inside the Playboy Mansion* (also known as *Inside the Playboy Mansion*), Arts and Entertainment, 2002.

Himself, *Steve McQueen: The Essence of Cool,* TNT and TCM, 2005.

Television Appearances; Awards Presentations:

Saturn Awards, 1981.

The Kennedy Center Honors: A Celebration of the Performing Arts (also known as *The 10th Annual Kennedy Center Honors: A Celebration of the Performing Arts*), CBS, 1988.

Presenter, *Thirteenth Annual Genesis Awards,* Animal Planet, 1999.

Television Appearances; Episodic:

"The Death of Socrates (399 B.C.)," *You Are There,* CBS, 1953.

"1984," *Studio One,* CBS, 1953.

Clint, "Nick and Letty," *Playwrights '56* (also known as *The Playwright Hour*), NBC, 1956.

Corporal Neville, "Operation Three Rs," *The United States Steel Hour* (also known as *The U.S. Steel Hour*), CBS, 1956.

Professor Teeling, "The Chevigny Man," *Star Tonight,* ABC, 1956.

"The Bridey Murphy Story," *The Big Story,* NBC, 1956.

"The Funny Heart," *The United States Steel Hour* (also known as *The U.S. Steel Hour*), CBS, 1956.

Clarence, "A Man Greatly Beloved," *Alfred Hitchcock Presents*, CBS, 1957.

Hoby Gilman, "Badge of Honor," *Zane Grey Theater* (also known as *Dick Powell's "Zane Grey Theater"* and *The Westerners*), CBS, 1957, pilot for the series *Trackdown*.

Himself, "The Airport," *The Jack Benny Program* (also known as *The Jack Benny Show*), CBS, 1957.

"Longing for to Go," *Robert Montgomery Presents* (also known as *Lucky Strike Theatre, Montgomery's "Summer Stock,"* and *The Robert Montgomery Summer Theater*), NBC, 1957.

"The Man Who Couldn't Say No," *Kraft Television Theatre* (also known as *Kraft Mystery Theatre* and *Kraft Theatre*), NBC, 1957.

Lamp unto My Feet, CBS, 1957.

"Flint and Fire," *The United States Steel Hour* (also known as *The U.S. Steel Hour*), CBS, 1958.

Himself, *The Ed Sullivan Show* (also known as *Toast of the Town*), CBS, 1958.

Abel, "Dead Man's Walk," *The Kraft Mystery Show* (also known as *The Chevy Mystery Show* and *Sunday Mystery Hour*), NBC, 1960.

Captain Masters, "The Patsy," *General Electric Theater* (also known as *G.E. Theater*), CBS, 1960.

Clay Horne, "Cave–In," *Johnny Ringo* (also known as *The Westerners*), CBS, 1960.

Colly Vane, "The Hero," *The Rifleman*, ABC, 1960.

Holgrave, "The House of the Seven Gables," *The Shirley Temple Theatre* (also known as *Shirley Temple's "Storybook"*), NBC, 1960.

Sam Applegate, "Calico Bait," *Zane Grey Theater* (also known as *Dick Powell's "Zane Grey Theater"* and *The Westerners*), CBS, 1960.

Sam Yadkin, "Thirty a Month," *Outlaws*, NBC, 1960.

Shad Hudson, "Morning Incident," *Zane Grey Theater* (also known as *Dick Powell's "Zane Grey Theater"* and *The Westerners*), CBS, 1960.

Shep Prescott, "Line Camp," *The Westerner* (also known as *The Westerners*), NBC, 1960.

Stuart Douglas, "So Dim the Light," *The June Allyson Show* (also known as *The DuPont Show Starring June Allyson* and *The DuPont Show with June Allyson*), CBS, 1960.

Tom Sandee (bounty hunter), "The Bounty Hunter," *Tate*, NBC, 1960.

Archie Bishop, "Josephine Little: Adventures in Happiness" (also known as "Adventures on Happiness Street"), *The Barbara Stanwyck Show*, NBC, 1961.

Craig Kern, "Incident at the Top of the World," *Rawhide*, CBS, 1961.

Ed Payson, "Broken Ballad," *Bonanza* (also known as *Ponderosa*), NBC, 1961.

Finletter, "The Guerrillas," *The Americans*, NBC, 1961.

Herbert Sanders, "Bad Apple," *The Detectives* (also known as *The Detectives Starring Robert Taylor, The Detectives, Starring Robert Taylor,* and *Robert Taylor's "Detectives"*), ABC, 1961.

Meeker, "To Wear a Badge," *Target: The Corruptors*, ABC, 1961.

Steven Gray, "The Specialist," *Hennessey*, CBS, 1961.

Thomas Burdue/Jesse Stuart, "Alias Jesse Stuart," *Death Valley Days* (also known as *Call of the West, The Pioneers, Trails West,* and *Western Star Theater*), syndicated, 1961.

"The Floater," *87th Precinct*, NBC, 1961.

Himself, *Here's Hollywood*, NBC, 1961.

Baylor Crowfoot, "The Baylor Crowfoot Story," *Wagon Train* (also known as *Major Adams, Trail Master*), NBC, 1962.

Dave Foley, "The Man from Salinas," *The Rifleman*, ABC, 1962.

Hank Shannon, "The Swinger," *Cain's Hundred*, NBC, 1962.

Kurt Yoder, "The Plush Jungle," *Cain's Hundred*, NBC, 1962.

Allen Leighton, "The Architects of Fear," *The Outer Limits*, ABC, 1963.

Guest panelist, "P.T. 109 Cast" (also known as "P.T. Boat 109 Cast"), *Pantomime Quiz* (also known as *Mike Stokey's "Pantomime Quiz"* and *Stump the Stars*), CBS, 1963.

Harry Lawrence, "Good–Bye, George," *The Alfred Hitchcock Hour*, CBS, 1963.

Jared Mace, "Where the Hawk Is Wheeling," *Empire* (also known as *Big G* and *Redigo*), NBC, 1963.

Matt Hendricks, "Face of Fear," *Dr. Kildare*, NBC, 1963.

Paul Cameron, "Corpus Earthling," *The Outer Limits*, ABC, 1963.

Richard Calder, "The Highest of Prizes," *Naked City*, ABC, 1963.

Sergeant John Metcalf, "Hill 256," *Combat!*, ABC, 1963.

Captain Shark, "The Shark Affair," *The Man from U.N.C.L.E.* (also known as *Ian Fleming's "Solo," Mr. Solo, Napoleon Solo, Solo,* and *0011 Napoleon Solo*), NBC, 1964.

Charles "Charlie" Orwell, "The Black Stallion," *The Virginian* (also known as *The Men from Shiloh*), NBC, 1964.

Eric Morgan, "Autumn without Red Leaves," *Ben Casey*, ABC, 1964.

Joe Costa, "Hung High," *Gunsmoke* (also known as *Gun Law* and *Marshal Dillon*), CBS, 1964.

Neil Herrick, "The Sound of One Hand Clapping," *Ben Casey*, ABC, 1964.

Peter Furgatch, "A Slow Fade to Black" (also known as "The Movie Maker"), *Bob Hope Presents the Chrysler Theater* (also known as *The Chrysler Theater* and *Universal Star Time*), NBC, 1964.

Sam Houston, "The Testing of Sam Houston," *The Great Adventure*, CBS, 1964.

Trent, "Demon with a Glass Hand," *The Outer Limits*, ABC, 1964.

Dr. Jesse Hartwood, "Do You Trust Our Doctor?," *Dr. Kildare*, NBC, 1965.

Frank Menlow, "The Tender Twigs," *Mr. Novak*, NBC, 1965.

Himself, *Dream Girl of '67*, ABC, 1967.

Himself, *Personality,* NBC, 1967.

Himself, *The Hollywood Squares,* NBC, multiple episodes, 1967–69.

(Uncredited) Waiter, "Die, Spy," *Get Smart,* NBC, 1968.

Guest performer, *Rowan & Martin's "Laugh–In"* (also known as *Laugh–In*), NBC, 1968 (multiple episodes).

Himself, *The Merv Griffin Show,* syndicated, 1968.

Dramatic reader, *The Hollywood Palace,* ABC, 1969.

Paul Tyler, "Cynthia Is Alive and Living in Avalon," *The Name of the Game,* NBC, 1970.

Paul Tyler, "Little Bear Died Running," *The Name of the Game,* NBC, 1970.

Himself, *The Mike Douglas Show,* syndicated, 1972.

Marshal Cunningham, "The Enforcers," *Shaft,* CBS, 1973.

"The Lie," *CBS Playhouse 90,* CBS, 1973.

Himself, *Match Game '73* (also known as *Match Game*), CBS, 1973.

Detective John Darrin, "Year of the Dragon: Parts 1 & 2," *Police Story,* NBC, 1975.

Himself, *Celebrity Bowling,* syndicated, 1975.

Himself, *V.I.P.–Schaukel,* 1975.

Himself, "Film '76 Episode 15," *The Film Programme* (also known as *Film '76*), BBC, 1976.

Joshua, "The Story of Joshua" (also known as "Joshua and the Battle of Jericho"), *The Greatest Heroes of the Bible,* NBC, 1978.

"D. H. Lawrence: A Restless Spirit," *Anyone for Tennyson?,* PBS, 1978.

Sergeant Price, "A Cry for Justice," *Police Story,* NBC, 1979.

"The Seduction Squad," *A Man Called Sloane,* NBC, 1979.

Major Ross Lathan, "Target Gopher/The Major's Wife/Strange Honeymoon/The Oilman Cometh," *The Love Boat,* ABC, 1980.

Guest host, *Saturday Night Live* (also known as *NBC's "Saturday Night," Saturday Night, Saturday Night Live '80, SNL,* and *SNL 25*), NBC, 1982.

Arthur Farnell, "School for Scandal," *Hardcastle and McCormick,* ABC, 1984.

"Richard Block," *An American Portrait,* CBS, 1985.

Norman Amberson, "Murder by Appointment Only," *Murder, She Wrote,* CBS, 1986.

Paul Fitzgerald, "Child's Play," *Hotel* (also known as *Arthur Hailey's "Hotel"*), ABC, 1986.

Daniel Kingsford, "Glass People," *Hotel* (also known as *Arthur Hailey's "Hotel"*), ABC, 1987.

Harrison Gregg, "The Man That Got Away," *Jake and the Fatman,* CBS, 1987.

Robert Irwin, "The Power Brokers: Parts 1 & 2," *Matlock,* NBC, 1987.

Ronald James, "Parents' Day," *Highway to Heaven,* NBC, 1987.

Scott Kelly, "Bald and Beautiful," *The Cosby Show,* NBC, 1987.

Hoey Babcock, "Member of the Club," *Doctor Doctor,* CBS, 1989.

Jason, "Gambling Jag," *Who's the Boss?,* ABC, 1989.

John Hathaway, "The Long Years," *The Ray Bradbury Theater* (also known as *The Bradbury Trilogy, Mystery Theatre, Ray Bradbury Theater, Le monde fantastique de Ray Bradbury,* and *Ray Bradbury presente*), USA Network, 1990.

Simon, "Like the Beep Beep Beep of the Tom Tom," *The Golden Girls* (also known as *Golden Girls, Miami Nice, Bnot Zahav, Cuori senza eta, Las chicas de oro, Les craquantes, Los anos dorados, Oereglanyok, Pantertanter,* and *Tyttoekullat*), NBC, 1990.

(In archive footage) William "Bill" Maxwell, "La audiencia tenia un precio," *Locos por la tele,* Television Espanola (TVE, Spain), 1990.

Harrison Gregg, "We'll Meet Again," *Jake and the Fatman,* CBS, 1991.

Elias "Doc Eli" Jackson, "The Great American Medicine Show," *Dr. Quinn, Medicine Woman,* CBS, 1993.

Ace Galvin, "The Wrong Stuff," *Wings,* NBC, 1994.

Cornelius Farnsworth, "O Western Wind" (also known as "O Western Wind: Part 1"), *Lonesome Dove: The Series,* CTV (Canada) and syndicated, 1994.

Cornelius Farnsworth, "Down Come Rain" (also known as "Down Come Rain: Part 2"), *Lonesome Dove: The Series,* CTV (Canada) and syndicated, 1994.

Cornelius Farnsworth, "When Wilt Thou Blow" (also known as "When Wilt Thou Blow: Part 3"), *Lonesome Dove: The Series,* CTV (Canada) and syndicated, 1994.

Stewart Babcock, "Ode to Barbara Joan (a.k.a. Daddy Dearest)," *The Nanny,* CBS, 1994.

Hiram Waters, "Who Killed the Sweet Smell of Success?," *Burke's Law,* CBS, 1995.

Lyle Pike, "Trust No One," *Walker, Texas Ranger* (also known as *Walker*), CBS, 1995.

Mr. Darryl, "Lucky Leon," *Lois & Clark: The New Adventures of Superman* (also known as *Lois & Clark* and *The New Adventures of Superman*), ABC, 1995.

Mr. Darryl, "Top Copy," *Lois & Clark: The New Adventures of Superman* (also known as *Lois & Clark* and *The New Adventures of Superman*), ABC, 1995.

Voice of Halcyon Renard, "Golem," *Gargoyles* (animated), syndicated, 1995.

Voice of Halcyon Renard, "The Gathering: Parts 1 & 2," *Gargoyles* (animated), syndicated, 1996.

Voice of Halcyon Renard, "Outfoxed," *Gargoyles* (animated), syndicated, 1996.

Narrator, *Sex and the Silver Screen,* Showtime, c. 1996.

(Uncredited) Crazed terrorist, "Why Spy?," *Spy Game,* ABC, 1997.

Dane Travis, "Discards," *Diagnosis Murder,* CBS, 1997.

Mark Bishop, "Cold Warriors," *Viper,* syndicated, 1997.

(Uncredited) Himself, "Judgement in LA: D–Girl," *Law & Order* (also known as *Law & Order Prime*), NBC, 1997.

Frank, "Guess Who's Not Coming to Dinner," *Holding the Baby,* Fox, 1998.

King Vog, "Red Sonja," *Conan* (also known as *Conan the Adventurer*), syndicated, 1998.

Kelly Robinson, "My Spy," *Cosby,* CBS, 1999.

Benjamin Quinn, "Devoted Attachment," *Chicago Hope,* CBS, 2000.

Himself, "African Americans in Television," *Inside TV Land* (also known as *Inside TV Land: African Americans in Television*), TV Land, 2002.

Himself, "Isaakland," *The Chris Isaak Show,* Showtime, 2002.

Jeffrey Grissom, "The Man Who Never Was," *The Dead Zone* (also known as *The Dark Half, Dead Zone, Stephen King's "Dead Zone," La morta zona, La zona morta, La zona muerta,* and *Zona smrti*), USA Network, 2003.

Himself, "Natalie Wood: Child of Hollywood," *Biography* (also known as *A&E Biography: Natalie Wood*), Arts and Entertainment, 2003.

(In archive footage) "Ice Bullet, Exploding Toilet, Who Gets Wetter?," *MythBusters,* The Discovery Channel, 2003.

Himself, *Hollywood Squares* (also known as *H2* and *H2: Hollywood Squares*), syndicated, 2004.

Voice of William "Bill" Maxwell, "Yancy the Yo–Yo Boy," *Robot Chicken* (animated), Cartoon Network, 2007.

(In archive footage) William "Bill" Maxwell, *La tele de tu vida,* Television Espanola (TVE, Spain), 2007.

Appeared in other programs, including *Accused,* ABC; *The Dick Powell Show,* NBC; and *The Kaiser Aluminum Hour,* NBC. Also appeared in "Al Tells the Truth," an unaired episode of *The Famous Teddy Z,* CBS.

Television Appearances; Pilots:

Hoby Gilman, *Trackdown,* CBS, 1957, broadcast as "Badge of Honor," an episode of *Zane Grey Theater* (also known as *Dick Powell's "Zane Grey Theater"* and *The Westerners*).

Now Is Tomorrow, 1958.

Modern knight–errant, *Tigero,* 1961.

Kelly Robinson, "So Long, Patrick Henry," *I Spy* (also known as *Danny Doyle*), NBC, 1965.

Colonel, "Married Alive," *On Stage,* syndicated and NBC, 1970.

William "Bill" Maxwell, "The Greatest American Hero," *The Greatest American Hero,* ABC, 1981.

Winston Goodhue, *Brothers–in–Law,* ABC, 1985.

Max Greene, *Early Bird,* NBC, 2005.

Television Work; Specials:

Director and producer, *Operation Breadbasket* (documentary), ABC, c. 1969.

Television Director; Episodic:

"Court of the Lion," *I Spy* (also known as *Danny Doyle*), NBC, 1966.

"Lilacs, Mr. Maxwell," *The Greatest American Hero,* ABC, 1982.

"Vanity, Says the Preacher," *The Greatest American Hero,* ABC, 1983.

Film Appearances:

Ensign George "Barney" Ross, *PT 109,* Warner Bros., 1963.

Russ Wilson, *Sunday in New York,* Metro–Goldwyn–Mayer, 1963.

Dr. Jim Hanlon, *Rhino!,* Metro–Goldwyn–Mayer, 1964.

James Butler "Wild Bill" Hickok, *The Raiders* (also known as *The Plainsmen*), Universal, 1964.

Bob Sanders, *Bob & Carol & Ted & Alice,* Columbia, 1969.

John Blake, *A Name for Evil* (also known as *The Face of Evil, The Grove,* and *There Is a Name for Evil*), Cinerama, 1970.

Thomas Luther Price, *Hannie Caulder* (also known as *Ana Caulder* and *Colt pour trois salopards*), Paramount, 1971.

Frank Boggs, *Hickey & Boggs,* United Artists, 1972.

Calvin Bryson (some sources cite role as Calvin Bronson), *The Castaway Cowboy,* Buena Vista, 1974.

Sly Wells, *Inside Out* (also known as *The Golden Heist, Hitler's Gold,* and *Ein Genialer Bluff*), Warner Bros., 1975.

Frank Sirrianni, *Breaking Point,* Twentieth Century–Fox, 1976.

Jack Colby, *The Great Scout & Cathouse Thursday* (also known as *Wildcat*), American International Pictures, 1976.

Jonas Bracken, *Sky Riders,* Twentieth Century–Fox, 1976.

Steve Esselton, *Goldengirl* (also known as *Golden–Girl* and *Golden Girl*), Avco–Embassy, 1979.

Paul Everest, "Success Wanters," *National Lampoon Goes to the Movies* (also known as *National Lampoon's "Movie Madness"*), Metro–Goldwyn–Mayer, 1981.

Mayor Tyler, *Turk 182!* (also known as *Turk 182*), Twentieth Century–Fox, 1985.

Daryl Pearson, *Big Bad Mama II,* Concorde Pictures, 1987.

Gregor, *Pucker Up and Bark Like a Dog,* Cinema Group International, 1989.

Lieutenant Connolly, *Silent Night Deadly Night 3: Better Watch Out!* (also known as *Blind Terror*), Quiet Films, 1989.

Mr. Phillips, *Timebomb,* Metro–Goldwyn–Mayer/Pathe, 1991.

Narrator, *That's Action* (documentary), Action International Pictures, 1991.

President of the United States, *The Pelican Brief,* Warner Bros., 1993.

Himself, *Warren Oates: Across the Border* (documentary), 1993.

Charles Garry, *Panther* (also known as *A fekete parduc, Les black panthers, Mustat pantterit,* and *Panteras negras*), Gramercy Pictures, 1995.

General Guardino, *Xtro 3: Watch the Skies* (also known as *Xtro: Watch the Skies*, *X–Tro 3*, and *XTRO 3: Watch the Skies*), Dorian/New Films International, 1995.

Businessperson, *Spy Hard* (also known as *Agent zero zero*, *Agent 00*, *Live and Let Spy*, *Agent 00—Mit der Lizenz zum Totlachen*, *Ciplak casus*, *Dragam add az eleted*, *Duro de espiar*, *Duro para espiar*, *Espia ... como puderes!*, *Espia como puedas*, *L'agent secret se decouvre*, *Mit der Lizenz zum Totlachen*, *Spia e lascia spiare*, *Spy Hard—Helt utan haemningar*, *Spy Hard—lupa laeikyttaeae*, *Szklanka po lapkach*, and *Tajni agent 000*), Buena Vista, 1996.

Donald Bickhart, *Most Wanted* (also known as *America's Most Wanted*), New Line Cinema, 1997.

Karl Thomassen, *Unconditional Love*, Horne Entertainment, 1999.

The chief, *Hunger*, Hunger Productions/Market Street Productions, 2000.

Judge McNamara, *NewsBreak*, Rojak Films, 2000.

Judge Winston, *Dark Summer* (also known as *The Innocents*), Santelmo Entertainment/Sceneries International, 2000.

Michael Reilly, *Farewell, My Love*, Win's Entertainment, 2001.

Isaac, *Blind Eye*, 2003.

The colonel, *The Almost Guys*, 2004, Karma Films, 2006.

Grandpa, *Santa's Slay*, Lions Gate Films, 2005.

Film Director:

Hickey & Boggs, United Artists, 1972.

Stage Appearances:

(As Robert M. Culp) Alan Draper, *The Prescott Proposals*, Broadhurst Theatre, New York City, 1953–54.

He, *He Who Gets Slapped*, Actors' Playhouse, New York City, 1956.

Ivan Gorodoulin, *Diary of a Scoundrel*, Phoenix Theatre, New York City, 1956.

Pete, *A Clearing in the Woods*, Belasco Theatre, New York City, 1957.

RECORDINGS

Videos:

(Narrator) Eminem, "Guilty Conscience," *Eminem: E*, 2000.

Himself, *Sex at 24 Frames per Second* (documentary; also known as *Playboy Presents "Sex at 24 Frames per Second: The Ultimate Journey through Sex in Cinema"*), Playboy Entertainment Group, 2003.

Music Videos:

(Narrator) Eminem with Dr. Dre, "Guilty Conscience," 1999.

Video Games:

Voice of Reed Hawke, *Voyeur*, 1994.

Voice of Dr. Wallace Breen, *Half–Life 2*, Sierra Studios, 2004.

Voice of Dr. Wallace Breen, *Half–Life 2: Episode One*, Electronic Arts, 2006.

Voice of Dr. Wallace Breen, *Half–Life 2: Episode Two*, Electronic Arts, 2007.

WRITINGS

Teleplays; Specials:

Operation Breadbasket (documentary), ABC, c. 1969.

Teleplays; Awards Presentations:

(With S. C. Dacy) *Saturn Awards*, 1981.

Teleplays; Episodic:

"Back to Crawford," *Trackdown*, NBC, 1959.

"The Swinger," *Cain's Hundred*, NBC, 1962.

"Waste: Parts 1 & 2," *The Rifleman*, ABC, 1962.

I Spy (also known as *Danny Doyle*), NBC, multiple episodes, 1965–68.

"Lilacs, Mr. Maxwell," *The Greatest American Hero*, ABC, 1982.

"Vanity, Says the Preacher," *The Greatest American Hero*, ABC, 1983.

Teleplays; Pilots:

"So Long, Patrick Henry," *I Spy* (also known as *Danny Doyle*), NBC, 1965.

Author of the pilot *Summer Soldiers* and other pilots.

Short Fiction:

Author of published short stories.

OTHER SOURCES

Periodicals:

Starlog, January, 1982, pp. 16–19, 64; February, 1982, pp. 44–48, 64.

TV Guide, November 8, 1997, pp. 24–27.

CURRY, Christopher 1948–
(Chris Curry)

PERSONAL

Original name, Christopher Root; born October 22, 1948, in Grand Rapids, MI.

Addresses: *Agent*—Silver Massetti & Szatmary, 8730 West Sunset Blvd., Suite 440, West Hollywood, CA 90069.

Career: Actor.

CREDITS

Film Appearances:

Hippie, *The Pursuit of D. B. Cooper* (also known as *Pursuit*), Universal, 1981.

Captain Bosch, *C.H.U.D.* (also known as *C.H.U.D.—New Yorkin alamaailma, C.H.U.D.—Panik in Manhattan,* and *New Yorkin alamaailma*), New World Pictures, 1984.

Mitchell, *F/X* (also known as *F/X—Murder by Illusion* and *Murder by Illusion*), Orion, 1986.

Larry's brother, *See You in the Morning*, Warner Bros., 1989.

Riot police officer, *Last Exit to Brooklyn* (also known as *Letzte Ausfahrt Brooklyn*), Cinecom International, 1989.

Chabon, *Desperate Hours*, Metro–Goldwyn–Mayer, 1990.

Officer, *The Laser Man* (also known as *The Laserman*), Original Cinema, 1990.

Tom Perkins, *The Return of Superfly*, Triton Pictures, 1990.

Father at McDonald's, *Bye Bye Love* (also known as *Au revoir mon amour, Mariti imperfetti, Tervemenoa, rakas,* and *Tres padres solteros*), Twentieth Century–Fox, 1995.

Trooper, *Bushwacked* (also known as *The Tenderfoot* and *Tenderfoots*), Twentieth Century–Fox, 1995.

Agent Stuckey, *Home Alone 3*, Twentieth Century–Fox, 1997.

Frank Sanders, *Matchbox Circus Train*, Beizer Productions/Mother Productions/Bouquet Multimedia, 1997.

Mr. Bill Rico, *Starship Troopers*, Sony Pictures Entertainment/TriStar, 1997.

Journalist, *Bulworth* (also known as *Tribulations, Bulworth—Candidato em perigo, Bulworth—Il senatore, El senador Bulworth, Koko kansan Bulworth,* and *Politicamente incorreto*), Twentieth Century–Fox, 1998.

Sam, *Summoning*, 2001.

Larry Luckman, *City of Ghosts*, Metro–Goldwyn–Mayer/United Artists, 2002.

Mr. Fisk, *Red Dragon* (also known as *A Voeroes sarkany, Den rode drage, Dragao vermelho, Dragon rojo, Dragon rouge, El dragon rojo, Punainen lohikaeaerme, Roed drake,* and *Roter Drache*), Universal, 2002.

Richard Ross, *All Your Difference*, Samuel Goldwyn Films, 2003.

Robert, *Shelter* (short film), University of Southern California, 2004.

Vice consul, *Dirt,* Mac Releasing, 2004.

Dr. Leonard Mahler, *Psychic Driving* (short film), Symerra Productions, 2005.

Voice, *Lincoln's Eyes* (short film), BRC Imagination Arts, 2005.

Ed Block, *Flags of Our Fathers*, DreamWorks/Warner Bros., 2006.

Dr. Taylor, *Crazy,* Spotlight Pictures, 2007.

Film Work:

Automated dialogue replacement voice, *Ging chaat goo si 3: Chiu kap ging chaat* (also known as *Police Story 3, Police Story 3—Supercop, Police Story 3: Supercop, Supercop, Jing cha gu shi III: Chao ji jing cha,* and *Supercop, a furia do relampago*), dubbed version released by Dimension Films, 1996, originally released by Golden Harvest Company, 1992.

Television Appearances; Miniseries:

(As Chris Curry) Officer McKenna, *The People vs. Jean Harris*, NBC, 1981.

(As Chris Curry) State trooper, *Internal Affairs*, CBS, 1988.

William Jennings Bryan, *Cross of Fire*, NBC, 1989.

(As Chris Curry) Harry Adams, *The Siege at Ruby Ridge* (also known as *Ruby Ridge: An American Tragedy*), CBS, 1996.

Television Appearances; Movies:

Laslo, *Too Young the Hero* (also known as *Too Young a Hero*), CBS, 1988.

Police officer number one, *The Boys* (also known as *The Guys*), ABC, 1991.

Captain Stevenson, *Betrayed by Love*, ABC, 1994.

Fritz Kohler, *The Song of the Lark,* broadcast as part of *The American Collection* on *Masterpiece Theatre* (also known as *ExxonMobil Masterpiece Theatre* and *Mobil Masterpiece Theatre*), PBS, 2001.

Walt Haney, *Taking Back Our Town* (also known as *A Few Good Hearts*), Lifetime, 2001.

Jackson Chandler, *Mystery Woman: Oh Baby,* The Hallmark Channel, 2006.

Television Appearances; Specials:

The Yanks Are Coming, ABC, 1974.

Surveyor, "The Almost Royal Family," *ABC Afterschool Specials*, ABC, 1984.

Television Appearances; Episodic:

Dr. Eilerton, "Life Class," *thirtysomething*, ABC, 1990.

Greg Dyson, "Aftermath," *DEA*, Fox, 1990, later known as *DEA: Special Task Force*.

Greg Dyson, "Jumping the Trampoline," *DEA*, Fox, 1990, later known as *DEA: Special Task Force*.

Greg Dyson, "Prime Mover," *DEA*, Fox, 1990, later known as *DEA: Special Task Force*.

Greg Dyson, "Under Presidential Seal," *DEA*, Fox, 1990, later known as *DEA: Special Task Force.*

Pete Florino, "Street Wise: Parts 1 & 2," *Hunter*, NBC, 1990.

"Bad Blood," *Paradise* (also known as *Guns of Paradise*), CBS, 1991.

Dr. Bruner, "Home to Roost," *Reasonable Doubts*, NBC, 1992.

Mr. Takin, "Trilogy: Part 2 (For Your Love)—June 14, 1966," *Quantum Leap*, NBC, 1992.

Brian McAlister, "That's Why the Lady Is a Stamp," *L.A. Law*, NBC, 1993.

Bitsy Mergere, "Poor Relations," *In the Heat of the Night*, CBS, 1994.

Bobby Young, "Moonlighting," *Wings*, NBC, 1994.

Special agent Tom Jerryman, "Genevieve and Fat Boy," *Chicago Hope*, CBS, 1994.

Dan Jacobs, "Dear Harris," *The Client* (also known as *John Grisham's "The Client"*), CBS, 1995.

Ronald Quantrell, "And Now for a Word," *Babylon 5* (also known as *B5*, *Babylon 5.*, and *Spacecenter Babylon 5*), syndicated, 1995.

Sheriff Chubb, "Frozen Stiff," *Murder, She Wrote*, CBS, 1995.

Captain Dykstra, "Ares," *JAG*, NBC, 1996.

Captain Dykstra, "Black Ops," *JAG*, NBC, 1996.

Jerry Wester, "Comic Relief," *Beverly Hills 90210*, Fox, 1997.

Jerry Wester, "Santa Knows," *Beverly Hills 90210*, Fox, 1997.

Jim Dolan, "All in the Family," *Chicago Hope*, CBS, 1997.

Kruger, "The Creeping Peril," *Dave's World*, CBS, 1997.

Voice of radio announcer, "Retreat and Surrender," *Malcolm & Eddie*, UPN, 1997.

Automobile driver, "11:59," *Star Trek: Voyager* (also known as *Voyager*), syndicated, 1999.

Jimm Keller, "Blue Christmas," *Crossing Jordan* (also known as *Untitled Tim Kring Project*), NBC, 2001.

Judge Langner, "Sacrifices," *Family Law*, CBS, 2001.

Colonel Lee, "We Killed Yamamoto," *The West Wing* (also known as *West Wing* and *El ala oeste de la Casablanca*), NBC, 2002.

Heinz Brucker, "Truth Takes Time," *Alias*, ABC, 2003.

Barry Henning, "Divorce Detective Style," *NYPD Blue*, ABC, 2004.

"Fractured," *Strong Medicine*, Lifetime, 2004.

Matt Stewart, "A Cornfield Grows in L.A.," *Huff* (also known as *!Huff* and *Huff—terapian tarpeessa*), Showtime, 2006.

Matt Stewart, "So ... What Brings You to Armageddon?," *Huff* (also known as *!Huff* and *Huff—terapian tarpeessa*), Showtime, 2006.

Matt Stewart, "Used, Abused, and Unenthused," *Huff* (also known as *!Huff* and *Huff—terapian tarpeessa*), Showtime, 2006.

Jared's father, "Bed, Bath and Be Gone," *General Hospital: Night Shift*, SOAPnet, 2007.

Jared's father, "Paternity Ward," *General Hospital: Night Shift*, SOAPnet, 2007.

Appeared as an attorney in "The Fifth" and "Separation Anxiety," both unaired episodes of *The Lyon's Den*, NBC.

Television Appearances; Pilots:
Daddy, *Love, American Style*, ABC, 1999.
Murray, *Patients*, 2004.

Television Work; Miniseries:
Voice–over, *Empires: The Roman Empire in the First Century* (documentary; also known as *The Roman Empire in the First Century*), PBS, 2001.

Stage Appearances:
The Spelling Bee, Playwrights Horizons Theatre, New York City, 1976.
Yasha, *The Cherry Orchard*, Roundabout Theatre Company Stage I, New York City, 1976.
Andre Beaunier, Heinrich Thode, and Stanislavky, *Isadora Duncan Sleeps with the Russian Navy*, American Place Theatre, New York City, 1977.
Jonathan Small, *The Crucifer of Blood*, Studio Arena Theatre, Buffalo, NY, 1978, and Helen Hayes Theatre, New York City, 1978–79.
Ian, *Mecca*, Quaigh Theatre, New York City, 1980.
Robert F. Kennedy, *Kennedy at Colonus*, Forty–Seventh Street Theatre, New York City, 1984.
Owen Musser, *The Foreigner*, Astor Place Theatre, New York City, 1984–86.
George Deever, *All My Sons*, Long Wharf Theatre, New Haven, CT, beginning 1986, and John Golden Theatre, New York City, 1987.
Griff, *House*, Falcon Theatre, Burbank, CA, 2001.
Dave G, *MAN.GOV*, Circus Theatricals Studio Theatre at the Hayworth, Los Angeles, c. 2005–2006.

RECORDINGS

Video Games:
Voice of Michael Paul Floyd (OSS), *Medal of Honor: Rising Sun*, Electronic Arts, 2003.
Voice, *Hitman: Blood Money*, Eidos Interactive, 2005.
Voices, *Ultimate Spider–Man*, Activision, 2005.

Screenplays; with Others:
(Uncredited) *C.H.U.D.* (also known as *C.H.U.D.—New Yorkin alamaailma*, *C.H.U.D.—Panik in Manhattan*, and *New Yorkin alamaailma*), New World Pictures, 1984.

CURRY, Mark 1964(?)–

PERSONAL

Full name, Mark G. Curry; born June 1, 1964 (some sources cite 1961), in Oakland, CA. *Education:* Studied journalism at California State University, Hayward (now

California State University, East Bay). *Avocational Interests:* Basketball, biking, old films.

Addresses: *Agent*—William Morris Agency, One William Morris Place, Beverly Hills, CA 90212.

Career: Actor, comedian, and writer. Contestant in talent competitions. Performer at various venues, including comedy clubs and Super Bowl XXV, Tampa, FL, 1991. Worked as a drugstore manager in San Francisco, CA. Affiliated with the East Oakland Youth Development Center.

Awards, Honors: Student Choice Award, 1993; named one of the best–loved stars on television, *TV Guide,* 1994.

CREDITS

Television Appearances; Series:
Host, *It's Showtime at the Apollo* (also known as *Showtime at the Apollo*), Showtime, 1992–93.
Mark Cooper, *Hangin' with Mr. Cooper* (also known as *Super Mr. Cooper, Echt super, Mr. Cooper, Mr. Cooper et nous,* and *Vivir con Mr. Cooper*), ABC, 1992–97.
Robert Soulard, a recurring role, *The Drew Carey Show,* ABC, 2000.
Host, *Don't Forget Your Toothbrush,* Comedy Central, beginning 2000.
Host, *Coming to the Stage,* Black Entertainment Television, 2003.
Host, *Animal Tails,* PAX TV, beginning 2003.
Host, *Bachelor Pad,* ABC Family Channel, 2004.
Himself (contestant), *Celebrity Mole: Yucatan* (also known as *Celebrity Mole*), ABC, 2004.
Comedian, *Poker Royale* (also known as *Poker Royale: Comedians vs. Pros*), Game Show Network (GSN), beginning 2005.

Television Appearances; Movies:
Bob Arness, *Motocrossed,* Disney Channel, 2001.
Norton Ballard, *The Poof Point,* Disney Channel, 2001.

Television Appearances; Specials:
Fox New Year's Eve Live, Fox, 1991.
Sinbad & Friends All the Way Live ... Almost, 1991.
Himself, *One Night Stand,* HBO, 1991, 2000.
Mark Cooper, *ABC Prime Time Preview Special,* ABC, 1992.
Cohost, *Dick Clark's "New Year's Rockin' Eve,"* ABC, 1992, 1993.
Mark Cooper, *ABC Saturday Morning Preview Special,* ABC, 1993.

Himself, *ABC Mark Curry & Delta Burke's "Back Lot Special,"* ABC, 1994.
Himself, *Comic Relief VI,* HBO, 1994.
Bob Hope's "Christmas Show: Hopes for the Holidays," NBC, 1994.
Host, *When Stars Were Kids,* 1995.
Himself, *Mark Curry: The Other Side,* HBO, 1996.
An Evening of Stars: A Celebration of Educational Excellence Benefitting the United Negro College Fund, 1998.
Himself, *Just for Laughs: Montreal Comedy Festival,* 1999.
Himself, *"Mark Curry," Comedy Central Presents,* Comedy Central, 1999.
Voice of giant, *The Valiant Little Tailor: An Animated Special from the "Happily Ever After: Fairy Tales for Every Child" Series* (animated), HBO, 2001.
Himself, *Platinum Comedy Series: Roasting Shaquille O'Neal,* 2002.
Host, *Bachelor Pad,* ABC Family Channel, 2004.
(In archive footage) Himself, *I Was a Network Star,* 2006.

Appeared in other programs, including *HBO Comedy Showcase,* HBO.

Television Appearances; Awards Presentations:
Presenter, *The Seventh Annual Soul Train Music Awards,* syndicated, 1993.
Apollo Theater Hall of Fame, 1993.
The Essence Awards, CBS, 1993.
Host, *Jim Thorpe Pro Sports Awards* (also known as *Jim Thorpe Pro Sports Awards Presented by Footlocker*), ABC, 1993, 1994, 1995.
Presenter, *Nickelodeon's "Eighth Annual Kids' Choice Awards"* (also known as *Kids' Choice Awards*), Nickelodeon, 1995.
The First Annual Soul Train Lady of Soul Awards (also known as *Soul Train Lady of Soul Awards*), 1995.
The Second Annual Soul Train Lady of Soul Awards (also known as *Soul Train Lady of Soul Awards*), syndicated, 1996.
Host, *Caribbean Music Awards,* syndicated, 1997.
Nickelodeon's "10th Annual Kids' Choice Awards" (also known as *Kids' Choice Awards*), Nickelodeon, 1997.
The 1997 ESPY Awards, ABC, 1997.

Television Appearances; Episodic:
Coach, *"Basketball Tryouts," My Brother and Me,* Nickelodeon, 1994.
Tony Ross, *"A Tale of Two Tattles," Living Single* (also known as *My Girls*), Fox, 1994.
Grandpa, *"I Remember Grandpa," Hangin' with Mr. Cooper* (also known as *Super Mr. Cooper, Echt super, Mr. Cooper, Mr. Cooper et nous,* and *Vivir con Mr. Cooper*), ABC, 1995.
Host, *Soul Train,* syndicated, 1995.

Himself, *The Rosie O'Donnell Show,* syndicated, 1996.

Ronnie Cochran, "Power to the People's Court," *Martin,* Fox, 1997.

Sergeant Easy, "Traffic School Daze," *The Jamie Foxx Show,* The WB, 1997.

Guest host, *MAD TV* (also known as *Mad TV* and *MADtv*), Fox, 1997.

Sergeant Easy, "I Am Too Sexy for This Shot," *The Jamie Foxx Show,* The WB, 1998.

Dr. Collins, "The Pregnant Pause," *For Your Love* (also known as *You Send Me, Foer kaerleks skull,* and *Tris di cuori*), The WB, 2000.

Himself, *The Daily Show* (also known as *The Daily Show with Jon Stewart, The Daily Show with Jon Stewart Global Edition, Ha–Daily Show,* and *I satira tou Jon Stewart*), Comedy Central, 2000.

Himself, *Intimate Portrait: Holly Robinson Peete,* Lifetime, 2000.

Himself, "Episode 101," *Comic Remix,* Comedy Central, 2002.

Himself, "Episode 109," *Comic Remix,* Comedy Central, 2002.

Himself, *Pyramid* (also known as *The $100,000 Pyramid*), syndicated, 2002, 2003.

Himself, *Hollywood Squares* (also known as *H2* and *H2: Hollywood Squares*), syndicated, 2004.

Himself, *On Air with Ryan Seacrest,* syndicated, 2004.

Himself, *101 Most Unforgettable SNL Moments 80–61* (also known as *E's "101"*), E! Entertainment Television, 2004.

Himself, *The Wayne Brady Show,* syndicated, 2004.

Shorties Watchin' Shorties (animated), Comedy Central, 2004.

Max Cooper, "Big Butts," *Fat Actress,* Showtime, 2005.

Max Cooper, "Hold This," *Fat Actress,* Showtime, 2005.

Morpheus, "Get Away," *Less Than Perfect,* ABC, 2005.

Himself, *The Daily Buzz,* syndicated, 2005.

Himself, "The 'Grammy' Goes to Camp: You're a Star & Kids Are Helping Kids," *In the Mix* (also known as *In the Cutz*), Urban American Channel, 2006.

Himself, "John at ESPY Awards," *Howard Stern on Demand* (also known as *Howard TV on Demand*), iN DEMAND, 2006.

Def Comedy Jam (also known as *Russell Simmons' "Def Comedy Jam"*), HBO, 2006.

Himself, "Betty White and Mark Curry," *Back to the Grind,* TV Land, 2007.

Himself, "Hitting Rock Bottom ... Life After," *The Montel Williams Show,* syndicated, 2007.

Also appeared in other programs, including *The Arsenio Hall Show* (also known as *Arsenio*), syndicated.

Television Appearances; Pilots:

Made a pilot for a talk show, The WB, c. 1996–97.

Television Work; Series:

Creative consultant, *Hangin' with Mr. Cooper* (also known as *Super Mr. Cooper, Echt super, Mr. Coo-* *per, Mr. Cooper et nous,* and *Vivir con Mr. Cooper*), ABC, 1992–93.

Executive consultant, *Hangin' with Mr. Cooper* (also known as *Super Mr. Cooper, Echt super, Mr. Coo- per, Mr. Cooper et nous,* and *Vivir con Mr. Cooper*), ABC, 1992–97.

Television Work; Specials:

Executive producer, *Mark Curry: The Other Side,* HBO, 1996.

Film Appearances:

Antonio, *Talkin' Dirty after Dark,* New Line Cinema, 1991.

Lombard, *Panther* (also known as *A fekete parduc, Les black panthers, Mustat pantterit,* and *Panteras negras*), Gramercy Pictures, 1995.

Fly Walker, *The Fanatics* (also known as *Fumbleheads*), 1997.

Robbie, *Switchback* (also known as *Going West* and *Going West in America*), Paramount, 1997.

Stu (the cab driver), *Armageddon* (also known as *Arma- geddon—Das juengste Gericht, Armageddon— giudizio finale,* and *Armagedon*), Buena Vista, 1998.

Jeff, *A Man Is Mostly Water,* Dog Park Productions, 2000.

Drew, *Bad Boy* (also known as *Dawg*), Wartex Interna- tional, 2002.

Stage Appearances:

Performer at comedy clubs and various venues and toured with a comedy revue headlined by Damon Wayans.

Radio Appearances:

Contributed the voice of a grandmother to a radio show in Oakland, CA.

RECORDINGS

Videos:

Himself, *Paul Mooney: Jesus Is Black—So Was Cleo- patra—Know Your History* (also known as *Paul Mooney: Know Your History—Jesus Was Black ... So Was Cleopatra*), Image Entertainment, 2007.

Appeared in other videos, including videos relating to *Def Comedy Jam* (also known as *Russell Simmons' "Def Comedy Jam"*).

WRITINGS

Teleplays; Stories for Series:

Hangin' with Mr. Cooper (also known as *Super Mr. Cooper, Echt super, Mr. Cooper, Mr. Cooper et nous,* and *Vivir con Mr. Cooper*), ABC, c. 1992–97.

Teleplays; Specials:
One Night Stand, HBO, 1991, 2000.
Mark Curry: The Other Side, HBO, 1996.
"Mark Curry," *Comedy Central Presents,* Comedy Central, 1999.

Contributed material for other programs, including *HBO Comedy Showcase,* HBO.

Teleplays; with Others; Episodic:
"Episode 101," *Comic Remix,* Comedy Central, 2002.
"Episode 109," *Comic Remix,* Comedy Central, 2002.
Shorties Watchin' Shorties (animated), Comedy Central, 2004.

Contributed material for episodes of other series.

Writings for the Stage:
Curry has written material that he has performed in comedy clubs and various venues and in a touring comedy revue headlined by Damon Wayans.

Videos:
Contributor of material that has appeared in videos.

OTHER SOURCES

Books:
Contemporary Black Biography, Volume 17, Gale, 1998.

Periodicals:
Essence, December, 1993, p. 52.

CURTIS, Oliver

PERSONAL

Son of Lion and Brenda Curtis; married Andi Marie d'Sa, February 15, 2002. *Education:* London College of Printing, B.A. *Avocational Interests:* Tennis, squash.

Addresses: *Agent*—International Creative Management, 76 Oxford St., London W1D 1BS United Kingdom.

Career: Cinematographer.

Member: British Society of Cinematographers.

Awards, Honors: Television Award nomination, best photography and lighting—fiction/entertainment, British Academy of Film and Television Arts, 1999, for *Vanity Fair.*

CREDITS

Film Cinematographer:
Ballad of Reading Gaol, Frameline Productions, 1988.
Flames of Passion, Frameline Productions, 1989.
Invisible City, 1991.
Madagascar Skin, International Film Circuit, 1995.
Red (short), British Film Institute, 1996.
Love and Death on Long Island (also known as *Amour et mort a Long Island*), Lions Gate Films, 1997.
(Second unit) *The Governess,* Sony Pictures Classics, 1998.
The Wisdom of Crocodiles (also known as *Immortality*), Miramax, 1998.
Saltwater, Artificial Eye, 2000.
The Final Curtain, Universal Focus, 2002.
Esther's Pool (short), 2002.
(Additional photography) *Calendar Girls,* Buena Vista, 2003.
Owning Mahowny (also known as *La double vie de Mahowny*), Sony Pictures Classics, 2003.
The Predator, 2004.
The Wedding Date, Universal, 2005.
Death at a Funeral (also known as *Sterben fur anfanger*), Metro–Goldwyn–Mayer, 2007.

Film Director:
Trotsky's Home Movies (documentary), 1990.
Affairs of the Heart (documentary), 1992.

Film Appearances:
Cinematographer Style, 2006.

Television Cinematographer; Miniseries:
Vanity Fair, BBC and Arts and Entertainment, 1998.

Television Cinematographer; Movies:
Our Boy, BBC, 1997.
Bait, ITV, 2002.
Uncle Adolph, 2005.

Television Director; Specials:
Pontecorvo: The Dictatorship of Truth (documentary), 1992.

D

D'ABO, Maryam 1960(?)–
  (Marymam D'Abo)

PERSONAL

Born December 27, 1960 (some sources cite 1961), in London, England; father, a banker; mother, a nonprofit executive; cousin of Olivia d'Abo (an actress) and Mike d'Abo (a singer); married Hugh Hudson (a director), November, 2003. *Education:* Attended the London College of Printing; studied at the Drama Centre, London. *Avocational Interests:* Chalk and pencil drawing, skiing, cycling.

Addresses: *Manager*—Polaris Entertainment, 8899 Beverly Blvd., Suite 812, West Hollywood, CA 90048.

Career: Actress, producer, and writer.

CREDITS

Film Appearances:

Analise Mercier, *Xtro,* New Line Cinema, 1983.
Nathalie, *Until September,* Metro–Goldwyn–Mayer, 1984.
French girlfriend, *White Nights* (also known as *Biale noce, Die Nacht der Entscheidung, Hvide naetter, Il sole a mezzanote, Noches del sol, O sol da meia–noite, O sol da meia noite, Sol de medianoche, Valkeat yoet, Vita naetter,* and *White Nights—Nacht der Entscheidung*), Columbia, 1985.
Kara Milovy, *The Living Daylights* (also known as *Ian Fleming's "The Living Daylights," Icecold Mission,* and *James Bond 007: The Living Daylights*), United Artists, 1987.
Sarah Walkins (some sources cite Sarah Watkins), *Money,* United International Pictures, 1991.

(As Marymam D'Abo) Madeleine, *Leon the Pig Farmer* (also known as *Leon*), Unapix Films/Cinevista, 1992.
Susan, *Immortal Sins* (also known as *Veil of Dreams, Vengeance with a Kiss,* and *Besos en la oscuridad*), 1992.
Beverly, *Tropical Heat* (also known as *Tropical Nights*), Prism Entertainment, 1993.
Cheryl, *Shootfighter: Fight to the Death* (also known as *Shootfighter*), New Films International/Vision International, 1993.
Jacki, *Tomcat: Dangerous Desires* (also known as *Dangerous Desires*), Republic Pictures, 1993.
Brooke Daniels, *Stalked* (also known as *Traquee*), Republic Pictures, 1994.
Caroline, *Solitaire for Two* (also known as *Solitaire for 2* and *The Tender Trap*), Trident Releasing, 1994.
Claire Burke, *Double Obsession* (also known as *Mirror Image*), 1994.
Diana, *The Browning Version,* Paramount, 1994.
Beatrice Baxter, *Savage Hearts,* August Entertainment/Bratton/Wavepower Navigation, 1995.
Sara number two, *Romance and Rejection* (also known as *So This Is Romance?*), Bloomsbury Films, 1996.
Geneveve, *An American Affair,* TSC, 1997.
Alison, *The Sea Change* (also known as *Cambio de rumbo*), Winchester Films, 1998.
Linda Bryce, *Trespassing* (also known as *Evil Remains*), Screen Media Ventures, 2004.
Margaux, *San–Antonio* (also known as *Spy Zone*), Pathe, 2004.
Julie, *L'enfer* (also known as *Hell*), Diaphana Films, 2005.
Queen Rosalind, *The Prince & Me II: The Royal Wedding,* First Look International, 2006.

Television Appearances; Series:

Ta'ra, *Something Is Out There,* NBC, 1988.

Television Appearances; Miniseries:

Dominique Masson, *Master of the Game,* CBS, 1984.

(As Marymam D'Abo) Solange, *If Tomorrow Comes*, CBS, 1986.

Martine, *The Man Who Lived at the Ritz*, syndicated, 1988.

Anne Summerton, *Not a Penny More, Not a Penny Less*, USA Network, 1990.

Amalia Guishar, *Doctor Zhivago* (also known as *Zhivago*), Granada Television, 2002, broadcast on *Masterpiece Theatre* (also known as *ExxonMobil Masterpiece Theatre* and *Mobil Masterpiece Theatre*), PBS, 2003.

Queen Hecuba, *Helen of Troy*, USA Network, 2003.

(And in archive footage) Herself, *James Bond Casino*, Veronica (the Netherlands), 2006.

Television Appearances; Movies:

Claudie DeBrille, *Behind Enemy Lines* (also known as *92 Grosvenor Street*), NBC, 1985.

Second court lady, *Arthur the King* (also known as *Merlin and the Sword* and *Merlin & the Sword*), CBS, 1985.

Angelique, *Nightlife*, USA Network, 1989.

Captain Jessie Teegs, *Timelock*, Sci–Fi Channel, 1996.

Francis Koln, *The Point Men* (also known as *Point Men*), Starz!, 2001.

Television Appearances; Specials:

(Uncredited) Kara Milovy, *The James Bond Story* (also known as *007: The James Bond Story*), American Movie Classics, 1999.

Herself, *James Bond: A BAFTA Tribute*, BBC, 2002.

Host and narrator, *Bond Girls Are Forever*, American Movie Classics, 2002, re–edited version known as *Bond Girls Are Forever 2006*.

Herself, *David Walliams: My Life with James Bond 007*, Independent Television (England), 2006.

Television Appearances; Episodic:

Lauren, "Previous Convictions," *TECX*, 1990.

Maggie, "L'epouvantail," *Les cadavres exquis de Patricia Highsmith* (also known as *Patricia Highsmith's "Tales"* and *Cadavres exquis*), BBC, 1990.

Barbara Calloway, "The Monte Carlo Murders," *Murder, She Wrote*, CBS, 1992.

Greta Kreutzel, "Well Cooked Hams," *Tales from the Crypt* (also known as *HBO's "Tales from the Crypt"*), HBO, 1993.

Zoe, "Another Woman's Lipstick," *Red Shoe Diaries* (also known as *Foxy Fantasies, Zalman King's "Red Shoe Diaries," Diarios del zapato rojo*, and *Skjulte laengsler*), Showtime, 1993, released on video as part of *Red Shoe Diaries 3: Another Woman's Lipstick*, 1993.

Cambria Elon, "Takeover," *Space Precinct* (also known as *Brigada espacial* and *Space Cops—Tatort Demeter City*), syndicated and Sky One, 1995.

(In archive footage) Jacki, "Brain–Damage Night," *Joe Bob's Drive–In Theater*, The Movie Channel, 1995.

Herself, "Bond Girls," *The E! True Hollywood Story* (also known as *Bond Girls: The E! True Hollywood Story* and *THS*), E! Entertainment Television, 1996.

(And in archive footage) Herself, "Bond Girls Are Forever/The Story of 'V'/A Moment with … Tristan Taormino," *SexTV*, 2004.

Television Guest Appearances; Episodic:

Today (also known as *NBC News Today* and *The Today Show*), NBC, 1987.

The Word, Channel 4 (England), 1990.

Breakfast with Frost, BBC, 2002.

Open House (also known as *Open House with Gloria Hunniford*), Channel 5 (England), 2002.

RI:SE, Channel 4, 2003.

The Terry and Gaby Show, Channel 5, 2003.

This Morning (also known as *This Morning with Richard and Judy*), Independent Television (England), 2003.

The Film Programme (also known as *Film 2006*), BBC, 2006.

This Week, BBC, 2006.

Television Appearances; Pilots:

Ta'ra, *Something Is Out There*, NBC, 1988.

Television Appearances; Other:

Marie, *Les idiots*, 1987.

Television Work; Specials:

Executive producer, *Bond Girls Are Forever*, American Movie Classics, 2002, re–edited version known as *Bond Girls Are Forever 2006*.

Creator and co–executive producer, *Bearing Witness*, Arts and Entertainment, 2005.

Stage Appearances:

Macon, *Abundance*, Riverside Studios Theatre, London, 1995.

Inessa Armand, *Lenin in Love*, New End Theatre, Hampstead, London, 2000.

Radio Appearances:

Appeared in radio programs, including an interview for BBC Radio Wiltshire, 2004.

RECORDINGS

Videos:

Girlfriend of main character in "Stay Alone," *Now Voyager*, 1992.

Zoe in episode "Another Woman's Lipstick," *Red Shoe Diaries 3: Another Woman's Lipstick,* 1993.

(In archive footage) Herself, *And the Word Was Bond,* 1999.

4Herself, *Inside "The Living Daylights"* (short), Sony Pictures Home Entertainment, 2000.

(In archive footage) Herself, *The Music of James Bond* (short), Metro–Goldwyn–Mayer/United Artists Home Entertainment, 2000.

(In archive footage) Herself, *Premiere Bond: Opening Nights* (short), Metro–Goldwyn–Mayer Home Entertainment, 2006.

WRITINGS

Teleplays; Specials:
Bond Girls Are Forever, American Movie Classics, 2002, re–edited version known as *Bond Girls Are Forever 2006.*

OTHER SOURCES

Periodicals:
Biography, April, 2003.
TV Guide, November 2, 2002, p. 8.

DALEY, John Francis 1985–
(John F. Daley)

PERSONAL

Born July 20, 1985, in Wheeling, IL; son of R. F. (an actor) and Nancy (a singer, pianist, and piano teacher) Daley. *Avocational Interests:* Playing piano and drums, Kung Fu (black belt).

Addresses: *Agent*—The Kohner Agency, 9300 Wilshire Blvd., Suite 555, Beverly Hills, CA 90212; Peters Fraser and Dunlop, 373 Park Ave. South, 5th Floor, New York, NY 10016. *Manager*—The Management Company, 2030 Pinehurst Rd., Los Angeles, CA 90068.

Career: Actor. Dayplayer (band), singer and keyboardist.

Awards, Honors: YoungStar Award nominations, best young actor or performer in a comedy television series and best young ensemble cast—television (with others), Young Artist Award nomination (with others), best performance in a television series—young ensemble,

2000, all for *Freaks and Geeks;* Young Artist Award nomination, best performance in a television comedy series—supporting young actor, 2001, for *The Geena Davis Show.*

CREDITS

Film Appearances:
Allerd Fishbein, *Allerd Fishbein's in Love* (short), 2000.
Rodney, *View from the Top,* Miramax, 2003.
Mitch, *Waiting ...,* Lions Gate Films, 2005.
Himself, *The Works* (documentary), Lions Gate Films Home Entertainment, 2006.
Tom, *Clark and Michael* (short), Innertube, 2006.
Himself, *A Recipe for Comedy* (documentary short), 2007.
Pat, *5–25–77,* 2007.

Film Director:
What Babies Do (short), 2001.

Television Appearances; Series:
Sam Weir, *Freaks and Geeks,* NBC, 1999–2000.
Anthony Ward, *Boston Public,* Fox, 2000–2001.
Carter Ryan, *The Geena Davis Show,* ABC, 2000–2001.
(As John F. Daley) Jim, *Kitchen Confidential,* Fox, 2005–2006.

Television Appearances; Specials:
Macy's Thanksgiving Day Parade, NBC, 1999.
Prism Awards 2000, syndicated, 2000.
100 Greatest Teen Stars, VH1, 2006.

Television Appearances; Pilots:
Tom Timlin, *The Call,* ABC, 2007.

Television Appearances; Episodic:
Panelist, *The List,* VH1, 1999.
Erik, "Walden Pond," *The Ellen Show,* CBS, 2001.
Spencer, "Eves Wide Open," *Spin City,* ABC, 2002.
Grant Binder, "Time and Punishment," *Regular Joe,* ABC, 2003.
Jace Crosby, "Roadhouse Blues," *Judging Amy,* CBS, 2004.
Kevin, "The Third Date," *Stacked,* Fox, 2006.

Major Tours:
Young Tommy, *The Who's "Tommy,"* U.S. and German cities, 1994.

RECORDINGS

Music Videos:
Abandoned Pools' "Mercy Kiss," 2001.

DAMON, Mark 1933–

PERSONAL

Original name, Alan Mark Harris; born April 22, 1933, in Chicago, IL; married; wife's name, Maggie; children: Jonathan Louis. *Education:* University of California, Los Angeles, B.A. and M.B.A.

Addresses: *Office*—MDP Worldwide, 1925 Century Park East, 17th Floor, Los Angeles, CA 90067–2701; Foresight Unlimited, 2934 1/2 Beverly Glen Circle, Suite 900, Bel Air, CA 90077.

Career: Producer, executive, and actor. Twentieth Century–Fox, contract actor, beginning 1950s; PAC (Italian film distribution company), head of foreign acquisitions department, beginning 1974; Producers Sales Organization, president, beginning 1977, chair and chief executive officer, beginning 1982; PSO/Delphia, chair and chief executive officer, beginning 1984; Vision Producers and Distributors Group, cofounder, 1987, chief executive officer and chair of Vision Productions and Vision International, 1987–93; MDP Worldwide (also known as Mark Damon Productions), Los Angeles, founder, 1993, and chair, beginning 1993; MDP/Behaviour Worldwide, founder, 1998; Behaviour Communications, chair and chief executive officer, beginning 2000; Foresight Unlimited, Bel Air, CA, principal.

Member: American Film Marketing Association (founding member).

Awards, Honors: Tied for Golden Globe Award, most promising male newcomer, 1961; Independent Spirit Award (with others), best first feature, Independent Feature Project/West, 2004, for *Monster.*

CREDITS

Film Executive Producer:
The Choirboys (also known as *Aenglarna*), Universal, 1977.
Das Boot (also known as *The Boat, A tengeralattjaro, El barco, El submarino (Das Boot), Le bateau, Sukellusvene U–96, To ypovryhio, U–baaten, U–Boot 96,* and *Ypovryhio U–96—Epistrofi stin Kolasi*), Columbia, 1981, subtitled version released by Triumph Releasing, 1982, extended version released as a miniseries on the German television networks Suddeutscher Rundfunk (SDR) and Westdeutscher Rundfunk (WDR), 1985, director's cut released in 1997.

Die unendliche Geschichte (also known as *The Never-Ending Story, A historia sem fim, Den oaendliga historien, Ha–Sippur Sh'Eino Nigmar, Historia interminavel, L'histoire sans fin, La historia interminable, La historia sin fin, La storia infinita, Niekonczaca sie opowiesc, Paeaettymaetoen tarina,* and *Vegtelen toertenet*), Warner Bros., 1984.
The Clan of the Cave Bear, Twentieth Century–Fox, 1986.
8 Million Ways to Die, TriStar, 1986.
Flight of the Navigator (also known as *Navigator* and *The Navigator*), Buena Vista, 1986.
Short Circuit, Twentieth Century–Fox, 1986.
Co–executive producer, *The Lost Boys,* Warner Bros., 1987.
High Spirits, TriStar, 1988.
Mac and Me, Orion, 1988.
I Come in Peace (also known as *Dark Angel*), Epic/Triumph Releasing, 1990.
Vietnam, Texas, Columbia, 1990.
Beastmaster 2: Through the Portal of Time (also known as *Beastmaster 2—Der Zeitspringer, Beastmaster 2—genom tidsbarriaeren, Beastmaster 2—petojen herra, Dar l'invincible 2—La puerta del tiempo, En senor de las bestias 2: La puerta del tiempo, O portal do tempo,* and *Wladca zwierzat 2*), New Line Cinema, 1991.
Diary of a Hitman, Columbia, 1991.
Inner Sanctum, Columbia, 1991.
Wild Orchid II: Two Shades of Blue (also known as *Blue Movie Blue* and *Wild Orchid 2: Blue Movie Blue*), Columbia, 1991.
Stalingrad, Entertainment/Senator Film, 1993, subtitled version, Strand Releasing, 1995.
The Jungle Book (also known as *Rudyard Kipling's "The Jungle Book"* and *El libro de la selva*), Buena Vista, 1994.
The Blackout, Trimark Pictures, 1997.
Deceiver (also known as *Liar*), Metro–Goldwyn–Mayer, 1997.
Loved, Imperial Entertainment, 1997.
Orgazmo, October Films, 1997.
The Second Jungle Book: Mowgli & Baloo (also known as *Jungle Book 2: Mowgli and Baloo* and *Rudyard Kipling's "The Second Jungle Book: Mowgli and Baloo"*), TriStar, 1997.
A Dog of Flanders, Warner Bros., 1999.
Grizzly Falls, Providence Entertainment, 1999.
Eye of the Beholder (also known as *Voyeur*), Destination Films, 2000.
Love & Sex, Lions Gate Films, 2000.
The Body (also known as *Das Geheimnisvolle Grab*), TriStar, 2001.
The Musketeer, Universal, 2001.
Extreme Ops (also known as *Extremist*), Paramount, 2002.
FeardotCom (also known as *Fear Dot Com*), Warner Bros., 2002.

The United States of Leland (also known as *State of Mind*), Manga Films, 2003, Paramount Classics, 2004.

11:14, 2003, New Line Cinema, 2005.

Beyond the Sea (also known as *Bobby Darin Biopic*), Lions Gate Films, 2004.

The Upside of Anger (also known as *An deiner Schulter*), New Line Cinema, 2005.

Film Producer:

The Arena (also known as *The Naked Warriors, La rivolta delle gladiatrici,* and *Livia, una virgine per l'impero*), New World Pictures, 1973.

9 1/2 Weeks (also known as *Nine 1/2 Weeks, 9 1/2 Weeks,* and *9-1/2 Weeks*), Metro–Goldwyn–Mayer/United Artists, 1986.

Coproducer, *Bat*21* (also known as *Air force—Bat 21* and *Bat 21*), TriStar, 1988.

Wild Orchid, Triumph Releasing, 1989.

Monster, Newmarket Films, 2003.

Coproducer, *O Jerusalem* (also known as *Beyond Friendship* and *O' Jerusalem*), Samuel Goldwyn Films, 2006.

Captivity, Lions Gate Films/After Dark Films, 2007.

Film Appearances:

Gregg Linden, *Inside Detroit,* Columbia, 1955.

Private Lambert, *Screaming Eagles,* Allied Artists, 1956.

Private Terry, *Between Heaven and Hell,* Twentieth Century–Fox, 1956.

Tommy Price, *Young and Dangerous,* Twentieth Century–Fox, 1957.

Russ Lippincott, *Life Begins at 17,* Columbia, 1958.

Twig Webster, *The Party Crashers,* Paramount, 1958.

Frank, *This Rebel Breed* (also known as *The Black Rebels* and *Three Shades of Love*), Warner Bros., 1960.

Philip Winthrop, *House of Usher* (also known as *The Fall of the House of Usher*), American International Pictures, 1960.

Aldo, *The Reluctant Saint* (also known as *Joseph Desa*), Davis/Royal, 1962.

(Uncredited) Private Harris, *The Longest Day* (also known as *The D. Day*), Twentieth Century–Fox, 1962.

Peccati d'estate (also known as *Island Affair*), 1962.

Il giorno piu corto (also known as *The Shortest Day* and *Il giorno piu corto commedia umoristica*), Titanus Distribuzione, 1962, dubbed version, Medallion Pictures, 1963.

Duke Eduardo, *Beauty and the Beast,* United Artists, 1963.

Stephen Children, *The Young Racers,* American International Pictures, 1963.

Vladimir d'Urfe, "The Wurdalak," *I tre volti della paura* (also known as *Black Christmas, Black Sabbath, The Three Faces of Fear, The Three Faces of Terror,* and *Les trois visages de la peur*), American International Pictures, 1963.

El Kebir, *Il figlio di Cleopatra* (also known as *Son of Cleopatra*), 1964.

Fernando Herrero, *I cento cavalieri* (also known as *Hundred Horsemen, 100 Horsemen, Son of El Cid, Die Hundert Ritter,* and *Los cien caballeros*), 1964.

Pietro I (king of Castile), *Sfida al re di Castiglia* (also known as *The Tyrant of Castile, El rey cruel,* and *Pedro el Cruel*), 1964.

Dr. Bardir, *Agente segreto 777—Operazione mistero* (also known as *Secret Agent 777*), 1966.

Johnny Oro and Ringo, *Ringo and His Golden Pistol* (also known as *Johnny Oro*), Sanson, 1966.

Luis, *Como te amo!* (also known as *How Do I Love You?* and *Dio, come ti amo*), 1966.

Brown, *Un treno per Durango* (also known as *Train for Durango* and *Un tren para Durango*), 1967.

Title role, *Johnny Yuma,* Clover, 1967.

Johnny, *Tutto per tutto* (also known as *All Out, Copperface, Go for Broke, One for All,* and *La hora del coraje*), 1967.

Lawrence, *La morte non conta i dollari* (also known as *Death at Owell Rock, Death Does Not Count the Dollars,* and *No Killing without Dollars*), 1967.

Vittorio, *Colpo doppio del camaleonte d'oro,* 1967.

American prisoner, *Kiedy milosc byla zbrodnia* (also known as *Rassenschande: When Love Was a Crime*), 1968.

Ferguson, *Requiescant* (also known as *Kill and Pray, Kill and Say Your Prayers, Let Them Rest,* and *Moegen sie in Frieden ruhen*), 1968.

Richard Barrett, *Nude ... si muore* (also known as *The Miniskirt Murders, Naked You Die, School Girl Killer, The Young, the Evil & the Savage,* and *Sette virgini per il diavolo*), American International Pictures, 1968.

Wally Richardson, *Lo sbarco di Anzio* (also known as *Anzio* and *The Battle for Anzio*), Columbia, 1968.

Quien grita venganza? (also known as *Cry for Revenge, Dead Men Don't Count!,* and *I morti non si contano*), 1968.

Temptation, [Italy], 1968.

Allen, *L'arciere di Sherwood* (also known as *Long Live Robin Hood, The Scalawag Bunch, El arquero de Sherwood, L'arciere di fuoco,* and *La grande chevauchee de Robin des bois*), 1970.

Ivanhoe, *La spada normanna* (also known as *The Norman Swordsman, La espada normanda,* and *Le retour d'Ivanhoe*), 1971.

Veritas, *Lo chiamavano Verita* (also known as *They Called Him Truth* and *They Call Him Veritas*), 1971.

Leoni di Petersburgo (also known as *Lions of St. Petersburg*), 1971.

Posate le pistole, reverendo (also known as *Pistol Packin' Preacher*), 1971.

Questa liberta de avere ... le ali bagnate, 1971.

Domenico, *Confessioni segrete di un convento di clausura,* 1972.

Felipe, *Monta in sella, figlio di ...!* (also known as *Great Treasure Hunt, Cinque per l'oro di los Quadros,* and *Repoker de bribones*), 1972.

Riano, *Little Mother* (also known as *Blood Queen, Don't Cry for Me, Little Mother, Immortal Mistress, Mother, Woman of the Year,* and *Sie nannten ihn kleine Mutter*), Audubon, 1972.

Duke Lionello Shandwell, *Byleth* (also known as *Byleth—il demone dell'incesto* and *Il demone dell'incesto*), 1973.

Karl Schiller, *Il plenilunio delle vergini* (also known as *The Devil's Wedding Night* and *Full Moon of the Virgins*), Dimension Films, 1973.

Peter, *La tumba de la isla maldita* (also known as *Crypt of the Living Dead, Vampire Woman, Vampire Women,* and *Young Hannah: Queen of the Vampires*), Atlas Films, 1973.

Fairbanks, *Es knallt—und die Engel singen* (also known as *Bang, and the Angels Sing, Do I Kill You or Do You Kill Me?, Les Humphries: Es knallt—und die Engel singen, Lo matas tu o lo mato yo,* and *Mena forte piu forte ... che mi piace!*), 1974.

George Thomas, *There Is No 13,* Film Ventures, 1974.

Member of Columbus's crew, *Stuck on You!,* Troma Entertainment, 1984.

Wayland's father, *Deceiver* (also known as *Liar*), Metro–Goldwyn–Mayer, 1997.

Also appeared in *A Scaffold for Django.*

Television Executive Producer; Miniseries:

Das Boot (also known as *The Boat* and *Le bateau;* extended version of the 1981 feature film *Das Boot*), Suddeutscher Rundfunk (SDR) and Westdeutscher Rundfunk (WDR), 1985.

War and Peace, multiple networks, 2007.

Television Executive Producer; Movies:

The Winner, The Movie Channel, 1997.

The I Inside, Starz!, 2003.

Television Executive Producer; Pilots:

Red Shoe Diaries (also known as *Red Shoe Diaries the Movie* and *Wild Orchid III: Red Shoe Diaries*), Showtime, 1992.

Television Appearances; Movies:

Miguel Serrano, "Zorro: The Postponed Wedding," *Walt Disney Presents* (also known as *Disneyland, Disneylandia, Disney's Wonderful World, The Disney Sunday Movie, The Magical World of Disney, Walt Disney, Walt Disney's Wonderful World of Color,* and *The Wonderful World of Disney*), ABC, 1961.

Television Appearances; Episodic:

Bill, "The Prison Within," *Cavalcade of America* (also known as *Cavalcade Theater, DuPont Cavalcade Theater, DuPont Presents the Cavalcade Theater,* and *DuPont Theater*), ABC, 1956.

Harold, "The Hefferan Family," *The 20th Century–Fox Hour* (also known as *The Fox Hour of Stars*), CBS, 1956.

Ray Clements, "Place of Shadows," *Alfred Hitchcock Presents,* CBS, 1956.

Rusty at the age of seventeen, "In Times Like These," *The 20th Century–Fox Hour* (also known as *The Fox Hour of Stars*), CBS, 1956.

"Star and Shield," *Cavalcade of America* (also known as *Cavalcade Theater, DuPont Cavalcade Theater, DuPont Presents the Cavalcade Theater,* and *DuPont Theater*), ABC, 1956.

Dave, "Patrol," *Panic!* (also known as *No Warning*), NBC, c. 1957.

Mickey, "East Side Story," *The Ann Sothern Show,* CBS, 1958.

Running Horse, "A Matter of Honor," *Tales of Wells Fargo* (also known as *Wells Fargo*), NBC, 1958.

Eugenio, "The Iron Box," *Zorro,* ABC, 1959.

"The Chinatown Story," *The Lineup* (also known as *San Francisco Beat*), CBS, 1959.

Cliff White, "The Lie," *The June Allyson Show* (also known as *The DuPont Show Starring June Allyson* and *The DuPont Show with June Allyson*), CBS, 1960.

Victor Winters, "The Big Shot," *National Velvet,* NBC, 1960.

"The Case of Corporal Newman," *Lock Up,* syndicated, 1960.

Carl Wakila, "Caves of Pele," *Hawaiian Eye,* ABC, 1961.

Nick Archer, "Decoy," *The Protectors,* syndicated, 1973.

Vendor, "Postcards from the Faultline," *Gabriel's Fire,* ABC, 1991.

Television Appearances; Pilots:

Calling CQ, 1960.

Artie Dale, *The McGonigle,* NBC, 1961.

RECORDINGS

Videos:

Himself, *Killing Priscilla,* 2000.

Himself, *A Life in Film* (short), Anchor Bay Entertainment, 2007.

OTHER SOURCES

Periodicals:

Forbes, February 27, 1984, pp. 154–56.

DANIELOVITCH, Issur
See DOUGLAS, Kirk

D'ARBANVILLE, Patti 1951–
(Patti D'Arbanville–Quinn, Patti D'Arbanville Quinn)

PERSONAL

Full name, Patricia D'Arbanville; born May 25, 1951, in New York, NY; daughter of George (a bartender) and Jean (an artist; maiden name, Egan) D'Arbanville; married Roger Miremont (an actor), August 1, 1975 (some sources cite 1976; divorced, 1980); married Steve Curry (an actor, singer, and farmer), April 26, 1980 (divorced, 1981); married Terry Quinn (a firefighter and bar owner), June 15, 1993 (divorced, March 12, 2002); children: (with Don Johnson, an actor) Jesse Wayne; (third marriage) Emmelyn, Alexandra, Liam. *Education:* Trained for the stage with Herbert Berghof, c. 1972.

Addresses: *Agent*—Ellis Talent Group, 4705 Laurel Canyon Blvd., Valley Village, CA 91607. *Manager*—Rob Kolker Management, 44 West 10th St., New York, NY 10011.

Career: Actress. Worked as a professional model and a disk jockey; appeared in advertisements. Worked at Le Figaro Cafe, New York City.

Awards, Honors: *DramaLogue* Award, best actress, c. 1987, for *Italian American Reconciliation; Soap Opera Digest* Award nomination, favorite scene stealer, 2000, for *Guiding Light.*

CREDITS

Film Appearances:
Tuesday and Blue Silk (short film), c. 1959.
Secretary, *Erotic Salad,* 1967.
Patti (Geri's lover), *Flesh* (also known as *Andy Warhol's "Flesh"*), Sherpix Productions, 1968.
La maison (also known as *The House*), 1970.
Hillary, *La saignee* (also known as *The Blood Letting, The Contract, Manhunt for Murder,* and *A denti stretti*), 1971.
Patti, *L'amour,* Altura, 1973.
Betty Fargo, *Rancho Deluxe,* United Artists, 1975.
Title role, *Bilitis,* Societe nouvelle de cinema, 1976.
The Crazy American Girl (also known as *La fille d'Amerique*), 1977.
Sally Johnson, *Big Wednesday* (also known as *Summer of Innocence*), Warner Bros., 1978.
Mai shen qi (also known as *The Contract* and *Maai san kai*), 1978.
Donna Washington, *The Main Event,* Warner Bros., 1979.

Shirley, *Time after Time,* Warner Bros., 1979.
Angie Barnes, *Hog Wild* (also known as *Les fous de la moto*), Avco–Embassy, 1980.
Cathy Burke, *The Fifth Floor,* Film Ventures, 1980.
Darcy, *Modern Problems,* Twentieth Century–Fox, 1981.
Herself, *Sois belle et tais–toi,* 1981.
Angie, *The Boys Next Door* (also known as *Big Shots* and *No Apparent Motive*), Republic Pictures/New World Pictures, 1985.
Sherry Nugil, *Real Genius,* TriStar, 1985.
Cori, *Call Me,* Vestron Pictures, 1988.
Jean, *Fresh Horses,* Columbia, 1988.
Cathy Smith, *Wired* (also known as *Belushi—Wired* and *John Belushi—Sex & Drugs in Hollywood*), Taurus Entertainment, 1989.
Barbara Griffin, *Frame–Up II: The Cover Up* (also known as *Deadly Conspiracy*), 1992.
(As Patti D'Arbanville–Quinn) Ellen Renard, *The Fan* (also known as *Fan*), Columbia/TriStar, 1996.
(Uncredited) Mrs. Shivers, *I Know What You Did Last Summer* (also known as *Last Summer*), Columbia, 1997.
Shirley Trainor, *Fathers' Day,* Warner Bros., 1997.
Elaine Tiger, *Archibald the Rainbow Painter* (also known as *The Homefront*), Empty Box Productions, 1998.
Iris, *Celebrity* (also known as *Woody Allen Fall Project 1997, Celebridades, Celebrity—kuuluisuus, Celebrity—schoen, reich, beruhmt, Diasimotites, Kaend-isliv,* and *Sztarral szemben*), Miramax, 1998.
Celia, *Personal Velocity: Three Portraits* (also known as *Personal Velocity*), Metro–Goldwyn–Mayer/United Artists, 2002.
Margie Bianco, *A Tale of Two Pizzas,* 2003, Cockeyed Caravan, 2005.
Donna's neighbor, *World Trade Center* (also known as *September* and *Untitled Oliver Stone September 11 Project*), Paramount, 2006.
Esmeralda, *Perfect Stranger,* Columbia, 2007.
Gladys, *You Belong to Me,* Mama's Boy Productions/Offhollywood Digital, 2007.
Sonya Weitzman, *The Marconi Bros.,* Blueprint Film Group/Old World Films, 2008.

Television Appearances; Series:
Amber Twine, *Wiseguy,* CBS, 1989.
Christy Carson, *Another World* (also known as *Another World: Bay City*), NBC, 1992–93.
Roxanne, *South Beach,* NBC, 1993.
(As Patti D'Arbanville–Quinn) Lieutenant Virginia Cooper, *New York Undercover* (also known as *Uptown Undercover*), Fox, 1994–97.
Selena Davis, *Guiding Light,* CBS, 1998–2000.
Rose Boscorelli, *Third Watch,* NBC, between 2000 and 2005.

Television Appearances; Miniseries:
Michele, *Once an Eagle,* NBC, 1976.

Television Appearances; Movies:
Lucy Conte, *Crossing the Mob* (also known as *Philly Boy*), NBC, 1988.
Lauren Crane, *Snow Kill,* USA Network, 1990.
Marilyn Wells, *Bad to the Bone,* ABC, 1997.

Television Appearances; Specials:
Lucinda, "Blind Spot," *Hallmark Hall of Fame,* CBS, 1993.

Television Appearances; Episodic:
Maggie, "The Great Boat Race," *Code R,* CBS, 1977.
"Where's There's Smoke," *Eddie Capra Mysteries,* NBC, 1978.
Bianca Blake, "Angels of the Deep," *Charlie's Angels,* ABC, 1980.
Jessica Collins, "Run to Death," *Barnaby Jones,* CBS, 1980.
Babette, "Guillotine," *Darkroom,* ABC, 1982.
Leslie Andler, "Hit, Run, and Homicide," *Murder, She Wrote,* NBC, 1984.
Mrs. Stone, "Back in the World," *Miami Vice* (also known as *Gold Coast* and *Miami Unworthiness*), NBC, 1985.
"Final Transmission," *Crime Story,* NBC, 1986.
Tough Cookies, CBS, 1986.
Jordan Sims, "Payback," *Midnight Caller,* NBC, 1988.
Theresa Demante, "How Will They Remember Me?," *Wiseguy,* CBS, 1989.
"Spinning Wheel," *The Hitchhiker* (also known as *Deadly Nightmares* and *Le voyageur*), USA Network, 1989.
Betty Drake, "Wedded Bliss," *Law & Order* (also known as *Law & Order Prime*), NBC, 1992.
(As Patti D'Arbanville–Quinn) Amber Vallon, "Guns and Gossip," *My So–Called Life* (also known as *Someone Like Me*), ABC, 1994.
(As D'Arbanville–Quinn) Amber Vallon, "On the Wagon," *My So–Called Life* (also known as *Someone Like Me*), ABC, 1994.
(As D'Arbanville–Quinn) Amber Vallon, "Other People's Mothers," *My So–Called Life* (also known as *Someone Like Me*), ABC, 1994.
Big Linda, "Death and Dishonor," *The John Larroquette Show* (also known as *Larroquette*), NBC, 1994.
(As Patti D'Arbanville Quinn) Caroline Hardy, "Dead Issue," *L.A. Law,* NBC, 1994.
(As D'Arbanville–Quinn) Herself, "Patti D'Arbanville–Quinn," *Lauren Hutton and ...,* 1995.
Darlene Everett, "The Twenty Percent Solution," *Homicide: Life on the Street* (also known as *H: LOTS* and *Homicide*), NBC, 1998.
Maggie, "The Cost of Freedom," *The Division* (also known as *Heart of the City*), Lifetime, 2003.
Wallace Forsythe, "Sofia Lopez," *Nip/Tuck,* FX Network, 2003.
Lorraine Calluzzo, "All Happy Families," *The Sopranos* (also known as *Made in Jersey, Sopranos, Die*

Sopranos, Familia Soprano, Les Soprano, Los Soprano, Maffiozok, and *Sopranod*), HBO, 2004.
Lorraine Calluzzo, "Rat Pack," *The Sopranos* (also known as *Made in Jersey, Sopranos, Die Sopranos, Familia Soprano, Les Soprano, Los Soprano, Maffiozok,* and *Sopranod*), HBO, 2004.
Lorraine Calluzzo, "Where's Johnny?," *The Sopranos* (also known as *Made in Jersey, Sopranos, Die Sopranos, Familia Soprano, Les Soprano, Los Soprano, Maffiozok,* and *Sopranod*), HBO, 2004.
Kathy, "See Ya Later, Investigator!," *Wild Card* (also known as *Zoe Busiek: Wild Card*), Lifetime, 2005.
Ellie, "Devil," *Rescue Me* (also known as *Rescue Me: FDNY*), FX Network, 2006.
Ellie, "Satisfaction," *Rescue Me* (also known as *Rescue Me: FDNY*), FX Network, 2006.
"Aquamom," *Entourage,* HBO, 2006.
Cecilia, "World's Fair," *Law & Order: Criminal Intent* (also known as *Law & Order: CI*), NBC, 2007.
Ellie, "Cycle," *Rescue Me* (also known as *Rescue Me: FDNY*), FX Network, 2007.

Stage Appearances:
Janice, *Italian American Reconciliation,* GNU Theatre, Los Angeles, 1987.

OTHER SOURCES

Periodicals:
People Weekly, April 3, 1989.
Playboy, December, 1989.
Vogue, October, 1988.

Electronic:
Patti D'Arbanville, http://www.pattidarbanville.com, October 7, 2007.

DARBO, Patrika 1948–

PERSONAL

Born April 6, 1948, in Jacksonville, FL; raised in Atlanta, GA; daughter of Chubby (a nightclub manager) and Patricia (a restaurant hostess); stepdaughter of Donald Davidson (a traveling secretary for a professional baseball team); married Rolf Darbo (a stage and film production manager), 1973 (some sources cite 1972). *Education:* Attended Georgia Southern University. *Avocational Interests:* Sewing, knitting, crocheting, shopping, watching old films.

Addresses: *Agent*—Michael Greene, Greene & Associates, 190 North Canon Dr., Suite 200, Beverly Hills, CA 90210.

Career: Actress. Appeared in advertisements. Also worked for a credit management firm.

Member: Actors' Equity Association.

Awards, Honors: Golden Cane Award, best actress, 10th Annual International Comedy Film Festival, 1990, for *Daddy's Dyin' … Who's Got the Will?*; *Soap Opera Digest* Award, outstanding female newcomer, 1999, named one of television's sexiest stars, *TV Guide*, 1999, and Daytime Emmy Award nomination, outstanding supporting actress in a drama series, 2000, all for *Days of Our Lives*.

CREDITS

Film Appearances:
Bimbo, *The Night Before*, 1988.
Dee Dee, *It Takes Two* (also known as *My New Car*), Metro–Goldwyn–Mayer, 1988.
Mar Vista troop leader, *Troop Beverly Hills*, Columbia, 1989.
Suzanne Weingartner, *The 'burbs* (also known as *The Burbs, The 'Burbs,* and *Life in the Burbs*), Universal, 1989.
Marlene, *Daddy's Dyin' … Who's Got the Will?*, Metro–Goldwyn–Mayer, 1990.
Mrs. Vanderspool, *Spaced Invaders* (also known as *Martians!!!*), Buena Vista, 1990.
Nurse number two, *Ghost Dad*, Universal, 1990.
Yogurt customer, *Gremlins 2: The New Batch* (also known as *Gremlins 2* and *Monolith*), Warner Bros., 1990.
Mrs. Walters, *The Willies*, 1991.
Waitress at greasy spoon, *Dutch* (also known as *Driving Me Crazy*), Twentieth Century–Fox, 1991.
Doattie, *The Vagrant*, Metro–Goldwyn–Mayer, 1992.
Sixty–six (66), *Leaving Normal* (also known as *Mary & Darly, Auf und Davon, Dos chicas en la carretera, Fuga per un sogno,* and *Tur och retur Alaska*), Universal, 1992.
Pam Magnus, *In the Line of Fire* (also known as *The Secret Service, B'Kav Ha–Esh, Dans la ligne de mire, Die zweite Chance, En la linea de fuego, En la linia de foc, I skottlinjen, In the Line of Fire—Die zweite Chance, Lige paa kornet, Na linha de fogo, Na linii ognia, Na ognjeni crti, Nel centro del mirino, Sur la ligne de feu,* and *Tulilinjalla*), Columbia, 1993.
Wilma (car hop), *Corrina, Corrina* (also known as *Corina, Corina* and *Corrina*), New Line Cinema, 1994.
Teebou, *Fast Money*, Orion, 1995.
Voice of sheep, *Babe* (also known as *Babe, the Gallant Pig*), Universal, 1995.
Cafeteria cashier, *House Arrest* (also known as *Perfect Family*), Metro–Goldwyn–Mayer/United Artists, 1996.

Ruby Fisher, *Speed 2: Cruise Control* (also known as *Speed: Cruise Control, Speed 2, Ca va clencher!, Fektelenuel 2., Fektelenuel 2.—Teljes goezzel, Hitrost 2—Brez zavor, Kiirus 2, Maxima velocidad 2, Speed 2: Cap sur le danger, Speed 2: Perigo a bordo, Speed 2—Vaara iskee vesillae,* and *Velocidade maxima 2*), Twentieth Century–Fox, 1997.
Sara Warren, *Midnight in the Garden of Good and Evil*, Warner Bros., 1997.
Mrs. Grey, *Durango Kids*, PorchLight Entertainment, 1999.
Herself, *Queen of the Whole Wide World* (documentary), 2001.
Betty, *Madhouse* (also known as *Mad Cannibal*), Lions Gate Films, 2004.
Fifties woman, *Mr. & Mrs. Smith*, Twentieth Century–Fox, 2005.
Patty, *Carpool Guy*, L.A. Ideas, 2005.
Auctioneer, *Charlie Wilson's War*, Universal, 2007.
Debbie, *Moving McAllister*, First Independent Pictures, 2007.
Mrs. Permatteo, *Hatchet*, Anchor Bay Entertainment, 2007.

Film Automated Dialogue Replacement Voices:
The Hot Spot (also known as *Hot Spot*), Orion, 1990.
Flesh and Bone, Paramount, 1993.

Television Appearances; Series:
Penny Baker, *Step by Step* (also known as *Eine Starke Familie, Kaos i familien, Notre belle famille, Paso a paso, Steg for Steg,* and *Una bionda per papa*), ABC, 1991–92.
Nancy Miller Wesley, *Days of Our Lives* (also known as *Cruise of Deception: Days of Our Lives, Days, DOOL, Des jours et des vies, Horton–sagaen, I gode og onde dager, Los dias de nuestras vidas, Meres agapis, Paeivien viemaeae, Vaara baesta aar, Zeit der Sehnsucht,* and *Zile din viata noastra*), NBC, 1999–2003 and sporadically after that.

Television Appearances; Movies:
Sara Murtry, *Nashville Beat*, The Nashville Network, 1989.
Arlene, *The Last Chance Detectives: Mystery Lights of Navajo Mesa*, 1994.
Leslie Holcomb, *Secret Sins of the Father* (also known as *Lethal Intent*), NBC, 1994.
Roseanne, *Roseanne and Tom: Behind the Scenes*, NBC, 1994.
Miss Jill Spencer, "Ruby Bridges," *The Wonderful World of Disney*, ABC, 1998.

Television Appearances; Specials:
(Uncredited; in archive footage) Nancy Miller Wesley, *Days of Our Lives' 35th Anniversary*, NBC, 2000.

Television Appearances; Awards Presentations:

The 15th Annual Soap Opera Digest Awards, NBC, 1999.

The 27th Annual Daytime Emmy Awards, ABC, 2000.

Television Appearances; Episodic:

Mother, "Kid's Stuff," *The Optimist,* 1983.

Female tourist, "Lost Link," *Misfits of Science,* NBC, 1985.

Mother, "Arnold Saves the Squirrel," *Diff'rent Strokes,* NBC, 1985.

Lady, "The Strike," *You Again?,* NBC, 1986.

Judy Jones, "Carnival," *Growing Pains,* ABC, 1987.

Estelle, "Graduation Day," *Growing Pains,* ABC, 1988.

Estelle, "How the West Was Won: Part 1," *Growing Pains,* ABC, 1988.

Kathy Goderegius, "Final Cut," *St. Elsewhere,* NBC, 1988.

Luella, "Fool for Love," *Growing Pains,* ABC, 1988.

Nancy, "Wimped Out," *Punky Brewster,* syndicated, 1988.

Nurse, "The Unkindest Cut of All," *Just the Ten of Us,* ABC, 1988.

Florence, "Reading the Riot Act," *Mama's Family,* syndicated, 1989.

Estelle, "Mike, the Teacher," *Growing Pains,* ABC, 1990.

Marge Dolman, "Dream Lover," *Roseanne,* ABC, 1990.

Mrs. Hatcher, "The Babysitters," *Saved by the Bell,* NBC, 1990.

"A Gang of Two," *The New Adam 12* (also known as *Adam 12, Adam–12,* and *New Adam–12*), syndicated, c. 1990.

Herself, *The Tonight Show Starring Johnny Carson* (also known as *The Best of Carson*), NBC, 1990, 1991.

Glenda, "The Revenge," *Seinfeld,* NBC, 1991.

Santa Barbara, NBC, 1991.

Ethel, "Take My Wife, Please," *Married ... with Children* (also known as *Not the Cosbys*), Fox, 1993.

Helene Morris, "I'm Looking through You," *Lois & Clark: The New Adventures of Superman* (also known as *Lois & Clark* and *The New Adventures of Superman*), ABC, 1993.

Pat, "The Dance," *Evening Shade,* CBS, 1993.

Rhonda, "Johnny Bago Free at Last," *Johnny Bago,* CBS, 1993.

(Uncredited) Woman at mailbox, "The Sniffing Accountant," *Seinfeld,* NBC, 1993.

Mrs. Littlewood, *The Boys,* CBS, 1993.

Waitress, "Memphis Bound," *Grace under Fire* (also known as *Grace under Pressure*), ABC, 1995.

Martha, "Housecleaning," *Sisters,* NBC, 1996.

"Past Imperfect," *The Client* (also known as *John Grisham's "The Client"*), CBS, 1996.

Phoebe Mosely, "Maybe It's You," *L.A. Doctors* (also known as *L.A. Docs, Kliniken, Kohtaloni Los Angeles,* and *Medicos de Los Angeles*), CBS, 1998.

Herself, *Who Knows You Best?,* 2000.

Waitress, "Help Wanted," *Gilmore Girls* (also known as *Gilmore Girls: Beginnings* and *The Gilmore Way*), The WB, 2002.

Irene, "Charity Ball," *Rodney* (also known as *That's Just Rodney* and *That's My Rodney*), ABC, 2005.

Herself, *SoapTalk,* SOAPnet, 2005, 2006.

Card store clerk, "Jackie Meets Her Match," *The Minor Accomplishments of Jackie Woodman,* Independent Film Channel, 2007.

Park ranger, "The Quest," *Unfabulous,* Nickelodeon, 2007.

Appeared as Jeannie, *The George Carlin Show,* Fox; also appeared in episodes of other programs, including *E!'s "Inside Word,"* E! Entertainment Television; *General Hospital* (also known as *Hopital central* and *Hospital general*), ABC; *The Tonight Show with Jay Leno,* NBC; and a show with Dennis Miller.

Television Appearances; Pilots:

Shelly, *One Night Band,* CBS, 1983.

Mildred Stubowitz, *Riptide,* NBC, 1984.

"B Men," *CBS Summer Playhouse,* CBS, c. 1989.

Penny Baker, *Step by Step* (also known as *Eine Starke Familie, Kaos i familien, Notre belle famille, Paso a paso, Steg for Steg,* and *Una bionda per papa*), ABC, 1991.

Dahlia O'Neill, *Arly Hanks,* CBS, 1993.

Edith Bretch, "For Whom the Bells Toll," *The Wedding Bells* (also known as *The Wedding Planners* and *The Wedding Store*), Fox, 2007.

Stage Appearances:

Anything Goes (musical), Burbank Little Theatre, Los Angeles, 1970.

Marlene, *Daddy's Dyin' ... Who's Got the Will?,* Theatre/Theater, Hollywood, CA, 1987–89.

Noleta Nethercott, *Sordid Lives,* Zephyr Theatre, Los Angeles, 2006.

Also appeared in various productions, including *The American Dream, Bottoms Up, Cat on a Hot Tin Roof, Cheatin', Club Indigo, Revisited, Don't Drink the Water, A Funny Thing Happened on the Way to the Forum* (musical), *George M!* (musical), *Never Too Late, Sleeping Beauty,* and *Wish You Were Here.* Performed with Theatre Atlanta.

WRITINGS

Nonfiction:

(With Lorraine Zenka) *365 Glorious Nights of Love and Romance,* ReganBooks, 2002.

OTHER SOURCES

Periodicals:

People Weekly, November 22, 1999, pp. 221–23.

TV Guide, August 7, 1999, p. 20.

DAVIDSON, Boaz 1943–

PERSONAL

Born August 11, 1943, in Tel Aviv, Palestine (now Israel). *Education:* Attended the London Film School.

Addresses: *Office*—Nu Image/Millennium Films, 6423 Wilshire Blvd., Los Angeles, CA 90048.

Career: Producer, director, actor, and screenwriter. Nu Image/Millennium Films, Los Angeles, CA, president (production and creative affairs).

Awards, Honors: Golden Berlin Bear Award nomination, 1978, for *Eskimo Limon.*

CREDITS

Film Second Unit Director:

Mivtza Yonatan (also known as *Entebbe: Operation Thunderbolt* and *Operation Thunderbolt*), Cinema Shares International, 1977.

The Alternate (also known as *Agent of Death*), Lions Gate Films, Inc., 1999.

Edison (also known as *Edison Force*), 2005.

The Wicker Man, 2006.

Mad Money, 2008.

Film Director:

Shablul (also known as *The Snail*), Hagar Films, 1971.

Hetzi Hetzi (also known as *Fifty Fifty*), 1971.

Azit Hakalba Hatzanhanit (also known as *Azit Shel Ha zanhanim* and *Azit, the Paratrooper Dog*), 1972.

Charlie Ve'hetzi (also known as *Charlie and a Half*), Tal–Shahar, 1974.

Hagiga B'Snucker (also known as *Festival at the Pool-room* and *Snooker*), 1975.

Mishpahat Tzan'ani (also known as *Tzanani Family*), 1976.

Lupo B'New York (also known as *Lupo Goes to New York*), 1976.

The Girl Who'll Do Anything, 1976.

Eskimo Limon (also known as *Going All the Way* and *Lemon Popsicle*), Noah Films, 1979.

Yotzim Kavua (also known as *Going Steady, Eis am Stiel 2: Feste Freundin, Greasy Kid Stuff,* and *Lemon Popsicle II*), Facets Video, 1979.

Seed of Innocence (also known as *Teen Mothers*), Cannon Film Distributors, 1980.

Shifshuf Naim (also known as *Eis am Stiel 3–Liebeleien, Hot Bubblegum,* and *Lemon Popsicle III*), 1981.

Hospital Massacre (also known as *Be My Valentine, or Else ...,* *Ward 13,* and *X–Ray*), Cannon Film Distributors, 1981.

The Last American Virgin, Cannon Film Distributors, 1982.

Saphies (also known as *Eis am Stiel 4–Hasenjagd, Lemon Popsicle IV,* and *Private Popsicle*), 1982.

Up Your Anchor, 1985.

Dutch Treat, Cannon Films, 1986.

Alex Holeh Ahavah (also known as *Alex in Love* and *Alex Is Lovesick*), 1986.

Going Bananas (also known as *My African Adventure*), Cannon Films, 1987.

Salsa, Cannon Group, 1988.

Lool, 1988.

Ochlim Lokshim (also known as *Crazy Camera*), 1989.

Lunarcop (also known as *Solar Force*), Astrocop Productions, 1994.

American Cyborg: Steel Warrior, Cannon Films, 1994.

(Uncredited) *Looking for Lola,* 1998.

Macarena, Dow Knut Productions, Inc., 1998.

(Uncredited) *Donuts,* 1998.

Film Producer:

Ochlim Lokshim (also known as *Crazy Camera*), 1989.

(With Christopher Pearce and Elie Cohn) *Human Shield,* 1991.

Tipat Mazal (also known as *A Bit of Luck*), 1992.

Lelakek Tatut (also known as *Licking the Raspberry*), 1992.

Hard Justice, 1995.

Macarena, Dow Knut Productions, Inc., 1998.

Shadrach, Columbia, 1998.

Looking for Lola, 1998.

Some Girl (also known as *Girl Talk* and *Men*), Scanbox Entertainment, 1998.

The 4th Floor, 1999.

Cold Harvest, 1999.

Bride of Dragons, 1999.

Spiders, Cobwester Corp., 2000.

Forever Lulu (also known as *Along for the Ride*), Millennium Films, 2000.

Crocodile, Flat Dog Corp., 2000.

For the Cause (also known as *Final Encounter*), Dimension Films, 2000.

Octopus, 2000.

Spiders II: Breeding Ground (also known as *Spiders 2*), Nu Image Films, 2001.

The Order, TriStar, 2001.

Octopus 2: River of Fear (also known as *Octopus II*), Nu Image Films, 2001.

Disaster (also known as *Cult of Fury* and *Sudden Damage*), Nu Image Films, 2001.

Cold Heart, 2001.

U.S. Seals II (also known as *U.S. Seals II: The Ultimate Force*), Artisan Entertainment, 2001.

Submarines, Nu Image Films, 2002.

Air Strike, Nu Image Films, 2002.

Derailed (also known as *Terror Train*), GAGA Communications, 2002.

Crocodile 2: Death Swamp (also known as *Crocodile 2: Death Roll*), Nu Image Films, 2002.

Shark Attack 3: Megalodon (also known as *Shark Attack III: Megalodon*), Nu Image Films, 2002.

Marines, Nu Image Films, 2003.

Special Forces, Starmedia Home Entertainment, 2003.

Alien Hunter, Columbia, 2003.

Air Marshal, Lions Gate Films Home Entertainment, 2003.

Shark Zone, DEJ Productions, 2003.

Unstoppable (also known as *9 Lives*), Columbia TriStar Home Entertainment, 2004.

Mozart and the Whale, Millennium Films, 2005.

Edison (also known as *Edison Force*), Sony Pictures Home Entertainment, 2005.

Lonely Hearts (also known as *Lonely Hearts Killer*), Roadside Attraction, 2006.

The Wicker Man, Warner Bros., 2006.

Wicked Little Things, Sony Pictures Entertainment, 2006.

Day of the Dead, Millennium Films, 2007.

Film Associate Producer:

Search and Destroy (also known as *The Four Rules*), October Films, 1995.

Armstrong, 1998.

Film Coproducer:

Wild Side, Metro Tartan, 1995.

The Maker, Maker Productions, Inc., 1997.

Plato's Run, Nu Image, 1997.

No Code of Conduct, Dimension Films, 1998.

The Contract, First Look International, 2006.

Film Executive Producer:

Dog Watch, Dog Watch Productions, 1996.

The Last Days of Frankie the Fly (also known as *Frankie the Fly*), Fly Productions, 1997.

American Perfekt, American Perfekt Productions, Inc., 1997.

Santa Fe, Absolute Unequivocal Productions, 1997.

Outside Ozona, TriStar/Sony Pictures Entertainment, 1998.

The Big Brass Ring, The Big Brass Ring, Inc., 1999.

Guinevere, Miramax, 1999.

Cold Heart, Nu Image, 2001.

Undisputed, Nu Image, 2001.

Ticker, Artisan Entertainment, 2001.

Panic (also known as *Air Panic*), Nu Image Films, 2001.

Edges of the Lord (also known as *Boze skrawski*), Miramax, 2001.

Replicant, Artisan Entertainment, 2001.

Diary of a Sex Addict, Nu Image Films, 2001.

The Order (also known as *Jihad Warrior*), TriStar, 2001.

Run for the Money (also known as *Hard Cash*), Millennium Films, 2002.

Undisputed (also known as *Undisputed—Sieg ohne Ruhm*), Miramax, 2002.

Try Seventeen (also known as *All I Want*), 2002.

Den of Lions, Millennium Films, 2003.

In Hell (also known as *The Savage* and *The Shu*), DEJ Productions, 2003.

Out for a Kill, Columbia TriStar Home Video, 2003.

Blind Horizon, Lions Gate Films, 2003.

Shadow of Fear, Millennium Film, 2004.

Control, Lions Gate Films, 2004.

Raging Sharks, Nu Image Films, 2005.

Mansquito (also known as *Mosquito Man*), First Look International, 2005.

Submerged, Nu Image Films, 2005.

The Mechanik (also known as *The Russian Specialist*), Sony Pictures Home Entertainment, 2005.

16 Blocks, Warner Bros., 2006.

End Game, Metro–Goldwyn–Mayer, 2006.

Undisputed II: Last Man Standing (also known as *Undisputed 2*), New Line Home Video, 2006.

Journey to the End of the Night, Nu Image Films, 2006.

Relative Strangers, First Look International, 2006.

The Black Dahlia (also known as *Black Dahlia*), Universal, 2006.

Wicked Little Things, AfterDark Films, 2006.

Home of the Brave, Metro–Goldwyn–Mayer, 2006.

King of California, First Look International, 2007.

88 Minutes, TriStar, 2007.

Until Death, Sony Pictures Home Entertainment, 2007.

The Death and Life of Bobby Z (also known as *Bobby Z* and *Let's Kill Bobby Z*), Sony Pictures Home Entertainment, 2007.

When Nietzsche Wept, 2007.

More Than You Know, Columbia, 2007.

Blonde Ambition, Sony Pictures Entertainment, 2007.

Hero Wanted, Nu Image Films, 2007.

Mad Money, Millennium Films, 2008.

John Rambo, Lionsgate, 2008.

Film Co–Executive Producer:

October 22, 1998.

Film Appearances:

Yisraelim Matzhikim (also known as *It's a Funny, Funny World*), 1978.

Ochlim Lokshim (also known as *Crazy Camera*), 1989.

Himself, *Creating "Larva"* (short), First Look International, 2005.

Television Work; Movies:

Director, *Blood Run* (also known as *Outside the Law*), 1994.

Producer, *Operation Delta Force,* 1997.

Executive producer, *Dogwatch,* 1997.

Producer, *Bridge of Dragons,* HBO, 1999.

Executive producer, *Skeleton Man,* 2004.

Producer, *Alien Lockdown* (also known as *Predator-Man*), Sci–Fi Channel, 2004.

Producer, *Larva* (also known as *MorphMan*), Sci–Fi Channel, 2005.

Producer, *The Snake King* (also known as *Snakeman*), Sci–Fi Channel, 2005.

Producer, *Hammerhead: Shark Frenzy* (also known as *Hammerhead* and *SharkMan*), Sci–Fi Channel, 2005.

Producer, *The Black Hole,* Sci–Fi Channel, 2006.

Executive producer, *Gryphon* (also known as *Attack of the Gryphon*), Sci–Fi Channel, 2007.

Producer, *MegaSnake,* Sci–Fi Channel, 2007.

Television Episodes:

Lool, 1969.

WRITINGS

Screenplays:

Shablul (also known as *The Snail*), 1971.

Hetzi Hetzi (also known as *Fifty Fifty*), 1971.

Azit Hakalba Hatzanhanit (also known as *Azit Shel Ha zanhanim* and *Azit, the Paratrooper Dog*), 1972.

Lupo B'New York (also known as *Lupo Goes to New York*), 1976.

Yisraelim Matzhikim (also known as *It's a Funny, Funny World*), 1978.

Eskimo Limon (also known as *Going All the Way* and *Lemon Popsicle*), Noah Films, 1979.

Yotzim Kavua (also known as *Going Steady, Eis am Stiel 2: Feste Freudin, Greasy Kid Stuff,* and *Lemon Popsicle II*), Facets Video, 1979.

Seed of Innocence (also known as *Teen Mothers*), Cannon Film Distributors, 1980.

Shifshuf Naim (also known as *Eis am Stiel 3–Liebeleien, Hot Bubblegum,* and *Lemon Popsicle III*), 1981.

The Last American Virgin, Cannon Film Distributors, 1982.

Saphies (also known as *Eis am Stiel 4–Hasenjagd, Lemon Popsicle IV, Hot Bubblegum,* and *Private Popsicle*), 1982.

Sababa (also known as *Lemon Popsicle, Eis am Stiel— Hasenjagd 2, Hasenjagd 2. Teil, Private Maneuver, Sababa—Wer hat mir die Butter vom Brto geklaut?,* and *Private Maneuvers*), 1983.

Roman Za'ir (also known as *Baby Love, Eis am Stiel 5 ie grosse Liebe, Hasenjagd II, Lemon Popsicle V,* and *Sababa er hat mir die Butter von Brot geklaut*), 1984.

Hot Resort, 1985.

Alex Holeh Ahavah (also known as *Alex in Love* and *Alex Is Lovesick*), 1986.

(And story) *Salsa,* 1988.

Delta Force 3: The Killing Game (also known as *Delta Force 3* and *Young Commandos*), 1991.

(Story only) *American Cyborg: Steel Warrior,* 1994.

(Story only) *Orion's Key* (also known as *Alien Chaser, Shadowchaster: The Gates of Time,* and *Project Shadowchaser 4*), Nu Image, 1996.

(Story only) *Looking for Lola,* 1998.

(Story only) *Macarena,* Dow Knut Productions, Inc., 1998.

(Story only) *Crocodile,* Nu Image, 2000.

(Story only) *Spiders,* 2000.

(Story only) *Octopus,* 2000.

(Story only) *Panic* (also known as *Air Panic*), 2001.

(Story only) *Disaster* (also known as *Cult of Fury* and *Sudden Damage*), Nu Image Films, 2001.

(Story only) *Spiders II: Breeding Ground* (also known as *Spiders 2*), Nu Image Films, 2001.

(Story only) *U.S. Seals II* (also known as *U.S. Seals II: The Ultimate Force*), Artisan Entertainment, 2001.

(Story only) *Octopus 2: River of Fear* (also known as *Octopus II*), Nu Image Films, 2001.

(Story only) *Air Strike,* Trimark Video, 2002.

(Story only) *Derailed* (also known as *Terror Train*), GAGA Communications, 2002.

(Story only) *Alien Hunter,* Columbia, 2003.

(Story only) *Rats,* 2003.

(Story only) *Mansquito* (also known as *Mosquitoman*), First Look International, 2005.

(Story only) *Wicked Little Things,* Lions Gate, 2006.

Television Movies:

(Story only) *Blood Run* (also known as *Outside the Law*), 1994.

(Story only) *Alien Lockdown* (also known as *Predator-Man*), Sci–Fi Channel, 2004.

(Story only) *Larva* (also known as *MorphMan*), Sci–Fi Channel, 2005.

(Story only) *The Snake King* (also known as *Snakeman*), Sci–Fi Channel, 2005.

(Story only) *Hammerhead: Shark Frenzy* (also known as *Hammerhead* and *SharkMan*), Sci–Fi Channel, 2005.

(And story) *Gryphon* (also known as *Attack of the Gryphon*), Sci–Fi Channel, 2007.

DAVIS, DeRay
(DeRay, De Ray)

PERSONAL

Full name, Antoine DeRay Davis.

Addresses: *Agent*—Global Artists Agency, 1648 N. Wilcox Ave., Los Angeles, CA 90028; The Gersh Agency, 232 North Canon Dr., Beverly Hills, CA 90210. *Manager*—Principato/Young Management, 9465 Wilshire Blvd., Suite 880, Beverly Hills, CA 90212.

Career: Actor and comedian.

CREDITS

Film Appearances:

Basketball player, *Frank McKlusky, C.I.,* Buena Vista, 2002.

Hustle guy, *Barbershop,* Metro–Goldwyn–Mayer, 2002.

Hustle guy, *Barbershop 2: Back in Business,* Metro–Goldwyn–Mayer, 2004.

Jamaican stoner, *Johnson Family Vacation,* Fox Searchlight Pictures, 2004.

E. J., *The Seat Filler,* DEJ Productions, 2004.

Mario "Fa Real" Greene, *Jiminy Glick in Lalawood,* Metro–Goldwyn–Mayer, 2004.

Spooner, *The Fog* (also known as *Le brouillard*), Columbia, 2005.

Marvin, *Scary Movie 4,* Dimension Films, 2006.

Dwayne, *Swap Meet,* Triumphant Pictures, 2006.

Bee Bee, *School for Scoundrels,* Weinstein Company, 2006.

June Bug, *Who Made the Potato Salad?,* Twentieth Century Fox Home Entertainment, 2006.

Ronnie, *Code Name: The Cleaner,* New Line Cinema, 2007.

Joel, *License to Wed,* Warner Bros., 2007.

Sirus, *The Hit,* 2007.

Omar, *Nite Tales: The Movie,* 2007.

Himself, *How She Move,* Paramount Vantage, 2007.

Motown, *Frankenhood,* Lionsgate, 2008.

Bee Bee Ellis, *Semi–Pro,* New Line Cinema, 2008.

Television Appearances; Series:

Himself, *Beef: The Series,* 2006.

Television Appearances; Movies:

Jaxx's bodyguard, *Play'd: A Hip Hop Story,* VH1, 2002.

Television Appearances; Episodic:

(As DeRay) Himself, *Premium Blend* (also known as *Comedy Central's "Premium Blend"*), Comedy Central, 2000.

(As De Ray) Himself, *Late Friday,* NBC, 2001.

R. J., "Working Relationship," *My Wife and Kids,* ABC, 2002.

R. J., "Jury Duty," *My Wife and Kids,* ABC, 2003.

R. J., "The Sweet Hairafter," *My Wife and Kids,* ABC, 2003.

R. J., "Jr. Executive," *My Wife and Kids,* ABC, 2003.

Hack, "Chinatown," *Entourage,* HBO, 2005.

Himself, "High Fidelity," *Love Lounge,* 2005.

Himself, "Getting It On–line," *Love Lounge,* 2005.

Himself, "Chris Brown: Yo," *Access Granted,* Black Entertainment Television, 2005.

Comedian, *Jamie Foxx's Laffapalooza,* Comedy Central, 2005.

Timpathy the criminal, " ... And the Installation is Free," *Reno 911!,* Comedy Central, 2005.

Junior the Third, "Dangle's Son," *Reno 911!,* Comedy Central, 2005.

Junior the Third, "CSI: Reno," *Reno 911!,* Comedy Central, 2005.

Himself, "DeRay," *Comedy Central Presents,* Comedy Central, 2006.

Various, "Young Buck," *Nick Cannon Presents: Wild 'N Out,* MTV, 2007.

Various, "Tara Reid," *Nick Cannon Presents: Wild 'N Out,* MTV, 2007.

Junior the Third, "The Department Gets a Corporate Sponsorship," *Reno 911!,* Comedy Central, 2007.

Campus Ladies, Oxygen, 2007.

Also appeared as himself, "Kanye West," *Nick Cannon Presents: Wild 'N Out,* MTV.

RECORDINGS

Videos:

Playboy: Queen of Clubs (documentary), Playboy Entertainment Group, 2004.

Music Videos:

(As DeRay) Himself, "Through the Wire" and "Two Words," *Kanye West: College Dropout—Video Anthology,* Universal Music, 2005.

Also appeared in R. Kelly's "The Truth."

WRITINGS

Television Episodes:

"DeRay," *Comedy Central Presents,* Comedy Central, 2006.

De LAURENTIIS, Raffaella 1954–

PERSONAL

Born June 28, 1954, in Italy; daughter of Dino De Laurentiis (a producer) and Silvana Mangano (an actress).

Addresses: *Office*—Raffaella Productions, 100 Universal City Plaza, Bungalow 5162, Universal City, CA, 91608–1085

Career: Producer. Began career as prop assistant and set dresser, c. 1969; later worked in art direction and costume design; De Laurentiis Entertainment Group, president of production, 1987; Raffaella Productions, Universal City, CA, founder and president, 1988—. Endowment Campaign Committee, Academy of Motion Picture Arts and Sciences Center for Motion Picture Study, member, 1990—.

CREDITS

Film Producer:
Beyond the Reef (also known as *Sea Killer* and *Shark Boy of Bora Bora*), Universal, 1981.
Conan the Barbarian, Universal, 1982.
Conan the Destroyer, Metro–Goldwyn–Mayer, 1984.
Dune, Universal, 1984.
Tai–Pan, De Laurentiis Group, 1986.
Prancer, Orion, 1989.
Timebomb, Metro–Goldwyn–Mayer, 1991.
Dragon: The Bruce Lee Story, Universal, 1993.
Trading Mom (also known as *The Mommy Market*), 1994.
Dragonheart, Universal, 1996.
Kull the Conqueror, MCA/Universal, 1997.
Black Dog, MCA/Universal, 1998.
Dragonheart: A New Beginning, Universal Home Entertainment, 2000.
The Last Legion (also known as *La derniere legion*), Weinstein Company, 2007.

Film Executive Producer:
Backdraft, Universal, 1991.
Daylight, Universal, 1996.
Prancer Returns (also known as *Le retour du petit renne*), USA Home Video, 2001.
Sky Captain and the World of Tomorrow, Paramount, 2004.
The Forbidden Kingdom, Weinstein Company, 2008.

Film Work; Other:
Assistant costume designer, *Ludwig* (also known as *Le crepuscule des dieux, Ludwig, Ludwig II,* and *Ludwig ... ou le crepuscule des dieux*), Metro–Goldwyn–Mayer, 1972.
Production assistant, *Hurricane* (also known as *Forbidden Paradise*), 1979.
Unit production manager, *Dragon: The Bruce Lee Story,* 1993.
Production manager, *Kull the Conqueror,* 1997.
Unit production manager, *Dragonheart: A New Beginning,* 2000.
Unit production manager, *The Last Legion* (also known as *La derniere legion*), Weinstein Company, 2007.

Film Appearances:
Herself, *The Making of "Dragonheart"* (documentary), Universal Studios Home Video, 1997.
Herself, *The Making of "Daylight"* (documentary short), Universal Studios Home Video, 1998.

Herself, *"Dune": Models and Miniatures* (documentary short), Universal Studios Home Video, 2006.
Herself, *Deleted "Dune"* (documentary short), Universal Studios Home Video, 2006.

Television Work; Series:
Executive producer, *Vanishing Son,* syndicated, 1995.
Producer, *The Guardian,* CBS, 1997.

Television Work; Miniseries:
Producer and executive producer, *Uprising,* NBC, 2001.

Television Executive Producer; Movies:
Vanishing Son, syndicated, 1994.
Vanishing Son II, syndicated, 1994.
Vanishing Son III, syndicated, 1994.
Vanishing Son IV, syndicated, 1994.
Prancer Returns, USA Network, 2001.
Stealing Christmas, USA Network, 2003.

Television Appearances; Specials:
Herself, *Dino De Laurentiis: The Last Movie Mogul,* BBC, 2001.

DERAY
　　See DAVIS, DeRay

DILLINGHAM, Jazzmine
　　See RAYCOLE, Jazz

DISCALA, Jamie–Lynn
　　See SIGLER, Jamie–Lynn

DISHY, Bob 1934(?)–
　　(Robert Dishy)

PERSONAL

Born in 1934 (some sources say 1933), in Brooklyn, NY; son of Nathan (a salesman) and Amy (maiden name, Barazani) Dishy; married Judy Graubart (an actress); children: Samuel Nathan. *Education:* Syracuse University, B.S., drama, 1955.

Addresses: *Agent*—International Creative Management, 10250 Constellation Way, 9th Floor, Los Angeles, CA 90067.

Career: Actor. Appeared with Second City Company, New York City, c. early 1960s; began directing with Second City, 1964. *Military:* U.S. Army, 1957–59.

Member: Academy of Motion Picture Arts and Sciences.

Awards, Honors: Antoinette Perry Award nomination, best featured actor in a play, Drama Desk Award, outstanding featured actor in play, 1977, both for *Sly Fox;* All–Army Entertainment Contest; Chancellor's Medal for Distinguished Achievement, Syracuse University.

CREDITS

Stage Appearances:
(Broadway debut) Rocky, *Damn Yankees,* 46th Street Theatre, 1955–56.
Chic, Orpheum Theatre, New York City, 1959.
Child, enemy, Fred, and Patsy, *From A to Z,* Plymouth Theatre, New York City, 1960.
Dig We Must, John Drew Theatre, East Hampton, NY, 1960.
Charlie Paal, *There Is a Play Tonight,* Theatre Marquee, New York City, 1961.
Theophile, *Can–Can,* City Center Theatre, New York City, 1962.
Medium Rare, Happy Medium Theatre, Chicago, IL, 1962.
Put It in Writing, Happy Medium Theatre, Chicago, IL, 1962.
When the Owl Screams Revue, Square East Theatre, New York City, 1963.
Open Season at Second City, Square East Theatre, 1964.
The Wrecking Ball, Square East Theatre, 1964.
Harry Toukarian, *Flora, the Red Menace,* Alvin Theatre, New York City, 1965.
Sapiens, *By Jupiter,* Theatre Four, New York City, 1967.
Inventor, *The Unknown Soldier and His Wife,* Vivian Beaumont Theatre, New York City, 1967.
Sheldon "Bud" Nemerov, *Something Different,* Cort Theatre, New York City, 1967–68.
Arthur Korman, *The Goodbye People,* Ethel Barrymore Theatre, New York City, 1968.
Alex Krieger, *A Way of Life,* American National Theatre Academy, New York City, 1969.
Adam, *The Creation of the World and Other Business,* Shubert Theatre, New York City, 1972.
Arnold Brody, *An American Millionaire,* Circle in the Square, New York City, 1974.
Abner Truckle, *Sly Fox,* Broadhurst Theatre, New York City, 1976.

Paul Miller, *Murder at the Howard Johnson's,* John Golden Theatre, New York City, 1979.
Jake, *Grownups,* American Repertory Theatre, Cambridge, MA, then Lyceum Theatre, New York City, both 1981, later Mark Taper Forum, Los Angeles, 1983.
Mort, *What's Wrong with This Picture?,* Manhattan Theatre Club, New York City, 1985.
Waiter, *Cafe Crown,* Brooks Atkinson Theatre, New York City, 1989.
Schlissel, *The Tenth Man,* Mitzi E. Newhouse Theatre, New York City, 1989–90.
Blue Light, 1994.
Simon Persky, *The Shawl,* Playhouse 91, New York City, 1996.
Gregory Soloman, *The Price,* Royal Theatre, New York City, 1999–2000.
Bob Dishy, *Morning's at Seven,* Lyceum Theatre, 2002.
Abner Truckle, *Sly Fox,* Barrymore Theatre, New York City, 2004.

Also appeared in *Twelfth Night,* Second City Company, New York City.

Major Tours:
Medium Rare, U.S. cities, 1960–61.

Stage Director:
The Wrecking Ball, Square East Theatre, New York City, 1964.

Also directed *Twelfth Night,* Second City Company, New York City.

Film Appearances:
Jerry, *The Tiger Makes Out,* Columbia, 1967.
(As Robert Dishy) Jerry, *Lovers and Other Strangers,* Cinerama, 1970.
Jordan Oliver, *I Wonder Who's Killing Her Now?* (also known as *Kill My Wife Please*), Lorimar, 1975.
Dr. Kurtz, *The Big Bus,* Paramount, 1976.
Howard, *Last Married Couple in America,* Universal, 1980.
Vice President Shockley, *The First Family,* Warner Bros., 1980.
Feinstein, *Author! Author!,* Twentieth Century–Fox, 1982.
Jack, *Brighton Beach Memoirs* (also known as *Neil Simon's "Brighton Beach Memoirs"*), Universal, 1986.
Dr. Foster, *Critical Condition,* Paramount, 1986.
Murray Seidenbaum, *Stay Tuned,* Warner Bros., 1992.
Jack, *Used People,* Twentieth Century–Fox, 1992.
Murray the gravedigger, *My Boyfriend's Back,* Buena Vista, 1993.
Dr. Paul Showalter, *Don Juan DeMarco,* New Line Cinema, 1995.

George Langston, *Jungle 2 Jungle* (also known as *Un Indien a New York*), Buena Vista, 1997.

Arthur Gold, *Judy Berlin,* Shooting Gallery, 1999.

Lou Moskowitz, *A Fish in the Bathtub,* Curb Entertainment, 1999.

Labor Pains, USA Home Video, 2000.

Irving Feffer, *Along Came Polly,* Universal, 2004.

Television Appearances; Series:

That Was the Week That Was, NBC, 1964–65.

Story Theatre, syndicated, 1971.

Television Appearances; Movies:

Rocky, *Damn Yankees!,* NBC, 1967.

Prisoner and aide, *The Police,* 1971.

Sergeant Frederic Wilson, *Columbo: The Greenhouse Jungle,* 1972.

Ed Huxley, *It Couldn't Happen to a Nicer Guy,* ABC, 1974.

Sargeant John J. Wilson, *Columbo: Now You See Him,* 1976.

Various roles, *The Good Doctor,* 1978.

Glen Schwartz, *Thicker Than Blood: The Larry McLinden Story* (also known as *The Larry McLinden Story*), CBS, 1994.

Television Appearances; Specials:

Pure Goldie, 1971.

Aaron, *The Cafeteria,* PBS, 1984.

Happy Birthday Oscar Wilde, BBC, 2004.

Television Appearances; Pilots:

Edward R Ace, *Ace,* ABC, 1976.

Dr. Friedman, *A.E.S. Hudson Street,* 1977.

Television Appearances; Episodic:

Officer Larry Tully, "Second Story Story," *Mary Tyler Moore* (also known as *The Mary Tyler Moore Show*), CBS, 1971.

David Green, "Maude," *All in the Family,* CBS, 1972.

"Love and the Love Nest," *Love, American Style,* ABC, 1972.

"Bless the Big Fish," *McCoy,* NBC, 1975.

Mr. Shine, "The Layoff," *Barney Miller,* ABC, 1975.

Pharmacist, "The Pharmacist," *Alice,* CBS, 1978.

Dr. Friedman, *A.E.S. Hudson Street,* ABC, 1978.

Sergeant Norris, "Word Games," *Mrs. Columbo* (also known as *Kate Columbo, Kate Loves a Mystery,* and *Kate the Detective*), NBC, 1979.

John Milford, "The Delegate," *Barney Miller,* 1980.

The Comedy Zone, CBS, 1984.

Harry/Shakespeare, "Act Break," *The Twilight Zone* (also known as *The New Twilight Zone*), CBS, 1985.

Mr. Terrific, "Mister Terrific," *The Golden Girls,* NBC, 1988.

Harry Gulliver, "The Passionate Painter Mystery," *Father Dowling Mysteries* (also known as *Father Dowling Investigates*), ABC, 1990.

Dr. Solomon, "The Heartbreak Id," *Flying Blind,* Fox, 1992.

Oscar Tredwell, "The P.I.," *Matlock,* ABC, 1994.

Dr. Schenkman, "The Maris Counselor," *Frasier,* NBC, 1998.

Mendel, "It's Hard to Meet Intelligent Women," *Welcome to New York,* CBS, 2000.

"Peter Falk: Just One More Thing," *Biography,* Arts and Entertainment, 2000.

Sol, "Man Up," *Jonny Zero,* Fox, 2005.

Television Director; Episodic:

Directed individual skits of *Story Theatre,* syndicated.

RECORDINGS

Albums:

Flora, the Red Menace, (original cast recording), RCA, 1965.

DOIG, Lexa 1973–

PERSONAL

Full name, Alexandra L. Doig; born June 8, 1973, in Toronto, Ontario, Canada; daughter of David and Gloria Doig; married Michael Shanks (an actor), August 2, 2003; children: Mia Tabitha, Samuel David. *Avocational Interests:* Reading, in–line skating, playing video games.

Addresses: *Manager*—Anthem Entertainment, 6100 Wilshire Blvd., Suite 1170, Los Angeles, CA 90069.

Career: Actress. Worked as a model and appeared in advertisements.

Awards, Honors: Nomination for Cinescape Genre Face of the Future Award, female category, Academy of Science Fiction, Fantasy, and Horror Films, 2002, for *Andromeda* and *Jason X.*

CREDITS

Television Appearances; Series:

Cohost, *Video & Arcade Top 10,* YTV (Canada), beginning c. 1991.

Cowgirl, *TekWar* (also known as *TekWar: The Series*), syndicated, 1994–96.

Voice of Dale Arden, *Flash Gordon* (animated), syndicated, c. 1996–97.

Tina Backus, *C15: The New Professionals*, Sky One (Canada), 1998, syndicated, 1999.

M. J. Sullivan, a recurring role, *Traders* (also known as *Haute finance*), CanWest Global Television (Canada) and Lifetime, 1999–2000.

Andromeda Ascendant, *Andromeda* (also known as *Gene Roddenberry's "Andromeda"*), syndicated, 2000–2005.

Dr. Carolyn Lam, *Stargate SG–1* (also known as *La porte des etoiles* and *Stargaate SG–1*), Sci–Fi Channel and syndicated, 2005–2007.

Television Appearances; Miniseries:

Rachel Sanders, *Human Cargo* (also known as *Third World*), CBC, 2004.

Television Appearances; Movies:

Cowgirl, *TekWar* (also known as *TekWar: The Movie* and *TekWar: The Original Movie*), syndicated, 1994.

Cowgirl, *TekWar: TekLords*, syndicated, 1994.

Mary Margaret "Tse Tse" McBride, *While My Pretty One Sleeps* (also known as *Mary Higgins Clark's "While My Pretty One Sleeps"*), Family Channel, 1997.

Camille, *No Alibi*, HBO, 2000.

Conchita Flores, *Code Name Phoenix* (also known as *Codename: Phoenix*, *Code Name—Phoenix*, *Codigo: Phoenix*, and *Koodinimi Phoenix*), UPN, 2000.

Kim Chang, *The Tracker* (also known as *Blood Chase*), HBO, 2000.

Jenny Morris, *Second Sight*, Lifetime and CanWest Global Television (Canada), 2007.

Ba'al, Sci–Fi Channel, 2008.

Television Appearances; Episodic:

Receptionist, "Glamour Girl," *Ready or Not* (also known as *Amanda und Betsy*, *Amigas para siempre*, *Les premieres fois*, and *Nu eller aldrig*), CanWest Global Television (Canada), 1993.

Second girl, "Marion & Jean," *The Hidden Room*, Lifetime, 1993.

Netta, "From Russia with Love," *Taking the Falls*, CTV (Canada), 1996.

Reporter, "French Kiss," *F/X: The Series* (also known as *F/X*, *F/X: Efeitos mortais*, *F/X*, *effets speciaux*, and *F/X—murha tilauksesta*), CTV (Canada) and syndicated, 1996.

Joan Price, "Abduction," *Earth: Final Conflict* (also known as *EFC*, *Gene Roddenberry's "Battleground Earth,"* *Gene Roddenberry's "Earth: Final Conflict,"* *Invasion planete Terre*, and *Mission Erde: Sie sind unter uns*), syndicated, 2000.

Detective Lucy Ramirez, "Home of the Brave," *The Chris Isaak Show*, Showtime, 2002.

Hospital doctor, "Forget Me Not," *Killer Instinct*, Fox, 2005.

Wendy Paulson, "As Fate Would Have It," *The 4400* (also known as *4400*), USA Network, 2005.

Wendy Paulson, "Hidden," *The 4400* (also known as *4400*), USA Network, 2005.

Wendy Paulson, "Voices Carry," *The 4400* (also known as *4400*), USA Network, 2005.

Wendy Paulson, "Weight of the World," *The 4400* (also known as *4400*), USA Network, 2005.

"Maneater," *Eureka* (also known as *A Town Called Eureka*), Sci–Fi Channel, 2007.

Film Appearances:

Spider, *Jungleground*, Norstar Releasing, 1995.

Mercedes, *Teen Sorcery*, Full Moon Entertainment, 1999.

Rowan, *Jason X* (also known as *Friday the 13th Part 10*, *Jason X: Friday the 13th Part 10*, *Jason 2000*, and *Jason 2000: Friday the 13th Part X*), New Line Cinema, 2001.

Stage Appearances:

Appeared in various productions, including *Arsenic and Old Lace* and *Romeo and Juliet*.

RECORDINGS

Videos:

Herself and Rowan, *By Any Means Necessary: The Making of "Jason X,"* New Line Home Video, 2002.

OTHER SOURCES

Periodicals:

Cult Times, August, 2003, pp. 20–23.

Cult Times Special, June, 2004, pp. 22–25.

Dreamwatch, December, 2002, pp. 20–21.

Starburst Special, February, 2004, pp. 120–25.

TV Zone, January, 2001, pp. 28–31; September, 2001, pp. 56–59.

TV Zone Special, January, 2003, pp. 6–10; January, 2006, pp. 44–45.

DOUGLAS, Kirk 1916–
(Issur Danielovitch; George Spelvin, Jr.)

PERSONAL

Original name, Issur Danielovitch Demsky (some sources cite name variously as Issur Danielovitch or Isadore Danielovitch Demsky); born December 9,

1916, in Amsterdam, NY; son of Harry (in business; some sources cite name as Jacob Danielovitch) and Bryna (maiden name, Sanglel) Demsky; married Diana Dill (an actress; also known as Diana Darrid and Diana Douglas Darrid), November 2, 1943 (divorced, February, 1950; some sources cite 1951); married Anne Buydens (a casting director, publicity agent, and producer), May 29, 1954; children: (first marriage) Michael (an actor and producer), Joel (a producer); (second marriage) Peter Vincent (a producer), Eric Anthony (an actor and comedian). *Education:* St. Lawrence University, A.B., English, 1938; American Academy of Dramatic Arts, graduated, 1941. *Religion:* Jewish. *Avocational Interests:* Collecting art, travel.

Addresses: *Agent*—Creative Artists Agency, 2000 Avenue of the Stars, Los Angeles, CA 90067. *Publicist*—Warren Cowan and Associates, 8899 Beverly Blvd., Suite 919, Los Angeles, CA 90048.

Career: Actor, producer, director, and writer. Greenwich House Settlement, New York City, drama coach, 1939–41; Bryna Productions (production company; also known as Bryna Company), founder, 1955, president, beginning 1955; Joel Productions, founder, 1962, president, beginning 1962; some sources state that Douglas has been affiliated with Brynapod Productions. Cannes International Film Festival, member of jury, 1970, and president of jury, 1980. Appeared in advertisements. Worked as a wrestler, janitor, waiter, usher, and bellhop. Heart Committee of the Motion Picture Industry, member; the Douglas Foundation, cofounder; Motion Picture Hospital and Country Home, endowed Harry's Haven (Alzheimer's wing) in honor of his father; affiliated with Access Theatre for the Handicapped, Cedars–Sinai Medical Center, and Anne Douglas Center for Women at Los Angeles Mission; contributed money to various organizations, institutions, and causes, including to St. Lawrence University, the Kirk Douglas Theatre, Center Theatre Group, Culver City, CA, and for the creation of parks and playgrounds; active in the fight against the blacklisting of entertainment industry figures with suspected ties to communism, 1950s–60s. *Military service:* U.S. Navy, beginning c. 1942; became lieutenant.

Member: Actors' Equity Association, Screen Actors Guild, American Federation of Television and Radio Artists, Directors Guild of America, Friars Club, United Nations Association (member of board of directors of Los Angeles chapter), National Student Federation of America, Honorary Society of Kixioc, Delta Kappa Alpha.

Awards, Honors: Golden Apple Award, most cooperative actor, Hollywood Women's Press Association, 1949; Academy Award nomination, best actor in a leading role, 1950, for *Champion;* Golden Laurel awards, Golden Laurel awards, Producers Guild of America, 1951, 1952, and 1956; Golden Globe Award nomination, best actor in a motion picture drama, 1952, for *Detective Story;* Academy Award nomination, best actor in a leading role, 1953, for *The Bad and the Beautiful;* Heart and Torch Award, American Heart Association, 1956; New York Film Critics Circle Award, best actor, 1956, Golden Globe Award, best actor in a motion picture drama, 1957, and Academy Award nomination, best actor in a leading role, 1957, all for *Lust for Life;* Special Award, Sant Jordi awards, 1957, for *The Juggler;* Splendid American Award of Merit, George Washington Carver Memorial Fund, 1957; Zulueta Prize, best actor, San Sebastian International Film Festival, 1958, for *The Vikings;* Golden Laurel Award nomination, top male action star, 1958, for *Gunfight at the O. K. Corral;* honorary D.F.A., St. Lawrence University, 1958; some sources cite a Golden Scissors Award, c. 1958; Golden Laurel Award nominations, top male star, 1960, 1961, 1962, and 1968; Golden Laurel Award, third place, top male dramatic performance, 1961, for *Spartacus;* Golden Laurel Award nomination, top action performance, 1962, for *The Last Sunset;* Golden Laurel Award, top action performance, and Film Award nomination, best foreign actor, British Academy of Film and Television Arts, both 1963, for *Lonely Are the Brave;* named U.S. goodwill ambassador to the United Nations, 1964 and 1983; Cecil B. DeMille Award, Golden Globe awards, Hollywood Foreign Press Association, 1968; nomination for Golden Berlin Bear, Berlin International Film Festival, 1975, for *Posse;* subject of *Kirk Douglas: An American Film Institute Seminar on His Work,* American Film Institute, 1970s; honorary Cesar Award, Academie des Arts et Techniques du Cinema, 1980; Saturn Award nomination, best actor, Academy of Science Fiction, Fantasy, and Horror Films, 1981, for *The Final Countdown;* Presidential Medal of Freedom, 1981; S. Roger Horchow Award, Jefferson awards, greatest public service by a private citizen, American Institute for Public Service, 1983; inducted into the Hall of Great Western Performers, National Cowboy and Western Heritage Museum, 1984; decorated knight of French Legion of Honor, 1985, designated an officier, 1990; Emmy Award nomination, outstanding lead actor in a miniseries or special, and Golden Globe Award nomination, best performance by an actor in a miniseries or motion picture made for television, both 1986, for *Amos;* German Goldene Kamera Award, 1987; Career Achievement Award, National Board of Review, 1988; Robert F. Meltzer Award, Writers Guild of America, 1991; Chaim Weizmann Award in Sciences and Humanities, for services to Israel, 1991; Lifetime Achievement awards, American Film Institute, 1991 and 1999; Douglas's performance in *The Secret* named the year's best performance by critics of the *Los Angeles Times,* c. 1992; Emmy Award nomination, outstanding lead actor in a drama series, and Annual CableACE Award nomination, National Cable Television Association, both 1992, for "Two–Fisted Tales," *Tales from the Crypt;* Einstein awards, National Dyslexia Research

Foundation, 1992 and 1995; Lifetime Achievement Award, ShoWest Convention, National Association of Theatre Owners, 1994; Kennedy Center Honors, John F. Kennedy Center for the Performing Arts, 1995, for contributions to U.S. cultural life; honorary Academy Award, lifetime achievement, 1996; Carl Foreman Prize, American Cinema Foundation, 1996; Lifetime Achievement Award, Hollywood Film Festival, 1997; named one of the top 100 movie stars of all time, *Empire* magazine, 1997, and *Entertainment Weekly;* Golden Boot Award (affiliated with the Motion Picture and Television Fund), 1998; Life Achievement Award, Screen Actors Guild, 1999; Spencer Tracy Award for outstanding achievement in drama, University of California, Los Angeles, 1999; Emmy Award nomination, outstanding guest actor in a drama series, 2000, for "Bar Mitzvah," *Touched by an Angel;* Lifetime Achievement awards, Wine Country Film Festival and Jerusalem Film Festival, both 2000; honorary Golden Berlin Bear, 2001; Milestone Award, Golden Laurel awards, Producers Guild of America, 2001; American National Medal of the Arts, National Endowment for the Arts, 2001; Medal of Honor, University of California, Los Angeles, 2002; Lifetime Achievement Award, Palm Springs International Film Festival, 2005; Kirk Douglas Way in Palm Springs, CA named in his honor, 2005; Excellence in Film Award, Santa Barbara International Film Festival, 2006; American Cinema Award, distinguished achievement in film; received a star on the Hollywood Walk of Fame; named one of the fifty greatest screen legends, American Film Institute; named Friars Club man of the year; Distinguished Contribution Award, American Labor Council; Bill of Rights Award, American Civil Liberties Union; other honors include the naming of a school in California in his honor.

CREDITS

Film Appearances:

Walter P. O'Neil, *The Strange Love of Martha Ivers,* Paramount, 1946.

Peter Niles, *Mourning Becomes Electra,* RKO Radio Pictures, 1947.

Whit Sterling, *Out of the Past* (also known as *Build My Gallows High*), RKO Radio Pictures, 1947.

George Phipps, *A Letter to Three Wives,* Twentieth Century–Fox, 1948.

Noll "Dink" Turner, *I Walk Alone,* Paramount, 1948.

Owen Waterbury, *My Dear Secretary,* United Artists, 1948.

Tucker Wedge, *The Walls of Jericho,* Twentieth Century–Fox, 1948.

Michael "Midge" Kelly, *Champion,* United Artists, 1949.

Jim O'Connor, *The Glass Menagerie,* Warner Bros., 1950.

Charles "Chuck" Tatum, *The Big Carnival* (also known as *Ace in the Hole* and *The Human Interest Story*), Paramount, 1951.

Detective James "Jim" McLeod, *Detective Story* (also known as *The Detective Story*), Paramount, 1951.

Marshal Len Merrick, *Along the Great Divide* (also known as *The Travelers*), Warner Bros., 1951.

Rick Martin, *Young Man with a Horn* (also known as *Young Man of Music* and *Young Man with a Trumpet*), Warner Bros., 1951.

Jim Deakins, *The Big Sky,* RKO Radio Pictures, 1952.

Jim (some sources cite John) Fallon, *The Big Trees* (also known as *Big Trees*), Warner Bros., 1952.

Jonathan Shields, *The Bad and the Beautiful* (also known as *Memorial to a Bad Man* and *Tribute to a Badman*), Metro–Goldwyn–Mayer, 1952.

Hans Muller, *The Juggler,* Columbia, 1953.

Pierre Narval, "Equilibrium," *The Story of Three Loves* (also known as *Equilibrium* and *Three Stories of Love*), Metro–Goldwyn–Mayer, 1953.

Robert Teller, *Un acte d'amour* (also known as *Act of Love* and *Quelque part dans le monde*), United Artists, 1953.

Ned Land, *20,000 Leagues under the Sea* (also known as *Jules Verne's "20,000 Leagues under the Sea"* and *Walt Disney's "20,000 Leagues under the Sea"*), Buena Vista, 1954.

Dempsey Rae, *Man without a Star,* Universal, 1955.

Gino Borgesa, *The Racers* (also known as *Such Men Are Dangerous*), Twentieth Century–Fox, 1955.

Johnny Hawks, *The Indian Fighter,* United Artists, 1955.

Ulysses, *Ulisse* (also known as *Ulysses*), Paramount, 1955.

(Uncredited) Himself, *Van Gogh: Darkness into Light* (short documentary), Metro–Goldwyn–Mayer, 1956.

Vincent van Gogh, *Lust for Life,* Metro–Goldwyn–Mayer, 1956.

Colonel Dax, *Paths of Glory,* United Artists, 1957.

John H. "Doc" Holliday, *Gunfight at the O. K. Corral,* Paramount, 1957.

Major general Melville A. Goodwin, *Top Secret Affair* (also known as *Their Secret Affair*), Warner Bros., 1957.

Einar, *The Vikings,* United Artists, 1958.

Marshal Matt Morgan, *Last Train from Gun Hill* (also known as *One Angry Day*), Paramount, 1959.

Richard "Dick" Dudgeon, *The Devil's Disciple,* United Artists, 1959.

Himself, *Premier Khrushchev in the USA* (documentary), 1959, Gala Film Distributors, 1960.

Larry Coe, *Strangers When We Meet,* Columbia, 1960.

Title role, *Spartacus* (also known as *Spartacus: Rebel against Rome*), Universal, 1960.

Brendan "Bren" O'Malley, *The Last Sunset,* Universal, 1961.

Major Steve Garrett, *Town without Pity* (also known as *Shocker, Stadt ohne Mitleid,* and *Ville sans pitie*), United Artists, 1961.

Jack Andrus, *Two Weeks in Another Town,* Metro–Goldwyn–Mayer, 1962.

John W. "Jack" Burns, *Lonely Are the Brave* (also known as *Last Hero*), Universal, 1962.

Sergeant P. J. Briscoe, *The Hook,* Metro–Goldwyn–Mayer, 1962.

Donald Kenneth "Deke" Gentry, *For Love or Money* (also known as *Three on a Match* and *A Three–Way Match*), Universal, 1963.

George Brougham, Vicar Atlee, Mr. Pythian, and Arthur Henderson, *The List of Adrian Messenger,* Universal, 1963.

(In archive footage) Himself, *Hollywood without Make–Up* (documentary), 1963.

Colonel Martin "Jiggs" Casey, *Seven Days in May,* Paramount, 1964.

Commander Paul Eddington, *In Harm's Way,* Paramount, 1965.

Dr. Rolf Pedersen, *The Heroes of Telemark* (also known as *Anthony Mann's "The Heroes of Telemark"*), Columbia, 1965.

Colonel David "Mickey" Marcus, *Cast a Giant Shadow,* United Artists, 1966.

General George S. Patton, Jr., *Paris brule–t–il?* (also known as *Is Paris Burning?*), Paramount, 1966.

Lomax, *The War Wagon,* Universal, 1967.

Senator William J. Tadlock, *The Way West,* United Artists, 1967.

Frank Ginetta, *The Brotherhood,* Paramount, 1968.

Jim Schuyler, *A Lovely Way to Die* (also known as *A Lovely Way to Go*), Universal, 1968.

Himself, *Once upon a Wheel* (documentary), 1968.

Himself, *Rowan & Martin at the Movies* (short), Metro–Goldwyn–Mayer, 1968.

Eddie Anderson (also known as Evangelos Arness and Evans Arness), *The Arrangement,* Warner Bros., 1969.

French Lunch (short film), 1969.

Paris Pitman, Jr., *There Was a Crooked Man,* Warner Bros., 1970.

Andrej, *To Catch a Spy* (also known as *Catch Me a Spy, Keep Your Fingers Crossed,* and *Les doigts croises*), Rank, 1971.

Will Denton, *The Light at the Edge of the World* (also known as *La luz del fin del mundo*), National General, 1971.

Will Tenneray, *A Gunfight* (also known as *Gunfight*), Paramount, 1971.

Peg, *Scalawag* (also known as *Jamie's Treasure Hunt, Protuva,* and *Un magnifico ceffo di galera*), Paramount, 1973.

Steve Wallace, *Un uomo da rispettare* (also known as *Hearts and Minds, A Man to Respect, The Master Touch,* and *Ein Achtbarer Mann*), Warner Bros., 1974.

Marshal Howard Nightingale, *Posse,* Paramount, 1975.

Mike Wayne, *Once Is Not Enough* (also known as *Jacqueline Susann's "Once Is Not Enough"*), Paramount, 1975.

Peter Sandza, *The Fury,* Twentieth Century–Fox, 1978.

Robert Caine, *Holocaust 2000* (also known as *The Chosen, The Hex Massacre,* and *Rain of Fire*), American International Pictures, 1978.

"Cactus Jack" Slade (title role), *The Villain* (also known as *Cactus Jack*), Columbia, 1979.

Dr. Tuttle (the Maestro), *Home Movies* (also known as *The Maestro*), United Artists, 1979.

Adam, *Saturn 3* (also known as *Saturn City* and *Saturn Three*), Associated Film Distributors, 1980.

Captain Matthew Yelland, *The Final Countdown* (also known as *U.S.S. Nimitz: Lost in the Pacific*), United Artists, 1980.

(In archive footage) Boss of three thugs, *Dead Men Don't Wear Plaid* (also known as *Bogart Jr.* and *Dead Men Wear No Plaid*), Universal, 1982.

Harrison and Spur, *The Man from Snowy River* (also known as *Snowy River, Czlowiek znad snieznej rzeki, El hombre del rio nevado, L'homme de la riviere d'argent, L'uomo del fiume nevoso, Lumisen joen mies,* and *Mannen fraan Snowy River*), Twentieth Century–Fox, 1982.

Carl "Buster" Marzack, *Eddie Macon's Run,* Universal, 1983.

Archie Long, *Tough Guys,* Buena Vista, 1986.

Host, *A Day in the Country: Impressionism and the French Landscape* (short documentary), c. 1989.

Eduardo Provolone, Sr., *Oscar* (also known as *A mala das trapalhadas, L'embrouille est dans le sac, Oscar czyli 60 klopotow na minute, Oscar—Minha filha quer casar, Oscar, quita las manos, Oscar—un fidanzato per due figlie,* and *Oscar—Vom Regen in die Traufe*), Buena Vista, 1991.

Quentin, *Veraz* (also known as *Welcome to Veraz* and *Bienvenido a Veraz*), 1991.

(In archive footage) *Rock Hudson's Home Movies* (documentary), Couch Potato Productions, c. 1993.

Himself, *A Century of Cinema* (documentary), Miramax, 1994.

Uncle Joe McTeague, *Greedy,* Universal, 1994.

Ed Reece, *Lies Boys Tell,* 1995, originally broadcast as the television movie *Take Me Home Again,* NBC, 1994.

Harry Agensky, *Diamonds* (also known as *Der Gauner mit dem Diamantenherz*), Miramax, 1999.

Mitchell Gromberg, *It Runs in the Family* (also known as *Family Business*), Metro–Goldwyn–Mayer, 2003.

Donal Baines, *Illusion* (also known as *The Illusion*), 2004, Awakened Media, 2006.

(Uncredited; in archive footage) Einar, *Cineastes contra magnats* (documentary), Canonigo Films, 2005.

Himself, *Trumbo* (documentary), Samuel Goldwyn Films, c. 2008.

Film Director:

Scalawag (also known as *Jamie's Treasure Hunt, Protuva,* and *Un magnifico ceffo di galera*), Paramount, 1973.

Posse, Paramount, 1975.

Film Executive Producer:

The Vikings, United Artists, 1958.

The Devil's Disciple, United Artists, 1959.

Spartacus (also known as *Spartacus: Rebel against Rome*), Universal, 1960.

The Last Sunset, Universal, 1961.

Grand Prix, Metro–Goldwyn–Mayer, 1966.

The Man from Snowy River (also known as *Snowy River, Czlowiek znad snieznej rzeki, El hombre del rio nevado, L'homme de la riviere d'argent, L'uomo del fiume nevoso, Lumisen joen mies,* and *Mannen fraan Snowy River*), Twentieth Century–Fox, 1982.

Eddie Macon's Run, Universal, 1983.

Film Producer:

The Indian Fighter, United Artists, 1955.

Paths of Glory, United Artists, 1957.

Lonely Are the Brave (also known as *Last Hero*), Universal, 1962.

The List of Adrian Messenger, Universal, 1963.

Seven Days in May, Paramount, 1964.

The Brotherhood, Paramount, 1968.

A Gunfight (also known as *Gunfight*), Paramount, 1971.

The Light at the Edge of the World (also known as *La luz del fin del mundo*), National General, 1971.

Summertree, Columbia, 1971.

Scalawag (also known as *Jamie's Treasure Hunt, Pro-tuva,* and *Un magnifico ceffo di galera*), Paramount, 1973.

Posse, Paramount, 1975.

Home Movies (also known as *The Maestro*), United Artists, 1979.

The Villain (also known as *Cactus Jack*), Columbia, 1979.

(With Peter Vincent Douglas) *The Final Countdown* (also known as *U.S.S. Nimitz: Lost in the Pacific*), United Artists, 1980.

Film Work; as Issur Danielovitch:

Production consultant, *Tough Guys,* Buena Vista, 1986.

Television Appearances; Miniseries:

Alex Vandervoort, *The Moneychangers* (also known as *Arthur Hailey's "The Moneychangers," Arthur Hailey's "The Money Changers,"* and *The Money Changers*), NBC, 1976.

David Konig, *Queenie,* ABC, 1987.

Television Appearances; Movies:

George Anderson, *Mousey* (also known as *Cat and Mouse*), ABC, 1974.

Hershel Vilnofsky, *Victory at Entebbe,* ABC, 1976.

Joe Rabin, *Remembrance of Love* (also known as *Holocaust Survivors ... Remembrance of Love*), NBC, 1982.

Harry H. "Handsome Harry" Holland, *Draw!,* HBO, 1984.

Amos Lasher (title role), *Amos,* CBS, 1985.

Matthew Harrison Brady, *Inherit the Wind,* NBC, 1988.

Mike Dunmore, *The Secret* (also known as *Family Secrets* and *What's the Matter with Danny Dunmore?*), CBS, 1992.

Ed Reece, *Take Me Home Again,* NBC, 1994, released theatrically in Europe as *Lies Boys Tell,* 1995.

Television Appearances; Specials:

Host and narrator, *The General Motors Fiftieth Anniversary Show,* NBC, 1957.

Narrator, *The Legend of Silent Night,* ABC, 1968.

Performer, *The Special London Bridge Special,* NBC, 1972.

Title roles, *Dr. Jekyll and Mr. Hyde,* NBC, 1973.

The Stars Salute Israel at Thirty, ABC, 1978.

Host and narrator, *I'd Rather Be Dead,* syndicated, 1979.

Himself, *Homage for the Duke,* ABC, 1979.

Johnny Cash: The First 25 Years, CBS, 1980.

(In archive footage) Himself, *Margret Duenser, auf der Suche nach den Besonderen,* 1981.

Himself, *Celebrity Daredevils,* ABC, 1983.

Himself, *James Bond: The First 21 Years,* 1983.

Himself, *Salute to Lady Liberty,* CBS, 1984.

Himself, *Bugs Bunny/Looney Tunes All–Star 50th Anniversary* (also known as *Looney Tunes 50th Anniversary*), CBS, 1986.

Liberty Weekend, ABC, 1986.

Host, *Circus of the Stars* (also known as *The 12th Annual Circus of the Stars*), CBS, 1987.

Narrator, *Korea: War at the 38th Parallel* (also known as *The War in Korea*), TBS and BBC, 1988.

The Music Center 25th Anniversary, PBS, 1990.

Himself, *Larry King TNT Extra,* TNT, 1992.

(In archive footage) Himself, *Rowan and Martin's "Laugh–In" 25th Anniversary* (also known as *Laugh–In's 25th Anniversary* and *Rowan and Martin's "Laugh–In" 25th Anniversary Reunion*), NBC, 1993.

(In archive footage) Himself, *The Best of the Don Lane Show,* 1994.

Great American Music: A Salute to Fast Cars, Family Channel, 1994.

Himself, *To Life! America Celebrates Israel's 50th,* CBS, 1998.

(In archive footage) Himself, *AFI's 100 Years, 100 Thrills: America's Most Heart–Pounding Movies,* 2001.

Himself, *FBI contre Hollywood,* 2001.

Himself, *Lana Turner ... a Daughter's Memoir,* 2001.

Himself, *Darkness at High Noon: The Carl Foreman Documents,* PBS, 2002.

(In archive footage) Himself, *Kirk Douglas and Vincente Minnelli,* 2002.

Himself, *AFI's 100 Years ... 100 Heroes & Villains* (also known as *AFI's 100 Years, 100 Heroes & Villains: America's Greatest Screen Characters*), CBS, 2003.

(In archive footage) Himself, *Anthony Quinn and Kirk Douglas,* 2003.

(Uncredited; in archive footage) Jonathan Shields, *Watch the Skies! Science Fiction, the 1950s, and Us* (also known as *Watch the Skies!*), TCM, 2005.

Himself, *… A Father … a Son … Once upon a Time in Hollywood,* HBO, 2005.

(In archive footage) Himself, *La marato 2005,* 2005.

Himself, *AFI's 100 Years … 100 Cheers: America's Most Inspiring Movies,* CBS, 2006.

(In archive footage) Himself, *Camara negra. Teatro Victoria Eugenia,* Television Espanola (TVE, Spain), 2007.

(In archive footage) Himself, *Ein Leben wie im Flug,* 2007.

(In archive footage) Himself, *100 Years of John Wayne,* Encore Westerns, 2007.

Television Appearances; Awards Presentations:

Presenter, *The 26th Annual Academy Awards,* NBC, 1954.

Presenter, *The 29th Annual Academy Awards,* NBC, 1957.

The 30th Annual Academy Awards, NBC, 1958.

The 31st Annual Academy Awards, NBC, 1959.

Presenter, *The 21st Annual Tony Awards,* ABC, 1967.

Show Business Salute to Milton Berle, NBC, 1973.

The American Film Institute Salute to James Cagney (also known as *The AFI Salute to James Cagney* and *American Film Institute Salutes James Cagney*), CBS, 1974.

Salute to Lew Grade, 1975.

Presenter, *The 50th Annual Academy Awards,* ABC, 1978.

The American Film Institute Salute to Henry Fonda (also known as *The AFI Salute to Henry Fonda* and *American Film Institute Salutes Henry Fonda*), CBS, 1978.

A Tribute to "Mr. Television," Milton Berle, NBC, 1978.

Presenter, *The 52nd Annual Academy Awards,* ABC, 1980.

Presenter, *The 57th Annual Academy Awards,* ABC, 1985.

The Kennedy Center Honors: A Celebration of the Performing Arts (also known as *The Seventh Annual Kennedy Center Honors: A Celebration of the Performing Arts*), CBS, 1985.

The 43rd Annual Golden Globe Awards, 1986.

America's Tribute to Bob Hope, NBC, 1988.

The 14th Annual People's Choice Awards, CBS, 1988.

Guest of honor, *The 19th Annual American Film Institute Lifetime Achievement Award: A Salute to Kirk Douglas* (also known as *The AFI Salute to Kirk Douglas* and *American Film Institute Salutes Kirk Douglas*), CBS, 1991.

Presenter, *The 46th Annual Tony Awards,* CBS, 1992.

Presenter, *The 66th Annual Academy Awards Presentation,* ABC, 1994.

Kennedy Center Honors: A Celebration of the Performing Arts (also known as *The 16th Annual Kennedy Center Honors: A Celebration of the Performing Arts*), CBS, 1994.

Presenter, *The 68th Annual Academy Awards,* ABC, 1996.

Fifth Annual Screen Actors Guild Awards (also known as *Screen Actors Guild Fifth Annual Awards*), TNT, 1999.

Presenter, *The 75th Annual Academy Awards,* ABC, 2003.

Presenter, *World Music Awards 2004,* ABC, 2004.

Presenter, *AFI Life Achievement Award: A Tribute to Al Pacino,* USA Network, 2007.

Television Appearances; Episodic:

Himself, *Floor Show* (also known as *Eddie Condon's "Floor Show"*), NBC, 1949.

Himself, *The Colgate Comedy Hour* (also known as *Colgate Summer Comedy Hour, The Colgate Variety Hour, Michael Todd Revue,* and *The NBC Comedy Hour*), NBC, 1952.

Himself, *The Ken Murray Show,* CBS, 1952.

Himself, *The Name's the Same,* ABC, 1953.

Himself, *What's My Line?,* CBS, 1953.

Himself, "The Disneyland Story," *Disneyland* (also known as *Disneylandia, The Disney Sunday Movie, Disney's Wonderful World, The Magical World of Disney, Walt Disney, Walt Disney Presents, Walt Disney's Wonderful World of Color,* and *The Wonderful World of Disney*), ABC, 1954.

Himself, "Jam Session at Jack's" (also known as "The Jam Session Show"), *The Jack Benny Program* (also known as *The Jack Benny Show*), CBS, 1954.

Himself, *Toast of the Town* (also known as *The Ed Sullivan Show*), CBS, 1954.

Himself, "Monsters of the Deep," *Disneyland* (also known as *Disneylandia, The Disney Sunday Movie, Disney's Wonderful World, The Magical World of Disney, Walt Disney, Walt Disney Presents, Walt Disney's Wonderful World of Color,* and *The Wonderful World of Disney*), ABC, 1955.

Awards presenter, *The Colgate Comedy Hour* (also known as *Colgate Summer Comedy Hour, The Colgate Variety Hour, Michael Todd Revue,* and *The NBC Comedy Hour*), NBC, 1955.

(In archive footage) Ulysses, *The Colgate Comedy Hour* (also known as *Colgate Summer Comedy Hour, The Colgate Variety Hour, Michael Todd Revue,* and *The NBC Comedy Hour*), NBC, 1955.

Himself, "Where Do the Stories Come From?," *Disneyland* (also known as *Disneylandia, The Disney Sunday Movie, Disney's Wonderful World, The Magical World of Disney, Walt Disney, Walt Disney Presents, Walt Disney's Wonderful World of Color,* and *The Wonderful World of Disney*), ABC, 1956.

Guest host, *The Ed Sullivan Show* (also known as *Toast of the Town*), CBS, 1956.

Himself, *The Ed Sullivan Show* (also known as *Toast of the Town*), CBS, 1956, 1957 (in archive footage), 1966.

Himself, "Hollywood around the World," *The Seven Lively Arts,* CBS, 1957.

Himself, *Person to Person,* CBS, 1957.

Himself, *The Steve Allen Show* (also known as *The Steve Allen Plymouth Show*), NBC, 1957, 1958.

Himself, "Kirk Douglas," *This Is Your Life,* NBC, 1958.

Mystery guest, *What's My Line?,* CBS, 1960.

The Best of Paar, NBC, 1960.

The Jack Paar Show, NBC, 1960.

Here's Hollywood, NBC, 1962.

Himself, *Cinepanorama,* 1962, 1964.

Himself, "Lucy Goes to a Hollywood Premiere," *The Lucy Show* (also known as *The Lucille Ball Show*), CBS, 1966.

Himself, *Reflets de Cannes,* 1966.

Narrator, "Cortez and the Legend," *Saga of Western Man,* syndicated, 1967.

Himself, *Rowan & Martin's "Laugh–In"* (also known as *Laugh–In*), NBC, 1968 (multiple episodes).

Himself, *The Johnny Cash Show,* ABC, 1970.

Himself, "Film Night Special: Kirk Douglas," *Film Night,* BBC–2, 1971.

Himself, *The Dick Cavett Show,* ABC, 1971.

Himself, *The Tonight Show Starring Johnny Carson* (also known as *The Best of Carson*), NBC, 1971.

Himself, "Don Rickles," *This Is Your Life,* 1972.

Himself, *V.I.P.–Schaukel,* 1972.

Himself, "Celebrity Roast: Kirk Douglas," *The Dean Martin Show* (also known as *The Dean Martin Comedy Hour*), NBC, 1973.

Himself, *Dinah's Place,* NBC, 1973.

Himself, "Celebrity Roast: Don Rickles," *The Dean Martin Show* (also known as *The Dean Martin Comedy Hour*), NBC, 1974.

Himself, *Dinah!* (also known as *Dinah* and *Dinah and Friends*), syndicated, 1975.

(In archive footage) Ned Land, "20,000 Leagues under the Sea," *The Wonderful World of Disney* (also known as *Disneyland, Disneylandia, The Disney Sunday Movie, Disney's Wonderful World, The Magical World of Disney, Walt Disney, Walt Disney Presents,* and *Walt Disney's Wonderful World of Color*), NBC, 1976.

Guest host, *Saturday Night Live* (also known as *NBC's "Saturday Night," Saturday Night, Saturday Night Live '80, SNL,* and *SNL 25*), NBC, 1980.

Himself, *Aspel & Company,* London Weekend Television, 1985.

Himself, *Good Morning Britain* (also known as *TV–am*), 1988.

Himself, *Mas estrellas que en el cielo,* 1989.

Champlin on Film, Bravo, 1989.

"Anthony Quinn," *Crazy about the Movies,* Cinemax, 1990.

General Calthrob, "Yellow," a segment of "Two–Fisted Tales," *Tales from the Crypt* (also known as *HBO's "Tales from the Crypt"*), HBO, 1991.

Himself, *Late Night with David Letterman,* NBC, 1992.

(Uncredited) Himself, "The Popcorn Bowl," *Coach,* ABC, 1994.

Himself, *Verstehen Sie Spass?,* 1995.

(In archive footage) Spartacus, "Athens City Academy for the Performing Bards," *Xena: Warrior Princess* (also known as *Xena*), syndicated, 1996.

Voice of Chester J. Lampwick, "The Day the Violence Died," *The Simpsons* (animated), Fox, 1996.

Himself, *Late Night with Conan O'Brien,* NBC, 1997.

Himself, *The Rosie O'Donnell Show,* syndicated, 1997.

Himself, "The Films of John Frankenheimer," *The Directors,* Encore, c. 1997.

Himself, *Intimate Portrait: Lauren Bacall,* Lifetime, 1998.

Himself, "Kirk Douglas: A Lust for Life," *Biography* (also known as *A&E Biography: Kirk Douglas*), Arts and Entertainment, 1999.

Himself, *Clive Anderson All Talk,* BBC, 1999.

Ross Burger, "Bar Mitzvah," *Touched by an Angel,* CBS, 2000.

Himself, "Jean Simmons: Picture Perfect," *Biography* (also known as *A&E Biography: Jean Simmons*), Arts and Entertainment, 2001.

Himself, *Parkinson,* 2001.

Himself, "Legends," *48 Hours* (also known as *48 Hours Investigates* and *48 Hours Mystery*), CBS, 2002.

Himself, *Larry King Live,* Cable News Network, 2002, 2005.

Himself, "Kirk Douglas," *The Hollywood Greats* (also known as *Hollywood Greats*), BBC, 2003.

Himself, *The Late Late Show with Craig Kilborn* (also known as *The Late Late Show*), CBS, 2003.

Himself, *The Oprah Winfrey Show* (also known as *Oprah*), syndicated, 2003 (multiple episodes).

(In archive footage) Himself, *Les 40 ans de la 2,* 2004.

Himself, *Entertainment Tonight* (also known as *Entertainment This Week, E.T., ET Weekend,* and *This Week in Entertainment*), syndicated, 2006, multiple episodes in 2007.

Himself, *Jimmy Kimmel Live!* (also known as *The Jimmy Kimmel Project*), ABC, 2007.

(In archive footage) Himself, *La tele de tu vida,* 2007.

Himself, *20 heures le journal,* 2007.

Appeared in other television programs, including *Storytime,* PBS.

Television Work:

Producer, *Tales of the Vikings* (series; also known as *The Vikings*), syndicated, c. 1959.

Director, *Mousey* (movie; also known as *Cat and Mouse*), ABC, 1974.

Stage Appearances:

(As George Spelvin, Jr.) Western Union boy, *Spring Again,* Henry Miller's Theatre, New York City, 1941.

Orderly, *The Three Sisters,* Ethel Barrymore Theatre, New York City, 1942–43.

Lieutenant Lenny Archer, *Kiss and Tell,* Biltmore Theatre, New York City, beginning c. 1943, also produced at the Bijou Theatre, New York City.

Star in the Window, c. 1944.

Ray Mackenzie, *Trio,* Belasco Theatre, New York City, 1944–45.

Soldier, *The Wind Is Ninety,* Booth Theatre, New York City, 1945.

Steve, *Alice in Arms,* National Theatre, New York City, 1945.

Hopkins, *Woman Bites Dog,* Belasco Theatre, 1946.

Detective James "Jim" McLeod, *Detective Story,* Sombrero Playhouse, Phoenix, AZ, 1951.

Randle Patrick "R. P." McMurphy, *One Flew over the Cuckoo's Nest,* Cort Theatre, New York City, 1963–64.

The Boys in Autumn, San Francisco, CA, 1981.

Appeared in other productions, including summer theatre productions, 1939–41.

Stage Producer; with Others:

One Flew over the Cuckoo's Nest, Cort Theatre, New York City, 1963–64.

Radio Appearances:

Appeared in radio programs, including appearances in radio soap operas.

RECORDINGS

Videos:

Himself, *The Racing Experience,* 1988.

Tee Vee Treasures, Volume Two, Rhino Home Video, 1991.

(In archive footage) Himself, *Kirk Douglas: Video Scrapbook,* 1994.

Himself, *Completely Cuckoo,* re–edited version known as *The Making of "One Flew over the Cuckoo's Nest,"* 1997.

Himself, *Frank Sinatra Memorial,* Passport Video, c. 2000.

Himself, *The Life and Times of Kirk Douglas* (short), Buena Vista Home Entertainment, 2000.

(In archive footage) Himself, *Pulp Cinema,* 2001.

(In archive footage) Himself, *The Definitive Elvis: The Hollywood Years—Part 1: 1956–1961,* Passport International Entertainment, 2002.

Himself, *The Making of "20,000 Leagues under the Sea,"* Buena Vista Home Entertainment, 2003.

Audiobooks:

Kirk Douglas, *The Ragman's Son,* Audioworks, 1988.

WRITINGS

Nonfiction; Autobiographies:

The Ragman's Son, Simon & Schuster, 1988.

Climbing the Mountain: My Search for Meaning, Simon & Schuster, 1997.

My Stroke of Luck, William Morrow, 2002.

Let's Face It: 90 Years of Living, Loving, and Learning, John Wiley and Sons, 2007.

Novels:

Dance with the Devil, Random House, 1990.

The Gift, Warner Books, 1992.

Last Tango in Brooklyn, Warner Books, 1994.

Writings for Children:

The Broken Mirror (novella), illustrated by Jenny Vasilyev, Simon & Schuster Children's Publishing, 1997.

Young Heroes of the Bible: A Book for Family Sharing (nonfiction; also known as *Kid Heroes of the Bible*), illustrated by Dom Lee, Simon & Schuster Children's Publishing, 1999.

OTHER SOURCES

Books:

Dictionary of Twentieth Century Culture, Volume 1: *American Culture after World War II,* Gale, 1994.

International Dictionary of Films and Filmmakers, Volume 3: *Actors and Actresses,* fourth edition, St. James Press, 2000.

Kaye, Annene and Jim Sclavunos, *Michael Douglas and the Douglas Clan,* 1989.

Lacourbe, Roland, *Kirk Douglas,* PAC, 1980.

McBride, Joseph, *Kirk Douglas,* Pyramid Publications, 1976.

Munn, Michael, *Kirk Douglas: The Man—The Actor,* St. Martin's Press, 1985.

Press, Skip, *Michael and Kirk Douglas,* Crestwood House, 1995.

Thomas, Tony, *The Films of Kirk Douglas,* Citadel, 1972.

Periodicals:

American Film, March, 1991.

Architectural Digest, April, 1990.

Cine Revue, July 12, 1984; September 27, 1984.

Daily News, October 28, 1991.

Empire, issue 61, 1994, pp. 86–93; October, 1997, p. 197.

Films and Filming, September, 1972.

Harper's Bazaar, June, 1990.

Interview, January, 2000, p. 44.

Ladies Home Journal, April, 1988.

New York Post, March 3, 1994.

New York Times, March 22, 1996.

Parade, January 23, 2000, p. 12.

People Weekly, October 3, 1988.

Premiere, July, 1991; December, 2002, p. 132.

Tikkun, September, 2000, p. 55.

Times (London), April 14, 2007.
TV Guide, March 6, 1999, pp. 32–35; August 7, 2005, pp. 34–35.
USA Today, December 14, 1994.
Washington Post, August 13, 2005.

DOWSE, Denise 1958–
(Denise Dowes, Denise Y. Dowse)

PERSONAL

Full name, Denise Yvonne Dowse; born February 21, 1958, in Honolulu, HI; father, a naval officer. *Education:* Norfolk State University, B.A., English and theatre (cum laude).

Addresses: *Office*—c/o Anthony Meindl's Actor's Lab, MetaTheater on Melrose, 7801 Melrose Ave., Los Angeles, CA 90046. *Agent*—Amsel, Eisenstadt & Frazier, 5055 Wilshire Blvd., Suite 865, Los Angeles, CA 90036. *Manager*—Sandra Siegal, The Siegal Company, 9025 Wilshire Blvd., Suite 400, Beverly Hills, CA 90211. *Publicist*—Celebrity Public Relations, 49 East 41st St., Suite 449, New York, NY 10165.

Career: Actress and director. Former member of the traveling performing group Up with People. Aschaffenburg Military Community Theatre (Germany), director; Amazing Grace Conservatory, Los Angeles, resident director and instructor of speech and acting; Anthony Meindl's Actor's Lab, Los Angeles, acting instructor.

Member: Actors' Equity Association.

Awards, Honors: *DramaLogue* Award, best director, 1995, and Image Award, best director, National Association for the Advancement of Colored People (NAACP), 1996, both for *The Chest;* Image Award, best director, c. 1996, for *Long Time Since Yesterday;* some sources cite an Image Award, best director, c. 1996, for *When Willows Weep in Foxholes.*

CREDITS

Television Appearances; Series:
Angela Quartermaine, *Almost There!,* 1988–89.
Mrs. Yvonne Teasley, *Beverly Hills 90210,* Fox, between 1991 and 2000.
Sylvia Watkins, *Built to Last,* NBC, 1997.
Judge Rebecca Damsen, *The Guardian* (also known as *El guardia, The Guardian—Retter mit Herz, Le protecteur, O allos mou eaftos, Ochita bengoshi Nick Fallin, Ochita bengoshi Nick Fallin 2,* and *Oikeuden puolesta*), CBS, 2001–2004.
Judge Jane Briar, *Shark,* CBS, beginning c. 2007.

Television Appearances; Miniseries:
Drug dealer, *Wild Palms,* ABC, 1993.

Television Appearances; Movies:
Board member, *Locked Up: A Mother's Rage,* 1991.
(As Denise Y. Dowse) Woman, *Murderous Vision,* USA Network, 1991.
(As Denise Y. Dowse) Dr. Jarvis, *The Enemy Within,* HBO, 1994.
Cristianne, *Kissing Miranda,* 1995.
Dispatcher, *Sketch Artist II: Hands That See* (also known as *A Feel for Murder* and *Sketch Artist II*), Showtime, 1995.
See Jane Run, ABC, 1995.
Detective Pruitt, *Killing Mr. Griffin* (also known as *Killing Griffin*), NBC, 1997.
Mom, *Book of Love* (also known as *Book of Love: The Definitive Reason Why Men Are Dogs*), Black Entertainment Television, c. 2002.
Mona, *What about Your Friends: Weekend Getaway,* UPN, 2002.
Voice of Officer Shirley, *Rocket Power: Reggie's Big "Beach" Break* (animated), Nickelodeon, 2003.

Television Appearances; Specials:
As a child, appeared in *A Dog Called Bum,* a televised play produced in the San Diego, CA area.

Television Appearances; Awards Presentations:
The 31st Annual People's Choice Awards, CBS, 2005.

Television Appearances; Episodic:
Fourth FBI agent, "Wanted: Dead or Alive," *ALF,* NBC, 1989.
Professor Harriet Welkman (some sources cite Harriet Strathmore), "The 17 Year Itch," *Beverly Hills 90210,* Fox, 1990.
Dr. Worthy, "Rock–A–Bye Baby: Parts 1 & 2," *Roc* (also known as *Roc Live*), Fox, 1991.
Maggie Day, "Come Along with Me," *Jake and the Fatman,* CBS, 1991.
Kim's mother, "Afternoon Delights," *Bodies of Evidence,* CBS, 1992.
Receptionist, "The Wallet," *Seinfeld,* NBC, 1992.
Mrs. Jacobs, "Be True to Your Pre–School," *Full House,* ABC, 1993.
Sergeant McBride, "Schoolhouse Rock," *California Dreams* (also known as *Dreams*), NBC, 1993.
Sergeant McBride, "Surfboards and Cycles," *California Dreams* (also known as *Dreams*), NBC, 1993.
"A Christmas Story," *Thea,* ABC, 1993.
Barbara Carter, *Dudley* (also known as *Modern Times*), CBS, 1993.
Mother, "The Couch," *Seinfeld,* NBC, 1994.

Second woman, "Brown vs. the Board of Education," *Murphy Brown,* CBS, 1994.

Judge Caldwell, "Flesh and Blood," *Touched by an Angel,* CBS, 1996.

Mrs. Carlson, "Drunken Proposal," *Men Behaving Badly* (also known as *It's a Man's World*), NBC, 1996.

Arthell, "Race Relations," *Tracey Takes On ...,* HBO, 1997.

Doris Harper, "On Golden Pons," *Chicago Hope,* CBS, 1997.

Mrs. Porter, "Logan's Run," *Ink,* CBS, 1997.

Ms. Miller, "Invisible Girl" (also known as "Out of Mind, Out of Sight"), *Buffy the Vampire Slayer* (also known as *BtVS, Buffy, Buffy the Vampire Slayer: The Series, Nightfall, Bafi, ubica vampira, Buffy, a vampirok reme, Buffy, cacadora de vampiros, Buffy contre les vampires, Buffy i vampirofonissa, Buffy—Im Bann der Daemonen, Buffy, l'ammazzavampiri, Buffy, la cazavampiros, Buffy och vampyrerna, Buffy—Vampyrdaeberen, Buffy vampyrdoedaren, Buffy—Vampyrenes skrekk, Buffy—Vampyrernes skraek,* and *Buffy, vampyyrintappaja*), The WB, 1997.

Adoption agent, "Look Who's Talking," *NewsRadio* (also known as *News Radio, The Station, Dias de radio,* and *Dies de radio*), NBC, 1998.

Alease, "The Domino Effect," *Sister, Sister,* The WB, 1998.

Claire's lawyer, "The Closure," *The Closer* (also known as *The Tom Selleck Show*), CBS, 1998.

Councilperson Rene Broussard, "No Comment," *Any Day Now,* Lifetime, 1998.

Judge Martin, "And Justice for Some," *Step by Step* (also known as *Eine Starke Familie, Kaos i familien, Notre belle famille, Paso a paso, Steg for Steg,* and *Una bionda per papa*), CBS, 1998.

Mrs. Lysell (some sources cite Mrs. Lydell), "Day for Knight," *ER* (also known as *Emergency Room*), NBC, 1998.

Nora, "Gifts," *Party of Five,* Fox, 1998.

(As Denise Dowes) Principal Groves, "What's in a Word," *Promised Land* (also known as *Home of the Brave*), CBS, 1999.

Arbitrator, "New Job," *Grown Ups,* UPN, 2000.

Aunt Mattie (some sources cite Aunt Hattie), "Secrets & Lies," *Moesha,* UPN, 2000.

Caroline, "The Thin Line," *The Practice,* ABC, 2001.

Emily Griffin, "The Burning Vagina Monologues," *Girlfriends,* UPN, 2001.

Janet Katz, "The Trouble with Harry," *Becker,* CBS, 2001.

Second doctor, "Drew and the Baby," *The Drew Carey Show,* ABC, 2001.

Mrs. Ray, "Little Big Man," *Without a Trace* (also known as *Vanished* and *W.A.T.*), CBS, 2002.

Ms. Shepherd, "Lost in the System," *Judging Amy,* CBS, 2002.

Sondra Herman, "Mojo Rising," *Philly,* ABC, 2002.

Juanita Hendrucks, "The Brass Ring," *Dragnet* (also known as *L.A. Dragnet*), ABC, 2003.

Juanita Hendrucks, "Redemption," *Dragnet* (also known as *L.A. Dragnet*), ABC, 2003.

Juanita Hendrucks, "Well Endowed," *Dragnet* (also known as *L.A. Dragnet*), ABC, 2003.

Lucyruth, "Inherit the Lynn," *Girlfriends,* UPN, 2003.

Cicily Sutherland, "Joel Gideon," *Nip/Tuck,* FX Network, 2004.

Laura Hoover, "The Birds and the Batteries," *Everwood* (also known as *Our New Life in Everwood*), The WB, 2004.

Counselor, "Let's Stay Together," *All of Us,* UPN, 2004.

Counselor, "Divorce Means Never Having to Say I'm Sorry," *All of Us,* UPN, 2005.

Counselor, "Focus," *All of Us,* UPN, 2005.

Dr. Margaret Johnson, "Progeny," *Threshold,* CBS, 2005.

Angel of Destiny, "Vaya con Leos," *Charmed,* The WB, 2005.

Angel of Destiny, "Forever Charmed," *Charmed,* The WB, 2006.

Angel of Destiny, "Kill Billie: Vol. 2," *Charmed,* The WB, 2006.

Dr. Shapiro, "The Hair Down There," *All of Us,* The CW, 2006.

Doctor, "Exercise in Fertility: Part 2," *The Bernie Mac Show,* Fox, 2006.

Judge Nora Glover, "Good Faith," *Law & Order* (also known as *Law & Order Prime*), NBC, 2007.

Judge, "To Whom It May Concern," *Gilmore Girls* (also known as *Gilmore Girls: Beginnings* and *The Gilmore Way*), The CW, 2007.

Appeared as Toni Worthington in "Wahunthra," an episode of *The Gregory Hines Show* (also known as *Gregory Hines, Gregory Hines Show, Square One,* and *Tal pai! Tal filho!*), CBS; and as Mrs. Hanson in an episode of *Me and the Boys,* ABC. Appeared in episodes of other series, including *The West Wing* (also known as *West Wing* and *El ala oeste de la Casablanca*), NBC; and appeared as Alice Godchaux in "Balls in Your Court," an unaired episode of *Inconceivable,* NBC.

Film Appearances:

Channing, *Coldfire,* 1991.

Bank teller, *Sneakers,* Universal, 1992.

Malik's mother, *Helicopter* (short film), 1993.

Neighborhood woman, *Out for Blood,* 1993.

Voice, *Theodore Rex* (also known as *T. Rex*), New Line Cinema, 1995.

Olivia Biggs, *Bio–Dome* (also known as *Biodome*), Metro–Goldwyn–Mayer, 1996.

Sky marshal Tehat Meru, *Starship Troopers,* Sony Pictures Entertainment, 1997.

Health teacher, *Pleasantville* (also known as *Color Of Heart*), New Line Cinema, 1998.

Judge Constance Mullen, *A Civil Action* (also known as *Civil Action* and *Prejudice*), Buena Vista, 1998.

Dr. Perkins, *K–911,* Universal Pictures Home Video, 1999.

Tyrone's mother, *Requiem for a Dream* (also known as *Delusion over Addiction*), Artisan Entertainment, 2000.

Secretary, *Dr. Dolittle 2* (also known as *Doctor Dolittle 2, DR2, DR.2, Docteur Dolittle 2, Elaeintohtori 2,* and *Il Dottor Dolittle 2*), Twentieth Century–Fox, 2001.

Matilda, *Rats* (also known as *Killer Rats*), Nu Image Films, 2003.

Derrick's mother, *The Seat Filler,* DEJ Productions, 2004.

Judge, *Eulogy,* Lions Gate Films, 2004.

Marlene Andres, *Ray* (also known as *Unchain My Heart: The Ray Charles Story*), Universal, 2004.

Lisa, *Guess Who* (also known as *Black/White* and *Untitled Bernie Mac/Ashton Kutcher Project*), Columbia, 2005.

Principal Garrison, *Coach Carter* (also known as *All Day Long*), Paramount, 2005.

Lisa, *Her Best Move,* Metro–Goldwyn–Mayer, 2007.

Psychiatric hospital therapist, *Reign over Me* (also known as *Empty City* and *Reign o'er Me*), Columbia, 2007.

Film Director:

Reflections: A Story of Redemption (short film), Brace Yourself, 2004.

Directed the filmed first act of *The Chocolate Factory* as well as the second half on stage. Some sources cite Dowse as the director a short film affiliated with the project *What about Us.*

Stage Appearances:

Ghost, player king, and Claudius, *Hamlet,* Los Angeles Women's Shakespeare Company, Santa Monica, CA, 1995.

Long Time since Yesterday, Los Angeles, 1995.

The Vagina Monologues, HerShe Group, 2006.

Also appeared in other productions in the Los Angeles area, including *Club Termina, The Darker Face of the Earth, The Jackie Robinson Story, Life and Death: The Vaudeville Show* (also produced in Cuba), *Othello,* and *South of Where We Live.* As a child, appeared in *A Dog Called Bum,* a production in the San Diego, CA area.

Stage Director:

Long Time Since Yesterday, Los Angeles, 1995.

The Chest, Los Angeles, c. 1995.

When Willows Weep in Foxholes, Hudson Theatre, c. 1996.

If I Knew Then …, A.S.K. Theater Projects, Common Ground Festival, 1999.

West Side Story (musical), Amazing Grace Conservatory, Los Angeles, 1999.

Love & Other Social Issues (solo show), Assistance League Playhouse, Los Angeles, 2007.

The Wiz (musical), Amazing Grace Conservatory, Nate Holden Performing Arts Center, Los Angeles, 2007.

Also directed *The Chocolate Factory* (multimedia production), *It's a Wonderful Life … Ain't It?, Little Shop of Horrors* (musical), *The Prodigal Sister,* and *What about Us,* all Amazing Grace Conservatory.

OTHER SOURCES

Electronic:

Denise Dowse, http://www.denisedowselive.com, October 7, 2007.

DRAPER, Polly 1955(?)–

PERSONAL

Full name Polly Carey Draper; born June 15, 1955 (some sources cite 1956), in Gary, IN (some sources cite Palo Alto, CA); daughter of William (a United Nations development official) and Phyllis (a Peace Corps administrator) Draper; married Kevin Wade (a writer), 1983 (divorced, 1990 [some sources cite 1988]); married Michael Wolff (a musician), 1993; children: (second marriage) Nathaniel Marvin Wolff (Nat; a musician and actor), Alexander Draper Wolff (Alex; a musician and actor). *Education:* Yale University, B.A., M.F.A.

Addresses: *Agent*—Innovative Artists Talent and Literary Agency, 1505 10th St., Santa Monica, CA 90401.

Career: Actress, director, producer, and writer. Provided voice work for advertisements. Drama instructor for children at MacLaren Hall, Los Angeles.

Member: Directors Guild of America.

Awards, Honors: Emmy Award nomination, outstanding supporting actress in a drama series, 1988, for *thirtysomething;* named best Broadway actress of the season, *New York,* c. 1994, for *Four Dogs and a Bone;* Bronze Gryphon, best actress, and Grand Jury Prize (with others), best picture, both Giffoni Film Festival, 1998, Audience Award (with others), most popular feature, Hamptons International Film Festival, 1999, Deutsches Kinderhilfswerk Grand Prix, best feature, and Glass Bear, best feature, both with others, both Berlin

International Film Festival, 1999, and Reel 2 Real International Film Festival (Vancouver) Award (with others), best picture, all for *The Tic Code.*

CREDITS

Television Appearances; Series:
Ellyn Warren, *thirtysomething,* ABC, 1987–91.
Elaine Hoffman, *Gideon's Crossing,* ABC, 2000–2001.
Narrator, *Maternity Ward,* The Learning Channel, c. 2001–2002.

Also appeared as Winnie Robin, *Ryan's Hope,* ABC.

Television Appearances; Movies:
Adrian Towers (some sources cite Adrian Townshed), *Danielle Steel's "Heartbeat"* (also known as *Heartbeat*), NBC, 1993.
Ella Sabin, *Broken Promises: Taking Emily Back* (also known as *Broken Promises*), CBS, 1993.
Pamela Sutton, *The Innocent* (also known as *Silent Witness*), NBC, 1994.
Claire Gardner, *Home Song* (also known as *LaVyrle Spencer's "Home Song"*), CBS, 1996.
Herself, *Naked Brothers Band Movie,* Nickelodeon, 2005.
Rose Livien, *Shooting Livien,* Showtime, 2005.
Beth, *Too Young to Marry,* Lifetime, 2007.

Television Appearances; Specials:
"Merrill Markoe's Guide to Glamorous Living," *Cinemax Comedy Experiment,* Cinemax, 1988.
Herself, *Inside "thirtysomething,"* Bravo, 2001.

Television Appearances; Episodic:
Aileen, "The Grave Robber," *Tales from the Darkside* (also known as *Beraettelser fraan andra siden, Histoires de l'autre monde, Historias del mas ella,* and *Keskiyoen kauhutarinoita*), syndicated, 1987.
"The Verdict," *The Hitchhiker* (also known as *Deadly Nightmares* and *Le voyageur*), USA Network, 1989.
The Arsenio Hall Show (also known as *Arsenio*), syndicated, 1989.
Dr. Monica Gordon, "Just the Perfect Blendship," *The Larry Sanders Show,* HBO, 1998.
Herself, *The View,* ABC, 1999.
Monique Lacroix, "Strange Death of Professor Marechal," *The Secret Adventures of Jules Verne,* Sci–Fi Channel, c. 1999.
Meryl Dimetrio, "Home," *The Guardian* (also known as *El guardia, The Guardian—Retter mit Herz, Le protecteur, O allos mou eaftos, Ochita bengoshi Nick Fallin, Ochita bengoshi Nick Fallin 2,* and *Oikeuden puolesta*), CBS, 2001.
Christine Wilkes, "Faith," *Law & Order: Criminal Intent* (also known as *Law & Order: CI*), NBC, 2002.

Rita Bronwyn, "Mr. Monk Takes a Vacation," *Monk,* USA Network, 2002.

Also appeared in episodes of other programs, including *Not Necessarily the News,* HBO.

Television Appearances; Pilots:
Bernadette Pascoe, *Adams Apple,* CBS, 1986.
Ellyn Warren, *thirtysomething,* ABC, 1987.

Television Work; Series:
Creator and executive producer, *The Naked Brothers Band,* Nickelodeon, 2007—.

Television Work; Movies:
Executive producer and director, *Naked Brothers Band Movie,* Nickelodeon, 2005.
Creator, executive producer, and director, *The Naked Brothers Band: Battle of the Bands,* Nickelodeon, 2007.

Television Work; Episodic:
Director, *The Naked Brothers Band,* Nickelodeon, various episodes, beginning 2007.

Stage Appearances:
Buried Child, Yale Repertory Theatre, New Haven, CT, 1978.
As You Like It, Yale Repertory Theatre, 1979.
Measure for Measure, Yale Repertory Theatre, 1979.
Jean, *Split,* Second Stage Theatre, McGinn–Cazale Theatre, New York City, 1980.
Caroline Lou Bingham, *The Stitch in Time,* American National Theatre and Academy (ANTA) Playhouse, New York City, 1980–81.
Gertrude Cayce, *The Freak,* Workshop of the Players Art (WPA) Theatre, New York City, 1981, then Douglas Fairbanks Theatre, New York City, 1982.
Meg, *The Actor's Nightmare* and Diane Symonds, *Sister Mary Ignatius Explains It All for You* (double–bill), Playwrights Horizons Theatre, New York City, 1981 and 1982, and Westside Theatre Downstairs, New York City, 1981–84.
Cheryl, *Hooters,* Hudson Guild Theatre, New York City, 1982.
Marlene, *Top Girls,* New York Shakespeare Festival, Joseph Papp Public Theater, Estelle R. Newman Theater, New York City, 1983.
Blake Upton, *Mr. and Mrs.,* Workshop of the Players Art (WPA) Theatre, 1984.
Fiona, "The Ground Zero Club," *The Young Playwrights Festival,* Playwrights Horizons Theatre, 1985.
Lucy, "Want Ad," Danny, "Folie a'deux," Heather, "Only a Woman," and Lois, "Separate Vacation/Grounds for Divorce/Sexual History," all in *Love as We Know It,* Manhattan Punch Line, INTAR Hispanic American Theatre, New York City, 1985.

Linda Seward, *Rum and Coke,* New York Shakespeare
Festival, Joseph Papp Public Theater, Susan Stein
Shiva Theater, New York City, 1986.
Melissa Gardner, *Love Letters,* Canon Theatre, Los
Angeles, 1990.
Yvette, *Crazy He Calls Me,* Walter Kerr Theatre, New
York City, 1992.
Collette, *Four Dogs and a Bone,* Manhattan Theatre
Club Stage II, New York City, 1993, then Lucille
Lortel Theatre, New York City, 1993–94.
Insignificance, Hudson Guild Theatre, New York City,
1996.
Anna, *Closer,* Music Box Theatre, New York City, 1999.
Dana Sue Kay, *Imagining Brad* (produced with *The
Author's Voice*), Greenwich House Theatre, New
York City, 1999.
Ginger, *Trudy Blue,* Manhattan Class Company Theatre,
New York City, 1999.
Mom, *Blur,* Manhattan Theatre Club Stage II, 2001.
The Guys, Flea Theater, New York City, 2002.
Nina Weiss, *Brooklyn Boy,* Manhattan Theatre Club,
Biltmore Theatre, New York City, 2005.

Appeared in other productions, including *Actors and
Actresses* and *Thorn Hill,* both New York City.

Film Appearances:
Aileen Moran Jones, *Seven Minutes in Heaven* (also
known as *Deslices de joventud*), Warner Bros.,
1986.
Pat, *The Pick–Up Artist,* Twentieth Century–Fox, 1987.
Suzy Duncan, *Making Mr. Right,* Orion, 1987.
Olivia Smith, *A Million to Juan* (also known as *A Mil-
lion to One*), Samuel Goldwyn Company, 1994.
Evelyn Hayes, *Schemes,* Bristol Entertainment, 1995.
Kate Easton, *Gold Diggers: The Secret of Bear Mountain*
(also known as *Le secret de Bear Mountain*),
Universal, 1995.
Donna Evans, *Always Say Goodbye* (also known as
Desperate Housewife: The Early Years and *A Little
Romance*), 1996.
Leslie, *Hudson River Blues* (also known as *Family
Blues*), 1997.
Laura Caraday, *The Tic Code,* Avalanche Releasing,
1998.
Marilyn, *18 Shades of Dust* (also known as *Hitman's
Journal* and *The Sicilian Code*), 1999.
Natalie Clemente, *Dinner Rush,* Access Motion Picture
Group, 2000.
Paula, *Second Best,* ThinkFilm/Velocity Films, 2004.
Dr. Weiss, *A Perfect Fit,* Polychrome Pictures, 2005.

Film Producer:
The Tic Code, Avalanche Releasing, 1998.

RECORDINGS

Audiobooks:
Nomi Eve, *The Family Orchard,* HarperAudio, 2001.

WRITINGS

Teleplays:
(And songs) *Naked Brothers Band Movie,* Nickelodeon,
2005.
The Naked Brothers Band (series), Nickelodeon,
2007—.

Also wrote scenes for episodes of *thirtysomething,* ABC.

Screenplays:
The Tic Code, Avalanche Releasing, 1998.

OTHER SOURCES

Periodicals:
Family Circle, March, 2007, p. 204.
TV Guide, January 29, 2007, p. 70.

DuMONT, James 1965–
   (James Dumont)

PERSONAL

Full name, James Kelton DuMont, Jr.; born August 12,
1965, in Chicago, IL; son of James Kelton and Judith
Katherine (maiden name, Johnson) DuMont; married
Wendell Faith Hall; children: Sinclair Marie, Kelton
Hall. *Education:* Attended Boston University, 1983–85.
Politics: Democrat. *Religion:* Buddhist. *Avocational
Interests:* Writing prose, short stories, plays, and
screenplays.

Addresses: *Agent*—Coast to Coast Talent, 3350 Barham
Blvd., Los Angeles, CA 90068. *Manager*—Steven Adams Entertainment, 2018 N. Vine St., Los Angeles, CA
90068.

Career: Actor and producer. Ensemble Studio Theatre,
New York City, member of company, 1989; National
Research Group, Hollywood, CA, field recruiter,
1993–2000; DuMont Entertainment Group, Hollywood, CA, president and chief executive officer, 1994;
L.A. Project, co–artistic director, 1996; PACE America,
Hollywood, CA, vice president sales and marketing,
2000–04; vice president sales and marketing for a website, 2005.

CREDITS

Film Appearances:
(Uncredited) Kid dancing in street, *The Blue Brothers,*
Universal, 1980.
(Uncredited) Mr. Simons, *Class,* Orion, 1983.

Ernie, *In a Shade Between Two Trees,* 1991.
Poet, *52nd St. Serenade,* 1992.
Bobby, *Time Expired* (short), Zeitgeist Films, 1992.
Cliff, *Park Tragedy,* 1993.
James, *Combination Platter,* Arrow, 1993.
Workman, *Speed,* Twentieth Century–Fox, 1994.
Dr. Braunmann, *Bombshell,* Trimark Pictures, 1996.
Young sniper, *The Peacemaker,* DreamWorks, 1997.
Mike, *In Quiet Night* (also known as *You Belong to Me Forever*), Curb Entertainment, 1998.
Confessor, *The Confession* (short), Big Film Shorts, 1998.
(Uncredited) Man number one in airport bar, *Primary Colors* (also known as *Mit aller macht*), MCA/Universal, 1998.
Ron, *Erasable You,* 1998.
Additional voices, *200 Cigarettes,* Paramount, 1999.
Lou, *Bellyfruit,* Seventh Art Releasing, 1999.
Reporter, *Love & Basketball* (also known as *Love and Basketball*), New Line Cinema, 2000.
(As James Dumont) FBI agent, *Catch Me If You Can,* DreamWorks, 2002.
Reporter Lewis, *Seabiscuit,* Universal, 2003.
Gus, *S.W.A.T.,* Columbia, 2003.
Larry, *Along Came Polly,* Universal, 2004.
Man in bookstore, *Miss Congeniality 2: Armed & Fabulous,* Warner Bros., 2005.
Lincoln's Eyes (short), 2005.
Well–meaning father, *War of the Worlds,* Paramount, 2005.
Vacuum salesman, *Dating Games People Play,* 2006.
Gas can guy, *Statistics,* 2006.
Security supervisor, *Ocean's Thirteen* (also known as *13*), Warner Bros., 2007.
Crew chief, *Fast Girl,* 2007.
Herman, *The Cellar Door,* Six Sense, 2007.

Film Work:
Producer, *The Confession* (short), Big Film Shorts, 1998.
Associate producer and coproducer, *Statistics,* 2006.
Coproducer, *The Cellar Door,* Six Sense, 2007.

Television Appearances; Series:
Voice of narrator, *The Simple Life,* Fox, 2005–2006.

Television Appearances; Miniseries:
Phil Duin, *Pandemic,* Hallmark Channel, 2007.

Television Appearances; Movies:
Dr. Braunmann, *Bombshell,* Sci–Fi Channel, 1997.
Young officer, *The Pentagon Wars,* HBO, 1998.
(Uncredited) Reporter, *Winchell,* HBO, 1998.
Mike, *You Belong to Me Forever,* Lifetime, 2000.
Alex, *Gotta Kick It Up!,* Disney Channel, 2002.

Television Appearances; Pilots:
Angry customer, *Sweet Potato Queens,* The WB, 2003.

Television Appearances; Episodic:
Desk clerk, "Conspiracy," *Law & Order,* NBC, 1992.
Marwood, "Story of My Life," *Sweet Justice,* NBC, 1994.
Cop number one, "George Tells the Truth," *The George Carlin Show,* Fox, 1995.
Leo, bookie priest, "Annie Get Your Armoire," *Can't Hurry Love,* CBS, 1995.
Short white cop, "Fearless," *Fallen Angels,* Showtime, 1995.
Orderly, *John Grisham's "The Client,"* CBS, 1995.
Uniform office, "The Nutty Confessor," *NYPD Blue,* ABC, 1996.
Tracy's show assistant director, "Fame," *Tracey Takes On …,* HBO, 1996.
Ralph, "Lord of the Flys," *Lois & Clark: The New Adventures of Superman* (also known as *Lois & Clark* and *The New Adventures of Superman*), ABC, 1996.
Ralph, "Stop the Presses," *Lois & Clark: The New Adventures of Superman* (also known as *Lois & Clark* and *The New Adventures of Superman*), ABC, 1996.
Ralph, "Twas the Night Before Myxymas," *Lois & Clark: The New Adventures of Superman* (also known as *Lois & Clark* and *The New Adventures of Superman*), ABC, 1996.
Gus, "Clash of the Taylors," *Home Improvement,* ABC, 1997.
Darryl Knopf, "Fans First," *Arli$$,* HBO, 1998.
Major Thompson, "Let Bartlet Be Bartlet," *The West Wing,* NBC, 2000.
Mr. Rigney, "One Wong Move," *Becker,* CBS, 2000.
Rudy, "The Smell of Success," *Titus,* Fox, 2001.
Bobby, "Bad Chemistry," *That's Life,* CBS, 2001.
Mr. Lowell, *That Was Then,* ABC, 2002.
Will Harnell, "Love Conquers All," *Cold Case,* CBS, 2003.
Mr. Haddick, "Coming of Rage," *CSI: Crime Scene Investigation* (also known as *C.S.I.* and *Les Experts*), 2003.
Clemens, "Damaged," *ER,* NBC, 2004.
George Lane, "Independence Day," *Joan of Arcadia,* CBS, 2005.
Steve Pinkus, "The Crossing," *Ghost Whisperer,* CBS, 2005.
Dave Simon, "Divine Directions," *Close to Home,* CBS, 2005.
George, "Skin Deep," *House M.D.* (also known as *House*), Fox, 2006.
Vendor, "Under Pressure," *Numb3rs* (also known as *Num3ers*), CBS, 2007.
Prison driver, "East Side Story," *Ugly Betty,* ABC, 2007.

Also appeared as Pat, "Then Came a Reasonable Division of Personal Property," *Then Came You,* ABC.

Stage Appearances:
Tony & Tina's Wedding, Off–Broadway production, 1989–90.

Hustler and understudy Ben, Doug, and Woody, *Six Degrees of Separation,* Vivian Beaumont Theatre, New York, City, 1990–92.

DUNCAN, Lindsay 1950–

PERSONAL

Full name, Lindsay Vere Duncan; born November 7, 1950, in Edinburgh, Scotland; married Hilton McRae (an actor); children: Callum. *Education:* Attended Central School for Speech and Drama, London.

Addresses: *Agent*—Conway Van Gelder, Ltd., 18–21 Jermyn St., Third Floor, London SW1Y 6HP, England. *Manager*—Larry Taube, Principal Entertainment, 1964 Westwood Blvd., Suite 400, Los Angeles, CA 90025.

Career: Actress. Performer with the National Theatre Company and the Royal Shakespeare Company; performed in repertory in East Anglia, England; Hampstead Theatre Club, London, member of the board of directors. Appeared in advertisements.

Awards, Honors: Obie Award, *Village Voice,* c. 1982, for *Top Girls;* Laurence Olivier Award, best actress in a new play, Society of West End Theatre, 1986, *Theatre World* Award, outstanding new performer, Drama League Award, best actress, and Antoinette Perry Award nomination, best actress, all 1987, for *Les Liaisons Dangereuses; Evening Standard* Award, best actress, 1988, for *Cat on a Hot Tin Roof;* Sitges—Catalonian International Film Festival Award, best actress, 1990, for *The Reflecting Skin;* F.I.P.A. Golden Award, Cannes International Film Festival, c. 1990, for *Traffik;* Television Award nomination, best actress, British Academy of Film and Television Arts, 1992, for *GBH;* Monte Carlo Television Festival Award, best actress, c. 1994, for *The Rector's Wife;* Television Award nomination, British Academy of Film and Television Arts, and Royal Television Society Award nomination, both best actress, 2000, for *Shooting the Past;* London Critics Circle Theatre Award, best actress in a drama, 2001, *Evening Standard* Award nomination, best actress, 2001, and Olivier Award nomination, best actress, 2002, all for *Mouth to Mouth; Evening Standard* Award nomination, best actress, 2001, and Laurence Olivier Award, Antoinette Perry Award, and Drama Desk Award, all best actress, 2002, and Stage Actress Award, Variety Club Showbusiness awards, 2002, all for *Private Lives;* Television Award nomination, best actress, British Academy of Film and Television Arts, 2002, for *Perfect Strangers;* Bratislava International Film Festival Award, best actress, 2004, for *AfterLife; Evening Standard* Award nomination, best actress, 2007, for *That Face.*

Stage Appearances:

Charlotta and Violette, *Don Juan,* Hampstead Theatre Club, London, 1976.

Lucy, *The Rivals,* Royal Exchange Theatre, Manchester, England, 1976.

Natalie, *The Prince of Homburg,* Royal Exchange Theatre, 1976.

Sally Teale, *Zack,* Royal Exchange Theatre, 1976.

The Script, Hampstead Theatre Club, 1976.

Geraldine Barclay, *What the Butler Saw,* Royal Exchange Theatre, 1976–77.

Anne, *The Deep Blue Sea,* Cambridge Theatre Company, Cambridge, England, 1977.

Daphne Stillington, *Present Laughter,* Royal Exchange Theatre, 1977.

Gladys, *The Skin of Our Teeth,* Royal Exchange Theatre, 1977.

Margaret, *The Ordeal of Gilbert Pinfold,* Royal Exchange Theatre, 1977, Round House Theatre, London, 1979.

Dorcas Frey, *Plenty,* National Theatre, Lyttelton Theatre, London, 1978.

Hilary, *Comings and Goings,* Hampstead Theatre Club, 1978.

Viola, *Twelfth Night* (also known as *Twelfth Night, or What You Will*), Royal Exchange Theatre, 1978.

Portia, *Julius Caesar,* Theatre at Riverside Studios, London, 1980.

Bellinda, *The Provok'd Wife,* National Theatre, London, 1980–81.

Lady Nijo and Win, *Top Girls,* Royal Court Theatre, London, and New York Shakespeare Festival, Joseph Papp Public Theater, Estelle R. Newman Theater, New York City, both 1982.

Incidents at Tulse Hill, Hampstead Theatre Club, 1982.

Ronnie, *Progress,* Bush Theatre, London, 1984.

Performer, *The Massacre at Paris,* Royal Shakespeare Company, The Other Place, Stratford–upon–Avon, England, 1985.

Alice Ford, *The Merry Wives of Windsor,* Royal Shakespeare Company, Royal Shakespeare Theatre, Stratford–upon–Avon, England, 1985, Barbican Theatre, London, 1986.

Helen of Troy, *Troilus and Cressida,* Royal Shakespeare Company, Royal Shakespeare Theatre, 1985, Barbican Theatre, 1986.

La marquise de Merteuil, *Les Liaisons Dangereuses,* Royal Shakespeare Company, The Other Place, 1985, The Pit, London, 1986, Ambassadors' Theatre, London, 1986, and Music Box Theatre, New York City, 1987.

Performer, *Blood on the Neck of the Cat,* Royal Shakespeare Company, Almeida Theatre, London, 1986.

Title role, *Hedda Gabler,* Hampstead Theatre Club, 1988.

Maggie, *Cat on a Hot Tin Roof,* National Theatre, Lyttelton Theatre, 1988.

Title role, *Berenice,* National Theatre, Cottesloe Theatre, London, 1990.

Barbara Boyle, *Three Hotels,* Tricycle Theatre, London, 1993.

Donny, *The Cryptogram,* Ambassadors' Theatre, 1994.

Hippolyta and Titania, *A Midsummer Night's Dream,* Royal Shakespeare Company, Barbican Theatre, 1995, Lunt–Fontanne Theatre, New York City, 1996.

Rebecca, *Ashes to Ashes,* Royal Court Theatre Upstairs, London, 1996, later Roundabout Theatre Company, Gramercy Theatre, New York City, 1999.

Ruth, *The Homecoming,* National Theatre, Lyttelton Theatre, c. 1997.

Prue, *The Celebration,* and Rose, *The Room* (double-bill), Almeida Theatre, 2000, then LaGuardia Drama Theatre, New York City.

Laura, *Mouth to Mouth,* Royal Court Theatre, Jerwood Theatre Downstairs, London, and Albery Theatre, both 2001.

Amanda, *Private Lives,* Albery Theatre, London, 2001, Richard Rodgers Theatre, New York City, 2002.

Martha, *That Face,* Royal Court Theatre, Jerwood Theatre Upstairs, London, 2007.

Appeared in other productions, including an appearance as Sylvia in *The Recruiting Officer,* Bristol Old Vic Theatre and Edinburgh Festival, Edinburgh, Scotland; also appeared in productions at Southwold and Crewe, England.

Major Tours:

Anne, *The Deep Blue Sea,* Cambridge Theatre Company, British cities, c. 1977.

Bellinda, *The Provok'd Wife,* National Theatre, English cities, c. 1981.

Hippolyta and Titania, *A Midsummer Night's Dream,* Royal Shakespeare Company, 1996.

Television Appearances; Series:

Alexandra, *Reilly—Ace of Spies,* Thames Television–Euston Films, 1983, broadcast on *Mystery!,* PBS, c. 1983.

Andrea, *Travelling Man,* Granada Television, 1984.

Pamela Scott, *Kit Curran,* Thames Television, 1986.

Barbara Douglas, *GBH,* Channel 4 (England), 1991.

Annie Mayle, *A Year in Provence,* BBC and Arts and Entertainment, 1993.

Monica, *Jake's Progress,* Channel 4, 1995.

Louise, *Get Real,* Independent Television (England), 1998.

Narrator, *Horizon,* BBC, c. 2000.

Reader, *A History of Britain,* BBC and History Channel, c. 2000–2002.

Alice, *Perfect Strangers* (also known as *Almost Strangers* and *Family Tree*), BBC–2, beginning 2001.

Servilla of the Junii, *Rome,* HBO, beginning 2005.

Television Appearances; Miniseries:

Dana, *Dead Head,* BBC–2, 1986.

Helen Rosshalde, *Traffik,* Channel 4 (England), 1989, broadcast on *Masterpiece Theatre* (also known as *ExxonMobil Masterpiece Theatre* and *Mobil Masterpiece Theatre*), PBS, 1990.

Anna Bouverie, *The Rector's Wife,* Channel 4, 1994, broadcast on *Masterpiece Theatre* (also known as *ExxonMobil Masterpiece Theatre* and *Mobil Masterpiece Theatre*), PBS, 1994.

Lady Bellaston, *The History of Tom Jones, a Foundling* (also known as *Henry Fielding's "The History of Tom Jones," Henry Fielding's "Tom Jones,"* and *Historia de Tom Jones enjeitado*), BBC, 1997, Arts and Entertainment, 1998.

Marilyn Truman, *Shooting the Past,* BBC, 1999, broadcast on *Masterpiece Theatre* (also known as *ExxonMobil Masterpiece Theatre* and *Mobil Masterpiece Theatre*), PBS, 1999.

Elizabeth Leeford, *Oliver Twist,* Harlech Television, 1999, broadcast on *Masterpiece Theatre* (also known as *ExxonMobil Masterpiece Theatre* and *Mobil Masterpiece Theatre*), PBS, 2000.

Lady Catherine de Bourgh, *Lost in Austen* (also known as *Inside Austen*), Independent Television (England), 2008.

Television Appearances; Movies:

Gutrune Day, *These Foolish Things,* BBC Scotland, 1989.

Kath Peachey, *Redemption,* BBC, 1991.

Alison, *Dirty Tricks,* Carlton Television, 2000.

Lady Elizabeth Longford, *Longford,* HBO, 2006.

Professor Jane Pretorius, *Frankenstein,* Independent Television (England), 2007.

Television Appearances; Specials:

Scrubba, *Further Up Pompeii!,* BBC, 1975.

Candice Marie, "Nuts in May," *Play for Today,* BBC, 1976.

Diane, "The Winkler," *ITV Playhouse,* Independent Television (England), 1979.

Christine Butcher, "Grown–Ups," *BBC–2 Playhouse,* BBC–2, 1980.

Helen Hale, "On Approval," *Play of the Month,* BBC, 1982.

Karen Miller, "Rainy Day Women," *Play for Today,* BBC, 1984.

Herself, *Victoria Wood with All the Trimmings,* BBC, 2000.

Narrator, *Witness of Truth: The Railway Murders,* [Great Britain], 2001.

Voices of Beryl and Gertrude, *Hamilton Mattress* (animated), BBC, 2001.

Rose, *Arena: Harold Pinter* (also known as "Harold Pinter," *Arena* and "Harold Pinter," *Arena: Theatre*), BBC, 2002.

Television Appearances; Awards Presentations:
The 41st Annual Tony Awards, CBS, 1987.
Charter 88 Bad Government Awards, Channel 4 (England), 1994.

Television Appearances; Episodic:
Jane, "Angels of Death," *The New Avengers* (also known as *The New Avengers in Canada* and *Chapeau melon et bottes de cuir*), Independent Television (England), 1977.
Catherine Langford, "Deadlier Than the Male," *Dick Turpin,* Independent Television, 1980.
Muck and Brass, Central Television (England), 1982.
Rosemary, "Enough," *Colin's Sandwich,* BBC, 1988.
Medea, "Theseus and the Minotaur," *The Storyteller: Greek Myths* (also known as *Jim Henson's "The Storyteller,"* *Jim Henson's "The Storyteller: Greek Myths,"* and *The Storyteller*), Channel 4 (England), 1988, HBO, 1997.
Laura Pellin, "Getting Personnel," *TECX,* Central Television, 1990.
Rosemary, "Zanzibar," *Colin's Sandwich,* BBC, 1990.
Lady Walton, "William Clears the Slums," *Just William,* BBC, 1995.
Herself, *Ruby,* BBC, 1999.
Herself, *Masterchef,* BBC, 2000.
Angela Wells, "Diana" (also known as "Episode 10"), *Spooks* (also known as *MI–5*), BBC and Arts and Entertainment, 2005.
Lady Tamplin, "The Mystery of the Blue Train," *Poirot* (also known as *Agatha Christie's "Poirot,"* *Hercule Poirot,* and *Poirot*), Arts and Entertainment and PBS, 2005, Independent Television, 2006.
Angela Wells, "One," *Spooks* (also known as *MI–5*), BBC and Arts and Entertainment, 2006.

Appeared in other programs, including *One Upmanship,* BBC.

Television Appearances; Other:
The Iron Frog, BBC, c. 1980.

Appeared in other programs, including *New Girl in Town,* Associated Television (England).

Film Appearances:
Sally, *Loose Connections,* Twentieth Century–Fox, 1983.
Alice Nankervis, *Samson and Delilah,* 1985.
Anthea Lahr, *Prick Up Your Ears,* Samuel Goldwyn Company, 1987.
Lily Sachor, *Manifesto* (also known as *A Night of Love*), Cannon, 1988.
Eirwen, *The Child Eater* (short film; also known as *The Childeater*), 1989.
Dolphin Blue, *The Reflecting Skin* (also known as *L'enfant miroir*), Prestige Films, c. 1990.

Dr. Alice (some sources cite Agatha) Webb, *Body Parts,* Paramount, 1991.
Hippolyta and Titania, *A Midsummer Night's Dream,* Miramax, 1996.
Sydney Pappas, *City Hall* (also known as *A sombra da corrupcao, City Hall—Conspiracao no alto escalao, City Hall. La sombra de la corrupcion, Complot dans la ville, Ludzie miasta, Maktspel, Mestna hisa, Minden gyanu felett,* and *Pormestari*), Columbia, 1996.
Lady Markby, *An Ideal Husband,* Miramax, 1999.
Mrs. Price and Lady Bertram, *Mansfield Park,* Miramax, 1999.
Voice of TC–14, *Star Wars: Episode I—The Phantom Menace* (also known as *The Phantom Menace, Star Wars: Episode I, Star Wars: Episode I—The Beginning, Star Wars I: The Phantom Menace, Csillagok haboruja I.—Baljos arnyak, Guerra nas estrelas—A ameaca fantasma, Guerre stellari: Episodio I, Gwiezdne wojny: Czesc I—Mroczne widmo, La amenaza fantasma, La guerra de las galaxias: Episodio I—La amenaza fantasma, Razboiul stelelor—Amenintarea fantomei, Star wars—det moerka hotet, Star Wars: Episodio I—A ameaca fantasma, Star wars: Episodio I—La amenaza fantasma, Star wars: Episode I—Den skjulte trussel, Star wars: Episode I—Den usynlige fjende, Star Wars: Episode I—Die dunkle Bedrohung, Star Wars: Episode I—La menace fantome, Star Wars: Episode 1—La menace fantome, Star wars episodi I: Pimeae uhka, Star wars: Episodio I—La minaccia fantasma, Star wars: H aorath apeilh, Suta wozu: Fantomu menasu,* and *Taehtien sota: Episodi I—Primeae uhka*), Twentieth Century–Fox, 1999.
Katherine, *Under the Tuscan Sun* (also known as *Bajo el sol de la Toscana, Bajo el sol de Toscana, Sob o sol da Toscana, Sotto il sole della Toscana, Sous le soleil de Toscane, Toscana paeikese all, Toscanan auringon alla, Under Toscanas sol,* and *Unter der Sonne der Toskana*), Buena Vista, 2003.
May Brogan, *AfterLife,* Soda Pictures, 2003.
Audrey Pretty, *The Queen of Sheba's Pearls,* CDI Films, 2004.
Rose Harbinson, *Starter for 10,* Picturehouse Entertainment, 2006.
Ice queen, *Burlesque Fairytales,* Double Barrel Productions, 2008.
How to Lose Friends & Alienate People, Channel 4 Films/Paramount Vantage, 2008.

Radio Appearances:
Voice of La marquise de Merteuil, *Les Liaisons Dangereuses,* BBC World Service, 1998.
Experiment with an Air–Pump, BBC Radio 3, 2001.

RECORDINGS

Audiobooks:
Peter Mayle, *A Year in Provence,* New Video Group, 1993.

Rosamunde Pilcher, *Voices in Summer,* Chivers Audio Books, 1994.

Pilcher, *The Empty House,* Chivers North America, 1996.

William Shakespeare, *Essential Shakespeare,* High-Bridge, 1996.

Jane Austen, *Pride and Prejudice,* Chivers Audio Books, 1998.

Pierre Choderlos de Laclos, *Les Liaisons Dangereuses,* BBC, 1998.

Brian Moore, *The Magician's Wife,* Chivers Audio Books, 1998.

Stella Tillyard, *Aristocrats: Caroline, Emily, Louisa, and Sarah Lennox, 1740–1832,* Chivers Audio Books, 2000.

Joanna Trollope, *Marrying the Mistress,* Chivers Audio Books, 2000.

Antonia Fraser, *Marie Antoinette,* Orion Publishing Group, 2001.

Videos:

Herself, *RSC Meets USA: Working Shakespeare,* 2006.

Video Games:

(Uncredited; in archive footage) Voice of TC–14, *Lego Star Wars: The Video Game,* LucasArts Entertainment, 2005.

OTHER SOURCES

Periodicals:

Radio Times, January 9, 1999, p. 146.

DUNNE, Griffin 1955–

PERSONAL

Full name, Thomas Griffin Dunne; born June 8, 1955, in New York, NY; son of Dominick (a writer, producer, and actor) and Ellen (maiden name, Griffin) Dunne; brother of Dominique Dunne (an actress); nephew of John Gregory Dunne and Joan Didion (both writers); married Kate Forte (a producer; marriage annulled); married Carey Lowell (an actress), December 9, 1989 (divorced, 1995); children: (second marriage) Hannah. *Education:* Trained for the stage at HB Studio and Neighborhood Playhouse, both New York City, and with Uta Hagen.

Addresses: *Office*—Abingdon Square Productions, 9 Desbrosses St., Second Floor, New York, NY 10013. *Agent*—Steve Rabineau, William Morris Agency, One William Morris Place, Beverly Hills, CA 90212; (voice work) Paul Doherty, Cunningham/Escott/Slevin &

Doherty Talent Agency, 10635 Santa Monica Blvd., Suite 140, Los Angeles, CA 90025. *Manager*—Media Talent Group, 9200 Sunset Blvd., Suite 550, West Hollywood, CA 90069.

Career: Actor, producer, director, and writer. Triple Play Productions, cofounder, 1977; Double Play Productions, founder (with Amy Robinson), 1983; Abingdon Square Productions, New York City, producer. Also a juror at film festivals.

Member: Artists' Equity Association, Screen Actors Guild, American Federation of Television and Radio Artists.

Awards, Honors: Independent Spirit Award (with Robert F. Colesberry and Amy Robinson), best feature, Independent Features Project West, and Golden Globe Award nomination, best performance by an actor in motion picture—comedy or musical, both 1986, for *After Hours; Theatre World* Award, outstanding new performer, 1992, for *Search and Destroy;* Academy Award nomination (with Thom Colwell), best short film, live action, 1996, for *Duke of Groove;* Emmy Award nomination, outstanding guest actor in a comedy series, 1996, for "The Friend," an episode of *Frasier;* Pioneer Filmmaker Award, Deep Ellum Film Festival, 2000.

CREDITS

Film Appearances:

Herbie Johnson, *The Other Side of the Mountain* (also known as *A Window to the Sky*), Universal, 1975.

Dr. Mark, *Head over Heels* (also known as *Chilly Scenes of Winter*), United Artists, 1979.

Jack Goodman, *An American Werewolf in London* (also known as *American Werewolf* and *The American Werewolf*), Universal, 1981.

Production assistant, *The Fan* (also known as *Trance*), Paramount, 1981.

Tom Christo, *Cold Feet,* Cinecom International, 1983.

Alex Boyer, *Almost You,* Twentieth Century–Fox, 1984.

(In archive footage) Jack, *Terror in the Aisles* (also known as *Time for Terror*), Universal, 1984.

Tommy Kelly, *Johnny Dangerously* (also known as *Gangster Kid*), Twentieth Century–Fox, 1984.

Paul Hackett, *After Hours* (also known as *Lies, A Night in SoHo, After Hours—quelle nuit de galere, Depois de horas, Despues de hora, Die Zeit nach Mitternacht, En Natt i New York, Fuori orario, Illasta aamuun, Jo, que noche!, Liderces orak, Meta ta mesanyhta, Natt paa Manhattan, Nova Iorque fora de horas, Po godzinach,* and *Quina nit!*), Warner Bros., 1985.

Doctor, "Hospital," *Amazon Women on the Moon* (also known as *Cheeseburger Film Sandwich*), Universal, 1987.

Loudon Trott, *Who's That Girl?* (also known as *Slammer* and *Who's That Girl*), Warner Bros., 1987.

Duffy, *Le grand bleu* (also known as *The Big Blue*), Columbia, 1988, other versions released as *Le grand bleu, version integrale* and *Le grand bleu, version longue.*

Bert Uttanzi, *Ich und Er* (also known as *Me and Him*), Columbia, 1990.

Mr. Jake Bixler, *My Girl,* Columbia, 1991.

Rob, *Once Around,* Universal, 1991.

Alan Riegart, *Straight Talk,* Buena Vista, 1992.

David Chartoff, *Big Girls Don't Cry … They Get Even* (also known as *Stepkids*), New Line Cinema, 1992.

(Uncredited) Planet Cleveland man, *The Pickle* (also known as *The Adventures of the Flying Pickle*), Columbia, 1993.

Account person, *Quiz Show* (also known as *Kviz, Kviz–show, Quiz Show—A verdade dos bastidores, Quiz Show—Der Skandal, Quiz Show—El dilema, Quiz show—El dilema, Quiz Show—tupla ja kuitti,* and *Sike*), Buena Vista, 1994.

Auditioner, *Naked in New York,* Fine Line Features, 1994.

Stephen Price, *I Like It Like That* (also known as *Black Out* and *Life Is Trouble*), Columbia, 1994.

Isle of Joy (short film), Double Play Productions, 1994.

Martin Mirkheim, *Search and Destroy* (also known as *The Four Rules*), October Films, 1995.

Man in bathroom, *Sam the Man,* 2000.

Agent, *Pinero,* Miramax, 2001.

Andrew, *Lisa Picard Is Famous* (also known as *Famous*), First Look Pictures Releasing, 2001.

Himself, *Perfume* (also known as *Dress to Kill*), Lions Gate Films, 2001.

Mr. Davis, *Cheats* (also known as *Chea+ers*), New Line Cinema/Destination Films, 2001.

Jerry Anderson, *40 Days and 40 Nights* (also known as *40 jours et 40 nuits*), Miramax, 2002.

Himself, *Stuck on You,* Twentieth Century–Fox, 2003.

Marie and Bruce, New Films International, 2004.

Elliott Litvak, *Game 6* (also known as *Game 6—Das Leben ist ein Spiel!*), Kindred Media Group, 2005.

Dr. Simon, *Bondage* (also known as *The Bondage*), Eccentric Cattle Entertainment, 2006.

(Uncredited) Himself, *My Date with Drew* (documentary), Warner Bros., 2006.

Johnathan Finerman, *The Great Buck Howard,* Long Shong Entertainment, 2007.

Don Parkinson, *Snow Angels,* Warner Independent Pictures, 2008.

Film Producer:

(With Amy Robinson and Mark Metcalf) *Head over Heels* (also known as *Chilly Scenes of Winter*), United Artists, 1979.

(With Robinson) *Baby It's You* (also known as *Baby, It's You, Baby, to jestes ty,* and *Promesse, promesse*), Paramount, 1983.

After Hours (also known as *Lies, A Night in SoHo, After Hours—quelle nuit de galere, Depois de horas, Despues de hora, Die Zeit nach Mitternacht, En Natt i New York, Fuori orario, Illasta aamuun, Jo, que noche!, Liderces orak, Meta ta mesanyhta, Natt paa Manhattan, Nova Iorque fora de horas, Po godzinach,* and *Quina nit!*), Warner Bros., 1985.

(With Robinson) *Running on Empty* (also known as *A bout de course, Ahava B'Milkud, Die Flucht ins Ungewisse, Elaemaenae pakotie, Flykt utan maal, O peso de um passado, Un lugar en ninguna parte,* and *Vivere in fuga*), Warner Bros., 1988.

(With Robinson and Mark Rosenberg) *White Palace,* Universal, 1990.

(With Robinson) *Once Around,* Universal, 1991.

Isle of Joy (short film), Double Play Productions, 1994.

Executive producer, *Joe's Apartment,* Warner Bros., 1996.

Fierce People, Lions Gate Films, 2005.

Game 6 (also known as *Game 6—Das Leben ist ein Spiel!*), Kindred Media Group, 2005.

Film Director:

Duke of Groove (short film), Chanticleer Films, 1995.

Addicted to Love (also known as *Forlorn*), Warner Bros., 1997.

Practical Magic, Warner Bros., 1998.

Lisa Picard Is Famous (also known as *Famous*), First Look Pictures Releasing, 2001.

Fierce People, Lions Gate Films, 2005.

Your Product Here (short film), 2006.

The Accidental Husband, Yari Film Group, 2008.

Television Appearances; Series:

Dr. Jeffrey (some sources cite Jerry) Cole, *3 lbs.,* CBS, 2006.

Television Appearances; Miniseries:

The playwright, *Blonde* (also known as *Marilyn Monroe*), CBS, 2001.

Television Appearances; Movies:

Mordecai Apt, *The Wall,* CBS, 1980.

Mordechai "Mordy" Vanunu, *Secret Weapon,* TNT, 1990.

Tom, *Love Matters,* Showtime, 1993.

William (Teach), *The Android Affair,* 1995.

Frank Zappa, *Warning: Parental Advisory,* VH1, 2002.

Television Appearances; Specials:

Himself, *The Making of "An American Werewolf in London,"* 1981.

Doctor at Stork Club, "From Here to Maternity," *Cinemax Comedy Experiment,* Cinemax, 1986.

Leonard "Len" Burdette, "Lip Service," *HBO Showcase,* HBO, 1988.

(Uncredited; in archive footage) Guest in segment, *Saturday Night Live: 15th Anniversary,* NBC, 1989.

Voice, *How Do You Spell God?,* HBO, 1996.

Saturday Night Live: 25th Anniversary (also known as *Saturday Night Live: 25th Anniversary Primetime Special*), NBC, 1999.

Himself, *Dominick Dunne: Murder He Wrote,* Arts and Entertainment, 2001.

Sounds from a Town I Love (short), 2001.

Himself, *Guilty Pleasure: The Extraordinary World of Dominick Dunne* (also known as *Guilty Pleasure: The Dominick Dunne Story*), Court TV, 2003.

Himself, *Alias Ricky Gervais,* [Great Britain], 2004.

Himself, *Dominick Dunne—Les crimes de la jet set* (also known as *Dominick Dunne in Search of Justice*), 2007.

Television Appearances; Awards Presentations:

Presenter, *15th Annual IFP/West Independent Spirit Awards,* Bravo and Independent Film Channel, 2000.

Television Appearances; Episodic:

Himself, *The Tonight Show Starring Johnny Carson* (also known as *The Best of Carson*), NBC, 1985.

Dick, "Secret Cinema," *Amazing Stories* (also known as *Steven Spielberg's "Amazing Stories"*), NBC, 1986.

Knoll, "The Jar," *Alfred Hitchcock Presents* (also known as *Alfred Hitchcock esittaeae, Alfred Hitchcock presenta, Alfred Hitchcock presente,* and *Alfred Hitchcock zeigt*), NBC, 1986.

(Uncredited) Frankie Toussaint, *Saturday Night Live* (also known as *NBC's "Saturday Night," Saturday Night, Saturday Night Live '80, SNL,* and *SNL 25*), NBC, 1986.

Guest host, *Saturday Night Live* (also known as *NBC's "Saturday Night," Saturday Night, Saturday Night Live '80, SNL,* and *SNL 25*), NBC, 1986.

David, "Hunger Chic," *Trying Times* (also known as *Trying Times: Hunger Chic*), PBS, 1989.

Gerard Samuels, "F.O.B.," *L.A. Law,* NBC, 1993.

Robert, "Getting Rid of Robby," *Hotel Room* (also known as *David Lynch's "Hotel Room"*), HBO, 1993.

Voice of Russell, "The Good Son," *Frasier* (also known as *Dr. Frasier Crane*), NBC, 1993.

Dean Robinson, "Partners," *Directed By,* Showtime, 1994.

Voice of Bob, "The Friend," *Frasier* (also known as *Dr. Frasier Crane*), NBC, 1996.

Himself, *Late Show with David Letterman* (also known as *The Late Show* and *Late Show Backstage*), CBS, 1997.

Himself, *The Rosie O'Donnell Show,* syndicated, 1997.

Himself, "Practical Magic," *HBO First Look,* HBO, 1998.

Henry Talbott, "Jones," *Law & Order: Criminal Intent* (also known as *Law & Order: CI*), NBC, 2001.

Nicolas Losseff, "Motherhunt: Parts 1 & 2," *A Nero Wolfe Mystery* (also known as *Nero Wolfe*), Arts and Entertainment, 2002.

Himself, *The Big Breakfast,* Channel 4 (England), 2002.

Himself, "Stuck on You," *HBO First Look,* HBO, 2003.

Himself, *Intimate Portrait: Rosanna Arquette,* Lifetime, 2003.

Leonid Lisenker, "Crossings," *Alias,* ABC, 2004.

Leonid Lisenker, "Facade," *Alias,* ABC, 2004.

Himself, "Fish Fry," *The Barry Z Show* (also known as *Z–TV*), 2005.

Himself, *Celebrity Charades,* American Movie Classics, 2005.

Himself, *Sunday Morning Shootout,* American Movie Classics, 2005.

Seamus Flaherty, "Country Crossover," *Law & Order: Criminal Intent* (also known as *Law & Order: CI*), NBC, 2006.

Seamus Flaherty, "Players," *Law & Order: Criminal Intent* (also known as *Law & Order: CI*), NBC, 2007.

Appeared in "The Films of Martin Scorsese," *The Directors,* Encore. Appeared in other programs, including *The Moth,* Trio.

Television Appearances; Pilots:

Toonces, the Cat Who Could Drive a Car (also known as *Toonces and Friends*), NBC, 1992.

Leonard, *What Leonard Comes Home To,* ABC, 2002.

Tony Mink, *Truth in Advertising,* TNT, 2008.

Also appeared in the pilot *Graham.*

Television Work:

Directed episodes of various programs, including *Going to California* (also known as *G2C* and *On the Road Again*), Showtime; also developed and produced other programs.

Stage Appearances:

Henry, Tim, and Ed, *Marie and Bruce,* New York Shakespeare Festival, Joseph Papp Public Theater, Estelle R. Newman Theater, New York City, 1980.

Coming Attractions, Playwrights Horizons Theatre, New York City, 1982.

Hooters, Hudson Guild Theatre, New York City, 1984.

Martin Mirkheim, *Search and Destroy,* Circle in the Square, New York City, 1992.

Mark, *The 24 Hour Plays 2003,* American Airlines Theatre, New York City, 2003.

Appeared in *Album, The Hotel Play,* and in other productions.

RECORDINGS

Videos:

Himself in audio commentary, *An American Werewolf in London* (also known as *American Werewolf* and *The American Werewolf*), Universal, 2001.

Himself, *Artists of Hell's Kitchen,* 2000, Transmission Films, 2002.

Himself and Paul Hackett, *Filming for Your Life: Making "After Hours,"* Warner Home Video, 2004.

Himself, *Making "Game 6"* (short), 2006.

Himself, *Beware the Moon: Remembering "An American Werewolf in London"* (documentary), Indywood Films, 2008.

WRITINGS

Screenplays:

(Story) *Isle of Joy* (short film), Double Play Productions, 1994.

Duke of Groove (short film), Chanticleer Films, 1995.

Worked on other screenplays, including *Not of This World.*

Teleplays:

Author of teleplays.

DURNING, Charles 1923–
(Charles Durnham)

PERSONAL

Born February 28, 1923, in Highland Falls, NY; married Carol (divorced, 1972); married Mary Ann Amelio, c. 1974; children: (first marriage) Michele (an actress), Douglas, Jeanine; (second marriage) two stepchildren. *Education:* Attended Columbia University and New York University; according to some sources, studied classical dance and martial arts.

Addresses: *Agent*—Paradigm, 360 North Crescent Dr., North Building, Beverly Hills, CA 90210.

Career: Actor. Worked as a nightclub singer and dancer, ballroom dancer, dance instructor, usher at a burlesque house, and as a boxer, cab driver, waiter, ironworker, construction worker, elevator operator, telegram delivery person, bartender, night watchman, and in factories. Some sources state that Durning spent time with the Alvin Ailey Dance Company. *Military service:* U.S. Army, Combat Infantry, served as a Ranger, served during World War II; received (according to various sources) three Purple Hearts, Silver Star, Bronze Star, and/or a Combat Infantryman's Badge.

Member: Actors' Equity Association, Screen Actors Guild, American Federation of Television and Radio Artists, American Film Institute.

Awards, Honors: Drama Desk Award and *Variety* poll winner, both 1972, for *That Championship Season;* Emmy Award nomination, outstanding lead actor in a special program—drama or comedy, 1975, for *Queen of the Stardust Ballroom;* National Board of Review Award, best supporting actor, 1975, and Golden Globe Award nomination, best supporting actor—motion picture, 1976, both for *Dog Day Afternoon;* Emmy Award nomination, outstanding single performance by a supporting actor in a comedy or drama series, and Golden Globe Award nomination, best supporting actor—television, both 1977, for *Captains and the Kings;* Emmy Award nomination, outstanding supporting actor in a limited series or special, 1980, for *Attica;* Academy Award nomination, best actor in a supporting role, 1983, for *The Best Little Whorehouse in Texas;* Academy Award nomination, best actor in a supporting role, and Golden Globe Award nomination, best performance by an actor in a supporting role in a motion picture, both 1984, for *To Be or Not to Be;* Emmy Award nomination, outstanding supporting actor in a miniseries or special, 1986, for *Death of a Salesman;* Annual CableACE Award nomination, best supporting actor in a movie or miniseries, National Cable Television Association, 1989, for *The Man Who Broke 1,000 Chains;* Antoinette Perry Award and Drama Desk Award, both best featured actor in a play, 1990, for *Cat on a Hot Tin Roof;* Golden Globe Award, best performance by an actor in a supporting role in a series, miniseries, or motion picture made for television, 1991, for *The Kennedys of Massachusetts;* Emmy Award nominations, outstanding supporting actor in a comedy series, 1991 and 1992, both for *Evening Shade;* Drama League Award, distinguished performance, c. 1997, for *The Gin Game;* Emmy Award nomination, outstanding guest actor in a drama series, 1998, for "Finnegan's Wake," an episode of *Homicide: Life on the Street;* inducted into the Theatre Hall of Fame, 1999; National Board of Review Award, 2000, Florida Film Critics Circle Award, 2001, and Online Film Critics Society Award nomination, 2001, all best ensemble performance, all with others, for *State and Main;* Emmy Award nomination, outstanding guest actor in a drama series, 2005, for *Navy NCIS: Naval Criminal Investigative Service;* Lucille Lortel Award, outstanding featured actor, League of Off–Broadway Theatres and Producers, 2006, for *Third;* Life Achievement Award, Screen Actors Guild, 2008.

CREDITS

Film Appearances:

Dooley, *Harvey Middleman, Fireman,* Columbia, 1965.

Stiletto, Avco–Embassy Pictures, 1969.

Deputy Wylie Hunnicutt, *I Walk the Line,* Columbia, 1970.

(As Charles Durnham) Superintendent, *Hi Mom!* (also known as *Blue Manhattan, Confessions of a Peeping John,* and *Son of Greetings*), Facets Multimedia, 1970.

Second guard, *The Pursuit of Happiness,* Columbia, 1971.

Murphy, *Dealing: Or the Berkeley–to–Boston Forty–Brick Lost–Bag Blues,* Warner Bros., 1972.

Red Ball rider, *Deadhead Miles,* Paramount, 1972.

Doomsday Voyage (also known as *Questions*), Futurama International, 1972.

Joseph Larch, *Sisters* (also known as *Blood Sisters*), American International Pictures, 1973.

Lieutenant William Snyder, *The Sting,* Universal, 1973.

Murphy, *The Front Page,* Universal, 1974.

Captain Pruss, *The Hindenburg,* Universal, 1975.

Detective sergeant Eugene Moretti, *Dog Day Afternoon,* Warner Bros., 1975.

Frank O'Brien, *Breakheart Pass,* Metro–Goldwyn–Mayer, 1975.

President David T. Stevens, *Twilight's Last Gleaming* (also known as *Nuclear Countdown, Das Ultimatum,* and *Todeskommando Feuerblitz Ultimatum*), Allied Artists, 1976.

Rufus T. Crisp, *Harry and Walter Go to New York,* Columbia, 1976.

Peter Stockmann, *An Enemy of the People* (also known as *Danger Plante Earth*), Warner Bros., 1977.

Spermwhale Whalen, *The Choirboys* (also known as *Aenglarna*), Universal, 1977.

Dr. Jim McKeever, *The Fury,* Twentieth Century–Fox, 1978.

Michael Russell, *The Greek Tycoon,* Universal, 1978.

Arnold, *Die Laughing,* Warner Bros., 1979.

Coach Johnson, *North Dallas Forty,* Paramount, 1979.

Doc Hopper, *The Muppet Movie,* Associated Film Distributors, 1979.

Harold "The Whale" Remmens, *Tilt,* Warner Bros., 1979.

John Clifford, *When A Stranger Calls,* Columbia, 1979.

Michael "Mickey" Potter, *Starting Over,* Paramount, 1979.

Senator Samuel Chapman, *The Final Countdown* (also known as *U.S.S. Nimitz: Lost in the Pacific*), United Artists, 1980.

Frisco, *Sharky's Machine,* Warner Bros., 1981.

Jack Amsterdam (some sources cite Jack Anderson), *True Confessions,* United Artists, 1981.

Governor, *The Best Little Whorehouse in Texas* (musical; also known as *The Best Little Cathouse in Texas*), Universal, 1982.

Leslie "Les" Nichols, *Tootsie,* Columbia, 1982.

Charlie, *Two of a Kind* (also known as *Second Chance*), Twentieth Century–Fox, 1983.

Colonel Erhardt, *To Be or Not to Be,* Twentieth Century–Fox, 1983.

(Uncredited) Voice of immigration official, *Scarface,* Universal, 1983.

Chucky Gorman, *Stick,* Universal, 1984.

Monsignor Thomas Burke, *Mass Appeal,* Universal, 1984.

Sam Crawford, *Hadley's Rebellion,* ADI Marketing, 1984.

Louis Thibadeau, *Stand Alone,* New World Pictures, 1985.

Ross, *The Man with One Red Shoe,* Twentieth Century–Fox, 1985.

Deke Yablonski, *Tough Guys,* Universal, 1986.

Father O'Reilly, *Where the River Runs Black,* Metro–Goldwyn–Mayer, 1986.

O'Mara, *Big Trouble,* Columbia, 1986.

The warden, *Solarbabies* (also known as *Solar Warriors*), Metro–Goldwyn–Mayer, 1986.

Charlie, *Happy New Year,* Columbia, 1987.

Father Ted Nabors, *The Rosary Murders* (also known as *Confession criminelle, Den sjaette doedssynden, Der Moerder mit dem Rosenkranz, I delitti del rosario, Los crimenes del rosario, O misterio do rosario negro,* and *Rukousnauhamurhaaja*), New Line Cinema, 1987.

(Uncredited) Pete (the doorman to Heaven), *Meatballs III: Summer Job* (also known as *Meatballs III* and *Meatballs III—Academie de vacances*), TMS (The Movie Store; also known as Moviestore Entertainment), 1987.

Bertrum, *Far North,* Alive Films, 1988.

Charlie Drumm, *A Tiger's Tale,* Atlantic Releasing, 1988.

Dutch Peltz, *Cop* (also known as *Blood on the Moon*), Atlantic Releasing, 1988.

Jiggs Scully, *Cat Chaser* (also known as *Short Run, Doedliga foerbindelser, El cazador de gatos, Hexenkessel Miami, Kocur, Macskafogo kommando, Oi synenohoi, Oltre ogni rischio, Progonitelj macaka,* and *Vaaran polttopisteessae*), Vestron Pictures, 1989.

Uncle Joshua, *Etoile* (also known as *Ballet*), 1989.

Editor Francis I. Livright, *Brenda Starr,* 1989, Triumph Releasing, 1992.

Chief Brandon, *Dick Tracy,* Buena Vista, 1990.

Colonel Clancy, *Project: Alien* (also known as *Fatal Sky* and *No Cause for Alarm*), 1991.

Lieutenant Bobby Mallory, *V. I. Warshawski* (also known as *V. I. Warshawski, Detective in High Heels*), Buena Vista, 1991.

Ozzie, *Dreamers,* 1991.

Bill Flower, *The Music of Chance,* IRS Releasing, 1993.

Louis Bamberger, *I.Q.* (also known as *A teoria do amor, Ahava Atomeat, Ask ve zeka, El genio del amor, Formula para amar, Genio per amore, I.Q.—A szerelem relativ, I.Q.—Liebe ist relativ, I.Q. (Q.I.), L'amour en equation,* and *Rakkauden yhtaeloe*), Paramount, 1994.

Waring Hudsucker, *The Hudsucker Proxy* (also known as *Mister Hula Hoop* and *Hudsucker–Der Grosse Sprung*), Warner Bros., 1994.

Mr. Henry Larson, *Home for the Holidays,* Paramount, 1995.

Reverend Gerald Hutchens, *The Last Supper,* Columbia, 1995.

Reverend Buster, *The Grass Harp,* 1995, Fine Line Features, 1996.

The director, *Spy Hard* (also known as *Agent zero zero, Agent 00, Live and Let Spy, Agent 00—Mit der Lizenz zum Totlachen, Ciplak casus, Dragam add az eleted, Duro de espiar, Duro para espiar, Espia … como puderes!, Espia como puedas, L'agent secret se decouvre, Mit der Lizenz zum Totlachen, Spia e lascia spiare, Spy Hard—Helt utan haemningar, Spy Hard—lupa laeikyttaeae, Szklanka po lapkach,* and *Tajni agent 000*), Buena Vista, 1996.

Lew, *One Fine Day,* Twentieth Century–Fox, 1996.

Voice of Archie, *The Land before Time IV: Journey through the Mists* (animated; also known as *The Land before Time 4: Journey through the Mists*), MCA Home Entertainment, 1996.

Recon, Wildtrack Productions, 1996.

Norbie Hess, *The Secret Life of Algernon,* Marano Productions/Phare–Est Productions, 1997.

Fatty, *Hi–Life,* Lions Gate Films, 1998.

Hunt for the Devil, Fries Film Group, 1999.

Mayor George Bailey, *State and Main* (also known as *Hollywood, Vermont* and *Sequences et consequences*), New Line Cinema/Fine Line Features, 2000.

Paddy Mulroney, *Very Mean Men,* Miracle Entertainment, 2000.

Pappy O'Daniel, *O Brother, Where Art Thou?* (also known as *O' Brother*), Buena Vista, 2000.

Bombshell, 2000.

Never Look Back, Giants Entertainment, 2000.

Big Philly Russo, *Turn of Faith,* CAOH Enterprises, 2001.

Himself, *A Constant Forge: The Life and Art of John Cassavetes* (documentary; also known as *A Constant Forge*), 2001.

Skippy, *Lakeboat,* Cowboy Booking International, 2001.

Stuart Steele, *L.A.P.D.: To Protect and to Serve* (also known as *LAPD, LAPD Conspiracy, Die Todesengel von L.A., LAPD: Policia de Los Angeles,* and *Policia de Los Angeles—Corrupcion total*), Fries Film Group, 2001.

Dylan Frier, *Pride & Loyalty,* Echelon Entertainment, 2002.

George, *Mother Ghost,* Imageworks Entertainment International, 2002.

John "Eagle Eye" Pennell, *The Last Man Club,* Cactus Films, 2002.

Congressperson Davenport, *The Naked Run* (short film), 2002, Weggee Productions, 2006.

Himself, *Broadway: The Golden Age, by the Legends Who Were There* (documentary; also known as *Broadway, Broadway: The Golden Age,* and *Broadway: The Movie*), Dada Films, 2003.

Jimmy Kerrigan, *Dead Canaries,* Showcase Entertainment, 2003.

Mr. Orlick, *One Last Ride,* Allumination Filmworks, 2003.

Performer, *The Education of Gore Vidal* (documentary), 2003.

Marshall Ledger, *Death and Texas,* Neofight Film, 2004.

Frank McNally, *Resurrection: The J. R. Richard Story,* Bellinger–Bethea X Films, 2005.

Murray Blythe, *River's End,* American World Pictures, 2005.

Victor Rasdale, *Dirty Deeds* (also known as *Dirtier Deeds*), Freestyle Releasing, 2005.

The Voyage of La Amistad: The Quest for Freedom, MPI Media Group, 2005.

Captain Pete, *Miracle Dogs Too,* Tag Entertainment, 2006.

Eddie O'Brien, *Forget about It,* Showcase Entertainment, 2006.

The lawyer, *The L.A. Riot Spectacular* (also known as *The L.A. Riot Show*), Visionbox Pictures, 2006.

Mr. Clark, *Unbeatable Harold,* Visual Factory, 2006.

Second innkeeper, *Descansos,* Film Arts Alliance, 2006.

Teddy the bartender, *Jesus, Mary and Joey* (also known as *Welcome Back Miss Mary*), Panorama Entertainment, 2006.

Yammi, *Local Color,* Media 8 Entertainment, 2006.

Alexander Hathaway, *Polycarp,* Vivendi Visual Entertainment, 2007.

Charlie, *Good Dick,* Morning Knight/Present Pictures, 2007.

Frank "the Handler" Maro, *The Waiter* (also known as *The Waiter: Chronicles of Purgatory*), Bacchus Entertainment, 2007.

Deal, Metro–Goldwyn–Mayer, 2007.

Audie & the Wolf, Brooklyn Reptyle Productions, c. 2008.

Grandpa, *Room and Board,* Hoboken Pictures, 2008.

John Bartlett, *Chatham* (also known as *The Golden Boys*), West Wind Productions, 2008.

Satan, *The Drum Beats Twice,* Justice for All Productions, 2008.

Television Appearances; Series:

Lieutenant Gil McGowan, *Another World* (also known as *Another World: Bay City*), NBC, 1972.

Officer Frank Murphy, *The Cop and the Kid,* NBC, 1975–76.

Oscar Poole, *Eye to Eye,* ABC, 1985.

Dr. Harlan Elldridge, *Evening Shade,* CBS, 1990–94.

Voice of Joseph Breen, *Sex, Censorship and the Silver Screen* (documentary; also known as *Sex and the Silver Screen*), Showtime, 1996.

Frank Vitelli, *Orleans,* CBS, 1997.

Father Hubley, *Everybody Loves Raymond* (also known as *Raymond, Alla aelskar Raymond, Alle elsker Raymond, Alle lieben Raymond, Kaikki rakastavat Raymondia, Svi vole Raymonda, Todo el mundo quiere a Raymond, Tothom estima en Raymond, Tout le monde aime Raymond,* and *Tutti amano Raymond*), CBS, between 1998 and 2002.

Justice Henry Hoskins, *First Monday,* CBS, 2002.

Tommy's father, *Rescue Me* (also known as *Rescue Me: FDNY*), FX Network, beginning 2004.

Television Appearances; Miniseries:

Ed Healey, *Captains and the Kings,* NBC, 1976.

Paddy Lonigan, *Studs Lonigan,* NBC, 1979.

Senator Henry Colton, *Kenny Rogers as The Gambler, Part III: The Legend Continues* (also known as *The Gambler III: The Legend Continues* and *Kenny Rogers as "The Gambler" III—The Legend Continues*), CBS, 1987.

John "Honey Fitz" Fitzgerald, *The Kennedys of Massachusetts* (also known as *The Fitzgeralds and the Kennedys*), ABC, 1990.

Papa Andrew Alcott, *A Woman of Independent Means* (also known as *Les tourments du destin, Mia anexartiti gynaika,* and *Wechselspiel des Lebens*), NBC, 1995.

Host and narrator, *America in the Forties: Sentimental Journey* (also known as *America in the Forties* and *America in the '40s*), PBS, 1998.

Voices, *Not for Ourselves Alone: The Story of Elizabeth Cady Stanton & Susan B. Anthony,* PBS, 1999.

Judge Harlan Radovich, *The Judge* (also known as *Steve Martini's "The Judge"*), NBC, 2001.

Voices, *Jazz,* PBS, 2001.

Tom Billingsley, *Desperation* (also known as *Stephen King's "Desperation"*), ABC, 2006.

Television Appearances; Movies:

Frank Devlin, *The Connection,* ABC, 1973.

Alvin "Al" Green, *Queen of the Stardust Ballroom,* CBS, 1975.

Budd Rogers, *The Trial of Chaplain Jensen,* ABC, 1975.

Carl Gallitzin, *Special Olympics* (also known as *A Special Kind of Love*), CBS, 1978.

Host, *One of the Missing,* 1979.

Bill Larson, *A Perfect Match,* CBS, 1980.

Commissioner Russell Oswald, *Attica,* ABC, 1980.

Frank Powell, *The Best Little Girl in the World,* ABC, 1981.

Jess Matthews, *Crisis at Central High,* 1981.

Otis P. Hazelrig, *Dark Night of the Scarecrow,* CBS, 1981.

Warden Hardy, *The Man Who Broke 1,000 Chains* (also known as *Unchained*), HBO, 1987.

Les Kabowski, *Case Closed* (also known as *Death by Diamonds*), CBS, 1988.

Reverend Samuel Corey, *Unholy Matrimony* (also known as *Deadly Vows*), CBS, 1988.

Dan Packard, *Dinner at Eight,* TNT, 1989.

Earl Mulcahaney, *Prime Target,* NBC, 1989.

Santa Claus, *It Nearly Wasn't Christmas* (also known as *The Nearly Wasn't Christmas*), syndicated, 1989.

(Uncredited) Judge, *The Story Lady,* NBC, 1991.

Roger Finn, *The Return of Eliot Ness,* NBC, 1991.

Tour guide, "The Water Engine," *TNT Screenworks* (also known as *Screenworks*), TNT, 1992.

John Clifford, *When a Stranger Calls Back,* Showtime, 1993.

Barney, *Roommates,* NBC, 1994.

Santa Claus, *Mrs. Santa Claus,* CBS, 1996.

Captain Robert Landis, *Shelter,* 1998.

Detective Charlie Duffy, *Hard Time,* TNT, 1998.

Earl Pulmer, *A Chance of Snow,* Lifetime, 1998.

Vic, *Jerry and Tom,* Showtime, 1998.

Detective Charlie Duffy, *Hard Time: Hostage Hotel* (also known as *Hostage Hotel*), TNT, 1999.

Detective Charlie Duffy, *Hard Time: The Premonition* (also known as *The Premonition*), TNT, 1999.

Moe Ryan, *Justice* (also known as *Backlash*), Cinemax, 1999.

Syd Wolf, *The Last Producer* (also known as *The Final Hit*), USA Network, 2000.

King Nicholas XX (Santa Claus), "Mr. St. Nick" (also known as "Mr. Saint Nick" and "Monsieur St–Nick"), *The Wonderful World of Disney,* ABC, 2002.

Scorekeeper Victor, *Bleacher Bums* (also known as *The Cheap Seats*), Showtime, 2002.

Ozzy Larson, *A Very Married Christmas,* CBS, 2004.

Santa Claus, *A Boyfriend for Christmas,* The Hallmark Channel, 2004.

Councilperson Max Ernst, *Detective* (also known as *Arthur Hailey's "Detective"*), Lifetime, 2005.

Television Appearances; Specials:

Will Pentland, *Look Homeward, Angel,* 1972.

Senator Stephen Douglas, "The Rivalry," *Hallmark Hall of Fame* (also known as *Hallmark Television Playhouse*), NBC, 1975.

"The Ashes of Mrs. Reasoner," *Hollywood Television Theatre,* PBS, 1976.

Cubby Doucette, "The Dancing Bear," *Visions,* PBS, 1977.

(Uncredited) Himself, *The Muppets Go Hollywood,* 1979.

Title role, "Casey Stengel," *Hallmark Hall of Fame* (also known as *Hallmark Television Playhouse*), PBS, 1981.

McMahon, "The Monument," *The Girls in Their Summer Dresses and Other Stories by Irwin Shaw,* PBS, 1981.

Himself, *The Best Little Special in Texas,* syndicated, 1982.

Retired man, "Working" (musical), *American Playhouse* (also known as *American Playhouse: Working*), PBS, 1982.

The captain, *Mr. Roberts,* NBC, 1984.

The Screen Actors Guild 50th Anniversary Celebration, 1984.

Himself, *The Night of 100 Stars II* (also known as *Night of One Hundred Stars*), ABC, 1985.

Charley, *Death of a Salesman* (also known as *Der Tod eines Handlungsreisenden*), CBS, 1985.

Dom DeLuise and Friends, Part 3, ABC, 1985.

Angelo Roncalli/Pope John XXIII, *I Would Be Called John: Pope John XXIII,* PBS, 1987.

Narrator and voice of Grandpa Yook, *The Butter Battle Book* (animated; also known as *Dr. Seuss' "The Butter Battle Book"*), TNT, 1989.

(Uncredited; in archive footage) Doc Hopper, *The Muppets Celebrate Jim Henson,* CBS, 1990.

Charles F. Money, *Tales from Hollywood,* BBC, 1992, broadcast on *American Playhouse,* PBS, 1992.

(Uncredited; in archive footage) Doc Hopper, "The World of Jim Henson," *Great Performances,* PBS, 1994.

Narrator, *Normandy: The Great Crusade,* The Discovery Channel, 1994.

Voice of Benjamin Franklin, *The American Revolution,* Arts and Entertainment, 1994.

Himself, *National Memorial Day Concert,* PBS, 1994, 1995, 1996, 1997, 1998, 1999, 2000, 2001, 2007.

Himself, *Jack Lemmon: America's Everyman,* Arts and Entertainment, 1996.

Santa Claus, *Elmo Saves Christmas* (also known as *Sesame Street—Elmo Saves Christmas*), PBS, 1996.

Himself, *Burt Reynolds,* 1998.

Voice of Mayor William Strong, *The City of Greater New York: The Story of Consolidation,* WNET (PBS affiliate), 1998.

Himself, *AFI's 100 Years, 100 Thrills: America's Most Heart–Pounding Movies* (also known as *AFI's 100 Years ... 100 Thrills*), CBS, 2001.

Television Appearances; Awards Presentations:

The American Film Institute Salute to Billy Wilder (also known as *The AFI Salute to Billy Wilder* and *American Film Institute Salutes Billy Wilder*), NBC, 1986.

The 40th Annual Tony Awards, CBS, 1986.

The Stuntman Awards, syndicated, 1986.

The 44th Annual Tony Awards, CBS, 1990.

The 17th Annual People's Choice Awards, CBS, 1991.

49th Annual Golden Globe Awards, TBS, 1992.

The American Film Institute Salute to Robert Wise (also known as *The AFI Salute to Robert Wise* and *American Film Institute Salutes Robert Wise*), NBC, 1998.

27th Annual People's Choice Awards, 2001.

American Veteran Awards, History Channel, 2002.

Appeared in other awards presentations and other programs.

Television Appearances; Episodic:

Bureaucrat, "Go Fight City Hall," *East Side, West Side,* CBS, 1963.

"A Question of Murder," *The Nurses* (also known as *The Doctors and the Nurses*), CBS, 1965.

"Old Gangsters Never Die," *N.Y.P.D.,* ABC, 1967.

Hewitt, "The Reluctant Deputy," *The High Chaparral,* NBC, 1970.

Sid Balinger, "The Midtown Beat," *Madigan,* NBC, 1972.

Detective, "Gloria the Victim," *All in the Family* (also known as *Justice for All* and *Those Were the Days*), CBS, 1973.

Himself, *The Tonight Show Starring Johnny Carson* (also known as *The Best of Carson*), NBC, 1973, 1975.

Don Corcoran, "The Deadly Conspiracy," *Cannon,* CBS, 1975.

Don Corcoran, "The Deadly Conspiracy: Part 2," *Barnaby Jones,* CBS, 1975.

Havens, "Retire in Sunny Hawaii—Forever," *Hawaii Five–O* (also known as *McGarrett*), CBS, 1975.

Jake Hatch, "Set Up City," *Baretta,* ABC, 1975.

Assistant to the boss, "Guilt Trip," *Amazing Stories* (also known as *Steven Spielberg's "Amazing Stories"*), NBC, 1985.

Doffue, "The Legend of Sleepy Hollow," *Shelley Duvall's "Tall Tales and Legends"* (also known as *Tall Tales and Legends*), Showtime, 1986.

Earl, "You Gotta Believe Me," *Amazing Stories* (also known as *Steven Spielberg's "Amazing Stories"*), NBC, 1986.

Himself, *Dolly,* ABC, 1987.

Himself, *A Conversation with Dinah,* The Nashville Network, 1990.

"Jessica Lange: It's Only Make Believe," *Crazy about the Movies,* Cinemax, 1991.

Dr. Futterman, "Leslie's Folly," *Directed By,* Showtime, 1994.

Vaughn, "Texan," *Directed By,* Showtime, 1994.

Himself, "The Films of Sydney Pollack," *The Directors* (also known as *The Directors: Sydney Pollack*), Encore, 1997.

Dr. Veckman, "A Regular Joe," *Early Edition,* CBS, 1997.

A. J. Sheridan, "Bakersfield," *Cybill,* CBS, 1998.

A. J. Sheridan, "Daddy," *Cybill,* CBS, 1998.

Stephen Donnell, "Passing Go," *The Practice,* ABC, 1998.

Thomas Finnegan, "Finnegan's Wake," *Homicide: Life on the Street* (also known as *Homicide* and *Homicide: HOTS*), NBC, 1998.

Himself, *Intimate Portrait: Jessica Lange,* Lifetime, 1998.

Voice of Francis Griffin, "Holy Crap," *Family Guy* (animated; also known as *Padre de familia* and *Padre del familia*), Fox, 1999.

"The Window," *Chicken Soup for the Soul,* PAX TV, 1999.

Judge Romick, "Time," *Early Edition,* CBS, 2000.

Stephen Donnell, "Death Penalties," *The Practice,* ABC, 2000.

Wes Connelly, "The Second Chance," *The Hoop Life,* Showtime, 2000.

Himself, "Jessica Lange: On Her Own Terms," *Biography* (also known as *A&E Biography: Jessica Lange*), Arts and Entertainment, 2001.

Clifford Connelly, "Three Days in November," *Citizen Baines* (also known as *The Second Act*), CBS, 2001.

Voice of Francis Griffin, "Mr. Saturday Knight," *Family Guy* (animated; also known as *Padre de familia* and *Padre del familia*), Fox, 2001.

"Fielding Offers," *Arli$$* (also known as *Arliss*), HBO, 2001.

Father Madden, "The Root of All Evil," *Touched by an Angel,* CBS, 2003.

Ernie Yost, "Call of Silence," *Navy NCIS: Naval Criminal Investigative Service* (also known as *Naval CIS, Navy CIS, Navy NCIS, NCIS,* and *NCIS: Naval Criminal Investigative Service*), CBS, 2004.

Himself, *Dinner for Five,* Independent Film Channel, 2004.

Voice of Francis Griffin, "The Father, the Son and the Holy Fonz," *Family Guy* (animated; also known as *Padre de familia* and *Padre del familia*), Fox, 2005.

Eugene "Gene" Brown, "Goodbye, Love," *Everwood* (also known as *Our New Life in Everwood*), The WB, 2006.

Eugene "Gene" Brown, "Reckoning," *Everwood* (also known as *Our New Life in Everwood*), The WB, 2006.

Hank Johansen, "Mr. Monk Goes to the Hospital," *Monk,* USA Network, 2007.

Also appeared in other programs, including *The Defenders,* CBS.

Television Appearances; Pilots:
District attorney Horn, *Rx for the Defense,* ABC, 1973.
Phil Beckman, *Switch,* CBS, 1975.
Nick, *Good Evening, He Lied,* NBC, 1984.
P. Oliver Pendergast, *P.O.P.,* NBC, 1984.
Harry Deegan, "Side by Side," *Comedy Factory,* ABC, 1985.
Dr. Harlan Elldridge, *Harlan & Merleen* (also known as *It's Never Too Late*), CBS, 1993.
Justice Henry Hoskins, *First Monday,* CBS, 2002.

Television Theme Song Performer; Pilots:
P.O.P., NBC, 1984.
"Side by Side," *Comedy Factory,* ABC, 1985.

Stage Appearances:
First servant to Cornwall, *King Lear,* New York Shakespeare Festival, Joseph Papp Public Theater, Delacorte Theater, New York City, 1962.

Lucius, *Julius Caesar,* New York Shakespeare Festival, Heckscher Theatre, New York City, 1962.

Porter and Seyton, *Macbeth,* New York Shakespeare Festival, Heckscher Theatre, 1962.

Stephano, *The Tempest,* New York Shakespeare Festival, Joseph Papp Public Theater, Delacorte Theater, 1962.

Clown, *Antony and Cleopatra,* New York Shakespeare Festival, Joseph Papp Public Theater, Delacorte Theater, 1963.

Clown, *The Winter's Tale,* New York Shakespeare Festival, Joseph Papp Public Theater, Delacorte Theater, 1963.

Corin, *As You Like It,* New York Shakespeare Festival, Joseph Papp Public Theater, Delacorte Theater, 1963.

Feste, *Twelfth Night* (also known as *Twelfth Night, or What You Will*), New York Shakespeare Festival, Heckscher Theatre, 1963.

Purser and a Cuban, *Too Much Johnson,* Phoenix Theatre, New York City, 1964.

Understudy for various roles, *Poor Bitos,* Cort Theatre, New York City, 1964.

Paul Rudd and understudy for various roles, *The Child Buyer,* The Theatre Guild, Garrick Theatre, New York City, 1964–65.

Grumio, *The Taming of the Shrew,* New York Shakespeare Festival, Joseph Papp Public Theater, Delacorte Mobile Theater, 1965.

Pincer, *Drat! The Cat!* (musical), Martin Beck Theatre, New York City, 1965.

Pistol, *King Henry V,* New York Shakespeare Festival, Joseph Papp Public Theater, Delacorte Mobile Theater, 1965.

Dean Steward and Maurice, *Pousse–Cafe* (musical), Forty–Sixth Street Theatre, New York City, 1966.

First murderer, *Richard III,* New York Shakespeare Festival, Joseph Papp Public Theater, Delacorte Theater, 1966.

Lavatch, *All's Well That Ends Well,* New York Shakespeare Festival, Joseph Papp Public Theater, Delacorte Theater, 1966.

Point and the discussion leader, *The World of Gunter Grass,* Pocket Theatre, New York City, 1966.

Pompey, *Measure for Measure,* New York Shakespeare Festival, Joseph Papp Public Theater, Delacorte Theater, 1966.

The Entertainer, Pittsburgh Playhouse, Pittsburgh, PA, 1966.

A Man's a Man, Pittsburgh Playhouse, 1966.

Dromio of Ephesus, *The Comedy of Errors,* New York Shakespeare Festival, Joseph Papp Public Theater, Delacorte Theater, 1967.

The Three Sisters, Pittsburgh Playhouse, 1967.

Louis Bonnard, *The Happy Time* (musical), Ahmanson Theatre, Los Angeles, 1967, then Broadway Theatre, New York City, 1967–68.

Daddy, *Huui, Huui,* New York Shakespeare Theatre, Joseph Papp Public Theater, New York City, 1968.

Feste, *Twelfth Night* (also known as *Twelfth Night, or What You Will*), New York Shakespeare Festival, Joseph Papp Public Theater, Delacorte Theater, 1969.

Rodicon the turnkey, *Invitation to a Beheading,* New York Shakespeare Festival, Joseph Papp Public Theater, 1969.

Ned Buntline, *Indians,* Brooks Atkinson Theatre, New York City, 1969–70.

Cade, *Chronicles of King Henry VI, Part II,* New York Shakespeare Festival, Joseph Papp Public Theater, Delacorte Theater, 1970.

Douglas, *Lemon Sky,* Studio Arena Theatre, Buffalo, NY, then Playhouse Theatre, New York City, 1970.

Mayor of London, *Chronicles of King Henry VI, Part 1,* New York Shakespeare Festival, Joseph Papp Public Theater, Delacorte Theater, 1970.

Orderly, *The Happiness Cage,* New York Shakespeare Festival, Joseph Papp Public Theater, Estelle R. Newman Theater, New York City, 1970.

First gravedigger, *Hamlet,* New York Shakespeare Festival, Joseph Papp Public Theater, Delacorte Theater, 1972.

George Sikowski, *That Championship Season,* New York Shakespeare Festival, Joseph Papp Public Theater, Estelle R. Newman Theater, then Booth Theatre, New York City, 1972–74.

Harold, *In the Boom Boom Room,* New York Shakespeare Festival, Lincoln Center, Vivian Beaumont Theater, New York City, 1973.

Eugene Hartigan, *The au Pair Man,* New York Shakespeare Festival, Lincoln Center, Vivian Beaumont Theater, 1973–74.

Cohn, *Knock, Knock,* Biltmore Theatre, New York City, 1976.

On Golden Pond, Mark Taper Forum, Los Angeles, 1980.

Charley, *Death of a Salesman,* Broadhurst Theatre, New York City, 1985.

The Night of 100 Stars II (also known as *Night of One Hundred Stars*), Theatre at Radio City Music Hall, New York City, 1985.

Sweet Bird of Youth, Royal Alexandra Theatre, Toronto, Ontario, Canada, 1988.

Big Daddy, *Cat on a Hot Tin Roof,* Playhouse Theatre, Wilmington, DE, then Eugene O'Neill Theatre, New York City, 1990.

Matthew Harrison Brady, *Inherit the Wind,* National Actors Theatre, Royale Theatre, New York City, 1996.

Weller Martin, *The Gin Game,* National Actors Theatre, Lyceum Theatre, New York City, 1997.

Former president Arthur Hockstader, *Gore Vidal's "The Best Man"* (also known as *The Best Man*), Virginia Theatre, New York City, 2000.

Old man, *Prelude to a Kiss* (staged reading), L.A. Theatre Works, Theatre at Skirball Cultural Center, Los Angeles, 2000.

Shelly Levine, *Glengarry Glen Ross,* McCarter Theatre, Princeton, NJ, 2000.

Village elder, *Brigadoon* (musical), Pittsburgh Civic Light Opera, Benedum Center, Pittsburgh, PA, 2001.

Old Dogsborough, *The Resistible Rise of Arturo Ui,* National Actors Theatre, Pace University, Michael Schimmel Center for the Arts, New York City, 2002.

Elwood P. Dowd, *Harvey,* Laguna Playhouse, Laguna Beach, CA, 2003.

Dalton Trumbo (title role), *Trumbo: Red, White & Blacklisted,* Westside Theatre Downstairs, New York City, 2003–2004.

Jack Jameson, *Third,* Lincoln Center, Mitzi E. Newhouse Theater, New York City, 2005.

Appeared as Trinculo, *The Tempest;* and as Sir Toby Belch, *Twelfth Night* (also known as *Twelfth Night, or What You Will*); also appeared in *King John* and *Two by Saroyan;* appeared in other productions of the New York Shakespeare Festival and in other productions, including productions in Brooklyn, New York City. Some sources cite an appearance in *The Eve of St. Mark,* Cort Theatre, c. 1943.

Major Tours:

The Andersonville Trial, U.S. cities, 1960.

Weller Martin, *The Gin Game,* U.S. cities, 1998–99.

Stage Work:

Stage manager, *The Child Buyer,* The Theatre Guild, Garrick Theatre, New York City, 1964–65.

Radio Appearances:

Radio appearances include the voice of an old man for *Prelude to a Kiss,* L.A. Theatre Works, KCRW (National Public Radio affiliate).

RECORDINGS

Videos:

Himself, *Sisters, l'autopsie* (short), Wild Side Video, 2004.

Himself, *The Art of "The Sting,"* Universal Studios Home Video, 2005.

(Uncredited; in archive footage) Doc Hopper, *Kermit: A Frog's Life* (short), Buena Vista Home Entertainment, 2005.

Himself, *"Dog Day Afternoon": Casting the Controversy* (short), Warner Home Video, 2006.

E–G

EBERSOLE, Christine 1953–

PERSONAL

Born February 21, 1953, in Chicago (some sources cite Winnetka), IL; daughter of Robert (an engineer and executive) and Marian (a psychiatric social worker) Ebersole; married Peter Bergman (an actor), c. 1977 (marriage ended, c. 1982); married Bill Moloney (a real estate agent and former drummer and musical director), 1988; children: (second marriage) Elijah, MaeMae (some sources cite name as May Dawn), Aron; aunt of Janel Moloney (an actress). *Education:* Attended Mac-Murray College; trained for the stage at American Academy of Dramatic Arts.

Addresses: *Agent*—Barry McPherson, Agency for the Performing Arts, 405 South Beverly Dr., Beverly Hills, CA 90212.

Career: Actress and singer. Performer at various venues, including cabarets and parades. Worked as a waitress and affiliated with benefits, charity functions, and fund–raisers.

Awards, Honors: Daytime Emmy Award nomination, outstanding actress in a supporting role in a daytime drama series, 1984, for *One Life to Live;* Antoinette Perry Award, Outer Critics Circle Award, and Drama Desk Award nomination, all best actress in a musical, 2001, for *42nd Street;* honorary doctorate, MacMurray College, 2002; Obie Award (with others), outstanding performance, *Village Voice,* and Drama Desk Award nomination, outstanding featured actress in a play, both 2003, for *Talking Heads;* Antoinette Perry Award nomination, best actress in a play, 2003, for *Dinner at Eight;* Obie Award, outstanding performance, Drama Desk Award and Outer Critics Circle Award, outstand-

ing actress in a musical, Drama League Award, best performance, and special citation, New York Drama Critics Circle, all 2006, and Antoinette Perry Award, best actress in a musical, 2007, all for *Grey Gardens.*

CREDITS

Stage Appearances:
Nancy, *Angel Street,* Lyceum Theatre, New York City, 1975–76.

Jan, *Angel Street,* Lyceum Theatre, 1976.

Dana, *Green Pond* (musical), Westside Theatre (Upstairs), Chelsea Theatre Center, New York City, 1977, also produced at the Brooklyn Academy of Music, Brooklyn, New York City.

I Love My Wife (musical), Ethel Barrymore Theatre, New York City, c. 1977–79.

Agnes, *On the Twentieth Century* (musical), St. James Theatre, New York City, 1978–79.

Margaret, *Gossip,* PAF Playhouse, New York City, 1979.

Ado Annie Carnes, *Oklahoma!* (musical), Palace Theatre, New York City, 1979–80, then John F. Kennedy Center for the Performing Arts, Washington, DC.

Guenevere, *Camelot* (musical), Lincoln Center, New York State Theater (some sources cite Palace Theatre), New York City, 1980.

Natasha, *The Three Sisters,* Manhattan Theatre Club Stage I, New York City, 1982–83.

Skye Bullene, *Geniuses,* Playwrights Horizons Theatre Company, Douglas Fairbanks Theatre, New York City, 1982–83.

Gerta Granville, *Harrigan 'n Hart* (musical), Longacre Theatre, New York City, 1985.

Beatrice, *Much Ado about Nothing,* Old Globe, San Diego, CA, 1986.

The Blue Dahlia, Court Theatre, Los Angeles, 1989.

The Marriage of Bette and Boo, Los Angeles Theatre Center, Los Angeles, 1989–90.

Miss Trixie Delight, *Paper Moon* (musical), Paper Mill Playhouse, Millburn, NJ, 1993.

Emily West, "Allegro" (concert), *Encores!* (also known as *Encores! Great American Musicals in Concert*), City Center Theatre, New York City, 1994.

Liza Elliott, "Lady in the Dark" (concert), *Encores!* (also known as *Encores! Great American Musicals in Concert*), City Center Theatre, 1994.

Dossie Lustig, *Getting Away with Murder*, Broadhurst Theatre, New York City, 1996.

Babe Williams, *The Pajama Game* (musical), Reprise! Broadway's Best in Concert, University of California, Los Angeles, Freud Playhouse, Los Angeles, 1998.

"Ziegfeld Follies of 1936" (concert), *Encores!* (also known as *Encores! Great American Musicals in Concert*), City Center Theatre, 1998.

Title role, *Mame* (musical), Paper Mill Playhouse, 1999.

Diana, *Current Events*, Manhattan Theatre Club Stage II, 2000.

Mabel Cantwell, *Gore Vidal's "The Best Man"* (also known as *The Best Man*), Virginia Theatre, New York City, 2000.

Guest, *Seth Rudetsky's "Broadway Chatterbox,"* Don't Tell MaMa (cabaret), New York City, 2000.

Fay Morgan and Morgan Le Fay, "A Connecticut Yankee" (concert), *Encores!* (also known as *Encores! Great American Musicals in Concert*), City Center Theatre, 2001.

Dorothy Brock, *42nd Street* (musical), Ford Center for the Performing Arts, New York City, 2001–2002.

Millicent Jordan, *Dinner at Eight*, Lincoln Center, Vivian Beaumont Theater, New York City, 2002–2003.

Irene Ruddock, "A Lady of Letters" (monologue), *Talking Heads*, Minetta Lane Theatre, New York City, 2003.

Aimee Semple McPherson (title role), *Hurricane Aimee* (readings of musical), c. 2003.

M'Lynn, *Steel Magnolias*, Lyceum Theatre, 2005.

Edith Ewing "Big Edie" Bouvier Beale and Edith "Little Edie" Bouvier Beale, *Grey Gardens* (musical), Playwrights Horizons Theatre, New York City, 2006, then Walter Kerr Theatre, New York City, 2006–2007.

Appeared in Los Angeles productions of *Into the Woods* (musical) and *Laughing Wild*. Appeared in the musicals *Evita*, *Guys and Dolls*, and *My Fair Lady*. Appeared in other productions, including a concert production of *Sunday in the Park with George* with the Eos Orchestra.

Television Appearances; Series:

Lily Darnell, *Ryan's Hope*, ABC, 1980.

Member of the ensemble, *Saturday Night Live* (also known as *NBC's "Saturday Night," Saturday Night, Saturday Night Live '80, SNL,* and *SNL 25*), NBC, 1981–82.

Maxie McDermott, *One Life to Live* (also known as *Between Heaven and Hell*), ABC, 1983–85.

Barbara Goodwin, *The Hogan Family* (also known as *The Hogans, Valerie,* and *Valerie's Family*), NBC, 1986.

Katherine "Kit" Cavanaugh, *The Cavanaughs*, CBS, 1986–89.

Voice of Mrs. Generic, *Bobby's World* (animated), Fox, 1990–98.

Title role, *Rachel Gunn, R.N.*, Fox, 1992, 2000.

Belinda Carhardt, *Ink*, CBS, 1996–97.

Renee, a recurring role, *Related,* The WB, 2005–2006.

Television Appearances; Movies:

Miss Vashinski, *The Dollmaker*, ABC, 1984.

Lee Snyder, *Acceptable Risks*, ABC, 1986.

Cheryl New, *Dying to Love You* (also known as *Lethal White Female*), 1993.

Tessie Tura, *Gypsy* (musical), CBS, 1993.

Ruth Whitney, *An Unexpected Family*, USA Network, 1996.

Ruth Whitney, *An Unexpected Life*, USA Network, 1998.

Peggy, *Double Platinum* (also known as *Double platine, Double Platinum—Doppel Platin!, Duo de platino,* and *Kaksi taehteae*), ABC, 1999.

Cecile Andrews, *Mary and Rhoda*, NBC, 2000.

Kathy Stanford, *Pros & Cons*, HBO, 2000.

Sandy, *An Unexpected Love* (also known as *This Much I Know*), Lifetime, 2003.

Television Appearances; Specials:

Herself, *Broadway Plays Washington on Kennedy Center Tonight*, 1982.

The Truth about Teachers (also known as *Raising Good Kids in Bad Times*), syndicated, 1989.

Herself, "Ira Gershwin at 100: A Celebration at Carnegie Hall," *Great Performances*, PBS, 1997.

Herself, "The Rodgers & Hart Story: Thou Swell, Thou Witty," *Great Performances*, PBS, 1999.

Dorothy Brock, *The Lullaby of Broadway: Opening Night on 42nd Street*, 2001.

Voice of Pat Dixon, *The Electric Piper* (animated rock opera), Nickelodeon, 2003.

(In archive footage) *Saturday Night Live in the '80s: Lost & Found*, NBC, 2005.

Herself, *Broadway under the Stars*, CBS, 2006.

Television Appearances; Awards Presentations:

Presenter, *The 60th Annual Tony Awards*, CBS, 2006.

Kennedy Center Honors: A Celebration of the Performing Arts, CBS, 2006.

The 61st Annual Tony Awards, CBS, 2007.

Television Appearances; Episodic:

"The Enormous Radio," *Tales from the Darkside* (also known as *Beraettelser fraan andra siden, Histoires de l'autre monde, Historias del mas ella,* and *Keskiyoen kauhutarinoita*), syndicated, 1987.

Dolly (also known as *The Dolly Show*), ABC, 1987.

Maddy, "The Bummer of 42," *Murphy Brown*, CBS, 1990.

Laura, "All about Harry," *Empty Nest,* NBC, 1991.

Voice of Lana Vail, "Heat/Snow," *Hey Arnold!* (animated; also known as *Hey, Arnold!*), Nickelodeon, 1996.

Margo Langhorne, "How Nina Got Her Groove Back," *Just Shoot Me!,* NBC, 1998.

Marie Stokes, "Just Looking," *Ally McBeal,* Fox, 1998.

Norma, "Remember?," *The Love Boat: The Next Wave,* UPN, 1998.

Herself, *The Rosie O'Donnell Show,* syndicated, multiple appearances, between 1998 and 2002.

"Three Guys, a Girl, and a Conversation Nook," *Madigan Men,* ABC, 2000.

Candy Pruitt, "Poker? I Don't Even Like Her," *Will & Grace,* NBC, 2001.

Herself, *Intimate Portrait: Rosie O'Donnell,* Lifetime, 2003.

Mrs. Maguire, "Fire in the Sky," *Crossing Jordan* (also known as *Untitled Tim Kring Project*), NBC, 2004.

Myra Hudson, "Tick Tock, Writer's Block," *Wild Card* (also known as *Zoe Busiek: Wild Card*), Lifetime, 2004.

Herself, "Production: Grey Gardens," *Working in the Theatre,* 2006.

Herself, *The View,* ABC, 2006.

(Uncredited; in archive footage) Edith Ewing "Big Edie" Bouvier Beale and Edith "Little Edie" Bouvier Beale, *La mandragora,* Television Espanola (TVE, Spain), 2007.

Herself, *Live with Regis & Kelly,* syndicated, 2007.

Television Appearances; Pilots:

Thea Jones (title role), *Miss Jones,* ABC, 1991.

Helen, *Breaking News,* Bravo, 2002.

Ruth Winterhalter, *The Mayor,* The WB, 2003.

Television Theme Performer:

Miss Jones (pilot), ABC, 1991.

"Working for a Living," *Rachel Gunn, R.N.* (series), Fox, 1992, 2000.

Film Appearances:

Linda, *Tootsie* (also known as *Would I Lie to You?*), Columbia, 1982.

Janie Pointer, *Thief of Hearts,* Paramount, 1984.

Katerina Cavalieri/Costanza, *Amadeus* (also known as *Peter Shaffer's "Amadeus"* and *Amadeusz*), Orion, 1984, director's cut released as *Amadeus: Director's Cut* (also known as *Peter Shaffer's "Amadeus": Director's Cut, Amadeus: El montaje del director, Amadeus—ohjaajan versio,* and *Amadeus—version integrale*).

Janet Cruise, *Mac and Me,* Orion, 1988.

Carol, *Ghost Dad,* Universal, 1990.

Lydia Larsen, *Dead Again,* Paramount, 1991.

Arlene Aldrich, *Folks!,* Twentieth Century–Fox, 1992.

Cynthia Lewis, *The Lounge People* (also known as *L–Dopa*), 1992.

Regina Rich, *Richie Rich,* Warner Bros., 1994.

Rose Zsigmond, *My Girl 2,* Columbia, 1994.

Governor Tracy, *Black Sheep,* Paramount, 1996.

Mom Dunlap, *Pie in the Sky* (also known as *Mr. Traffic*), Fine Line Features, 1996.

Beebee Moss, *'Til There Was You* (also known as *Ate tu apareceres ..., Ha–Dereh el Ha–Osher, Hasta que te encontre, Idoeszamitasom eloett, L'amour de ma vie, Si on s'aimait, Solo se ilm destino,* and *Zwei Singles in L.A.*), Paramount, 1997.

Bridget Rossiter, *True Crime* (also known as *True Crimes, Crimenes verdaderos, Ein Wahres Verbrechen, Ejecucion inminente, Fino a prova contraria, Juge coupable, Oegonblicket foere tystnaden, Pahin rikos,* and *Um crime real*), Warner Bros., 1999.

Mrs. Loralie Brown, *My Favorite Martian* (also known as *My Favourite Martian*), Buena Vista, 1999.

Miriam Prigusivac, *Love Comes to the Executioner,* Velocity Home Entertainment, 2006.

Herself, *Grey Gardens: From East Hampton to Broadway* (documentary), East of Doheny, 2007.

Herself, *Dying for Change* (documentary), Scott Goldberg Films, c. 2007.

Herself, *Wrangler: Anatomy of an Icon* (documentary), Automat Pictures, 2008.

RECORDINGS

Albums:

Live at the Cinegrill, Footlight Records, 1998.

(With Billy Stritch) *In Your Dreams* (also known as *In Your Dreams, Christine Ebersole with Billy Stritch*), Ghostlight Records, 2004.

Appeared in cast recordings.

OTHER SOURCES

Books:

Newsmakers, issue 2, Gale, 2007.

Periodicals:

New York Times, June 3, 2007.

Parade, August 26, 2001, p. 17.

Playbill, December 31, 2001, pp. 22, 24; July 31, 2003, pp. 15–16.

TV Guide, August 27, 1988, p. 2.

ECKHOLDT, Steven 1961–
   (Stephen Eckholdt, Steve Eckholdt)

PERSONAL

Born September 6, 1961, in Los Angeles, CA; married Kirsten Getchell (an actress).

Addresses: *Agent*—Innovative Artists Talent and Literary Agency, 1505 10th St., Santa Monica, CA 90401.

Career: Actor. Appeared in advertisements.

Awards, Honors: Camie Award (with others), Character and Morality in Entertainment awards, 2005, for *Secret Santa*.

CREDITS

Television Appearances; Series:
Rick Singer, *WIOU*, CBS, 1990–91.
(Sometimes credited as Steve Eckholdt) Kenny Stollmark, Jr., a recurring role, *Life Goes On* (also known as *Glenbrook*), ABC, 1992.
Thumper Klein, *Grapevine*, CBS, 1992.
Robert Wilson, a recurring role, *Melrose Place*, Fox, 1993–94.
Patrick Flanagan, a recurring role, *L.A. Law*, NBC, 1994.
James Monroe, *The Monroes*, ABC, 1995.
Mark Robinson, a recurring role, *Friends* (also known as *Across the Hall*, *Friends Like Us*, *Insomnia Cafe*, and *Six of One*), NBC, 1997.
Robbie Graham, *It's Like, You Know ...*, ABC, 1999–2000.
David Klein, *Grapevine*, CBS, 2000.
Joe Connelly, a recurring role, *Providence*, NBC, 2001.
Thomas Miller, *My Big Fat Greek Life*, CBS, 2003.
Doug Westin, *The West Wing* (also known as *West Wing* and *El ala oeste de la Casablanca*), NBC, between 2003 and 2006.
Henry, a recurring role, *The L Word* (also known as *Earthlings*), Showtime, 2006–2007.

Television Appearances; Miniseries:
Peter Wilson, *Message from Nam* (also known as *Danielle Steel's "Message from Nam"*), NBC, 1993.
Colm Connolly, *And Never Let Her Go*, CBS, 2001.

Television Appearances; Movies:
(As Steve Eckholdt) Student in Jack Parrish's class, *Between the Darkness and the Dawn*, NBC, 1985.
(As Steve Eckholdt) Danny Forndexter as an adult, "14 Going on 30," *The Disney Sunday Movie* (also known as *Disneyland*, *Disneylandia*, *Disney's Wonderful World*, *The Magical World of Disney*, *Walt Disney*, *Walt Disney Presents*, *Walt Disney's Wonderful World of Color*, and *The Wonderful World of Disney*), ABC, 1988.
Jeff, *Go to the Light* (also known as *Go toward the Light*), 1988.
Robert Stethem, *The Taking of Flight 847: The Uli Derickson Story* (also known as *The Flight* and *The Taking of Flight 847*), NBC, 1988.

Tommy Cox, *Condition: Critical* (also known as *Final Pulse*), 1992.
Detective Bill Rounder, *The Stranger beside Me*, ABC, 1995.
Chris Lallek, *Family Blessings* (also known as *LaVyrle Spencer's "Family Blessings"*), CBS, 1996.
Detective Richard Younger, *I Know What You Did* (also known as *Crimes of Passion: I Know What You Did* and *In Defense of Murder*), ABC, 1998.
Peter Albright, "Santa Who?" (also known as "Leslie Nielsen's Santa Claus"), *The Wonderful World of Disney*, ABC, 2000.
John Martin Carter, *Secret Santa*, NBC, 2003.
Sam Keller, *Comfort and Joy*, Lifetime, 2003.

Television Appearances; Episodic:
Dino Perelli, "Brand New Bag," *St. Elsewhere*, NBC, 1986.
(As Steve Eckholdt) Dennis, "What I Did for Love," *Day by Day*, NBC, 1988.
(As Steve Eckholdt) Mike, "Birth of a Salesman," *The Charmings*, ABC, 1988.
Andrew Garrison, "Cruise Ship," *Baywatch* (also known as *Baywatch Hawaii* and *Baywatch Hawai'i*), NBC, 1989.
(As Steve Eckholdt) Brian Lander, "Investment in Death," *Hunter*, NBC, 1989.
Lance, "Shirts and Skins," *21 Jump Street*, Fox, 1990.
(As Steve Eckholdt) Mark Carter, "The Student," *Matlock*, NBC, 1990.
Cleland, "Pump It Up," *L.A. Law*, NBC, 1991.
Richard, "It Never Entered My Mind," *Jake and the Fatman*, CBS, 1991.
Connor, "Exit Laughing," *Wings*, NBC, 1993.
Daniel, "Woman Loses Space Alien, Finds God!," *The Naked Truth* (also known as *Wilde Again*), ABC, 1996.
David, "For Art's Sake," *Champs*, ABC, 1996.
David, "It's Must Have Been Gridlock," *Champs*, ABC, 1996.
Assistant district attorney Chris Kelton, "The Blessing," *The Practice*, ABC, 1997.
Assistant district attorney Chris Kelton, "Part VI," *The Practice*, ABC, 1997.
(As Stephen Eckholdt) Assistant district attorney Chris Kelton, "Sex, Lies and Monkeys," *The Practice*, ABC, 1997.
Chip Stoody, "The Thanksgiving Show," *George & Leo*, CBS, 1997.
Richard, "The Puppy Episode: Parts 1 & 2," *Ellen* (also known as *These Friends of Mine*), ABC, 1997.
Dr. Kevin Michaels, "A Little Tail," *Maximum Bob*, ABC, 1998.
Professor Dwyer, "Bad Hair Week," *That's Life*, CBS, 2000.
Professor Dwyer, "The Tell–Tale Uterus," *That's Life*, CBS, 2000.
Alex Hall, "The Liar's Club: Parts 1 & 2," *Family Law*, CBS, 2001.

Alex Hall, "Soul Custody," *Family Law,* CBS, 2001.

Mark Robinson, "The One with Princess Consuela," *Friends* (also known as *Across the Hall, Friends Like Us, Insomnia Cafe,* and *Six of One*), NBC, 2004.

Officer Rick Thompson, "Come In, Stranger," *Desperate Housewives* (also known as *Beautes desespereees, Desperate housewives—I segreti di Wisteria Lane, Desupareto na tsuma tachi, Esposas desesperadas, Frustrerte fruer, Gotowe na wszystko, Kucanice, Meeleheitel koduperenaised, Mujeres desesperadas, Noikokyres se apognosi, Szueletett felesegek,* and *Taeydelliset naiset*), ABC, 2004.

Commander Dr. Brad Pitt, "SWAK," *CSI: Crime Scene Investigation* (also known as *C.S.I., CSI: Las Vegas, CSI Weekends,* and *Les experts*), CBS, 2005.

Dale Livingston, "From the Grave," *CSI: Miami,* CBS, 2005.

Gus Mason, "The Big Frozen Assets Episode," *Half & Half,* UPN, 2005.

Gus Mason, "The Big Training Day Episode," *Half & Half,* UPN, 2005.

Senator Billy Cole, "One Nation, under Surveillance," *Las Vegas* (also known as *Casino Eye*), NBC, 2005.

Assistant district attorney Richard Kelton, "Word Salad Days," *Boston Legal* (also known as *Fleet Street, The Practice: Fleet Street,* and *The Untitled Practice*), ABC, 2006.

Dr. Mitchell Sterling, "Dr. Feelbad," *Shark,* CBS, 2006.

Gus Mason, "The Big Take Me as I Am Episode," *Half & Half,* UPN, 2006.

Steve, "Four," *Smith,* CBS, 2007.

Television Appearances; Pilots:

Lyle "Buck" Buchanan, *The Bakery,* CBS, 1990.

Rick Singer, *WIOU,* CBS, 1990.

Gavin Travers, *Daytona Beach,* ABC, 1996.

Executive, *Dads,* 1997.

Guy, "Love and the Blind Date," *Love American Style,* ABC, 1999.

Robbie Graham, *It's Like, You Know ...,* ABC, 1999.

David Klein, *Grapevine,* CBS, 2000.

Professor Dwyer, *That's Life,* CBS, 2000.

Man, *Fourplay,* CBS, c. 2000.

Steve, *Smith,* CBS, 2006.

Ted Brennan, *Split Decision,* The CW, 2006.

Appeared as Matt, *Plan B,* ABC.

Film Appearances:

George in Daytona, *The Wraith,* New Century/Vista Film Company, 1986.

Man in bar, *About Last Night ...* (also known as *Sexual Perversity in Chicago*), Columbia/TriStar, 1986.

(As Steve Eckholdt) Ronald, *For Keeps* (also known as *For Keeps?* and *Maybe Baby*), TriStar, 1988.

Shaun, *The Runnin' Kind,* United Artists, 1989.

(As Steve Eckholdt) Jake Bedford, *Just in Time,* Leucadia Films, 1997.

Steve, *Making Sandwiches,* Fortis Films, 1998.

David Osborne, *Message in a Bottle,* Warner Bros., 1999.

Oliver, *Leaving Drew* (short film), 2000.

Film Producer:

Leaving Drew (short film), 2000.

OTHER SOURCES

Periodicals:

TV Guide, February 22, 2003, p. 20.

FIRESIGN THEATRE
   See PROCTOR, Phil

FOGLER, Dan 1977–

PERSONAL

Full name, Daniel Kevin Fogler; born October 20, 1977, in Brooklyn, NY; father, a surgeon; mother, an English teacher. *Education:* Graduated from Boston University. *Religion:* Jewish. *Avocational Interests:* Sculpting.

Addresses: *Agent*—William Morris Agency, One William Morris Pl., Beverly Hills, CA 90212.

Career: Actor. 2nd Rate (band), member; Stage 13 Theater Company, founding member; performed as a stand–up comedian at such clubs as Caroline's Comedy Club, Gotham Comedy Club, Stand Up NY, and New York Comedy Club.

Awards, Honors: Lucille Lortel Award, outstanding featured actor, League of Off–Broadway Theatres and Producers, *Theatre World* Award, Outer Critics Circle Award, outstanding featured actor in a play, Antoinette Perry Award, best featured actor in a musical, 2005, all for *The 25th Annual Putnam County Spelling Bee.*

CREDITS

Film Appearances:

Melvin Mittman, *Brooklyn Thrill Killers* (short), 1999.

Charlie, *Home Field Advantage,* 2000.

Charlie, *Bust a Move* (short), Native Pictures Productions, 2000.
Lenny, *Hyper* (short), Apollo Cinema, 2002.
Crafty, *Slippery Slope,* 2006.
Carmine Marconi, *The Marconi Bros.,* 2006.
Zack, *School for Scoundrels,* Weinstein Company, 2006.
Stu, *Good Luck Chuck,* Lions Gate Films, 2007.
Randy Daytona, *Balls of Fury,* Rogue Pictures, 2007.
Barry Nathan, *Kids in America,* Universal, 2008.
Hutch, *Fanboys,* Weinstein Company, 2008.
Voice of Yummo, *Horton Hears a Who* (animated), Twentieth Century–Fox, 2008.
Rapunzel (animated), Buena Vista, forthcoming.

Television Appearances; Specials:
The 59th Annual Tony Awards, CBS, 2005.
Broadway Under the Stars, CBS, 2005.

Stage Appearances:
Joe Fearless, Ford Theatre, New York City, 2000.
Interrogator, *Bobby Gould in Hell,* Theatre Row, 2004.
William Barfee, *C–R–E–P–U–S–C–U–L–E,* Theatorium, New York City, 2004.
William Barfee, *25th Annual Spelling Bee,* Circle in the Square, New York City, 2005–2006.

Also appeared in *The 25th Annual Putnam County Spelling Bee,* Barrington Stage Company, Pittsfield, MA; *Bridges and Harmonies,* New York City Drama League, New York City; *The Detective Sketches,* Lincoln Center, New York City; as Bane Barrington/Bill, *The Voyage of the Carcass,* Greenwich Street Theatre, New York City.

Major Tours:
Toured in *Warner Brothers' "Scooby Doo/Stage Fright,"* U.S. cities.

Stage Director:
Elephant in the Room!, New York International Fringe Festival, 2007.

WRITINGS

Stage Plays:
Elephant in the Room!, New York International Fringe Festival, 2007.

OTHER SOURCES

Periodicals:
BackStage Magazine, September 14, 2007.

FRIED, Robert N. 1959(?)–
(Rob Fried, Robert Fried)

PERSONAL

Born c. 1959; brother of Daniel Fried (a producer); married Nancy Travis (an actress), 1994.

Addresses: *Office*—Fried Films, 212 26th St., Suite 148, Santa Monica, CA 90402.

Career: Producer and executive. Columbia Pictures, past executive vice president; Savoy Pictures, past president and chief executive officer; Fried Films, Santa Monica, CA, principal. WhatsHotNow.com (Internet service producer for the licensing business), founder, 1996, past chief executive officer, founder of WHN Exchange, 2000.

Awards, Honors: Christopher Award, 1992, for *Rudy;* Academy Award (with Seth Winston), best short, live–action film, 1992, for *Session Man.*

CREDITS

Film Producer:
So I Married an Axe Murderer, TriStar, 1993.
Rudy, TriStar, 1993.
Only You (also known as *Him* and *Just in Time*), TriStar, 1994.
My Teacher's Wife, Savoy Pictures/Trimark Pictures, 1995.
(As Robert Fried) *The Boondock Saints* (also known as *Mission des dieux*), Indican Pictures, 2000.
(As Rob Fried) *The Man* (also known as *Cool & Fool— Mein partner mit der grossen Schnauze*), New Line Cinema, 2005.
Weapons, After Dark Films, 2007.

Film Executive Producer:
Co–executive producer, *Godzilla,* TriStar, 1998.
Two Can Play That Game, C4 Pictures/Screen Gems, 2001.
(As Rob Fried) *Collateral,* DreamWorks, 2004.
(As Rob Fried) *Man of the Year,* Universal, 2006.

Television Executive Producer; Movies:
Black Cat Run, HBO, 1998.
(As Rob Fried) *Winchell,* HBO, 1998.
Swing Vote (also known as *The Ninth Justice*), ABC, 1999.

Television Executive Producer; Specials:
Conquering Space, Showtime, 1990.
The Letters from Moab, Showtime, 1991.
Sapphire Man, Showtime, 1991.
Once in a Blue Moon, Showtime, 1991.
Missing Parents, Showtime, 1991.
Hearts of Stone, Showtime, 1991.
(As Rob Fried) *Without a Pass,* Showtime, 1991.
The Washing Machine Man, Showtime, 1991.
Hogg's Heaven, Showtime, 1992.
Traveler's Rest, Showtime, 1993.
Contact, Showtime, 1993.

Television Producer; Specials:
Session Man, Showtime, 1991.
Under the Car, Showtime, 1993.

Television Work; Other:
(As Rob Fried) Executive producer, *Fifteenth Phase of the Moon,* 1992.

GARNER, James 1928–

PERSONAL

Original name, James Scott Baumgarner, born April 7, 1928, in Norman, OK; son of Weldon Baumgarner (a construction worker); married Lois Clarke, August 17, 1956; children: Kimberly, Gretta "Gigi" (an actress and author), Scott. *Education:* Attended University of Oklahoma; studied acting at Herbert Berghof Studios, New York. *Avocational Interests:* Playing golf and humanitarian causes.

Addresses: *Agent*—Paradigm, 360 North Crescent Dr., North Bldg., Beverly Hills, CA 90210; Cunningham, Escott, Slevin and Doherty Talent Agency, 10635 Santa Monica Blvd., Suite 140, Los Angeles, CA 90025. *Manager*—Bill Robinson Management, PO Box 6284, Malibu, CA 90264. *Publicist*—PMK/HBH Public Relations, 700 San Vicente Blvd., Suite G910, West Hollywood, CA 90069.

Career: Actor, producer, director, and song performer. Cherokee Productions, founder and president; appeared in television commercials for Polaroid, Xerox, Chevrolet Camaro, 10–10–9000 long distance service, Williams (Energy Solutions), Chevy Suburban, Financial Freedom reverse mortgage, and Chevy Tahoe. Previously worked as a salesman, oil field worker, carpet layer, swim trunks model, lifeguard, and truck driver. Pace car driver in the Indianapolis 500 in 1975, 1977, and 1985. Native American Rights Fund's National Support Committee member; United States High School Golf Association, member of national advisory board; Save the Children volunteer. *Military service:* Merchant Marines, U.S. Army; served during Korean conflict; received Purple Heart.

Awards, Honors: Golden Globe Award, most promising newcomer, 1958; Emmy Award nomination, outstanding lead actor in a drama series, 1976, Emmy Award, outstanding lead actor in a drama series, 1977, and Golden Globe Award nominations, best television actor—drama, 1978, 1979, 1980, all for *The Rockford Files;* Clio Award, 1978, for Polaroid commercials; Advertising Age Star Presenter of the Year, 1978; Golden Globe Award nomination, best performance by an actor in a television series—comedy or musical, 1982, for *Bret Maverick;* Emmy Award nomination, outstanding leading actor in a limited series or special, and Golden Globe Award nomination, best performance by an actor in a miniseries or motion picture made for television, both 1985, for *Heartsounds;* Academy Award nomination, best actor, and Golden Globe Award nomination, best performance by an actor in a motion picture—comedy or musical, both 1986, for *Murphy's Romance;* Oklahoma Hall of Fame, inductee, 1986; Emmy Award (with Peter K. Duchow), outstanding special, and Golden Globe Award nomination, best performance by an actor in a miniseries or motion picture made for television, both 1987, for "Promise," *Hallmark Hall of Fame;* Emmy Award nominations, outstanding supporting actor in a miniseries or special, and outstanding drama or comedy special (with Duchow), both 1989, for "My Name Is Bill W.," *Hallmark Hall of Fame;* National Cowboy and Western Heritage Museum, inductee, 1990; Academy of Television Arts and Sciences' Hall of Fame, inductee, 1991; Golden Globe Award, best performance by an actor in a miniseries or motion picture made for television, 1991, for "Decoration Day," *Hallmark Hall of Fame;* Golden Globe Award, best performance by an actor in a miniseries or motion picture made for television, 1994, for *Barbarians at the Gate;* Golden Globe Award nomination, best performance by an actor in a miniseries or motion picture made for television, 1995, for *Breathing Lessons;* Screen Actors Guild Award nomination, outstanding performance by a male actor in a television movie or miniseries, 1995, for *The Rockford Files: I Still Love L.A.;* Screen Actors Guild Award nomination, outstanding performance by a male actor in a television movie or miniseries, 1996, for *The Rockford Files: A Blessing in Disguise;* Screen Actors Guild Award nomination, outstanding performance by a male actor in a television movie or miniseries, 1999, for *Legalese;* Golden Boot Award, Motion Picture and Television Fund, 1999; Blockbuster Entertainment Award nomination (with others), favorite action team (Internet only), 2001, for *Space Cowboys;* Lifetime Achievement Award, Screen Actors Guild, 2005; Screen Actors Guild Award nomination, outstanding performance by a male actor in a supporting role, 2005, for *The Notebook;* Star on Hollywood Walk of Fame, 2005.

CREDITS

Film Appearances:

Tumblers, *Joan of Arc,* RKO Radio Pictures, 1948.

Preston, *The Girl He Left Behind,* Warner Bros., 1956.

Major Joe Craven, *Toward the Unknown* (also known as *Brink of Hell*), Warner Bros., 1956.

Captain Mike Baily, *Sayonara,* Warner Bros., 1957.

John Maitland, *Shoot–Out at Medicine Bend,* Warner Bros., 1957.

(Uncredited) Voice of anchor, search and rescue operation, *Bombers B–52* (also known as *No Sleep Till Dawn*), 1957.

Major William Darby, *Darby's Rangers* (also known as *William A. Wellman's "Darby's Rangers"* and *Young Invaders*), Warner Bros., 1958.

Bret Maverick, *Alias Jesse James,* United Artists, 1959.

Lieutenant Ken Braden, *Up Periscope,* Warner Bros., 1959.

Title role, *Cash McCall,* Warner Bros., 1960.

Dr. Joe Cardin, *The Children's Hour* (also known as *The Loudest Whisper*), United Artists, 1961.

Fred Williams, *Boys' Night Out,* Metro–Goldwyn–Mayer, 1962.

Flight Lieutenant Bob Anthony Hendley, "The Scrounger," *The Great Escape,* United Artists, 1963.

Nicholas Arden, *Move Over Darling,* Twentieth Century–Fox, 1963.

Dr. Gerald Boyer, *The Thrill of It All,* Universal, 1963.

Henry Tyroon, *The Wheeler Dealers* (also known as *Separate Beds*), Filmways, 1963.

Lieutenant Commander Charles Madison, *The Americanization of Emily* (also known as *Emily*), Metro–Goldwyn–Mayer, 1964.

Himself, *Action on the Beach,* 1964.

Casey Barnett, *The Art of Love,* Universal, 1965.

Major Jefferson Pike, *36 Hours,* Metro–Goldwyn–Mayer, 1965.

Jess Remsberg, *Duel at Diablo* (also known as *Ralph Nelson's "Duel at Diablo"*), United Artists, 1966.

William Beddoes, *A Man Could Get Killed* (also known as *Welcome, Mr. Beddoes*), Universal, 1966.

Pete Aron, *Grand Prix,* 1966.

(Uncredited) Himself, *"Grand Prix": Challenge of Champions,* 1966.

Title role, *Mr. Buddwing* (also known as *Woman Without a Face*), Metro–Goldwyn–Mayer, 1966.

Wyatt Earp, *Hour of the Gun,* United Artists, 1967.

Grif Henderson, *How Sweet It Is!,* New General Pictures, 1968.

Ben Morris, *The Pink Jungle,* Universal, 1968.

(Uncredited) Himself, *The Man Who Makes the Difference,* 1968.

Philip Marlowe, *Marlowe,* Metro–Goldwyn–Mayer, 1969.

Himself, *The Racing Scene,* 1969.

Jason McCullough, *Support Your Local Sheriff,* United Artists, 1969.

Luther Sledge, *A Man Called Sledge* (also known as *Sledge*), Columbia, 1971.

Quincy Drew, *The Skin Game,* Warner Bros., 1971.

Latigo Smith, *Support Your Local Gunfighter,* United Artists, 1971.

Police Chief Abel Marsh, *They Only Kill Their Masters,* Metro–Goldwyn–Mayer, 1972.

Corporal Clint Keys, *One Little Indian,* Buena Vista, 1973.

Lincoln Costain, *The Castaway Cowboy,* Buena Vista, 1974.

Harry Wolff, *Health* (also known as *H.E.A.L.T.H.*), Twentieth Century–Fox, 1980.

Jake Berman, *The Fan* (also known as *Trance*), Paramount, 1981.

King, *Victor/Victoria,* United Artists, 1982.

Commander Sergeant Major Zack Carey, *Tank,* Universal, 1984.

Murphy Jones, *Murphy's Romance,* Columbia, 1985.

Wyatt Earp, *Sunset* (also known as *Catalina*), TriStar, 1988.

Jeff Johnson, *The Distinguished Gentleman,* 1992.

Sheriff Frank Watters, *Fire in the Sky,* 1993.

Himself, *Return to "The Great Escape"* (documentary short), Metro–Goldwyn–Mayer Home Entertainment,1993.

Zane Cooper, *Maverick,* 1994.

Matt Douglas, *My Fellow Americans,* Warner Bros., 1996.

Himself, *Wild Bill: Hollywood Maverick* (documentary; also known as *Wild Bill, Hollywood Maverick: The Life and Times of William A. Wellman*), Turner Pictures, 1996.

Narrator, *The Hidden Dimension* (documentary), 1997.

Voice of homeowner, *4 Million Houseguests,* 1997.

Raymond Hope, *Twilight,* Paramount, 1998.

Tank Sullivan, *Space Cowboys,* Warner Bros., 2000.

Voice of Captain Rourke, *Atlantis: The Lost Empire* (animated), Buena Vista, 2001.

Shepard James "Shep" Walker, *Divine Secrets of the Ya-Ya Sisterhood,* Warner Bros., 2002.

Voice of Pat, *The Land Before Time X: The Great Longneck Migration* (animated), Universal, 2003.

Duke, *The Notebook,* New Line Cinema, 2004.

Title role, *Al Roach: Private Insectigator,* 2004.

Himself, *James Garner On–Camera Interview "Rockford Files" Season 1 DVD* (documentary short), Universal Studios, 2005.

Himself, *The Trail of Tears: Cherokee Legacy* (documentary), 2006.

Himself, *Pushing the Limit: The Making of "Grand Prix"* (documentary short), Warner Home video, 2006.

Red Stevens, *The Ultimate Gift,* FoxFaith, 2006.

Also appeared in *Hawaiian Cowboy.*

Film Work:

Executive producer, *Grand Prix,* 1966.

Television Appearances; Series:
Bret Maverick, *Maverick*, ABC, 1957–60.
Title role, *Nichols* (also known as *James Garner* and *James Garner as Nichols*), NBC, 1971–72.
Jim Rockford, *The Rockford Files* (also known as *Jim Rockford, Private Investigator*), NBC, 1974–80.
Title role, *Bret Maverick*, NBC, 1981–82.
Councilman Jim Doyle, *Man of the People*, 1991.
Hubert Miller, *Chicago Hope*, CBS, 2000.
Voice of God, *God, the Devil and Bob* (animated), NBC, 2000.
Chief Justice Thomas Brankin, *First Monday*, 2002.
Jim Egan, *8 Simple Rules ... for Dating My Teenage Daughter* (also known as *8 Simple Rules*), ABC, 2003–2005.

Television Appearances; Miniseries:
Norman Grant, *Space* (also known as *James A. Michener's "Space"*), CBS, 1987.
Captain Woodrow F. Call, *Streets of Laredo* (also known as *Larry McMurtry's "Streets of Laredo"*), CBS, 1995.
Host, *A Century of Country*, CBS, 1999.
Shake, Rattle and Roll: An American Love Story, 1999.

Television Appearances; Movies:
Jim Rockford, *The Rockford Files* (also known as *The Rockford Files: Backlash of the Hunter*), NBC, 1974.
Bret Maverick, *The New Maverick*, ABC, 1978.
Bret Maverick and Edmund Trueblood, federal bank examiner, *Bret Maverick* (also known as *Bret Maverick: The Lazy Ace*), 1981.
George Adams, *The Long Summer of George Adams*, NBC, 1982.
Dr. Harold Lear, *Heartsounds*, ABC, 1984.
Al Mackay, *The Glitter Dome*, HBO, 1984.
F. Ross Johnson, *Barbarians at the Gate*, HBO, 1993.
Ira Moran, *Breathing Lessons*, CBS, 1994.
Jim Rockford, *The Rockford Files: I Still Love L.A.*, CBS, 1994.
Jim Rockford, *The Rockford Files: A Blessing in Disguise*, CBS, 1995.
Jim Rockford, *The Rockford Files: If the Frame Fits ...*, CBS, 1996.
Jim Rockford, *The Rockford Files: Godfather Knows Best*, CBS, 1996.
Jim Rockford, *The Rockford Files: Friends and Foul Play*, CBS, 1996.
Jim Rockford, *The Rockford Files: Crime and Punishment*, CBS, 1996.
John Potter, *Dead Silence* (also known as *Silence de mort*), Fox, 1997.
Jim Rockford, *The Rockford Files: Murders and Misdemeanors*, CBS, 1997.
Norman Keane, *Legalese*, TNT, 1998.
Jim Rockford, *The Rockford Files: If It Bleeds ... It Leads*, CBS, 1999.
Robert Woodward, *One Special Night*, CBS, 1999.

Mike Howley, *The Last Debate*, Showtime, 2000.
Samuel Clemens/Mark Twain, *Roughing It* (also known as *Mark Twain's "Roughing It"*), Hallmark Channel, 2002.

Television Appearances; Specials:
The Bing Crosby Special, ABC, 1959.
The Bob Hope Show, NBC, 1960, 1961, 1963, 1965.
Presenter, *The 38th Annual Academy Awards*, ABC, 1966.
The Tonight Show Starring Johnny Carson, NBC, 1968, 1971, 1972, 1973, 1986, 1991.
Superstunt, NBC, 1977.
The American Film Institute Salute to Henry Fonda, CBS, 1978.
Superstunt, 1978.
James Garner, *Waylon*, 1980.
Host, *60 Years of Seduction*, ABC, 1981.
Bret Maverick, *Lily for President?*, CBS, 1982.
Bob Beuhler, "Promise," *Hallmark Hall of Fame*, 1986.
The 12th Annual People's Choice Awards, 1986.
The 58th Annual Academy Awards, ABC, 1986.
Presenter, *The 60th Annual Academy Awards Presentation*, 1988.
Dr Robert "Dr. Bob" Holbrook Smith, "My Name Is Bill W.," *Hallmark Hall of Fame*, ABC, 1989.
Albert Sidney Finch, "Decoration Day," *Hallmark Hall of Fame*, NBC, 1990.
Dinah Comes Home Again, 1990.
Host, *Take Me To Your Leaders*, 1990.
Michael Landon: Memories with Laughter and Love, 1991.
Voice of General Dwight Eisenhower, *The Year of the Generals*, 1992.
The Great Ones: The National Sports Awards, 1993.
Behind Closed Doors with Joan Lunden, ABC, 1994.
100 Years of the Hollywood Western, 1994.
Golf: The Greatest Game, 1994.
Julie Andrews: Back on Broadway, PBS, 1995.
Host, *Big Guns Talk: The Story of the Western*, TNT, 1997.
Presenter, *The 50th Emmy Awards*, 1998.
Doris Day: It's Magic, Arts and Entertainment, 1998.
Hollywood Salutes Jodie Foster: An American Cinematheque Tribute, TNT, 1999.
Clint Eastwood: Out of the Shadows, PBS, 2000.
The Making of "Space Cowboys," 2000.
The 2000 Blockbuster Entertainment Awards, Fox, 2000.
Private Screenings: James Garner, TCM, 2001.
Intimate Portrait: Suzannne Pleshette, Lifetime, 2002.
TV Land Moguls, TV Land, 2004.
The 11th Annual Screen Actor Guild Awards, TNT, 2005.

Television Appearances; Pilots:
Councilman Jim Doyle, *Man of the People*, 1991.

Television Appearances; Episodic:
Forsythe, "Mountain Fortress," *Cheyenne,* 1955.
"The Black Hawk War," *Cheyenne,* 1956.
Bret, "The Last Train West," *Cheyenne,* 1956.
Lieutenant Lee Rogers, "Decision," *Cheyenne,* 1956.
Lieutenant Jim Collins, "Stars over Texas," *Zane Grey Theater* (also known as *The Westerners* and *Dick Powell's "Zane Grey Theater"*), 1956.
Jim Curtis, "The People Against McQuade," *Conflict,* ABC, 1956.
Jim Curtis, "The Man from 1997," *Conflict,* ABC, 1956.
"Explosion," *Warner Brothers Presents,* 1956.
Peake, "War Party," *Cheyenne,* 1957.
Bret Maverick, "Misfire," *Sugarfoot* (also known as *Tenderfoot*), 1957.
"Girl on the Subway," *Conflict,* ABC, 1957.
"The Western," *Wide Wide World,* 1958.
"James Garner," *This Is Your Life,* 1958.
Himself, "Downbeat," *77 Sunset Strip,* 1959.
Beau "Pappy" Maverick, "Pappy," *Maverick,* ABC, 1959.
I've Got a Secret, 1962.
Here's Hollywood, 1962.
Mystery guest, *What's My Line?,* 1964.
Rowan & Martin's Laugh–In (also known as *Laugh–In*), 1968, 1969, 1970.
The Andy Williams Show, 1969.
Toast of the Town (also known as *The Ed Sullivan Show*), 1969.
The Carol Burnett Show (also known as *Carol Burnett and Friends*), 1978.
Bret Maverick, "Clancy," *Young Maverick,* CBS, 1979.
A Conversation with Dinah, 1989.
"Doris Day: It's Magic," *Biography,* Arts and Entertainment, 1998.
The Rosie O'Donnell Show, syndicated, 1998, 1999, 2002.
The Howard Stern Radio Show, 1999.
"James Garner: Hollywood Maverick," *Biography,* Arts and Entertainment, 2000.
"Jack Webb: Just the Facts Ma'am," *Biography,* Arts and Entertainment, 2000.
Hubert "Hue" Miller, "Devoted Attachment," *Chicago Hope,* CBS, 2000.
Hubert "Hue" Miller, "Miller Time," *Chicago Hope,* CBS, 2000.
Hubert "Hue" Miller, "Thoughts of You," *Chicago Hope,* CBS, 2000.
Hubert "Hue" Miller, "Everybody's Special at Chicago Hope," *Chicago Hope,* CBS, 2000.
Hubert "Hue" Miller, "Have I Got a Deal for You," *Chicago Hope,* CBS, 2000.
"Clint Eastwood: Out of the Shadows," *American Masters,* PBS, 2000.
"Rod Steiger," *Bravo Profiles,* Bravo, 2001.
"James Garner," *Private Screenings,* TCM, 2001.
The Tonight Show Starring Jay Leno, NBC, 2002, 2005.
Entertainment Tonight (also known as *E.T.*), syndicated, 2003.
TV Land Moguls, TV Land, 2003.
Larry King Live, CNN, 2004.

Late Night with Conan O'Brien, NBC, 2004.
Jimmy Kimmel Live, ABC, 2004.
"Jack Lemmon," *The Hollywood Greats* (also known as *Hollywood Greats*), BBC1, 2006.
"Marlon Brando," *The Hollywood Greats* (also known as *Hollywood Greats*), BBC1, 2006.

Also appeared in "James Garner," *Celebrity Golf* (also known as *The Golf Channel Presents "Celebrity Golf" with Sam Snead*).

Television Executive Producer; Movies:
The Rockford Files: I Still Love L.A., CBS, 1994.
The Rockford Files: A Blessing in Disguise, CBS, 1995.
The Rockford Files: If the Frame Fits …, CBS, 1996.
The Rockford Files: Godfather Knows Best, CBS, 1996.
The Rockford Files: Friends and Foul Play, CBS, 1996.
The Rockford Files: Crime and Punishment, CBS, 1996.
The Rockford Files: Murders and Misdemeanors, CBS, 1997.
The Rockford Files: If It Bleeds … It Leads, CBS, 1999.

Television Executive Producer; Specials:
(With Peter K. Duchow) "Promise," *Hallmark Hall of Fame,* 1986.
(With Duchow) "My Name Is Bill W.," *Hallmark Hall of Fame,* ABC, 1989.

Television Director; Episodic:
"The Girl in the Bay City Boys' Club," *The Rockford Files* (also known as *Jim Rockford, Private Investigator*), NBC, 1975.

Also directed episodes of *Maverick,* ABC.

Stage Appearances:
The Caine Mutiny Court–Martial, Plymouth Theatre, New York City, 1954.

RECORDINGS

Albums:
Recorded an album with Waylon Jennings in 1980.

Videos:
Himself, *Amy Grant: Building the House of Love* (documentary), A&M Video, 1994.

OTHER SOURCES

Books:
International Dictionary of Films and Filmmakers, Volume 3: *Actors and Actresses,* St. James Press, 1996.

Periodicals:
Entertainment Weekly, November 1, 1999, p. 139.
People Weekly, February 7, 2007, p. 95.

GILBERT, Melissa 1964–
(Melissa Gilbert Brinkman, Melissa Gilbert–Boxleitner, Melissa Gilbert–Brinkman)

PERSONAL

Full name, Melissa Ellen Gilbert; born May 8, 1964, in Los Angeles, CA; daughter of Paul Gilbert (a comedian) and Barbara Gilbert Cowan (a dancer, actress, talent manager, and producer; maiden name, Crane; some sources cite another surname of Yudko); stepdaughter of Warren Cowan (a publicist); granddaughter of Harry Crane (a writer and actor) and Julia Crane (a dancer); sister of Sara Gilbert (an actress, director, and writer); half sister of Jonathan Gilbert (an actor); married Bo Brinkman (an actor, producer, and writer), February 21, 1988 (divorced, 1992 [some sources cite 1994]); married Bruce Boxleitner (an actor), January 1, 1995; children: (first marriage) Dakota "Cody" Paul; (second marriage) Michael Garrett; stepsons: Sam, Lee Davis. *Education:* Attended the University of Southern California. *Politics:* Democrat.

Addresses: *Agent*—Jonathan Howard, Innovative Artists Talent and Literary Agency, 1505 10th St., Santa Monica, CA 90401.

Career: Actress, director, and producer. Appeared in advertisements, infomercials, and public service announcements, including the public service announcement series *The More You Know,* NBC. Also known as Melissa Gilbert–Boxleitner.

Member: Screen Actors Guild (member of board of directors, 2000; president, 2001–05), Directors Guild of America.

Awards, Honors: Emmy Award nomination, outstanding lead actress in a limited series or special, 1980, for *The Miracle Worker;* Young Artist Award nomination, best juvenile actress in a television series or special, Young Artist Foundation, 1980, Golden Globe Award nomination, best performance by an actress in a television series—drama, 1981, Young Artist awards, best young actress in a drama series, 1983 and 1984, and TV Land Award (with Dean Butler), most memorable kiss, 2006, all for *Little House on the Prairie;* Young Artist Award nomination, best young actress in a television special, 1982, for *Splendor in the Grass;* Outer

Critics Circle Award, best debut performance, and *Theatre World* Award, outstanding new performer, both 1988, for *A Shayna Maidel;* Gilbert and other members of the *Little House on the Prairie* cast were named to the Hall of the Great Western Performers, National Cowboy and Western Heritage Museum, 1998; Golden Boot Award (affiliated with the Motion Picture and Television Fund), 2000; named one the one hundred greatest teen stars, VH1, 2006; received a star on the Hollywood Walk of Fame.

CREDITS

Television Appearances; Series:
Laura Elizabeth Ingalls Wilder, *Little House on the Prairie* (also known as *Little House: A New Beginning*), NBC, 1974–83.
(As Melissa Gilbert–Brinkman) Rochelle Dunphy, *Stand by Your Man,* Fox, 1992.
Voice of Batgirl/Barbara Gordon, *Batman* (animated; also known as *The Adventures of Batman & Robin* and *Batman: The Animated Series*), Fox, between 1992 and 1994.
Kate Delacroy, *Sweet Justice,* NBC, 1994–95.
Host, *Adoption,* The Hallmark Channel, beginning 2002.

Television Appearances; Miniseries:
Zoya Ossipov (title role), *Zoya* (also known as *Danielle Steel's "Zoya"*), NBC, 1995.
Herself (teen star number thirty–one), *100 Greatest Teen Stars,* VH1, 2006.

Television Appearances; Movies:
Kelly Sullivan, *Christmas Miracle in Caufield, U.S.A.* (also known as *The Christmas Coal Mine Miracle*), NBC, 1977.
Helen Keller, *The Miracle Worker,* NBC, 1979.
Laura Elizabeth Ingalls Wilder, *Little House Years,* NBC, 1979.
Anne Frank, *The Diary of Anne Frank,* NBC, 1980.
Wilma Dean "Deanie" Loomis, *Splendor in the Grass,* NBC, 1981.
Jean Donovan, *Choices of the Heart* (also known as *In December the Roses Will Bloom Again*), NBC, 1983.
Laura Elizabeth Ingalls Wilder, *Little House: Look Back to Yesterday,* NBC, 1983.
Laura Elizabeth Ingalls Wilder, *Little House: Bless All the Dear Children,* NBC, 1984.
Laura Elizabeth Ingalls Wilder, *Little House: The Last Farewell,* NBC, 1984.
Sara Calloway, *Family Secrets,* NBC, 1984.
Leah Furman, *The Penalty Phase,* CBS, 1986.
Terry Granger, *Choices,* ABC, 1986.
Marian Winslow, *Blood Vows: The Story of a Mafia Wife* (also known as *The Godfather's Wife* and *The Story of a Mafia Wife*), NBC, 1987.

Dr. Lisa DeVito, *Killer Instinct* (also known as *Deadly Observation* and *Over the Edge*), NBC, 1988.

(As Melissa Gilbert–Brinkman) Claudia Cassara, *Joshua's Heart,* NBC, 1990.

(As Gilbert–Brinkman) Dr. Kristine Lipton, *Donor,* CBS, 1990.

Emily Briggs, *Without Her Consent* (also known as *A Matter of Trust*), NBC, 1990.

(As Gilbert–Brinkman) Gina Crandall and Jennifer Crandall, *The Lookalike,* USA Network, 1990.

Judith Shapiro, *Forbidden Nights* (also known as *China Love Story* and *China Nights*), CBS, 1990.

(As Melissa Gilbert Brinkman) Janet King (some sources cite Gena King) and Vanessa, *With a Vengeance* (also known as *Undesirable*), CBS, 1992.

Julie, *A Family of Strangers* (also known as *Nee de pere inconnu*), CBS, 1993.

Lynn Matthews, *Dying to Remember,* USA Network, 1993.

Marion Ravinel, *House of Secrets* (also known as *Conspiracy of Terror*), NBC, 1993.

Miranda Berkley, *With Hostile Intent* (also known as *Two Cops, Two Cops: The Long Beach Sexual Harassment Case,* and *With Hostile Intent: Sisters in Black and Blue*), CBS, 1993.

Shari Karney, *Shattered Trust: The Shari Karney Story* (also known as *Conspiracy of Silence: The Shari Karney Story* and *Shattered Trust*), NBC, 1993.

Karen Barth, *Cries from the Heart* (also known as *Touch of Truth*), CBS, 1994.

Mary Bennett, *The Babymaker: The Dr. Cecil Jacobson Story* (also known as *Seeds of Deception*), CBS, 1994.

Melissa Prentice, *Against Her Will: The Carrie Buck Story,* Lifetime, 1994.

Emma Murphy, *Christmas in My Hometown* (also known as *A Holiday for Love*), CBS, 1996.

Karen Carlson, *Childhood Sweetheart?,* CBS, 1997.

Sarah Jenks, *Seduction in a Small Town* (also known as *Harvest of Lies*), ABC, 1997.

Meredith Saunders, *Her Own Rules* (also known as *Barbara Taylor Bradford's "Her Own Rules"*), CBS, 1998.

Gwen Todson, *Murder at 75 Birch,* CBS, 1999.

Rebecca, *The Soul Collector,* CBS, 1999.

Sarah Barlow, *Switched at Birth* (also known as *Mistaken Identity* and *Two Babies: Switched at Birth*), CBS, 1999.

Donielle, *A Vision of Murder: The Story of Donielle,* CBS, 2000.

Jo Ellen Hathaway, *Sanctuary* (also known as *Nora Roberts' "Sanctuary"*), CBS, 2001.

Taylor Singer, *Hollywood Wives: The New Generation* (also known as *Jackie Collins' "Hollywood Wives: The New Generation"* and *Femmes a Hollywood*), CBS, 2003.

Cassie Brodbeck, *Heart of the Storm,* Lifetime, 2004.

Natalie Jones, *Thicker Than Water,* The Hallmark Channel, 2005.

Katelyn Weston, *Spring Thaw* (also known as *Sacrifices of the Heart*), The Hallmark Channel, 2007.

Television Appearances; Specials:

Cohost, *Circus Lions, Tigers and Melissas Too,* NBC, 1977.

Herself, "NBC Salutes the 25th Anniversary of the Wonderful World of Disney," *The Wonderful World of Disney* (also known as *Disneyland, Disneylandia, The Disney Sunday Movie, Disney's Wonderful World, The Magical World of Disney, Walt Disney, Walt Disney Presents,* and *Walt Disney's Wonderful World of Color*), NBC, 1978.

NBC team member, *Battle of the Network Stars IV* (also known as *Battle of the Network Stars*), ABC, 1978.

NBC team member, *Battle of the Network Stars VII* (also known as *Battle of the Network Stars*), ABC, 1979.

Celebrity Challenge of the Sexes 5 (also known as *Celebrity Challenge of the Sexes*), CBS, 1980.

NBC team member, *Battle of the Network Stars X* (also known as *Battle of the Network Stars*), ABC, 1981.

NBC team member, *Battle of the Network Stars XI* (also known as *Battle of the Network Stars*), ABC, 1982.

NBC team member, *Battle of the Network Stars XIII* (also known as *Battle of the Network Stars*), ABC, 1982.

Night of 100 Stars (also known as *Night of One Hundred Stars*), ABC, 1982.

The Dean Martin Celebrity Roast, NBC, 1984.

Herself, *NBC's 60th Anniversary Celebration* (also known as *NBC 60th Anniversary Celebration*), NBC, 1986.

Drug Free Kids: A Parents' Guide, PBS, 1988.

(As Melissa Gilbert–Brinkman) *Michael Landon: Memories with Laughter and Love* (also known as *Michael Landon: Memorias, risas y gran amor*), c. 1992.

People's 20th Birthday, ABC, 1994.

Barney's First Adventures, 1998.

Herself, *Michael Landon,* 1999.

Herself, *Child Stars: Their Story* (also known as *Child Stars*), Arts and Entertainment, 2000.

Segment host, *The '70s: The Decade That Changed Television,* ABC, 2000.

Herself, *NBC 75th Anniversary Special* (also known as *NBC 75th Anniversary Celebration*), NBC, 2002.

Television Appearances; Awards Presentations:

(As Melissa Gilbert–Brinkman) *The 43rd Annual Primetime Emmy Awards Presentation,* Fox, 1991.

Presenter, *The 21st Annual People's Choice Awards,* CBS, 1995.

Eighth Annual Screen Actors Guild Awards (also known as *Screen Actors Guild Eighth Annual Awards*), TNT, 2002.

Presenter, *Ninth Annual Screen Actors Guild Awards* (also known as *Screen Actors Guild Ninth Annual Awards*), TNT, 2003.

Presenter, *10th Annual Screen Actors Guild Awards* (also known as *Screen Actors Guild 10th Annual Awards*), TNT, 2004.

Presenter, *11th Annual Screen Actors Guild Awards* (also known as *Screen Actors Guild 11th Annual Awards*), TNT, 2005.

Television Appearances; Episodic:

Jenny, "Dinner Date," *Emergency!* (also known as *Emergency One* and *Emergencia*), NBC, 1972.

Jenny, "Helpful," *Emergency!* (also known as *Emergency One* and *Emergencia*), NBC, 1972.

Spratt's child, "The Judgment," *Gunsmoke* (also known as *Gun Law* and *Marshal Dillon*), CBS, 1972.

Tenafly, NBC, c. 1972.

Herself, *Dinah!* (also known as *Dinah* and *Dinah and Friends*), syndicated, 1975.

Herself, "Oral Smoke Alarm," *America 2Night*, syndicated, 1978.

Rocky (young teenage tomboy), "Julie's Dilemma/ Who's Who/Rocky," *The Love Boat*, ABC, 1978.

The Hanna–Barbera Happy Hour, NBC, 1978.

Gerda (title role), "The Snow Queen," *Faerie Tale Theater* (also known as *Shelley Duvall's "Faerie Tale Theater"*), Showtime, 1985.

"Matthew Henson," *An American Portrait*, CBS, 1986.

"Japanese Literature," *American Treasury*, CBS, 1989.

"New Sweden," *American Treasury*, CBS, 1989.

"Stereographics," *American Treasury*, CBS, 1989.

"Thanksgiving and FDR," *American Treasury*, CBS, 1989.

Live with Regis and Kathie Lee, syndicated, 1989.

"The Spirit Cabinet," *The Hidden Room*, Lifetime, 1991.

Herself, *The Howard Stern Interview* (also known as *The Howard Stern "Interview"*), 1993.

Herself, *Howard Stern*, 1994.

Herself, *Late Night with Conan O'Brien*, NBC, 1994.

Anna Sheridan, "Shadow Dancing," *Babylon 5* (also known as *B5*, *Babylon 5.*, and *Spacecenter Babylon 5*), syndicated, 1996.

Anna Sheridan, "Z'ha'dum," *Babylon 5* (also known as *B5*, *Babylon 5.*, and *Spacecenter Babylon 5*), syndicated, 1996.

(Uncredited) Voice of Anna Sheridan, "War without End: Part 2," *Babylon 5* (also known as *B5*, *Babylon 5.*, and *Spacecenter Babylon 5*), syndicated, 1996.

Herself, "Michael Landon," *The E! True Hollywood Story* (also known as *Michael Landon: The E! True Hollywood Story* and *THS*), E! Entertainment Television, 1997.

Guest host, *The Vicki Lawrence Show* (also known as *Fox after Breakfast*), Fox, 1997 (multiple episodes).

Michelle Tanner, "The Peacemaker," *Touched by an Angel*, CBS, 1998.

Theresa Janovitch, "Relativity Theory," *The Outer Limits* (also known as *The New Outer Limits*), Showtime, Sci-Fi Channel, and syndicated, 1998.

Herself, *Intimate Portrait: Melissa Gilbert*, Lifetime, 1998.

Herself, *The Daily Show* (also known as *The Daily Show with Jon Stewart*, *The Daily Show with Jon Stewart Global Edition*, *Ha–Daily Show*, and *I satira tou Jon Stewart*), Comedy Central, 1999.

Herself, *The Howard Stern Radio Show*, 1999.

Herself, "Melissa Gilbert," *Celebrity Profile* (also known as *E! Celebrity Profile*, *Celebrity Profile: Melissa Gilbert*, and *E! Celebrity Profile: Melissa Gilbert*), E! Entertainment Television, c. 1999.

Herself, *Hollywood Squares* (also known as *H2* and *H2: Hollywood Squares*), syndicated, 2000.

Herself, "Melissa Gilbert," *Biography* (also known as *A&E Biography: Melissa Gilbert*), Arts and Entertainment, 2001.

Herself, *Intimate Portrait: Melissa Sue Anderson*, Lifetime, 2001.

Herself, *Intimate Portrait: Patty Duke*, Lifetime, 2001.

Herself, *MAD TV* (also known as *Mad TV* and *MADtv*), Fox, 2001.

Herself, *Who Wants to Be a Millionaire*, ABC, 2001.

Grace Bennett, "Once upon a Family," *Presidio Med*, CBS, 2002.

Lorna Berlin, "Smoke and Mirrors," *Providence*, NBC, 2002.

Herself, *The Oprah Winfrey Show* (also known as *Oprah*), syndicated, 2002.

Herself, *Intimate Portrait: Young Hollywood*, Lifetime, c. 2002.

Herself, *The View*, ABC, 2003.

Herself, "Melissa Gilbert," *Biography for Kids*, Biography Channel, 2004.

Marie Wagner, "Honor Thy Mother," *7th Heaven* (also known as *Seventh Heaven* and *7th Heaven: Beginnings*), The WB, 2005.

Herself, "Charlies Angels or Too Pooped to Pop," *Fat Actress*, Showtime, 2005.

Herself, "1974: Melissa Gilbert," *Class of ...*, Biography Channel, 2005.

Herself, *Sunday Morning Shootout*, American Movie Classics, 2005.

Guest, *Good Day Live*, syndicated, 2005, 2006.

Title role, "Shari Noble," *Nip/Tuck*, FX Network, 2006.

(In archive footage) Laura Elizabeth Ingalls Wilder, *Como estan ustedes?*, Television Espanola (TVE, Spain), 2006.

(In archive footage) Laura Elizabeth Ingalls Wilder, *Corazon, corazon*, Television Espanola (TVE, Spain), 2006.

(In archive footage) Laura Elizabeth Ingalls Wilder, *La imagen de tu vida*, 2006.

(In archive footage) Laura Elizabeth Ingalls Wilder, *Today* (also known as *NBC News Today* and *The Today Show*), NBC, 2007.

Herself, *Le syndicate des acteurs a Hollywood*, 2007.

Appeared in other programs.

Television Appearances; Pilots:

Laura Elizabeth Ingalls, *Little House on the Prairie*, NBC, 1974.

Like Magic, CBS, 1981.
Chameleons, 1989.
Kate Delacroy, *Sweet Justice,* NBC, 1994.
Jennifer Bastian, *Finally Home,* The WB, c. 2000.
Host, "Adoption," *Adoption,* The Hallmark Channel, 2002.
Devon Jones–Thomas, *Then Came Jones,* ABC, 2003.

Appeared as the host of *Reunion,* CBS.

Television Work; Specials:
Director, "Me and My Hormones," *ABC Afterschool Specials,* ABC, 1997.
Director and executive producer, *Child Stars: Their Story* (also known as *Child Stars*), Arts and Entertainment, 2000.

Film Appearances:
Voice of Clara, *Nutcracker Fantasy* (animated), Sanrio Communications, 1979.
Herself, *Hollywood's Children* (documentary), Janson Media, 1982.
Charlie, *Sylvester,* Columbia, 1985.
Actress in "Who Gave You the Ten Cents?," *Funny,* Original Cinema, 1989.
Kay, *Ice House,* Upfront Films, 1989.
(Uncredited) Herself, *Lisa Picard Is Famous* (also known as *Famous*), First Look Pictures Releasing, 2001.
Ophelia, *Safe Harbour* (also known as *Danielle Steel's "Safe Harbour"*), New Line Cinema, 2007.

Stage Appearances:
Night of 100 Stars (also known as *Night of One Hundred Stars*), Theatre at Radio City Music Hall, New York City, 1982.
Laura Wingfield, *The Glass Menagerie,* Chautauqua, NY, 1985.
Rose Weiss, *A Shayna Maidel,* Westside Theatre (Downstairs), New York City, 1987–89.

Radio Appearances; Episodic:
Herself, *Howard Stern,* 1994.
Herself, *The Howard Stern Radio Show,* 1999.

RECORDINGS

Videos:
Herself, *A Little House Conversation,* 2006.

Music Videos:
Ray Parker, Jr., "Ghostbusters," 1984.

OTHER SOURCES

Periodicals:
Entertainment Weekly, October 17, 2003, p. 88.
McCall's, August, 1993, p. 114.

People Weekly, March 17, 2003, p. 113.
TV Guide, April 7, 1990, p. 17.

Electronic:
The Official Melissa & Bruce Site, http://www. gilbertboxleitner.com, October 8, 2007.

GILBERT–BRINKMAN, Melissa
   See GILBERT, Melissa

GINTER, Lindsey
   (L. L. Ginter, Lindsay Ginter, Lindsay Lee Ginter, Lindsey Lee Ginter)

PERSONAL

Some sources cite original name as Lindsay Lee Ginter. *Education:* California State University, Los Angeles, graduated.

Career: Actor. Circle West Group, Los Angeles, member of company; Circle Repertory Company, New York City, member of company. California State University, Los Angeles, theatre arts instructor. Also known as Lindsay Ginter.

Member: Actors' Equity Association.

CREDITS

Television Appearances; Miniseries:
Major Hugo Rotterdam, *Trade Winds,* ABC, 1993.
Frankel, *The Invaders,* The WB, 1995.

Television Appearances; Movies:
John Rayborn, *Rita Hayworth: The Love Goddess,* CBS, 1983.
George Renan, *Getting Up and Going Home* (also known as *Unfaithful*), Lifetime, 1992.
Woody Jackson, *In the Line of Duty: Siege at Marion* (also known as *Children of Fury*), NBC, 1992.
Detective Bayer, *Darkness before Dawn,* NBC, 1993.
Officer Weldon, *Eye of the Stalker* (also known as *Eye of the Stalker: A Moment of Truth Movie*), NBC, 1995.
Ike Ringo, *Mars,* 1996.
Hydra, *Acts of Betrayal,* HBO, 1997.
Klinge, *Mercenary,* HBO and Cinemax, 1997.
Alan Houston, *The Outsider* (also known as *Gangster World*), 1998.

Television Appearances; Episodic:

Ed, "In the Dog House," *Knots Landing,* CBS, 1991.

Garbage collector, "The Lost Hour," *Eerie, Indiana,* NBC, 1991.

Rolf, "Where or When: Parts 1 & 2," *Jake and the Fatman,* CBS, 1991.

Thomas Hardin, "Legacy: Parts 1 & 2," *Street Justice,* syndicated, 1991.

(As Lindsay Lee Ginter) Jonathan Bruner, "Try to Be Nice—What Does It Get You?," *Reasonable Doubts,* NBC, 1992.

Mickey Morgan, "92 Seconds to Midnight," *The Hat Squad,* CBS, 1992.

Thomas Hardin, "Back from the Dead Again," *Street Justice,* syndicated, 1992.

Mr. Collasurdo, "Cold Shower," *L.A. Law,* NBC, 1993.

Chuck Woodley, "Murderer's Row: Parts 1 & 2," *Renegade,* USA Network and syndicated, 1994.

The cleaner, "The Erlenmeyer Flask," *The X–Files,* Fox, 1994.

The cleaner, "Red Museum," *The X–Files,* Fox, 1994.

Jack Sharpe, "The Quest," *Hawkeye,* syndicated, 1994.

Troy Cochran, "Rampage," *Walker, Texas Ranger* (also known as *Walker),* CBS, 1994.

Commander, "Lucky Leon," *Lois & Clark: The New Adventures of Superman* (also known as *Lois & Clark* and *The New Adventures of Superman),* ABC, 1995.

Detective Tom Banning, "St. Valentine's Day Massacre," *Melrose Place,* Fox, 1995.

Marine sergeant, "The Camp Counselor: Part 2," *Deadly Games,* UPN, 1995.

(As Lindsay Lee Ginter) "Baby Makes Three," *Renegade,* USA Network and syndicated, 1996.

(As Lindsey Lee Ginter) Captain Horace McNamara, "Cowboys & Cossacks," *JAG,* CBS, 1997.

Cassus, "A Rock and a Hard Place," *Hercules: The Legendary Journeys* (also known as *Hercules),* syndicated, 1997.

(As Lindsey Lee Ginter) Gary Wilder, "Is Paris Burning?," *NYPD Blue,* ABC, 1997.

(As Lindsey Lee Ginter) Sergeant Linson, "Bloodlines," *Dark Skies* (also known as *Cielo negro, Dark Skies—l'impossible verite, Dark Skies—Oscure presenze,* and *Dark Skies—Toedliche Bedrohung),* NBC, 1997.

(As L. L. Ginter) Dirk Morgan, "Code of the West," *Walker, Texas Ranger* (also known as *Walker),* CBS, 1998.

Frank Kozell, "Soldiers of Misfortune," *Pensacola: Wings of Gold,* syndicated, 1998.

(As L. L. Ginter) John Schramm, "Body Count," *The Practice,* ABC, 1998.

(As L. L. Ginter) John Schramm, "The Defenders," *The Practice,* ABC, 1998.

"Episode 13," *Beyond Belief: Fact or Fiction* (also known as *Beyond Belief* and *Strange Truth: Fact or Fiction),* Fox, 1998.

(As L. L. Ginter) "Exposing Johnson," *Brooklyn South* (also known as *A esquadra de Brooklyn* and *Brooklyn Sud),* CBS, 1998.

(As L. L. Ginter) Dr. Willard Spence, "PTB," *The Pretender,* NBC, 1999.

(As L. L. Ginter) Ivan, "American Gulag," *Air America,* syndicated, 1999.

(As L. L. Ginter) Roy Atkins, "Infidelity," *Profiler,* NBC, 1999.

(As L. L. Ginter) Alan Gorman, "Outside Chance," *18 Wheels of Justice* (also known as *Highway to Hell—18 Rader aus Stahl, La loi du fugitif,* and *Oikeutta tien paeaell),* The National Network, 2000.

(As L. L. Ginter) Saavedra, "Memorial," *Star Trek: Voyager* (also known as *Voyager),* UPN, 2000.

(As L. L. Ginter) "How They Lived," *The District* (also known as *Washington Police, The District—Einsatz in Washington, Mannions distrikt,* and *Poliisipaeaellikkkoe Mannion),* CBS, 2000.

Man, "Children Are the Most Important Thing," *Any Day Now,* Lifetime, 2001.

Boo, "Tears, Bones & Desire," *Six Feet Under,* HBO, 2003.

Mr. Jones, "A Free Agent," *Alias,* ABC, 2003.

Captain Renquist, "Reese Joins the Army: Part 2," *Malcolm in the Middle* (also known as *Fighting in Underpants),* Fox, 2004.

Commander Petrie, "Why We Fight," *Angel* (also known as *Angel: The Series, Angel—Jaeger der Finsternis,* and *Skoteinos angelos),* The WB, 2004.

Detective Mark Johnston, "Slade's Chophouse," *Judging Amy,* CBS, 2004.

Chris Daniels, "Gum Drops," *CSI: Crime Scene Investigation* (also known as *C.S.I., CSI: Las Vegas, CSI Weekends,* and *Les experts),* CBS, 2005.

Sergeant Sam Austen, "What Kate Did," *Lost,* ABC, 2005.

Sheriff Paddon, "The Bogie Man," *Without a Trace* (also known as *Vanished* and *W.A.T.),* CBS, 2005.

"Dying Inside," *Strong Medicine,* Lifetime, 2005.

Sergeant Sam Austen, "One of Them," *Lost,* ABC, 2006.

Television Appearances; Pilots:

Some sources cite an appearance in the pilot for *Silk Stalkings,* CBS and USA Network.

Film Appearances:

Officer Young, *Bound by Honor* (also known as *Blood In ... Blood Out* and *Blood In, Blood Out ... Bound by Honor),* Buena Vista, 1993.

Holloway, *Beverly Hills Cop III,* Paramount, 1994.

Commando leader, *Timemaster* (also known as *Time Master),* 1995.

(As Lindsey Lee Ginter) Mission commander, *Gattaca* (also known as *The Eighth Day),* Sony Pictures Entertainment, 1997.

(As L. L. Ginter) Peter Burrell, *Mercury Rising* (also known as *Code Mercury, Mercury Falling, Simon, Simon Says,* and *Simple Simon*), Universal, 1998.

(As L. L. Ginter) Submarine captain Low, *Pearl Harbor* (also known as *Pearl Harbour*), Buena Vista, 2001.

Agent Hauser, *S.W.A.T.,* Columbia, 2003.

Jury foreperson, *The L.A. Riot Spectacular* (also known as *The L.A. Riot Show*), Visionbox Pictures, 2006.

FBI agent, *Radio Free Albemuth,* Discovery Productions/Open Pictures/Rhino Films, 2008.

Stage Appearances:

Bellievre, *Mary Stuart,* Circle Repertory Company, New York City, 1979–80.

Kenneth Talley, Jr. and understudy for roles of Weston Hurley and John Landis, *Fifth of July,* New Apollo Theatre, New York City, c. 1980–82.

Emmet Young, *A Tale Told* (later known as *Talley & Son*), Circle Repertory Company, 1981.

Augie Belfast, *The Man Who Had All the Luck,* Antaeus Company, North Hollywood, CA, 2000.

Five Mojo Secrets White Bird, Los Angeles, 2001.

Faust, The Artists' Collective and California State University, Los Angeles, 2007.

Also appeared in other productions, including *Exploding Mother,* Blank Theatre Company, Hollywood, CA; and in *Hamlet,* Circle Repertory Company, New York City.

GLICKMAN, Jonathan 1969–

PERSONAL

Born May 18, 1969, in Wichita, KS; son of Daniel Robert "Dan" (chief executive officer of the Motion Picture Association of America) and Rhoda (maiden name, Yura) Glickman. *Education:* Attended the University of Southern California School of Cinematic Arts.

Addresses: *Office*—Spyglass Entertainment Holdings, 10900 Wilshire Blvd., 10th Floor, Los Angeles, CA 90024.

Career: Producer and studio executive. Caravan Pictures, began as intern, 1993, became president, 1997; Spyglass Entertainment Holdings, Los Angeles, president, 2002—.

Member: Academy of Motion Picture Arts and Sciences.

CREDITS

Film Executive Producer:

Celtic Pride (also known as *Dunk Brothers*), Buena Vista, 1996.

Grosse Pointe Blank (also known as *Ein Mann, ein Mord, Grosse Pointe Blank—aeven en loennmoerdare behoever en traeff ibland, Grosse Pointe Blank: Ein Mann—Ein Mord, Grosse Pointe Blank—Erst der Mord, dann das Vergnuegen, Grosse pointe blank—palkkamurhaaja pikkukaupungissa, Le tueur de grosse pointe, L'ultimo contratto, O ultimo contrato, Placanec, Tiro al blanco, Tueurs a gages, Tueurs a gages et robes de balles, Un asesino algo especial,* and *Zabijanie na sniadanie*), Buena Vista, 1997.

RocketMan (also known as *Rocket Man*), Buena Vista, 1997.

Holy Man (also known as *Mister G.*), Buena Vista, 1998.

Inspector Gadget (also known as *Gadget, Go! Go! Gadget, The Real Inspector Gadget, Etsivae Gadget, Inspecteur Gadget, Inspektor Gadget,* and *Inspetor Bugiganga*), Buena Vista, 1999.

Keeping the Faith, Buena Vista, 2000.

Out Cold (also known as *Cool Border, Snowbiz!, Snow, Sex and Sun, Ten to One,* and *10 to 1*), Buena Vista, 2001.

Reign of Fire (also known as *Salamander*), Buena Vista, 2002.

The Recruit (also known as *The Farm*), Buena Vista, 2003.

Mr. 3000, Buena Vista, 2004.

Stay Alive (also known as *Death Game*), Buena Vista, 2006.

Stick It, Buena Vista, 2006.

The Lookout (also known as *Vigilante*), Miramax, 2007.

Flash of Genius, Universal, 2008.

Film Producer:

Rush Hour, New Line Cinema, 1998.

Shanghai Noon (also known as *Shanghai Kid* and *Shaolin Cowboy*), Buena Vista, 2000.

Rush Hour 2, New Line Cinema, 2001.

The Count of Monte Cristo (also known as *Alexandre Dumas' "The Count of Monte Cristo," Montecristo,* and *Monte Cristo*), Buena Vista, 2002.

Shanghai Knights (also known as *Shanghai kid II* and *Shanghai Noon 2*), Buena Vista, 2003.

Connie and Carla (also known as *Connie & Carla* and *Connie and Carla Do L.A.*), Universal, 2004.

The Perfect Score (also known as *Voll gepunktet*), Paramount, 2004.

The Hitchhiker's Guide to the Galaxy, Buena Vista, 2005.

The Pacifier (also known as *Captain Wolfe, Gnome,* and *Le pacificateur*), Buena Vista, 2005.

Balls of Fury, Rogue Pictures, 2007.

The Invisible (also known as *Invisible*), Hollywood Pictures, 2007.

Rush Hour 3, New Line Cinema, 2007.

Underdog, Buena Vista, 2007.

Four Christmases, New Line Cinema, 2008.

27 Dresses, Fox 2000 Pictures, 2008.

Film Associate Producer:

The Jerky Boys, Buena Vista, 1995.
While You Were Sleeping, Buena Vista, 1995.
Before and After, Buena Vista, 1996.

Film Studio Executive:

Out Cold (also known as *Cool Border, Snowbiz!, Snow, Sex and Sun, Ten to One,* and *10 to 1*), Buena Vista, 2001.
(Uncredited) *The Recruit* (also known as *The Farm*), Buena Vista, 2003.

Studio executive for other film projects.

Television Work:

Executive producer for the pilot *The Wedding Planner,* CBS.

GOLDBERG, Daniel
   (Dan Goldberg)

PERSONAL

Addresses: *Office*—Todd Phillips Company, 4000 Warner Blvd., Bldg. 66, Burbank, CA 91522.

Career: Producer and writer. McMaster Film Board, McMaster University, Hamilton, Ontario, Canada, vice president, then president; Northern Lights Entertainment, partner; Todd Phillips Company, Burbank, CA, producer.

Awards, Honors: Genie Awards, Golden Reel Award (with Ivan Reitman) and best screenplay—original (with others), Academy of Canadian Cinema and Television, Genie Award nomination (with others), best motion picture, 1980, all for *Meatballs;* Emmy Award nomination (with others), outstanding made for television movie, 1996, for *The Late Shift;* Golden Satellite Award nomination (with others), best motion picture—animated or mixed media, International Press Academy, 1997, for *Space Jam.*

CREDITS

Film Producer:

The Columbus of Sex (also known as *My Secret Life*), Howard Mahler Films, 1969.
Cannibal Girls (also known as *Des filles cannibales*), American International Pictures, 1973.

(As Dan Goldberg) *Meatballs* (also known as *Arrete de ramer, t'es sur le sable* and *Summer Camp*), Paramount, 1979.
(As Dan Goldberg) *Stripes,* Columbia, 1981.
Space Jam, Warner Bros., 1996.
Commandments, Gramercy Pictures, 1997.
Road Trip, DreamWorks, 2000.
Evolution, DreamWorks, 2001.
Old School, DreamWorks, 2003.
EuropTrip, DreamWorks, 2004.
School for Scoundrels, Weinstein Company, 2006.

Film Executive Producer:

Junior, Universal, 1994.
Private Parts (also known as *Howard Stern's "Private Parts"*), Paramount, 1997.
Fathers' Day, Warner Bros., 1997.
Mummies Alive! The Legend Begins (animated), Buena Vista Home Video, 1998.
Six Days Seven Nights (also known as *6 Days 7 Nights*), Buena Vista, 1998.
Killing Me Softly, Metro–Goldwyn–Mayer, 2002.

Film Work; Other:

Editor, *Cannibal Girls* (also known as *Des filles cannibales*), American International Pictures, 1973.
Sound designer, *Death Weekend* (also known as *Fin de semaine infernale* and *The House by the Lake*), American International Pictures, 1976.
Director, *No Nukes* (documentary; also known as *The Muse Concert: No Nukes*), Warner Bros., 1980.
Post–production supervisor, *Heavy Metal,* Columbia, 1981.
(As Dan Goldberg) Director, *Feds,* Warner Bros., 1988.
Second unit director, *Junior,* Universal, 1994.

Film Appearances:

Orientation (short), Twentieth Century–Fox, 1968.
Himself, *Imagining "Heavy Metal"* (documentary short), Columbia TriStar Home Video, 1999.
(As Dan Goldberg) Himself, *"Old School" Orientation* (short), DreamWorks Home Entertainment, 2003.
Himself, *Stars and Stripes 1* (documentary short), Columbia TriStar Home Video, 2004.
Himself, *Stars and Stripes 2* (documentary short), Columbia TriStar Home Video, 2004.

Television Work; Series:

Executive producer, *Extreme Ghostbusters,* 1997.
Executive producer, *Mummies Alive!,* UPN, 2001.
Executive producer, *Alienators: Evolution Continues,* Fox, 2001.

Television Work; Movies:

Co–executive producer, *The Late Shift,* HBO, 1996.

Television Work; Pilots:
Executive producer, *The First Gentleman,* CBS, 1994.

Television Appearances; Specials:
Living in America, VH1, 1991.
Hollywood, D.C.: A Tale of Two Cities, Bravo, 2000.

Television Appearances; Episodic:
(As Dan Goldberg) *Howard Stern,* E! Entertainment Television, 1997.

WRITINGS

Screenplays:
(As Dan Goldberg) *Meatballs* (also known as *Arrete de ramer, t'es sur le sable* and *Summer Camp*), Paramount, 1979.
(As Dan Goldberg) *Stripes,* Columbia, 1981.
Heavy Metal, Columbia, 1981.
Spacehunter: Adventures in the Forbidden Zone (also know as *Adventures in the Creep Zone* and *Road Gangs*), Columbia Pictures Industries, 1983.
(As Dan Goldberg) *Feds,* Warner Bros., 1988.

Film Stories:
Cannibal Girls (also known as *Des filles cannibales*), American International Pictures, 1973.

GONZALEZ, Clifton Gonzalez
    See COLLINS, Clifton, Jr.

GOODING, Cuba, Jr. 1968–

PERSONAL

Full name, Cuba M. Gooding, Jr.; born January 2, 1968, in the Bronx, New York, NY; son of Cuba, Sr. (a singer) and Shirley (a singer) Gooding; brother of Omar Gooding (an actor); married Sara Kapfer (a teacher), March 13, 1994; children: Spencer, Mason, Piper. *Education:* Studied martial arts. *Religion:* Christian.

Addresses: *Agent*—Creative Artists Agency, 2000 Avenue of the Stars, Los Angeles, CA 90067. *Manager*—Michael Rotenberg, 3 Arts Entertainment, 9460 Wilshire Blvd., Seventh Floor, Beverly Hills, CA 90212.

Career: Actor. Goodbro Picture Entertainment, co-founder; Feel Good Films, partner. Worked as a backup dancer. As a member of the Majestic Vision Breakdanc-

ers, dancer at the closing ceremonies of the Olympic Games, Los Angeles, 1984. Appeared in advertisements. Held various jobs.

Member: Screen Actors Guild.

Awards, Honors: Winner and second place finisher in various competitions affiliated with the Drama Teachers' Association of Southern California; Young Artist Award nomination, best young actor guest starring in a television series, Young Artist Foundation, 1990, for *MacGyver;* named one of the promising new actors of 1991, *John Willis' Screen World,* 1991; Special Award, newcomer of the year, ShoWest Convention, National Association of Theatre Owners, 1992; Image Award nomination, outstanding supporting actor in a motion picture, National Association for the Advancement of Colored People (NAACP), 1996, for *Outbreak;* Image Award nomination, outstanding actor in a television movie, miniseries, or drama special, 1996, for *The Tuskegee Airmen;* Academy Award, best actor in a supporting role, Screen Actors Guild Award, outstanding performance by a male actor in a supporting role, Broadcast Film Critics Association Award and Chicago Film Critics Award, both best supporting actor, Golden Satellite Award, best performance by an actor in a supporting role in a motion picture—comedy or musical, International Press Academy, American Comedy Award, funniest supporting actor in a motion picture, Blockbuster Entertainment Award, favorite supporting actor—comedy/romance, Golden Globe Award nomination, best performance by an actor in a supporting role in a motion picture, and Image Award nomination, outstanding lead actor in a motion picture, all 1997, for *Jerry Maguire;* Special Award, supporting actor of the year, ShoWest Convention, 1997; Golden Satellite Award nomination, best performance by an actor in a supporting role in a motion picture—comedy or musical, 1998, for *As Good as It Gets;* Blockbuster Entertainment Award, favorite supporting actor—drama/romance, and Image Award nomination, outstanding supporting actor in a motion picture, both 1999, for *What Dreams May Come;* Image Award nomination, outstanding actor in a motion picture, and Black Reel Award nomination, best theatrical actor, both 2001, for *Men of Honor;* received a star on the Hollywood Walk of Fame, 2002; Image Award, outstanding actor in a motion picture, 2004, and Camie award (with others), Character and Morality in Entertainment awards, 2005, both for *Radio;* Black Movie Award nomination, outstanding performance by an actor in a leading role, 2006, for *Shadowboxer;* Screen Actors Guild Award nomination (with others), outstanding performance by a cast in a motion picture, 2008, for *American Gangster.*

CREDITS

Film Appearances:
Boy getting haircut, *Coming to America* (also known as *Prince in New York*), Paramount, 1988.

Stanley (Stan), *Sing* (musical), TriStar, 1989.

Tre Styles, *Boyz n the Hood* (also known as *Boys in the Hood, A malta do bairro, Boyz n the Hood—Jungs im Viertel, Boyz n the Hood—kulman kundit, Boyz n the Hood—strade violente, Fekete videk, La loi de la rue, Los chicos del barrio, Os donos da rua,* and *Ta paidia tis geitonias*), Columbia, 1991.

Abraham Lincoln Haynes, *Gladiator,* Columbia, 1992.

Corporal Carl Edward Hammaker, *A Few Good Men,* Columbia, 1992.

Officer Alvarez, *Hitz* (also known as *Judgment*), Vidmark Entertainment, 1992.

Mike Peterson, *Judgment Night,* Universal, 1993.

Ben Doyle, *Lightning Jack* (also known as *Jack colpo di fulmine, Jack, o relampago, Relampago Jack,* and *Salama–Jack*), Savoy Pictures, 1994.

(Uncredited) Tony, *Blown Away,* Metro–Goldwyn–Mayer, 1994.

Eddie Hughes, *Losing Isaiah,* Paramount, 1995.

Major Salt, *Outbreak* (also known as *A virus, Alerte!, Epidemia, Esclat, Estallido, Fora de controlo, Hitpar'tzoot, I farozonen, Izbruh, Outbreak—I farozonen, Outbreak—Lautlose Killer, Tehdit, Tuntematon uhka,* and *Virus letale*), Warner Bros., 1995.

Rod Tidwell, *Jerry Maguire* (also known as *The Agent*), TriStar, 1996.

Frank Sachs, *As Good as It Gets* (also known as *Old Friends*), Sony Pictures Entertainment, 1997.

Liquor store clerk, *Do Me a Favor* (also known as *Dead End* and *Trading Favors*), Imperial Entertainment, 1997.

Albert Lewis, *What Dreams May Come,* PolyGram Filmed Entertainment, 1998.

Himself, *Welcome to Hollywood,* Phaedra Cinema/PM Entertainment Group, 1998.

Arlo, *Chill Factor,* Warner Bros., 1999.

Theo Calder, *Instinct* (also known as *Ishmael*), Buena Vista, 1999.

Chief Carl Brashear, *Men of Honor* (also known as *The Diver, Men of Honour, Navy Diver, Barbati de onoare, Ferfibecsuelet, Hombres de honor, Homens de honra, Kunnian puolesta, Les chemins de la dignite, L'honneur a tout prix, Maend af aere,* and *Men of Honor—L'onore degli uomini*), Twentieth Century–Fox, 2000.

Himself, *Zoolander* (also known as *Derek Zoolander*), Paramount, 2001.

Draven, *In the Shadows,* Lions Gate Films, 2001.

Owen Templeton, *Rat Race* (also known as *No Brain Race, Course folle, Der Nackte Wahnsinn, El mundo esta loco loco, Esta tudo louco!, Rat Race—Der nackte Wahnsinn, Rat Race—Sk(r)attjakten, Ratas a la carrera, Rottaralli, Sk(r)attjakten, Ta todo mundo louco! Uma corrida por milhoe$,* and *Ueldoezesi mania*), Paramount, 2001.

Petty officer Doris "Dorie" Miller, *Pearl Harbor* (also known as *Pearl Harbour*), Buena Vista, 2001.

Dr. Ted Brooks, *Snow Dogs* (also known as *Winterdance, Aventuras en Alaska, Chiens des neiges, Det store slaedelob, Frio de perros, Heranca canina,* *Kutyababajnok, Lumihauvat, Neve pra cachorro, Snow Dogs—Acht Helden auf vier Pfoten,* and *Snowdogs—Acht Helden auf vier Pfoten*), Buena Vista, 2002.

Jerry Robinson, *Boat Trip,* Motion Picture Corporation of America, 2002.

Darrin Hill, *The Fighting Temptations* (also known as *Lucha de tentaciones, Resistindo as tentacoes,* and *Taivaallinen viettelys*), Paramount, 2003.

James Robert "Radio" Kennedy, *Radio,* Columbia, 2003.

Voice of Buck, *A Dairy Tale* (animated short film), Walt Disney Home Video, 2004.

Voice of Buck, *Home on the Range* (animated; also known as *Sweating Bullets*), Buena Vista, 2004.

Officer Salim Adel, *Dirty,* Silver Nitrate Releasing, 2005.

Alex Thomas, *End Game,* Metro–Goldwyn–Mayer, 2006.

Mikey, *Shadowboxer* (also known as *The Contract*), Freestyle Releasing, 2006.

Lightfield's Home Videos, Big Screen Entertainment Group, 2006.

Charlie Hinton, *Daddy Day Camp,* TriStar, 2007.

Himself, *Hollywood on Fire* (documentary), Saylor Brothers Entertainment/Outlast Innertainment, 2007.

Deion Hughes, *Norbit,* DreamWorks, 2007.

Liam Case, *Hero Wanted,* Nu Image Films, 2007.

Nicky Barnes, *American Gangster* (also known as *The Return of Superfly* and *Tru Blu*), Universal, 2007.

Tom, *What Love Is,* Big Sky Motion Pictures, 2007.

Voice of Loofah, *The Land before Time XIII: The Wisdom of Friends* (animated), Universal, 2007.

Michael Dixon, *Linewatch,* Sony Pictures Entertainment, 2008.

School janitor, *Harold,* City Lights Pictures, 2008.

The Way of War, Story Teller Pictures, 2008.

Appeared in other film projects.

Film Work:

Producer, *Harold,* City Lights Pictures, 2008.

Television Appearances; Series:

Himself, *The Entertainment Business* (documentary; also known as *Bravo Profiles: The Entertainment Business*), BBC and Bravo, 1998.

Television Appearances; Miniseries:

Himself, *I Love the '80s,* VH1, 2002.

Television Appearances; Movies:

Kill or Be Killed, NBC, 1990.

Tyree, *Murder with Motive: The Edmund Perry Story* (also known as *Best Intentions*), NBC, 1992.

Torch, *Daybreak* (also known as *Bloodstream*), HBO, 1993.

Billy "A–Train" Roberts, *The Tuskegee Airmen*, HBO, 1995.

Russell Lawson (some sources cite role as Lawson Russell), *A Murder of Crows* (also known as *Confession, Murder of Crows, A Murder of Crows— Diabolische Versuchung, Analisi di un delitto, L'empreinte des corbeaux, Murhat kovissa kansissa, Nido de cuervos,* and *Relatos de um crime*), Cinemax, 1999.

Television Appearances; Specials:

Paul, "No Means No," *CBS Schoolbreak Special*, CBS, 1988.

Cool People, Hot Places, ABC and syndicated, 1993.

Himself, *America: A Tribute to Heroes*, multiple networks, 2001.

Himself, *Christmas in Tinseltown*, BBC, 2001.

Himself, *Journey to the Screen: The Making of "Pearl Harbor"* (also known as *Pearl Harbor: A Journey to the Screen*), Black Entertainment Television, 2001.

Narrator, *Above and Beyond: The U.S. Air Force Experience*, PAX TV, 2001.

Himself, *Muhammad Ali's All–Star 60th Birthday Celebration!*, CBS, 2002.

Host, *Rockin' for the U.S.A.: A National Tribute to the U.S. Military*, CBS, 2002.

Oscar Countdown 2003, ABC, 2003.

Himself, *A Capitol Fourth*, PBS, 2006.

(In archive footage) Himself, *Celebrity Debut*, ABC and Independent Television 2 (England), 2006.

Host, *When Parents Are Deployed*, PBS, 2006.

(Uncredited; in archive footage) Tre Styles, *Boffo! Tinseltown's Bombs and Blockbusters*, HBO and The Movie Network (Canada), 2006.

Himself, *Movies Rock*, CBS, 2007.

(Uncredited; in archive footage) Himself, *Saturday Night Live in the '90s: Pop Culture Nation*, NBC, 2007.

Presenter, *Fashion Rocks*, CBS, 2007.

Television Appearances; Awards Presentations:

The Fourth Annual Desi Awards, syndicated, 1992.

Blockbuster Entertainment Awards, UPN, 1997.

The ShoWest Awards, TNT, 1997.

The 69th Annual Academy Awards, ABC, 1997.

Presenter, *The 70th Annual Academy Awards*, ABC, 1998.

The 24th Annual People's Choice Awards, CBS, 1998.

Fifth Annual Screen Actors Guild Awards (also known as *Screen Actors Guild Fifth Annual Awards*), TNT, 1999.

Host, *VH1/Vogue Fashion Awards*, VH1, 2000.

The 32nd Annual NAACP Image Awards, Fox, 2001.

E! Entertainer of the Year 2003, E! Entertainment Television, 2003.

The 75th Annual Academy Awards, ABC, 2003.

Presenter, *The 46th Annual Grammy Awards*, CBS, 2004.

Presenter, *The 30th Annual People's Choice Awards*, CBS, 2004.

35th NAACP Image Awards, Fox, 2004.

(In archive footage) *Ceremonia de clausura*, Television Espanola (TVE, Spain), 2005.

Premio Donostia a Willem Dafoe, 2005.

Host, *37th NAACP Image Awards*, Fox, 2006.

Presenter, *The 2006 Black Movie Awards—A Celebration of Black Cinema: Past, Present & Future* (also known as *The 2006 Black Movie Awards*), TNT, 2006.

Presenter, *The 12th Annual Critics Choice Awards*, E! Entertainment Television, 2007.

Presenter, *The 2007 Film Independent Spirit Awards* (also known as *Film Independent's 2007 Spirit Awards*), Independent Film Channel, 2007.

Television Appearances; Episodic:

Ethan Dillon, "Suitcase," *Hill Street Blues*, NBC, 1986.

Contestant, *The New Dating Game* (also known as *The Dating Game*), syndicated, c. 1986.

Bobby Devlin, "It's Hard to Be a Saint in the City," *The Bronx Zoo*, NBC, 1987.

Second gang member, "Days of Swine and Roses," *Hill Street Blues*, NBC, 1987.

Kenny, "Thelma's Handyman," *Amen*, NBC, 1988.

Billy Colton, "Black Rhino," *MacGyver*, ABC, 1989.

Ray Collins, "The Challenge," *MacGyver*, ABC, 1989.

Skater, "The Real Decoys," *227*, NBC, 1989.

Billy Colton, "Serenity," *MacGyver*, ABC, 1990.

"Night of the Living Shred," *Mancuso F.B.I.*, NBC, 1990.

Billy Colton, "The Coltons," *MacGyver*, ABC, 1991.

Himself, "Coralie, Jr.," *The E! True Hollywood Story* (also known as *Coralie, Jr.: The E! True Hollywood Story* and *Hollywood Outsider: Coralie, Jr.: The E! True Hollywood Story*), E! Entertainment Television, 1999.

Guest host, *Saturday Night Live* (also known as *NBC's "Saturday Night," Saturday Night, Saturday Night Live '80, SNL,* and *SNL 25*), NBC, 1999.

Himself, "The Making of 'Men of Honor,'" *HBO First Look*, HBO, 2000.

Himself, "Filmen 'Pearl Harbor,'" *Nyhetsmorgon*, TV4 Sweden, 2001.

Himself, "Pearl Harbor," *Beyond the Movie* (also known as *National Geographic Beyond the Movie: Pearl Harbor* and *Beyond the Movie: Pearl Harbor*), National Geographic Channel, 2001.

Himself, "Pearl Harbor," *History vs. Hollywood* (also known as *History through the Lens* and *History vs. Hollywood: Pearl Harbor*), History Channel, 2001.

Himself, "Steal vs Slashers & Bouncers vs Rumble," *Slamball*, The National Network, 2002.

(In archive footage) Himself, *Celebrities Uncensored*, E! Entertainment Television, 2003.

Himself, *MAD TV* (also known as *Mad TV* and *MADtv*), Fox, 2003.

(Uncredited) Himself, "Season Finale," *The Contender*, NBC, 2005.

Himself, "American Gangster," *HBO First Look,* HBO, 2007.

Himself, "Norbit," *HBO First Look,* HBO, 2007.

Appeared as Tommy Taylor in *The Untouchables,* syndicated; also appeared in other programs, including *Jake and the Fatman,* CBS.

Television Guest Appearances; Episodic:

The Dennis Miller Show, syndicated, 1992.

The Arsenio Hall Show (also known as *Arsenio*), syndicated, 1993.

The Rosie O'Donnell Show, syndicated, 1996.

Mundo VIP, SIC Televisao (Portugal), 1999.

The Tonight Show with Jay Leno, NBC, multiple appearances, beginning 2001.

This Hour Has 22 Minutes, CBC, 2002.

The Daily Show (also known as *The Daily Show with Jon Stewart, The Daily Show with Jon Stewart Global Edition, Ha–Daily Show,* and *I satira tou Jon Stewart*), Comedy Central, 2003.

Extra (also known as *Extra: The Entertainment Magazine*), syndicated, 2003 (multiple episodes).

Richard & Judy, Channel 4 (England), 2003.

Tinseltown TV (also known as *Tinseltown.TV*), International Channel, 2003.

V Graham Norton, Channel 4, 2003.

Sunday Morning Shootout, American Movie Classics, 2003, multiple episodes in 2004, 2006.

Entertainment Tonight (also known as *Entertainment This Week, E.T., ET Weekend,* and *This Week in Entertainment*), syndicated, 2003, multiple episodes in 2007.

Oprah (also known as *The Oprah Winfrey Show*), syndicated, 2004.

Magacine, [Spain], 2005.

Corazon de ..., Television Espanola (TVE, Spain), 2006 (multiple episodes).

ESPN Hollywood, ESPN, 2006.

Howard Stern on Demand (also known as *Howard TV* and *Howard TV on Demand*), iN DEMAND, 2006 (multiple episodes).

In the Mix (also known as *In the Cutz*), Urban America, 2006.

The Late Late Show with Craig Ferguson (also known as *The Late Late Show*), CBS, 2006, 2007.

Caiga quien caiga, Telecino (Spain), 2007.

Late Night with Conan O'Brien, NBC, 2007 (multiple episodes).

Live with Regis & Kelly, syndicated, 2007.

Television Work; Movies:

Producer, *A Murder of Crows* (also known as *Confession, Murder of Crows, A Murder of Crows— Diabolische Versuchung, Analisi di un delitto, L'empreinte des corbeaux, Murhat kovissa kansissa, Nido de cuervos,* and *Relatos de um crime*), Cinemax, 1999.

Stage Appearances:

Title role, *Othello,* California Shakespeare Festival, 1986.

Radio Appearances; Episodic:

Himself, *The Howard Stern Show,* Howard 100 (Sirius Satellite Radio), 2006 (multiple episodes).

RECORDINGS

Videos:

Host, *Get a Grip* (driver's education video), 1992.

(In archive footage) Himself, *Lord Stanley's Cup: Hockey's Ultimate Prize,* 2000.

Himself, *Making "Rat Race"* (short), Paramount, 2001.

Himself, *Friendly Fire: Making an Urban Legend* (short; also known as *Boyz n the Hood: Friendly Fire— Making an Urban Legend*), Columbia/TriStar Home Entertainment, 2003.

Himself, *Gettin' Dirty* (short), Sony Pictures Entertainment, 2006.

Audiobooks:

Inspired by ... The Bible Experience: New Testament, Zondervan, 2006.

Inspired by ... The Bible Experience: The Complete Bible, Zondervan, 2007.

Inspired by ... The Bible Experience: The Easter Story (also known as *The Easter Story: The Bible Experience*), Zondervan, 2007.

Inspired by ... The Bible Experience: Old Testament, Zondervan, 2007.

OTHER SOURCES

Books:

Contemporary Black Biography, Volume 16, Gale, 1997.

Newsmakers 1997, issue 4, Gale, 1997.

Periodicals:

American Visions, October/November, 1993, p. 40.

Ebony, June, 1997, p. 44.

Entertainment Weekly, February 21, 1997, p. 92; October 31, 2003, pp. 14–15; February 31, 2006, p. 84.

Jet, April 14, 1997, p. 58.

Los Angeles Times, January 5, 1997.

People Weekly, May 12, 1997, p. 76.

Premiere, January, 1997, p. 37.

Rolling Stone, April 3, 1997.

Sun–Times (Chicago), May 31, 1999.

Total Film, April, 1997, p. 42.

Washington Post, May 30, 1999.

GUMBA, Vinnie
   See PROCTOR, Phil

H

PERSONAL

Full name, Taylor Edwin Hackford; born December 31, 1944 (some sources cite December 3 or 1945), in Santa Barbara, CA; son of Joseph and Mary (a waitress; maiden name, Taylor) Hackford; married Georgie Lowres (divorced); married Lynne Littman (a producer and director), May 7, 1977 (divorced); married Helen Mirren (an actress, producer, and director), December 31, 1997; children: (first marriage) Rio D; (second marriage) Alexander Littman. *Education:* University of Southern California, B.A., 1968.

Addresses: *Agent*—Scott Greenberg, Creative Artists Agency, 2000 Avenue of the Stars, Los Angeles, CA 90067.

Career: Director and producer. KCET–TV (PBS affiliate), Los Angeles, began as mailroom clerk, became director, producer, investigative reporter, and writer, 1970–77; Hackford–Littman Films, Los Angeles, director, producer, and writer, 1977–79; New Visions, Inc., founder, mid–1970s; New Visions Pictures, partner and chair, 1988–91; Venice International Film Festival, jury member, 2000 and 2001; U.S. Peace Corps, volunteer in Bolivia, 1968–69.

Member: Directors Guild of America (vice president), Writers Guild of America, West.

Awards, Honors: Silver Reel Award, San Francisco International Film Festival, 1972; local Emmy awards, investigative reporting category, 1974 and 1977; Academy Award, best live–action short film, 1979, for *Teenage Father;* ShoWest Award, director of the year, National Association of Theatre Owners, 1983; Directors Guild of America Award nomination, outstanding directorial achievement in motion pictures, 1983, for *An Officer and a Gentleman;* Tokyo International Film Festival Award, best director, 1993, for *Bound by Honor;* Film Society Award for Lifetime Achievement in Directing, San Francisco International Film Festival, 2005; Academy Award nomination, Golden Satellite Award nomination, International Press Academy, and Critics Choice Award nomination, Broadcast Film Critics Association, all best director, Directors Guild of America Award nomination, outstanding directorial achievement in motion pictures, Academy Award nomination (with others), best motion picture of the year, and David di Donatello Award nomination, best foreign film, all 2005, and Grammy Award (with others), best compilation soundtrack album for motion picture, television, or other visual media, National Academy of Recording Arts and Sciences, 2006, all for *Ray;* Best of Show Award, Music DVD awards, *Home Media* magazine, 2007, for *Hail! Hail! Rock 'n' Roll;* Robert B. Aldrich Achievement Award (with Paris Barclay), Directors Guild of America, 2007.

CREDITS

Film Director:
Teenage Father (short film), New Visions, 1978.
The Idolmaker (also known as *Rock machine*), United Artists, 1980.
An Officer and a Gentleman, Paramount, 1982.
Against All Odds, Columbia, 1984.
White Nights (also known as *Biale noce, Die Nacht der Entscheidung, Hvide naetter, Il sole a mezzanote, Noches del sol, O sol da meia–noite, O sol da meia noite, Sol de medianoche, Valkeat yoet, Vita naetter,* and *White Nights—Nacht der Entscheidung*), Columbia, 1985.
Hail! Hail! Rock 'n' Roll (music documentary; also known as *Chuck Berry Hail! Hail! Rock 'n' Roll* and *Chuck Berry: Hail! Hail! Rock 'n' Roll*), Universal, 1987.

Everybody's All American (also known as *When I Fall in Love*), Warner Bros., 1988.
Bound by Honor (also known as *Blood In ... Blood Out* and *Blood In, Blood Out ... Bound by Honor*), Buena Vista, 1993.
Dolores Claiborne (also known as *Dolores, Eclipse Total, Eclipse total, Eclipse total (Dolores Claiborne), Stephen Kings Dolores,* and *Stephen Kings Dolores Claiborne*), Columbia, 1995.
The Devil's Advocate (also known as *Devil's Advocate* and *Im Auftrag des Teufels*), Warner Bros., 1997.
Proof of Life, Warner Bros., 2000.
Ray (also known as *Unchain My Heart: The Ray Charles Story*), Universal, 2004.

Film Executive Producer:

Rooftops (also known as *Combat Dance*), New Visions, 1989.
The Long Walk Home, Miramax, 1990.
Defenseless, New Visions/Seven Arts Pictures, 1991.
Mortal Thoughts, Columbia, 1991.
Queens Logic, Seven Arts Pictures, 1991.
Sweet Talker (also known as *Confidence*), New Visions, 1991.
The Devil's Advocate (also known as *Devil's Advocate* and *Im Auftrag des Teufels*), Warner Bros., 1997.

Film Producer:

Bukowski (documentary; also known as *Bukowski: A Film by Taylor Hackford and Richard Davies*), 1973.
Teenage Father (short film), New Visions, 1978.
Against All Odds, Columbia, 1984.
White Nights (also known as *Biale noce, Die Nacht der Entscheidung, Hvide naetter, Il sole a mezzanote, Noches del sol, O sol da meia–noite, O sol da meia noite, Sol de medianoche, Valkeat yoet, Vita naetter,* and *White Nights—Nacht der Entscheidung*), Columbia, 1985.
La Bamba (also known as *Let's Go*), Columbia, 1987.
Everybody's All American (also known as *When I Fall in Love*), Warner Bros., 1988.
Bound by Honor (also known as *Blood In ... Blood Out* and *Blood In, Blood Out ... Bound by Honor*), Buena Vista, 1993.
Dolores Claiborne (also known as *Dolores, Eclipse Total, Eclipse total, Eclipse total (Dolores Claiborne), Stephen Kings Dolores,* and *Stephen Kings Dolores Claiborne*), Columbia, 1995.
When We Were Kings (documentary), Gramercy Pictures, 1996.
G:MT Greenwich Mean Time (also known as *G:mt*), Icon Film Distribution, 1999.
Proof of Life, Warner Bros., 2000.
Ray (also known as *Unchain My Heart: The Ray Charles Story*), Universal, 2004.

Film Work; Other:

Film editor, *When We Were Kings* (documentary), Gramercy Pictures, 1996.

Film Appearances:

The director, *To Grandma with Love* (short film), Total Sol Films, 2003.
Himself, *Bukowski: Born into This* (documentary), Magnolia Pictures, 2004.
Vince Vaughn's "Wild West Comedy Show: 30 Days & 30 Nights—Hollywood to the Heartland" (documentary; also known as *Wild West Comedy Show: 30 Days & 30 Nights—Hollywood to the Heartland*), 2006, Picturehouse Entertainment, 2008.

Television Producer; Specials:

Bonnie Raitt and Paul Butterfield, PBS, 1974.
Rick Nelson: It's All Right Now, The Nashville Network, 1990.
Executive producer, *Genius: A Night for Ray Charles,* CBS, 2004.

Also worked on programs about various other musicians, including John Prine, Sonny Rollins, Leon Russell, and Cat Stevens.

Television Work; Pilots:

Executive producer and director, *E–Ring* (also known as *Pentagon, D.O.S.—Division des operations speciales,* and *E–Ring—Aporrites apostoles*), NBC, 2005.

Television Work; Other:

Director, *Economic Love–In,* KCET–TV (PBS affiliate), 1973.

Television Appearances; Specials:

Himself, *The Score,* Trio, 2003.
Himself, *Bleep! Censoring Hollywood,* American Movie Classics, 2005.
Himself, *Budd Boetticher: A Man Can Do That,* TCM, 2005.

Television Appearances; Awards Presentations:

(In archive footage) *The 77th Annual Academy Awards,* ABC, 2005.
36th NAACP Image Awards, Fox, 2005.
The 59th Primetime Emmy Awards, Fox, 2007.
The 64th Annual Golden Globe Awards, NBC, 2007.

Television Appearances; Episodic:

Himself, *First Works* (also known as *Firstworks*), 1989.
Himself, *"The Making of 'Proof of Life,'"* *HBO First Look,* HBO, 2000.
Himself, *"Richard Gere," Biography* (also known as *A&E Biography: Richard Gere*), Arts and Entertainment, 2004.
Himself, *Sunday Morning Shootout,* American Movie Classics, 2004.

RECORDINGS

Videos:
Director, "Say You, Say Me," *The Lionel Richie Collection*, Universal Music & Video Distribution, 2003.

Himself, *Pas de Deux: Making "White Nights"* (short), Columbia/TriStar Home Video, 2004.

Himself, *Budd Boetticher: An American Original*, Paramount Home Video, 2005.

Himself, *An Officer and a Gentleman: 25 Years Later* (short), Paramount Home Entertainment, 2007.

Music Video Director:
Phil Collins, "Against All Odds," 1984.

Lionel Richie, "Say You, Say Me," 1985.

WRITINGS

Screenplays:
Bukowski (documentary; also known as *Bukowski: A Film by Taylor Hackford and Richard Davies*), 1973.

Teenage Father (short film), New Visions, 1978.

Song "Show Me Your Tattoo," *The Devil's Advocate* (also known as *Devil's Advocate* and *Im Auftrag des Teufels*), Warner Bros., 1997.

(Story) *Ray* (also known as *Unchain My Heart: The Ray Charles Story*), Universal, 2004.

Author of other screenplays, including *Cry Dance.*

OTHER SOURCES

Periodicals:
Entertainment Weekly, February 4, 2005, p. 92.

Movieline, November, 2000, pp. 70–74.

People Weekly, November 3, 1997, p. 153; January 19, 1998, p. 102.

Variety, February 14, 2005, p. S34.

Washington Post, October 29, 2004, p. C4.

HALL, Craig

PERSONAL

Addresses: *Manager*—Sanders Armstrong Caserta Management, 2120 Colorado Blvd., Suite 120, Santa Monica, CA 90404.

Career: Actor.

CREDITS

Film Appearances:
Soldier, *Siren* (short), 1996.

Dean Savage, *Savage Honeymoon,* 2000.

Antarctic Angel, *The World's Fastest Indian,* Magnolia Pictures, 2005.

Mike, *King Kong* (also known as *Kong: The Eighth Wonder of the World* and *Peter Jackson's "King Kong"*), Universal, 2005.

Dominic, *Perfect Creature,* Twentieth Century–Fox, 2006.

Shane, *Knife Shift* (short), 2006.

Jonathan, *Embers* (short), 2006.

Doug Davis, *Eagle vs. Shark,* Miramax, 2007.

Chris Hamilton, *The Ferryman,* First Look International, 2007.

Wilson Buloson, *30 Days of Night,* Sony, 2007.

Charlie MacMorrow, *The Water Horse: Legend of the Deep,* Columbia, 2007.

Television Appearances; Series:
Leo Kenny, *Shortland Street,* TVNZ, 1992.

Clint, *The Strip,* 2002.

Television Appearances; Movies:
Darren, *The Chosen,* 1998.

Melvin, *The Vector File,* 2002.

Alex, *Raising Waylon,* CBS, 2004.

Corporal William Hayes, *Ike: Countdown to D–Day,* Arts and Entertainment, 2004.

Television Appearances; Episodic:
Timuron, "Highway to Hades," *Hercules: The Legendary Journeys,* syndicated, 1995.

Jason Bridges, "Death in Paradise," *Duggan,* Television One, 1997.

Guard, "Mind Games," *Cleopatra 2525,* syndicated, 2000.

Justin Lynch, "Heroin Chic," *Street Legal,* TV2, 2000.

Raczar, "Dangerous Prey," *Xena: Warrior Princess* (also known as *Xena*), syndicated, 2001.

Private Tatts, "The Lost Tribe," *Mataku,* 2002.

Joseph of Arimathea, "The Good Samaritan," *Revelations,* Sci–Fi Channel, 2003.

Ryan, "The Day That the Rain Came Down," *Mercy Peak,* TVNZ, 2003.

Jason Sumner, "As If Nothing Had Happened," *Interrogation,* 2005.

HALLIDAY, Kene
　　See HOLLIDAY, Kene

HARGETT, Hester
(Hester Hargett–Aupetit)

PERSONAL

Born in Los Angeles, CA. *Education:* University of Southern California, B.F.A., masters, film producing.

Career: Producer and unit production manager. De Laurentiis Entertainment Group, employee; Raffaella Productions, executive vice president and coproducer.

CREDITS

Film Work:
Production assistant, *Dune,* Universal, 1984.
Executive assistant to producers, *Tai–Pan,* De Laurentiis Company, 1986.
Associate producer, *Prancer,* Orion, 1989.
Associate producer, *Timebomb,* Metro–Goldwyn–Mayer, 1991.
Associate producer and second assistant director, *Dragon: The Bruce Lee Story,* Universal, 1993.
Line producer, *Trading Mom* (also known as *The Mommy Market*), 1994.
Coproducer and second assistant director, *Dragonheart,* Universal, 1996.
Coproducer, *Daylight,* Universal, 1996.
Coproducer, *Kull the Conqueror,* MCA/Universal, 1997.
Coproducer and unit production manager, *Black Dog,* MCA/Universal, 1998.
Executive producer, *Dragonheart: A New Beginning,* Universal Home Entertainment, 2000.
Coproducer and unit production manager, *Kingdom Come,* Fox Searchlight, 2001.
(As Hester Hargett–Aupetit) Coproducer, *Sky Captain and the World of Tomorrow,* Paramount, 2004.
Line producer, *The Last Legion* (also known as *La derniere legion*), Weinstein Company, 2007.
Line producer and unit production manager, *The Forbidden Kingdom,* Weinstein Company, 2008.

Film Appearances:
FBI technician, *Black Dog,* MCA/Universal, 1998.

Television Work; Miniseries:
Coproducer and unit production manager, *Uprising,* NBC, 1992.

Television Work; Movies:
Associate producer, *Vanishing Son,* syndicated, 1994.
Associate producer, *Vanishing Son II,* syndicated, 1994.
Associate producer, *Vanishing Son III,* syndicated, 1994.
Delegate producer, *Vanishing Son IV,* syndicated, 1994.
Unit production manager, *Uprising,* 2001.

HAYWARD, David
(David T. Hayward)

PERSONAL

Career: Actor.

CREDITS

Film Appearances:
Time to Run, WorldWide Pictures, 1973.
Kenny Fraiser, *Nashville,* Paramount, 1975.
The cowboy, *Eaten Alive* (also known as *Death Trap, Horror Hotel, Horror Hotel Massacre, Legend of the Bayou, Murder on the Bayou,* and *Starlight Slaughter*), Virgo International Pictures, 1977.
Carl Lewis, *The Hazing* (also known as *Here Come the Delts, The Campus Corpse,* and *The Curious Case of the Campus Corpse*), Vestron Video, 1977.
Leon Barnes "Chooch," *Van Nuys Blvd.,* Crown International Pictures, 1979.
Cannonball McCall, *Fast Charlie ... the Moonbeam Rider* (also known as *Fast Charlie and the Moonbeam*), Universal, 1979.
Jeffrey Fraser, *Delusion* (also known as *The House Where Death Lives*), New American Films, 1980.
Collins, *The Legend of the Lone Ranger,* Universal, 1981.
Laufman, *Slayground,* Universal, 1983.
George, *The Big Picture,* Columbia, 1989.
Cal, *Eve of Destruction,* Orion, 1991.
Ohio, *Thousand Pieces of Gold,* Greycat Films, 1991.
Pete, *View from the Top,* Miramax, 2003.

Television Appearances; Series:
David, *Knots Landing,* CBS, 1988–89.
Kevin Weaver, *Beverly Hills, 90210,* Fox, 1994–95.

Also appeared in *All My Children,* ABC.

Television Appearances; Miniseries:
Timothy Oates, *The Chisholms,* CBS, 1979.

Television Appearances; Movies:
Brady, *Little Ladies of the Night* (also known as *Diamond Alley*), ABC, 1977.
Larry Cadwell, *Red Alert,* CBS, 1977.

Bob Garver, *Who'll Save Our Children?,* CBS, 1978.

Red Brody, *11th Victim* (also known as *The Lakeside Killer*), CBS, 1979.

Dennis, *Fallen Angel,* CBS, 1981.

Gary Snyder, *Love on the Run,* NBC, 1985.

Bill Harlow, *Northstar,* ABC, 1986.

Jack, *Body of Evidence,* CBS, 1988.

Coach Hudson, *For the Very First Time* (also known as *Til I Kissed Ya*), NBC, 1991.

Darren Gaines, *A Case of Murder,* USA Network, 1993.

Jonathan Holtman, *Accidental Meeting,* USA Network, 1994.

Television Appearances; Pilots:

Burt Stahl, *Flying High,* CBS, 1978.

Temple Boone, *The Cherokee Trail* (also known as *Louis L'Amour's "The Cherokee Trail"*), CBS, 1981.

Television Appearances; Pilots:

Marco, *The Georgia Peaches* (movie; also known as *Follow That Car*), CBS, 1980.

Television Appearances; Episodic:

Georgie, "Log 103: A Sound Like Thunder," *Adam–12,* NBC, 1969.

Hurley, "The Weary Willies," *Bonanza* (also known as *Ponderosa*), NBC, 1970.

Messenger, "Today I am a Ma'am," *Mary Tyler Moore* (also known as *The Mary Tyler Moore Show*), CBS, 1970.

Delivery boy, "1040 or Fight," *Mary Tyler Moore* (also known as *The Mary Tyler Moore Show*), CBS, 1970.

Young Larry, "Serena's Youth Pill," *Bewitched,* ABC, 1972.

Chet Boyle, "Love and the Old–Fashioned Father," *Love, American Style,* ABC, 1972.

Voice of Chet Boyle, "The Victim," *Wait Till Your Father Gets Home* (animated), syndicated, 1972.

"The Case of the Violent Valley," *The New Perry Mason,* CBS, 1974.

"The Last Days," *Lincoln* (also known as *Sandburg's "Lincoln"*), 1974.

Scott, "A House of Prayer, a Den of Thieves," *Kojak,* CBS, 1975.

Turk Foley, "Luke's Love Story," *The Dukes of Hazzard,* CBS, 1979.

Richard, "Angels on Campus," *Charlie's Angels,* ABC, 1979.

Slim, *Soap,* ABC, 1980.

Andy Whitman, "Home Fires Burning," *CHiPs* (also known as *CHiPs Patrol*), NBC, 1981.

David Barnes, "Rhinestone Harts," *Hart to Hart,* ABC, 1981.

Roger Dillon, "Tempered Steele," *Remington Steele,* NBC, 1982.

Trainer, "The Close Call," *Dynasty,* ABC, 1985.

Mark, "Dreams for Sale," *The Twilight Zone* (also known as *The New Twilight Zone*), CBS, 1985.

Reporter, "A Saucer of Loneliness," *The Twilight Zone* (also known as *The New Twilight Zone*), CBS, 1986.

David McCall, "Florence Bravo," *Tales from the Darkside,* syndicated, 1986.

Brian Willis, "Peregrine," *Starman,* ABC, 1986.

Kenneth Myers, "Return of White Cloud," *Hunter,* NBC, 1989.

"The Return of Johnny Ryan," *Paradise* (also known as *Guns of Paradise*), 1989.

Lieutenant Judd Myerson, "Nowhere to Turn," *Matlock,* NBC, 1990.

Dempsey, "The Leap Home: Part 2 (Vietnam)—April 7, 1970," *Quantum Leap,* NBC, 1990.

Coach Redding, "Requiem for an Urkel," *Family Matters,* ABC, 1990.

Coach Redding, "Brain over Brawn," *Family Matters,* ABC, 1991.

Farmer, *Wings,* NBC, 1991.

Gilbert Webber, "Echoes in the Dark," *Bodies of Evidence,* CBS, 1992.

Lonnie Hill, *Diagnosis Murder,* CBS, 1995.

"Tribes," *ER,* NBC, 1997.

Jack Wilson, "Flight Risk," *JAG,* CBS, 2000.

"Chaos Theory," *ER,* NBC, 2002.

Television Work; Specials:

Production staff member, *Billboard's Rock 'n' Roll New Year's Eve,* Fox, 2000.

Production staff, *TV Land Awards: A Celebration of Classic TV,* TV Land, 2003.

Production manager, *The Nick at Nite Holiday Special,* 2003.

HOFFMAN, Gus 1991–

PERSONAL

Full name, Augustus Paul Hoffman; born August 26, 1991, in Colorado Springs, CO.

Career: Actor.

CREDITS

Film Appearances:

Goggles, *Rebound,* Twentieth Century–Fox, 2005.

Young Clyde, *Welcome Home Roscoe Jenkins,* Universal, 2008.

Television Appearances; Series:

Ty, *Just Jordan,* Nickelodeon, 2007.

Johnny Nightingale, *Lincoln Heights,* ABC Family, 2007.

Television Appearances; Movies:

Henry, *What's Stevie Thinking?,* 2007.

Television Appearances; Episodic:

Jorge, "You Say Toe–Mato," *Phil of the Future,* Disney Channel, 2004.

Heavyset kid, "Sk8erboyz," *George Lopez,* ABC, 2004.

Mason, "Jack & Jacqueline," *The Bernie Mac Show,* Fox, 2005.

Ninth grade boy, "Election," *Zoey 101,* Nickelodeon, 2005.

Sean, "Danger," *Sex, Love and Secrets,* UPN, 2005.

Sean, "Molting," *Sex, Love and Secrets,* UPN, 2005.

Sean, "Territorial Defense," *Sex, Love and Secrets,* UPN, 2005.

Caroler number one, "All About Christmas Eve," *ER,* NBC, 2005.

Warren, "Cody Goes to Camp," *The Suite Life of Zack and Cody* (also known as *TSL*), Disney Channel, 2006.

Warren, "Odd Couples," *The Suite Life of Zack and Cody* (also known as *TSL*), Disney Channel, 2006.

Warren, "Forever Plaid," *The Suite Life of Zack and Cody* (also known as *TSL*), Disney Channel, 2006.

Warren, "Ah, Wilderness," *The Suite Life of Zack and Cody* (also known as *TSL*), Disney Channel, 2006.

HOGAN, Hulk 1953–

(Mr. America, Terry Bollea, Terry Gene Bollea, Hollywood Hogan, Hollywood Hulk Hogan, Terry Hogan, Terry "Hulk" Hogan, the Incredible Hulk Hogan, the Hulkster)

PERSONAL

Original name, Terrence (Terry) Gene Bollea; born August 11, 1953, in Augusta, GA (some sources cite Tampa, FL); son of Peter (a construction foreman) and Ruth (a dance teacher and homemaker) Bollea; married Linda Claridge, December 18, 1983; children: Brooke (a singer), Nicholas Allan (Nick). *Education:* Attended Hillsborough Community College and the University of South Florida.

Addresses: *Agent*—Peter Young, Sovereign Talent Group, 10474 Santa Monica Blvd., Suite 301, Los Angeles, CA 90025.

Career: Professional wrestler and actor. Worked as a dockworker, beginning 1976; bass guitarist, and played in the rock band Ruckus, 1970s; worked as a bodyguard for the singer Cyndi Lauper; professional wrestler, beginning 1978, using professional names Mr. America, Sterling Golden, Super Destroyer, Terry Boulder, and Terry "the Hulk" Boulder, before adopting the name Hulk Hogan and other similar names; affiliated with World Wrestling Federation (later known as World Wrestling Entertainment), beginning 1979, and later World Championship Wrestling and New World Order; also a member of the Wrestling Boot Band. Worked as a spokesperson, appeared in advertisements and on merchandise, and involved in the Hulkamania phenomenon. Also known as Terry Gene Bollea, Terry Hogan, the Incredible Hulk Hogan, and the Hulkster.

Awards, Honors: Named most inspirational wrestler by *Pro Wrestling Illustrated,* 1983, followed by most popular wrestler, 1985, 1989, and 1990, and pro wrestler of the year, 1987, 1994, and 1997, and named number one in the PWI 500 for the years 1979–99; inducted into the Professional Wrestling Hall of Fame, 2003, and the World Wrestling Entertainment Hall of Fame, 2005; Teen Choice Award nomination, television—choice reality star (male), 2006, for *Hogan Knows Best;* multiple heavyweight championships, World Wrestling Federation (later known as World Wrestling Entertainment), World Championship Wrestling, International Wrestling Grand Prix, and others; some sources state that Hogan was the first professional wrestler on the cover of *Sports Illustrated.*

CREDITS

Television Appearances; Series:

Himself, *AWA All–Star Wrestling,* syndicated, 1981–83.

Himself, *WWF Superstars of Wrestling,* syndicated, beginning 1984.

(As Terry "Hulk" Hogan) *Rock 'n' Wrestling* (animated and live action; also known as *Hulk Hogan's "Rock 'n' Wrestling!"* and *Rock 'n' Wrestling Saturday Spectacular*), CBS, 1985–87.

Himself, *Saturday Night's Main Event* (also known as *The Main Event* and *Saturday Night Main Event*), NBC, 1985–92, Fox, 1992.

(As Terry "Hulk" Hogan) Randolph J. "Hurricane" Spencer, *Thunder in Paradise,* syndicated, 1994–95, selected episodes later combined to form films.

(As Hollywood Hogan) Himself, *WCW Saturday Night* (also known as *WCW Saturday Morning*), syndicated, 1994–2000.

(Sometimes billed as Hollywood Hogan) Himself, *WCW Monday Nitro* (also known as *nWo Nitro, WCW Monday Nitro Live!,* and *World Championship Wrestling Monday Nitro*), TNT, 1995–2000.

(As Hollywood Hogan) Himself, *WCW Thunder,* TBS, 1998–2000.

Himself, *WWE Velocity,* The National Network, 2002–2003.

Mr. America, *WWE Velocity,* The National Network, 2003.

(Some sources cite billing as Terry Bollea) Himself, *Hogan Knows Best,* VH1, beginning 2005.

Host, *American Gladiators,* NBC, beginning 2008.

Television Appearances; Miniseries:

Himself, *I Love the '90s,* VH1, 2004.

Himself, *I Love the '90s: Part Deux,* VH1, 2005.

Television Appearances; Movies:

(As Terry "Hulk" Hogan) Mike McBride, *Assault on Devil's Island* (also known as *Shadow Warriors*), TNT, 1997.

Mike McBride, *Shadow Warriors II: Hunt for the Death Merchant* (also known as *Assault on Death Mountain* and *Shadow Warriors 2*), TNT, 1998.

Television Appearances; Specials:

Himself, *WrestleMania* (also known as *WrestleMania* and *WWF WrestleMania*), pay–per–view, 1985.

Himself, *WWF Wrestling Classic* (also known as *Wrestlevision* and *The Wrestling Classic*), pay–per–view, 1985.

Himself, *WrestleMania 2,* pay–per–view, 1985, Showtime, 1986.

Himself, *WrestleMania III,* pay–per–view, 1987.

Himself, *Survivor Series* (also known as *WWF Survivor Series*), pay–per–view, 1987, 1988, 1989, 1990, 1991.

Himself, *WrestleMania IV,* pay–per–view, 1988.

Himself, *Summerslam,* pay–per–view, 1988, 1989, 1990.

Himself, *Royal Rumble* (also known as *WWF Royal Rumble*), pay–per–view, 1988, 1989, 1990, 1991, 1992.

Himself, *WrestleMania V* (also known as *WWF WrestleMania V*), pay–per–view, 1989.

The Valvoline National Driving Test, CBS, 1989.

Himself, *Happy Birthday, Bugs! 50 Looney Years* (also known as *Hollywood Celebrates Bugs Bunny's 50th Birthday*), CBS, 1990.

Sinatra 75: The Best Is Yet to Come (also known as *Frank Sinatra: 75th Birthday Celebration*), CBS, 1990.

The 25th Anniversary MDA Jerry Lewis Labor Day Telethon, syndicated, 1990.

WrestleMania VI, pay–per–view, 1990.

Himself, *Hulk Hogan: A Real American Story,* pay–per–view, 1991.

Himself, *Stories from Growing Up,* Nickelodeon, 1991.

Himself, *Summerslam* (also known as *Summerslam '91*), pay–per–view, 1991.

Himself, *Tuesday in Texas* (also known as *WWF Tuesday in Texas*), pay–per–view, 1991.

Himself, *WrestleMania VII,* pay–per–view, 1991.

Himself, *WWF UK Rampage '91,* pay–per–view, 1991.

Himself, *WrestleMania VIII,* pay–per–view, 1992.

Florida host, *Circus of the Stars Gives Kids the World* (also known as *Circus of the Stars #18*), CBS, 1993.

Himself, *WrestleMania IX,* pay–per–view, 1993.

In a New Light '93, ABC, 1993.

Himself, *King of the Ring* (also known as *WWF King of the Ring*), pay–per–view, c. 1993.

Himself, *Clash of the Champions XXIX,* TBS, 1994.

Himself, *Starrcade* (also known as *WCW Starrcade*), pay–per–view, 1994, 1996, 1997.

Himself, *Halloween Havoc* (also known as *WCW Halloween Havoc*), pay–per–view, 1994, 1995, 1996, 1997, 1998.

Himself, *Kids against Crime,* Trinity Broadcasting Network (TBN), 1995.

(As Hollywood Hulk Hogan) Himself, *WCW Bash at the Beach,* pay–per–view, 1995, 1996, 1998.

Himself, *WCW Fall Brawl,* pay–per–view, 1995, 1998.

Himself, *WCW Hog Wild,* pay–per–view, 1996.

(As Hollywood Hogan) Himself, *WCW Uncensored* (also known as *Uncensored 1996*), pay–per–view, 1996.

(As Hollywood Hogan) Himself, *WCW Road Wild '97,* pay–per–view, 1997.

(As Hollywood Hogan) Himself, *WCW SuperBrawl VII* (also known as *WCW SuperBrawl*), pay–per–view, 1997.

Himself, *The Unreal Story of Professional Wrestling,* Arts and Entertainment, 1998.

(As Hollywood Hulk Hogan) Himself, *WCW Road Wild '98,* pay–per–view, 1998.

(As Hollywood Hogan) Himself, *WCW Souled Out* (also known as *WCW Souled Out 1998*), pay–per–view, 1998.

(As Hollywood Hogan) Himself, *WCW Superbrawl VIII* (also known as *WCW SuperBrawl*), pay–per–view, 1998.

Himself, *WCW Road Wild '99,* pay–per–view, 1999.

(As Hollywood Hogan) Himself, *WCW Souled Out* (also known as *WCW Souled Out 1999*), pay–per–view, 1999.

(As Hollywood Hogan) Himself, *WCW Uncensored* (also known as *Uncensored 1999*), pay–per–view, 1999.

(As Hollywood Hulk Hogan) Himself, *King of the Ring* (also known as *WWE King of the Ring*), iN DEMAND, 2002.

(As Hollywood Hulk Hogan) Himself, *WrestleMania X-8* (also known as *WrestleMania X-VIII* and *WWF WrestleMania X-8*), pay–per–view, 2002.

(As Hollywood Hulk Hogan) Himself, *WWE Backlash* (also known as *Backlash*), pay–per–view, 2002.

Himself, *WWE Judgment Day,* pay–per–view, 2002.

(As Hollywood Hulk Hogan) Himself, *WWE No Way Out* (also known as *No Way Out*), pay–per–view, 2002.

Himself, *WWE Vengeance,* iN DEMAND, 2002.

Himself, *WrestleMania XIX,* pay–per–view, 2003.

(As Mr. America) *WWE Judgment Day,* pay–per–view, 2003.

Himself, *WWE No Way Out* (also known as *No Way Out*), iN DEMAND, 2003.

(Uncredited; in archive footage) Himself, *Cheating Death, Stealing Life: The Eddie Guerrero Story,* UPN, 2004.

Himself, *Hope Rocks: The Concert with a Cause,* Fox, 2005.

(In archive footage) Himself, *Saturday Night Live in the '80s: Lost & Found,* NBC, 2005.

Himself, *Summerslam* (also known as *WWE Summerslam*), iN DEMAND, 2005.

Himself, *WrestleMania 21,* pay–per–view, 2005.

Himself, *WWE Backlash* (also known as *Backlash*), iN DEMAND, 2005.

Himself, *WWE Great American Bash* (also known as *Great American Bash 2005*), iN DEMAND, 2005.

(In archive footage) Himself, *WWE Unforgiven,* pay–per–view, 2005.

Host, *20 Greatest Celebreality Moments,* VH1, 2006.

Himself, *75th Annual Hollywood Christmas Parade,* The CW, 2006.

Himself, *Summerslam* (also known as *Summerslam DX*), pay–per–view, 2006.

Himself, *WWE Cyber Sunday,* pay–per–view, 2006.

Himself, *WWE Great American Bash* (also known as *Great American Bash 2006*), pay–per–view, 2006.

(In archive footage) Himself, *WWE Royal Rumble,* pay–per–view, 2006.

Himself, *WWE Saturday Night's Main Event* (also known as *Saturday Night Main Event, Saturday Night's Main Event,* and *WWE Saturday Night Main Event*), NBC, 2006.

Himself, *WWE Draft Special* (also known as *WWE Monday Night RAW WWE Draft Special*), USA Network, 2007.

(In archive footage) Voice of Abraham Lincoln, "Bush's Jedi Powers," *Robot Chicken: Star Wars* (animated), Cartoon Network, 2007.

Television Appearances; Awards Presentations:

2004 Radio Music Awards, NBC, 2004.

Presenter, *VH1 Big in 05* (also known as *Big in 2005, VH1 Big in 2005,* and *VH1 Big in '05 Awards*), VH1, 2005.

The Teen Choice Awards 2005, Fox, 2005.

The 2005 Billboard Music Awards, Fox, 2005.

2005 Taurus World Stunt Awards, 2005.

(Uncredited) *MTV Video Music Awards 2006,* MTV, 2006.

Television Appearances; Episodic:

Himself, "Body Slam," *The A Team,* NBC, 1985.

Guest host, *Saturday Night Live* (also known as *NBC's "Saturday Night," Saturday Night, Saturday Night Live '80, SNL,* and *SNL 25*), NBC, 1985.

Himself, *Hot Properties,* Lifetime, 1985.

Himself, *Search for Tomorrow* (also known as *Search for Happiness*), NBC, 1985.

Himself, "The Trouble with Harry," *The A Team,* NBC, 1986.

"Miss Mom/Who's the Champ/Gopher's Delusion," *The Love Boat,* ABC, 1986.

Starlight Starbright, *Dolly* (also known as *The Dolly Show*), ABC, 1987.

Himself, *WWE Monday Night RAW,* USA Network, multiple episodes in 1993, 2005, and 2006, also 2007.

Himself, *Larry King Live,* Cable News Network, 1994, 2005, 2007.

Voice of himself, "Sleeper," *Space Ghost Coast to Coast* (live action and animated; also known as *SGC2C*), Cartoon Network, 1995.

The Big Breakfast, Channel 4 (England), 1995.

(As Terry "Hulk" Hogan) Himself, "Bash at the Beach," *Baywatch* (also known as *Baywatch Hawaii* and *Baywatch Hawai'i*), syndicated, 1996.

Himself, *Howard Stern,* 1997.

(In archive footage) Himself, "Andre the Giant," *Biography* (also known as *A&E Biography: Andre the Giant*), Arts and Entertainment, 1999.

Himself, "Hulk Hogan," *The E! True Hollywood Story* (also known as *Hulk Hogan: The E! True Hollywood Story* and *THS*), E! Entertainment Television, 1999.

(As Hollywood Hogan) Himself, "In This Corner ... Susan Keane! Parts 1 & 2," *Suddenly Susan,* NBC, 1999.

(In archive footage) Himself, "The Life and Death of Owen Hart," *Biography* (also known as *A&E Biography: Owen Hart*), Arts and Entertainment, 1999, also broadcast on TVOntario.

Himself, "Hulk Hogan: American Made," *Biography* (also known as *A&E Biography: Hulk Hogan*), Arts and Entertainment, 2000.

Himself, *Cribs* (also known as *MTV Cribs*), MTV, 2000.

(As Terry "Hulk" Hogan) Boomer Night, "Division Street," *Walker, Texas Ranger* (also known as *Walker*), CBS, 2001.

Himself, *Friday Night Smackdown!* (also known as *Smackdown!, Smackdown! Xtreme, World Wrestling Federation Smackdown!, WWE Smackdown!,* and *WWF Smackdown!*), UPN (later The CW), multiple episodes, beginning 2002.

Himself, *Hollywood Squares* (also known as *H2* and *H2: Hollywood Squares*), syndicated, 2002, 2004.

Himself, *Sunday Night Heat* (also known as *WWE Heat, WWE Sunday Night Heat,* and *WWF Sunday Night Heat*), MTV, 2002, 2005.

Himself, *WWF Raw Is War* (also known as *Raw Is War, WWE Raw,* and *WWF Raw*), The Nashville Network, 2002, USA Network, 2005.

(In archive footage) Himself, *WWE Confidential,* Spike TV, 2003.

Himself, "Hulk Hogan, Stage Dad," *(Inside)Out* (also known as *VH1 (Inside)Out* and *VH1 (Inside)Out: Hulk Hogan, Stage Dad*), VH1, 2004.

Himself, *Life & Style,* 2004.

(In archive footage) Himself, *TNA Impact! Wrestling,* USA Network, 2004 (multiple episodes).

Himself, "Adjusted Gross," *Kathy Griffin: My Life on the D–List,* Bravo, 2005.

Himself, "Ashlee Turns 20," *The Ashlee Simpson Show,* MTV, 2005.

Himself, "The Priceless Egg," *Damage Control,* MTV, 2005.

(Uncredited) Himself, "Series Finale," *The Contender,* NBC, 2005.

Himself, *Jimmy Kimmel Live!* (also known as *The Jimmy Kimmel Project*), ABC, 2005 (multiple episodes).

Himself, *MAD TV* (also known as *Mad TV* and *MADtv*), Fox, 2005.

Himself, *The Big Idea with Donny Deutsch,* CNBC, 2005 (multiple episodes), 2006.

Himself, *Live with Regis & Kelly,* syndicated, 2005, 2006 (multiple episodes), 2008.

Himself, "Semi Final Results," *Dancing with the Stars,* ABC, 2006.

Voices of himself and Abraham Lincoln, "Massage Chair," *Robot Chicken* (animated), Cartoon Network, 2006.

Voices of himself and a bartender, "Metal Militia," *Robot Chicken* (animated), Cartoon Network, 2006.

Himself, *Quite Frankly with Stephen A. Smith,* ESPN, 2006.

Himself, *The Tonight Show with Jay Leno,* NBC, 2006.

(And in archive footage) Himself, *Howard Stern on Demand* (also known as *Howard TV* and *Howard TV on Demand*), iN DEMAND, multiple episodes, beginning 2006.

(In archive footage) Himself, *WWE Monday Night RAW,* USA Network, multiple episodes, 2006 and 2007.

Appeared in other programs, including *The Arsenio Hall Show* (also known as *Arsenio*), syndicated.

Television Appearances; Pilots:
(As Terry "Hulk" Hogan) Mac MacKenna, *Goldie and the Bears,* ABC, 1985.

(As Terry "Hulk" Hogan) Randolph J. "Hurricane" Spencer, *Thunder in Paradise,* syndicated, 1994.

Host, *American Gladiators,* NBC, 2008.

Television Work; Series:
(As Terry "Hulk" Hogan) Executive producer, *Thunder in Paradise,* syndicated, 1994–95, selected episodes later combined to form films.

Television Producer; Movies:
(As Terry Bollea) Executive producer, *Assault on Devil's Island* (also known as *Shadow Warriors*), TNT, 1997.

(As Bollea) Producer, *Shadow Warriors II: Hunt for the Death Merchant* (also known as *Assault on Death Mountain* and *Shadow Warriors 2*), TNT, 1998.

Television Music Performer; Episodic:
Performer of song "Real American," "Killing Time," *Beavis and Butt–Head* (animated; also known as *The Bad Boys* and *Beavis and Butt–head*), MTV, 1994.

Music performer for various episodes, *WCW Monday Nitro* (also known as *nWo Nitro, WCW Monday Nitro Live!,* and *World Championship Wrestling Monday Nitro*), TNT, c. 1995–2000.

Television Work; Pilots:
Executive producer, *Thunder in Paradise,* syndicated, 1994.

Film Appearances:
Thunder Lips (some sources cite as Thunderlips), *Rocky III* (also known as *Rocky III, the Eye of the Tiger*), Metro–Goldwyn–Mayer, 1982.

Bimini Code (also known as *Raiders of the Lost Code*), American National Enterprises, 1984.

Rip Thomas, *No Holds Barred,* New Line Cinema, 1989.

Himself, *Gremlins 2: The New Batch* (also known as *Gremlins 2* and *Monolith*), Warner Bros., 1990.

Shep Ramsey, *Suburban Commando* (also known as *Urban Commando*), New Line Cinema, 1991.

(As Terry "Hulk" Hogan) Sean Armstrong, *Mr. Nanny* (also known as *Mr. Babysitter* and *Rough Stuff*), New Line Cinema, 1993.

(As Terry "Hulk" Hogan) Randolph J. "Hurricane" Spencer, *Thunder in Paradise II* (consists of episodes of television series), Vidmark Entertainment, 1994.

(As Terry "Hulk" Hogan) Randolph J. "Hurricane" Spencer, *Thunder in Paradise 3* (consists of episodes of television series), Trimark Pictures, 1995.

Blake Thorne, *Santa with Muscles,* Legacy Releasing, 1996.

Ray Chase, *The Secret Agent Club,* Cabin Fever Entertainment, 1996.

Steele's other tag team member, *Spy Hard* (also known as *Agent zero zero, Agent 00, Live and Let Spy, Agent 00—Mit der Lizenz zum Totlachen, Ciplak casus, Dragam add az eleted, Duro de espiar, Duro para espiar, Espia … como puderes!, Espia como puedas, L'agent secret se decouvre, Mit der Lizenz zum Totlachen, Spia e lascia spiare, Spy Hard—Helt utan haemningar, Spy Hard—lupa laeikyttaeae, Szklanka po lapkach,* and *Tajni agent 000*), Buena Vista, 1996.

Ben Cutter, *The Ultimate Weapon,* New City Releasing, 1998.

David "Dave" Dragon, *3 Ninjas: High Noon at Mega Mountain* (also known as *Mega Mountain Mission, 3 Ninjas: Showdown at Mega Mountain, 3 Ninjas 4, 3 Ninjas 4: High Noon at Mega Mountain,* and *3 Ninjas 4: Showdown at Mega Mountain*), TriStar, 1998.

Himself, *Jefftowne* (documentary), 1998.

(As Terry "Hulk" Hogan) Joe McGray, *McCinsey's Island,* Big Island Productions, 1998.

(As Hollywood Hogan) Man in black, *Muppets from Space* (also known as *Muppets in Space*), Columbia, 1999.

Himself, *Luscious Johnny: The Wrestler* (documentary), 2005.

Zeus, *Little Hercules in 3–D,* Little Hercules, 2007.

Film Producer:

Executive producer, *No Holds Barred,* New Line Cinema, 1989.

Executive producer, *Suburban Commando* (also known as *Urban Commando*), New Line Cinema, 1991.

(As Terry "Hulk" Hogan) Executive producer, *Thunder in Paradise II* (consists of episodes of television series), Vidmark Entertainment, 1994.

(As Terry "Hulk" Hogan) Executive producer, *Thunder in Paradise 3* (consists of episodes of television series), Trimark Pictures, 1995.

Associate producer, *Remainder,* Xtra Medium Productions, 2005.

Radio Appearances; Episodic:

Himself, *Howard Stern,* 1997.

Himself, *The Howard Stern Show,* Howard 100 (Sirius Satellite Radio), multiple episodes, beginning 2006.

Appeared in various radio programs.

RECORDINGS

Videos:

Himself, *Wrestling's Country Boys,* Coliseum Video, 1985.

(In archive footage) Himself, *WWF Greatest Matches,* 1986.

Himself, *Hulkamania 4* (also known as *WWF Hulkamania 4*), Coliseum Video, 1989.

Himself, *Best of Saturday Night's Main Event,* 1991.

Himself, *Hulkamania 6* (also known as *WWF Hulkamania 6*), Coliseum Video, 1991.

Himself, *WCW/NWO Superstar Series: Diamond Dallas Page—Feel the Bang!,* 1998.

(In archive footage) Himself, *Andre the Giant: Larger than Life* (also known as *Andre the Giant* and *WWF—Andre the Giant: Larger than Life*), 1999.

Himself, *WCW Superstar Series: Mayhem,* Turner Home Entertainment, 1999.

Himself, *Hollywood Hulk Hogan: Hulk Still Rules,* Koch Vision, 2002.

(As Hollywood Hulk Hogan) Himself, *WWE Back in Black: NWO New World Order* (also known as *WWE Back in Black*), Silver Vision Video, 2002.

(In archive footage) Himself, *The Ultimate Ric Flair Collection,* 2003.

Himself, *WWE: Brock Lesnar, Here Comes the Pain,* World Wrestling Federation Entertainment, 2003.

(In archive footage) Himself, *John Cena: Word Life,* 2004.

(In archive footage) Himself, *The Monday Night War: WWE RAW vs. WCW Nitro* (also known as *The Monday Night War: WWE RAW Is WAR vs. WCW Monday Nitro*), World Wrestling Entertainment Home Video, 2004.

Himself, *Sting: Moment of Truth,* Dove Canyon Films, 2004.

(In archive footage) Himself, *WWE: The Rise & Fall of ECW,* 2004.

(In archive footage) Himself, *The Bret Hart Story: The Best There Is, Was, and Ever Will Be,* 2005.

Himself, *Jake "The Snake" Roberts: Pick Your Poison,* World Wrestling Entertainment, 2005.

(In archive footage) Himself, *Road Warriors: The Life and Death of Wrestling's Most Dominant Tag Team,* 2005.

Himself, *The Self Destruction of the Ultimate Warrior,* World Wrestling Entertainment Home Video, 2005.

Himself, *Tombstone: The History of the Undertaker,* World Wrestling Entertainment Home Video, 2005.

Himself, *WWE Hall of Fame 2005,* World Wrestling Entertainment Home Video, 2005.

Himself, *WWE Legends: Greatest Wrestling Stars of the '80s,* World Wrestling Entertainment Home Video, 2005.

Himself, *Hulk Hogan: The Ultimate Anthology,* 2006.

Himself, *WWE Hall of Fame 2006,* World Wrestling Entertainment Home Video, 2006.

Albums; with Others:

(With the Wrestling Boot Band) *Hulk Rules* (also known as *Hulk Hogan: Hulk Rules*), Select Records, 1995.

Some sources cite other recordings.

Music Videos:

Brooke Hogan, "For a Moment," c. 2006.

Video Games:

Himself, *WWF Superstars,* 1989.

Himself, *WWF WrestleMania Challenge,* 1990.

Voice of himself, *WCW: Nitro* (also known as *Nitro*), THQ, 1997.

Voice of himself, *WCW/NWO Thunder,* 1998.

Himself, *Legends of Wrestling,* 2001.

Himself, *WWE SmackDown! Shut Your Mouth,* THQ, 2002.

(As Hollywood Hogan) Himself, *WWE WrestleMania X–8,* THQ, 2002.

Himself, *WWE Crush Hour,* 2003.

Himself, *WWE Day of Reckoning 2,* THQ, 2005.

Voice of himself, *WWE SmackDown! vs. RAW 2006,* THQ, 2005.

Voice of himself, *WWE SmackDown! vs. RAW 2007,* THQ, 2006.

WRITINGS

Teleplays; with Others; Series:
WCW Monday Nitro (also known as *nWo Nitro, WCW Monday Nitro Live!,* and *World Championship Wrestling Monday Nitro*), TNT, 1995–2000.

Created material used in other programs.

Nonfiction:
(With Michael Jan Friedman) *Hollywood Hulk Hogan* (autobiography), Pocket Star, 2002.

Author of articles.

Albums; with Others:
(With the Wrestling Boot Band) *Hulk Rules* (also known as *Hulk Hogan: Hulk Rules*), Select Records, 1995.

Some sources cite other recordings.

Songs; with Others:
Created the wrestling entrance music "Ravishing: The Hulk Hogan Theme," an adaptation from the song "Ravishing" by Jim Steinman.

OTHER SOURCES

Books:
Contemporary Newsmakers 1987, issue cumulation, Gale, 1988.
St. James Encyclopedia of Popular Culture, St. James Press, 2000.

Periodicals:
Fortune, December 7, 1998, p. 40.
People Weekly, October 14, 1991, p. 61; March 23, 1992, p. 91; July 25, 2005, p. 95.
USA Today, October 4, 1991.

HOLCOMB, Rod
(Alan Smithee)

PERSONAL

Addresses: *Agent*—Cori Wellins, William Morris Agency, One William Morris Place, Beverly Hills, CA 90212.

Career: Director and producer.

Member: Directors Guild of America (member of the board of directors).

Awards, Honors: Emmy Award nomination, outstanding directing in a drama series, 1988, and Directors Guild of America Award nomination, outstanding directorial achievement in dramatic specials, 1989, both for the pilot episode of *China Beach;* Directors Guild of America Award (with others), outstanding directorial achievement in dramatic specials, and Emmy Award nomination, outstanding individual achievement in directing for a drama series, both 1995, for the pilot episode of *ER;* Emmy Award nomination, outstanding directing for a drama series, 1997, for "Last Call," an episode of *ER;* Directors Guild of America Award nomination, outstanding directorial achievement in movies for television, 2004, for *The Pentagon Papers.*

CREDITS

Television Producer; Series:
Supervising producer, *China Beach,* ABC, 1988–91.
Executive producer, *The Division* (also known as *Heart of the City*), Lifetime, 1996–97.
Executive producer and producer, *The Education of Max Bickford* (also known as *Max Bickford*), CBS, 2001–2002.
Executive producer, *Shark,* CBS, beginning 2006.
Executive producer, *Moonlight* (also known as *Twilight*), CBS, beginning 2007.

Television Director; Miniseries:
Thanks of a Grateful Nation (also known as *The Gulf War*), Showtime, 1998.

Television Director; Movies:
Captain America, CBS, 1979.
Midnight Offerings, 1981.
The Cartier Affair, 1984.
No Man's Land, NBC, 1984.
The Red Light Sting (also known as *The Whorehouse Sting*), CBS, 1984.
Chase, CBS, 1985.
Two Fathers' Justice, 1985.
Blind Justice, CBS, 1986.
The Long Journey Home (also known as *Bloody Home*), CBS, 1987.
Stillwatch, CBS, 1987.
A Promise to Keep (also known as *Angels without Wings* and *Promises to Keep*), NBC, 1990.
Chains of Gold, Showtime, 1991.
Finding the Way Home (also known as *Mittelmann's Hardware*), ABC, 1991.
A Message from Holly, CBS, 1992.

Donato and Daughter (also known as *Dead to Rights* and *Under Threat*), CBS, 1993.
Royce, Showtime, 1994.
Convict Cowboy, Showtime, 1995.
The Prosecutors, 1996.
Songs in Ordinary Time, CBS, 2000.
The Pentagon Papers, FX Network, 2003.
Code Breakers, ESPN, 2005.

Television Producer; Movies:
Producer, *No Man's Land,* NBC, 1984.
Producer, *Finding the Way Home* (also known as *Mittelmann's Hardware*), ABC, 1991.
Executive producer, *The Prosecutors,* 1996.
Supervising producer, *The Pentagon Papers,* FX Network, 2003.

Television Director; Episodic:
"Bigfoot V," *The Six Million Dollar Man* (also known as *Cyborg, De Man van zes miljoen, Der sechs Millionen Dollar Mann, El hombre de los seis millones de dolares, Kuuden miljoonan dollarin mies, L'homme qui valait 3 milliards,* and *L'uomo da sei milioni di dollari*), ABC, 1977.
"The Cancelled Czech," *The American Girls* (also known as *Have Girls, Will Travel*), CBS, 1978.
"Date with Danger: Parts 1 & 2," *The Six Million Dollar Man* (also known as *Cyborg, De Man van zes miljoen, Der sechs Millionen Dollar Mann, El hombre de los seis millones de dolares, Kuuden miljoonan dollarin mies, L'homme qui valait 3 milliards,* and *L'uomo da sei milioni di dollari*), ABC, 1978.
Battlestar Galactica (also known as *Galactica*), ABC, multiple episodes, 1978–79.
"Mode of Death," *Quincy, M.E.* (also known as *Quincy*), NBC, 1979.
"The Money Plague," *Quincy, M.E.* (also known as *Quincy*), NBC, 1979.
"The Murphy Contingent," *B. J. and the Bear,* NBC, 1979.
Big Shamus, Little Shamus, CBS, 1979.
"Aphrodite/Dr. Jeckyll and Miss Hyde," *Fantasy Island,* ABC, 1980.
"Loose Larry's List of Losers," *Tenspeed and Brownshoe,* ABC, 1980.
"My Brother's Keeper," *Beyond Westworld,* CBS, 1980.
"Riot," *Quincy, M.E.* (also known as *Quincy*), NBC, 1980.
"Unholy Wedlock/Elizabeth," *Fantasy Island,* ABC, 1980.
"Untitled," *Tenspeed and Brownshoe,* ABC, 1980.
"What Do You People Want from Me?," *Stone,* ABC, 1980.
"Fruits of the Poisonous Tree," *Hill Street Blues,* NBC, 1981.
"Welcome to Sweetwater," *Bret Maverick,* NBC, 1981.
The Greatest American Hero, ABC, multiple episodes, 1981–82.

"The French Detective," *The Devlin Connection,* NBC, 1982.
Chicago Story, NBC, 1982.
"The First Time," *Scarecrow and Mrs. King,* CBS, 1983.
"Mexican Slayride: Parts 1 & 2," *The A Team,* NBC, 1983.
"There Goes the Neighborhood," *Scarecrow and Mrs. King,* CBS, 1983.
"To Catch a Mongoose," *Scarecrow and Mrs. King,* CBS, 1984.
"The Defector," *The Equalizer,* CBS, 1985.
Detective in the House, CBS, 1985.
"The Game's Not Over, 'til the Fat Lady Sings," *Spies,* CBS, 1987.
"Home," *China Beach,* ABC, 1988.
"Somewhere over the Radio," *China Beach,* ABC, 1988.
"On the Run," *Wolf,* CBS, 1989.
ER (also known as *Emergency Room*), NBC, multiple episodes, between 1994 and 1998.
"In a Yellow Wood," *Trinity,* NBC, 1998.
"Hearts and Minds," *The Education of Max Bickford* (also known as *Max Bickford*), CBS, 2001.
"Herding Cats," *The Education of Max Bickford* (also known as *Max Bickford*), CBS, 2001.
"The Most Dangerous Job," *The District* (also known as *Washington Police, The District—Einsatz in Washington, Mannions distrikt,* and *Poliisipaeaellikkkoe Mannion*), CBS, 2001.
"The Good, the Bad and the Lawyers," *The Education of Max Bickford* (also known as *Max Bickford*), CBS, 2002.
"Fish Story," *Invasion,* ABC, 2005.
"Hearts and Minds," *Lost,* ABC, 2005.
"Ninety Miles Away," *The West Wing* (also known as *West Wing* and *El ala oeste de la Casablanca*), NBC, 2005.
"Deja Vu All Over Again," *Shark,* CBS, 2006.
"LAPD Blue," *Shark,* CBS, 2006.
"The OG," *Numb3rs* (also known as *Numbers* and *Num3ers*), CBS, 2006.
"Teacher's Pet," *Shark,* CBS, 2007.

Also directed episodes of other programs, including *The Division* (also known as *Heart of the City*), Lifetime.

Television Associate Producer; Episodic:
"Fausta, the Nazi Wonder Woman," *Wonder Woman* (also known as *The New Adventures of Wonder Woman* and *The New Original Wonder Woman*), ABC, 1976.
"Wonder Woman Meets Baroness Von Gunther" (also known as "Wonder Woman Meets Baroness Paula Von Gunther"), *Wonder Woman* (also known as *The New Adventures of Wonder Woman* and *The New Original Wonder Woman*), ABC, 1976.
"Just a Matter of Time," *The Six Million Dollar Man* (also known as *Cyborg, De Man van zes miljoen, Der sechs Millionen Dollar Mann, El hombre de los seis*

millones de dolares, Kuuden miljoonan dollarin mies, L'homme qui valait 3 milliards, and *L'uomo da sei milioni di dollari*), ABC, 1978.

Television Director; Pilots:
"The Greatest American Hero," *The Greatest American Hero,* ABC, 1981.
(As Alan Smithee) *Moonlight,* CBS, 1982.
The Quest, ABC, 1982.
Scene of the Crime, NBC, 1984.
"The Equalizer," *The Equalizer,* CBS, 1985.
Stark (also known as *Las Vegas Cop*), CBS, 1985.
Wiseguy, CBS, 1987.
China Beach, ABC, 1988.
(And cocreator) *Wolf,* CBS, 1989.
Silverfox (also known as *Double Old 7* and *Our Man James*), ABC, 1991.
Angel Street (also known as *Polish Hill*), CBS, 1992.
"24 Hours," *ER* (also known as *Emergency Room*), NBC, 1994.
The Underworld, NBC, 1997.
Hopewell, CBS, 2000.
The Education of Max Bickford (also known as *Max Bickford*), CBS, 2001.
Bradford, CBS, c. 2001.
The Lyon's Den (also known as *I lovens hule* and *Lain luola*), NBC, 2003.
Bounty Hunters, CBS, 2005.
Lancaster, CBS, c. 2005.
The Way, CBS, 2006.
"No Such Thing as Vampires," *Moonlight* (also known as *Twilight*), CBS, 2007.

Director for other pilot projects, including *Allies,* CBS; and *Match,* ABC.

Television Producer; Pilots:
Associate producer, *The Man with the Power,* NBC, 1977.
Associate producer, *Mandrake,* NBC, 1979.
Producer, *Wiseguy,* CBS, 1987.
Producer and cocreator, *Wolf,* CBS, 1989.
Supervising producer, *Silverfox* (also known as *Double Old 7* and *Our Man James*), ABC, 1991.
Executive producer, *Bradford,* CBS, c. 2001.
Executive producer, *The Lyon's Den* (also known as *I lovens hule* and *Lain luola*), NBC, 2003.
Executive producer, *Bounty Hunters,* CBS, 2005.

Executive producer for other pilot projects, including *Allies,* CBS; and *Match,* ABC.

Television Appearances; Episodic:
Himself, *TV Land Moguls,* TV Land, 2004.

Film Director:
(As Alan Smithee) *Stitches,* International Film Marketing, 1985.

RECORDINGS

Videos:
Himself, *Remembering "Battlestar Galactica,"* Universal Studios Home Video, 2004.

WRITINGS

Nonfiction:
Some sources state that Holcomb wrote the article that was the basis for the made–for–television movie *The Red Light Sting* (also known as *The Whorehouse Sting*), CBS, 1984.

HOLLIDAY, Kene 1949–
(Kene Halliday)

PERSONAL

Born June 25, 1949, in Copiague, NY; married Linda Copling. *Education:* University of Maryland, degree in speech and drama; studied with Moto Jicho.

Addresses: *Agent*—The Irv Schechter Company, 9300 Wilshire Blvd., Suite 400, Beverly Hills, CA 90212.

Career: Actor. Associated with Robert Hooks' D.C. Black Repertory Company; stage manager for the Smithsonian–sponsored U.S. tour of Ghanaian entertainers, 1975.

Awards, Honors: Best Actor Award, best male performance, Newport International Film Festival, 2007, for *Great World of Sound.*

CREDITS

Film Appearances:
Walt Cronin, *No Small Affair,* Columbia, 1984.
Major Clark, *The Philadelphia Experiment,* New World, 1984.
Voice of Roadblock, *G.I. Joe: The Movie* (also known as *Action Force: The Movie*), 1987.
Man in church number one, *Bulworth,* 1998.
Simon, *The Immaculate Misconception,* 2006.

Clarence, *Great World of Sound,* Magnolia Pictures, 2007.

Television Appearances; Series:
Host, *Burglar Proofing,* 1974.
Sergeant Curtis Baker, *Country* (also known as *Carter Country*), ABC, 1977–79.
Eddie Dawson, *Soap,* ABC, 1977–81.
Voice of Roadblock, *G.I. Joe* (animated; also known as *Action Force* and *Chijo saikyo no Expert Team G.I. Joe*), 1985.
Tyler Hudson, *Matlock,* NBC, 1986–87, 1989–90.

Television Appearances; Miniseries:
Detroit, *Roots: The Next Generations,* 1979.

Television Appearances; Movies:
Doug, *The Last Song,* 1980.
Andy Murphy, *The Two Lives of Carol Letner,* 1981.
Ron Dixon, *Farrell for The People,* 1982.
Bill Washington, *Dangerous Company,* 1982.
Voice of Roadblock, *"G.I. Joe": The Revenge of Cobra,* 1984.
Albert Washington, *Badge of the Assassin,* 1985.
Tyler Hudson, *Diary of a Perfect Murder,* NBC, 1986.
Bob Sperling, *If It's Tuesday, It Still Must Be Belgium,* NBC, 1987.
Joe Dillon, *Perry Mason: The Case of the Silenced Singer,* NBC, 1990.
Sidney Bechet, *The Josephine Baker Story,* HBO, 1991.
Rasheed Wilkes, *Stormy Weathers,* ABC, 1992.
Jack Calloway, *Miracle on the Mountain: The Kincaide Family Story,* 2000.

Television Appearances; Pilots:
Dr. Jeffrey House, *The Chicago Story,* NBC, 1981.
Sergeant Alvin Sykes, *Momma the Detective* (also known as *See China and Die*), NBC, 1981.
Don Kingman, *The Best of Times* (also known as *Changing Times*), CBS, 1983.
Al Stark, *The Sheriff and the Astronaut,* CBS, 1984.
Voice of Roadblock, *"G.I. Joe": Arise, Serpentor, Arise!* (animated; also known as *Action Force: Arise, Serpentor, Arise!*), 1986.

Television Appearances; Specials:
ABC team member, *Battle of the Network Stars IV,* ABC, 1978.
Coach Sanford, "A Special Gift," *ABC Afterschool Specials,* ABC, 1979.
Bill Washington, "Dangerous Company," *CBS Afternoon Playhouse,* CBS, 1982.

Television Appearances; Episodic:
"Love and the Pill," *Love, American Style,* 1969.

"Love and the Second Time," *Love, American Style,* 1971.
Assistant district attorney Dunn, "A Shield for Murder; Parts 1 & 2," *Kojak,* 1976.
Paul, "Earthquakes Happen," *The Incredible Hulk,* 1978.
Himself, "Going, Going, Going," *What's Happening!!,* 1978.
J. D., "Slammer," *Lou Grant,* 1979.
Father Tony Hamilton, "Never a Child," *Quincy M.E.* (also known as *Quincy*), 1979.
Earl DuBois, "Takin' It to the Streets," *Benson,* ABC, 1980.
District attorney Arnold Turner, "The Hit Car," *The Greatest American Hero,* 1981.
William Dean, "Hart and Sole," *Hart to Hart,* 1982.
Officer Kenwood, "Lesson in Love," *The Jeffersons,* 1982.
Vernon Lee, "Of Mouse and Men," *Hill Street Blues,* 1982.
Vernon Lee, "Zen and the Art of Law Enforcement," *Hill Street Blues,* 1982.
Vernon Lee, "The Young, the Beautiful and the Degraded," *Hill Street Blues,* 1982.
Ballentine, "Space Ranger," *The Greatest American Hero,* 1983.
Earl DuBois, "The Reunion," *Benson,* ABC, 1984.
Pablo Jackson, "You're in Alice's," *Hill Street Blues,* 1985.
Lieutenant Joe Budd, "In His Shadow," *The Fall Guy,* 1986.
"Truth and Consequences," *Doogie Howser, M.D.,* 1991.
Burke's producer, "Fmurder," *Diagnosis Murder,* CBS, 1996.
Melvin, "Sid, Lies, and Videotape," *Sparks,* UPN, 1996.
Reverend Washington, "Family Ties," *Dangerous Minds,* 1996.
Harold, "The Return of the Temptones," *The Wayans Bros.,* The WB, 1996.
Anthony Fleming, "All in the Family," *The Profiler,* NBC, 1999.
(As Kene Halliday) "Family Is Family," *Any Day Now,* 1999.
George Simmons, "Pot Scrubbers," *The District,* CBS, 2000.
Guard, "Charley's Baseball," *Hope & Faith,* ABC, 2004.
Coach Venezano, "Ripped," *Law & Order: Special Victims Unit* (also known as *Law & Order: SVU* and *Special Victims Unit*), NBC, 2005.

Stage Appearances:
Dionysus Wants You, Folger Theatre Group, Astor Place Showcase Theatre, New York City, 1970.
(Off-Broadway debut) Carlyle, *Streamers,* New York Shakespeare Festival, Mitzi E. Newhouse Theatre, New York City, 1976–77.
Private Tony Smalls, *A Soldier's Play,* Center Theatre Group, Mark Taper Forum, Los Angeles, 1981–82.

Vantyle Mayfield, *Joe Louis Blues,* Los Angeles Theatre Center, Los Angeles, 1992.

HOSEA, Bobby

PERSONAL

Original name, Willie Samuel Hosea, Jr.; father, an Air Force sergeant; mother, a nurse; married Marcia Hairston, 1980; children: Ranae, Steven. *Education:* Attended University of California at Los Angeles.

Addresses: *Agent*—Metropolitan Talent Agency, 4500 Wilshire Blvd., 2nd Floor, Los Angeles, CA 90010.

Career: Actor. Previously played professional football in the United States Football League and the Canadian Football League.

CREDITS

Film Appearances:
Tom Dellerton, *Jack's Back,* Paramount, 1988.
The Runnin' Kind, 1989.
Hutch, *Rock–A–Die Baby,* 1989.
Why Colors?, 1992.
The Colors of Love, 1992.
Steve, *Boiling Point* (also known as *L'extreme limite*), Warner Bros., 1993.
Major Danowitz, *Independence Day* (also known as *ID4*), Twentieth Century–Fox, 1996.
Rickles, *Judas Kiss,* Moonlight Films, 1998.
Going Back, 2001.
Greg, *All About You,* 2001.
Detective, *The Dead Girl,* First Look International, 2006.

Television Appearances; Series:
Private "Sweetness" Elroy, *China Beach,* ABC, 1988–90.
Mitchell Patterson, *Singer & Sons,* NBC, 1990.
Marine Pilot Major Reggie Warren, *The Cape,* syndicated, 1996–97.
Major MacArthur "Hammer" Lewis, Jr., *Pensacola: Wings of Gold,* syndicated, 1998–2000.
Jonathan Snow, *18 Wheels of Justice,* TNN, 2001.

Television Appearances; Movies:
Football player, *Her Life as a Man,* 1984.
First reporter, *Second Serve,* 1986.
Reporter number two, *Warm Hearts, Cold Feet,* CBS, 1987.
Rhodes, *Angel in Green,* CBS, 1987.

Glory Years (also known as *Wacky Weekend*), 1987.
Coach Webster, *What Price Victory,* 1988.
Devaux, *French Silk,* ABC, 1994.
O. J. Simpson, *The O. J. Simpson Story,* Fox, 1995.
Sheriff R. J. Turnage, *Nightscream* (also known as *Night Scream*), NBC, 1997.
Colonel Wayne, *Gargantua,* Fox, 1998.
Tom McMillian, *Wie Stark muss eine liebe sein,* 1998.
Elston Howard, *61** (also known as *61* and *Home Run Race*), HBO, 2001.
Ray, *Going Back* (also known as *Freres de guerre* and *Under Heavy Fire*), 2001.
John Muhammad, *D.C. Sniper: 23 Days of Fear,* USA Network, 2003.
Ray Watson, *The Veteran,* 2006.

Television Appearances; Specials:
Yellow gang, *Why Colors?,* 1995.

Television Appearances; Pilots:
Sweetness, *China Beach,* ABC, 1988.
Emory Hacker, *The Heat,* CBS, 1989.
Greg, *Jackee,* NBC, 1989.
Yuri Barnes, *M.A.N.T.I.S.,* 1994.
Marine Pilot Major Reggie Warren, *The Cape,* 1996.
Sergeant Joe Hernandez, *Standoff,* Fox, 2006.
Born in the USA, Fox, 2007.

Television Appearances; Episodic:
1st and Ten, HBO, c. 1985.
The sheriff, "Benson the Hero," *Benson,* 1985.
Reporter, "Aftershocks," *Knots Landing,* CBS, 1985.
Reporter, "His Brother's Keeper," *Knots Landing,* CBS, 1986.
Customer number two, "Knock, Knock, Who's There?," *Perfect Strangers,* ABC, 1986.
Stretcher Bearer, "The Junction," *The Twilight Zone* (also known as *The New Twilight Zone*), CBS, 1987.
"What about Love?," *21 Jump Street,* Fox, 1989.
Hacker, "The Heat," *CBS Summer Playhouse,* CBS, 1989.
Danny, "Conspiracy," *Mancuso, FBI,* 1990.
Terrence Moses, "The Day That Moses Came to Town," *Coach,* ABC, 1990.
Officer Kevin Bryce, "Night Fears," *Murder, She Wrote,* CBS, 1991.
Dr. Alec Hudson, "Community Action," *The Fresh Prince of Bel–Air,* NBC, 1992.
William, "The Presentation," *Hangin' with Mr. Cooper,* ABC, 1992.
Tyrell, *Rhythm & Blues,* 1992.
Guy Stewart, "Guy Perfect," *Sirens,* ABC, 1993.
Lawrence, "U.N.I.T.Y. or Five Card Stud," *Living Single* (also known as *My Girls*), Fox, 1994.
Lawrence, "A Hair–Razing Experience," *Living Single* (also known as *My Girls*), Fox, 1994.
Lawrence, "He Works Hard for the Money," *Living Single* (also known as *My Girls*), Fox, 1995.

Dr. Gregory Talbot, "Playing for Keeps," *Diagnosis Murder,* CBS, 1995.

John McCarver, "Game, Set, Murder," *Murder, She Wrote,* CBS, 1995.

Ray, "Lock and Load, Babe," *Vanishing Son,* 1995.

Marcus, "The Path Not Taken," *Xena: Warrior Princess,* syndicated, 1995.

Marcus, "Mortal Beloved," *Xena: Warrior Princess,* syndicated, 1996.

Chief Petty Officer, "Black Ops," *JAG,* NBC, 1996.

Lieutenant Colonel Robert Turner, "The Court–Martial of Sandra Gilbert," *JAG,* CBS, 1997.

"Hired Guns," *Soldier of Fortune, Inc.* (also known as *S.O.F. Special Ops Force, S.O.F., Inc.,* and *SOF, Inc.*), 1998.

Mr. Johnson, "The Dust of Life," *Any Day Now,* Lifetime, 2000.

"Saving Private Irons," *V.I.P.* (also known as *V.I.P.—Die Bodyguards*), syndicated, 2002.

David Blake, "Scared Straight," *Crossing Jordan,* NBC, 2002.

Gordon Beecham, "Untouchable," *The District,* CBS, 2003.

Gordon Beecham, "Blindsided," *The District,* CBS, 2003.

Kenneth Holmes, "Alpha–126," *Threat Matrix,* ABC, 2003.

Greg Haymer, "The Hole–in–the–Wall Gang," *Boomtown,* NBC, 2003.

F. Robert Chapin, "Water," *The Mountain,* The WB, 2004.

F. Robert Chapin, "Masquerade," *The Mountain,* The WB, 2004.

F. Robert Chapin, "Best Laid Plans," *The Mountain,* The WB, 2004.

Rich Rebba, "Mea Culpa," *CSI: Crime Scene Investigation* (also known as *C.S.I., CSI: Las Vegas,* and *Les Experts*), CBS, 2004.

Officer Joey Brown, "The Score," *CSI: Miami,* CBS, 2006.

Terrell Tisdale, "Fireflies," *Cold Case,* CBS, 2006.

Sarge, "Croatoan," *Supernatural,* The CW, 2006.

Greek, ABC Family, 2006.

Detective, "Godsend," *Heroes,* NBC, 2007.

Bartender, "Here Comes the Judge," *Shark,* CBS, 2007.

Detective Franklin, "Manchild," *Lincoln Heights,* ABC Family, 2007.

Detective Franklin, "Blowback," *Lincoln Heights,* ABC Family, 2007.

Detective Franklin, "Tricks and Treats," *Lincoln Heights,* ABC Family, 2007.

Detective Franklin, "The Feeling That We Have," *Lincoln Heights,* ABC Family, 2007.

OTHER SOURCES

Periodicals:

People Weekly, February 6, 1995, p. 75.

HUBAND, David 1958–

PERSONAL

Born in 1958, in Winnipeg, Manitoba, Canada.

Addresses: *Manager*—Edna Talent Management, Ltd., 318 Dundas St. West, Toronto, Ontario MST 1G5 Canada.

Career: Actor and writer. Appeared in television commercials.

Awards, Honors: Canadian Comedy Award nomination, film–writing—adapted, Gemini Award, best dramatic short, Academy of Canadian Cinema and Television, 2000, both for *The Dane.*

CREDITS

Film Appearances:

Cadet Hedges, *Police Academy 3: Back in Training,* Warner Bros., 1986.

Gas attendant, *Tommy Boy,* Paramount, 1995.

Shecky Bernstein, *Frame by Frame,* 1995.

Dr. Ceyes, *No One Could Protect Her,* 1996.

William Gilmer, *What Kind of Mother Are You?,* 1996.

Cop, *That Old Feeling,* Unit International Pictures, 1997.

David, *Seven Gates,* 1997.

Buckland, *Motel,* 1998.

Effects of a Decent Man, 1999.

Oscar, *Chez amore,* 2000.

Lounge bartender, *Frequency,* New Line Cinema, 2000.

Frank, *The Ladies Man* (also known as *The Ladies' Man*), Paramount, 2000.

Bob Wilikers, *Truth in Advertising,* 2001.

Maitre'd—Serge, *Down to Earth* (also known as *Einmal Himmel und zuruck*), 2001.

Trooper, *Wrong Turn,* Twentieth Century–Fox, 2003.

Xavier MacDonald, *Love, Sex and Eating the Bones,* THINKFilm, 2003.

Sammy, *The Republic of Love,* Seville Pictures, 2003.

Ralph Stipes, *The Straightjacket Lottery* (short), 2004.

Dodd, *Club Zero,* Lions Gate Films, 2004.

Ford Bond, *Cinderella Man,* Universal, 2005.

Dodd, *Re–Entering the Nightmare* (documentary short), Savage Dog Film & Digitals, 2005.

Photographer, *Breach,* Universal, 2007.

Mr. Tuttle, *The Lookout,* Miramax, 2007.

Mr. Sulsky, *Hank and Mike,* Christal Films, 2008.

Television Appearances; Series:

Douglas Hendrychuck, *The Red Green Show* (also known as *The New Red Green Show*), CBC, 1991.

Voice of Grant Campbell, Serena's dad, *Sailor Moon* (animated; also known as *English Sailor Moon, Sailor Moon S,* and *Sailor Moon Super S*), syndicated, 1995–98.

Bruce, *The Newsroom,* CBC, 1996.

Morty Storkowitz, *Birdz,* CBS, 1998.

Voice of Vice Principal Zeigler, *Pelswick* (animated), Nickelodeon and CBC, 2000.

Coach, *Ace Lightening,* CBC, 2002.

Blue Jay, *Peep and the Big Wide World,* 2004.

Television Appearances; Miniseries:

Photographer, *J.F.K.: Reckless Youth,* ABC, 1993.

Michael Longwill, *And Never Let Her Go,* CBS, 2001.

Charley/Customs, *The Path to 9/11,* ABC, 2006.

Warden, *The State Within,* BBC, 2006.

Television Appearances; Movies:

Cheston, *The Diamond Fleece,* USA Network, 1992.

Racine, *Fatal Vows: The Alexandra O'Hara Story,* CBS, 1994.

Dr. Roge, *Against Their Will: Women in Prison* (also known as *Against Their Will* and *Cage Seduction: The Shocking True Story*), ABC, 1994.

Engineer Craig, *Almost Golden: The Jessica Savitch Story* (also known as *Almost Golden*), Lifetime, 1995.

Holiday Affair, USA Network, 1996.

Shecky Bernstein, *Conundrum* (also known as *Frame by Frame*), Showtime, 1996.

Warm–up guy, *Dead Husbands* (also known as *Last Man on the List*), USA Network, 1998.

Stan, *Ultimate Deception* (also known as *Ultimate Betrayal*), USA Network, 1999.

Skip Humphrey, *The Jesse Ventura Story,* NBC, 1999.

Hardware convention emcee, *Ricky Nelson: Original Teen Idol* (also known as *Ricky Nelson* and *The Ricky Nelson Story*), VH1, 1999.

Sirkin, *Dirty Pictures,* Showtime, 2000.

Wardley, *WW3,* Fox, 2001.

Sportsweek photographer, *The Red Sneakers,* Showtime, 2002.

Reporter, *RFK,* FX Channel, 2002.

Bruce, *Escape from the Newsroom,* CBC, 2002.

Rolly Fox, *Terry,* CTV, 2005.

Television Appearances; Specials:

The 2000 Canadian Comedy Awards (also known as *The CCAs*), Comedy Network, 2000.

Buck Calder, *The Buck Calder Experience,* 2006.

Television Appearance; Pilots:

Intense man, *1–800–MISSING* (also known as *Missing*), Lifetime, 2003.

Artemis Jones, *Dead Lawyers,* Sci–Fi Channel, 2004.

Television Appearances; Episodic:

Cop, "Birds of a Feather," *Street Legal,* CBC, 1986.

"Another Point of View," *Seeing Things,* CBC, 1987.

"Race against Time," *Katts and Dog* (also known as *Rin Tin Tin: K–9 Cop*), CTV and Family Channel, 1988.

"Under Siege," *Katts and Dog* (also known as *Rin Tin Tin: K–9 Cop*), CTV and Family Channel, 1992.

Jerry, "What Money Can't Buy," *RoboCop* (also known as *RoboCop: The Series*), syndicated, 1994.

Jerry, "Nanno," *RoboCop* (also known as *RoboCop: The Series*), syndicated, 1994.

Peter McCann, "Leave My Burn Alone," *Side Effects,* CBC, 1995.

Nigel, "Flying Fists of Fury II," *Kung Fu: The Legend Continues,* syndicated, 1995.

"Rumours," *Traders,* Global, 1996.

Uncle Jim, "Plane Crash on Christmas Day," *Real Kids, Real Adventures,* Global, 1998.

Barry Lloyd, "Six Little Letters," *Exhibit A: A Secrets of Forensic Science* (also known as *Secrets of Forensic Science*), 1998.

Dick Twitty, "Vootie–Muck–a–Heev," *The Famous Jett Jackson,* Disney Channel, 1998.

Mr. Wilmott, "New Directions," *Wind at My Back,* CBC, 1999.

Peter Lawyer, "The Trial," *Foolish Heart,* CBC, 1999.

Gavin, "Ethaniel's Story," *Code Name: Eternity* (also known as *Code: Eternity*), syndicated, 2000.

Judge (Kirk Trial), *Monk,* USA Network, 2001.

Colin, "The War of 1812," *Made in Canada* (also known as *The Industry*), CBC, 2002.

"Search Party," *Blue Murder* (also known as *En quete de preuves*), Global, 2003.

"Eyewitness," *Blue Murder* (also known as *En quete de preuves*), Global, 2003.

"Swimmers," *The Eleventh Hour,* CTV, 2004.

Ralph "Bucky" Buckram, "Shuffle Up and Deal," *Tilt,* ESPN, 2005.

Bert Bart, "The Lovely Fred," *Puppets Who Kill,* Comedy Central, 2005.

Kid's dad, "Trees a Crowd," *Corner Gas,* CTV, 2005.

"Taming of the Bitch," *The Shakespeare Comedy Show,* Comedy Network, 2006.

Doctor Richard, "Richard III," *The Shakespeare Comedy Show,* Comedy Network, 2006.

"The Titus Andronicus Show," *The Shakespeare Comedy Show,* Comedy Network, 2006.

Steve–O, "Two of a Kind," *Naturally, Sadie* (also known as *The Complete Freaks of Nature*), Disney Channel, 2006.

Warden Slake, *The State Within,* 2006.

Television Work; Episodic:

Segment director, *Canadian Comedy Shorts,* Comedy Network, 2006.

Producer, *The Shakespeare Comedy Show,* Comedy Network, 2006.

Stage Appearances:
Retribution, Toronto Fringe Festival, Toronto, Ontario, Canada, 1997.
The Dane, 1998.
Demetrius, *A Midsummer Night's Dream,* Festival Theatre, 1999.

Also appeared in *The Illustrated Men.*

Radio Appearances; Specials:
Daniel and cop, *Jacob Two—Two's First Spy Case,* CBC 4 Kids: Radio Festival, 1997.

Radio Appearances; Plays:
Appeared in "A Dream Play," *Great Plays of the Millennium,* CBC.

RECORDINGS

Video Games:
(English version) Voice of inspector, *Rokkuman DASH* (also known as *Mega Man 64, Mega Man Legends, Rockman DASH,* and *Rokkuman DASH: Hagane no boukenshin*), 1997.
Voice, *Aura: Fate of the Ages,* The Adventure Company, 2004.

WRITINGS

Plays:
The Big Victim, 1998.
Johnny Pacheco, 1998.

Screenplays:
The Dane, 1997.
Seven Gates, 1997.

Television Episodes:
The Shakespeare Comedy Show, Comedy Network, 2006.
Canadian Comedy Shorts, Comedy Network, 2006.

HURT, Mary Beth 1948(?)–
    (Mary–Beth Hurt)

PERSONAL

Original name, Mary Beth Supinger; name is sometimes spelled MaryBeth or Marybeth; born September 26, 1948 (some sources cite 1946), in Marshalltown, IA; daughter of Forrest Clayton and Delores Lenore (maiden name, Andre) Supinger; married William Hurt (an actor), 1971 (divorced, 1981 [some sources cite 1982]); married Paul Schrader (a director, producer, actor, writer, and critic), August 6, 1983; children: (second marriage) Molly Johanna, Sam. *Education:* University of Iowa, B.A., 1968; graduate study at New York University, 1971.

Addresses: *Agent*—Paul Martino, International Creative Management, 825 Eighth Ave., New York, NY 10019.

Career: Actress. Appeared in advertisements.

Member: Actors' Equity Association, Screen Actors Guild.

Awards, Honors: Clarence Derwent Award, Actors' Equity Association, 1975, for *Love for Love;* Antoinette Perry Award nomination, best featured actress in a play, 1976, for *Trelawny of the "Wells";* Film Award nomination, best newcomer, British Academy of Film and Television Arts, 1979, for *Interiors;* Obie Award, *Village Voice,* Antoinette Perry Award nomination, and Drama Desk Award nomination, all best actress in a play, 1981, for *Crimes of the Heart;* Antoinette Perry Award nomination, best actress in a play, 1986, for *Benefactors;* Drama Desk Award nomination (with others), outstanding ensemble, 1988, for *The Day Room;* Joe A. Callaway Award, Actors' Equity Association, 1991, for *Othello;* Independent Spirit Award nomination, best supporting female, Independent Features Project/West, 2007, for *The Dead Girl.*

CREDITS

Stage Appearances:
Celia, *As You Like It,* New York Shakespeare Festival, Joseph Papp Public Theater, Delacorte Theater, New York City, 1973.
New Girl in Town, Equity Library Theatre, New York City, 1973.
Nurse and Uncle Remus, *More Than You Deserve,* New York Shakespeare Festival, Joseph Papp Public Theater, Estelle R. Newman Theater, New York City, 1973–74.
Marina, *Pericles, Prince of Tyre* (also known as *Pericles*), New York Shakespeare Festival, Joseph Papp Public Theater, Delacorte Theater, 1974.
Miss Prue, *Love for Love,* New Phoenix Theatre Company, Helen Hayes Theatre, New York City, 1974.
Understudy for Clara, *The Rules of the Game,* New Phoenix Repertory Company, Helen Hayes Theatre, 1974.
Frankie Addams, *Member of the Wedding,* New Phoenix Theatre Company, Helen Hayes Theatre, 1974–75.

Rose Trelawny (title role), *Trelawny of the "Wells,"* Lincoln Center, Vivian Beaumont Theater, New York City, 1975.

Caroline Mitford, *Secret Service,* Playhouse Theatre, New York City, 1976.

Susie, *Boy Meets Girl,* Playhouse Theatre, 1976.

Anya, *The Cherry Orchard,* New York Shakespeare Festival, Lincoln Center, Vivian Beaumont Theater, 1977.

Vi, *Dusa, Fish, Stas, and Vi,* Mark Taper Forum, Los Angeles, 1978.

All–Shakespeare Concert, Lincoln Center, Theater at Alice Tully Hall, New York City, 1978.

Estelle, *Father's Day,* American Place Theatre, New York City, 1979.

Meg Magrath, *Crimes of the Heart,* Manhattan Theatre Club, New York City, 1980, John Golden Theatre, New York City, 1981–82, and Ahmanson Theatre, Los Angeles, 1983.

Lizzie, *The Rainmaker,* Berkshire Theatre Festival, Stockbridge, MA, 1981.

Celimene, *The Misanthrope,* Circle in the Square, New York City, 1983.

Iskra, *The Nest of the Wood Grouse,* New York Shakespeare Festival, Lincoln Center, Estelle R. Newman Theater, 1984.

Sheila, *Benefactors,* Brooks Atkinson Theatre, New York City, 1985–86.

Nurse Walker and Lynette, *The Day Room,* Manhattan Theatre Club Stage I, New York City, 1987–88.

Katherine Glass, *The Secret Rapture,* Ethel Barrymore Theatre, New York City, 1989.

Melissa Gardner, *Love Letters,* Promenade Theatre, New York City, 1989.

Emilia, *Othello,* New York Shakespeare Festival, Joseph Papp Public Theater, Delacorte Theater, 1991.

Dinah, *One Shoe Off,* Second Stage Theatre Company, Joseph Papp Public Theater, Anspacher Theater, New York City, 1993.

Patti, *Oblivion Postponed,* Second Stage Theatre Company, McGinn–Cazale Theatre, New York City, 1995–96.

Julia, *A Delicate Balance,* Plymouth Theatre, New York City, 1996.

Saulina Webb and Sally Webster, *Old Money,* Lincoln Center, Mitzi E. Newhouse Theater, New York City, 2000–2001.

Mercy Lott, *Humble Boy,* Manhattan Theatre Club Stage I, 2003.

Also appeared in other productions, including *The Drunkard* and *Three Wishes for Jamie.* Some sources cite an appearance in *On the Town* (musical).

Film Appearances:

Joey, *Interiors* (also known as *Innenleben, Interieurs, Interiores, Intimidade, Sisaekuvia,* and *Vivodasok*), United Artists, 1978.

Laura Connolly, *Head over Heels* (also known as *Chilly Scenes of Winter*), United Artists, 1979.

Kasey Evans, *A Change of Seasons,* Twentieth Century–Fox, 1980.

Helen Holm, *The World According to Garp,* Warner Bros., 1982.

Joyce Richardson, *D.A.R.Y.L.,* Paramount, 1985.

Peg Tuccio, *Compromising Positions,* Paramount, 1985.

Lily Laemle, *Parents* (also known as *Morgue ao domicilio, O que ha para jantar?, Pfui Teufel!—Daddy ist ein Kannibale,* and *Pranzo misterioso*), Vestron Pictures, 1989.

Ginger Booth, *Slaves of New York,* TriStar, 1990.

Ellie Seldes, *Defenseless,* New Visions/Seven Arts Pictures, 1991.

Kitty, *Six Degrees of Separation,* Metro–Goldwyn–Mayer, 1993.

Mrs. Dingle, *My Boyfriend's Back* (also known as *Johnny Zombie*), Buena Vista, 1993.

Regina Beaufort, *The Age of Innocence,* Columbia, 1993.

Teresa Aranow, *Light Sleeper,* Fine Line Features, 1993.

Jane Gudmanson, *Alkali, Iowa* (short film), Strand Releasing, 1995, edited into *Boys Life 2.*

Jean Seberg, *From the Journals of Jean Seberg* (documentary), 1995, Planet Pictures, 1996.

June Gudmanson, *Boys Life 2* (includes an edited version of *Alkali, Iowa*), Strand Releasing, 1997.

Narrator, *Noisy Nora* (animated short film), c. 1997.

Lillian, *Affliction,* 1997, Lions Gate Films, 1998.

Nurse Constance, *Bringing out the Dead,* Paramount, 1999.

Adelle, *The Family Man* (also known as *Family Man*), Universal, 2000.

Dr. Sibley, *Autumn in New York* (also known as *Amar em Nova Iorque, Es begann im September, Fthinoporo sti Nea Yorki, Hoest i New York, Host i New York, New York en automne, Otono en Nueva York, Outono em Nova York, Syksy New Yorkissa, Toamna la New York,* and *Un automne a New York*), Metro–Goldwyn–Mayer, 2000.

Narrator, *Leo the Late Bloomer* (animated short film), 2001.

(Uncredited) Museum curator, *Red Dragon* (also known as *A Voeroes sarkany, Den rode drage, Dragao vermelho, Dragon rojo, Dragon rouge, El dragon rojo, Punainen lohikaeaerme, Roed drake,* and *Roter Drache*), Universal, 2002.

Judge Brewster, *The Exorcism of Emily Rose* (also known as *The Exorcism of Anneliese Michel* and *Untitled Scott Derrickson Project*), Screen Gems, 2005.

Dorothy Marshall, *Perception,* 2005, Empire Pictures, 2006.

Mrs. Bell, *Lady in the Water,* Warner Bros., 2006.

Ruth, *The Dead Girl,* First Look International, 2006.

Chrissie Morgan, *The Walker,* ThinkFilm, 2007.

Stella Marsh, *Untraceable* (also known as *Streaming Evil*), Screen Gems, 2008.

Television Appearances; Series:
Sheila Bradley, *Tattinger's,* NBC, 1988–89.
Sheila Bradley, *Nick & Hillary,* NBC, 1989.
Andy, *Working It Out* (also known as *The Jane Curtin Show*), NBC, 1990.

Television Appearances; Miniseries:
Voice of Annie Ellis, *The Wild West* (documentary), syndicated, 1993.

Television Appearances; Movies:
Wendy Scott, *Baby Girl Scott,* CBS, 1987.
Dr. Amanda Gordon, *After Amy* (also known as *No Ordinary Baby*), Lifetime, 2001.

Television Appearances; Specials:
Caroline Mitford, "Secret Service," *American Playhouse,* PBS, 1977.
Jane Dent, "The 5:48," *3 by Cheever* (also known as "The Five Forty–Eight," *3 by Cheever* and *3 by Cheever: The 5:48*), broadcast on *Great Performances,* PBS, 1979.
"It's the Willingness," *Visions,* KCET (PBS affiliate), c. 1980.
Mother, "Shimmer," *American Playhouse,* PBS, 1995.

Television Appearances; Episodic:
Karen Foster, "A Shield for Murder: Parts 1 & 2," *Kojak,* CBS, 1976.
Emily Dickinson, "I'm Nobody, Who Are You?," *thirtysomething,* ABC, 1990.
Sela Dixon, "Deceit," *Law & Order* (also known as *Law & Order Prime*), NBC, 1996.
Eleanor Waclawek, "Someone to Watch over Me," *The Beat* (also known as *Flesh & Blood*), UPN, 2000.
Jessica Blaine–Todd, "Greed," *Law & Order: Special Victims Unit* (also known as *Law & Order's Sex Crimes, Law & Order: SVU,* and *Special Victims Unit*), NBC, 2002.

Appeared in other programs, including an appearance as Adelaide in "The Brother of the Bride," an unaired episode of *Monty,* Fox.

Television Appearances; Pilots:
(As Mary–Beth Hurt) *Ann in Blue,* ABC, 1974.
Susan Mabry, *Royce,* CBS, 1976.

RECORDINGS

Audiobooks; Reader:
Kevin Henkes, *A Weekend with Wendell,* Scholastic, 1986.
Barbara Taylor Bradford, *Remember,* Random House Audio, 1991.

Teresa Carpenter, *Mob Girl: A Woman's Life in the Underworld* (also known as *Mob Girl*), HarperCollins, 1992.
Alice Miller, *The Drama of the Gifted Child: The Search for the True Self,* HarperCollins, 1992.
Anne Wilson Schaef, *Beyond Therapy beyond Science,* HarperCollins, 1992.
Louisa May Alcott, *Little Women,* Random House Audio, 1994.
Jane Hamilton, *A Map of the World,* Random House Audio, 1995.
Cathleen Schine, *The Love Letter,* Random House Audio, 1996.
Elizabeth Richards, *Every Day,* Random House Audio, 1997.
Jane Langton, *The Fledgling,* Listening Library, 2000.
Jane Smiley, *Horse Heaven,* Random House Audio, 2000.
Nicholas Sparks, *The Rescue,* Hachette Audio, 2000.
Russell Banks, *The Darling,* Sound Library, 2004.
Ann Rule, *Bitter Harvest: A Woman's Fury, a Mother's Sacrifice,* Simon & Schuster Audio, 2005.
Elizabeth George Speare, *The Witch of Blackbird Pond,* Listening Library, 2007.

Videos:
Herself, *Reflections of Lady in the Water* (short), Warner Home Video, 2006.

OTHER SOURCES

Periodicals:
New York Times, November 2, 1989.
New York Times Biographical Service, February 2, 1986, pp. 170–71.
Oui, December, 1980, p. 161.

HUSS, Toby 1966–

PERSONAL

Born December 9, 1966, in Marshalltown, IA; married; children: one daughter. *Education:* Attended the University of Iowa.

Addresses: *Agent*—The Agency Group, 1880 Century Park East, Suite 711, Century City, CA 90067.

Career: Actor, voice performer, and comedian. Appeared in several promotional spots for MTV. Also a painter.

CREDITS

Television Appearances; Series:

Artie (the strongest man in the world), *The Adventures of Pete & Pete* (also known as *Pete and Pete* and *Pete & Pete*), Nickelodeon, 1993–95.

Voices of Todd and others, *Beavis and Butt–Head* (animated; also known as *The Bad Boys* and *Beavis and Butt–head*), MTV, 1993–97.

Voices of Kahn Souphanousinphone, Sr., Joe Jack, Cotton Hill, and others, *King of the Hill* (animated), Fox, beginning 1997.

Corporal Rusty Link, *The Army Show,* The WB, 1998.

Himself, *The Martin Short Show,* syndicated, 1999–2000.

Jupiter, *Nikki,* The WB, 2000–2002.

Hank, a recurring role, *One on One,* UPN, 2002–2003.

Felix "Stumpy" Dreifuss, *Carnivale,* HBO, 2003–2005.

Big Mike and other characters, *Reno 911!,* Comedy Central, beginning 2003.

Also appeared as Dr. Eric Singleton, *Days of Our Lives* (also known as *Cruise of Deception: Days of Our Lives, Days, DOOL, Des jours et des vies, Horton–sagaen, I gode og onde dager, Los dias de nuestras vidas, Meres agapis, Paeivien viemaeae, Vaara baesta aar, Zeit der Sehnsucht,* and *Zile din viata noastra*), NBC.

Television Appearances; Miniseries:

Stewart, *Pilot Season,* Trio, 2004.

Television Appearances; Movies:

Ansel Adams, *Windy City Heat,* Comedy Central, 2003.

Television Appearances; Specials:

Artie (the strongest man in the world), *What We Did on Our Summer Vacation* (also known as *The Adventures of Pete and Pete: What We Did on Our Summer Vacation*), Nickelodeon, 1991.

Artie (the strongest man in the world), *Apocalypse Pete* (also known as *The Adventures of Pete and Pete: Apocalypse Pete*), Nickelodeon, 1992.

Artie (the strongest man in the world), *Space, Geeks and Johnny Unitas* (also known as *The Adventures of Pete and Pete: Space, Geeks and Johnny Unitas*), Nickelodeon, 1992.

Artie (the strongest man in the world), *New Year's Pete* (also known as *The Adventures of Pete and Pete: New Year's Pete*), Nickelodeon, 1993.

Felix "Stumpy" Dreifuss, *Making "Carnivale": The Show behind the Show,* HBO, 2003.

Television Appearances; Awards Presentations:

1994 MTV Movie Awards, MTV, 1994.

Television Appearances; Episodic:

Performer of "Reverend Tex Stoveheadbottom," "Spoken Word II," *Unplugged* (also known as *MTV Unplugged*), MTV, 1994.

Junior, "Xmas Story," *NewsRadio* (also known as *News Radio, The Station, Dias de radio,* and *Dies de radio*), NBC, 1995.

Second guard, "Friends," *NewsRadio* (also known as *News Radio, The Station, Dias de radio,* and *Dies de radio*), NBC, 1995.

Jack, "The Junk Mail," *Seinfeld* (also known as *The Seinfeld Chronicles* and *Stand–Up*), NBC, 1997.

Voice of Terror, "Hercules and the Owl of Athens," *Hercules* (animated; also known as *Disney's "Hercules"*), ABC and syndicated, 1998.

Jack Frost, "Stinkbutt," *NewsRadio* (also known as *News Radio, The Station, Dias de radio,* and *Dies de radio*), NBC, 1999.

Voices of Rikki and pirate rats, "Beavemaster/Deck Poops," *The Angry Beavers* (animated), Nickelodeon, 2001.

Voice of coach and floating head, "Shore Leave," *Home Movies* (animated), Cartoon Network, 2002.

Voice, "Hip Hop to the Godfather," *Kid Notorious* (animated), Comedy Central, 2003.

Voice of Ernie Devlin, "The Devlin Made Me Do It," *Harvey Birdman, Attorney at Law* (animated), Cartoon Network, 2004.

Voices of Ernie Devlin and Shado, "Harvey's Civvy," *Harvey Birdman, Attorney at Law* (animated), Cartoon Network, 2005.

Lenny, "The Mattress," *Help Me Help You,* ABC, 2006.

Lenny, "Perseverance," *Help Me Help You,* ABC, 2006.

Voice of Ernie Devlin, "Grodin," *Harvey Birdman, Attorney at Law* (animated), Cartoon Network, 2006.

Limousine driver, "The Freak Book," *Curb Your Enthusiasm* (also known as *Curb*), HBO, 2007.

Appeared in other programs, including an appearance as Roy Kretchmar in "35 Hours," an episode of *The Adventures of Pete & Pete* (also known as *Pete and Pete* and *Pete & Pete*), Nickelodeon.

Television Appearances; Pilots:

The Duplex, NBC, 1999.

Three Strikes, Comedy Central, 2006.

Television Additional Voices; Series:

King of the Hill (animated), Fox, beginning 1997.

Film Appearances:

Patrick Schliesman, *The Adventures of Roo* (short film), 1984.

Clerk, *Zadar! Cow from Hell,* 1989.

Himself, *Cracking Up,* c. 1993, Phaedra Cinema, 1998.

Ted, *Hand Gun* (also known as *Handgun*), Shooting Gallery/Odessa Motion Picture Corporation, 1994.

The Salesman and Other Adventures (short film), 1994.

Kenny, *The Basketball Diaries* (also known as *Basketball Diaries* and *The Streets of New York*), New Line Cinema, 1995.

Doubting Thomas minister, *Dear God* (also known as *Cher bon Dieu, Deus nos Acuda!, Hej gud, Hilfe, ich Komm' in den Himmel, Querido Deus, Suoraan sydaemestae,* and *Un timador con alas*), Paramount, 1996.

Sammy Cybernowski, *Dogs: The Rise and Fall of an All–Girl Bookie Joint,* The Asylum, 1996.

Seaman Nitro Mike, *Down Periscope* (also known as *Abajo el periscopio, Cilgin denizalti, Giu le mani dal mio periscopio, Locos a bordo, Mission—Rohr frei!, Nagi peryskop, Nao mexas no meu periscopio, Periskope dol!, Perskooppi pystyyn, Titta, vi dyker!, Touche pas a mon periscope, Tuez a viz ala,* and *Y a–t–il un commandant pour sauver la Navy?*), Twentieth Century–Fox, 1996.

Steve Remo, *Jerry Maguire* (also known as *The Agent*), TriStar, 1996.

Voices of second television thief, concierge, bellboy, and male television reporter, *Beavis and Butt–head Do America* (animated; also known as *Beavis and Butt–Head*), Paramount, 1996.

(Uncredited) Fake ID salesperson, *Vegas Vacation* (also known as *National Lampoon's "Las Vegas Vacation"* and *National Lampoon's "Vegas Vacation"*), Warner Bros., 1997.

Cameron, *Still Breathing,* October Films, 1998.

Donut shop patron, *Shock Television* (also known as *Shock TV*), Filmmakers Alliance, 1998.

Rastus, *Clubland,* Legacy Releasing, 1999.

Red, *The Mod Squad,* Metro–Goldwyn–Mayer, 1999.

Voice of AmeriShine, *A Good Baby,* Curb Entertainment, 1999.

The Wetonkawa Flash, 1999, Indican Pictures, 2006.

Lance, Jerry, Alejandro, beach jock, and Jerry Turner, *Bedazzled* (also known as *Teuflisch*), Twentieth Century–Fox, 2000.

Dykes, *Beyond the City Limits* (also known as *Rip It Off* and *Rip Off*), Spartan Home Entertainment, 2001.

Puff's father, *Human Nature,* Fine Line Features, 2001.

Voice of Tennessee, *The Country Bears* (also known as *The Bears, Beary e os ursos campos, Beary—karhun suuri seikkailu, Die country Bears—Hier tobt der Baer, La grand aventura de Beary,* and *Les country bears*), Buena Vista, 2002.

Spook, *Rescue Dawn,* Metro–Goldwyn–Mayer, 2006.

Glen the desk clerk, *Reno 911!: Miami* (also known as *Reno 911!: Miami: The Movie*), Twentieth Century–Fox, 2007.

Groundskeeper, *Balls of Fury,* Rogue Pictures, 2007.

RECORDINGS

Videos:

Frank Sinatra impersonator, *I Want My MTV* (animated short film), MTV Home Video/Sony Music Entertainment, 1996.

Himself, *The Making of "King of the Hill,"* Twentieth Century–Fox Home Entertainment, 2003.

Commentator, *The Adventures of Pete & Pete,* season two, Nickelodeon/Paramount, 2005.

Music Videos:

Sheryl Crow, "A Change Would Do You Good," 1997.

Video Games:

Voice, *Beavis and Butt–Head in Virtual Stupidity,* Viacom, 1995.

WRITINGS

Teleplays; with Others; Episodic:

The Martin Short Show, syndicated, 1999–2000.

HUSSEY, Olivia 1951–

PERSONAL

Original name, Olivia Osuna; born April 17, 1951, in Buenos Aires, Argentina; daughter of Andreas Osuna (a singer; also known as Isvaldo Ribo) and Joy Alma Hussey (a legal secretary); married Dean Paul Martin (an actor and musician), April 17, 1971 (divorced, 1978); married Paul Ryan (a songwriter), 1978 (some sources cite 1979; divorced); married Akira Fuse (a singer and composer), February 18, 1980 (divorced, 1989); married David Glenn Eisley (a musician, actor, and stunt performer), 1991; children: (first marriage) Alexander (an actor); (third marriage) Max; (fourth marriage) India Joy. *Education:* Studied acting at the Italia Conti Stage School, London.

Addresses: *Agent*—Diverse Talent Group, 1875 Century Park East, Suite 2250, Los Angeles, CA 90067. *Manager*—Richard Schwartz, Richard Schwartz Management, 2934 1/2 Beverly Glen Circle, Suite 107, Bel Air, CA 90077.

Career: Actress, voice performer, and lyricist. Appeared in advertisements.

Awards, Honors: Golden Globe Award, most promising newcomer—female, New York Film Critics Award, best actress, and Targa d'Oro, most promising actress, and best actress, David DiDonatello awards, all 1969, and nomination for Golden Laurel Award, best female new face, Producers Guild of America, 1970, all for *Romeo and Juliet;* Annie Award nomination, outstanding individual achievement for voice acting by a female performer in an animated television production, International Animated Film Society, 2001, for "Out of the Past," *Batman Beyond.*

CREDITS

Film Appearances:
Donna, *The Battle of the Villa Fiorita* (also known as *Affair at the Villa Fiorita*), Warner Bros., 1965.

Jinny as a child, *Cup Fever,* CFF, 1965.

Juliet, *Romeo and Juliet* (also known as *Romeo e Giulietta*), Paramount, 1968.

Val, *All the Right Noises,* 1969, Twentieth Century–Fox, 1973.

H–Bomb (also known as *Great Friday* and *Operation Alpha*), 1971.

Maria, *Lost Horizon,* Columbia, 1973.

Tania Scarlotti, *Un verano para matar* (also known as *The Summertime Killer, Meurtres au soleil,* and *Ricatto alla mala*), Avco–Embassy Pictures, 1973.

Jessica "Jess" Bradford, *Black Christmas* (also known as *Silent Night, Evil Night, Stranger in the House,* and *Noel tragique*), Ambassador Film Distributors/ Warner Bros., 1974.

Rosalie Otterbourne, *Death on the Nile* (also known as *Agatha Christie's "Death on the Nile," Assassinio sul Nilo, Doden paa Nilen, Doeden paa Nilen, Eglima sto Neilo, Kuolema Niilillae, Morte no Nilo, Morte sobre o Nilo, Mort sur le Nil, Smierc Nilu,* and *Tod auf dem Nil*), Paramount, 1978.

Cicily Young, *The Cat and the Canary,* Cinema Shares, 1979.

Elsa Borsht, *The Man with Bogart's Face* (also known as *Sam Marlowe, Private Eye*), Twentieth Century–Fox, 1980.

Marit, *Fukkatsu no hi* (also known as *Day of Resurrection, The End,* and *Virus*), Media, 1980.

Chris Walters, *Turkey Shoot* (also known as *Blood Camp Thatcher* and *Escape 2000*), New World Pictures, 1983.

Amy Marks, *Distortions,* Cori, 1987.

Therese, *La bottega dell'orefice* (also known as *Bonds of Love, The Jeweller's Shop, Der Laden des Goldschmieds,* and *La boutique de l'orfevre*), Alliance Entertainment, 1988.

Rebecca Eche, *Sheng zhan feng yun* (also known as *Undeclared War, La guerre sans om,* and *Sing chin fung wan*), 1990.

Gail, *Save Me,* Entertainment in Video, 1993.

The Mannerjay, *Quest of the Delta Knights,* Hemdale Home Video, 1994.

Nurse Wharton, *Ice Cream Man,* A–pix Entertainment, 1995.

Bad English I: Tales of a Son of a Brit, Bad English Productions, 1995.

Jewel, *Seven Days of Grace* (also known as *Saving Grace*), Picture Perfect Productions, 1996.

Voice of the Ancients, *The Dark Mist* (also known as *Lord Protector*), Alpine Releasing/Smooth Pictures, 1996.

Mrs. Carter, *The Gardener* (also known as *The Garden of Evil* and *Silent Screams*), 1998.

Laura, *El grito* (also known as *Bloody Proof*), 2000.

Catherine Gaits, *Island Prey,* 2001.

Dr. Karen Murphy, *Headspace,* Freestyle Releasing, 2006.

Rachel, *Three Priests,* Gum Spirits Productions, 2007.

Harvest Moon, Capricorn 23 Productions/ThunderBall Films, 2007.

Petra, *Tortilla Heaven,* Archangel Entertainment, 2007.

Mrs. Duncan, *Chinaman's Chance,* Mustardseed–Films/ Crafted Films, 2008.

Television Appearances; Miniseries:
Virgin Mary, *Jesus of Nazareth* (also known as *Gesu di Nazareth*), NBC, 1977.

Alicia, *The Bastard* (also known as *The Kent Chronicles* and *Kent Family Chronicles*), Operation Prime Time, 1978.

Leila, *The Pirate* (also known as *Harold Robbins' "The Pirate"*), CBS, 1978.

Ione, *The Last Days of Pompeii,* ABC, 1984.

Audra Phillips Denbrough, *It* (also known as *Stephen King's "It"*), ABC, 1990.

Herself, *The 100 Scariest Movie Moments,* Bravo, 2004.

Television Appearances; Movies:
Mrs. Ken's daughter, *The Crunch,* 1964.

Annamaria de Guidice, *The Corsican Brothers* (also known as *Vendetta*), CBS, 1985.

Norma Bates, *Psycho IV: The Beginning,* Showtime, 1990.

Rosie, *Dead Man's Island,* CBS, 1996.

Therapist, *Shame, Shame, Shame* (also known as *Climax*), The Movie Channel, 1998.

Mother Teresa (title role), *Madre Teresa* (also known as *Mother Teresa, Mother Teresa of Calcutta,* and *Teresa*), 2003.

Television Appearances; Specials:
(In archive footage) Rosalie Otterbourne, *Death on the Nile: Making of Featurette,* 1978.

Esther, *The Thirteenth Day: The Story of Esther* (also known as *The Bible*), ABC, 1979.

Rebecca, "Ivanhoe," *Hallmark Hall of Fame,* CBS, 1982.

Judge, *Miss Hollywood, 1986,* CBS, 1986.

Herself, *The Great Christmas Movies,* American Movie Classics, 1998.

Television Appearances; Episodic:
Herself, *The Tonight Show Starring Johnny Carson* (also known as *The Best of Carson*), NBC, 1973.

Kitty Trumbull, "Sing a Song of Murder," *Murder, She Wrote,* CBS, 1985.

Olivia Jessup, "Firebrand," *Lonesome Dove: The Series* (also known as *Lonesome Dove*), CTV (Canada) and syndicated, 1993.

Olivia Jessup, "Law and Order," *Lonesome Dove: The Series* (also known as *Lonesome Dove*), CTV and syndicated, 1993.

Olivia Jessup, "Where the Heart Is," *Lonesome Dove: The Series* (also known as *Lonesome Dove*), CTV and syndicated, 1993.

Aunt Prudence Curtis, "A Long Walk to Pittsburgh: Part 2," *Boy Meets World* (also known as *Cory si restul lumii, Crescere che fatica, Das Leben und ich, De wereld om de hoek, Du store verden!, Et gutteliv, Incorigible Cory, Isojen poikien leikit, O mundo e dos jovens, O rapaz e o mundo,* and *Yo y el mundo*), ABC, 1997.

Herself, "Anthony Perkins," *The E! True Hollywood Story* (also known as *Anthony Perkins: The E! True Hollywood Story* and *THS*), E! Entertainment Television, 1998.

Voice of the queen, "Brainie the Poo/Melancholy Brain," *Pinky & the Brain* (animated), The WB, 1998.

Voice of Talia, "The Demon Reborn," *Superman* (animated; also known as *The New Batman/Superman Adventures* and *Superman: The Animated Series*), The WB, 1998.

Voice of Talia, "Out of the Past," *Batman Beyond* (animated; also known as *Batman of the Future, Batman Tomorrow, Batman del futuro, Batman do futuro,* and *Fremtidens Batman*), The WB, 2000.

Herself, "Malibu Charity Bash," *I Married a Princess,* Lifetime, 2005.

Stage Appearances:

Jenny, *The Prime of Miss Jean Brodie,* Theatre Royal, Brighton, England, 1966, Wyndham's Theatre, London, beginning 1966.

Some sources cite appearances in other productions.

RECORDINGS

Videos:

"Liberian Girl," *Michael Jackson: HIStory on Film—Volume II,* Epic Music Video/Sony Music, 1997.

Herself, *The 12 Days of "Black Christmas,"* Critical Mass Productions, 2006.

Herself, *The 21st Annual Genesis Awards,* 2007.

Music Videos:

Michael Jackson, "Liberian Girl," 1989.

Video Games:

Voice of Kasan Moor, *Star Wars: Rogue Squadron,* 1998.

Voices of AT–AA driver and Abridon refugee, *Star Wars: Force Commander,* 2000.

WRITINGS

Song Lyrics:

Wrote lyrics for songs published in Japan.

OTHER SOURCES

Periodicals:

People Weekly, March 16, 1992, pp. 53–55.

J

JOHNSON, Shelly

PERSONAL

Born in Pasadena, CA. *Education:* Pasadena Art Center College of Design, graduated, 1980.

Career: Cinematographer. Also worked as camera operator and photographer. Painter, with work exhibited in galleries and national shows, and at the Ventura County Museum.

Member: American Society of Cinematographers.

Awards, Honors: American Society of Cinematographers Award nominations, outstanding achievement in cinematography in a movie of the week or pilot, 1990, for *Everybody's Baby: The Rescue of Jessica McClure,* and 1998, for *The Inheritance;* American Society of Cinematographers Award nomination, outstanding achievement in cinematography in episodic television series, 2001, for *The Others;* has won awards for his paintings.

CREDITS

Film Cinematographer:
Maid to Order, New Century/Vista Film Company, 1987.
Nightflyers (also known as *Nightfliers* and *Night Flyers*), New Century/Vista Film Company, 1987.
Jack's Back, Paramount, 1988.
Hitz (also known as *Judgement* and *Judgment*), Vidmark Entertainment, c. 1992.
True Lies, Twentieth Century–Fox, 1994.
Amanda, Sony Pictures Entertainment, 1996.
Jurassic Park III (also known as *The Extinction: Jurassic Park 3, JP3, Jurassic Park 3, Jurassic Park 3: Breakout, Jurassic Park 3: The Extinction, Return to the Island: Jurassic Park 3, Jurassic Park III: Parque jurasico III, Jurski park 3, Le parc jurassique III,* and *Parc jurassic III*), Universal, 2001.
The Last Castle (also known as *The Castle* and *Untitled Rod Lurie Project*), DreamWorks, 2001.
Hidalgo (also known as *Dash* and *Ocean of Fire*), Buena Vista, 2004.
I Know What Boys Like, Columbia, 2008.
They Came from Upstairs, Twentieth Century–Fox, 2008.

Film Director of Photography:
Teenage Mutant Ninja Turtles II: The Secret of the Ooze (also known as *Mutant Ninja Turtles 2* and *Teenage Mutant Ninja Turtles 2*), New Line Cinema, 1991.
Sky High, Buena Vista, 2005.
Jurassic Park IV (also known as *JP4, Jurassic Park 4,* and *Jurassic Park IV: The Extinction*), Universal, 2008.

Film Work; Other:
Additional photographer, *Native Son,* Cinecom Pictures, 1986.
Camera operator for snow unit, *True Lies,* Twentieth Century–Fox, 1994.

Television Director of Photography; Series:
Charlie Grace, ABC, 1995.
Turks, CBS, 1999.
The Others, NBC, 2000.

Television Camera Operator; Series:
The Grand Tour, beginning c. 1985.

Television Director of Photography; Miniseries:
The Fire Next Time (also known as *American Inferno*), CBS, 1993.

Ride with the Wind, ABC, 1994.

Naomi & Wynonna: Love Can Build a Bridge (also known as *Love Can Build a Bridge*), NBC, 1995.

The Shining (also known as *Shining, Stephen King "Shining,"* and *Stephen King's "The Shining"*), ABC, 1997.

Television Director of Photography; Movies:

Red River, CBS, 1988.

Unholy Matrimony (also known as *Deadly Vows*), CBS, 1988.

Everybody's Baby: The Rescue of Jessica McClure, ABC, 1989.

Love and Betrayal (also known as *Throw Away Wives*), Fox, 1989.

Angel of Death (also known as *Intimate Terror: Angel of Death*), CBS, 1990.

The Girl Who Came between Them (also known as *Victim of Innocence*), NBC, 1990.

Joshua's Heart, NBC, 1990.

Keeper of the City (also known as *Lethal Justice*), Showtime, 1991.

Back to the Streets of San Francisco, NBC, 1992.

Grave Secrets: The Legacy of Hilltop Drive (also known as *Grave Secrets*), CBS, 1992.

Something to Live for: The Alison Gertz Story (also known as *Fatal Love*), ABC, 1992.

Judgment Day: The John List Story, CBS, 1993.

Murder of Innocence, CBS, 1993.

Relentless: Mind of a Killer, NBC, 1993.

Nowhere to Hide, ABC, 1994.

Trick of the Eye (also known as *Primal Secrets*), CBS, 1994.

The Yarn Princess (also known as *More Than a Miracle*), ABC, 1994.

Alien Nation: Body and Soul (also known as *Alien Nation—Die neue Generation, Muukalaiset—ruumis ja sielu, Os novos invasores de corpo e alma,* and *Przybysze—Cialo i dusza*), Fox, 1995.

In the Line of Duty: Kidnapped (also known as *Kidnapped: In the Line of Duty*), NBC, 1995.

Alien Nation: Millennium, Fox, 1996.

Blue Rodeo, CBS, 1996.

The Devil's Child (also known as *Devil to Pay*), ABC, 1997.

The Inheritance (also known as *Louisa May Alcott's "The Inheritance"*), CBS, 1997.

Quicksilver Highway, Fox, 1997.

Tell Me No Secrets, ABC, 1997.

Virtual Obsession (also known as *Host*), ABC, 1998.

Come On, Get Happy: The Partridge Family Story (also known as *C'Mon, Get Happy: The Partridge Family Story, Come on, get happy—Die Partridge Familie, Den sanna historien om familjen Partridge,* and *Partridge familyn tarina*), ABC, 1999.

Additional director of photography, *Manhood*, Showtime, 2003.

Television Director of Photography; Specials:

Cartoon All-Stars to the Rescue, multiple networks, 1990.

"Saint Maybe" (also known as "Anne Tyler's 'Saint Maybe'"), *Hallmark Hall of Fame*, CBS, 1998.

"Durango" (also known as "A Rose for Annie"), *Hallmark Hall of Fame*, CBS, 1999.

"A Season for Miracles," *Hallmark Hall of Fame* (also known as *Hallmark Hall of Fame: A Season for Miracles*), CBS, 1999.

Television Photographer; Specials:

"Malcolm Takes a Shot," *CBS Schoolbreak Special*, CBS, 1990.

Television Director of Photography; Episodic:

"Korman's Kalamity," *Tales from the Crypt* (also known as *HBO's "Tales from the Crypt"*), HBO, 1990.

Television Director of Photography; Pilots:

Grand Slam, syndicated, 1990.

Nick's Game, 1993.

Frogmen, NBC, 1994.

JOINER, Rusty 1972–

PERSONAL

Full name, Jason Russell Joiner; born December 11, 1972, in Montgomery, AL. *Education:* Attended Georgia Southern University.

Career: Actor. Former model, appearing in runway work and campaigns for Abercrombie and Fitch, Prada, American Eagle, Levi's, Rips Underwear, Jockey, Naya Spring Water, and Powerade sports drinks; official Structure Underwear Model, 1998–2000; appeared on numerous magazine covers, including Men's Fitness Magazine eleven times. Active in charitable work for Project Angel Food and the Leukemia and Lymphoma Society.

CREDITS

Film Appearances:

Blade, *Dodgeball: A True Underdog Story* (also known as *Dodgeball* and *Voll auf die nusse*), Twentieth Century–Fox, 2004.

Bruce Stein, *Idol*, Indie–Pictures, 2006.

Eddie, *Resident Evil: Extinction*, Screen Gems, 2007.

Television Appearances; Movies:

Costar, *The Commuters*, 2005.

Television Appearances; Specials:
CMT: The Greatest—Sexiest Southern Women, Country Music Television, 2006.
CMT: The Greatest—Sexiest Southern Men, Country Music Television, 2006.
CMT: The Greatest—20 Sexiest Videos of 2006, Country Music Television, 2006.

Television Appearances; Episodic:
Man in store, "All the Wrong Moves," *Spin City,* ABC, 2000.
Pretty blonde boy, "Rap Sheet," *CSI: Miami,* CBS, 2004.
Ronny, "Dead Man, Live Bet," *Dr. Vegas,* CBS, 2004.
Rock–climbing instructor Brett, "Shot in the Dark," *ER,* NBC, 2004.
Charlie, "The Man in the Bear," *Bones,* Fox, 2005.
Matthew Toobin, "Maternal Instinct," *Close to Home,* CBS, 2007.
Danny Jones, "Manhunt," *The Closer,* TNT, 2007.

OTHER SOURCES

Electronic:
Rusty Joiner Website, http://www.rustyjoiner.com, October 20, 2007.

JONES, Gary 1958–

PERSONAL

Born January 4, 1958, in Swansea, Wales; married Meg Cameron; children: three. *Education:* Attended schools in Swansea, Wales.

Career: Actor and writer. Vancouver TheatreSports League (improvisational group), Vancouver, British Columbia, Canada, actor and writer. Appeared at conventions, including serving as the host of a panel at Comic–Con International, San Diego, CA, 2007. Worked as an art director for a newspaper in Burlington, Ontario, Canada; also worked at an advertising agency in Hamilton, Ontario, Canada.

Awards, Honors: Jessie Richardson Theatre Award (with Shawn MacDonald), Vancouver Professional Theatre Alliance, 1997, for *Fear Not;* Leo Award nomination for comedy writing, Motion Picture Arts and Sciences Foundation of British Columbia.

CREDITS

Television Appearances; Series:
(And sometimes in archive footage) Walter Harriman, *Stargate SG–1* (also known as *La porte des etoiles* and *Stargaate SG–1*), Showtime and syndicated, 1997–2002, Sci–Fi Channel and syndicated, 2002–2007.
Walter Harriman, *Stargate: Atlantis* (also known as *La porte d'Atlantis*), Sci–Fi Channel, beginning 2004.

Television Appearances; Miniseries:
J. Schroeder, *And the Sea Will Tell* (also known as *Nur die See kennt die Warheit*), CBS, 1991.

Television Appearances; Movies:
Bernard Brewster, *Double, Double, Toil and Trouble* (also known as *Abracadabra*), 1993.
Elliott, *The Substitute,* 1993.
Mr. Green, *Relentless: Mind of a Killer* (also known as *Mood Indigo*), NBC, 1993.
X–ray technician, *When a Stranger Calls Back,* Showtime, 1993.
Carriage driver, *This Can't Be Love* (also known as *Liebe ist Nicht Bloss ein Wort*), 1994.
Floor manager, *Ebbie,* Lifetime, 1995.
Production assistant, *A Dream Is a Wish Your Heart Makes: The Annette Funicello Story* (also known as *A Dream Is a Wish Your Heart Makes*), CBS, 1995.
Third reporter, *Bye Bye, Birdie* (musical), ABC, 1995.
First Alberta Railway police officer, *Heck's Way Home* (also known as *Kalte Schnauze–treues Herz* and *Un drole de cabot*), 1996.
Leonard Drake, *Murder at My Door,* 1996.
Television host, *Bloodhounds II* (also known as *Blood-Hounds 2*), USA Network, 1996.
Attendant, "Angels in the Endzone," *The Wonderful World of Disney,* ABC, 1997.
Gil Naspeth, *Doomsday Rock* (also known as *Cosmic Shock* and *Asteroidenfeuer—Die Erede explodiert*), Family Channel, 1997.
Nick Smythe, *Cabin Pressure* (also known as *Hijack'd*), PAX TV, 2001.
Television standards executive, *Behind the Camera: The Unauthorized Story of "Charlie's Angels,"* NBC, 2004.
Dr. Lycar, *12 Hours to Live,* Lifetime, 2006.
Ron Isley, *Christmas on Chestnut Street* (also known as *The Competition*), Lifetime, 2006.

Television Appearances; Specials:
Sailor, *H.M.S. Pinafore* (opera; also known as *H.M.S. Pinafore: The Lass That Loved a Sailor* and *The Lass That Loved a Sailor*), [Australia and New Zealand], 1997.
Sketch comedian, *The Western Alienation Comedy Hour,* CBC, 2002.
Himself, *Sci Fi Inside: Stargate SG–1 200th Episode,* Sci–Fi Channel, 2006.

Television Appearances; Episodic:
Video director, "Aquarium Rock," *Danger Bay,* CBC and Disney Channel, 1986.

Computer technician, "Rogue Warrior," *Airwolf* (also known as *Airwolf II*), USA Network, 1987.

Shadow, "Heir to the Throne," *Wiseguy,* CBS, 1989.

Shadow, "Sins of the Father," *Wiseguy,* CBS, 1989.

Mr. Roberts, "Rounding Third," *21 Jump Street,* Fox, 1990.

Reporter, "Hi Mom," *21 Jump Street,* Fox, 1990.

Third reporter, "Crazy," *Booker* (also known as *Booker, P.I.*), Fox, 1990.

Veterinarian, "The Big Fix," *The Black Stallion* (also known as *The Adventures of the Black Stallion, The New Adventures of the Black Stallion,* and *L'etalon noir*), YTV (Canada) and Family Channel, 1990.

"Tammy Tell Me True," *Glory Days,* Fox, 1990.

Driver, "Guns and Sons" (also known as "Kinderhand am Abzug"), *The Commish,* ABC, 1992.

Klein, "Bad Day in Building A," *Highlander* (also known as *Highlander: The Series*), syndicated, 1992.

Himself, *Friday Night with Ralph Benmergui,* 1993.

Reporter, "Sons and Mudders," *Birdland,* ABC, 1994.

Accountant, "Rainbow Comix," *The Marshal,* ABC, 1995.

Michael Hurley, "The Prince of Wails," *Sliders,* Fox, 1995.

Television host, "If These Walls Could Talk," *The Outer Limits* (also known as *The New Outer Limits*), Showtime, Sci–Fi Channel, and syndicated, 1995.

Duncan, "A Stitch in Time," *The Outer Limits* (also known as *The New Outer Limits*), Showtime, Sci–Fi Channel, and syndicated, 1996.

Hotel guest, "The End of Innocence," *Highlander* (also known as *Highlander: The Series*), syndicated, 1996.

Michael Hurley, "Time Again and World," *Sliders,* Fox, 1996.

Mr. Jones, "Vendetta," *The Sentinel,* UPN, 1997.

Ed Barker, "The Internment" (also known as "Die verfluchte Stadt"), *Poltergeist: The Legacy* (also known as *Poltergeist, El legado, Poltergeist—Die unheimliche Macht, Poltergeist: El legado,* and *Poltergeist, les aventuriers du surnaturel*), Showtime and syndicated, 1998.

Poker player, "Pay the Line," *The Net,* USA Network, 1999.

"Sit, Duke," *Hollywood Off–Ramp,* E! Entertainment Television, 2000.

Dr. Ludlow, "Gather Up All the Little People," *Da Vinci's Inquest,* CBC, 2002.

Bill, "Bob & Carol & Len & Ali," *Cold Squad* (also known as *Files from the Past, Cold Squad, brigade speciale,* and *Halott uegyek*), CTV (Canada), 2003.

Chuck, "Reaping Havoc," *Dead Like Me* (also known as *Dead Girl, Mitt liv som doed,* and *Tan muertos como yo*), Showtime, 2003.

Woody, "Abridging the Devil's Divide," *Andromeda* (also known as *Gene Roddenberry's "Andromeda"*), syndicated, 2004.

Eric Beener, "Loneliest Number," *The L Word* (also known as *Earthlings*), Showtime, 2005.

Roger Ballchant, "The Girl from Upper Gaborski," *Young Blades,* i (Independent Television), 2005.

Himself, *RoundTable,* [Canada], 2005.

Dr. Erich Saunders, "Trial by Fire," *Painkiller Jane,* Sci–Fi Channel, 2007.

Appeared in other programs, including an appearance as La May in "Overage," an episode of *Palace Guard,* CBS.

Television Appearances; Pilots:

Glory Days, Fox, 1990.

Captain Michael Hurley, *Sliders,* Fox, 1995.

Walter Davis, *Stargate SG–1: Children of the Gods* (also known as *Stargate SG–1, La porte des etoiles,* and *Stargaate SG–1*), Showtime and syndicated, 1997.

Television Appearances; Other:

Channel 92, 1995.

Television Work; Series:

Story editor, *Big Sound,* CanWest Global Television, 2000–2001.

Film Appearances:

Fan at party, *Postcards from the Edge,* Columbia, 1990.

Jackson, *Bingo!* (also known as *Bingo*), TriStar, 1991.

Lance Tindall, *Andre* (also known as *Andre the Seal, Andre—den fantastiska saelungen, Andre—Die kleine Robbe, Andre, una foca en mi casa, Saelen Andre,* and *Una foca en mi casa*), Paramount, 1994.

Loan officer, *Sleeping with Strangers,* 1994.

Step magazine man, *Intersection* (also known as *Begegnungen*), Paramount, 1994.

Milk man, *Once in a Blue Moon* (also known as *Rendez–vous sur la lune*), Brainstorm Media, 1995.

Baggage handler, *Homeward Bound II: Lost in San Francisco* (also known as *Ein tierisches Trio*), Buena Vista, 1996.

Gertz, *The Sixth Man* (also known as *The 6th Man* and *Der Teamgeist*), Buena Vista, 1997.

William Shatner, *William Shatner Lent Me His Hairpiece: An Untrue Story* (short film), 1997.

First lobbyist, *Trixie,* Sony Pictures Classics, 2000.

Bernie, *Head over Heels,* Universal, 2001.

Teacher, *The Santa Clause 2* (also known as *Santa Clause 2, The Santa Clause 2: The Mrs. Clause,* and *SC2*), Buena Vista, 2002.

Murray, *The Delicate Art of Parking,* Horizon Entertainment/Cinema Libre, 2003.

Bartender, *Connie and Carla* (also known as *Connie & Carla* and *Connie and Carla Do L.A.*), Universal, 2004.

Colin Jenkins, *Snakehead Terror,* Artsy Fartsy Pictures/Cinetel Films, 2004.

Hockey referee Scotty Buttons, *Raising Helen* (also known as *Educando a Helen, Eine Liebe auf Umwegen, Fashion maman, Heleni kasvatamine, Helens smaa underverk, Kasvukipuja, Liebe auf Umwegen, Mama a la fuerza, Quando meno te lo aspetti,* and *Um presente para Helen*), Buena Vista, 2004.

Charles, *The French Guy,* IndustryWorks Distribution, 2005.

Principal, *Dr. Dolittle 3,* Twentieth Century–Fox Home Entertainment, 2006.

Stage Appearances:

Captain, *Star Trick: The Musical* (musical), Vancouver TheatreSports League, Vancouver, British Columbia, Canada, beginning c. 1991, eventually evolved into the production *Star Trick: The Next Improvisation.*

Babes in the Wood, 1997.

Fear Not, Vancouver, British Columbia, Canada, 1997.

Lawrence and Holloman, 1998.

The History of Things to Come, 1999.

Mission Improvable, 1999.

A Town Called Hockey, 2000.

RECORDINGS

Video Games:

Voice of Walter Harriman, *Stargate SG–1: The Alliance,* 2005.

WRITINGS

Teleplays; with Others; Specials:

The Western Alienation Comedy Hour, CBC, 2002.

Teleplays; with Others; Episodic:

Big Sound, CanWest Global Television, episodes from 2000–2001.

Silverwing (animated), TeleToon (Canada) and Disney Channel, multiple episodes in 2003.

(With Richard Side) "The Comic," *The Collector,* Space Television and City TV, 2005.

Teleplays; with Others; Pilots:

(With Richard Side; and story with Side) "A Glimpse of the Son," *Silverwing* (animated), TeleToon (Canada) and Disney Channel, 2003.

Writings for the Stage; with Others:

Star Trick: The Musical (musical), Vancouver Theatre-Sports League, Vancouver, British Columbia, Canada, beginning c. 1991, eventually evolved into the production *Star Trick: The Next Improvisation.*

(With Shawn MacDonald) *Fear Not,* Vancouver, British Columbia, Canada, 1997.

(With MacDonald and Morris Panych) *The History of Things to Come,* 1999.

Mission Improvable, 1999.

Author of material with the Vancouver TheatreSports League.

OTHER SOURCES

Periodicals:

Stargate, August 23, 2005, pp. 38–41.

TV Zone Special, August, 2000, p. 43; January, 2006, pp. 42–43.

Electronic:

Gary Jones—The Official Website, http://www.galaxyofstars.co.uk/garyjones, October 9, 2007.

JOYCE, Ella 1954–

PERSONAL

Original name, Cherron Hoye; born June 12, 1954, in Chicago, IL; raised in Detroit, MI; daughter of Bunnie Hoye; married Dan Martin (an actor, director, and producer). *Education:* Graduated from Lewis Cass Technical High School (Detroit, MI; also known as Cass Tech), 1972; attended Eastern Michigan University and a business college; studied acting with Lloyd Richards at Yale Repertory Theatre; trained for the stage at Corner Loft Studio, Frank Silvera's Workshop, Al Fann's Theatrical Ensemble, and Lembeck Comedy Workshop; trained in dance with Broadway Dance Center and Los Angeles Dance Center; studied voice with Thom Bridell, Jr. *Avocational Interests:* Gardening.

Career: Actress, producer, and writer. Miss Thing Productions, founder, 1992, and principal. Affiliated with the National Black Theatre Festival, Winston–Salem, NC. Participated in conferences and book tours. Also worked as a secretary for Ford Motor Company.

Member: Women in Film.

Awards, Honors: Audelco Award, Audience Development Committee, 1985, for *Odessa;* Theatre of Renewal Award, best actress in a drama, 1986, for *Not a Single Blade of Grass;* Audelco Award, best dramatic actress, c. 1995, Jeff Award, actress in a supporting role, Joseph Jefferson awards Committee, 2006, and Hattie

McDaniel Award, best featured actress in a play (drama or comedy), Black Theatre Alliance awards, 2006, all for *Crumbs from the Table of Joy;* Image Award nominations, National Association for the Advancement of Colored People, for *Roc* and *Story Porch;* Theatre of Renewal Award, best dramatic actress, off–Broadway category; named to the Lewis Cass Technical High School (Cass Tech) Hall of Fame.

CREDITS

Television Appearances; Series:
Eleanor Emerson, *Roc* (also known as *Roc Live*), Fox, 1991–94.
Jasmine Scott (Vanessa's mother), *My Wife and Kids* (also known as *Wife and Kids*), ABC, 2003–2004.

Television Appearances; Miniseries:
Common Ground, CBS, 1990.

Television Appearances; Movies:
Herself, *Choices,* 1992.
Betty Webb, "Selma Lord Selma," *The Wonderful World of Disney,* ABC, 1999.
Dr. Solomon, *Her Married Lover* (also known as *A Clean Kill*), 1999.
Doodle Alderidge, *Stranger Inside,* 2001.
Juanita, *What about Your Friends: Weekend Getaway,* UPN, 2002.

Television Appearances; Specials:
The African American Collegiate Beauty Pageant, 1993.
Waitress, "The Old Settler," *PBS Hollywood Presents,* PBS, 2001.
Herself, *Bid Whist Party Throwdown,* TV One, 2005.

Television Appearances; Awards Presentations:
The Seventh Annual Stellar Gospel Music Awards (also known as *The Stellar Gospel Music Awards*), syndicated, 1992.
The 12th Annual Stellar Gospel Music Awards (also known as *The Stellar Gospel Music Awards*), syndicated, 1997.

Television Appearances; Episodic:
"Officer Down," *Katts and Dog* (also known as *Rin Tin Tin: K–9 Cop*), CTV (Canada) and Family Channel, 1989.
Guest host, "Lisa Lisa/Masta Ace/Smooth Sylk," *Soul Train,* syndicated, 1994.
Alice Ward, "Them That Has …," *John Grisham's "The Client"* (also known as *The Client*), CBS, 1995.
Mrs. Bogzigian, "Bundt Friday," *Sabrina, the Teenage Witch* (also known as *Sabrina* and *Sabrina Goes to College*), ABC, 1996.

Dean Jones, "The Voice," *Seinfeld* (also known as *The Seinfeld Chronicles* and *Stand–Up*), NBC, 1997.
Annabeth, "Convent–ional Gifts," *The Jamie Foxx Show,* The WB, 1998.
Porsche Langford, "My Pest Friend's Wedding," *In the House,* UPN, 1998.
Mama Pearl, "Dateless in Miami," *Eve* (also known as *The Opposite Sex*), UPN, 2004.

Appeared as herself in *The Dating Game* (also known as *The New Dating Game*) and *The Newlywed Game,* both syndicated. Appeared in other programs, including *One Life to Live* (also known as *Between Heaven and Hell*), ABC; *Search for Tomorrow* (also known as *Search for Happiness*), CBS and NBC; *Story Porch,* Black Entertainment Television; and *The Precinct.*

Television Appearances; Pilots:
Eleanor Emerson, *Roc* (also known as *Roc Live*), Fox, 1991.
Catherine Duke, *NewsRadio* (also known as *News Radio, The Station, Dias de radio,* and *Dies de radio*), NBC, 1995.
Judge, *Dangerous Minds,* ABC, 1996.

Stage Appearances:
Odessa, c. 1985.
Not a Single Blade of Grass, c. 1986.
Risa, *Two Trains Running,* Yale Repertory Theatre, New Haven, CT, beginning 1990.
Medea, *Medea and the Doll,* New Ivar Theatre, Hollywood, CA, 1995.
Checkmates, International Bermuda Arts Festival, c. 1995–96.
Lily Ann "Sister" Green, *Crumbs from the Table of Joy,* Second Stage Theatre Company, McGinn–Cazale Theatre, New York City, 1995, and Goodman Theatre, Owen Theatre, Chicago, IL, 2006.
Ruby McCollum (also known as *The Ruby McCollum Story*), L.A. Theatre Works, Los Angeles, c. 1996, released as an audio recording.
The Last Street Play, 1997.
Tonya, *King Hedley II,* Pittsburgh Public Theater, Pittsburgh, PA, 1999–2000.
Valaida Snow, *Hot Snow! In Search of Snow* (also known as *Hot Snow!*), Company of Character, National Black Theatre Festival, Wake Forest University, Brendle Recital Hall, Winston–Salem, NC, 2001.
Professor Hill, *Unquestioned Integrity: The Hill/Thomas Hearings,* L.A. Theatre Works, c. 2001, released as an audio recording.
The Vagina Monologues, Coronet Theatre, Los Angeles, 2002.
Barefoot in the Park, National Black Theatre Festival, Winston–Salem, NC, 2003.
Jingles in a Broken Tongue, Red Program, Juneteenth Jamboree of New Plays, Juneteenth Legacy Theatre, Louisville, KY, 2003.

Willie and Esther, Red Program, Juneteenth Jamboree of New Plays, Juneteenth Legacy Theatre, 2003.

Rosa Parks, *A Rose among Thorns: A Dramatic Tribute to Rosa Parks* (solo show), Richard Allen Center for Culture & Art, Shooting Star Theatre, New York City, 2006, and Lucy Florence Cultural Center, Los Angeles, 2007.

The Vagina Monologues, 2008.

Appeared as Bianca, *Brothers and Sisters, Husbands and Wives,* Houston Music Hall, Houston, TX; as Barbara Ann and Claudette, *Don't Get God Started* (musical), Pantages Theater, Los Angeles, and Paramount Theatre, Oakland, CA; and in *Fences,* National Black Theatre Festival. Also appeared in other productions, including *Anna Lucasta, Chapter, The First Breeze of Summer, Home, Ma Rainey's Black Bottom, Milestones in Drama, Split Second,* and *Steppin' into Tomorrow.*

Major Tours:

Risa, *Two Trains Running,* U.S. cities, 1989–91.

Rosa Parks, *A Rose among Thorns: A Dramatic Tribute to Rosa Parks* (solo show), U.S. cities, beginning 2007.

Stage Work:

Creator and researcher, *A Rose among Thorns: A Dramatic Tribute to Rosa Parks* (solo show), Richard Allen Center for Culture & Art, Shooting Star Theatre, New York City, 2006, Lucy Florence Cultural Center, Los Angeles, 2007, then tour of U.S. cities, beginning 2007.

Film Appearances:

McCabe, *Stop! Or My Mom Will Shoot,* Universal, 1992.

(Uncredited) Libby Cumba, *Reality Bites,* Universal, 1994.

Detective Waller, *Set It Off,* New Line Cinema, 1996.

Attorney Ross, *Frozen Hot,* 1999.

Sonya Brignone, *Clockin' Green* (also known as *Playing Both Sides*), 2000.

Auntie Reed, *Salvation* (short film), Worn Path Productions, 2003.

The nurse, *Bubba Ho–tep,* 2002, Vitagraph Films, 2003.

Herself, *My Nappy Roots: A Journey through Black Hair–itage* (documentary; also known as *My Nappy ROOTS*), Virgin Moon Entertainment, 2005.

Minister's wife, *Forbidden Fruits,* Product Productions, 2006.

Mrs. Jenkins, *Who Made the Potato Salad?,* Twentieth Century–Fox Home Entertainment, 2006.

Mary, *A Simple Promise,* Marlo Productions, 2007.

Mother, *City Teacher,* Drummond and Smith Entertainment, 2007.

Romeo's mother, *Uncle P,* New Line Home Video, 2007.

Nancy Caulderbank, *Lost Signal,* Lionsgate, 2008.

Film Producer:

Producer, *Frozen Hot,* 1999.

Associate producer, *Clockin' Green* (also known as *Playing Both Sides*), 2000.

RECORDINGS

Videos:

Herself, *Making of "Bubba Ho–tep"* (short), Metro–Goldwyn–Mayer/United Artists Home Entertainment, 2004.

Music Videos:

Tupac Shakur (also known as 2Pac), "If My Homie Calls," 1991.

TLC, "Waterfalls," 1994.

Audiobooks:

Ron Milner, Steve Albrezzi, and William Bradford Huie, *Ruby McCollum* (also known as *The Ruby McCollum Story*), L.A. Theatre Works, c. 1996.

Mame Hunt, *Unquestioned Integrity: The Hill/Thomas Hearings,* L.A. Theatre Works, c. 2001.

WRITINGS

Writings for the Stage:

A Rose among Thorns: A Dramatic Tribute to Rosa Parks (solo show), Richard Allen Center for Culture & Art, Shooting Star Theatre, New York City, 2006, Lucy Florence Cultural Center, Los Angeles, 2007, then tour of U.S. cities, beginning 2007.

Nonfiction:

Kink Phobia: Journey through a Black Woman's Hair, different versions self–published and published by FirstPublish, 2002.

OTHER SOURCES

Books:

Who's Who among African Americans, twentieth edition, Gale, 2007.

Periodicals:

Jet, April 12, 1993, p. 54.

K

KAGAN, Elaine

PERSONAL

Full name, Elaine Goren Kagan; born in St. Louis, MO; daughter of Earl and Milly; children: Eve (an actress). *Education:* Attended the University of Missouri.

Career: Actress and writer.

Member: Screen Actors Guild, Writers Guild of America, West.

CREDITS

Television Appearances; Series:
Carole Kravitz, *The Trials of Rosie O'Neill,* CBS, 1990–92.

Television Appearances; Miniseries:
House of Frankenstein (also known as *House of Frankenstein 1997*), NBC, 1997.
Woman in red, *The 70s* (also known as *Los 70* and *Os anos 70*), NBC, 2000.

Television Appearances; Movies:
Dr. Wilde, *Love Can Be Murder* (also known as *Kindred Spirits*), NBC, 1992.
Esperanza, *There Was a Little Boy,* CBS, 1993.
Dr. Patricia Raines, *Sharon's Secret* (also known as *Into the Fire*), USA Network, 1995.
Susan Brownmiller, *Hefner: Unauthorized* (also known as *Hugh Hefner: The True Story*), USA Network, 1999.

Mrs. Flagg, *The Ballad of Lucy Whipple* (also known as *California Gold*), CBS, 2001.

Television Appearances; Specials:
Mother Davitch, "Back When We Were Grownups," *Hallmark Hall of Fame,* CBS, 2004.

Television Appearances; Episodic:
The old psychic lady with the evil eye who reads fortunes and knows everything before it happens, "The Great Hereafter," *The Super Mario Bros., Super Show!* (live action and animated; also known as *Club Mario* and *The Super Mario Bros., Super Show*), syndicated, 1989.
Barbara Todd, "Death and Taxes," *Mancuso F.B.I.,* NBC, 1990.
"On the Toad Again," *L.A. Law,* NBC, 1991.
"Since I Fell for You," *L.A. Law,* NBC, 1991.
Harriet Bridges, "Mr. Dreeb Comes to Town," *Picket Fences* (also known as *Smalltown USA, High Secret City—La ville du grand secret, La famiglia Brock, Picket Fences—Tatort Gartenzaun, Rome—Stadt im Zwielicht, Rooman sheriffi, Sheriffen, Smaastadsliv,* and *Un drole de sherif*), CBS, 1992.
Dr. Katherine Goodman, "The Man of Steel Bars," *Lois and Clark: The New Adventures of Superman* (also known as *Lois and Clark* and *The New Adventures of Superman*), ABC, 1993.
Mrs. Shearer, "Hit and Run," *ER* (also known as *Emergency Room*), NBC, 1994.
Vicki Hackett, "Food Chains," *Chicago Hope,* CBS, 1994.
Linda, "Thanksgiving," *Townies,* ABC, 1996.
"The Spirit of 76th & Park," *Dream On,* HBO, 1996, also broadcast on Fox.
Arleen Rosenfeld, "Who's Poppa?," *Total Security* (also known as *Os vigilantes* and *Taeyttae turvaa*), ABC, 1997.
Mrs. Fishbein, "A Very P.C. Christmas (Holiday)" (also known as "A Very P.C. Holiday"), *Clueless* (also

known as *Clueless—Die wichtigen Dinge des Lebens, Clueless—Huolettomat,* and *Ni idea!*), UPN, 1997.

Nurse Jo, "Miles to Go Before I Sleep," *Touched by an Angel,* CBS, 1998.

Therapist, "Sexual Healing," *Get Real* (also known as *Asuntos de familia, Helt aerligt!, Irti arjesta, La famille Green, Realitatile vietii,* and *Sechs unter einem Dach*), Fox, 1999.

Professor Mary Morton, "The Biggest Deal There Is," *Felicity,* The WB, 2000.

Professor Mary Morton, "Final Answer," *Felicity,* The WB, 2000.

Professor Mary Morton, "One Ball, Two Strikes," *Felicity,* The WB, 2000.

"Paradise Inn," *Providence,* NBC, 2000.

Judge Marilyn Change, "The Liars Club: Part 1," *Family Law,* CBS, 2001.

June Litvack, "Color–Blind," *Alias,* ABC, 2001.

June Litvack, "Parity," *Alias,* ABC, 2001.

June Litvack, "Time Will Tell," *Alias,* ABC, 2001.

Mrs. Clemonds, "Sounds of Silence," *C.S.I.: Crime Scene Investigation* (also known as *C.S.I., CSI, CSI: Las Vegas, CSI Weekends,* and *Les experts*), CBS, 2001.

Celia (Eve's boss), "Between the Cracks," *Without a Trace* (also known as *Vanished* and *W.A.T.*), CBS, 2002.

June Litvack, "Almost Thirty Years," *Alias,* ABC, 2002.

Cynthia, "Bewitched, Bothered and Bewildered," *The Division* (also known as *Heart of the City*), Lifetime, 2003.

Cynthia, "Cost of Freedom," *The Division* (also known as *Heart of the City*), Lifetime, 2003.

Cynthia, "Misdirection," *The Division* (also known as *Heart of the City*), Lifetime, 2003.

Freda Genow, "Meet the Grandparents," *NYPD Blue,* ABC, 2003.

Freda Genow, "Yo, Adrian," *NYPD Blue,* ABC, 2003.

Eileen Goldberg, "Dancing for Me," *Six Feet Under,* HBO, 2005.

Gina Carroll (2005), "Yo, Adrian," *Cold Case* (also known as *Anexihniastes ypothesis, Caso abierto, Cold case—affaires classees, Cold Case—Kein Opfer ist je vergessen, Doegloett aktak, Kalla spaar, Todistettavasti syyllinen,* and *Victimes du passe*), CBS, 2005.

Mrs. Griswold, "Something to Talk About," *Grey's Anatomy* (also known as *Complications, Procedure, Surgeons, Under the Knife,* and *Grey's Anatomy— Die jungen Aerzte*), ABC, 2005.

Angela Bardem, "All the Lonely People," *Everwood* (also known as *Our New Life in Everwood*), The WB, 2006.

Judge Driscoll, "Light the Lights," *Brothers & Sisters,* ABC, 2006.

Justice Elizabeth Mulray, "The Proffer," *Vanished,* Fox, 2006.

Myra Schlike, "Coyote Ugly," *Las Vegas* (also known as *Casino Eye*), NBC, 2006.

Appeared in other programs, including an appearance as Linda in "The Life of Ryan," an unaired episode of *Townies,* ABC.

Television Appearances; Pilots:

Woman on train, *Dharma & Greg,* ABC, 1997.

Film Appearances:

Attendee, *Someone to Love,* International Rainbow, 1987.

Telegraph lady, *Coming to America* (also known as *Prince in New York*), Paramount, 1988.

Prosecuting attorney, *Big Man on Campus* (also known as *The Hunchback Hairball of L.A.* and *The Hunchback of UCLA*), Regency International Pictures, 1989.

Mrs. Hill (Henry's mother), *GoodFellas* (also known as *Goodfellas* and *Wise Guy*), Warner Bros., 1990.

Stan's receptionist, *Impulse,* Warner Bros., 1990.

Rachel, *By the Sword,* Hansen Entertainment, 1991.

Frannie Bergman, *Innocent Blood* (also known as *Bloody Marie* and *A French Vampire in America*), Warner Bros., 1992.

Aunt Jean, *Angie,* Buena Vista, 1994.

Milly, *Babyfever* (also known as *Babyfever: For Those Who Hear Their Clock Ticking*), Rainbow Releasing, 1994.

Sanderson's secretary, *Beverly Hills Cop III,* Paramount, 1994.

Pretty woman at gas station, *The Sunchaser* (also known as *Sunchaser*), Warner Bros., 1996.

Valerie, *Absolute Power,* Warner Bros., 1997.

Myrna, *My Giant,* Columbia, 1998.

Judge Evelyn Reed, *Traffic* (also known as *Traffic—Die Macht des Kartells*), USA Films, 2000.

Judge, *Undisputed* (also known as *Dead Lock, Ice Man, Invincible, Contraataque, Invicto, O imbativel, So um sera vencedor, Teraeskehae, Un seul deviendra invincible,* and *Undisputed—Sieg ohne Ruhm*), Miramax, 2002.

WRITINGS

Novels:

The Girls, Knopf, 1994.

Blue Heaven, Knopf, 1996.

Somebody's Baby, William Morrow, 1998.

Jenny's Baby, Rowohlt, Reinbek, 2000.

No Goodbyes (also known as *No Good–Byes* and *No Good–byes*), William Morrow, 2000.

Losing Mr. North, William Morrow, 2002.

Nonfiction:
With others, featured in Bonnie Miller Rubin's book *Fifty on Fifty: Wisdom, Inspiration, and Reflections on Women's Lives Well Lived,* Warner Books, 1998.

KANAN, Sean 1966–

PERSONAL

Original name, Sean Perelman; born November 2, 1966, in Cleveland, OH; raised in New Castle, PA; son of Dale (an owner of a chain of jewelry stores) and Michele (a real estate agent) Perelman; married Athena Ubach, September 26, 1999 (divorced, 2001); children: (with Gladys Jiminez, an actress) Simone Andrea. *Education:* University of California, Los Angeles, B.A., political science; also attended Boston University. *Avocational Interests:* Collecting baseball cards from the 1940s and 1950s, martial arts.

Addresses: *Agent*—Seth Lawrence, Rebel Entertainment Partners, Inc., 5700 Wilshire Blvd., Suite 456, Los Angeles, CA 90036. *Manager*—Kim Matuka, Online Talent Group, 1522 North Formosa, Suite 211, Los Angeles, CA 90046.

Career: Actor, producer, and writer. Worked in comedy clubs as a stand–up comedian; entertainer at various venues, including performing for U.S. military personnel in Bosnia and Kosovo, 1999. Appeared in advertisements. Kanan/Hammerschlag Productions, founder and partner. Public speaker at various venues. Also worked in restaurants and bars.

Awards, Honors: *Soap Opera Digest* Award nomination, outstanding male newcomer, 1994, for *General Hospital;* Golden Boomerang Award (with Adrienne Frantz), best couple in daytime television, *TV Soap* magazine, 2002, Special Fan Award nomination (with Katherine Kelly Lang), America's favorite couple, Daytime Emmy awards, 2002, and *Soap Opera Digest* Award nomination, outstanding supporting actor, 2005, all for *The Bold and the Beautiful.*

CREDITS

Television Appearances; Series:
Gregg Parker, *The Outsiders,* Fox, 1990.
Alan "A. J." Quartermaine, Jr., *General Hospital* (also known as *Hopital central* and *Hospital general*), ABC, 1993–97.
Jude Cavanaugh, *Sunset Beach,* NBC, 1999.

Deacon Sharp, *The Bold and the Beautiful* (also known as *Glamour, Rags, Top Models,* and *Belleza y poder*), CBS, 2000–2005.
Judge, *The Little Talent Show,* MTV, beginning 2006.
Himself (dance competitor), *Ballando con le stelle* (Italian version of *Dancing with the Stars*), Radiotelevisione Italiana (RAI), beginning 2006.

Television Appearances; Miniseries:
(Uncredited) Jacob, *Wild Palms,* ABC, 1993.

Television Appearances; Movies:
Jeff Sorrento, *Perry Mason: The Case of the Maligned Mobster* (also known as *The Case of the Maligned Mobster*), NBC, 1991.
Mark Stratton (some sources cite role of Mark Shaw), *Perry Mason: The Case of the Killer Kiss,* NBC, 1993.
Jay, *The Chaos Factor* (also known as *Chaos Factor*), HBO, 2000.

Television Appearances; Specials:
Hot Summer Soaps (also known as *ABC's "Hot Summer Soaps"*), ABC, 1995.
Alan "A. J." Quartermaine, Jr., *General Hospital: Twist of Fate,* ABC, 1996.

Television Appearances; Awards Presentations:
Presenter, *The 28th Annual Daytime Emmy Awards,* NBC, 2001.

Television Appearances; Episodic:
Scott, "X–y–l–o–p–h–o–n–e," *Baby Boom,* NBC, 1989.
Charlie, "Take Me Back to the Ballgame," *Who's the Boss?,* ABC, 1990.
Michael, "Sister Act," *Step by Step* (also known as *Eine Starke Familie, Kaos i familien, Notre belle famille, Paso a paso, Steg for Steg,* and *Una bionda per papa*), ABC, 1993.
Vince, "Shock the Monkey," *Dead at 21,* MTV, 1994.
Contestant, *Family Feud* (also known as *The New Family Feud*), syndicated, c. 1994.
Himself, "The Secret Crush Show," *Night Stand* (also known as *Nightstand* and *Night Stand with Dick Dietrick*), syndicated, 1995.
Steve Law, "Super Mann," *Lois & Clark: The New Adventures of Superman* (also known as *Lois & Clark* and *The New Adventures of Superman*), ABC, 1995.
Mike McMullen, "The Cradle Robbers," *The Nanny,* CBS, 1996.
Brad Alt, "Eyes of a Ranger," *Walker, Texas Ranger* (also known as *Walker*), CBS, 1998.
Stu Solomon, "Three Days to a Kill," *V.I.P.* (also known as *V.I.P.—Die Bodyguards*), syndicated, 1999.
Celebrity contestant, "Cancun (III)," *Search Party,* E! Entertainment Television, 2000.

Celebrity contestant, "Cancun (V)," *Search Party,* E! Entertainment Television, 2000.

Himself, *The Test,* FX Network, 2001.

"Surf's Up, Thumbs Down," *Rendez–View,* syndicated, 2002.

Himself, *Pyramid* (also known as *The $100,000 Pyramid*), syndicated, 2004.

Himself, *Soap Talk,* SOAPnet, 2004.

Steve Mulroy, "Eligible Bachelor," *Freddie,* ABC, 2006.

Appeared as Alex Roggin (some source spell name Alex Rogan), *Likely Suspects,* Fox. Appeared in other programs, including *Spenser: For Hire,* ABC; and in *Werewolf.* Fox.

Television Appearances; Pilots:

Gregg Parker, *The Outsiders,* Fox, 1990.

Todd Channing, *Revenge of the Nerds,* 1991.

Film Appearances:

John Robbins, *Hide and Go Shriek,* New Star Entertainment, 1988.

Mike Barnes, *The Karate Kid, Part III* (also known as *Karate kid III* and *The Karate Kid III*), Columbia, 1989.

Jeffrey, *Rich Girl,* Studio Three Film Corporation, 1990.

Oasis Cafe (short film), 1994.

Don Spengler, *Crash Point Zero* (also known as *Extreme Limits* and *Final Crash*), New City Releasing, 2000.

Alex Patterson, *Chasing Holden* (also known as *Christmas with J. D.*), Lions Gate Films, 2001.

Craig, *10 Attitudes,* Michael Gallant Entertainment, 2001.

Julian March (title role), *March,* 2001.

Tom, *Carpool Guy,* L.A. Ideas, 2005.

Michele Morri, *Sons of Italy,* Sunstar Productions, 2006.

Vincent King, *Hack!,* Smithfield Street Productions/Autumn Entertainment/Tomorrow's Horizons, 2007.

Adam McNeil, *Jack Rio,* Black Hat Productions/GruntWorks Entertainment, 2008.

Some sources cite an appearance in *The Fear: Resurrection* (also known as *The Fear 2, The Fear: Halloween Night,* and *The Fear II: Happy Halloween*), A–pix Entertainment, 1999.

Film Producer:

Oasis Cafe (short film), 1994.

Executive producer, *Chasing Holden* (also known as *Christmas with J. D.*), Lions Gate Films, 2001.

March, 2001.

Hack!, Smithfield Street Productions/Autumn Entertainment/Tomorrow's Horizons, 2007.

Jack Rio, Black Hat Productions/GruntWorks Entertainment, 2008.

Stage Appearances:

Appeared as Austin, *True West,* Zephyr Theatre, Los Angeles; and in *Irish Coffee,* Burbage Theatre, Los Angeles.

Stage Work:

Produced *True West,* Zephyr Theatre, Los Angeles.

WRITINGS

Screenplays:

Oasis Cafe (short film), 1994.

Chasing Holden (also known as *Christmas with J. D.*), Lions Gate Films, 2001.

OTHER SOURCES

Periodicals:

Entertainment Weekly, October 21, 1994, p. 54.

People Weekly, July 17, 1989.

Soap Opera, December 28, 1993.

Soap Opera Digest, August 31, 1993; October 24, 2000.

Soap Opera Update, April 20, 1993.

Soap Opera Weekly, September 28, 1993; August 24, 1999.

Soap World, May, 2001; March, 2003.

Teen Beat, September, 1989.

TV Guide, June 21, 1997, p. 34.

KASSIR, John 1957(?)–

(Johnny Kassir, Jon Kassir)

PERSONAL

Born October 24, 1957 (some sources cite 1962), in Baltimore, MD; married Julie Benz (an actress), May 30, 1998. *Education:* Attended Towson State University.

Addresses: *Agent*—Danis, Panaro & Nist, 9201 West Olympic Blvd., Beverly Hills, CA 90212.

Career: Actor, voice performer, and comedian. As a comedian, was the opening act for various performers, including the Temptations, the Four Tops, and Lou Rawls. Worked as a street performer in New York City. Appeared in advertisements. Provided the voice of the cryptkeeper (from *Tales from the Crypt*), for various productions, albums, and clubs.

Awards, Honors: Drama Desk Award nomination (with others), outstanding ensemble performance, 1985, and Outer Critics Circle Award nomination, c. 1985, both for *3 Guys Naked from the Waist Down;* Ovation Award, best ensemble performance, LA Stage Alliance, and Garland Award, best ensemble cast, *Back Stage West,* both with others, 1999, for *Reefer Madness.*

CREDITS

Television Appearances; Series:
Comedian contestant, *Star Search,* syndicated, 1984–85.

Zagreb Shkenusky, *1st & Ten* (also known as *1st & Ten: The Bulls Mean Business, 1st and Ten: The Championship, 1st & Ten: Do It Again, 1st & Ten: Going for Broke, 1st & Ten: In Your Face?,* and *1st & Ten, Training Camp: The Bulls Are Back*), HBO, c. 1984–91.

Don Tupsouni, *FM,* NBC, 1989–90.

Voice of the cryptkeeper, *Tales from the Crypt* (also known as *HBO's "Tales from the Crypt"*), HBO, 1989–96.

Voice of Buster J. Bunny, *Tiny Toon Adventures* (animated; also known as *Steven Spielberg Presents ... "Tiny Toon Adventures"* and *Tiny Tunes*), syndicated, 1990–92, Fox, 1992–93.

Voice of Buster J. Bunny, *The Plucky Duck Show* (animated), Fox, 1992.

Voices of Yoji and Murph, *Problem Child* (animated), USA Network, 1993.

Voice of Draconis, *Exosquad* (animated; also known as *EXO Squad*), syndicated, 1993–95.

Voice of the cryptkeeper, *Tales from the Cryptkeeper* (animated; also known as *New Tales from the Cryptkeeper*), ABC, 1993–97.

Voices of Snott and Henchrat, *Earthworm Jim* (animated), The WB, 1995–96.

Voice of the cryptkeeper, *Secrets of the Cryptkeeper's Haunted House,* CBS, 1996–97.

Voice of Plato, *Team Knight Rider* (also known as *El equipo fantastico, Nom de code: TKR, Oi ippotes tis asfaltou,* and *Ritariaessaet*), ABC, 1997–98.

Johnny, *Johnnytime,* USA Network, c. 1997–99.

(As Johnny Kassir) Member of ensemble, *The Amanda Show* (also known as *Amanda*), Nickelodeon, 1999–2002.

(Sometimes known as Jon Kassir) Voices of Ray "Raymundo" Rocket and Animal, *Rocket Power* (animated; also known as *RocketPower*), Nickelodeon, 1999–2004.

Voices of Winston and other characters, *As Told by Ginger* (animated; also known as *Gingers Welt* and *To imerologio tis Ginger*), Nickelodeon, 2000–2001.

Voice of Falbot, *Danger Rangers* (animated), beginning 2005.

(As Jon Kassir) Voice of Soshun, *Afro Samurai* (anime; also known as *Afuro zamurai*), Spike, 2007, also broadcast on the Internet.

Television Appearances; Movies:
Voice of Haman, *Scooby–Doo in Arabian Nights* (animated; also known as *Arabian Nights* and *Scooby Doo's Arabian Nights*), 1994.

Jean Michel, *Encino Woman* (also known as *California Woman*), ABC, 1996.

Shemp Howard (one of the title roles), *The Three Stooges,* ABC, 2000.

Danny Doyle, *McBride: Tune in for Murder,* The Hallmark Channel, 2005.

Voice on public address system, *Casper's Scare School* (animated), Cartoon Network, 2006.

Television Appearances; Specials:
Host, *TV 2000,* syndicated, 1985.

Announcer, *Heartstoppers: Horror at the Movies,* 1992.

Himself, *Jonathan Winters: Spaced Out* (also known as *Spaced Out!*), Showtime, 1992.

Voice of Buster J. Bunny, *It's a Wonderful Tiny Toons Christmas Special* (animated), Fox, 1992.

Voice, *Eek! the Cat Christmas Special* (animated; also known as *Eek! the Cat Christmas* and *It's a Very Merry Eek's–mas*), Fox, 1993.

Voice of Buster J. Bunny, *Tiny Toon Adventures: Night Ghoulery* (animated), Fox, 1995.

Himself, *Halloween Homes,* Home & Garden Television (HGTV), 1998.

Voice of Ray "Raymundo" Rocket, *Rocket Power: Double–O Twistervision/Womp Race 2000* (animated; also known as *Double–O Twistervision/ Womp Race 2000*), Nickelodeon, 2001.

Voices of concierge, bartender, border guard, and florist, *The Flintstones: On the Rocks* (animated), Cartoon Network, 2001.

Voice of Ray "Raymundo" Rocket, *Rocket Power: Race across New Zealand* (animated; also known as *Race across New Zealand*), Nickelodeon, 2002.

Voices of Randy and first riot man, *The Ugly Duck–Thing* (animated), Nickelodeon, 2002.

Voice of Ray "Raymundo" Rocket, *Rocket Power: A Rocket X–Mas* (animated; also known as *A Rocket X–Mas*), Nickelodeon, 2003.

Voice of Winston, *As Told by Ginger: Far from Home (aka Foutley's on Ice)* (animated; also known as *As Told by Ginger: Far from Home, Far from Home,* and *Far from Home (aka Foutley's on Ice)*), Nickelodeon, 2003.

Voices of Ray "Raymundo" Rocket and television executive, *Rocket Power: Reggie's Big (Beach) Break* (animated; also known as *Reggie's Big (Beach) Break*), Nickelodeon, 2003.

Voice of Ray "Raymundo" Rocket, *Rocket Power: The Big Day* (animated; also known as *The Big Day*), Nickelodeon, 2004.

Voice of Ray "Raymundo" Rocket, *Rocket Power: Island of the Menehune* (animated; also known as *Island of the Menehune*), Nickelodeon, 2004.

Voice of Ray "Raymundo" Rocket, *Rocket Power: Maximum Rocket Power Games* (animated; also known as *Rocket Power: Maximum Rocket Power Games*), Nickelodeon, 2004.

Voice of Ray "Raymundo" Rocket, *Rocket Power: Twist of Fate* (animated; also known as *Twist of Fate*), Nickelodeon, 2004.

Himself, *Reefer Madness: Grass Roots,* Showtime, 2005.

Television Appearances; Awards Presentations:
Voice of the cryptkeeper, *The Horror Hall of Fame,* syndicated, 1990.

Television Appearances; Episodic:
Peter Macy, "Yours, Very Deadly," *Moonlighting,* ABC, 1986.

Himself (comedian), *It's Showtime at the Apollo* (also known as *Showtime at the Apollo*), syndicated, 1987.

Andre, "Let's Face the Music," *The Facts of Life,* NBC, 1988.

Lenny Pilchowski, "Popular Forces," *Tour of Duty,* CBS, 1989.

Max, *Lenny,* CBS, 1990.

Chuck, "The Guilty Party," *Dream On,* HBO, 1992, also broadcast on Fox.

Morgue man, "Moss Dies," *The New WKRP in Cincinnati,* syndicated, 1992.

Voice of Buster J. Bunny, "Noah's Lark," *Animaniacs* (animated; also known as *Animania* and *Steven Spielberg Presents "Animaniacs"*), The WB, 1993.

Voice, "T.V. or Not to Be," *Duckman* (animated; also known as *Duckman: Private Dick/Family Man*), USA Network, 1994.

Voice of Rats, "Scuttle," *The Little Mermaid* (animated), CBS, 1994.

Maitre d', "Gift," *The Single Guy,* NBC, 1995.

Maitre d', "Midnight," *The Single Guy,* NBC, 1995.

Voice of leopard, "Johnny Bravo/Jungle Boy in "Mr. Monkeyman"/Johnny Bravo and the Amazon Women," *Johnny Bravo* (animated), Cartoon Network, 1995.

Maitre d', "Communication," *The Single Guy,* NBC, 1996.

Voice, "The Malladarian Candidate," *Duckman* (animated; also known as *Duckman: Private Dick/Family Man*), USA Network, 1996.

Voice of Beldar, "The Return of Astroth," *Mighty Ducks* (animated; also known as *Disney's "Mighty Ducks"* and *Mighty Ducks: The Animated Series*), ABC, 1996.

Voice of crazy Aunt Gretion, "The Big Question/The Big Answer," *Rocko's Modern Life* (animated), Nickelodeon, 1996.

Voice of Katty, "Color Me Cave Kid" (also known as "Color Me Cavekid"), *Cave Kids* (animated), Cartoon Network, 1996.

Voices of second and third men and second kid, "Jurassic Pooch/Dial M for Monkey: Orgon Grinder/Dimwit Dexter," *Dexter's Laboratory* (animated; also known as *Dexter's Lab, Dexters Labor,* and *Dexter de Shiyanshi*), Cartoon Network, 1996.

Waiter, "Kept Man," *The Single Guy,* NBC, 1996.

Frankie Gunderson, "I. D. Endow," *Boston Common,* NBC, 1997.

Mr. Kotter, "The Welcome Back Show," *Mr. Rhodes,* NBC, 1997.

Photographer, "Getting Personal," *Hangin' with Mr. Cooper* (also known as *Super Mr. Cooper, Echt super, Mr. Cooper, Mr. Cooper et nous,* and *Vivir con Mr. Cooper*), ABC, 1997.

Rooster, "Jingle Fever," *Malcolm & Eddie,* UPN, 1997.

Voice of Sweetcheecks, "Super Duped/Bungled in the Jungle/Bearly Enough Time," *Johnny Bravo* (animated), Cartoon Network, 1997.

(As Jon Kassir) Arnold Potts, "Lipschitz Live!," *Sliders,* Sci–Fi Channel, 1998.

Kenny, "Help Me Rwanda" (also known as "Help Me, Help Me, Rwanda"), *Ask Harriet,* Fox, 1998.

Voice of El Gordita, "Blood Sisters," *The Wild Thornberrys* (animated; also known as *The Thornberrys*), Nickelodeon, 1998.

Voice of Hobart, "Hobart in The Weedkeeper," *Oh Yeah! Cartoons!* (animated), Nickelodeon, 1998.

Voices of Dunglop and Mervis, "Fetch," *CatDog* (animated), Nickelodeon, 1998.

Voices of messenger and asp, "Dirty Laundry/Grizzly Bear Safari/I. M. Weasel: Queen of DeNile," *Cow and Chicken* (animated), Cartoon Network, 1998.

Dmitri Shishtokovich, "Cuba," *The Love Boat: The Next Wave,* UPN, 1999.

Jerzy Carpathian, "The Fourth Carpathian," *Early Edition,* CBS, 1999.

Stanley, "The One with Joey's Big Break," *Friends* (also known as *Across the Hall, Friends Like Us, Insomnia Cafe,* and *Six of One*), NBC, 1999.

Voice of Fred the flying fish, "Fred the Flying Fish/CatDog Divided," *CatDog* (animated), Nickelodeon, 1999.

Voice of lifeguard, "Rocket Girls/Father's Day Off," *Rocket Power* (animated; also known as *Rocket-Power*), Nickelodeon, 1999.

Voice of possum, "Marge Simpson in 'Screaming Yellow Honkers,'" *The Simpsons* (animated), Fox, 1999.

Voices of waiter and doorman, "Dem Bones/Winslow's Home Videos/You're Fired," *CatDog* (animated), Nickelodeon, 1999.

Gar, "Critical Care," *Star Trek: Voyager* (also known as *Voyager*), syndicated, 2000.

Voice of Marl, "Downloaded," *Buzz Lightyear of Star Command* (animated; also known as *Captain Buzz Lightyear* and *Disney/Pixar's "Buzz Lightyear of Star Command"*), UPN and syndicated, 2000.

Voice of Marl, "Mira's Wedding," *Buzz Lightyear of Star Command* (animated; also known as *Captain Buzz Lightyear* and *Disney/Pixar's "Buzz Lightyear of Star Command"*), UPN and syndicated, 2000.

Voice of Marl, "Star Crossed," *Buzz Lightyear of Star Command* (animated; also known as *Captain Buzz Lightyear* and *Disney/Pixar's "Buzz Lightyear of Star Command"*), UPN and syndicated, 2000.

Voice of second mover, "Twisting Away/Spot Remover," *Rocket Power* (animated; also known as *Rocket-Power*), Nickelodeon, 2000.

Voices of Evan Zarl, Snark, and Zinko, "Large Target," *Buzz Lightyear of Star Command* (animated; also known as *Captain Buzz Lightyear* and *Disney/Pixar's "Buzz Lightyear of Star Command"*), UPN and syndicated, 2000.

Voice of pie man, "Seeing Eye Dog/Beware of Cliff," *CatDog* (animated), Nickelodeon, 2001.

Voice of submarine pilot Dimitri, "The Deep Blue Sea," *The Mummy: The Animated Series* (animated; also known as *The Mummy: Secrets of the Medjai*), The WB, 2001.

Voices of Alfred Nobel and Rasputin, "White House Weirdness/Nobel Peace Surprise," *Time Squad* (animated), broadcast as part of the Cartoon Cartoons programming block, 2001.

Voices of man from *It's a Wonderful Life* and second kid, "A Very Special Family Guy Freakin' Christmas," *Family Guy* (animated; also known as *Padre de familia* and *Padre del familia*), Fox, 2001.

Voices of medieval man and others, "Stuck in the Middle Ages with You," *Totally Spies!* (animated; also known as *Totally Spies* and *Totally Spies Undercover!*), ABC Family Channel and TeleToon (Canada), 2001.

Arnie Kellogg, "Meat Me in Philly," *Philly,* ABC, 2002.

Musgrove, "Eddie and This Guy with Diamonds," *Grounded for Life* (also known as *Freaky Finnertys, Familietrobbel, Keine Gnade fuer Dad,* and *Parents a tout prix*), Fox, 2002.

Roger Weiss, "Betrayal," *The Job,* ABC, 2002.

Various animal sounds, "Jaws Wired Shut," *The Simpsons* (animated), Fox, 2002.

Voice of Scissorsmith, "XXI: Jack and the Farting Dragon," *Samurai Jack* (animated), Cartoon Network, 2002.

Voice of Thomas Jefferson, "Pasteur Packs o' Punch/Floundering Fathers," *Time Squad* (animated), broadcast as part of the Cartoon Cartoons programming block, Cartoon Network, 2002.

Voices of first McCoy boy, Randall McCoy, and McCoy teenager, "Houdini Whodunnit?!/Feud for Thought," *Time Squad* (animated), broadcast as part of the Cartoon Cartoons programming block, Cartoon Network, 2002.

Charlie, "Off the Edge," *The Handler,* CBS, 2003.

Hotel guest, "Assume Nothing," *CSI: Crime Scene Investigation* (also known as *C.S.I., CSI, CSI: Las Vegas, CSI: Weekends,* and *Les experts*), CBS, 2003.

Mime/God, "The Fire and the Wood," *Joan of Arcadia,* CBS, 2003.

Various animal sounds, "Old Yeller Belly," *The Simpsons* (animated), Fox, 2003.

Voice, "Day of the Snowmen," *Kim Possible* (animated; also known as *Disney's "Kim Possible"*), Disney Channel, 2003.

Voices of coach, second nerd, and second player, "Hostile Makeover/Grid Iron Glory," *My Life as a Teenage Robot* (animated), Nickelodeon, 2003.

Voices of Hammer brothers and first man, "Sibling Tsunami/I Was a Preschool Dropout," *My Life as a Teenage Robot* (animated), Nickelodeon, 2003.

Farley Wheeler, "Crime Wave," *CSI: Miami,* CBS, 2004.

Kip Krowley (2004), "Greed (a.k.a. Greed Is Good)," *Cold Case* (also known as *Anexihniastes ypothesis, Caso abierto, Cold case—affaires classees, Cold Case—Kein Opfer ist je vergessen, Doegloett aktak, Kalla spaar, Todistettavasti syyllinen,* and *Victimes du passe*), CBS, 2004.

Voice of Lord Woldybutt, "Nigel Planter and the Chamber Pot of Secrets/Circus of Fear," *Grim & Evil* (animated; also known as *The Grim Adventures of Billy & Mandy*), Cartoon Network, 2004.

The alchemist, "Death Becomes Them," *Charmed,* The WB, 2005.

Voice of Chey, "The Deserter," *Avatar: The Last Airbender* (animated; also known as *Avatar—Der Herr der Elemente*), Nickelodeon, 2005.

Lawrence Melvoy, "The Girl in Suite 2103," *Bones* (also known as *Brennan, Bones—Die Knochenjaegerin, Dr. Csont,* and *Kondid*), Fox, 2006.

Voice of Wigglenog, "Meet the Wigglenog," *Super Robot Monkey Team Hyperforce Go!* (animated; also known as *SRMTHG* and *Super Robot Monkey*), ABC Family Channel, 2006, also broadcast on the Disney Channel.

Voices of carrion beetle, second newscaster, and television announcer, "Billy and Mandy vs. the Martians," *Grim & Evil* (animated; also known as *The Grim Adventures of Billy & Mandy*), Cartoon Network, 2006.

Voices of Cube and Pinface, "Everything Breaks/The Show That Dare Not Speak Its Name," *Grim & Evil* (animated; also known as *The Grim Adventures of Billy & Mandy*), Cartoon Network, 2006.

Voices of donkey, salesperson, and manager, "Herbicidal Maniac/Chaos Theory," *Grim & Evil* (animated; also known as *The Grim Adventures of Billy & Mandy*), Cartoon Network, 2006.

Voices of first thief and Zombozo, "Last Laugh," *Ben 10* (animated), Cartoon Network, 2006.

Voices of Dugly Uckling and Kung Pao Bunny, "Dugly Uckling's Treasure Quest," *Random! Cartoons* (animated), Nickelodeon, 2007.

Voices of Flynn, a villain, and a security guard, "Rat Traps," *All Grown Up* (animated; also known as *Rugrats All Grown Up, Les razbitume, Los nuevos rugrats,* and *Rugratazo*), Nickelodeon, 2007.

Voices of ice king and fire element, "Adventure Time," *Random! Cartoons* (animated), Nickelodeon, 2007.

Appeared as the cryptkeeper, *Brotherly Love,* NBC; and as Bob (a disc jockey), *The Visitor,* Fox; appeared in episodes of other programs, including *In Living Color,* Fox; also appeared as Chaz in "A Girl's Gotta Go Vogue," an unaired episode of *Jenny,* NBC.

Television Appearances; Pilots:
Lester Plotz, *Vidiots,* CBS, 1991.
Rooster, *Malcolm & Eddie,* UPN, 1996.
Ray Palmer/The Atom, *Justice League of America,* CBS, 1997.
Kevin Maloney, *Buddy Faro,* CBS, 1998.

Television Additional Voices; Series:
Eek! the Cat (animated; also known as *Eek! and the Terrible Thunderlizards, Eek!Stravaganza,* and *The Six and a Half Lives of Eek the Cat),* Fox, 1992–97.
(As Jon Kassir) *Sonic the Hedgehog* (animated; also known as *Sonic),* ABC and syndicated, 1993–95.
(As Jon Kassir) *Hercules* (animated; also known as *Disney's "Hercules"),* ABC and syndicated, 1998–99.

Television Creator, Executive Producer, and Puppeteer; Series:
Johnnytime, USA Network, c. 1997–99.

Film Appearances:
Himself, *New Wave Comedy,* 1986.
Igor, *Monster Mash: The Movie* (also known as *Frankenstein Sings),* Prism Pictures, 1995.
Tripwire, *Cyber–Tracker 2* (also known as *Cybertracker 2),* PM Entertainment Group, 1995.
Voice of the cryptkeeper, *Casper* (live action and animated; also known as *Casper, the Friendly Ghost),* Universal, 1995.
Voice of the cryptkeeper, *Tales from the Crypt: Demon Knight* (also known as *Demon Keeper, Demon Knight,* and *Tales from the Crypt Presents Demon Knight),* Universal, 1995.
Voice of dragon, *The Tales of Tillie's Dragon* (short animated film), 1995.
Voice of Meeko, *Pocahontas* (animated), Buena Vista, 1995.
Rancor guard at intercom, *Spy Hard* (also known as *Agent zero zero, Agent 00, Live and Let Spy, Agent 00—Mit der Lizenz zum Totlachen, Ciplak casus, Dragam add az eleted, Duro de espiar, Duro para espiar, Espia … como puderes!, Espia como puedas, L'agent secret se decouvre, Mit der Lizenz zum Totlachen, Spia e lascia spiare, Spy Hard—Helt utan haemningar, Spy Hard—lupa laeikyttaeae, Szklanka po lapkach,* and *Tajni agent 000),* Buena Vista, 1996.

Voice of the cryptkeeper, *Bordello of Blood* (also known as *Dead Easy* and *Tales from the Crypt Presents: "Bordello of Blood"),* Universal, 1996.
Voice of Meeko, *Pocahontas II: Journey to a New World* (animated; also known as *Disney's "Pocahontas II: Journey to a New World"* and *Pocahontas: Journey to a New World),* Walt Disney Home Video, 1998.
John, *The Glass Jar,* Sterling Pacific Films, 1999.
Voice of Scuttlebutt, *An American Tail: The Treasure of Manhattan Island* (animated; also known as *American Story 3* and *An American Tail 3: The Treasure of Manhattan Island),* Universal Pictures Home Video, 2000.
Voice of the cryptkeeper, *Ritual* (also known as *Revelation, Tales from the Crypt Presents: Revelation, Tales from the Crypt Presents: Voodoo,* and *Voodoo Ritual),* Miramax/Dimension Films, 2001.
Simon Thaddeus Mulberry Pew, *Who Slew Simon Thaddeus Mulberry Pew* (short film), Image Entertainment, 2002.
Voice of squirrel, *The Wild Thornberrys Movie* (animated), Paramount, 2002.
B list director, *The Midget Stays in the Picture* (short film), 2003.
Voices of Rocky and Armando, *George of the Jungle 2* (also known as *Jungle George 2),* Walt Disney Pictures, 2003.
Quint, *Soccer Dog: European Cup,* Columbia/TriStar Home Entertainment, 2004.
Moe Moebius, *Dr. Rage* (also known as *The Last Patient, Nightmare Hostel,* and *The Straun House),* Providence Productions, 2005.
Ralph Wiley and Uncle Sam, *Reefer Madness: The Movie Musical* (musical; also known as *Reefer Madness* and *Kifferwahn),* 2005.
Himself and the cryptkeeper, *American Scary* (documentary), Z–Team Productions, 2006.
Walter, *Channels,* OllieWood Films, 2008.

Film Additional Voices:
The Wild (animated; also known as *Jungle City, Aivan villit, Divocina, Helt vildt, I zoungla, La vie sauvage, Salvaje, Selvagem, Tierisch wild, Vashi doga, Vida salvaje, Vilddjuren,* and *Villdyr),* Buena Vista, 2006.

Film Director:
First assistant director of second unit, *Forbidden Games* (also known as *Games),* PM Entertainment Group, 1995.

Stage Appearances; Musicals:
Kenny Brewster, *3 Guys Naked from the Waist Down,* Minetta Lane Theatre, New York City, 1985.
Ralph, *Reefer Madness,* Hudson Backstage Theatre, Hollywood, CA, 1999–2000, and Variety Arts Theatre, New York City, 2001.
Teddy, *The Gift,* Tiffany Theater, Hollywood, CA, 2000.

Dottore, *The Glorious Ones,* Lincoln Center, Mitzi E. Newhouse Theater, New York City, 2007–2008.

Internet Appearances:
Voice of the cryptkeeper, *Tales from the Crypt* (Internet radio series), http://www.scifi.com/set/tales, beginning 2000.

(As Jon Kassir) Voice of Soshun, *Afro Samurai* (anime series; also known as *Afuro zamurai*), 2007, also broadcast as a television series on Spike, 2007.

RECORDINGS

Albums; Cast Recordings; with Others:
3 Guys Naked from the Waist Down, Jay Records, 1993.
The Gift—Live from the Tiffany, Interscope Records, 2000.
Reefer Madness, 2000.

Albums; with Others:
Voice of the cryptkeeper, *Tales from the Crypt: Have Yourself a Scary Little Christmas,* Capitol, 1994.

Video Games:
Voices, *Bouncers,* Dynamix, Inc., 1994.
Voice, *Sacrifice,* Interplay Productions, 2000.
Voices of Belhifet, Poquelin, and others, *Forgotten Realms: Icewind Dale,* 2000.
Voices, *Min'na no gorufu 3: Everybody's Gold* (also known as *Hot Shots Golf 3*), Sony Computer Entertainment America, 2001.
Voice of Jibolba, *Tak and the Power of Juju,* Nickelodeon Productions, 2003.
Voices, *Freelancer,* Microsoft, 2003.
Voices, *Min'na no gorufu 4* (also known as *Hot Shots of Golf Fore!* and *Minna Golf 4*), Sony Computer Entertainment America, 2003.
Voice, *The Punisher,* THQ, 2004.
Voice of Jibolba, *Tak 2: The Staff of Dreams,* THQ, 2004.
Voice of marine, *Halo 2,* Microsoft, 2004.
Voices of Zohar, officer, FBI officer, copilot, and Birchim, *Syphon Filter: The Omega Strain* (also known as *Syphon Filter 4*), Sony Computer Entertainment America, 2004.
Multiple voices, *EverQuest II,* Sony Online Entertainment, 2004.
Multiple voices, *Minna no gorufu portable,* Sony Computer Entertainment America, 2004.
Voice of Jibolba, *Tak 3: The Great Juju Challenge,* THQ, 2005.
Voices of lemur, taxi driver, and man on cellular phone, *Madagascar,* Activision, 2005.
Voices of Pyro, Sauron, and Deadpool, *X–Men Legends II: Rise of Apocalypse,* Activision, 2005.
Voices, *Ultimate Spider–Man,* Activision, 2005.

Voice of Deadpool, *Marvel: Ultimate Alliance,* Activision, 2006.
Voices of Adam MacIntyre and others, *Dead Rising,* Capcom Entertainment, 2006.
Voices, *Spider–Man 3,* Activision, 2007.

WRITINGS

Teleplays; with Others; Series:
Johnnytime, USA Network, c. 1997–99.

OTHER SOURCES

Periodicals:
TV Guide, April 15, 2000.

KELLEHER, Tim

PERSONAL

Born in the Bronx, NY.

Addresses: *Agent*—Venture IAB, 2509 Wilshire Blvd., Los Angeles, CA 90057; William Morris Agency, One William Morris Pl., Beverly Hills, CA 90212.

Career: Actor.

CREDITS

Film Appearances:
Duke/Larry, *The Understudy: Graveyard Shift II,* Virgin Vision, 1988.
Bobby, *Black Rain,* Paramount, 1989.
Man at catering truck, *Late for Dinner,* Columbia Pictures, 1991.
Cop at Harlem station, *Malcolm X* (also known as *X*), Warner Bros., 1992.
Voice of Raphael, *Teenage Mutant Ninja Turtles III,* New Line Cinema, 1993.
Jump Junkie number one, *Terminal Velocity,* Buena Vista, 1994.
C–123 pilot, *Operation Dumbo Drop* (also known as *Dumbo Drop*), Buena Vista, 1995.
Narc number two, *Clockers,* Universal, 1995.
Wabash, *Never Talk to Strangers* (also known as *Spiel mit dem feuer* and *L'inconnu*), TriStar Pictures, 1995.
Waiter in club, *The Birdcage* (also known as *Birds of a Feather*), United Artists, 1996.

Bulldog, *Executive Decision* (also known as *Critical Decision*), Warner Bros., 1996.

Technician, *Independence Day* (also known as *ID4*), Twentieth Century–Fox, 1996.

Helicopter pilot, *Desperate Measures*, TriStar, 1998.

Argento, *The Negotiator* (also known as *Verhandlungssache*), Warner Bros., 1998.

Deputy Conley, *Made Men*, New City Releasing, 1999.

Ted Sorensen, *Thirteen Days*, New Line Cinema, 2000.

Bishop, *Matchstick Men*, Warner Bros., 2003.

Flash of Genius, 2008.

Television Appearances; Series:

Jim Steele, *Dark Skies*, NBC, 1996–97.

Television Appearances; Movies:

Voice, *Say What?*, CBS, 1992.

Monty, *Love, Lies & Lullabies* (also known as *Sad Inheritance*), ABC, 1993.

Detective Cahill, *A Family Torn Apart* (also known as *Sudden Fury: A Family Torn Apart*), NBC, 1993.

Lieutenant Wesley, *The Tuskegee Airmen*, HBO, 1995.

Booster, *Apollo 11* (also known as *Apollo 11: The Movie*), The Family Channel, 1996.

Wayne Kennedy, *A Murder on Shadow Mountain*, 1999.

David Sonenberg, *Meat Loaf: To Hell and Back*, VH1, 2000.

Television Appearances; Pilots:

Driver cop, *NYPD Blue*, ABC, 1993.

Television Appearances; Episodic:

Intern, "Subterranean Homeboy Blues," *Law & Order*, NBC, 1990.

"Second Chance," *Human Target*, 1992.

Dale Rudolph, "Apocrypha," *Law & Order*, NBC, 1993.

Commando/Bowman, "Nothing But the Truth," *SeaQuest DSV* (also known as *SeaQuest 2032*), NBC, 1994.

Ensign Gaines, "All Good Things," *Star Trek: The Next Generation* (also known as *Star Trek: TNG*), syndicated, 1994.

Howard, "Booktopus," *All–American Girl*, ABC, 1994.

Lieutenant Moore, "Pilot Error," *JAG*, NBC, 1995.

Jason's dad, "If You Have to Ask the Price," *High Sierra Search and Rescue*, 1995.

Lieutenant Morgan Fine, "Disclosure," *The Crow: Stairway to Heaven*, syndicated, 1999.

Nick Bekins, "Guys and Dolls," *Providence*, NBC, 1999.

Four of Nine, "Survival Instinct," *Star Trek: Voyager* (also known as *Voyager*), UPN, 1999.

Dr. Fillmore, "Hold On Tight," *Judging Amy*, CBS, 2001.

Willie Parnell, "Outcomes," *Strong Medicine*, Lifetime, 2002.

Lieutenant Pell, "The Communicator," *Enterprise* (also known as *Star Trek: Enterprise*), UPN, 2002.

Axel, "Sand Francisco Dreamin'," *Charmed*, The WB, 2003.

Mr. McKeon—Vorcon, "War, Inc.," *The Agency*, CBS, 2003.

U.S. embassy officer, "The Lost," *ER*, NBC, 2003.

Internal Affairs Bureau officer, "Paper or Plastic?," *CSI: Crime Scene Investigation* (also known as *C.S.I.*, *CSI: Las Vegas*, and *Les Experts*), CBS, 2004.

Kenneth Hart, "The People vs. Oliver C. Handley," *The D.A.*, ABC, 2004.

NCIS Agent Chris Pacci, "Bete Noire," *Navy NCIS: Naval Criminal Investigative Service* (also known as *NCIS* and *NCIS: Naval Criminal Investigative Service*), CBS, 2004.

NCIS Agent Chris Pacci, "UnSEALed," *Navy NCIS: Naval Criminal Investigative Service* (also known as *NCIS* and *NCIS: Naval Criminal Investigative Service*), CBS, 2004.

NCIS Agent Chris Pacci, "Dead Man Talking," *Navy NCIS: Naval Criminal Investigative Service* (also known as *NCIS* and *NCIS: Naval Criminal Investigative Service*), CBS, 2004.

Ed Pisarchik, "Who's Your Daddy?," *NYPD Blue*, ABC, 2004.

Joel Morrison, "The Dare," *Six Feet Under*, HBO, 2004.

Security guard Burns, "Murder in a Flash," *CSI: Miami*, CBS, 2004.

Duane Burdick, "Nickel and Dimed: Parts 1 & 2," *Without a Trace* (also known as *W.A.T.*), CBS, 2004.

Dylan Clark, "Things Fall Apart," *The West Wing*, NBC, 2005.

Dylan Clark, "2162 Votes," *The West Wing*, NBC, 2005.

Greg Merfield, "Day 4: 1:00 a.m.–2:00 a.m.," *24*, Fox, 2005.

Drug enforcement agent, "The Ex–Games," *North Shore*, Fox, 2005.

D agent, "The End," *North Shore*, Fox, 2005.

Adrian Bale, "Won't Get Fooled Again," *Criminal Minds*, CBS, 2005.

Ray Jamison, "Shanghai'd," *Standoff*, Fox, 2006.

KIMBALL, Jeffrey L. 1943–
(Jeffrey Kimball)

PERSONAL

Born May 29, 1943, in Wichita, KS; son of Richard Pearl and Macel (maiden name, Kidson) Kimball; married Eileen Sue Fisher, February 24, 1978; children: Chelsea, Sarah Beth. *Education:* Graduated from North Texas State University with degrees in psychology and music. *Avocational Interests:* Horse breeding and horseback riding, skiing, photography, fishing.

Addresses: *Agent*—Endeavor, 9601 Wilshire Blvd., 3rd Floor, Beverly Hills, CA 90210; The Mack Agency, 4705 Laurel Canyon Blvd., Suite 204, Valley Village, CA 91607.

Career: Cinematographer. Warner Bros., worked as photography trainee; worked with still photographer Bill Langley, Dallas, TX, 1963–65; director of photography for various companies in Los Angeles, CA, 1965—; director of photography for numerous commercials, including advertisements for Oil of Olay skin care products, Marlboro and Lark cigarettes, Diet Coke soft drink, Estee Lauder cosmetics, and Federal Express delivery service.

Member: American Society of Cinematographers.

Awards, Honors: Golden Satellite Award nomination, best cinematography, 2001, International Press Academy for *Mission: Impossible II.*

CREDITS

Film Cinematographer:
(Second unit) *Hell Raiders,* 1965.
On the Line, 1971.
(Second unit) *It's Alive,* 1974.
(As Jeffrey Kimball; second unit) *Cat People,* 1982.
Legend of Billy Jean, TriStar, 1985.
(As Jeffrey Kimball) *Top Gun,* Paramount, 1986.
Beverly Hills Cop II, Paramount, 1987.
(As Jeffrey Kimball) *Revenge,* New World, 1990.
Jacob's Ladder (also known as *Dante's Inferno*), TriStar, 1990.
Curly Sue, Warner Bros., 1991.
True Romance (also known as *Breakaway*), Warner Bros., 1993.
The Specialist (also known as *El Especialista*), Warner Bros., 1994.
Lolita, 1996.
Wild Things (also known as *wildthings*), Columbia, 1998.
Stigmata, Metro–Goldwyn–Mayer, 1999.
Mission: Impossible II (also known as *M:I–2*), Paramount, 2000.
Windtalkers, Metro–Goldwyn–Mayer, 2001.
(As Jeffrey Kimball) *Hostage* (short; also known as *The Hire: Hostage*), 2002.
Star Trek: Nemesis, Paramount, 2002.
Paycheck, Paramount, 2003.
The Big Bounce, Warner Bros., 2004.
Be Cool, Metro–Goldwyn–Mayer, 2005.
Glory Road, Buena Vista, 2006.
Bonneville, Twentieth Century Fox Home Entertainment, 2006.
Old Dogs, Walt Disney Pictures, 2008.
The Camel Wars, 2008.

Film Work; Other:
Camera operator; second unit, *Cat People,* 1982.

OTHER SOURCES

Periodicals:
American Cinematographer, March, 1993, p. 25.

KING, Arthur
    See **LOCKE, Peter**

KNOX, Terence 1946–
    (Terrence Knox, Terry Knox)

PERSONAL

Original name, Terry Davis; born December 16, 1946, in Richland, WA; father, a construction worker; mother, a secretary; married Susie Davis (divorced). *Education:* Earned an English degree from Washington State University.

Addresses: *Agent*—House of Representatives, 400 South Beverly Dr., Suite 101, Beverly Hills, CA 90212.

Career: Actor. Was a former Inland Gloves champion.

Awards, Honors: Founder's Award, Viewers for Quality Television, 1989, for *Tour of Duty.*

CREDITS

Film Appearances:
(As Terrence Knox) Reese, *Used Cars,* Columbia, 1980.
Jack's friend, *Heart Like a Wheel,* Twentieth Century–Fox, 1983.
Circle of Power (also known as *Brainwash, Mystique,* and *The Naked Weekend*), 1983.
Eric Macklin, *Lies,* Alpha, 1984.
Buddy, *Truckin' Buddy McCoy,* Bedford Entertainment, 1984.
Hightower and McHugh, *Rebel Love* (also known as *Shadow Waltz*), Troma, 1986.
Burt, *The Offspring* (also known as *From a Whisper to a Scream*), 1986.
Paul Elliott, *Distortions,* Cori, 1988.
Twist of Fate, 1990.
Jack DeForest, *Tripwire,* 1990.
Wallace Reid, *Forever,* 1993.

John Garrett, *Children of the Corn II: The Final Sacrifice* (also known as *Children of the Corn: Deadly Harvest*), Miramax, 1993.

Jonathan "J. B." Brandels, *The Spy Within* (also known as *Flight of the Dove*), Tanglewood, 1995.

Construction foreman, *At Face Value,* 1999.

Fardum Gaspro the Bounty Hunter, *Space Banda,* 2001.

Detective Ben Bannister, *An Ordinary Killer,* Anthem Pictures, 2003.

Himself, *Beyond Ordinary: The Making of "An Ordinary Killer"* (documentary), Anthem Pictures, 2004.

Sam Preston, *Obsession* (short), 2006.

Mayor Emerson Rogers, *Ghost Town: The Obsession,* 2007.

Grandpa Jack, *The House That Jack Built,* FourTwoFive Films, 2007.

Himself, *Interviews "Ghost Town: The Movie"* (documentary), 2007.

Himself, *Behind the Scenes of "Ghost Town: The Movie"* (documentary), Collective Development, 2007.

Also appeared in *Violent Blade.*

Television Appearances; Series:

Dr. Peter White, *St. Elsewhere,* NBC, 1982–85.

Matt Russell, *All Is Forgiven,* NBC, 1986.

Sergeant Zeke Anderson, *Tour of Duty,* CBS, 1987–90.

Jack Matson, *The Road Home,* CBS, 1994.

Matt "Siggy" Sigalos, *Under One Roof,* CBS, 1995.

Griffith, *Rescue 77,* 1999.

Television Appearances; Miniseries:

Martin Anderson, *Murder Ordained* (also known as *Broken Commandments* and *Kansas Gothic*), CBS, 1987.

Coyle, *The Invaders,* Fox, 1995.

Television Appearances; Movies:

Leo Kalb, *City Killer,* NBC, 1984.

Craig Phelan, *Chase,* CBS, 1985.

Dan Casey, *Unspeakable Acts,* ABC, 1990.

Clayton Thorpe, *Snow Kill* (also known as *Over the Edge*), USA Network, 1990.

Vince Slade, *Angel of Death* (also known as *Intimate Terror: "Angel of Death"*), CBS, 1990.

Nick Moore, *Lucky Day,* ABC, 1991.

Nick Kasten, *Overexposed,* ABC, 1992.

Dr. Eric Foretich, *A Mother's Right: The Elizabeth Morgan Story* (also known as *With Reason to Suspect* and *Shattered Silence*), ABC, 1992.

Frank Del Pzzo, *Nick's Game,* 1993.

Bobby Ballew, *Poisoned by Love: The Kern County Murders* (also known as *Blind Angel* and *Murder So Sweet*), CBS, 1993.

Jed Harris, *Stolen Innocence,* CBS, 1995.

919 Fifth Avenue (also known as *Dominick Dunne's "919 Fifth Avenue"*), 1995.

University Blues, 1996.

Mike, *Love in Another Town* (also known as *Barbara Taylor Bradford's "Love in Another Town"*), CBS, 1997.

Television Appearances; Pilots:

Dr. Michael Rourke, *J.O.E. and the Colonel* (also known as *Humanoid Defender*), ABC, 1985.

Television Appearances; Specials:

Steve Grenowski, "Mighty Pawns," *Wonderworks,* PBS, 1987.

Host (Toronto), *CBS All-American Thanksgiving Day Parade,* CBS, 1989.

Television Appearances; Episodic:

Officer Bright, "The Hitchhiker," *Knots Landing,* 1980.

Rafe Logan, "New Deputy in Town," *The Dukes of Hazzard,* 1981.

Himself, *Just Men,* 1983.

Alan Davis, "The Rescue," *V* (also known as *V: The Series*), 1985.

Fred Hampton, "Bystanders," *Hotel* (also known as *Arthur Hailey's "Hotel"*), 1985.

Steve Pascal, "Murder Takes the Bus," *Murder, She Wrote,* CBS, 1985.

Mr. Teckett, "The Next Best Thing to Winning," *Sidekicks,* 1987.

Thomas Bartin, "The Cold Equations," *The Twilight Zone* (also known as *The New Twilight Zone*), 1988.

Attitudes, 1989.

"Life Without Possibility: Parts 1 & 2," *Midnight Caller,* 1990.

Leon, "Made in Paris," *The Hitchhiker* (also known as *Deadly Nightmares* and *Le Voyageur*), 1990.

Elroy Bunch, "Lifelines: Parts 1 & 2," *Reasonable Doubts,* 1992.

Jason Trask, "Strange Visitor (From Another Planet)," *Lois & Clark: The New Adventures of Superman,* ABC, 1993.

Jason Trask, "The Green, Green Glow of Home," *Lois & Clark: The New Adventures of Superman* (also known as *Lois & Clark* and *The New Adventures of Superman*), ABC, 1993.

Jack, "Nowhere to Run," *Cobra,* 1993.

John Penner, "Love Never Dies," *Silk Stalkings,* 1993.

Bobby Noonan, *Traps,* CBS, 1994.

Commander Van Camp, "Second Chance," *SeaQuest DSV* (also known as *SeaQuest 2032*), NBC, 1995.

Martin Cavanaugh, "University Blues: Parts 1 & 2," *High Tide,* 1996.

Douglas Fournier, "Chapter Nineteen," *Murder One,* ABC, 1996.

Douglas Fournier, "Chapter Twenty-Two," *Murder One,* ABC, 1996.

Tom Matthews, "Flyer," *The Pretender,* NBC, 1996.

Martin Cavanaugh, "University Blues: Parts 1 & 2," *High Tide,* 1996.

Major Reed, "Secret in the Neighborhood," *The Burning Zone,* UPN, 1997.

Zack Torrence, "Soft Targets," *Pacific Blues,* USA Network, 1997.

Lieutenant Colonel Dan Ballinger, "Yesterday, Upon the Stairs: Part 1," *Pensacola: Wings of Gold,* syndicated, 1997.

Coach Marsh, *Push,* 1998.

"Don't Say Anything," *Any Day Now,* 1999.

Garrett Pope, "Desperate Measures," *Walker, Texas Ranger* (also known as *Walker*), CBS, 2001.

Larry Wadd, "An Open Book," *Six Feet Under,* HBO, 2001.

Porter, "Val in Space," *V.I.P.* (also known as *V.I.P.—Die Bodyguards*), syndicated, 2001.

Detective Al Stein, "Live and Leg Die," *Philly,* ABC, 2001.

(As Terrence Knox) "Moo," *The Agency,* 2002.

"Sex Pistols," *Wanted,* TNT, 2005.

Also appeared in *The Pat Sajack Show.*

Stage Appearances:

Brick, *Cat on a Hot Tin Roof,* Coconut Grove Playhouse, Coconut Grove, FL, 1985.

Teddy, *When You Comin' Back, Red Ryder?,* Coconut Grove Playhouse, 1985.

Also appeared in *Rosencrantz and Guildenstern Are Dead; A Streetcar Named Desire.*

RECORDINGS

Video Games:

Dr. D. Boss, *Emergency Room 2,* 1999.

OTHER SOURCES

Electronic:

Terence Knox Website, http://www.terenceknox.com, December 7, 2007.

KNUDSEN, Erik 1988–
   (Eric Knudsen)

PERSONAL

Born March 25, 1988, in Toronto, Ontario, Canada. *Education:* Studied improvisation at Second City. *Avocational Interests:* Drums, hockey, rollerblading, swimming, paintball, skate boarding, and fishing.

Addresses: *Agent*—Fountainhead Talent, Inc., 131 Davenport Rd., Toronto, ON M5R 1H8 Canada. *Manager*—Burstein Company, 15304 Sunset Blvd., Suite 208, Pacific Palisades, CA 90272.

Career: Actor.

Member: Alliance of Canadian Cinema, Television and Radio Artists, Screen Actors Guild.

Awards, Honors: Young Artist Award nomination, best performance in a television drama series—guest starring young actor, 2002, for *The Guardian.*

CREDITS

Film Appearances:

Young Tom Canboro, *Tribulation,* Con Dios Entertainment, 2000.

Rog Ryan at age thirteen, *The Prize Winner of Defiance, Ohio,* DreamWorks, 2005.

Daniel Matthews, *Saw II,* Lions Gate Films, 2005.

Arthur Thomson, *Booky Makes Her Mark,* Shaftesbury Sales Company, 2006.

Jonathan Ward, *Bon Cop, Bad Cop,* Alliance Atlantis Home Video, 2006.

(As Eric Knudsen) Timmy Brock, *A Lobster Tale,* 2006.

Television Appearances; Series:

Donovan Mackay, *Mental Block,* YTV, 2003.

Dale Turner, *Jericho,* CBS, 2006—.

Television Appearances; Movies:

Young Johnny Burroughs, *Common Ground,* Showtime, 2000.

Nasty boy, *Santa Who?,* ABC, 2000.

Ian Robbins, *Blackout,* CBS, 2001.

Young Chris Welch, *The Familiar Stranger* (also known as *My Husband's Double Life*), Lifetime, 2001.

Tommy, *Stolen Miracle,* Lifetime, 2001.

T. J. Murphy, *Full–Court Miracle,* Disney Channel, 2003.

Television Appearances; Pilots:

Hunter Reed, *The Guardian,* CBS, 2001.

Dale Turner, *Jericho,* CBS, 2006.

Television Appearances; Episodic:

Alex Shreffler, "Heimlich Hero: The Michelle Shreffler Story," *Real Kids, Real Adventures,* Global, 1999.

"First Impressions," *Doc,* PAX, 2001.

Hunter Reed, "Reunion," *The Guardian,* CBS, 2001.

Hunter Reed, "Home," *The Guardian,* CBS, 2001.

Hunter Reed, "The Beginning," *The Guardian,* CBS, 2002.

(As Eric Knudsen) Jake Green, "Janet Green," *Blue Murder* (also known as *En quete de preuves*), Global, 2004.

Ryan Stallinger, "Losing Isn't Everything," *Kevin Hill,* UPN, 2005.

KOPELSON, Anne

PERSONAL

Original name, Anne Feinberg; married Arnold Kopelson; children: Peter, Evan, Stephanie.

Addresses: *Office*—Kopelson Entertainment, 1900 Avenue of the Stars, Suite 500, Los Angeles, CA 90067.

Career: Producer. Kopelson Entertainment, Los Angeles, CA, co–chairman. American Film Marketing Association, founding member and member of board of directors; American Film Export Association, member of executive council; Academy of Motion Picture Arts and Sciences, member of executive committee of the executive producers branch; University of California at Los Angeles Producers Program Advisory Board, member.

Member: Academy of Motion Picture Arts and Sciences (producers branch).

Awards, Honors: *Variety's* Show Biz Expo Hall of Fame, inductee, 1997.

CREDITS

Film Producer:
Eraser, Warner Bros., 1996.
Mad City, Warner Bros., 1997.
The Devil's Advocate (also known as *Devil's Advocate* and *Im Auftrag des teufels*), Warner Bros., 1997.
U.S. Marshals, Warner Bros., 1998.
A Perfect Murder, Warner Bros., 1998.
Don't Say a Word, Twentieth Century–Fox, 2001.
Joe Somebody, Twentieth Century–Fox, 2001.
Twisted, Paramount, 2004.

Film Executive Producer:
Outbreak, Warner Bros., 1995.
Se7en, New Line Cinema, 1995.
Murder at 1600, Warner Bros., 1997.

Television Executive Producer; Series:
The Fugitive, CBS, 2000.
Thieves, ABC, 2001.

Television Executive Producer; Movies:
Past Tense, Showtime, 1994.

L

LADD, Alan, Jr. 1937–

PERSONAL

Full name, Alan Walbridge Ladd, Jr.; born October 22, 1937, in Los Angeles, CA; son of Alan Walbridge (an actor) and Marjorie Jane (maiden name, Harrold) Ladd; married Patricia Ann Beazley, August 30, 1959 (divorced, 1983); married Cindra Kay, July 13, 1985; children: (first marriage) Kelliann, Tracy Elizabeth, Amanda Sue.

Addresses: *Office*—The Ladd Company, 9465 Wilshire Blvd., Suite 910, Beverly Hills, CA 90210.

Career: Studio executive and producer. Creative Management, Los Angeles, CA, motion picture agent, 1963–69; independent producer, 1969–73; Twentieth Century–Fox Film Corp., Los Angeles, vice president for production, 1973–74; Worldwide Productions Division, Beverly Hills, CA, senior vice president, 1974–76; Twentieth Century–Fox Pictures, president, 1976–79; Ladd Co., Burbank, CA, president, 1979–83; Metro–Goldwyn–Mayer/United Artists Entertainment Co., president and chief operating officer, 1983–86, chief executive officer, beginning 1986, and chair of board of directors; Metro–Goldwyn–Mayer Pictures, Inc., Culver City, CA, chair and chief executive officer, 1986–88, co–chair, 1990–93; Pathe Entertainment, Los Angeles, president and chair, 1989–90; MGM–Pathe, Los Angeles, co–chair, 1990–93; developed and produced films for Paramount, The Ladd Company, Beverly Hills, CA, founder and president, 1993—. *Military service:* U.S. Air Force, 1961–63.

Awards, Honors: Academy Award (with others), best picture, 1996, for *Braveheart*.

CREDITS

Film Producer:
The Walking Stick, Metro–Goldwyn–Mayer, 1970.
Tam Lin (also known as *The Ballad of Tam–Lin, The Devil's Widow,* and *The Devil's Woman*), 1970.
A Severed Head, Columbia, 1971.
(With Jay Kanter) *Villain,* 1971.
(With Stanley Mann) *The Devil's Widow* (also known as *Tamlin*), British International, 1972.
(With Kanter) *X Y and Zee* (also known as *Zee and Co.*), Columbia, 1972.
The Nightcomers, Avco Embassy, 1972.
(With Kanter) *Fear Is the Key,* Paramount, 1973.
Braveheart, 1995.
The Phantom, 1996.
A Very Brady Sequel, 1996.
An Unfinished Life (also known as *Ein ungezahmtes leben*), Miramax, 2005.
Gone Baby Gone, Miramax, 2007.

Film Executive Producer:
Vice Versa, Columbia, 1988.
The Russia House, 1990.
Quigley Down Under, 1990.
The Brady Bunch Movie, 1995.
The Man in the Iron Mask, 1998.

Film Appearances:
Himself, *The Beat Within: The Making of "Alien"* (documentary), Twentieth Century Fox Home Entertainment, 2003.
Himself, *The Last Mogul* (documentary; also known as *The Last Mogul: Life and Times of Lew Wasserman*), THINKFilm, 2005.
Himself, *Dangerous Days: Making "Blade Runner"* (documentary), Warner Home Video, 2007.

Television Appearances; Specials:
The 68th Annual Academy Awards, ABC, 1996.

Mel Gibson's "Braveheart": A Filmmaker's Passion, 2000.

Twentieth Century Fox: The Blockbuster Years, AMC, 2000.

The "Omen" Legacy, AMC, 2001.

(Uncredited) *The "Alien" Saga,* 2002.

Empire of Dreams: The Story of the "Star Wars" Trilogy (documentary), Arts and Entertainment, 2004.

When "Star Wars" Rules the World, VH1, 2004.

Television Appearances; Episodic:

"Braveheart," *History Vs. Hollywood,* History Channel, 2001.

"Science Fiction," *Film Genre* (also known as *Hollywood History*), 2002.

OTHER SOURCES

Periodicals:

Business Week, August 14, 1991, p. 65.

LANDON, Michael, Jr. 1964–

PERSONAL

Full name, Michael Graham Landon; born June 20, 1964, in Encino, CA; son of Michael (an actor, producer, director, and writer) and Marjorie Lynn (maiden name, Noe) Landon; brother of Christopher B. Landon (a writer, producer, and director) and Leslie Landon (an actress); married Sharee Gregory (an actress), December, 1987; children: three.

Addresses: *Agent*—Mark Lichtman, Lichtman Group, 14621 Mulholland Blvd., Los Angeles, CA 90077.

Career: Director, producer, writer, and actor.

Awards, Honors: Camie Award (with others), Character and Morality in Entertainment Awards, 2003, for *Love Comes Softly;* Camie Award (with others), 2005, for *Love's Enduring Promise;* Camie Award (with others), 2006, for *Love's Long Journey.*

CREDITS

Film Director:

(And co–executive producer) *Love's Abiding Joy,* Bigger Picture, 2006.

(And producer and editor) *The Last Sin Eater,* Twentieth Century–Fox, 2007.

(And producer) *Saving Sarah Cain,* FoxFaith/Bigger Picture, 2007.

The Velveteen Rabbit, Visiplex Family Entertainment, 2007.

Television Work; Movies:

Executive producer and director, *Michael Landon, the Father I Knew* (also known as *A Father's Son*), CBS, 1999.

Co–executive producer and director, *Love Comes Softly,* Hallmark Channel, 2003.

Co–executive producer and director, *Love's Enduring Promise,* Hallmark Channel, 2004.

Co–executive producer and director, *Love's Long Journey,* Hallmark Channel, 2005.

Co–executive producer, *Love's Unending Legacy,* Hallmark Channel, 2007.

Television Work; Specials:

Producer, *Michael Landon: Memories with Laughter and Love,* NBC, 1991.

Television Appearances; Movies:

Benjamin "Benj" Cartwright, *Bonanza: The Next Generation* (also known as *Bonanza: The Movie*), syndicated, 1988.

Benjamin "Benj" Cartwright, *Bonanza: The Return,* NBC, 1993.

Benjamin "Benj" Cartwright, *Bonanza: Under Attack,* NBC, 1995.

Television Appearances; Specials:

Michael Landon: Memories with Laughter and Love, NBC, 1991.

Host, *Back to Bonanza,* NBC, 1993.

Television Appearances; Episodic:

Jim, "The Election," *Little House on the Prairie,* NBC, 1977.

Stretch, "The Fixer," *Superboy* (also known as *The Adventures of Superboy*), syndicated, 1988.

WRITINGS

Screenplays:

Love's Abiding Joy (also based on story by Landon), Bigger Picture, 2006.

The Last Sin Eater, Twentieth Century–Fox, 2007.

Television Movies:

Love Comes Softly, Hallmark Channel, 2003.

Love's Enduring Promise, Hallmark Channel, 2004.

Love's Long Journey, Hallmark Channel, 2005.
Love's Unending Legacy, Hallmark Channel, 2007.
Love's Unfolding Dream, Hallmark Channel, 2007.

ADAPTATIONS

The 1991 television special *Bonanza: The Return* was based on a story by Landon; the 1999 television special *Michael Landon, the Father I Knew* was also based on a story by Landon.

LANSBURY, David 1961–
(David Landsbury)

PERSONAL

Born February 25, 1961; married Ally Sheedy (an actress), October 10, 1992; children: Rebecca Elizabeth.

Career: Actor.

CREDITS

Film Appearances:

Larry, *Gorillas in the Mist: The Story of Dian Fossey* (also known as *Gorillas in the Mist*), Universal, 1988.

(As David Landsbury) Hamlet Humphrey, *Gas, Food, Lodging,* IRS Media, 1992.

Michael, *Scent of a Woman,* Universal, 1992.

Charlie Kinneson, *Stranger in the Kingdom,* Ardustry Home Entertainment, 1998.

Max and Macduff, *Macbeth in Manhattan,* The Asylum, 1999.

U.S. court prosecutor, *The Hurricane,* Universal, 1999.

Brian Schwartzbaum, *From Other Worlds,* Shoreline Entertainment, 2004.

Timmy Clayton, *Michael Clayton,* Warner Bros., 2007.

Television Appearances; Movies:

Bob Morgan, *Empty Cradle,* ABC, 1993.
Timy Farley, *Parallel Lives,* Showtime, 1994.
Lieutenant Jim Pendergast, *Truman,* HBO, 1995.
Philip, *Cupid & Cate,* CBS, 2000.

Television Appearances; Pilots:

Stone Paxton, *Swift Justice,* UPN, 1996.

Television Appearances; Episodic:

Douglas Philips, "The Wages of Love," *Law & Order,* NBC, 1991.

Brad Hellman, "Moving Violation," *Murder, She Wrote,* CBS, 1991.

Brian Singer, "Murder on the Madison Avenue," *Murder, She Wrote,* CBS, 1992.

Randall, "Love Lost," *Swamp Thing,* USA Network, 1992.

Peter Morgan, "Threshold of Fear," *Murder, She Wrote,* CBS, 1993.

Jimmy Blake, *Crime & Punishment,* NBC, 1993.

Rob Norman, "Cybill's Fifteen Minutes," *Cybill,* CBS, 1995.

Bill Parker, "Civil Wars," *Promised Land* (also known as *Home of the Brave*), CBS, 1997.

Robert Sippel, "Animal Farm," *Oz,* HBO, 1998.

Robert Sippel, "Escape from Oz," *OZ,* HBO, 1998.

Kevin, "The Fuck Buddy," *Sex and the City,* HBO, 1999.

David, "Are We Sluts?," *Sex and the City,* HBO, 2000.

Officer Michael Stovic, "Crazy," *Law & Order: Criminal Intent* (also known as *Law & Order: CI*), NBC, 2002.

Larry Purcell, "Contagious," *Law & Order: Special Victims Unit* (also known as *Law & Order: SVU* and *Special Victims Unit*), NBC, 2005.

Stage Appearances:

Desmond, "Twice Shy," *Young Playwrights Festival,* Playwrights Horizons Theatre, New York City, 1989.

Peter Patrone, *The Heidi Chronicles,* Plymouth Theatre, New York City, 1989–90.

Brat, *Advice from a Caterpillar,* Lucille Lortel Theatre, New York City, 1991.

Ridley, *Hapgood,* Mitzi E. Newhouse Theatre, New York City, 1994–95.

West Bright, Frazier Tidings, David Bloom, and Pinky Wheelock, *Pride's Crossing,* Mitzi E. Newhouse Theatre, New York City, 1997–98.

Bill Walker, *Major Barbara,* American Airlines Theatre, New York City, 2001.

Eilert Lovborg, *Hedda Gabler,* Ambassador Theatre, New York City, 2001–2002.

George McBrain, *Comedians,* Samuel Beckett Theatre, New York City, 2003.

Long, *The Hairy Ape,* Irish Repertory Theatre, New York City, 2006.

J. J., *Defender of the Faith,* Irish Repertory Theatre, New York City, 2007.

George McBrain, *Comedians,* Samuel Beckett Theatre, New York City, 2003.

Also appeared in *Cymbeline,* Old Globe Theatre, San Diego, CA; *Henry IV, Parts I & II,* Old Globe Theatre, Princeton, NJ; *A Doll's House,* McCarter Theatre; *The Glass Menagerie,* Birmingham Repertory Theatre,

Birmingham, England; *Jane Eyre,* Birmingham Repertory Theatre; *Julius Caesar,* Birmingham Repertory Theatre; *Saved,* Birmingham Repertory Theatre.

LANTIERI, Michael
(Mike Lantieri)

PERSONAL

Born in Los Angeles, CA; children: son, one stepson, two stepdaughters. *Education:* Attended Art Center College of Design and University of California at Los Angeles.

Addresses: *Contact*—c/o IATSE Local 44, 11500 Burbank Blvd., North Hollywood, CA 91601–2308.

Career: Special effects supervisor, special effects coordinator, and special effects technician. Universal Studios, special effects shop employee working on television shows, 1974–81; helped create Disneyland's ride "Pirates of the Caribbean."

Member: International Alliance of Theatrical Stage Employees (IATSE).

Awards, Honors: Saturn Award nomination (with Ken Ralston), Academy of Science Fiction, Fantasy, and Horror Films, best special effects, 1987, for *Star Trek IV: The Voyage Home;* Film Award (with others), best special effects, British Academy of Film and Television Arts, Saturn Award nomination, best special effects, 1988, both for *The Witches of Eastwick;* Film Award (with others), best special effects, British Academy of Film and Television Arts, and Academy Award nomination (with others), best effects—visual effects, 1990, both for *Back to the Future Part II;* Academy Award nomination (with others), best effects—visual effects, 1992, for *Hook;* Film Award (with others), best special effects, British Academy of Film and Television Arts, 1993, for *Death Becomes Her;* Film Award nomination (with others), best special effects, British Academy of Film and Television Arts, 1994, for *Dracula;* Academy Award (with others), best effects—visual effects, Film Award (with others), best special effects, British Academy of Film and Television Arts, Saturn Award (with others), best special effects, Academy of Science Fiction, Fantasy and Horror Films, 1994, all for *Jurassic Park;* Saturn Award nomination (with others), best special effects, Academy of Science Fiction, Fantasy and Horror Films, 1996, for *Congo;* Saturn Award nomination (with others), best special effects, Academy of Science Fiction, Fantasy and Horror Films, 1997, for

Mars Attacks!; Academy Award nomination, best effects—visual effects, Saturn Award nomination (with others), best special effects, Academy of Science Fiction, Fantasy and Horror Films, 1998, both for *The Lost World: Jurassic Park;* Saturn Award nomination (with David Drzewiecki), best special effects, Academy of Science Fiction, Fantasy and Horror Films, 2001, both for *The 6th Day;* Academy Award nomination (with others), best effects, visual effects, Phoenix Film Critics Society Award nomination (with others), best visual effects, Film Award nomination (with others), best achievement in special visual effects, British Academy of Film and Television Arts, Saturn Award (with others), best special effects, Academy of Science Fiction, Fantasy and Horror Films, 2002, all for *Artificial Intelligence: AI;* Phoenix Film Critics Society Award nomination (with others), best visual effects, Online Film Critics Society Award nomination, best visual effects, Film Award nomination (with others), best achievement in special visual effects, British Academy of Film and Television Arts, Saturn Award nomination (with others), best special effects, Academy of Science Fiction, Fantasy and Horror Films, 2003, all for *Minority Report;* Saturn Award nomination, best special effects, Academy of Science Fiction, Fantasy and Horror Films, 2004, for *Hulk.*

CREDITS

Film Special Effects:
Flashdance, Paramount, 1983.
Thief of Hearts, Paramount, 1984.
The Last Starfighter, Universal, 1984.
The Women in Red, 1984.
Fright Night, Columbia Pictures, 1985.
Moving, 1988.
The Indian in the Cupboard, Paramount, 1995.
Mr. Payback: An Interactive Movie (also known as *Mr. Payback*), A.e.c., 1995.
Mousehunt, DreamWorks Distribution, 1997.

Film Special Effects Coordinator:
Poltergeist II: The Other Side (also known as *Poltergeist II* and *Poltergeist 2*), 1986.
Twins, 1988.
(Uncredited) *Paulie,* DreamWorks Distribution, 1998.
Deep Impact, Paramount, 1998.
Jurassic Park III (also known as *JP3*), Universal, 2001.
Seabiscuit, Universal, 2003.
House of Sand and Fog, DreamWorks, 2003.
The Polar Express (animated), Warner Bros., 2004.
Pirates of the Caribbean: Dead Man's Chest (also known as *P.O.T.C. 2* and *Pirates 2*), Buena Vista, 2006.
Beowulf, Warner Bros., 2007.

Film Special Effects Supervisor:
Back to School, Orion, 1986.

Star Trek IV: The Voyage Home (also known as *The Voyage Home: Star Trek IV*), Paramount, 1986.

(As Mike Lanteri) *The Witches of Eastwick,* Warner Bros., 1987.

Who Framed Roger Rabbit, 1988.

Caddyshack II, 1988.

(As Mike Lantieri) *Indiana Jones and the Last Crusade,* Paramount, 1989.

Back to the Future Part II, Universal, 1989.

Hook, TriStar Pictures, 1991.

Nothing But Trouble, 1991.

Death Becomes Her, Universal, 1992.

The Flintstones, Universal, 1994.

Casper, Universal, 1995.

Matilda (also known as *Roald Dahl's "Matilda"*), Sony Pictures Entertainment, 1996.

Mars Attacks!, Warner Bros., 1996.

Wild Wild West, Warner Bros., 1999.

The Astronaut's Wife, New Line Cinema, 1999.

(Los Angeles tank crew) *Snow Falling on Cedars,* 1999.

The 6th Day (also known as *Le sixieme jour*), Sony Pictures Entertainment, 2000.

A.I. Artificial Intelligence (also known as *Artificial Intelligence: AI*), 2001.

Minority Report, Twentieth Century–Fox, 2002.

Hulk, Universal, 2003.

Starship Troopers 2: Hero of Freedom, Columbia TriStar Home Video, 2004.

Lemony Snicket's "A Series of Unfortunate Events" (also known as *Lemony Snicket—Ratselhafte Ereignisse*), Paramount, 2004.

The Spiderwick Chronicles, Paramount, 2008.

Get Smart, Warner Bros., 2008.

Film Work; Other:

(As Mike Lanteri) Phil's remote operator, *Heartbeeps,* Universal, 1981.

Special mechanical effects supervisor, *My Science Project,* 1985.

Mechanical effects supervisor, *Back to the Future Part III,* Universal, 1990.

Special mechanical effects supervisor, *Dracula* (also known as *Bram Stoker's "Dracula"*), Columbia, 1992.

Special effects consultant, *Alive* (also known as *Alive: The Miracle of the Andes*), 1993.

Special dinosaur effects, *Jurassic Park* (also known as *JP*), Universal, 1993.

Physical effects supervisor, *Congo,* Paramount, 1995.

Special dinosaur effects, *The Lost World: Jurassic Park,* Universal, 1997.

Director, *Komodo,* Komodo Film Productions Pty Ltd., 1999.

Special effects consultant, *Jurassic Park III* (also known as *JPIII*), 2001.

Special effects director, *The Terminal,* DreamWorks, 2004.

Special effects consultant, *Monster House* (animated; also known as *Neighbourhood Crimes & Peepers*), Columbia, 2006.

Film Appearances:

Himself, *The Making of "Jurassic Park"* (documentary), Universal Home Video, 1995.

Himself, *The Making of "Lost World"* (documentary), Universal Studios Home Video, 1997.

Himself, *Beyond "Jurassic Park"* (documentary), Universal Home Video, 2001.

Himself, *The Special Effects of "Jurassic Park III"* (documentary short), Universal Studios Home Video, 2001.

Himself, *The Making of "Jurassic Park III"* (documentary short), Universal Studios Home Video, 2001.

Himself, *AI/FX* (documentary short), DreamWorks Home Entertainment, 2002.

Himself, *Creating "AI"* (documentary short), 2002.

Himself, *Deconstructing Precrime and Precogs* (short), DreamWorks Home Entertainment, 2002.

Himself, *Deconstructing Vehicles of the Future* (short), DreamWorks Home Entertainment, 2002.

Himself, *The Making of "Hulk"* (documentary short), Universal Studios Home Video, 2003.

Himself, *Behind the Ears: The True Story of "Roger Rabbit"* (documentary short), Buena Vista Home Entertainment, 2003.

Himself, *The Making of "Seabiscuit"* (documentary short; also known as *Bringing the Legend to Life: The Making of "Seabiscuit"*), Universal Studios Home Video, 2003.

Himself, *A Terrible Tragedy: Alarming Evidence from the Making of the Film—A Woeful World* (documentary), Paramount, 2004.

Television Appearances; Specials:

"Hulk": The Lowdown, Sci–Fi Channel, 2003.

Television Appearances; Episodic:

"Creating Environments: Out of This World," *Movie Magic,* Discovery Channel, 1997.

"Blockbuster Visual FX," *Space Top 10 Countdown,* Space Channel, 2006.

RECORDINGS

Video Games (Appearances):

Voice of himself and special effects supervisor, *Steven Spielberg's "Director's Chair,"* 1996.

Video Games (Work):

Special effects, *Superman Returns,* Electronic Arts, 2006.

LEISURE, David 1950–

PERSONAL

Full name, David Russell Leisure; born November 16, 1950, in San Diego, CA; married Flora Kleinfeld, November 29, 1975 (divorced); married Kelly Hutchinson, 1989 (divorced, 1994); married Patricia Bunch (a makeup artist), June 14, 1997; children: (first marriage) Maya. *Education:* Studied drama at Grossmont College; San Diego State University, graduated with a degree in fine arts.

Addresses: *Agent*—Cunningham, Escott, Slevin and Doherty Talent Agency, 10635 Santa Monica Blvd., Suite 140, Los Angeles, CA 90025.

Career: Actor. Appeared in more than sixty television commercials, including appearing as Joe Isuzu, the spokesperson for Isuzu cars and trucks, and as Joe Friday, for Bell Atlantic Yellow Pages.

Member: Screen Actors Guild.

CREDITS

Film Appearances:
First Krishna, *Airplane!* (also known as *Flying High* and *Flying High!*), Paramount, 1980.
Religious zealot, *Airplane II: The Sequel* (also known as *Flying High II* and *Flying High II: The Sequel*), Paramount, 1982.
Police sergeant, *Say Yes,* 1986.
Peter Newcomb, *You Can't Hurry Love* (also known as *Greetings from L.A.* and *Lovestruck*), Lightning, 1988.
Jason, *The Brady Bunch Movie,* 1995.
Pal Acres, *Dogmatic,* 1996.
Egg and Ducky's Dad, *Nowhere,* Fine Line, 1997.
Troy Johnson, *Hollywood Safari,* 1997.
Baby Huey's Great Easter Adventure, Columbia TriStar Home Video, 1998.
Mr. Johnson, *Right Hand Woman,* 1998.
Peter Colgrove, Amanda's boss, *Fallout,* 1998.
Pal Acres, *Dogmatic,* 1999.
Mr. Chapin, *10 Things I Hate About You,* Buena Vista, 1999.
District attorney, *3 Strikes,* Metro–Goldwyn–Mayer, 2000.
Charles, *Downward Angel* (also known as *The Guild*), 2000.
A Package for Me, 2001.
Voice of Bus Org, *Power Rangers Wild Force: Curse of the Wolf,* 2002.

Hold–in–the–Head Elvis, *Elvis Has Left the Building,* Lookalike Productions LLC, 2004.
Elliott Faydo, *Welcome to September,* 2005.
Your golf guide, *Teed Off* (also known as *National Lampoon's "Teed Off: Just Fore Laughs"*), Another Television Discovery, 2005.
Himself, *Teed Off: Behind the Tees* (documentary short; also known as *National Lampoon's "Teed Off: Behind the Tees"*), Another Television Discovery, 2005.
Your golf guide, *Teed Off Too* (also known as *National Lampoon's "Teed Off Too"*), Another Television Discovery, 2006.

Television Appearances; Series:
Charley, *Empty Nest,* NBC, 1988–91.

Television Appearances; Movies:
Andrew Selsky, *If It's Tuesday, It Still Must Be Belgium* (also known as *If It's Tuesday, It Must Be Belgium*), NBC, 1987.
Jimmy, *Goddess of Love,* NBC, 1988.
Derek, *Perfect People,* ABC, 1988.
Newscaster/game show host, *Mother Goose Rock 'n Rhyme,* Disney Channel, 1990.
"Hart to Hart": Old Friends Never Die, 1994.
Dr. Greenstreet, *The Outsider* (also known as *Gangster World*), 1998.
Pal Acres, *Dogmatic,* 1999.
Dr. Vaughn, *Ghost Dog: A Detective Tail,* PAX, 2003.

Television Appearances; Specials:
Policeman, *Wait Until Dark,* HBO, 1982.
NBC Presents the American Film Institute Comedy Special (also known as *American Film Institute Comedy Special*), NBC, 1987.
Host, *All–American Sports Nuts,* 1988.
The 14th Annual Circus of the Stars, CBS, 1989.
The 4th Annual American Comedy Awards, ABC, 1990.
Host, *Live! The World's Greatest Stunts,* Fox, 1990.
Host, *The World's Funniest, Cleverest, Most Imaginative Commercials,* CBS, 1990.
Super Bloopers & New Practical Jokes, 1990.
Segment host, *Live! The World's Greatest Stunts,* 1990.
Tube Test Two, ABC, 1991.
The 61st Annual Hollywood Christmas Parade, syndicated, 1992.
Circus of the Stars Goes to Disneyland, 1994.
TV's Funniest Friends & Neighbors, 1995.
The Greatest Commercials of All Time, 1999.
Intimate Portrait: Park Overall, Lifetime, 2000.

Television Appearances; Episodic:
Waiter, "The Betrayal," *Falcon Crest,* 1983.
Man in restaurant, "Dead Drop," *The Equalizer,* CBS, 1986.
Ben Fairley, "Shootout," *T. J. Hooker,* 1986.

Vigilante, "Magnum Farce," *Sledge Hammer!* (also known as *Sledge Hammer: The Early Years*), 1986.

Oliver, "Empty Nests," *The Golden Girls,* 1987.

Brandon Tartikoff, "Crime Time," *ALF,* 1987.

Brandon Tartikoff, "The Gambler," *ALF,* 1987.

Chester, "Hammer Hits the Rock," *Sledge Hammer!* (also known as *Sledge Hammer: The Early Years*), 1987.

Pery, "The Audit," *227,* NBC, 1987.

Bink Winkleman, "Just Married … with Children," *Married … with Children,* Fox, 1988.

Host, "All–American Sports Nuts" (also known as "The All–American Sports Comedy Hour"), *The Magical World of Disney,* NBC, 1988.

Mark's replacement, "Championship Game," *First in Ten: In Your Face!* (also known as *1st & Ten*), HBO, 1990.

Super Bloopers and New Practical Jokes, NBC, 1990.

Voice of Mr. Teddy Wolfe, "What 'Sexual Harris' Meant," *Dinosaurs,* 1991.

Charlie Dietz, "Questions and Answers," *The Golden Girls,* CBS, 1992.

Himself, "The Making of the President," *Blossom,* NBC, 1992.

Charlie Dietz, "Moon Over Miami," *Nurses,* 1992.

Charlie Dietz, "Jack's Indecent Proposal," *Nurses,* 1993.

Stormy Gilliss, "Who Killed the Anchorman?" *Burke's Law,* CBS, 1994.

Spencer Spencer, "Ordinary People," *Lois & Clark: The New Adventures of Superman* (also known as *Lois & Clark* and *The New Adventures of Superman*), ABC, 1995.

Nick Adams, "Tony's 15 Minutes," *Hudson Street,* 1996.

Derek Devlin/Mr. Success, "Mr. Success," *Renegade,* 1996.

Councilman Hinkley, "Angel of Death," *Touched by an Angel,* CBS, 1997.

William Tilbrook, "Given the Heir," *Perversions of Science,* HBO, 1997.

Fred, "Caroline and the Used Car Salesman," *Caroline in the City,* NBC, 1997.

Bud, "Stand Up Guy," *The Wayans Bros.,* 1997.

Dean's boss, "The Endangered Species," *For Your Love,* 1999.

Voice of Guy McMahon, "The Beauty Contest," *Recess* (animated), ABC, 1999.

"Honey, It's the Ghostest with the Mostest," *Honey, I Shrunk the Kids: The TV Show,* 1999.

Game show host, "Integrity to Block," *The Parent 'Hood,* 1999.

Lenny Rosen, "The Roast," *Diagnosis Murder,* CBS, 1999.

Himself, "Lights, Camera, Action," *Action,* Fox, 1999.

(Uncredited) Himself, "Love Sucks," *Action,* Fox, 2000.

"Chasing Anna," *V.I.P.* (also known as *V.I.P.—Die Bodyguards*), syndicated, 2001.

Frank, "Tame Me, I'm the Shrew," *One on One,* UPN, 2002.

Voice of Bus Org, "Predazord, Awaken," *Power Rangers Wild Force,* Fox, 2002.

Reverend Grace, *General Hospital,* ABC, 2002.

Purser/Bob Bermuda, "What a Witch Wants," *Sabrina, the Teenage Witch* (also known as *Sabrina* and *Sabrina Goes to College*), The WB, 2003.

Also appeared as cohost, *Hour Magazine,* syndicated; in *Super Password,* ABC; "Money Grubbers," *Too Something* (also known as *New York Daze*), Fox.

Stage Appearances:

Emery, *The Boys in the Band,* San Diego, CA, 1972.

Also appeared in *Richard III,* Old Globe Theatre, San Diego, CA; *The Trial of the Catonsville 9,* Old Globe Theatre, San Diego, CA; *Pal Joey; Lenny.*

OTHER SOURCES

Periodicals:

New York Daily News, January 28, 1988.
New York Newsday, October 31, 1988.
People, November 10, 1986.

LEVIN, Peter

PERSONAL

Original name, Daniel Levin; born in Trenton, NJ; son of Max (a merchant) and Katherine (maiden name, Klempner) Levin; married Audrey Davis (a writer). *Education:* Carnegie–Mellon University, B.F.A., 1954; trained for the stage at the Webber–Douglas School of Drama, London, and with Lee Strasberg.

Addresses: *Agent*—Paradigm, 360 North Crescent Dr., North Bldg., Beverly Hills, CA 90210.

Career: Director, producer, and actor.

Member: Actors' Equity Association, Directors Guild of America, Academy of Television Arts and Sciences.

Awards, Honors: Shakespeare Cup, 1954–55; Emmy Award nomination, achievement by an individual in a daytime drama, 1972, for *Love Is a Many Splendored Thing;* Daytime Emmy Award nomination, best director, daytime special program, 1974, for *The Other Woman;* Emmy Award nomination, outstanding directing in a drama series, 1980, for *Lou Grant;* Christopher Award (with others), television and cable, 2004, for *Homeless to Harvard: The Liz Murray Story;* Fulbright scholarship; Norman Apell Award; Webber Cup.

CREDITS

Television Work; Series:
Producer, *Sons and Daughters,* CBS, 1991.
Consultant, *Love Potion No. 9,* 1992.

Television Director; Miniseries:
And Never Let Her Go, CBS, 2001.

Television Director; Movies:
Heart in Hiding, 1973.
The Other Woman, ABC, 1973.
"Ashes of Mrs. Reasoner," *Hollywood Television Theatre,* 1976.
The Comeback Kid, ABC, 1979.
Rape and Marriage: The Rideout Case, 1980.
Palmerstown, USA, CBS, 1980.
Washington Mistress, 1981.
The Marva Collins Story, CBS, 1981.
The Royal Romance of Charles and Diana, CBS, 1982.
A Doctor's Story, 1983.
A Reason to Live, 1984.
Call to Glory: J. F. K., 1985.
Between the Darkness and the Dawn, 1985.
Northstar, 1986.
"Popeye" Doyle, 1986.
Houston: The Legend of Texas, 1987.
Sworn to Silence, ABC, 1987.
Hostage (also known as *Against Her Will*), CBS, 1988.
The Littlest Victims, CBS, 1989.
Lady in a Corner, NBC, 1989.
A Killer Among Us, NBC, 1990.
My Son Johnny (also known as *Bad Seed*), CBS, 1991.
Overkill: The Aileen Wuornos Story, CBS, 1992.
Deliver Them from Evil: The Taking of Alta View (also known as *Take Down* and *Under Pressure*), CBS, 1992.
The Man with Three Wives, CBS, 1993.
Precious Victims, 1993.
Fighting for My Daughter, 1995.
A Stranger in Town, 1995.
A Stranger to Love, CBS, 1996.
The Perfect Mother (also known as *The Mother–In–Law*), 1997.
Two Voices (also known as *Two Small Voices*), 1997.
Little Girl Fly Away (also known as *The Poet*), CBS, 1998.
My Father's Shadow: The Sam Sheppard Story (also known as *Death in the Shadows*), CBS, 1998.
To Love, Honor & Betray, 1999.
In the Name of the Pope, 2000.
Homeless to Harvard: The Liz Murray Story, Lifetime, 2003.

In from the Night, CBS, 2006.
A Perfect Day, TNT, 2006.
Queen Sized, Lifetime, 2008.

Other Television Work; Movies:
Executive producer, *Heartless,* 1997.
Executive producer, *High Voltage,* 1998.
Co–executive producer, *To Love, Honor & Betray,* 1999.

Television Director; Pilots:
Joshua's World, CBS, 1980.
Palmerstown, U.S.A., 1980.
Knots Landing, CBS, 1983.
In the Heat of the Night, NBC, 1988.
The Bakery, CBS, 1990.

Television Director; Specials:
Monkey, Monkey, Bottle of Beer, How Many Monkeys Have We Here?, PBS, 1974.
Sojourner, CBS, 1975.
Zalmen: or, The Madness of God (also known as *Zalmen*), PBS, 1975.
Secret Service, PBS, 1977.

Television Director; Episodic:
Love Is a Many Splendored Thing, CBS, 1972.
"Circuit of Death," *The Starlost,* 1973.
"The Other Woman," *The ABC Afternoon Playbreak* (also known as *ABC Matinee Today*), ABC, 1973.
"Heart in Hiding," *The ABC Afternoon Playbreak* (also known as *ABC Matinee Today*), ABC, 1975.
Beacon Hill, CBS, 1975.
Starsky and Hutch, 1975.
Lovers and Friends, NBC, 1977.
Lou Grant, CBS, 1977.
James at 15 (also known as *James at 16*), NBC, 1977.
Kaz, CBS, 1977–78.
Paper Chase, CBS, 1978.
"Just Friends," *Family,* ABC, 1978.
"Malicious Mischief," *Family,* ABC, 1979.
Married: The First Year, 1979.
Lou Grant, 1979–82.
"Scandal," *Palmerstown, U.S.A.,* 1981.
"Words," *Fame,* NBC, 1982.
"Homecoming," *Fame,* 1982.
Cagney & Lacey, CBS, 1982–83.
Ryan's Four, ABC, 1983.
Seven Brides for Seven Brothers, CBS, 1983.
Trauma Center, ABC, 1983.
Emerald Point, N.A.S., CBS, 1983–84.
AfterMASH, CBS, 1984.
Boone, NBC, 1984.
Two Marriages, ABC, 1984.
Call to Glory, ABC, 1984–85.
The Best Times, NBC, 1985.
Hell Town, NBC, 1985.

"But Not for Me," *Midnight Caller*, NBC, 1988.

In the Heat of the Night, 1988–89.

"Blame It On Midnight," *Midnight Caller*, NBC, 1989.

"The Reverend Soundbite," *Midnight Caller*, NBC, 1990.

Sons and Daughters, CBS, 1991.

Reasonable Doubts, 1991.

"Blood Is Thicker ...," *Law & Order*, NBC, 1992.

The Client (also known as *John Grisham's "The Client"*), CBS, 1995.

Dellaventura, 1997.

Chicago Hope, CBS, 1999.

"The Men from the Boys," *The Guardian*, CBS, 2001.

"Boston Terriers from France," *Judging Amy*, CBS, 2002.

"Every Stranger's Face I See," *Judging Amy*, CBS, 2002.

"Requiem," *Judging Amy*, CBS, 2003.

"Tricks of the Trade," *Judging Amy*, CBS, 2003.

"Death Be Not Whatever," *Joan of Arcadia*, CBS, 2003.

The Lyon's Den, NBC, 2003.

Also directed "The Madness of God," *Theatre in America*, PBS; *Best of Families*, ABC; *Another World*.

Television Appearances; Series:

Sam Holliday, *Goodnight, Beantown*, CBS, 1983.

Stage Appearances:

Peter, *The Diary of Anne Frank*, Cort Theatre, New York City, 1955.

Orlando, *As You Like It*, San Diego Shakespeare Festival, San Diego, CA, 1960.

Octavius Caesar, *Julius Caesar*, San Diego Shakespeare Festival, 1960.

Horatio, *Hamlet*, San Diego Shakespeare Festival, 1960.

Parritt, *The Iceman Cometh*, Arena Stage, Washington, DC, 1960.

Orlando, *As You Like It*, Shakespeare Festival, Princeton, NJ, 1961.

Stage Director:

Hardware Poets, Playhouse Theatre, New York City, 1962–66.

The Show Off, Long Wharf Theatre, New Haven, CT, 1975.

Also directed *Real Inspector Hound* and *A Memory of Two Mondays*, Guildhall School, London; *You Never Can Tell*, Arlington Heights, IL, then Chicago, IL.

Major Tours:

Directed a tour of *Hamlet*, U.S. cities.

WRITINGS

Television Series:

Emerald Point, N. A. S., CBS, 1983–84.

LINDENLAUB, Karl Walter 1957–
(Walter Lindenlaub)

PERSONAL

Born June 19, 1957, in Bremen, Germany. *Education:* Graduated from Munich Film and Television School; also studied at National Film and Television School, England, and Royal Film Academy.

Addresses: *Agent*—International Creative Management, 10250 Constellation Way, 9th Floor, Los Angeles, CA 90067.

Career: Cinematographer and camera operator. Also shot commercials and documentaries.

Member: American Society of Cinematographers.

Awards, Honors: Promotional Award, best feature film, German Camera Award, 1990, for *Moon 44*; Apex Award, best cinematography—fantasy/science fiction/horror, 1994, for *Stargate*; Universe Reader's Choice Award, best cinematography for a genre motion picture, Sci–Fi Universe Magazine, 1996, for *Independence Day*.

CREDITS

Film Cinematographer:

Alleingang, 1981.

Tango im Bauch, 1985.

Lebe kreuz und sterbe quer, 1985.

Der Flieger (also known as *The Flyer*), 1986.

Hollywood–Monster (also known as *Ghost Chase*), Image Entertainment, Inc., 1987.

Tele–Vision, 1988.

Im Jahr der schildkrote (also known as *Year of the Turtle*), 1989.

Todesvisionen—Geisterstunde (also known as *Strange Encounters*), 1989.

Moon 44 (also known as *Intruder*), 1990.

Der Schonste busen der welt (also known as *The Most Beautiful Breasts in the World*), 1990.

Eye of the Storm, 1991.

Das Tatowierte Herz (also known as *The Tattooed Heart*), 1991.

Celibidache (also known as *You Don't Do Anything, You Just Let It Evolve*), 1992.

Universal Soldier, TriStar Pictures, 1992.

CB4, 1993.

Polski Crash, 1993.

(And cinematographer: model unit), *Stargate* (also known as *Stargate, la porte des etoiles*), Metro–Goldwyn–Mayer/United Artists, 1994.

Rob Roy, United Artists, 1995.

Last of the Dogmen, Savoy Pictures, 1995.

Up Close and Personal, Buena Vista, 1996.

Independence Day (also known as *ID4*), Twentieth Century–Fox, 1996.

Red Corner, Metro–Goldwyn–Mayer/United Artists, 1997.

The Jackal (also known as *Le chacal* and *Der Schakal*), Universal, 1997.

The Haunting (also known as *La maldicion*), Dream-Works Distribution, 1999.

(And second unit cinematographer) *Isn't She Great* (also known as *Ist sie nicht groBartig?*), Universal, 2000.

One Night at McCool's, USA Films, 2001.

The Princess Diaries (also known as *The Princess of Tribeca*), Buena Vista, 2001.

City by the Sea (also known as *The Suspect*), Warner Bros., 2001.

The Banger Sisters, Fox Searchlight, 2002.

Maid in Manhattan (also known as *Made in New York*), Columbia, 2002.

Because of Winn–Dixie, Twentieth Century–Fox, 2005.

Guess Who, Columbia, 2005.

Zwartboek (also known as *Black Book*), Sony Pictures Classics, 2006.

Georgia Rule, Universal Pictures, 2007.

The Chronicles of Narnia: Prince Caspian, Buena Vista, 2008.

Film Work; Other:

Sound assistant, *Stachel im fleisch,* 1980.

Camera assistant, *Unser Mann im dschungel* (also known as *Amazonas Mission*), 1985.

Camera operator: second unit, *The NeverEnding Story II: The Next Chapter,* 1990.

Television Cinematographer; Series:

Leo und Charlotte, 1991.

Television Cinematographer; Movies:

(As Walter Lindenlaub) *Altosax,* 1980.

Casualties of Love: The "Long Island Lolita" Story, CBS, 1993.

(Additional photography) *Attack of the 50 Ft. Woman,* 1993.

Television Cinematographer; Specials:

Celibiedach Rehearses Bruckner (documentary), 1991.

WRITINGS

Television Movies:

(As Walter Lindenlaub) *Altosax,* 1980.

LINSON, Art 1942–

PERSONAL

Full name, Arthur Larry Linson; born March 16, 1942, in Chicago, IL; married second wife, c. 1995; children: John (a producer). *Education:* University of California, Los Angeles, law degree, 1967; also attended University of California, Berkeley.

Addresses: *Office*—Linson Films, 210 Palisades Ave., Santa Monica, CA 90402. *Agent*—John Burnham, International Creative Management, 10250 Constellation Way, Ninth Floor, Los Angeles, CA 90067.

Career: Producer, director, and writer. Art Linson Productions, principal; Linson Films, Santa Monica, CA, principal; Indelible Pictures, Los Angeles, principal (with David Fincher), beginning 2000. Spin Dizzy (record company), former owner; also worked as a rock music manager with Lou Adler.

Member: Directors Guild of America, Writers Guild of America, West.

CREDITS

Film Producer:

(With Michael Gruskoff) *Rafferty and the Gold Dust Twins* (also known as *Rafferty and the Highway Hustlers*), Warner Bros., 1975.

(With Gary Stromberg) *Car Wash,* Universal, 1976.

American Hot Wax, Paramount, 1978.

(With Don Phillips) *Melvin and Howard,* Universal, 1980.

Where the Buffalo Roam, Universal, 1980.

(With Irving Azoff) *Fast Times at Ridgemont High* (also known as *Fast Times*), Universal, 1982.

(With Cameron Crowe and Phillips) *The Wild Life,* Universal, 1984.

The Untouchables, Paramount, 1987.

(With Richard Donner and Ray Hartwick) *Scrooged,* Paramount, 1988.

(With Fred Caruso) *Casualties of War* (also known as *Outrages*), Columbia, 1989.

We're No Angels, Paramount, 1989.

Point of No Return (also known as *The Assassin, The Assassin—(Point of No Return), Codename—Nina, Codename: Nina, Girl No. 5, Nina,* and *The Specialist*), Warner Bros., 1993.

This Boy's Life, Warner Bros., 1993.

Heat (also known as *Tension*), Warner Bros., 1995.

The Edge (also known as *The Bear and the Brain, Bookworm,* and *The Wild*), Twentieth Century–Fox, 1997.

Great Expectations, Twentieth Century–Fox, 1998.

Fight Club, Twentieth Century–Fox, 1999.

Pushing Tin (also known as *Turbulenzen—und andere Katastrophen*), Twentieth Century–Fox, 2000.

Sunset Strip (also known as *Untitled Sunset Strip Project*), Twentieth Century–Fox, 2000.

Heist (also known as *Professional* and *Le vol*), Warner Bros., 2001.

Imaginary Heroes, Sony Pictures Classics, 2004.

Spartan, Warner Bros., 2004.

Neverwas, Senator Films, 2005.

The Black Dahlia, Universal, 2006.

Into the Wild, Paramount Vantage, 2007.

Producer of other projects.

Film Executive Producer:

(With Barrie M. Osborne and Floyd Mutrux) *Dick Tracy,* Buena Vista, 1990.

Singles, Warner Bros., 1992.

Lords of Dogtown (also known as *American Knights* and *Dogtown Boys*), TriStar, 2005.

Film Director:

Where the Buffalo Roam, Universal, 1980.

The Wild Life, Universal, 1984.

Television Executive Producer; Series:

The Untouchables, syndicated, 1993–94.

Television Executive Producer; Pilots:

Sons of Anarchy (also known as *Charming, CA* and *Forever Sam Crow*), FX Network, c. 2008.

What Just Happened?, HBO, c. 2008.

Television Appearances; Specials:

The New Hollywood, NBC, 1990.

Himself, *Buy the Ticket, Take the Ride: Hunter S. Thompson on Film,* Starz!, 2006.

Television Appearances; Episodic:

Himself, *Sunday Morning Shootout,* American Movie Classics, 2004.

RECORDINGS

Videos:

Himself, *The Making of "Casualties of War"* (short), Columbia/TriStar Home Entertainment, 2001.

Himself, *The Untouchables: The Classic* (short), Paramount Home Video, 2004.

Himself, *The Untouchables: Re–inventing the Genre* (short), Paramount Home Video, 2004.

Himself, *The Untouchables: The Script, the Cast* (short), Paramount Home Video, 2004.

Himself, *The Making of "Heat,"* Warner Home Video, 2005.

Video Work:

Still photographer, *The Making of "Heat,"* Warner Home Video, 2005.

WRITINGS

Screenplays:

(Story) *American Hot Wax,* Paramount, 1978.

(With Cameron Crowe) *The Wild Life,* Universal, 1984.

(Story) *Sunset Strip* (also known as *Untitled Sunset Strip Project*), Twentieth Century–Fox, 2000.

Wrote the screenplay *Cover Me.* Provided the stories for other films.

Teleplays; Pilots:

(With William Finkelstein) *What Just Happened?* (based on his book *What Just Happened? Bitter Hollywood Tales from the Front Line*), HBO, c. 2008.

Nonfiction:

A Pound of Flesh: Perilous Tales of How to Produce Movies in Europe, Grove Press, 1993.

What Just Happened? Bitter Hollywood Tales from the Front Line, Bloomsbury, 2002.

LIVELY, Blake 1987–

PERSONAL

Full name, Blake Christina Lively; born August 25, 1987, in Tarzana, CA; daughter of Ernie (an actor) and Elaine (a manager and coach of child actors) Lively; sister of Eric Lively (an actor), Jason Lively (an actor), Lori Lively (an actress), and Robyn Lively (an actress).

Addresses: *Agent*—Alex Yarosh, Gersh Agency, 232 North Canon Dr., Beverly Hills, CA 90210; (voice work), Special Artists Agency, 9465 Wilshire Blvd., Suite 890, Beverly Hills, CA 90212.

Career: Actress.

Awards, Honors: Teen Choice Award nomination, choice female movie breakout performance, 2005, for *The Sisterhood of the Traveling Pants.*

CREDITS

Film Appearances:
Trixie (tooth fairy), *Sandman,* Black Lion Records, 1998.
Bridget, *The Sisterhood of the Traveling Pants* (also known as *The Sisterhood of the Travelling Pants*), Warner Bros., 2005.
Monica, *Accepted,* Universal, 2006.
Jenny, *Simon Says,* Dark Moon Pictures, 2006.
Anabelle, *Elvis and Anabelle,* Goldcrest Films International, 2006.
Bridget, *The Sisterhood of the Traveling Pants 2,* Warner Bros., 2008.

Television Appearances; Series:
Serena van der Woodsen, *Gossip Girl,* CW Network, 2007.

Television Guest Appearances; Episodic:
The View, ABC, 2005.
Today (also known as *NBC News Today* and *The Today Show*), NBC, 2005.
Entertainment Tonight (also known as *Entertainment This Week, E.T., ET Weekend,* and *This Week in Entertainment*), syndicated, 2007.
Live with Regis and Kelly, syndicated, 2007.

RECORDINGS

Videos:
Reject Rejection: The Making of "Accepted," Universal Studios Home Entertainment, 2006.

OTHER SOURCES

Periodicals:
Atlanta Journal–Constitution, June 3, 2005.
Hollywood Life, July, 2006, p. 42.

LOCHART, Ann
    See **LOCKHART, Anne**

LOCKE, Peter
    (Arthur King, Abe Snake)

PERSONAL

Married Liz Torres (an actress, comedian, and vocalist).

Addresses: *Office*—Peter Locke Co., 846 Woodacres Rd., Santa Monica, CA 90402; Kushner–Locke Co., 280 South Beverly Dr., Suite 205, Beverly Hills, CA 90212.

Career: Executive, producer, director, writer, actor. Peter Locke Co., Santa Monica, CA, producer; Kushner–Locke Co., Beverly Hills, CA, partner; Castel Film Studios, Bucharest, Romania, co–owner.

Awards, Honors: Emmy Award nomination, outstanding animated program (with others), 1988, for *The Brave Little Toaster.*

CREDITS

Film Executive Producer:
Dorothy Meets Ozma of Oz (animated), A–KOM Productions/Atlanta–Kushner–Locke/Prairie Rose Productions, 1987.
Andre, Paramount, 1994.
Lady in Waiting (also known as *Hollywood Madam*), Atlantic Group Films, 1994.
Last Gasp, Warner Bros., 1995.
The Whole Wide World, Sony Pictures Classics, 1996.
The Grave, Kushner–Locke/New City Releasing, 1996.
The Adventures of Pinocchio (also known as *Carlo Collodi's "Pinocchio," Pinocchio,* and *Die Legende von Pinocchio*), New Line Cinema, 1996.
Small Time (also known as *Waiting for the Man*), Manga Films, 1996.
The Brave Little Toaster to the Rescue (animated), Walt Disney Home Video, 1997.
The Last Time I Committed Suicide, New City Releasing/Roxie Releasing, 1997.
Little Ghost, Paramount Home Video, 1997.
The Midas Touch, Full Moon Entertainment, 1997.
Jungle Book: Lost Treasure (also known as *Jungle Book: Search for the Lost Treasure* and *Mowgli's First Adventure: In Search of the Elephant Eye Diamond*), Le Monde Entertainment, 1998.
The Secret Kingdom, Amazing Film Entertainment, 1998.
Girl, Kushner–Locke, 1998.
The Brave Little Toaster Goes to Mars (animated), Walt Disney Home Video, 1998.
Basil, Kushner–Locke, 1998.
Possums, HSX Films, 1998.
The Shrunken City, Amazing Fantasy Entertainment, 1998.
Ringmaster, Artisan Entertainment, 1998.
The Boy with the X–Ray Eyes (also known as *X–Ray Boy* and *X–treme Teens*), Amazing Fantasy Entertainment, 1999.
Phantom Town, Amazing Fantasy Entertainment/Full Moon Entertainment, 1999.
Beowulf, Miramax/Dimension Films, 1999.
Shapeshifter, Full Moon Entertainment, 1999.

The Incredible Genie, New Films International, 1999.
Blood Dolls, Full Moon Entertainment, 1999.
Freeway II: Confessions of a Trickbaby, Full Moon Entertainment/Trick Productions, 1999.
But I'm a Cheerleader, Lions Gate Films, 1999.
Picking Up the Pieces, Kushner–Locke/Miraculous Hand Productions, 2000.
Task Force 201 (also known as *Spy High*), 2000.
Train Quest, Kushner–Locke, 2001.
Harvard Man, Lions Gate Films, 2001.
Snuff–Movie, Lions Gate Films, 2005.

Film Producer:
(And director and film editor) *You've Got to Walk It Like You Talk It or You'll Lost That Beat,* J.E.R. Pictures, 1971.
The Hills Have Eyes (also known as *Wes Craven's "The Hills Have Eyes"*), Vanguard, 1977.
The Hills Have Eyes Part II, Castle Hill, 1985.
Nutcracker: The Motion Picture, Atlantic Releasing, 1986.
The Brave Little Toaster (animated), Buena Vista/Hyperion Pictures, 1987.
Pound Puppies and the Legend of Big Paw (animated), TriStar, 1988.
The Hills Have Eyes, Fox Searchlight, 2006.
The Hills Have Eyes II, Twentieth Century–Fox, 2007.

Also producer of adult films.

Film Director:
It Happened in Hollywood, J.E.R. Pictures, 1973.
The Carhops (also known as *California Drive–in Girls* and *Kitty Can't Help It*), N.M.D. Film Distributing, 1975.

Director of adult material, credited as Abe Snake.

Film Appearances:
Shoe thief and purse snatcher, *You've Got to Walk It Like You Talk It or You'll Lost That Beat,* J.E.R. Pictures, 1971.
King, *It Happened in Hollywood,* J.E.R. Pictures, 1973.
(As Arthur King) Mercury, *The Hills Have Eyes* (also known as *Wes Craven's "The Hills Have Eyes"*), Vanguard, 1977.
Voice of unseen aristocracy, *The Adventures of Pinocchio* (also known as *Carlo Collodi's "Pinocchio,"* *Pinocchio,* and *Die Legende von Pinocchio*), New Line Cinema, 1996.

Television Executive Producer; Movies:
Liberace: Behind the Music, CBS, 1988.
Your Mother Wears Combat Boots, NBC, 1989.
Sweet Bird of Youth (also known as *Tennessee Williams's "Sweet Bird of Youth"*), NBC, 1989.

Murder C.O.D., NBC, 1990.
Good Cops, Bad Cops: The Biggest Heist in History, NBC, 1990.
Carolina Skeletons, NBC, 1991.
Fire in the Dark, CBS, 1991.
Father & Son: Dangerous Relations (also known as *Dangerous Relations* and *On the Streets of L.A.*), NBC, 1993.
Getting Gotti, CBS, 1994.
Dangerous Intentions, CBS, 1995.
Wes Craven Presents "Mind Ripper," HBO, 1995.
Lady Killer, CBS, 1995.
A Husband, a Wife, and a Lover (also known as *A Strange Affair*), CBS, 1996.
Serpent's Lair, HBO, 1996.
Princess in Love, CBS, 1996.
Jack Reed: A Killer amongst Us, NBC, 1996.
Unlikely Angel, CBS, 1996.
Echo (also known as *Deadly Echo*), ABC, 1997.
Jack Reed: Death and Vengeance, NBC, 1997.
Johnny Mysto: Boy Wizard, HBO, 1997.
Teen Knight, HBO, 1998.
Denial (also known as *Something about Sex*), Cinemax, 1998.
Clockmaker, HBO, 1998.
Susan's Plan (also known as *Dying to Get Rich*), Cinemax, 1998.
Bone Daddy (also known as *Palmer's Bones* and *L'affaire Palmer*), HBO, 1998.
Black and White, HBO, 1999.
Murdercycle, Cinemax, 1999.
Dragonworld: The Legend Continues (also known as *Dragonworld II* and *Shadow of the Knight*), 1999.
Search for the Jewel of Polaris: Mysterious Museum, 1999.
Alien Arsenal, Cinemax, 2000.
They Nest (also known as *Creepy Crawlers*), USA Network, 2000.
Dark Prince: The True Story of Dracula (also known as *Dark Prince: Legend of Dracula* and *Dracula: The Dark Prince*), USA Network, 2000.
The Last Producer (also known as *The Final Hit*), USA Network, 2000.
Wolf Girl (also known as *Blood Moon*), USA Network, 2001.

Television Executive Producer; Series:
1st & Ten (also known as *1st & Ten: Do It Again, 1st & Ten: Going for Broke, 1st & Ten: In Your Face!, 1st & Ten: The Bulls Mean Business, 1st & Ten: The Championship,* and *1st & Ten, Training Camp: The Bulls Are Back*), HBO, 1984.
The Investigators, HBO, 1984.
The Spiral Zone, syndicated, 1987.
Glory Years, HBO, 1987.
Relatively Speaking, syndicated, 1988.
Sweating Bullets, CBS, 1990–91.
TrialWatch, NBC, 1991.
The Barbara DeAngelis Show, CBS, 1991.

Night Games, CBS, 1991.
Harts of the West, CBS, 1991.
Cracker, ABC, 1997.
Thrills, 2001.

Television Executive Producer; Episodic:

"Gatten vs. Gatten," *Divorce Court,* syndicated, 1988.
"Columbus Day," *Gun* (also known as *Robert Altman's "Gun"*), ABC, 1997.
"All the President's Women," *Gun* (also known as *Robert Altman's "Gun"*), ABC, 1997.

Television Producer; Pilots:

Love at First Sight, CBS, 1980.
Automan, ABC, 1983.
Stopwatch: Thirty Minutes of Investigative Ticking, HBO, 1983.
Executive producer, *Glory Years* (also known as *Wacky Weekend*), HBO, 1987.

Television Producer; Other:

Supervising producer, *Just Friends* (series), CBS, 1979.
A Gun in the House (movie), CBS, 1981.
The Star Maker (miniseries), NBC, 1981.
Executive producer, *The Hunt for Stolen War Treasures ... Live* (special), syndicated, 1989.
Every Woman's Dream (movie), CBS, 1996.

Television Appearances; Specials:

Interviewee, *The Perfect Pitch* (also known as *Brilliant but Cancelled: The Perfect Pitch*), Trio, 2002.

RECORDINGS

Videos:

Looking Back at "The Hills Have Eyes," Anchor Bay Entertainment, 2003.
Surviving the Hills: Making of "The Hills Have Eyes," Twentieth Century–Fox, 2006.

WRITINGS

Films:

You've Got to Walk It Like You Talk It or You'll Lost That Beat, J.E.R. Pictures, 1971.
It Happened in Hollywood, J.E.R. Pictures, 1973.

Writer of adult material, credited as Abe Snake.

LOCKHART, Anne 1953–
(Ann Lochart)

PERSONAL

Full name, Anne Kathleen Maloney; born September 6, 1953, in New York, NY; daughter of John F. Maloney (a doctor) and June Lockhart (an actress); married Adam C. Taylor, December 24, 1986 (died, June 4, 1994); children: Carlyle, Zane.

Career: Actress and automated dialogue replacement (ADR) voice. Champion horsewoman in cutting, reining, team penning, and barrel racing; Pro–Celebrity Rodeos, co–founder, 1983.

CREDITS

Film Appearances:

Dora, *Jory,* AVCO Embassy, 1973.
Tina, *Slashed Dreams* (also known as *Sunburst*), Cinema Financial, 1975.
Cindy Young, *Joyride,* American International Pictures, 1977.
Additional voice, *Beyond and Back* (documentary), Sunn Classic Pictures, 1978.
(Uncredited) Dispatcher, *Convoy,* United Artists, 1978.
Kris, *Just Tell Me You Love Me* (also known as *Hawaii Heat* and *Maui*), 1980.
(Uncredited) Mom, *Earthbound,* Taft International Pictures, 1981.
(Uncredited) Barmaid, *Cannery Row* (also known as *John Steinbeck's "Cannery Row"*), Metro–Goldwyn–Mayer, 1982.
(Uncredited) Nurse, *E. T.: The Extra–Terrestrial* (also known as *E. T.*), Universal, 1982.
(Uncredited) Murder victim, *10 to Midnight,* Cannon, 1983.
(Uncredited) Babysitter, *Risky Business,* Warner Bros., 1983.
Lucy, *Young Warriors* (also known as *The Graduates of Malibu High*), Cannon, 1983.
Anna, *The Oasis* (also known as *Savage Hunger*), 1984.
Roberta Radcliffe, *Hambone and Hillie,* New World Pictures, 1984.
The Serpent Warriors, 1985.
(Uncredited) Wife, *Flesh+Blood* (also known as *Los senores del acero* and *The Rose and the Sword*), Orion, 1985.
(Uncredited) Secretary, *Head Office,* TriStar, 1985.
Young Eunice St. Clair, *Troll,* Empire Pictures, 1986.
(Uncredited) Police officer, *8 Million Ways to Die,* TriStar, 1986.
(Uncredited) Club patron, *Blue City,* Paramount, 1986.
Elaine, *Dark Tower,* Fries Distribution, 1987.
(Uncredited) Assistant district attorney and hotel guest, *Black Widow* (also known as *Bullseye*), Twentieth Century–Fox, 1987.
Voiceover, *Cherry 2000,* Orion, 1987.
Additional voices, *The Little Mermaid* (animated), Buena Vista, 1989.
Lady police officer, *Big Bad John,* Red River Films, 1990.
Additional voices, *Total Recall,* TriStar, 1990.

(Uncredited) Party guest, *Wishman,* Curb/Esquire Films, 1991.

Voice, *Scenes from a Mall,* Buena Vista, 1991.

(Uncredited) Ranch hand and passenger, *City Slickers,* Columbia, 1991.

(Uncredited) Football mom, *The Last Boy Scout,* Warner Bros., 1991.

(Uncredited) Disco patron, *Basic Instinct* (also known as *Ice Cold Desire*), TriStar, 1992.

(Uncredited) Soccer mom, *Ladybugs,* Paramount, 1992.

(Uncredited) Prisoner, *Caged Fear* (also known as *Hotel Oklahoma, Innocent Young Female,* and *Jail Force*), Asso Film, 1992.

Voice performer, *Theodore Rex* (also known as *T. Rex*), New Line Cinema, 1995.

Cammie Griffin, *Bug Buster,* DMG Entertainment, 1998.

Mary Webster, *A Dog's Tale,* Majestic Family Film I, 1999.

Mrs. Warner, *Daybreak* (also known as *Rapid Transit*), Off Track Productions, 2000.

Sylvie, *Cahoots,* 2001.

Additional character voice, *Osmosis Jones,* Warner Bros., 2001.

Dave's mom, *Last Ride,* Liberty International Entertainment, 2001.

Radio dispatcher, *Route 666,* Lions Gate Films, 2001.

Jackie, *Disconnected* (short), American Film Institute, 2002.

(Uncredited) Additional character voice, *Dickie Roberts: Former Child Star* (also known as *Dickie Roberts: (Former) Child Star*), Paramount, 2003.

Miss Connors, *Big Chuck, Little Chuck,* Maricopa Films, 2004.

Herself, *Working with the Daggit of "Battlestar Galactica"* (documentary short), 2004.

Herself, *Remembering "Battlestar Galactica"* (documentary), Universal Studios Home Video, 2004.

Additional voices, *Chicken Little* (animated), Buena Vista, 2005.

(Uncredited) Gymnastic coach and mom, *Stick It,* Buena Vista, 2006.

Celeste, *Revamped,* Millennium Concepts, 2007.

Lady Moroni, *Deadly Sins,* 2007.

Film Additional Automated Dialogue Replacement (ADR) Artist:

(Uncredited) *Newsies* (also known as *Newsboys*), Buena Vista, 1992.

(Uncredited) *White Sands,* Warner Bros., 1992.

(Uncredited) *Lethal Weapon 3,* Warner Bros., 1992.

(Uncredited) *Unforgiven,* Warner Bros., 1992.

(Uncredited) *The Gun in Betty Lou's Handbag,* Buena Vista, 1992.

(Uncredited) *Matinee,* MCA/Universal Home Video, 1993.

(Uncredited) *The Crush,* Warner Bros., 1993.

(Uncredited) *The Pickle* (also known as *The Adventures of the Flying Pickle*), Columbia, 1993.

(Uncredited) *Son in Law,* Buena Vista, 1993.

(Uncredited) *Hocus Pocus,* Buena Vista, 1993.

(Uncredited) *Hearts and Souls,* Universal, 1993.

(Uncredited) *Undercover Blues,* Metro–Goldwyn–Mayer, 1993.

(Uncredited) *Airborne,* Warner Bros., 1993.

(Uncredited) *The Three Musketeers,* Buena Vista, 1993.

(Uncredited) *A Perfect World,* Warner Bros., 1993.

(Uncredited) *Young and Younger,* 1993.

(Uncredited) *Maverick,* Warner Bros., 1994.

(Uncredited) *Little Big League,* Columbia, 1994.

(Uncredited) *Pentathlon,* Live Entertainment, 1994.

(Uncredited) *The War,* Universal, 1994.

(Uncredited) *Irving,* 1995.

(Uncredited) *Heavy Weights,* Buena Vista, 1995.

(Uncredited) *Gordy,* Miramax, 1995.

(Uncredited) *The Stars Fall on Henrietta,* Warner Bros., 1995.

Stick It, Buena Vista, 2006.

(Uncredited) *First Snow,* Yari Film Group Releasing, 2006.

(Uncredited) *Everyone's Hero* (animated), Twentieth Century–Fox, 2006.

(Uncredited) *Employee of the Month,* Lions Gate, 2006.

(Uncredited) *Running with Scissors,* TriStar, 2006.

(Uncredited) *The Santa Clause 3: The Escape Clause* (also known as *Pretender*), Buena Vista, 2006.

(Uncredited) *The Fox and the Hound 2* (animated), Buena Vista, 2006.

(Uncredited) *Deck the Halls,* Twentieth Century–Fox, 2006.

(Uncredited) *Walk the Talk,* 2007.

(Uncredited) *Wild Hogs* (also known as *Blackberry*), Buena Vista, 2007.

Film Work; Other:

Automated dialogue replacement (ADR), *Turner & Hooch,* Buena Vista, 1986.

Vocalization (chimp), *Project X,* Twentieth Century–Fox, 1987.

(As Ann Lochart) ADR, *Scenes from a Mall,* 1991.

ADR, *Ladybugs,* Paramount, 1992.

ADR, *The River Wild,* Universal, 1994.

ADR, *The Trigger Effect,* Gramercy Pictures, 1996.

ADR, *This World, Then the Fireworks,* Orion Classics, 1997.

ADR, *Antz* (animated), DreamWorks, 1998.

ADR, *The Prince of Egypt* (animated), DreamWorks, 1998.

ADR, *The Road to El Dorado* (animated), DreamWorks, 2000.

Co–producer, *Cahoots,* 2001.

ADR, *Flightplan,* Buena Vista, 2005.

ADR, *Everyone's Hero,* Twentieth Century–Fox, 2006.

ADR (Todd AO), *Employee of the Month,* Lionsgate, 2006.

Television Appearances; Series:

Sheba, *Battlestar Galactica,* ABC, 1978–79.

Television Appearances; Movies:

Karen Jorgenson, "Fire on Kelly Mountain," *Disneyland* (also known as *Disney's Wonderful World, The Disney Sunday Movie, The Magical World of Disney, The Wonderful World of Disney, Walt Disney, Walt Disney Presents,* and *Walt Disney's Wonderful World of Color*), NBC, 1973.

Elizabeth Frazer, "Lisa, Bright and Dark," *Hallmark Hall of Fame* (also known as *Hallmark Television Playhouse*), NBC, 1973.

Lieutenant Sheba, *Mission Galactica: The Cylon Attack,* 1978.

Additional voice, *Daddy, I Don't Like It Like This,* CBS, 1978.

Additional voice, *Donner Pass: The Road to Survival,* NBC, 1978.

Additional voice, *The Deerslayer,* 1978.

Larue Powell, *Gidget's Summer Reunion,* syndicated, 1985.

(Uncredited) Reporter, *Classified Love,* CBS, 1986.

Additional voice, *Under the Influence,* CBS, 1986.

(Uncredited) Juror, *Act of Betrayal,* 1988.

(Uncredited) Wedding guest, *An "Eight Is Enough" Wedding,* NBC, 1989.

Carolyn MacNamara, *Bionic Ever After?* (also known as *Bionic Breakdown*), CBS, 1994.

Megan Glenneyre, *"Simon & Simon": In Trouble Again,* CBS, 1995.

(Uncredited) Housewife, *Not In This Town,* 1997.

(Uncredited) Cult member, *The Spring,* NBC, 2000.

Television Appearances; Pilots:

Mary Rose Coogan, *The Magician* (movie), NBC, 1973.

Ginger Forehead, *Washingtoon,* Showtime, 1985.

Television Appearances; Specials:

All Commercials ... A Steve Martin Special, NBC, 1980.

Voice of teacher and barmaid, "Miss Switch to the Rescue," *ABC Weekend Specials,* ABC, 1982.

Television Appearances; Episodic:

(Uncredited) Little girl, "The UNICEF Story," *Lassie* (also known as *Jeff's Collie* and *Timmy and Lassie*), CBS, 1959.

(Uncredited) Little girl, "Lassie's Ordeal," *Lassie* (also known as *Jeff's Collie* and *Timmy and Lassie*), CBS, 1962.

(Uncredited) Little girl, "Lassie and the Girl in the Canyon," *Lassie* (also known as *Jeff's Collie* and *Timmy and Lassie*), CBS, 1965.

Street urchin, "Magic Locket," *Death Valley Days* (also known as *Call of the West, The Pioneers, Trails West,* and *Western Star Theater*), syndicated, 1965.

(Uncredited) Little girl, "Little Dog Lost," *Lassie* (also known as *Jeff's Collie* and *Timmy and Lassie*), CBS, 1965.

Tabby, "A Deadly Quiet Town," *Cannon,* CBS, 1972.

Diana, "Dear Joan: We're Going to Scare You to Death," *The Sixth Sense,* ABC, 1972.

Bobbi, "Bullet from the Grave," *Get Christie Love!,* ABC, 1974.

"Ride on a Red Balloon," *Three for the Road,* CBS, 1975.

Marcia, "Three on a Porch," *Happy Days* (also known as *Happy Days Again*), ABC, 1975.

Wendy Millikan, "Death Beat," *Barnaby Jones,* CBS, 1977.

Sarah Masters, "The Mystery of the African Safari," *The Hardy Boys/Nancy Drew Mysteries* (also known as *The Nancy Drew Mysteries*), ABC, 1977.

Jess, "The Last Kiss of Summer: Parts 1 & 2," *The Hardy Boys/Nancy Drew Mysteries* (also known as *The Nancy Drew Mysteries*), ABC, 1978.

Sue Adams, "The Steel Inferno," *Emergency!* (also known as *Emergencia* and *Emergency One*), NBC, 1978.

"A Chance to Live," *Police Story,* NBC, 1978.

Ann Booth, "Sighting 4019: The Believe It or Not Incident," *Project U.F.O.* (also known as *Project Blue Book*), NBC, 1978.

"Breakout to Murder," *The Eddie Capra Mysteries,* NBC, 1978.

Beyond Reason, CBC, 1979.

Marcia, "Mork Returns," *Happy Days,* ABC, 1979.

All Star Secrets, NBC, 1979.

The $1.98 Beauty Show, syndicated, 1979.

Making Me Laugh, syndicated, 1979.

The Tonight Show with Johnny Carson, NBC, 1979.

Kathy Mulligan, "Return of the Supercycle," *CHiPs* (also known as *CHiPs Patrol*), NBC, 1979.

Lillian Pogovich, "Pogo Lil," *B. J. and the Bear,* NBC, 1979.

Karen Mitchell, "Captive Night," *The Incredible Hulk,* 1979.

Lillian Pogovich, "Fire in the Hole," *B. J. and the Bear,* NBC, 1980.

Voices, *Thundarr the Barbarian* (animated), NBC, 1980.

Jennifer/Leila Markeson, "A Dream of Jennifer," *Buck Rogers in the 25th Century,* NBC, 1980.

Leila/Jennifer, "Testimony of a Traitor," *Buck Rogers in the 25th Century,* NBC, 1981.

Audrey, "The Phenom," *The Incredible Hulk,* CBS, 1981.

Diane Westmore, "Lest We Forget," *Magnum P.I.,* CBS, 1981.

Voices, *Spider–Man and His Amazing Friends* (animated), 1981.

Voices, *Goldie Gold and Action Jack* (animated), ABC, 1981.

Brenda McCutchen and Cassie McCutchen, "Flashback," *Magnum, P.I.,* CBS, 1982.

Martha, "The Lady and the Tiger," *Tales of the Gold Monkey* (also known as *Tales of the Golden Monkey*), ABC, 1982.

Amy Jones, "Merry Christmas, Bogg," *Voyagers!,* NBC, 1982.

"Exit Line," *Darkroom,* ABC, 1982.

Sherry Benson, "Good Day at White Rock," *Knight Rider,* NBC, 1982.

Robin Stevens, "The Snow Job," *The Fall Guy,* ABC, 1982.

Sally, "Inside, Outside," *The Fall Guy,* ABC, 1983.

Jennifer Shell, "Return to Cadiz," *Knight Rider,* NBC, 1983.

"Cinderella," *The Paper Chase,* Showtime, 1983.

Lori Lightbody, "What's in a Gnome?," *Simon & Simon,* CBS, 1983.

Jo McFarland, "Yes, Virginia, There Is a Liberace," *Simon & Simon,* CBS, 1984.

Ellen Butler, "Hot Property," *T. J. Hooker,* ABC, 1984.

Tracy Morgan, "Death by Design," *Automan,* ABC, 1984.

"Minneapolis: Six Months Down," *Lottery!,* ABC, 1984.

"The Babysitter," *Scene of the Crime,* NBC, 1984.

Detective Sergeant Anne Brannen, "Random Target," *Airwolf* (also known as *Lobo del aire*), CBS, 1984.

Grace Earl Lamont, "Deadly Lady," *Murder, She Wrote,* CBS, 1984.

Mrs. Cooper, *Scene of the Crime,* NBC, 1984.

Veronica Harrold, "Widow, Weep for Me," *Murder, She Wrote,* CBS, 1985.

"Home for Dinner," *George Burns Comedy Week,* CBS, 1985.

Herself, "Home for Christmas," *George Burns Comedy Week,* CBS, 1985.

Navy Lieutenant Yvonne Wilkes/The Iron Maiden, "A.W.O.L.," *Simon & Simon,* CBS, 1986.

Mrs. Meechum, "Meechun vs. Meechum," *Divorce Court,* syndicated, 1986.

"Love–a–Gram/Love and the Apartment," *New Love, American Style,* ABC, 1986.

"Love and the Last Chance Cafe," *New Love, American Style,* ABC, 1986.

"Love and the Acting Class," *New Love, American Style,* ABC, 1986.

"Love and the Carterre," *New Love, American Style,* ABC, 1986.

Tess Dixon, "Day of Jeopardy," *Airwolf* (also known as *Lobo del aire*), CBS, 1986.

Dr. Tracy Kinsington, "A Town for Hire," *Airwolf* (also known as *Lobo del aire*), CBS, 1987.

Audrey Kensington, "A Town for Hire," *Airwolf* (also known as *Airwolf II*), USA Network, 1987.

Shelly North, "Road Ranger," *The Highwayman,* NBC, 1988.

Rachel Kelley, "Heartbreak Hotel," *Freddy's Nightmare* (also known as *Freddy's Nightmares: A Nightmare on Elm Street: The Series*), syndicated, 1989.

Roz Briggs, "Three Strikes, You're Out," *Murder, She Wrote,* CBS, 1989.

"Doogie's Wager," *Doogie Howser, M.D.,* ABC, 1991.

Eva Stoddard, "Star Light, Star Bright—May 21, 1966," *Quantum Leap,* NBC, 1992.

Maureen, "Where the Heart Is: Part 1 & 2," *Dr. Quinn, Medicine Woman,* CBS, 1993.

Karen Banks, "Terminal Island," *One West Waikiki,* CBS, 1994.

Norma Willens, "Fatal Paradise," *Murder, She Wrote,* CBS, 1994.

Stacy Pardcek, "Manhunt," *Kung Fu: The Legend Continues,* syndicated, 1995.

"Past, Present," *High Sierra Search and Rescue,* NBC, 1995.

The Bold and the Beautiful (also known as *Belleza y poder*), CBS, 1996.

Andrea Rivers, "Murder in the Family," *Diagnosis Murder,* CBS, 1996.

Maureen, "Colleen's Paper," *Dr. Quinn, Medicine Woman,* CBS, 1997.

Kay Borgstrom, "St. Russell," *Promised Land* (also known as *Home of the Brave*), CBS, 1997.

Dr. Linda Morgan, "Brainchild," *Walker, Texas Ranger* (also known as *Walker*), CBS, 1997.

Mrs. Mathers, "Smash and Grab," *L.A. Heat,* syndicated, 1999.

Navy Rear Admiral Scotchel, "Psychic Warrior," *JAG,* CBS, 1999.

"Sciography," *Sciography,* 2000.

Jean Malone, "Frontier Dad," *Diagnosis Murder,* CBS, 2000.

(Uncredited) Police officer, "Redemption," *Dragnet* (also known as *L.A. Dragnet*), ABC, 2003.

Television Work; Series:

(Uncredited) Additional automated dialogue replacement (ADR), *Cover Up,* 1984.

(Uncredited) Additional ADR, *The Cosby Mysteries* (also known as *Guy Hanks I*), NBC, 1994.

(Uncredited) Additional ADR, *Deadly Games,* UPN, 1995.

Additional ADR, *Grosse Pointe,* The WB, 2000.

Additional ADR, *The Twilight Zone,* UPN, 2002.

Additional ADR, *Dragnet* (also known as *L.A. Dragnet*), ABC, 2003.

Television Work; Movies:

(Uncredited) Additional automated dialogue replacement (ADR), *The Good Old Boys,* TNT, 1995.

ADR, *Menno's Mind* (also known as *Power.com*), Showtime, 1996.

Television Additional Automated Dialogue Replacement (ADR) Artist; Episodic:

(Uncredited) "Fault," *Law & Order: Special Victims Unit* (also known as *Law & Order: SVU* and *Special Victims Unit*), NBC, 2006.

(Uncredited) "Heart of Darkness," *Law & Order,* NBC, 2006.

(Uncredited) "Cost of Capital," *Law & Order,* NBC, 2006.

(Uncredited) "Thinking Makes It So," *Law & Order,* NBC, 2006.

(Uncredited) "Home Sweet," *Law & Order,* NBC, 2006.

(Uncredited) "Ravenous," *Navy NCIS: Naval Criminal Investigative Service* (also known as *NCIS* and *NCIS: Naval Criminal Investigative Service*), CBS, 2006.

(Uncredited) "Escaped," *Navy NCIS: Naval Criminal Investigative Service* (also known as *NCIS* and *NCIS: Naval Criminal Investigative Service*), CBS, 2006.

(Uncredited) "Faking It," *Navy NCIS: Naval Criminal Investigative Service* (also known as *NCIS* and *NCIS: Naval Criminal Investigative Service*), CBS, 2006.

Television Director; Episodic:
Directed episodes of *The Heartbreak Cafe.*

Stage Appearances:
Various roles, *War of the Worlds,* Forum Theatre, Thousand Oaks, CA, 1998.

Melissa Santa Susanna, *Love Letters,* Repertory Company, Scherr Forum Theatre, Thousand Oaks, CA 1998.

Melissa, *Love Letters,* Mariott Theatre, Indianapolis, IN, 1999.

Melissa, *Love Letters,* Rubicon Theatre Company, Laurel Theatre, Ventura, CA, 2000.

Frenchy McCormick, *The Legend, Lore and Legacy of Texas,* Texas and Southwest Cattle Raisers, Astrodome, Houston, TX, 2000.

Maxine, *The Night of the Iguana,* Central Methodist College, Fayette, MO, 2000.

Various, *Your's Truly, Johnny Dollar,* Gold Coast Performing Arts Center, Thousand Oaks, CA, 2001.

Mrs. Cratchit, *A Christmas Carol,* Santa Sisanna Repertory Company, Scherr Forum Theatre, 2002.

Frenchy McCormick, *The Soul of the West,* Lisner Theatre, George Washington University, Washington, DC, 2002.

Mrs. Cratchit, *A Christmas Carol,* Santa Susanna Repertory Company, Scherr Forum Theatre, 2003.

Frenchy McCormick, *The Ballad of Frenchy McCormick,* McCormick Poetry Gathering, Boy's Ranch, TX, 2003.

Calpurnia, *Julius Caesar,* Kingsmen Shakespeare Festival, Thousand Oaks, CA, 2003.

Maria, *Twelfth Night,* Kingsmen Shakespeare Festival, 2003.

Mistress Quickly and Queen of France, *Henry V,* Kingsmen Shakespeare Festival, 2004.

Poetry reader, *Green River Preservation Society,* MET Theatre, Hollywood, CA, 2004.

Nurse (*Romeo & Juliet*), Maria (*Twelfth Night*), and sonnet reader, *Wine, Women and Shakespeare,* Gardens of the World, Thousand Oaks, CA, 2004.

Frenchy McCormick, *The Soul of the West,* Bass Performance Hall, Ft. Worth, TX, 2004.

A Christmas Carol, Santa Susanna Repertory Company, Scherr Forum Theatre, 2004.

Nurse, *Romeo and Juliet,* Kingsmen Shakespeare Festival, 2004, 2005.

Mistress Quickly, *The Merry Wives of Windsor,* Kingsmen Shakespeare Festival, 2005.

Queen Margaret, *Richard III,* Kingsmen Shakespeare Festival, 2005.

Mrs. Cratchit, *A Christmas Carol,* Santa Susana Repertory Company, Scherr Forum Theatre, 2006.

Frenchy McCormick, *The Soul of the West,* Pioneer Theatre, Palo Duro, TX, 2006.

Emilia, *Othello,* Kingsmen Shakespeare Festival, 2006.

LONDON, Todd

PERSONAL

Son of Jerry London (a producer and director). *Education:* University of California, Los Angeles, B.A.S., 1985. *Avocational Interests:* Building home theatre systems, Harley Davidson motorcycles.

Career: Producer and actor. Aaron Spelling Productions, Hollywood, CA, apprentice editor, then associate producer, between 1986 and 1988; Universal Studios, producer; also worked as post–production supervisor.

Member: Motion Picture and Video Tape Editors Guild, Academy of Television Arts and Sciences, Screen Actors Guild.

CREDITS

Television Associate Producer; Series:
The Burning Zone, UPN, 1996.
Roar, Fox, 1997.
V.I.P. (also known as *V.I.P.—Die Bodyguards*), syndicated, 1998–99.
Manhattan, AZ, USA Network, 2000.
Grosse Pointe, The WB, 2000.
Method & Red, Fox, 2004–2005.

Television Coproducer; Series:
Murder, She Wrote, CBS, 1992–96.
Get Real, Fox, 1999.
Robbery Homicide Division (also known as *R.H.D./L.A.: Robbery Homicide Division/Los Angeles*), CBS, 2002–2003.
Carnivale, HBO, 2003–2005.
Rome, HBO, 2005.

Television Producer; Series:
Rome, HBO, 2007.
Mad Men, AMC, 2007.

Television Associate Producer; Pilots:
Harry's Hong Kong, ABC, 1987.
Black Jaq, ABC, 1998.
Action, Fox, 1999.

Television Coproducer; Pilots:
Born in Brooklyn, ABC, 2001.
The Third Degree, Fox, 2001.
Miracles, ABC, 2003.
House M.D. (also known as *House*), Fox, 2004.

Television Associate Producer; Other:
Manhunt for Claude Dallas (movie), CBS, 1986.
Crossings (miniseries), ABC, 1986.

Associate producer of ten movies featuring police detective Columbo, ABC, 1989–90; also coproducer of five "Columbo" movies, ABC, 1990–92.

Television Appearances; Episodic:
Stan, "Canyon of Death," *The Bionic Woman,* ABC, 1976.

Television Appearances; Other:
The Gift of Life (movie), CBS, 1982.
Jason Fielder, *Hotel* (pilot), ABC, 1983.

OTHER SOURCES

Electronic:
Todd London Official Site, http://www.toddlondon.com, November 7, 2007.

LONDON, Todd

PERSONAL

Companion of Karen Hartman (a playwright); children: Guthrie, Grisha (son). *Education:* Boston University, M.F.A.; American University, Ph.D.

Addresses: *Contact*—c/o Theatre Communications Group, 520 Eighth Ave., 24th Floor, New York, NY 10018–4156.

Career: Artistic director, educator, magazine editor, critic, and novelist. Classic Stage Company, New York City, associate artistic director, 1987–88; New Dramatists (nonprofit center), New York City, artistic director. Yale University, faculty member; Harvard University,

visiting lecturer. Theatre Development Fund, director of Playwrights Project; New York State Council on the Arts, past chair of theatre panel; member of board of directors, Theatre Communications Group, John Golden Fund, and Talking Band. *American Theatre,* past managing editor.

Awards, Honors: George Jean Nathan Award for Dramatic Criticism, for essays in *American Theatre.*

WRITINGS

Published Works:
The Artistic Home: Discussions with Artistic Directors of America's Institutional Theatres, Theatre Communications Group, 1988.
(Editor) *Contemporary American Monologues for Men,* Theatre Communications Group, 1998.
(Editor) *Contemporary American Monologues for Women,* Theatre Communications Group, 1998.
The World's Room (novel), Steerforth Press, 2001.
(Editor) *New Dramatists: The Best Plays by the Graduating Class of 2000,* Smith & Kraus, 2002.
(Editor) *New Dramatists: The Best Plays by the Graduating Class of 2001,* Smith & Kraus, 2003.

Contributor to other books. Contributor of articles and essays to periodicals in the United States and around the world.

LOWERY, Marcella 1946–
  (Marcella Lowry)

PERSONAL

Born April 27, 1946, in Queens, NY.

Career: Actress. Portrayed professional football player Donovan McNabb's mother in Chunky Soup commercials; also appeared in commercials for Wendy's restaurants, 1995, 2003, Sudafed medications, 2003, and Verizon telecommunications, 2004.

Awards, Honors: Image Award nomination, outstanding performance in a youth or children's series/special, National Association for the Advancement of Colored People, 2000, for *City Guys.*

CREDITS

Film Appearances:
Bag woman's daughter, *Super Spook,* Levitt–Pickman, 1975.

(As Marcella Lowry) Harriet, Martha's maid, *Arthur,* Orion, 1981.

Sargeant Rocco, *Without a Trace,* Twentieth Century–Fox, 1983.

Mrs. Richards, *Lean on Me,* Warner Bros., 1989.

Selma, *Fletch Lives,* Universal, 1989.

Woman in hallway, *New Jack City,* Warner Bros., 1991.

Betty, switchboard operator, *What About Bob?,* Buena Vista, 1991.

Anna Eldridge, *The Preacher's Wife,* Buena Vista, 1996.

Nurse, *Vibrations* (also known as *Cyberstorm*), Dimension Films, 1996.

Jacked, York Entertainment, 2003.

Nurse, *Second Best,* THINKFilm, 2004.

Nurse, *Twelve and Holding,* IFC Films, 2005.

Nurse Hardaway, *Waltzing Anna,* Kindred Media Group, 2006.

Mrs. Washington, *School for Scoundrels,* Weinstein Company, 2006.

Television Appearances; Series:

Francine Tibideaux, *The Cosby Show,* NBC, 1988–89.

Grandma Jenkins, *Ghostwriter,* PBS, 1992–95.

Ms. Karen Coretta Noble, *City Guys,* NBC, 1997–2001.

Television Appearances; Movies:

(Uncredited) Stranger, *Just Me and You,* NBC, 1978.

Ruby, *3 by Cheever: The Sorrows of Gin* (also known as *The Sorrows of Gin*), 1979.

Fast food customer, *Strapped,* 1993.

Marcia, *Angel Rodriguez,* HBO, 2007.

Television Appearances; Specials:

Voice of Harriet Jacobs, *Christmas and the Civil War,* 2007.

Television Appearances; Pilots:

Smitty, *How to Succeed in Business Without Really Trying,* ABC, 1975.

Television Appearances; Episodic:

(As Marcella Lowry) "Hello, Yetta," *Love, Sidney,* NBC, 1981.

Mom, "My Zombie Lover," *Monsters,* syndicated, 1988.

Professor Lowery, "Life About Death," *A Man Called Hawk,* ABC, 1989.

Nurse, "Sonata for Solo Organ," *Law & Order,* NBC, 1991.

Sheridan, "Breeder," *Law & Order,* NBC, 1994.

Van Buren's attorney, "Competence," *Law & Order,* NBC, 1994.

Postal worker, "Knock You Out," *New York Undercover* (also known as *Uptown Undercover*), Fox, 1995.

Miss Crilley, "Big Brother Is Watching," *The Cosby Mysteries,* NBC, 1995.

"Broadway Joe," *New York News,* CBS, 1995.

Receptionist, *Matt Waters,* CBS, 1996.

Rose, *Michael Hayes,* CBS, 1997.

Lois Barker, "Sheltered," *Law & Order,* NBC, 2003.

Stage Appearances:

Aunt Shoo and Clara, *Americana Pastoral,* Greenwich Mews Theatre, New York City, 1968.

Sister Laura and understudy Berenice Sadie Brown, *The Member of the Wedding,* Helen Hayes Theatre, New York City, 1974–75.

Lou Mae, *Welcome to Black River,* St. Mark's Playhouse, New York City, 1975.

Louise, *Lolita,* Brooks Atkinson Theatre, New York City, 1981.

Janelle, *Baseball Wives,* Harold Clurman Theatre, New York City, 1982.

Ladies, Theatre at St. Clement's Church, New York City, 1989.

Maybelle, *Before It Hits Home,* Joseph Papp Public Theatre, New York City, 1992.

M

MAHON, John

PERSONAL

Education: Graduated from the University of Scranton with a degree in classical languages.

Addresses: *Agent*—House of Representatives, 400 South Beverly Dr., Suite 101, Beverly Hills, CA 90212.

Career: Actor, producer, director, and writer. Previously worked as a chemical engineer.

Awards, Honors: New York Drama Critics Award nomination, for *Nobody Hears a Broken Drum;* won directing award for *That Championship Season.*

CREDITS

Film Appearances:
(Uncredited) Language lab director, *The Exorcist* (also known as *"The Exorcist": The Version You Haven't Seen Yet, "The Exorcist: The Version You've Never Seen,* and *William Peter Blatty's "The Exorcist"*), Warner Bros. 1973.
Police captain, *The Couch Trip,* Orion, 1988.
Dr. Fielding, *Bad Influence,* Triumph Releasing Corp., 1990.
Chief Jenkins, *One False Move,* IRS Media, 1991.
Police Sergeant, *The People Under the Stairs* (also known as *Wes Craven's "The People Under the Stairs"*), Universal, 1992.
Chairman of the Joint Chiefs, *The American President,* Universal, 1995.
Police chief, *L.A. Confidential,* Warner Bros., 1997.
Karl, *Armageddon,* Buena Vista, 1998.

NATO Colonel, *Austin Powers: The Spy Who Shagged Me* (also known as *Austin Powers 2: The Spy Who Shagged Me*), New Line Cinema, 1999.
Riverside captain, *Zodiac,* Paramount, 2007.
Knight Fever, Sunn Classic Pictures, 2008.

Film Producer:
Brother of the Wind (also known as *Frere du vent*), Sun International, 1972.

Television Appearances; Series:
George, *Studio 60 on the Sunset Strip* (also known as *Studio 60*), NBC, 2006–2007.

Television Appearances; Miniseries:
Mr. Cleaves, *Sinatra,* CBS, 1992.

Television Appearances; Movies:
General Hoyt Vandenburg, *Collision Course: Truman vs. MacArthur* (also known as *Collision Course*), 1976.
Detective Shoup, *A Killing Affair* (also known as *Behind the Badge*), CBS, 1977.
Frimsin, *Someone's Watching Me!* (also known as *High Rise*), NBC, 1978.
Victim for Victims: The Theresa Saldana Story (also known as *Victims for Victims*), 1984.
Betrayed by Innocence (also known as *Jailbait: Betrayed by Innocence*), 1986.
Convicted: A Mother's Story, 1987.
Officer Bill Miller, *Six Against the Rock,* 1987.
Deputy Chief Evans, *Shakedown on the Sunset Strip,* CBS, 1988.
Police captain, *The Couch Trip,* 1988.
Inspector Hedges, *Murder without Motive: The Edmund Perry Story* (also known as *Best Intentions*), NBC, 1992.
LMU coach, *Final Shot: The Hank Gathers Story,* syndicated, 1992.
Lifepod, Fox, 1993.

Coach Dickler, *Natural Selection* (also known as *Dark Reflection*), 1994.

Red Hat vet, *Roswell* (also known as *Incident at Roswell* and *Roswell: The U.F.O. Cover–Up*), Showtime, 1994.

Judge Ferguson, *Just Ask My Children*, Lifetime, 2001.

Television Appearances; Specials:
Billy Crystal: Midnight Train to Moscow, 1989.
"The Promise of Steve Wilkins," *Rock the Vote*, 1992.

Television Appearances; Episodic:
SWAT Commander, "To Kill a Tank," *The Blue Knight*, 1976.

Todd Morris, "Foul on the First Play," *The Rockford Files* (also known as *Jim Rockford, Private Investigator*), NBC, 1976.

Lieutenant Hayes, "Return to the Thirty–eighth Parallel," *The Rockford Files* (also known as *Jim Rockford, Private Investigator*), NBC, 1976.

Victor Sherman, "There's One in Every Port," *The Rockford Files* (also known as *Jim Rockford, Private Investigator*), NBC, 1977.

Man, "Breath of the Dragon," *Manimal*, NBC, 1983.

"Remembrance of Things Past," *Scarecrow and Mrs. King*, CBS, 1984.

Policeman, "Zippers," *Automan*, ABC, 1984.

Mr. Zewecki, "The Chicago Connection," *T. J. Hooker*, ABC, 1985.

Military police, "Guess What's Coming to Dinner," *Misfits of Science*, NBC, 1985.

Vendor, "The Prodigal," *MacGyver*, ABC, 1985.

Police officer, "Cheers," *St. Elsewhere*, 1985.

Alfie Girdler, "Knight Rider," *Knight Rider*, 1985.

Det. McConnell, "Dr. Hoof and Mouth," *Hill Street Blues*, 1985.

Mario, "Say It as It Plays," *Hill Street Blues*, 1986.

Desk sergeant, "Sometimes You Gotta Sing the Blues," *Stingray*, NBC, 1986.

"Dead Pigeon," *Mike Hammer* (also known as *Mickey Spillane's "Mike Hammer"* and *The New Mike Hammer*), 1986.

Chapell, "Aria da Capo," *Hooperman*, ABC, 1987.

"Shoot to Kill," *Hunter*, NBC, 1989.

Arnold Anderson, "The Cretin of the Shallows," *Baywatch*, NBC, 1989.

Captain Holgar, "A Tale of Two Cities," *Dallas*, CBS, 1990.

"Adamant Eve," *Mancuso, FBI*, 1990.

Surveillant, "The Grim Reaper," *Knots Landing*, CBS, 1990.

Superior, "Wrong for Each Other," *Knots Landing*, CBS, 1990.

Investigator, "The Fan Club," *Knots Landing*, CBS, 1990.

"You Took Advantage of Me," *Jake and the Fatman*, CBS, 1990.

Bus driver, "When the Stars Begin to Fall," *Homefront*, 1992.

"Death before Dishonor," *Space Rangers*, CBS, 1993.

Dave, *Cutters*, 1993.

Detective Spitz, "Blue Highway," *Profiler*, NBC, 1997.

Eugene Clark, "A Stand–Up Guy," *The Pretender*, NBC, 1998.

Gene Donovan, "Dead Man Sleeping," *Brooklyn South*, CBS, 1998.

Fire chief, "Resurrection: Part 1," *Diagnosis Murder*, CBS, 1998.

General Wegman, "Dreamland: Parts 1 & 2," *The X–Files*, Fox, 1998.

Uncle Walter "Walt" Crane, "Beware of Greeks," *Frasier*, NBC, 1999.

"You Gotta Love This Game," *Arli$$*, 1999.

Alan Drake, "Blackmail Photographer," *Just Shoot Me*, NBC, 1999.

Trevor Lockley, "Sense and Sensitivity," *Angel*, The WB, 1999.

Sergeant Staley, *Martial Law*, CBS, 1999.

Trevor Lockley, "The Prodigal," *Angel*, The WB, 2000.

Wally, "A Clown's Prayer," *Touched by an Angel*, CBS, 2000.

"A Separate Peace: Part 2," *JAG*, CBS, 2000.

Leo, "Touched by a Biker," *That's Life*, 2001.

Barry Constansas, "What Sharp Teeth You Have," *The Division* (also known as *Heart of the City*), 2001.

Agent Milton, "The Devil Still Holds My Hand," *Strange World*, ABC, 2002.

"Payback," *Crossing Jordan*, NBC, 2002.

Colonel, "The Plan," *Cold Case*, CBS, 2004.

Mr. Bradford, "Prank Week," *Zoey 101*, Nickelodeon, 2005.

Admiral Gardner, "In a Mirror, Darkly: Part 2," *Enterprise* (also known as *Star Trek: Enterprise*), UPN, 2005.

Also appeared as Paul Catteo, "What the Past Will Bring," *Bull*.

Stage Appearances:
Understudy Mr. Stein, Joe, Stanley, Joe, and Adam, *Monopoly*, Stage 73, New York City, 1966.

Pequod, Mercury Theatre, New York City, 1969.

Lebedev, *Subject to Fits*, Public Theatre, New York City, 1971.

Alderman, bearer, citizen, Anthony Woodville, Earl Rivers, and John Howard, *King Richard III*, Cort Theatre, New York City, 1979.

Also appeared in *Arturo Vi*, New York Shakespeare Festival, New York City; *Subject to Fits*, New York Shakespeare Festival; *Nobody Hears a Broken Drum*, New York City; *The Prime of Miss Jean Brodie*, U.S. cities.

Stage Director:
Directed productions of *Camelot, Hair; Who's Afraid of Virginia Wolf; That Championship Season*.

WRITINGS

Screenplays:
Brother of the Wind (also known as *Frere du vent*), Sun International, 1972.

MAILER, Stephen 1966–

PERSONAL

Full name, Stephen McLeod Mailer; born March 10, 1966, in New York, NY; son of Norman Mailer (a writer) and Beverly Bentley (an actress); married Lindsay Marx (a producer); children: one. *Education:* Attended Middlebury College and New York University.

Addresses: *Agent*—Stone Manners Agency 8436 West Third St., Suite 740, Los Angeles, CA 90048.

Career: Actor.

CREDITS

Film Appearances:
Sevek, *War and Love* (also known as *The Children's War*), Cannon, 1985.
Young Paul, *Another Woman*, 1988.
Baldwin, *Cry–Baby*, Universal, 1990.
Elon Dershowitz, *Reversal of Fortune*, 1990.
Kit's date in bar, *A League of Their Own*, Columbia, 1992.
Gabriel Higgs, *Getting In* (also known as *Student Body*), Trimark Pictures, 1994.
Patrick, *Quiet Days in Hollywood* (also known as *The Way We Are*), Overseas Film Group, 1997.
Chris, *Red Meat*, Peninsula Films, 1997.
Guy's Guide to Money, 1998.
Keith, *24 Nights*, 1999.
Babe Hudspeth, *Ride with the Devil*, USA Films, 1999.
What I Came For (short), 2004.
Himself, *It Came from Baltimore* (documentary short), Universal Home Entertainment, 2005.
Band leader, *Kettle of Fish*, Blue Sky Media, 2006.

Television Appearances; Movies:
In the Line of Duty: Ambush in Waco, NBC, 1993.

Television Appearances; Specials:
T. J., "Robbers, Rooftops and Witches," *CBS Schoolbreak Special*, CBS, 1982.
Mickey, "Divorced Kids' Blues," *ABC Afterschool Specials*, ABC, 1987.

Ben Griffin, "Love and Other Sorrows," *American Playhouse*, PBS, 1989.
Paul Darrow, "Darrow," *American Playhouse*, PBS, 1991.
Leo Spitzer, "The Hollow Boy," *American Playhouse*, PBS, 1991.

Television Appearances; Episodic:
Greg Jarman, "The Serpent's Tooth," *Law & Order*, NBC, 1991.
Steve, "The Fat Boys of Summer," *A League of Their Own*, 1993.
Mr. McGuire, "Desperate," *Law & Order: Special Victims Unit* (also known as *Law & Order: SVU* and *Special Victims Unit*), NBC, 2003.
Josh Davies, "Norman Mailer, I'm Pregnant!," *Gilmore Girls*, The WB, 2004.
Dr. Cutler, *As the World Turns*, CBS, 2007.

Stage Appearances:
Minor Demons, Harold Prince Theatre, Annenberg Center, Philadelphia, PA, 1988.
(Off–Broadway debut) Sam, *For Dear Life*, New York Shakespeare Festival, Public Theatre, Martinson Hall, New York City, 1989.
Artie, *What's Wrong with This Picture?*, Jewish Repertory Theatre, New York City, 1990.
Morris Singer, *Peacetime*, Workshop of the Players Arts Theatre, New York City, 1990.
Bill, *Innocents' Crusade*, City Center Stage II, New York City, 1992.
Lucas, *Laughter on the 23rd Floor*, Richard Rodgers Theatre, New York City, 1993–94.
Ralph Berger, *Awake and Sing!*, Jewish Repertory Theatre, New York City, 1995.

Also appeared in productions at Philadelphia Festival Theatre, Pittsburgh's Public Theatre, The Actor's Studio, and the Ensemble Theatre in New York City.

Major Tours:
Appeared in *Broadway Bound*, U.S. cities.

McCARTHY, Julianna 1929–
    (Juliana McCarthy)

PERSONAL

Born August 17, 1929, in Erie, PA; married Michael Constantine (an actor), October 5, 1953 (divorced, 1969); children: two

Addresses: *Agent*—Stone Manners Agency, 8436 West Third St., Suite 740, Los Angeles, CA 90048–4100.

Career: Actress.

CREDITS

Film Appearances:

Sister Nadine, *Seed of Innocence* (also known as *Teen Mothers*), Cannon Film Distributors, 1980.

Counselor, *The Last American Virgin,* Cannon Film Distributors, 1982.

Elderly lady, *Maid to Order,* New Century Vista Film Company, 1987.

Nurse number one, *Bad Dreams,* Twentieth Century–Fox, 1988.

Grandmother, *The First Power* (also known as *Pentagram, Possessed, Possessed by Evil,* and *Transit*), Orion, 1990.

Mrs. O'Hara, *Satan's Princess* (also known as *Malediction*), Paramount Home Video, 1990.

(As Juliana McCarthy) Woman, *L.A. Story,* TriStar Pictures, 1991.

Blue–haired lady, *The Distinguished Gentleman,* Buena Vista, 1992.

Mrs. Voss, *When the Bough Breaks* (also known as *Missing Victims* and *Two Rivers*), Turner Home Entertainment, 1993.

Judge Helen Kramer, *Striking Distance,* Columbia Pictures, 1993.

Wilma, *Lightening in a Bottle,* 1993.

Old Lady Bradley, *The Frighteners* (also known as *Robert Zemeckis Presents: "The Frighteners"*), Universal, 1996.

Old woman, *Skeletons,* 1996.

Expert number one, *Starship Troopers,* Sony Pictures Entertainment, 1997.

(As Juliana McCarthy) Bingo lady, *Kill the Man,* 1999.

Nana, *The Girls' Room,* 2000.

Professor, *Ted Bundy* (also known as *Bundy*), First Look International, 2002.

Television Appearances; Series:

Elizabeth "Liz" Foster Brooks, *The Young and the Restless* (also known as *Y&R*), CBS, 1973–88.

Margaret the bank clerk, *Paradise,* CBS, 1988–89.

Mrs. Sarah Loomis Johnson and Aunt Abigail Collins, *Dark Shadows* (also known as *Dark Shadows Revival*), NBC, 1991.

Liz Foster, *The Young and the Restless* (also known as *Y&R*), CBS, 2004.

Television Appearances; Miniseries:

(As Juliana McCarthy) Mrs. Sarah Loomis Johnson, *Dark Shadows,* NBC, 1990.

Television Appearances; Movies:

Thelma Grine, *A Gun in the House,* 1981.

Ellen, *A House of Secrets and Lies,* CBS, 1992.

Adele Loring, *Donato and Daughter* (also known as *Dead to Rights* and *Under Threat*), CBS, 1993.

Mrs. Swicker, *Bucket of Blood* (also known as *Dark Secrets, The Death Artist,* and *Roger Corman Presents "Bucket of Blood"*), Showtime, 1995.

Interviewee, *Alien Avengers* (also known as *Roger Corman Presents "Alien Avengers"* and *Welcome to Planet Earth*), Showtime, 1996.

Eileen Hunter, *The Sleepwalker Killing* (also known as *Crimes of Passion: "Sleepwalker"* and *From the Files of Unsolved Mysteries: "The Sleepwalker Killing"*), NBC, 1997.

Mrs. D., *Poodle Springs,* HBO, 1998.

Dorothy, *Mystery Woman: Mystery Weekend,* Hallmark Channel, 2005.

Grandma, *Shredderman Rules,* Nickelodeon, 2006.

Television Appearances; Episodic:

Augusta, "Search," *Lou Grant,* 1981.

Dr. Davis, "Up in Arms," *Hill Street Blues,* NBC, 1981.

Frances Clifford, "Slum Enchanted Evening," *L.A. Law,* NBC, 1986.

Ruth Daniela, "Echoes," *Stingray,* 1987.

Annie, "Easy Does It," *Cagney & Lacey,* 1987.

Flo, "The Inner Limits," *Highway to Heaven,* NBC, 1989.

Vera Rose, "The Lady in Red," *Jake and the Fatman,* CBS, 1989.

Lucille, "Pinup Mama," *Mama's Family,* 1990.

"Dust on the Wind," *Paradise,* CBS, 1990.

Mrs. Abbot, "The Dame," *Matlock,* NBC, 1991.

Mrs. Raskin, "24 Hours," *ER,* NBC, 1994.

Housekeeper Mila, "Improbable Cause," *Star Trek: Deep Space Nine* (also known as *DS9, Deep Space Nine,* and *Star Trek: DS9*), syndicated, 1995.

Susanne Foster, "Parentnapping," *Land's End,* syndicated, 1995.

Henrietta Gaines, "Sympathy for the Devil," *The Client* (also known as *John Grisham's "The Client"*), CBS, 1996.

Mabel, "The Circle of Strife," *Melrose Place,* Fox, 1996.

Jessie, "Inmate 78," *The Magnificent Seven,* CBS, 1998.

"Sub–Conscious," *Sleepwalkers,* 1998.

Agnes McMillan, "Coronation," *Profiler,* NBC, 1998.

Housekeeper Mila, "The Dogs of War," *Star Trek: Deep Space Nine* (also known as *DS9, Deep Space Nine,* and *Star Trek: DS9*), syndicated, 1999.

Housekeeper Mila, "What You Leave Behind," *Star Trek: Deep Space Nine* (also known as *DS9, Deep Space Nine,* and *Star Trek: DS9*), syndicated, 1999.

Dog's owner, "Who Murders Sleep," *NYPD Blue,* ABC, 2000.

Nana, "The Other End of the Telescope," *Once and Again,* 2001.

Catherine Knight, "Holy of Holies," *Touched by an Angel,* CBS, 2001.

Beatrice, "Out, Out, Brief Candle," *Six Feet Under,* HBO, 2002.

Mrs. Raskin, "Orion in the Sky," *ER,* NBC, 2002.

Margaret, "Old Home Week," *The Unit,* CBS, 2006.

Stage Appearances:
Hedda Gabler, Mark Taper Forum, Los Angeles, 1985.

RECORDINGS

Taped Readings:
Read (with others) *Four Last Songs by Martha Morehead,* California Artists Radio Theatre.

McCURDY, Jennette 1992–
(Jeanette McCurdy, Jenette McCurdy)

PERSONAL

Born June 26, 1992. *Avocational Interests:* Dance, karate, ice skating, piano, cooking, reading, watching movies, and collecting stuffed animals, hats, books, and crafts.

Addresses: *Manager*—Curtis Talent Management, 9607 Arby Dr., Beverly Hills, CA 90210.

Career: Actress. Appeared in commercials for Sprint PCS, Simon Malls, Dominos Pizza, Dinkie Robots, and Dental World.

Awards, Honors: Young Artist Award nomination, best performance in a television series—guest starring young actress, 2005, for *Young Medicine.*

CREDITS

Film Appearances:
Anna Markov, *Shadow Fury,* Lions Gate Films, 2001.
Mary Fields, *My Daughter's Tears* (also known as *Against All Evidence* and *Meine Tochter ist keine morderin*), Beta Film, 2002.
Van family daughter, *Hollywood Homicide,* Columbia, 2003.
The little girl, *Breaking Dawn,* Lions Gate Films Home Entertainment, 2004.
Lucy Randall, *See Anthony Run* (short), 2005.
Aria Krait, *Proving Ground: From the Adventures of Captain Redlocks,* 2008.

Television Appearances; Series:
Sam Puckett, *iCarly,* Nickelodeon, 2007—.

Television Appearances; Movies:
Kiley Dolan, *Tiger Cruise,* Disney Channel, 2004.

Dory Sorenson, *The Last Day of Summer,* Nickelodeon, 2007.

Television Appearances; Specials:
Meredith, *Against Type,* 2006.

Television Appearances; Episodic:
Cassidy Gifford, *Mad TV,* Fox, 2000.
Jackie Trent, "Cats in the Cradle," *CSI: Crime Scene Investigation* (also known as *C.S.I., CSI: Las Vegas,* and *Les Experts*), CBS, 2002.
Daisy Wilkerson, "If Boys Were Girls," *Malcolm in the Middle,* Fox, 2003.
Josephina "Josie" Boyle, "No One's Girl," *Karen Sisco,* ABC, 2004.
Haley Campos, "Selective Breeding," *Strong Medicine,* Lifetime, 2004.
Holly Purcell, "Contagious," *Law & Order: Special Victims Unit* (also known as *Law & Order: SVU* and *Special Victims Unit*), NBC, 2005.
Sara Crewson, "Coded," *Medium,* NBC, 2005.
Amber Reid, "My Name Is Amy Gray ...," *Judging Amy,* CBS, 2005.
Penelope, "Buseys Take a Hostage," *Malcolm in the Middle,* Fox, 2005.
(As Jenette McCurdy) Madison St. Clair, "Everything Nice," *The Inside,* Fox, 2005.
Lynn, "Situation Normal," *Over There,* FX Channel, 2005.
Trisha Kirby, "Bad Girl," *Zoey 101,* Nickelodeon, 2005.
Lisa, "Von Trapped," *Will & Grace,* NBC, 2006.
Stacey Johnson, "Escape," *Close to Home,* CBS, 2006.
Becky, "Betrayal," *Lincoln Heights,* ABC Family, 2007.
Becky, "Tricks and Treats," *Lincoln Heights,* ABC Family, 2007.
Becky, "House Arrest," *Lincoln Heights,* ABC Family, 2007.

Also appeared as herself, *Sesame Street,* PBS.

RECORDINGS

Music Videos:
Appeared in Wild Horses' "Safely Home"; Faith Hill's "The Way You Love Me."

OTHER SOURCES

Electronic:
Jennette McCurdy Website, http://www.jennette mccurdy.com, December 1, 2007.

McGARVEY, Seamus 1967–

PERSONAL

Born June 29, 1967, in Armagh, Northern Ireland; son of Jimmy ad Peggy McGarvey. *Education:* Graduated from a film school in London, 1988.

Addresses: *Agent*—Casarotto Marsh, Ltd., National House 60–66 Wardour St., London W1V 4ND United Kingdom; Sandra Marsh Management, 9150 Wilshire Blvd., Suite 220, Beverly Hills, CA 90212.

Career: Cinematographer. Began career as a still photographer; worked as a cinematographer and director on over 100 music videos; worked as a cinematographer on television commercials. Solo exhibitions at the City Centre Art Gallery, Dublin, Ireland, including Armagh in a New Light, 1984, and Eternity Where?, 1989; London Film School, board of governors. Previously worked as an usher at the Institute of Contemporary Art's cinemas.

Member: British Society of Cinematographers, International Alliance of Theatrical Stage Employees 600 (USA cinematography unit), British Academy of Film and Television Arts, Academy of Motion Picture Arts and Sciences.

Awards, Honors: *Evening Standard* British Film Award, best technical/artistic achievement, 2004, for *The Hours;* Lumiere Medal, Royal Photographic Society, 2004, for his contributions to the art of cinematography; Irish Film and Television Award, best cinematography, 2005, for *Sahara;* Irish Film and Television Award, best cinematography, 2007, for *World Trade Center;* Royal Television Society Award nomination, for *Skin.*

CREDITS

Film Cinematographer:
Memoranda (short), 1990.
Mad Bad Mortal Beings (short), 1991.
The Winding Sheet—A Documentary About Guilt (documentary), 1992.
Damsel Jam (documentary), 1992.
Taking Liberties with Mr. Simpson (short), 1993.
Marooned (short), 1993.
The Take Out (short), British Film Institute, 1994.
A Sort of Homecoming (short), British Film Institute, 1994.
Skin Tight (short), 1994.
Look Me in the Eye, 1994.
Butterfly Kiss (also known as *Killer on the Road*), 1995.

This Charming Man (documentary short), British Film Institute, 1995.
Magic Moments, 1997.
Flying Saucer Rock'n'Roll (short), 1997.
Harald (also known as *Harald—Der Chaot aus dem weltall*), Sales Company, 1997.
Jump the Gun, 1997.
The Winter Guest, Image Entertainment, 1997.
The Slab Boys, 1997.
The End (short), 1998.
The War Zone (also known as *Tim Roth's "The War Zone"* and *Zona di guerra*), Lot 47 Films, 1999.
I Could Read the Sky, Artificial Eye, 1999.
A Map of the World (also known as *Unschuldig verfolgt*), USA Films, 1999.
The Big Tease, Warner Bros., 1999.
The Name of This Film is Dogme95 (documentary), 2000.
High Fidelity, Buena Vista, 2000.
Enigma (also known as *Enigma—Das Geheimnis*), Manhattan Pictures International, 2001.
The Hours, Paramount, 2002.
The Actors, Miramax, 2003.
Rolling Stones: Tip of the Tongue (documentary), TGA, 2003.
Along Came Polly, Universal, 2004.
Sahara (also known as *Sahara—Abenteuer in der wuste*), Paramount, 2005.
"Death Valley," *Destricted,* IFC Films, 2006.
World Trade Center, Paramount, 2006.
Charlotte's Web (also known as *Schweinchen Wilbur und seine freunde*), Paramount, 2006.
Atonement, Focus Features, 2007.
The No. 1 Ladies Detective Agency, Weinstein Company, 2008.

Film Work; Other:
Camera trainee, *December Bride,* MD Wax/Courier Films, 1990.
Second assistant camera, *Dakota Road,* 1991.
Focus puller, *Floating,* 1991.
Assistant camera, *Projections,* Substance Video, 1993.
Second unit camera operator, *Jude,* 1996.
Additional camera operator, *Ali G Indahouse* (also known as *Ali G in da House, Ali G,* and *Ali G Indahouse: The Movie*), Universal Focus, 2002.

Film Appearances:
Himself, *Visualizing "Sahara"* (documentary short), Paramount Home Video, 2005.
Himself, *The Making of "World Trade Center"* (documentary), Paramount Home Video, 2006.
Himself, *"Charlotte's Web": Making Some Movies* (documentary short), 2007.

Television Cinematographer; Movies:
Shooting to Stardom, 1993.
Out of the Deep Pan, 1995.

Stand and Deliver, 1997.
Wit, HBO, 2001.

Television Work; Specials:
35mm camera operator (documentary crew), *U2's Beautiful Day,* CBS, 2002.

Television Cinematographer; Episodic:
"Look Me in the Eye," *Screen Two,* BBC, 1993.
Murder Most Horrid, 1994.
"The Maids," *Blow Your Mind: See a Show,* 1995.
"Macbeth," *Blow Your Mind: See a Show,* 1995.
"One Man Show Dramatic: The Art of Steven Berkoff," *Blow Your Mind: See a Show,* 1995.

RECORDINGS

Music Videos:
Directed and/or worked as cinematographer on music videos for U2, the Rolling Stones, P J Harvey, Robbie Williams, Paul McCartney, Dusty Springfield, Natalie Imbruglia, Pet Shop Boys, Elton John, The Cure, David Stewart, Terry Hall, Orbital, UB40, and Coldplay.

OTHER SOURCES

Electronic:
Seamus McGarvey Website, http://www.seamusmcgarvey.com, November 10, 2007.

McHATTIE, Stephen 1947(?)–
(Steve McHattie, Steven McHattie, Stephen Smith)

PERSONAL

Full name, Stephen McHattie Smith; born February 3, 1947 (some sources cite 1946), in Antigonish, Nova Scotia, Canada; married Meg Foster (an actress; divorced); married Lisa Houle (an actress); children: (second marriage) one. *Education:* Attended Acadia University; trained for the stage at the American Academy of Dramatic Arts.

Addresses: *Agent*—Characters Talent Agency, 8 Elm St., Second Floor, Toronto, Ontario M5G 1G7, Canada; Kazarian/Spencer and Associates, 11365 Ventura Blvd., Suite 100, Studio City, CA 91604. *Manager*—Wright Entertainment, 3207 Winnie Dr., Los Angeles, CA 90068.

Career: Actor. Also known as Stephen Smith.

Member: Actors' Equity Association, Screen Actors Guild, American Federation of Television and Radio Artists.

Awards, Honors: Obie Award, performance, *Village Voice,* 1984, for *Mensch Meier;* Drama Desk Award, outstanding actor, 1989, for *Ghetto;* Gemini Award, best performance by an actor in a leading role in a dramatic program or miniseries, Academy of Canadian Cinema and Television, 1995, for *Life with Billy;* Gemini Award nomination, best performance by an actor in a continuing leading dramatic role, 1998, for *Emily of New Moon;* Gemini Award nomination, best performance by an actor in a leading role in a dramatic program or miniseries, 1999, for *American Whiskey Bar;* Genie Award, best performance by an actor in a supporting role, Academy of Canadian Cinema and Television, 2007, for *Maurice Richard.*

CREDITS

Film Appearances:
Artie Mason, *The People Next Door,* Avco–Embassy, 1970.
(As Steve McHattie) Werner Voss, *Von Richtofen and Brown* (also known as *The Red Baron*), United Artists, 1970.
Robert, *The Ultimate Warrior* (also known as *The Barony* and *The Last Warrior*), Warner Bros., 1975.
Eddie Moore, *Moving Violation,* Twentieth Century–Fox, 1976.
Murphy, *Gray Lady Down,* Universal, 1977.
Frank, *Tomorrow Never Comes,* Rank, 1978.
Hal, *Death Valley,* Universal, 1982.
Brett Munro, *Best Revenge* (also known as *Misdeal*), 1982, RKR Releasing, 1984.
James Willoughby, *Belizaire the Cajun,* Skouras Pictures/Norstar, 1985.
Reverend Edward Randall, *Salvation!* (also known as *Have You Said Your Prayers Today?* and *Salvation! Have You Said Your Prayers Today?*), Circle Releasing, 1987.
Whitehale, *Caribe,* Miramax, 1987.
Eddie (some sources cite Sam), *Sticky Fingers,* Spectrafilm, 1988.
(As Steven McHattie) Jellybean, *Call Me,* Vestron Pictures, 1988.
Erik, *One Man Out* (also known as *Erik*), Creswin, 1989.
Red Henry, *Bloodhounds of Broadway,* Columbia, 1989.
Schoonover, *Geronimo: An American Legend,* Columbia, 1993.
Dr. Egbert Drum, *Pterodactyl Woman from Beverly Hills,* Troma Team Video, 1994.

Gary "Hunter" Henderson, *The Dark,* Imperial Entertainment, 1994.

Hyena, *Art Deco Detective,* Trident Releasing, 1994.

Steve Fulbright, *Beverly Hills Cop III,* Paramount, 1994.

Alex's father, *Nonnie & Alex,* PolyGram Filmed Entertainment, 1995.

Edge, *Theodore Rex* (also known as *T. Rex*), New Line Cinema, 1995.

Curt, *My Friend Joe* (also known as *Mein Freund Joe*), Gemini/Portman Entertainment Group/Promedia, 1996.

Jack McLaglin, *The Climb* (also known as *Le defi*), Panorama Entertainment/Banner Entertainment, 1998.

Narrator, *BASEketball* (also known as *Baseketball*), Universal, 1998.

Frank Drake, *The Highwayman,* Lions Gate Films, 1999.

Burt Holloway, *Secretary,* Lions Gate Films, 2002.

Chief prosecutor William Warner, *The Lazarus Child,* Warner Bros., 2004.

Senator, *Twist,* Strand Releasing/Christal Films, 2004.

Dick Irvin, *Maurice Richard* (also known as *The Rocket, The Rocket: The Legend of Rocket Richard,* and *The Rocket: The Maurice Richard Story*), Alliance Atlantis Vivafilm/Palm Pictures, 2005.

Leland, *A History of Violence,* New Line Cinema, 2005.

Grand inquisitor Silecio, *The Fountain,* Warner Bros., 2006.

James Danvers, *The Covenant,* Columbia, 2006.

Loyalist, *300,* Warner Bros., 2006, IMAX version released as *300: The IMAX Experience.*

The Astounding Lew, *Cursing Hanley* (short film), Canadian Film Centre, 2007.

Dr. Robert Parker, *Medium Raw,* Fantastic Films International/Decade Distribution, 2007.

Earl Stanton, *All Hat,* Odeon Films, 2007.

Hammerson, *Shoot 'Em Up,* New Line Cinema, 2007.

Uncle Joe, *Poor Boy's Game,* TLA Releasing, 2007.

Fisk, *The Timekeeper,* Christal Films, 2008.

Watchmen, Warner Bros., 2009.

Some sources cite an appearance in *Straight from the Heart,* c. 1997.

Television Appearances; Series:
Reverend Ian Glenville, *Highcliffe Manor,* NBC, 1979.

Rick, *Mariah* (also known as *Equations, Mariah State,* and *Mariah State Prison*), ABC, 1987.

Gabriel, a recurring role, *Beauty and the Beast* (also known as *A Szepseg es a szoernyeteg, Die Schoene und das Biest, I pentamorfi kai to teras, La bella e la bestia, La bella y la bestia, La belle et la bete,* and *Skonheden og udyret*), CBS, 1989–90.

Regular performer, *Scene of the Crime* (also known as *L'heure du crime*), CBS, 1991–94.

Jimmy Woolner Murray, *Emily of New Moon,* CBC, 1998–2000.

Sergeant Frank Coscarella, *Cold Squad* (also known as *Files from the Past, Cold Squad, brigade speciale,* and *Halott uegyek*), CTV (Canada), c. 1998–2005.

Chief Gil Brewer, *Sabbatical,* CTV (Canada), beginning 2007.

Television Appearances; Miniseries:
Temple Franklin, "The Statesman," *Benjamin Franklin,* CBS, 1976.

Jacques "Jake" Pasquinel, *Centennial,* NBC, 1979.

Roy Bethke, *Roughnecks,* syndicated, 1980.

Billy Stafford, *Life with Billy,* CBC, 1994.

General Issac Brock, *Canada: A People's History* (also known as *Le Canada: Une histoire populaire*), CBC, 2000.

Edgar (some sources cite Edgard) Powell, *Killer Wave,* ION Television, 2007.

Jack Shea, *The Trojan Horse* (also known as *H2O II: The Trojan Horse*), CBC, 2007.

Would Be Kings, CTV (Canada), c. 2007.

General Carrington, *XIII* (also known as *XIII: The Conspiracy*), 2008.

Tate, *The Summit,* CBC, 2008.

Guns, CBC, 2008.

Television Appearances; Movies:
Willie Longfellow, *Search for the Gods,* ABC, 1975.

Adrian and Andrew, *Look What's Happened to Rosemary's Baby* (also known as *Rosemary's Baby II*), ABC, 1976.

Title role, *James Dean* (also known as *The Legend*), NBC, 1976.

Judah, *Mary and Joseph: A Story of Faith* (also known as *Story of Faith*), NBC, 1979.

Darnell, *Terror on Track 9* (also known as *Janek: The Grand Central Murders*), CBS, 1992.

Lieutenant Durant, *Jonathan Stone: Threat of Innocence* (also known as *Frame Up*), NBC, 1994.

Bryan English, *Visitors of the Night,* 1995.

Chief Nat Coogan, *Remember Me* (also known as *Mary Higgins Clark's "Remember Me"* and *Souviens–toi*), Family Channel, 1995.

Jack Claremont, *Deadlocked: Escape from Zone 14* (also known as *Deadlock 2*), 1995.

Jagges Neff, *Convict Cowboy,* Showtime, 1995.

Sean O'Connor, *Deadly Love,* 1995.

A, *American Whiskey Bar,* CITY–TV, 1998.

Lieutenant Jack Kelly, *Alptraum im Airport* (also known as *Midnight Flight*), 1998.

Pierce, *Die Abzocker—Eine eiskalte Affaere* (also known as *The Hustle* and *A Sordid Affair*), 1999.

Hugh, *Wall of Secrets* (also known as *Le mur des secrets*), Lifetime, 2003.

Admiral Lawrence, *Solar Strike* (also known as *Solar Attack*), Sci–Fi Channel, 2005.

Captain Healy, *Stone Cold* (also known as *Jesse Stone: Stone Cold* and *Robert B. Parker's "Stone Cold"*), CBS, 2005.

Captain Healy, *Jesse Stone: Death in Paradise,* CBS, 2006.

Captain Healy, *Jesse Stone: Night Passage,* CBS, 2006.

Mike Lloyd, *Absolution,* Lifetime, 2006.

Police field commander, *One Dead Indian,* CTV (Canada), 2006.

Captain Healy, *Jesse Stone: Sea Change,* CBS, 2007.

Captain Healy, *Jesse Stone: Thin Ice,* CBS, 2007.

Clyde, *Kaw,* Sci–Fi Channel, 2007.

Duncan Albright, *The Dark Room,* CBC, 2007.

Captain Healy, *Jesse Stone: Thin Ice,* CBS, 2008.

Television Appearances; Specials:

Nicholas, "The Lady's Not for Burning," *Hollywood Television Theatre,* PBS, 1974.

Hank, "Life under Water," *American Playhouse,* PBS, 1989.

Ice Age Columbus: Who Were the First Americans, The Discovery Channel, 2005.

Himself, *Maurice Richard: The Legend, the Story, the Movie,* 2006.

Television Appearances; Episodic:

Paul Nelson, "Slay Ride," *Kojak,* CBS, 1974.

Skip, "Roll Call," *Adam–12,* NBC, 1974.

William Michael Desmond, "Terror on the Docks," *Starsky and Hutch,* ABC, 1975.

"The Summer of '69: Parts 1 & 2," *Kojak,* CBS, 1977.

Curtis Folger, "Frame–Up," *Lou Grant,* CBS, 1979.

Officer Jerry Nash, "Chipped Beef," *Hill Street Blues,* NBC, 1981.

Officer Jerry Nash, "Cranky Streets," *Hill Street Blues,* NBC, 1981.

Tales of the Klondike (also known as *Jack London's "Klondike Tales"* and *Jack London's "Tales of the Klondike"*), CBC, 1981.

Joe Caldwell, "A Time for Rifles," *The Hitchhiker* (also known as *Deadly Nightmares* and *Le voyageur*), HBO, 1985.

Johnny, "Nightshift," *The Hitchhiker* (also known as *Deadly Nightmares* and *Le voyageur*), HBO, 1985.

Corbett, "Brother to Dragons," *Spenser: For Hire,* ABC, 1986.

Eddie Washburn, "Out of the Past," *The Equalizer,* CBS, 1986.

Carlo Mastrangelo, "The Senator, the Movie Star, and the Mob," *Crime Story,* NBC, 1987.

Robert Perry, "Family Reunion," *Tales from the Darkside* (also known as *Beraettelser fraan andra siden, Histoires de l'autre monde, Historias del mas ella,* and *Keskiyoen kauhutarinoita*), syndicated, 1988.

Death, "Rendezvous in a Dark Place," *The Twilight Zone* (also known as *The New Twilight Zone*), CBS, 1989.

Sam Boyle, "Fruit of the Poison Tree," *Miami Vice* (also known as *Gold Coast* and *Miami Unworthiness*), NBC, 1989.

Joe Pilefsky, "The Torrents of Greed: Parts 1 & 2," *Law & Order* (also known as *Law & Order Prime*), NBC, 1991.

Nick, "Going Home," *Counterstrike* (also known as *Auf eigene Faust, Contraataque, Contragolpe,* and *Force de frappe*), CTV (Canada) and USA Network, 1991.

Dr. Reston, "The Pitch," *Seinfeld,* NBC, 1992.

Dr. Reston, "The Ticket," *Seinfeld,* NBC, 1992.

Dr. Reston, "The Wallet," *Seinfeld,* NBC, 1992.

Dr. Reston, "The Watch," *Seinfeld,* NBC, 1992.

Gordon Reeve, "Hello and Goodbye," *L.A. Law,* NBC, 1993.

Jack, "Love Crimes," *The Hidden Room,* Lifetime, 1993.

Stawpah, "Mirror Image—August 8, 1953," *Quantum Leap,* NBC, 1993.

Sweet, "The High Cost of Loving/Impostors," *Secret Service,* NBC, 1993.

Diablo the Deceiver, "Magic Trick," *Kung Fu: The Legend Continues,* syndicated, 1994.

Gerald Ravens, "Switches," *M.A.N.T.I.S.,* Fox, 1994.

Michael Kent, "The Samurai," *Highlander* (also known as *Highlander: The Series*), syndicated, 1994.

Turk Tortelli, "Fish Story," *Northern Exposure,* CBS, 1994.

Red–haired man, "Nisei," *The X–Files,* Fox, 1995.

Red–haired man, "731," *The X–Files,* Fox, 1995.

Dr. Sherrick, "Beyond the Veil," *The Outer Limits* (also known as *The New Outer Limits*), Showtime, Sci–Fi Channel, and syndicated, 1996.

Gunnery sergeant Ray Crockett, "High Ground," *JAG,* NBC, 1996.

Karl Mayes, "Redemption," *Walker, Texas Ranger* (also known as *Walker*), CBS, 1996.

Mac, "Purgatory," *The Lazarus Man,* syndicated, 1996.

Cletus Fowler, "Nemesis," *The Magnificent Seven,* CBS, 1998.

Commander E. K. Moss, "Lyekka," *Lexx* (also known as *Lexx: The Series* and *Tales from a Parallel Universe*), Sci–Fi Channel and syndicated, 1998.

Leigh Noir, "The Prodigy," *Poltergeist: The Legacy* (also known as *Poltergeist, El legado, Poltergeist—Die unheimliche Macht, Poltergeist: El legado,* and *Poltergeist, les aventuriers du surnaturel*), Showtime and syndicated, 1998.

Romulan senator Vreenak, "In the Pale Moonlight," *Star Trek: Deep Space Nine* (also known as *Deep Space Nine, DS9,* and *Star Trek: DS9*), syndicated, 1998.

Strike, "The Face of Helene Bournouw," *The Hunger,* Showtime, 1998.

Thomas Openshaw, "In Harm's Way: Parts 1 & 2," *Walker, Texas Ranger* (also known as *Walker*), CBS, 1999.

Willie Kane, "Sympathy for the Devil," *La Femme Nikita* (also known as *Nikita*), USA Network, 2000.

Aaron Gaumont, "Power Play," *Mutant X,* syndicated, 2002.

Al Hawke, "Sins of the Mother," *Birds of Prey* (also known as *BOP*), The WB, 2002.

Commander E. K. Moss, "Moss," *Lexx* (also known as *Lexx: The Series* and *Tales from a Parallel Universe*), Sci–Fi Channel and syndicated, 2002.

Commander E. K. Moss, "Prime Ridge," *Lexx* (also known as *Lexx: The Series* and *Tales from a Parallel Universe*), Sci–Fi Channel and syndicated, 2002.

Lieutenant Adam Kirk, "Mr. Monk Goes to the Carnival," *Monk*, USA Network, 2002.

Voice of Shade, "Fury: Part 1," *Justice League* (animated; also known as *JL, JLA, Justice League of America,* and *Justice League Unlimited*), Cartoon Network, 2002.

Voice of Shade, "Injustice for All: Parts 1 & 2," *Justice League* (animated; also known as *JL, JLA, Justice League of America,* and *Justice League Unlimited*), Cartoon Network, 2002.

Alien foreman, "The Xindi," *Enterprise* (also known as *Star Trek: Enterprise, Star Trek: Series V,* and *Star Trek: Untitled Fifth Series*), UPN, 2003.

Voice of Shade, "Secret Society: Parts 1 & 2," *Justice League* (animated; also known as *JL, JLA, Justice League of America,* and *Justice League Unlimited*), Cartoon Network, 2003.

"Ambush," *Blue Murder* (also known as *En quete de preuves*), CanWest Global Television, 2003.

Dravitt, "Voices Carry," *The 4400* (also known as *4400*), USA Network, 2005.

Mr. Swain, "The Rival House," *Puppets Who Kill,* The Comedy Network (Canada), 2006.

Television Appearances; Pilots:

Lester, *Bullet Hearts,* Fox, c. 1996.

Stage Appearances:

Edmond Mortimer, *Henry IV Part 1,* New York Shakespeare Festival, Joseph Papp Public Theater, Delacorte Theater, New York City, 1968.

Lord Bardoll, *Henry IV Part 2,* New York Shakespeare Festival, Joseph Papp Public Theater, Delacorte Theater, 1968.

The American Dream, Billy Rose Theatre, New York City, 1968.

Xerxes, *The Persians,* St. George's Church, New York City, 1970.

John Caside, *Pictures in the Hallway,* Forum Theatre, New York City, 1971.

Orin Mannon, *Mourning Becomes Electra,* Circle in the Square, New York City, 1972.

Sebastian, *Twelfth Night* (also known as *Twelfth Night, or What You Will*), Lincoln Center, Vivian Beaumont Theater, New York City, 1972.

Don Parritt, *The Iceman Cometh,* Circle in the Square, 1973.

James Dean, *Alive and Well in Argentina,* St. Clement's Church Theatre, New York City, 1974.

Carver, *The Winter Dancers,* Phoenix Theatre, Marymount Manhattan College, New York City, 1979.

Mark Crawford, *Casualties,* Playhouse 46, New York City, 1980.

Mortimer, *Mary Stuart,* Center Theatre Group, Ahmanson Theatre, Los Angeles, 1981.

Vasily Vasilevich Solyony, *The Three Sisters,* Manhattan Theatre Club, New York City, 1982–83.

Alceste, *The Misanthrope,* Circle in the Square, 1983.

Hotspur, *Henry IV Part 1,* Old Globe, San Diego, CA, 1983.

Macduff, *Macbeth,* Old Globe, 1983.

Hector Hushabye, *Heartbreak House,* Circle in the Square, 1983–84.

Otto Meier, *Mensch Meier,* Manhattan Theatre Club, 1984.

Petruchio, *The Taming of the Shrew,* Great Lakes Theater Festival, Cleveland, OH, 1984.

Danton's Death, Center Stage, Baltimore, MD, 1984.

Jack, *Haven,* South Street Theatre, New York City, 1985.

Little Eyolf, Yale Repertory Theatre, New Haven, CT, 1985.

Mr. Bohun, *You Never Can Tell,* Circle in the Square, 1986–87.

Christopher Glander, *The Milk Train Doesn't Stop Here Anymore,* Workshop of the Performing Arts (WPA) Theatre, New York City, 1987.

Faber, *American Notes,* New York Shakespeare Festival, Joseph Papp Public Theater, Susan Stein Shiva Theater, New York City, 1988.

Kittel, *Ghetto,* Circle in the Square, 1989.

Title role, *Macbeth,* Riverside Shakespeare Company, Playhouse 91, New York City, 1991.

Dr. Waxling, *Search and Destroy,* Circle in the Square, 1992.

Appeared in New York City productions of *Anna K, Now There's Just the Three of Us,* and *Richard III.*

RECORDINGS

Videos:

Himself, *Acts of Violence,* New Line Home Video, 2006.

Himself, *Inside "The Fountain": Death and Rebirth,* Warner Home Video, 2007.

Video Games:

Voice of Pascal, *The Chronicles of Riddick: Escape from Butcher Bay,* Vivendi Universal Games, 2004.

McKEON, Nancy 1966(?)–

PERSONAL

Full name, Nancy Justine McKeon; born April 4, 1966 (some sources cite 1967), in Westbury, NY; daughter of Don (a travel agent) and Barbara McKeon; sister of

Philip McKeon (an actor, a producer, and director); married Marc Andrus (a key grip), June 8, 2003; children: Aurora, one son. *Education:* Attended college.

Addresses: *Agent*—The Gersh Agency, 232 North Canon Dr., Beverly Hills, CA 90210.

Career: Actress, director, and producer. Worked as a model and appeared in television advertisements and public service announcements, including One to Grow On, a series of public service announcements.

Member: Directors Guild of America.

Awards, Honors: Young Artist Award nomination, best young comedienne—motion picture or television, Young Artist Foundation, 1982, Young Artist Award, best young actress in a comedy series, 1983, Young Artist Award nomination, best young actress in a comedy series, 1984, and nomination for When Bad Teens Go Good Award, TV Land awards, 2007, all for *The Facts of Life;* Young Artist Award, best young actress in a movie made for television, 1983, for *The Facts of Life Goes to Paris;* Young Artist Award, best young actress in a television special, 1983, for "Please Don't Hit Me, Mom," *ABC Afterschool Specials;* Crystal Palm Award, best first short film, and Audience Award, best short drama, both Marco Island Film Festival, 2000, for *A Wakening;* Prism Award nominations, performance in a drama series and performance in a drama series episode, both 2003, and performance in a drama series multiepisode storyline, 2004, all for *The Division;* named one the one hundred greatest teen stars, VH1, 2006.

CREDITS

Television Appearances; Series:
Jill Stone, *Stone,* ABC, 1980.
Joanna Marie "Jo" Polniaszek Bonner, *The Facts of Life,* NBC, 1980–88.
Voice of Dolly, *The Scooby and Scrappy–Doo Puppy Hour* (animated; also known as *Scooby & Scrappy–Doo: The Puppy's New Adventures* and *The Scooby–Doo Puppy Hour*), ABC, beginning 1982.
Annie O'Donnell, *Can't Hurry Love,* CBS, 1995–96.
Jane Sokol, *Style and Substance* (also known as *Style & Substance*), CBS, 1998.
Inspector Jinny Exstead, *The Division* (also known as *Heart of the City*), Lifetime, 2001–2004.

Television Appearances; Miniseries:
Rosalie Profaci Bonnano, *Love, Honor & Obey: The Last Mafia Marriage* (also known as *Mafia Marriage*), CBS, 1993.

Amy Harkin, *Category 6: Day of Destruction* (also known as *Overload*), CBS, 2004.
Herself (teen star number eighty–one), *100 Greatest Teen Stars,* VH1, 2006.

Television Appearances; Movies:
Susan Moreland, *A Question of Love* (also known as *A Purely Legal Matter*), NBC, 1978.
Joanna Marie "Jo" Polniaszek Bonner, *The Facts of Life Goes to Paris,* NBC, 1982.
Kimberly Downs, *This Child Is Mine,* NBC, 1985.
Rhonda Malone, *Poison Ivy,* NBC, 1985.
Cindy Fralick, *Firefighter* (also known as *Greater Alarm* and *The Lady in Firehouse 109*), CBS, 1986.
Joanna Marie "Jo" Polniaszek, *The Facts of Life Down Under,* NBC, 1987.
Nicole "Nikki" Glover, *Strange Voices,* NBC, 1987.
Tracy Thurman, *A Cry for Help: The Tracy Thurman Story* (also known as *Under the Law: The Tracy Thurman Story*), NBC, 1989.
Martha Townsend, *Lightning Field* (also known as *The Lightning Incident*), USA Network, 1991.
Karen Williams, *Baby Snatcher,* CBS, 1992.
Margaret Deal, *A Mother's Gift* (also known as *A Lantern in Her Hand*), CBS, 1995.
Joan Connor, *In My Sister's Shadow,* CBS, 1997.
Jane Berry, *Comfort and Joy,* Lifetime, 2003.
Emily, *Wild Hearts,* The Hallmark Channel, 2006.

Television Appearances; Specials:
Voice of Dolly, "The Puppy's Great Adventure" (animated), *ABC Weekend Specials,* ABC, 1979.
Lucy Twining, "Schoolboy Father," *ABC Afterschool Specials,* ABC, 1980.
Voice of Amelia Matilda Daley, "The Trouble with Miss Switch" (animated), *ABC Weekend Specials,* ABC, 1980.
Voice of Dolly, "The Puppy's Amazing Rescue" (animated), *ABC Weekend Specials,* ABC, 1980.
Voice of Scruffy, "Scruffy" (animated), *ABC Weekend Specials,* ABC, 1980.
Nancy Parks, "Please Don't Hit Me, Mom," *ABC Afterschool Specials,* ABC, 1981.
Voice of Amelia Matilda Daley, "Miss Switch to the Rescue" (animated), *ABC Weekend Specials,* ABC, 1981.
Voice of Dolly, "The Puppy Saves the Circus" (animated), *ABC Weekend Specials,* ABC, 1981.
Herself (NBC team contestant), *Battle of the Network Stars XII* (also known as *Battle of the Network Stars*), ABC, 1982.
Herself (NBC team contestant), *Battle of the Network Stars XIV* (also known as *Battle of the Network Stars*), ABC, 1983.
Voice of Dolly, "The Puppy's Further Adventures" (animated), *ABC Weekend Specials,* ABC, 1983.
Herself (NBC team contestant), *Battle of the Network Stars XVII* (also known as *Battle of the Network Stars*), ABC, 1985.

The Golden Globe's 50th Anniversary Celebration, NBC, 1994.

(In archive footage) Herself, *50 Cutest Child Stars: All Grown Up,* E! Entertainment Television, 2005.

Television Appearances; Awards Presentations:

Presenter, *Lifetime Presents Disney's "American Teacher Awards"* (also known as *American Teacher Awards*), Lifetime, 2000.

Television Appearances; Episodic:

Guest at birthday party, *Another World* (also known as *Another World: Bay City*), NBC, 1975.

Vikki Mayer, "The Crying Child," *Starsky and Hutch,* ABC, 1977.

"Who Ordered the Hot Turkey?," *Alice,* CBS, 1978.

Penney Barrett, "The Brotherhood of the Sea/Letter to Babycakes/Daddy's Pride," *The Love Boat,* ABC, 1979.

Voice of Tai, "Harvest of Doom," *Thundarr the Barbarian* (animated), ABC, 1980.

Voice of Tai, "Last Train to Doomsday," *Thundarr the Barbarian* (animated), ABC, 1981.

Kimberly, "Alice's Halloween Surprise," *Alice,* CBS, 1981.

Herself, *The Tonight Show Starring Johnny Carson* (also known as *The Best of Carson*), NBC, 1985.

Frizzo, "52 Pick Up," *The Facts of Life,* NBC, 1987.

"New Dawn," *The Hitchhiker* (also known as *Deadly Nightmares* and *Le voyageur*), USA Network, 1990.

Herself, "Nancy McKeon," *Lauren Hutton and ...,* 1995.

Rachel Waters, "The Last Day of the Rest of Your Life," *Touched by an Angel,* CBS, 1999.

Herself, *Intimate Portrait: Nancy McKeon,* Lifetime, 2001.

Herself, *The Rosie O'Donnell Show,* syndicated, 2001, 2002.

Herself, "Michael J. Fox," *The E! True Hollywood Story* (also known as *Michael J. Fox: The E! True Hollywood Story* and *THS*), E! Entertainment Television, 2006.

Herself, *Today* (also known as *NBC News Today* and *The Today Show*), NBC, 2006.

Gail Sweeney, "Absalom," *Without a Trace* (also known as *Vanished* and *W.A.T.*), CBS, 2007.

Television Appearances; Pilots:

Ann, *Return to Fantasy Island* (also known as *Fantasy Island II*), ABC, 1978.

Jill Stone, *Stone,* ABC, 1979.

Beth Franklin, *High School U.S.A.,* ABC, 1983.

Slugger, *Dusty,* NBC, 1983.

Cohost, *Candid Kids,* NBC, 1985.

Television Producer; Series:

Can't Hurry Love, CBS, 1995–96.

Television Additional Voices; Series:

Scooby–Doo and Scrappy–Doo (animated), ABC, beginning 1979.

Television Executive Producer; Movies:

Firefighter (also known as *Greater Alarm* and *The Lady in Firehouse 109*), CBS, 1986.

Strange Voices, NBC, 1987.

Television Director; Episodic:

"Full Moon," *The Division* (also known as *Heart of the City*), Lifetime, 2002.

"The Cost of Freedom," *The Division* (also known as *Heart of the City*), Lifetime, 2003.

Film Appearances:

Vikki, *Where the Day Takes You,* New Line Cinema, 1992.

Sara, *Teresa's Tattoo* (also known as *Mystery Model*), Trimark Pictures, 1994.

Melanie Brooke, *The Wrong Woman,* Allegro Films/The Image Organization, 1995.

Bride, *Just Write* (also known as *Just Right*), 1997, Heartland Film Releasing, 1998.

Film Work:

Director and producer, *A Wakening* (short film), 1999.

RECORDINGS

Videos:

(In archive footage) Herself, *Candid Camera: 5 Decades of Smiles,* Rhino, 2005.

WRITINGS

Screenplays:

A Wakening (short film), 1999.

OTHER SOURCES

Periodicals:

People Weekly, October 22, 2001, p. 105.

TV Guide, October 7, 1995, pp. 24–25.

McLAGLEN, Mary

PERSONAL

Daughter of Andrew V. McLaglen.

Career: Production manager, producer, and production coordinator.

CREDITS

Film Work:

Production coordinator, *Girls Just Want to Have Fun,* New World Pictures, 1985.

Production coordinator, *Runaway Train,* Cannon Group, 1985.

Production coordinator, *Nomads,* Metro–Goldwyn–Mayer, 1986.

Production coordinator, *Back to School,* Orion, 1986.

Production executive, *Inside Out,* Hemdale Film, 1987.

Production coordinator, *And God Created Woman,* Vestron Pictures, 1988.

Unit manager, *A Time of Destiny,* Columbia, 1988.

Production manager, *Jack's Back,* Paramount, 1988.

Production manager, *The Prince of Pennsylvania,* New Line Cinema, 1988.

Producer, *Cold Feet,* Avenue Pictures Productions, 1989.

Unit production manager, *Drop Dead Fred* (also known as *My Special Friend*), New Line Cinema, 1991.

Unit production manager, *Zandalee,* 1991.

Unit production manager, *My Cousin Vinny,* Twentieth Century–Fox, 1992.

Unit production manager, *That Night* (also known as *One Hot Summer*), Warner Bros., 1992.

Coproducer and unit production manager, *Sommersby,* Warner Bros., 1993.

Coproducer and unit production manager, *The Client,* Warner Bros., 1994.

Coproducer and unit production manager, *Sgt. Bilko* (also known as *Sergeant Bilko*), Universal, 1996.

Coproducer and unit production manager, *One Fine Day,* Twentieth Century–Fox, 1996.

Executive producer, assistant director, and unit production manager, *Hope Floats,* Twentieth Century–Fox, 1998.

Executive producer and unit production manager, *Practical Magic,* Warner Bros., 1998.

Executive producer and unit production manager, *Pay It Forward,* Warner Bros., 2000.

Executive producer and unit production manager, *Divine Secrets of the Ya–Ya Sisterhood,* Warner Bros., 2002.

Executive producer and unit production manager, *Two Weeks Notice,* Warner Bros., 2002.

Executive producer, *Envy,* Columbia, 2004.

Executive producer and unit production manager, *Dodgeball: A True Underdog Story* (also known as *Dodgeball* and *Voll auf die nusse*), Twentieth Century–Fox, 2004.

Executive producer and unit production manager, *Miss Congeniality 2: Armed & Fabulous,* Warner Bros., 2005.

Executive producer, *The Lake House,* Warner Bros., 2006.

Executive producer and unit production manager, *All About Steve,* Fox 2000, 2008.

Film Appearances:

(Uncredited) *Chisum,* Warner Bros., 1970.

Television Work; Movies:

Production coordinator, *Uncle Tom's Cabin,* Showtime, 1987.

Producer, *Last Light,* Showtime, 1993.

Coproducer, *Moonlight and Valentino,* 1995.

McNAMARA, William 1965–
(Billy McNamara)

PERSONAL

Full name, William West McNamara; born March 31, 1965, in Dallas, TX; father, a professional race car driver; mother, an interior designer. *Education:* Attended Columbia University; studied acting at the Lee Strasberg Institute; studied acting with Kim Stanley.

Addresses: *Agent*—Ellis Talent Group, 4705 Laurel Canyon Blvd., Valley Village, CA 91607. *Manager*—Entertainment Management Group, 8265 West Sunset Blvd., Suite 203, West Hollywood, CA 90046.

Career: Actor. Williamstown Theatre Festival, Williamstown, MA, member of Act I theatre group, c. 1986. Appeared in advertisements. Worked as a production assistant at Twentieth Century–Fox.

Awards, Honors: Annual CableAce Award nomination, actor in a movie or miniseries, National Cable Television Association, 1993, for *Wildflower.*

CREDITS

Film Appearances:

Stefano (some sources cite Urbano), *Opera* (also known as *Terror at the Opera*), 1987, South Gate Entertainment, 1991.

Billy Kane, *The Beat* (also known as *The Conjurer*), Vestron Pictures, 1988.

Teenage Billy Wyatt, *Stealing Home,* Warner Bros., 1988.

Joel, *Dream a Little Dream* (also known as *Long before Tomorrow*), Vestron Pictures, 1989.

Dickie Jackson, *Texasville,* Columbia, 1990.

Pat Robbins, *Stella* (also known as *A minha mae Stella* and *Stella—ensam mor*), Buena Vista, 1990.

Dave Ritchie, *Aspen Extreme* (also known as *Aspen—Dinheiro, seducao e perigo, Aspen extreme, Aspen—miljonaarien paratiisi, Aspen—Sci estremo, Fuera de pistas, Ski radical,* and *Zwei Asse im Schnee*), Buena Vista, 1993.

(Uncredited) Mark Franklin, *Extreme Justice* (also known as *S.I.S.—Extreme Justice*), Trimark Pictures, 1993.

Derek Wolfe, Jr., *Surviving the Game,* New Line Cinema, 1994.

Eddie Devane, *Chasers,* Warner Bros., 1994.

Peter Foley, *Copycat* (also known as *Copykill* and *Imitator*), Warner Bros., 1995.

Prince Arthur, *Storybook* (animated; also known as *Adventure Land*), PM Entertainment Group, 1995.

Rick Davis, *Girl in the Cadillac,* Columbia/TriStar Home Video, 1995.

Damon, *Dead Girl,* Cinetel Films, 1996.

Sam Gunn, *The Brylcreem Boys,* Downtown Pictures, 1996.

Shakley, *Snitch,* Cargo Films, 1996.

Kevin, *The Deli,* Golden Monkey Pictures, 1997.

Sonny Daye, *Glam* (also known as *Gangster Glam*), 1997, Storm Entertainment, 2001.

Mike Lewis, *Something to Believe in,* Warner Bros., 1998.

Stan Bleeker, *Sweet Jane,* Phaedra Cinema, 1998.

Troy Davenport, *Ringmaster* (also known as *Jerry Springer: Ringmaster* and *Springers*), Artisan Entertainment, 1998.

Daniel, *Just Sue Me,* Award Entertainment, c. 1999.

Laurence McCoy, *Paper Bullets* (also known as *American Samurai*), 2000.

Michael DeMarco, *Knockout,* Legacy Releasing, 2000.

Clayton Pirce, *Time Lapse* (also known as *Past Tense*), Trimark Video, 2001.

Bobby Murky, *The Calling* (also known as *Man of Faith*), Sabeva Film Distribution, 2002.

Chris Parmel, *The Kings of Brooklyn* (also known as *License to Steal*), 2004.

Gerard, *The Iron Man,* Karim Movies, 2006.

David, *April Moon,* April Moon Productions, 2007.

Hugh Babcock, *The Grift* (also known as *The Fallen*), Hemisphere Entertainment, 2007.

James Fisher, *A Dance for Bethany,* Raise the Bar Productions, 2007.

Teacher, *The Still Life,* Polychrome Pictures, 2007.

Television Appearances; Series:

Sam "Pono" Kulani, *Island Son* (also known as *The Hawaiian* and *Kahuna*), CBS, 1989–90.

Brad Advail, *Beggars and Choosers* (also known as *TV business*), Showtime, 1999–2001.

Television Appearances; Miniseries:

Philip, *Il segreto del Sahara* (also known as *The Secret of the Sahara, Das Geheimnis der Sahara,* and *El secreto del Sahara*), multiple networks, 1989.

Montgomery Clift, *Liz: The Elizabeth Taylor Story* (also known as *Liz Taylor Story*), NBC, 1995.

Ricky Nelson, "You Know They Got a Hell of a Band" segment, *Nightmares and Dreamscapes: From the Stories of Stephen King,* TNT, 2006.

Television Appearances; Movies:

Sammy Perkins, *Wildflower,* Lifetime, 1991.

Chris Pritchard, *Honor Thy Mother,* CBS, 1992.

Matt Carter, *Doing Time on Maple Drive* (also known as *Faces in the Mirror*), Fox, 1992.

(As Billy McNamara) Michael Burke, *Sworn to Vengeance* (also known as *Careless Whispers* and *Secret Vows*), CBS, 1993.

Matthew Anderson, *Radio Inside,* Showtime, 1994.

Jeremy Harper, *Natural Enemy,* 1997.

Jon DiCapri, *Stag,* 1997.

Tom Baker, *Implicated,* 1998.

C. Whitmore Evans, *Trapped,* USA Network, 2001.

Tony Harriman, *McBride: Murder Past Midnight,* The Hallmark Channel, 2005.

Wilford, *American Black Beauty,* 2005.

Television Appearances; Specials:

Jay Medford, "Soldier Boys," *CBS Schoolbreak Specials,* CBS, 1987.

"Indian Poker," *The Edge,* HBO, 1989.

Johnny Dumont, "It's Only Rock & Roll," *ABC Afterschool Specials,* ABC, 1991.

Judge, *The 2000 Miss Teen USA Pageant,* CBS, 2000.

Himself, *Shooting the Police: Cops on Film,* Starz!, 2006.

Television Appearances; Episodic:

Clay Edwards, "The Brotherhood," *Silk Stalkings,* CBS and USA Network, 1992.

Nick Boyer, "Given the Heir," *Perversions of Science,* HBO, 1997.

Gilbert "Gil" Jax, "Encore," *Brimstone* (also known as *Brimstone: el pacto* and *Le damne*), Fox, 1998.

Q. M., "Blue Champagne Resort," *Welcome to Paradox* (also known as *Betaville*), Sci-Fi Channel, 1998.

Kimble, "Better Luck Next Time," *The Outer Limits* (also known as *The New Outer Limits*), Showtime, Sci-Fi Channel, and syndicated, 1999.

Kent Johanssen, "Approaching Desdemona," *The Hunger,* Showtime, 2000.

(As Billy McNamara) Detective Sam Bishop, "Pandora," *Law & Order: Special Victims Unit* (also known as *Law & Order's Sex Crimes, Law & Order: SVU,* and *Special Victims Unit*), NBC, 2003.

Richard Pencava, "Old Man Quiver," *NYPD Blue,* ABC, 2005.

Richard, "Waving Goodbye," *Beyond the Break* (also known as *Boarding School*), The N (Noggin), 2006.

Television Appearances; Pilots:

Mikey Wyatt, *The Wyatts,* Fox, 1994.

Stage Appearances:
Affiliated with productions of the Williamstown Theatre Festival, Williamstown, MA, 1986.

RECORDINGS

Videos:
Himself, *Living the Still Life* (short), Polychrome Pictures, 2007.

OTHER SOURCES

Electronic:
William McNamara Official Website, http://www.williammcnamara.com, October 12, 2007.

McNEIL, Scott 1962–
  (Scott McNeill, Scott McNiel)

PERSONAL

Born September 15, 1962, in Brisbane, Queensland, Australia. *Education:* Studied theatre.

Addresses: *Agent*—Lauren Levitt & Associates, 1525 West Eighth Ave., Third Floor, Vancouver, British Columbia V6J 1T5, Canada.

Career: Actor and voice artist. Provided the voice of Hack for the theme park attraction *ReBoot: The Ride* (also known as *Journey into Chaos*), IMAX Corporation. Appeared in conventions, including AnimeFest, Dallas, TX.

CREDITS

Television Appearances; Animated Series:
Voice of Ganpachi Chabane, *Kyofun no byoningen saishu kyoshi* (anime; also known as *Fearsome Bio Human: The Last Teacher, The Scary Bionic Man: The Ultimate Teacher, Ultimate Teacher,* and *Kyofun no bio–ningen*), Central Park Media, originally broadcast in Japan, beginning 1988.
Voices of Principal Kuno, Captain Daitokuji, and Ushinoske Chomanme, *Ranma 1/2* (anime; also known as *Ranma nibun no ichi*), originally released in Japan by Fuji Television Network, 1989–92.
Voice of Zorran, *Salty's Lighthouse,* The Learning Channel, c. 1989–95.

Voices of uncle and munchkins, *The Wizard of Oz* (anime; also known as *Sugar & Spice: The Wizard of Oz* and *Oz no Mahou Tsukai*), beginning c. 1990, originally broadcast in Japan, 1986–87.
Voices of Flipshot, Butthead, Krex, and Captain Zang, *The New Adventures of He–Man* (also known as *Il nuovo viaggio de Musclor*), syndicated, 1990–91.
Voice of Cobra commander, *G.I. Joe* (also known as *G.I. Joe: A Great American Hero*), syndicated, 1990–92.
Voices of Deadeye Duck, Frax, and others, *Bucky O'Hare and the Toad Wars,* syndicated, 1991–92.
Voices of Adder and Bubba, *The Adventures of T–Rex,* syndicated, 1992.
Voices of police officer and fisherman, *Denei shoujo Ai* (anime; also known as *Video Girl Ai* and *Den'ei shoujo*), originally broadcast in Japan, 1992.
Voices of Sir Lancelot, Sir Gallop, Sir Tone, Sir Trunk, and others, *King Arthur and the Knights of Justice* (anime; also known as *King Arthur & the Knights of Justice* and *El rei Artur* and *Entaku no Kishi Monogatari: Moero Arthur*), syndicated, 1992–93, originally broadcast in Japan, 1979–80.
Voice of Greywolf, *Conan: The Adventurer* (also known as *Conan l'aventurier*), Fox, 1992–93.
Voices of Motofuji Hikita and Hachiro Kanamari, *Hakkenden shin sho* (anime; also known as *Hakkenden, Hakkenden: Legend of the Dog Warriors,* and *The Legend of the Dog Warriors: The Hakkenden*), AIC, beginning c. 1993, originally broadcast in Japan, 1990–91, 1993–95.
Voices of Jimmy Lee, Shadow Boss, and Sickle, *Double Dragon,* syndicated, 1993–94.
Voices of Cal Casey and Genghis Kahn, *Hurricanes,* syndicated, c. 1993–97.
Voice, *Stone Protectors,* syndicated, beginning c. 1994.
Voice of Dak, *Dino Babies* (also known as *Dinobabies*), BBC, c. 1994–96, YTV (Canada), Fox Family Channel, and syndicated, beginning 1996.
Voices of Hack and Specky, *ReBoot,* ABC, 1994–96, Cartoon Network, 1999–2001, also broadcast on YTV (Canada).
Voices of Lord Raptor, Anakaris, and Rikuo, *Darkstalkers* (also known as *Dark Stalkers*), UPN, 1995.
Voice of El Gado, *Final Flight,* beginning 1995.
Voices of Dr. Albert Wily, Proto Man, Brain Bot, and Eddie, *Megaman* (anime; also known as *Mega Man* and *Rockman*), ABC Family Channel and syndicated, beginning 1995.
Voices, *The Littlest Pet Shop,* syndicated, 1995–96.
Voice of Kale, *Ronin Warriors* (anime; also known as *Legendary Armor Samurai Troopers, Samurai Warriors,* and *Yoroiden Samurai Trooper*), Cartoon Network and Sci–Fi Channel, beginning 1995, originally broadcast in Japan by Nagoya Broadcasting Network, 1988–89.
Voice of Cobra commander, *G.I. Joe Extreme,* syndicated, 1995–97.
Voices of Blanka, Ken Masters, Rolento, and Rory, *Street Fighter: The Animated Series,* syndicated, 1995–97.

Voice of Stinger, *Vortech: Undercover Conversion Squad* (also known as *Vor–Tech*), Fox, beginning c. 1996, also broadcast as part of The Power Block, ABC.

Voice of Rinzo, *Saber Marionette J* (anime), Animax and TV Tokyo, 1996–97.

Voices of Piccolo, Jeice, Nappa, and others, *Dragon Ball Z* (anime; also known as *DBZ*), Showtime and syndicated, 1996–98, Cartoon Network, 1999–2003, also broadcast on YTV (Canada), originally broadcast in Japan by Fuji Television Network, 1989–96.

Voices of Dinobot, Rattrap, Silverbolt (also known as Grifo), and Waspinator, *Beast Wars: Transformers* (anime; also known as *Beasties, Beasties: Transformers, Transformers: Beast Wars,* and *Beast wars chou seimeitai transformers*), YTV (Canada) and syndicated, 1996–99, originally broadcast in Japan.

Voice of Galbraith, *Ehrgeiz* (anime; also known as *Ehrgeiz: The Next War, Next Senki Ehrgeiz,* and *Next War Chronicle Ehrgeiz*), originally broadcast by TV Tokyo, 1997.

Voice of T–Bone, *Extreme Dinosaurs,* syndicated, 1997.

Voices of Rath, Set, and Bob the police officer, *Mummies Alive!,* syndicated, 1997.

Voice of Amanda Banshee, *The Wacky World of Tex Avery* (also known as *Tex Avery Theater*), Cartoon Network and syndicated, beginning 1997.

Voice of Bonesteel, *Ninja Turtles: The Next Mutation* (also known as *Hero Turtles: The Next Mutation, Saban's "Hero Turtles: The Next Mutation,"* and *Saban's "Ninja Turtles: The Next Mutation"*), Fox, 1997–98.

Voices of Lord Raptor (Zabel Zarock), the zombie, and others, *Vampire Hunter: The Animated Series* (anime; also known as *Night Warriors: Darkstalkers' Revenge* and *Vampire Hunter*), originally broadcast in Japan, 1997–98.

Voice of evil genetic mutant monster, *Silent Moebius* (anime; also known as *Silent Mobius*), TechTV, originally broadcast in Japan by TV Tokyo, beginning 1998.

Voices of Pelvus and Blokk, *Shadow Raiders* (also known as *ShadowRaiders* and *War Planets*), YTV (Canada) and syndicated, 1998–99.

Voices of Lord Refang, Milesight, guardian, and general, *Monkey Magic* (anime), beginning 1998, TV Tokyo, 1998–2000.

Voice of principal, *3 Friends and Jerry,* Australian Broadcasting Corporation, 1998–2000.

Voice of Nick Logan, *Roswell Conspiracies: Aliens, Myths & Legends* (also known as *The Roswell Conspiracies*), syndicated, 1999–2000.

Voice of Rattrap, *Beast Machines Transformers* (also known as *Beast Machines* and *Beast Machines: Battle for the Sparks*), Fox, 1999–2000.

Voices of Daddy–O Chassis, Davey, and Killer McBash, *Weird–Ohs* (animated), Fox and YTV (Canada), 1999–2000.

Voices of Captain Black Dino and others, *Monster Farm: Enbanseki no himitsu* (anime; also known as *Monster Farm, Monster Farmer,* and *Monster Rancher*), Fox and syndicated, 1999–2001, also broadcast on YTV (Canada), also broadcast in Japan by TBS, 1999–2000.

Voice of Duo Maxwell, *Shin kido senki Gundam W* (also known as *Gundam W, Gundam Wing, New Mobile Report Gundam W,* and *New Mobile War Chronicle Gundam W*), Cartoon Network, beginning 2000, originally broadcast in Japan, beginning 1995.

Voices of King Aston and Jajuka, *Escaflowne* (anime; also known as *Escaflowne of the Heavens, FoxKids Escaflowne, The Vision of Escaflowne,* and *Tenku no Escaflowne*), Fox, 2000–2001, also broadcast in YTV (Canada), originally broadcast in Japan by TV Tokyo, beginning 1996.

Voice of Duo Maxwell, *Mobile Suit Gundam Wing: Endless Waltz* (anime; also known as *Endless Waltz, Gundam Wing Endless Waltz, Mobile Suit Gundam Wing: Endless Waltz, New Mobile Report Gundam W: Endless Waltz, New Mobile War Chronicle Gundam Wing: Endless Waltz,* and *Shin kidou senki Gundam Wing Endless Waltz*), Cartoon Network, beginning 2000, also broadcast by YTV (Canada), originally broadcast in Japan, 1997.

Voice of Master D, *Bionic Commando,* beginning 2000.

Voice, *D'Myna Leagues,* YTV (Canada), beginning 2000.

Voice of Eric "Tan" Tannenbaum IV, *Kong: The Animated Series,* multiple networks, including TeleToon (Canada), beginning c. 2000.

Voices of Duo Maxwell and Teniente Reed, *Mobile Suit Gundam Wing* (anime; also known as *First Gundam, Gundam, Gundam Wing, Mobile Suit Gundam, Mobile Suit Gundam 0079, Space Fighter Team Gunboy, Kido senshi Gundam,* and *Kido senshi Gundamu*), Cartoon Network, 2000–2001, also broadcast by YTV (Canada), originally broadcast in Japan, 1979–80.

Voice of Nub, *Generation O!,* The WB and YTV (Canada), 2000–2001.

Voice of Lyle "The Collector" Owens, *NASCAR Racers* (also known as *NASCAR Superchargers*), Fox, 2000–2001, ABC Family Channel, beginning 2002.

Voice of Wolverine/Logan, *X–Men: Evolution,* The WB, 2000–2003.

Multiple voices, *Zoids/ZERO* (anime; also known as *Zoids, ZOIDS New Century/Zero, Kiju shinseiki Zoid,* and *Zoids shinseiki/zero*), Cartoon Network, YTV (Canada), and broadcast in Japan, beginning 2001.

Voice of Arnold the alligator, *Sitting Ducks,* Cartoon Network, 2001–2004.

Voices of Mr. Yoshi, Melanie Foster's father, and Mr. Cluck, *Hamtaro* (anime; also known as *Trotting Hamtaro* and *Tottoko Hamutaro*), Cartoon Network, beginning 2002, also broadcast by YTV (Canada), originally broadcast by TV Tokyo, 2000–2006.

Voices of Saizou Toki, Magna, and Guan–Coo's aide, *Dragon Drive* (anime), originally broadcast by TV Tokyo, 2002–2003.

Voice of Jetfire, *Transformers: Armada* (also known as *Super Living–Robot Transformer The Legend of Micron Transformers: Micron Legend*, *Cho robotto seimeitai transformer micron densetsu*, and *Toransufoma: Arumada*), Cartoon Network, 2002–2003, also broadcast by YTV (Canada), and broadcast by TV Tokyo, beginning 2003.

Voices of Beast Man, Clawful, Mer–Man, Ram Man, Stratos, and Kobra Khan, *He–Man and the Masters of the Universe* (also known as *He–Man and Masters of the Universe vs. the Snake Men*), Cartoon Network, 2002–2004.

(As Scott McNeill) Voices of Mr. Spongy's spongecake man, Francis of the forest, and Senior Hasbeena, *Mucha Lucha!* (also known as *Mucha Lucha! Gigante!*), The WB, 2002–2005.

Voices of Koga/Kouga, Hoshiyomi, and others, *Inuyasha* (anime; also known as *Inu Yasha*), Cartoon Network, 2002–2006, also broadcast on YTV (Canada), originally broadcast in Asia.

Voices of Walter and others, *Master Keaton* (anime), beginning c. 2003, originally broadcast by NHK and NTV, 1998–99.

Voice of Professor Crazyhair, *Yakkity Yak*, Nickelodeon, beginning 2003.

Voice, *Hot Wheels Highway 35 World Race* (also known as *Hot Wheels Highway 35*), Cartoon Network, beginning 2003.

Multiple voices, *Zoids: Fuzors* (anime), Cartoon Network, 2003, TV Tokyo, 2004–2005.

Voices of GutsMan, all six CutMan brothers, KingMan, and ShadeMan.

MegaMan: NT Warrior (anime; also known as *MegaMan: NT Warrior Axess*, *Rockman.EXE*, and *Rockman.exe Axess*), Cartoon Network, The WB, and TeleToon (Canada), 2003–2004, originally broadcast in Japan by TV Tokyo, 2002–2003.

Voices of Gerard Garcia, Koopman, and others, *Kido senshi Gundam Seed* (anime; also known as *Gundam Seed* and *Mobile Suit Gundam SEED*), Cartoon Network and YTV (Canada), beginning 2004, originally broadcast in Japan, 2002–2003.

Voice of Cain, *Dragon Booster*, ABC Family Channel and Disney Channel, beginning 2004, also broadcast on CBC.

Voices of Jetfire, Strongarm, and Omega Supreme, *Transformers: Super Link* (also known as *Transformer: Energon*), TV Tokyo and Cartoon Network, 2004–2005.

Voice of Hohenheim Elric, *Hagane no renkinjutsushi* (anime; also known as *Fullmetal Alchemist* and *Hagaren*), Cartoon Network, 2004–2006, also broadcast on YTV (Canada) and Rapture (Great Britain), originally broadcast in Japan, 2003–2004.

Voice of Ultrox, *Alien Racers*, TeleToon (Canada), beginning 2005.

Voices of Ignatius and Ace the Bathound, *Krypto the Superdog*, Cartoon Network, beginning 2005.

(Uncredited) Voices of Snarl and Backstop, *Transformers: Cybertron* (anime; also known as *Transformers: Galaxy Force*), Cartoon Network, The WB, and YTV (Canada), and broadcast in Japan, beginning 2005.

Voices of Mr. White and others, *Johnny Test*, The WB, 2005–2006, The CW, beginning 2006.

Voices of Grandpa and Shimano, *Hikaru no Go* (anime; also known as *Hikago* and *Hikaru's Go*), ImaginAsian, beginning 2006, originally broadcast by TV Tokyo.

Voices of Tanomo and others, *Samurai 7* (anime), Independent Film Channel, beginning 2006, originally broadcast in Japan, beginning 2004.

Voice of Unato Seiran, *Mobile Suit Gundam Seed Destiny Special Edition* (anime), broadcast in Japan, 2006.

Voice of Atlas, *Class of the Titans*, TeleToon (Canada), beginning 2006.

Voice of ramen vendor, *Human Crossing* (anime), ImaginAsian, beginning 2007, originally broadcast by TV Tokyo, 2003.

Voice of Unato Ema Seiran, *Mobile Suit Gundam Seed Destiny* (anime; also known as *Gundam Seed Destiny* and *Kido senshi Gundam SEED DESTINY*), YTV (Canada), beginning 2007, originally broadcast in Japan, 2004–2005.

Voices of Beazon, pirate, and rich man, *Elemental Gelade* (anime; also known as *Erementar Gerad*), ImaginAsian, beginning 2007, originally broadcast by TV Tokyo, beginning 2005.

Voices of Yoshiyuki Sakai, cat, and gatekeeper, *Ayakashi–Samurai Horror Tales* (anime; also known as *Ayakashi—Japanese Classic Horror*), ImaginAsian, beginning 2007, originally broadcast in Japan by Fuji Television Network, beginning 2006.

Voice of Funshine Bear, *Care Bears: Adventures in Care–a–Lot*, CBS, beginning 2007.

Voice of Mr. Fischberger, *Ricky Sprocket, Showbiz Boy*, TeleToon (Canada) and Nicktoons, beginning 2007.

Voices of Stork, Repton, Luegy, and others, *Storm Hawks*, Cartoon Network, beginning 2007.

Voice of Verrocchio, *Black Lagoon: The Second Barrage* (anime; also known as *The Second Barrage*), G4techTV Canada, beginning c. 2008, originally broadcast in Japan, beginning 2006.

Provided the voices of Dr. Albert Wily and Beat, *Megaman: Upon a Star* (anime; also known as *Mega Man*, *Rockman: Wishing upon a Star*, and *Rockman: Hoshi ni Nagai wo*). Provided the voice of Prince Brad for *Mix Master* (anime), broadcast in English, originally broadcast in South Korea. Provided voices for other programs, including *Aeon Kid*. McNeil appears in several video compilations of Japanese television series.

Television Appearances; Live Action Series:
Voice of Lightningborg, *Beetleborgs Metallix* (also known as *Saban's "Beetleborgs Metallix"*), Fox, 1996–98.

Television Appearances; Animated Movies:

Voice of Shere Khan, *The Adventures of Mowgli,* c. 1996.

Voice of Piccolo, *Dragon Ball Z The Movie 1: The Deadzone* (also known as *Dead Zone, Dragon Ball Z: The Movie—Dead Zone, Dragon Ball Z: Return My Gohan!!, Dragon Ball Z: Son Goku Super Star,* and *Dragon Ball Z: Ora no Gohan wo Kaese!!*), Cartoon Network, and YTV (Canada), 2000, originally broadcast in Japan, 1989.

Voices of Piccolo and turtle, *Dragon Ball Z Movie 2: The World's Strongest* (anime; also known as *Dragon Ball Z: The Movie—The World's Strongest, Dragon Ball Z: The Strongest Guy in the World, Dragon Ball Z: The World's Strongest Man, Bola de Drac Z: el mes fort del mon, Doragon boru Z 2: Kono yo de ichigan tsuyoi yatsu,* and *Dragon Ball Z: Konoyo de ichibaniyatsu*), Cartoon Network and YTV (Canada), 2000, originally broadcast in Japan, 1990.

Voices of Piccolo and Daizu, *Dragon Ball Z Movie 3: The Tree of Might* (anime; also known as *Dragon Ball Z: The Movie—The Tree of Might, Dragon Ball Z: Super Battle in the World, Dragon Ball Z: The Tree of Might, Dragon Ball Z 3: Ultimate Decisive Battle for Earth, The Tree of Might, Dragon Ball Z: Chikyuu marugoto chou kessen,* and *Doragon boru Z 3: Chikyu marugoto cho kessen*), Cartoon Network and YTV (Canada), 2000, originally broadcast in Japan, 1990.

Voice of Duo Maxwell, *Gundam Wing Endless Waltz Special Edition* (consists of enhanced episodes of anime series *Mobile Suit Gundam Wing: Endless Waltz;* also known as *Endless Waltz, Gundam Wing: The Movie—Endless Waltz, Mobile Suit Gundam Wing: The Movie—Endless Waltz, New Mobile Report: Gundam-W Endless Waltz, New Mobile War Chronicle Gundam Wing: Endless Waltz Special Edition,* and *Shin kidou senki Gundam Wing Endless Waltz*), The WB, 2000, originally broadcast in Japan, 1998.

Voice of Gloom, *Lion of Oz* (also known as *Lion of Oz and the Badge of Courage* and *Le lion d'Oz*), Disney Channel, 2000.

Voices of Hack and Specky, *ReBoot: Daemon Rising* (consists of episodes of the television series), Cartoon Network, 2001.

Voices of Hack and Specky, *ReBoot: My Two Bobs* (consists of episodes of the television series; also known as *ReBoot: The Movie II*), Cartoon Network, 2001.

English voices of Lyle, shuttle pilot, and Londo Bell technician, *Kido senshi Gandamu: Gyakushu no Sha* (anime; also known as *Gundam: Char's Counter Attack, Mobile Suit Gundam: Char's Counterattack,* and *Mobile Suit Gundam: The Counteractive Char*), Cartoon Network, 2002, originally broadcast in Japan by Bandai Channel and NHK, 1988.

Voice of Destro, *G.I. Joe: Spy Troops the Movie,* Cartoon Network, 2003.

Voices of Amergan, Gregor, and lab director, *Highlander: The Search for Vengeance* (also known as *Highlander: Vengeance* and *Untitled Yoshiaki Kawajiri/Highlander Project*), Sci-Fi Channel, 2007.

Television Appearances; Live Action Movies:

Seasons of the Heart, NBC, 1994.

Someone Else's Child (also known as *Lost and Found*), ABC, 1994.

Harry Maxwell, *Sleeping Dogs,* Sci-Fi Channel, 1998.

Master of ceremonies, "Ladies and the Champ," *The Wonderful World of Disney,* ABC, 2001.

Temptor, *I Was a Teenage Faust,* Showtime, 2002.

Victor Kirk, *12 Hours to Live,* Lifetime, 2006.

Television Appearances; Animated Specials:

(As Scott McNiel) Voice, *Christopher the Christmas Tree,* Fox, 1994.

Voice of Loopy, *Santa Mouse and the Ratdeer,* Fox Family Channel, 2000.

Voice of Stretch, *Casper's Haunted Christmas* (also known as *Le Noel hante de Casper*), USA Network, 2000.

Voice, *Grandma Got Run Over by a Reindeer,* 2000.

Voice of Wolfman, *Monster Mash* (animated musical), [United States and Italy], c. 2000.

Multiple voices, *Donner,* ABC Family Channel, 2001.

Voice of Lenny the elf foreman, *The Christmas Orange,* TeleToon (Canada) and ABC Family Channel, 2002.

Voices of Skully Pettibone and Count Max, *Scary Godmother Halloween Spooktakular,* Cartoon Network, 2003.

Voices of Skully Pettibone and Count Max, *Scary Godmother: The Revenge of Jimmy,* Cartoon Network, 2005.

Television Appearances; Animated Episodes:

Voice of Syd Sycamore, "Emmy's Dream House/Dragon Sails," *Dragon Tales,* PBS, 1999.

Voice of Syd Sycamore, "Sky Pirates/Four Little Pigs," *Dragon Tales,* PBS, 1999.

Voice of Syd Sycamore, "Zak and the Beanstalk/A Feat on Her Feet," *Dragon Tales,* PBS, 1999.

Voice of Arlo, "Finders Keepers/Remember the Pillow Fort," *Dragon Tales,* PBS, 2000.

Voice of Arlo, "Out with the Garbage/Lights, Camera, Dragon," *Dragon Tales,* PBS, 2000.

Voice of baby eggplant, "Revenge of the Chicken from Outer Space/Journey to the Center of Nowhere," *Courage the Cowardly Dog,* Cartoon Network, 2000.

Voice of Syd Sycamore, "Ord Sees the Light/The Ugly Dragling," *Dragon Tales,* PBS, 2000.

Voice of Syd Sycamore, "To Do or Not to Do/Much Ado about Nodlings," *Dragon Tales,* PBS, 2000.

Voice of clown, "Clown," *The Weekenders* (also known as *Disney's "The Weekenders"*), Disney Channel, 2001.

Voice of Electro, "Ill–Met by Moonlight," *Spider–Man Unlimited* (also known as *Spiderman Unlimited*), Fox, 2001.

Voice of homeless person, "Mortgages and Marbles," *Home Movies,* Cartoon Network, 2001.

Voice of Lester, "Sustenance," *Spider–Man Unlimited* (also known as *Spiderman Unlimited*), Fox, 2001.

Voice of Speedy, "Teasing Is Not Pleasing/Team Work," *Dragon Tales,* PBS, 2001.

Voice of Syd Sycamore, "Dragonberry Drought/A Snowman for All Seasons," *Dragon Tales,* PBS, 2001.

Voice of Syd Sycamore, "A New Friend/Have No Fear," *Dragon Tales,* PBS, 2001.

Voice of Syd Sycamore, "One Big Wish/Breaking Up Is Hard to Do," *Dragon Tales,* PBS, 2001.

Voice of the Vulture, "Cry Vulture," *Spider–Man Unlimited* (also known as *Spiderman Unlimited*), Fox, 2001.

Voice of Arlo, "The Grudge Won't Budge/Putting the Fun in Fun Houses," *Dragon Tales,* PBS, 2002.

Voices, "Picket, Picket/Sick Daze," *The Cramp Twins,* Fox, YTV (Canada), and BBC, 2003.

Voice of pastel Mr. Shin, "Don't Give Up Sumi High Baseball Team," *Oh! Supa Miruku–chan* (anime; also known as *Oh! Super Milk–Chan, The Super Milk–Chan Show,* and *Vintage Milk–Chan*), Cartoon Network, 2004, originally broadcast in Japan.

Voice of pastel Mr. Shin, "The Mysterious Case of Red Wine Tide Vintage 1961," *Oh! Supa Miruku–chan* (anime; also known as *Oh! Super Milk–Chan, The Super Milk–Chan Show,* and *Vintage Milk–Chan*), Cartoon Network, 2004, originally broadcast in Japan.

Voices of official and first biker, "Triker Trouble/Heart Wrench," *The Cramp Twins,* Fox, YTV (Canada), and BBC, 2004.

Voices of Turnip Shoot and Rawhide Bear, "Little Big Man/Flag Boy," *The Cramp Twins,* Fox, YTV (Canada), and BBC, 2004.

Voice of Captain Scaliwag, "A New Friend/El Dia del Maestro," *Dragon Tales,* PBS, 2005.

Voice of Captain Scaliwag, "Teasing Is Not Pleasing/ Down the Drain," *Dragon Tales,* PBS, 2005.

Voice of Syd Sycamore, "To Fly with a New Friend: Parts 1 & 2," *Dragon Tales,* PBS, 2005.

Voice of Annihilus, "Annihilation," *Fantastic Four: World's Greatest Heroes* (also known as *Fantastic Four* and *Les quatre fantastiques*), Cartoon Network, 2006.

Voice of Ashton Kutcher, "The Last Ashton Kutcher," *Where My Dogs at?,* MTV2, 2006.

Voice of man in television commercial, "Planet of the Imps," *Being Ian,* YTV (Canada), 2006.

Voice of Orgon, *Shakugan no Shana* (anime; also known as *Shana* and *Shana of the Burning Eyes*), broadcast in Japan, 2006 (multiple episodes).

Voice of Verrocchio, "Ring–Ding Ship Chase," *Burakku ragun* (anime; also known as *Black Lagoon*), c. 2006, originally broadcast by TV Tokyo, c. 2006.

Voice of beefy ape, "The Snoring/George's Day Off," *George of the Jungle,* Cartoon Network, 2007.

Television Appearances; Live Action Episodes:
Crack house drug abuser, "Parenthood," *Street Justice,* syndicated, 1992.

Dennis, "The Sea Witch," *Highlander* (also known as *Highlander: The Series*), syndicated, 1992.

Mike Surnac, "The Puck Stops Here," *The Commish,* ABC, 1992.

Photographer, "Safe at Home," *Neon Rider,* syndicated, 1993.

"The Traitor," *Hawkeye,* syndicated, 1994.

Robert MacLeod, "Homeland," *Highlander* (also known as *Highlander: The Series*), syndicated, 1995.

Astronaut, "Trial by Fire," *The Outer Limits* (also known as *The New Outer Limits*), Showtime, Sci–Fi Channel, and syndicated, 1996.

Judd, "Breakout," *Viper,* syndicated, 1998.

Lane Cassidy, "Foreign Exchange," *The Sentinel,* UPN, 1998.

Robbie Laine, "Room Service," *Strange Frequency,* VH1, 2001.

Voices of Silloin and Linna, "Think Like a Dinosaur," *The Outer Limits* (also known as *The New Outer Limits*), Showtime, Sci–Fi Channel, and syndicated, 2001.

Townsperson, "Nightwalkers," *Stargate SG–1* (also known as *La porte des etoiles* and *Stargaate SG–1*), Sci–Fi Channel and syndicated, 2002.

Voices of the hoodlum and henchmen, "Republic Commando, CSI: Miami, Iron Phoenix and More!," *X–Play,* G4techTV, 2005.

Kefflin, "Company of Thieves," *Stargate SG–1* (also known as *La porte des etoiles* and *Stargaate SG–1*), Sci–Fi Channel and syndicated, 2006.

Television Appearances; Animated Pilots:
Voice of General Slaughter, *Battletoads,* UPN, 1991.

Voice, *NASCAR Racers: The Movie,* 1999.

Voices of Ram Man, Stratos, Mer–Man, and Clawful, "The Beginning," *He–Man and the Masters of the Universe* (also known as *He–Man and the Masters of the Universe: The Beginning*), Cartoon Network, 2002.

Voice of Chinese man, "The Black Lagoon," *Burakku ragun* (anime; also known as *Black Lagoon*), c. 2006, originally broadcast by TV Tokyo, 2006.

Television Appearances; Live Action Pilots:
Douglas, *The Ranch,* Showtime, 2004.

Television Additional Voices; Animated Series:
Sonic the Hedgehog (also known as *Sonic*), ABC and syndicated, 1993–95.

Action Man, UPN and syndicated, 1995–97, broadcast as part of the programming block Amazin' Adventures (also known as Bohbot Kids Network and BKN).

Mobile Suit Gundam Wing (anime; also known as *First Gundam, Gundam, Gundam Wing, Mobile Suit Gundam, Mobile Suit Gundam 0079, Space Fighter Team Gunboy, Kido senshi Gundam,* and *Kido senshi Gundamu*), Cartoon Network, 2000–2001, also broadcast by YTV (Canada), originally broadcast in Japan, 1979–80.

X–Men: Evolution, The WB, 2000–2003.

Aaagh! It's the Mr. Hell Show!, Showtime and other networks, 2001–2002.

Firehouse Tales, Cartoon Network, beginning 2005, broadcast as part of the programming block Tickle U.

Television Work; Episodic:

Director and coproducer, "Sypher," *Loonatics Unleashed* (animated; also known as *Super Looney Tunes*), The WB (later The CW), 2005.

Animated Film Appearances:

Voice of Harlock, *Ginga tetsudo Three–Nine* (anime; also known as *Galaxy Express 999, Galaxy Express 999: The Signature Edition,* and *Ginga tetsudo 999*), Viz Media, originally released, 1979.

Voice of Harlock, *Sayonara, ginga tetsudo Suri–Nain: Andromeda shuchakueki* (anime; also known as *Adieu, Galaxy Express 999, Adieu, Galaxy Express 999: Last Stop Andromeda, Adieu, Galaxy Express 999: The Signature Edition, Galaxy Express 999, Adieu, Goodbye Galaxy Express 999: Andromeda Terminal,* and *Sayonara, ginga tetsudo 999: Andromeda shuchakueki*), Viz Media, originally released in Japan, 1981.

Voices of Lee and trooper, *Grey: Digital Target* (anime; also known as *Grey—Cible digitale*), Viz Media, originally broadcast in Japan, 1986.

Voice of Captain Napolipolita, *Project A–ko 2: Daitokuji zaibatsu no inbou* (anime; also known as *Project A–Ko 2: Plot of the Daitokuji Financial Group*), Central Park Media, originally released in Japan, 1987.

Voice of Cobra commander, *G.I. Joe: Sgt. Savage and His Screaming Eagles,* 1994.

Voice, *Cinderella* (also known as *La Cenicienta*), GoodTimes Home Video, 1994.

Voice, *Leo the Lion: King of the Jungle* (also known as *Leo Leon*), 1994.

Voice, *The Nutcracker,* GoodTimes Home Video, 1994.

Voice, *Pocahontas* (also known as *The Adventures of Pocahontas: Indian Princess*), GoodTimes Home Video, 1994.

Voice, *Sleeping Beauty* (also known as *La bella durmiente*), GoodTimes Home Video, 1994.

Voice, *Alice in Wonderland* (also known as *Alicia en el pais de las maravillas*), GoodTimes Home Video, 1995.

Voice, *Black Beauty* (also known as *Hermoso negro*), GoodTimes Home Video, 1995.

Voice, *Curly: The Littlest Puppy,* GoodTimes Home Video, 1995.

Voice, *Hercules,* Goodtimes Entertainment, 1995.

Voice, *Jungle Book* (also known as *El libro de la selva*), GoodTimes Home Video, 1995.

Voice, *Little Red Riding Hood,* GoodTimes Home Video, 1995.

Voice, *Magic Gift of the Snowman* (also known as *El regalo magico del muneco de nieve*), GoodTimes Home Video, 1995.

Voice, *Snow White* (also known as *Blancanieves*), 1995.

Voice of Harlock, *Galaxy Express 999* (anime; also known as *Galaxy Express* and *Ginga tetsudo 999*), Viz Video, 1996, released in Japan, 1979.

Voice of Tokai, *Sanctuary* (anime), Viz Media, 1996.

Voice, *The Hunchback of Notre Dame,* GoodTimes Home Video, 1996.

Voices of Chester and Buster, *A Tale of Two Kitties* (also known as *Good Housekeeping Kids—A Tale of Two Kitties*), Simitar, c. 1997.

Voices, *Mummies Alive! The Legend Begins* (consists of episodes of the television series), Buena Vista Home Video, 1998.

English voices of demon king and Solid Gold, *Xiao qian* (anime; also known as *Chinese Ghost Story, A Chinese Ghost Story: The Tsui Hark Animation,* and *Siu–sin*), Geneon Entertainment, 2000, originally released in China, 1997.

Voice of Seabass for English version, *Hjaelp, jeg er en fisk* (also known as *A Fish Tale, Help! I'm a Fish,* and *Hilfe! Ich bin ein Fisch*), 2000.

Voices of Hermey the elf, Boomerang, Yukon Cornelius, Coach Comet, and Duck, *Rudolph the Red–Nosed Reindeer & the Island of Misfit Toys* (also known as *Rudolph & the Island of Misfit Toys*), Golden Books Family Entertainment, 2001.

Voice of Jajuka, *Escaflowne* (anime; also known as *Escaflowne: The Movie, A Girl in Gaea,* and *Vision of Escaflowne: A Girl in Gaea*), Bandai Entertainment, 2002, originally released in Japan by Omega Project, 2000.

Voice of Jesus, *Ben–Hur,* Agamemnon Films, 2003.

Voice of peddler, *Barbie of Swan Lake,* Artisan Entertainment, 2003.

Voices of Toa Tahu, Toa Onua, Grallock the ash bear, and others, *Bionicle: Mask of Light* (also known as *Bionicle: Mask of Light—the Movie*), Buena Vista Home Video/Miramax Home Entertainment, 2003.

Voice of Quinn, *Ark* (anime), Creative Light Worldwide, 2004.

Voices of Destro and Gung Ho, *G.I. Joe: Valor vs. Venom,* Paramount Home Video, 2004.

Voices of Mortmottimes, Bugkus Bill, and Timebomb Tom, *In Search of Santa,* Buena Vista Home Video/Miramax Home Entertainment, 2004.

English voices of Captain Napolipolita and Kei, *Project A–ko 3: Cinderella Rhapsody* (anime), Central Park Media, 2005, originally released in 1988.

English voices of Captain Napolipolita and Kei, *Project A–ko 4: Final* (anime; also known as *Project A–ko 4: Kanketsuron*), Central Park Media, 2005, originally released in Japan, 1989.

Voice of Bomonga, *Bionicle 3: Web of Shadows,* Buena Vista Home Video/Miramax Home Entertainment, 2005.

Voice of Elementor, *Max Steel: Forces of Nature,* Mattel Entertainment, 2005.

Voice of Eric "Tan" Tannenbaum IV, *Kong: King of Atlantis,* Warner Home Video, 2005.

Voice of Ruby, *Barbie: Fairytopia,* Lions Gate Films, 2005.

Voice of Senor Hasbeena and sound of alarm, *Mucha Lucha! The Return of El Malefico,* Warner Bros., 2005.

Voices of King Kandy and Licorice Bite, *Candyland: Great Lollipop Adventure,* Hasbro, 2005.

Voice of Dogg, *The Condor* (also known as *Stan Lee Presents: "The Condor"*), Starz Media, 2006.

Voices of Mr. Bullwraith and landlord, *Mosaic* (also known as *Stan Lee Presents "Mosaic"*), Anchor Bay Entertainment, 2006.

Voice of Hoenheim Elric, *Gekijo–ban hagane no ren-kinjutsushu: Shanbara wo yuku mono* (anime; also known as *Fullmetal Alchemist the Movie: Conquerer of Shamballa, Fullmetal Alchemist: The Movie—Conqueror of Shamballa,* and *HagaRen the Movie*), National CineMedia, 2007, originally released in Japan, 2005.

Live Action Film Appearances:

Rex, *Crackerjack,* Excalibur Pictures, 1994.

Todd Warren, *Sleeping with Strangers,* Skouras Pictures, 1994.

Voice of Yun, *Warriors of Virtue* (also known as *Creature Zone* and *Magic warriors*), Metro–Goldwyn–Mayer, 1997.

Himself, *Invasion: Anime* (documentary), Tempest Productions, 2002.

Evil masked figure, *Scooby–Doo 2: Monsters Unleashed* (also known as *Scooby–Doo 2, Scooby–Doo 2: Monster Panic, Scooby Too,* and *Scooby 2*), Warner Bros., 2004.

Ben Holm, *The Green Chain,* Christal Films, 2007.

Film Work:

Additional voices for English version, *Jin–Ro* (anime; also known as *Jin Roh: The Wolf Brigade, Kerberos Panzer Cops,* and *Wolf Brigade*), Bandai, c. 1998.

Internet Appearances; Series:

Voice of Mars, *Broken Saints,* http://bs.brokensaints.com, 2001–2003.

RECORDINGS

Videos:

Himself, *Making of "Bionicle: Mask of Light"* (live action), Buena Vista Home Entertainment, 2006.

McNeil appears in several video compilations of Japanese anime series.

Video Games:

Voices of Rattrap, Silverbolt (also known as Grifo), and Waspinator, *Transformer Beast Wars Metals: Geki-totsu! Gangan Battle,* Bay Area Multi Media, 2000.

(Uncredited) Voice of Duo Maxwell, *Gundam: Battle Assault 2,* Bandai Games, 2002.

Voices of Lumpy and high–tech elder, *Frogger Beyond,* 2002.

Voice of Luce Kassel, *Kido senshi Gundam: Meguriai sora* (also known as *Mobile Suit Gundam: Encounters in Space*), Bandai Games, 2003.

Voices of hoodlums, *Rayman 3: Hoodlum Havoc,* Ubi Soft, 2003.

Voices of Raba, Ryug, Cloa, Toksa, Mikhail, Emilio, Napishtim, and Mannan, *Ys: The Ark of Napishtim,* Konami Digital Entertainment America, 2003.

Voice of evil masked figure, *Scooby–Doo 2: Monsters Unleashed,* VoiceWorks Productions, 2004.

Voice of hero (Cocky), *Def Jam Fight for NY,* Electronic Arts, 2004.

Voice of Koga, *Inuyasha: Juso no kamen* (also known as *Inuyasha: The Secret of the Cursed Mask*), Bandai Games, 2004.

Voices of Lord Bale, Sorcerer Sindri, space marine Sergeant Mattias, daemon Prince Sindri, and Servitor, *Warhammer 40,000: Dawn of War,* THQ, 2004.

Voices of young man, Carlos Oliveira, pickpocket, karate champion, yuppie, old man, and Cosmi, Sr., *Meiwaku seijin: Panic Maker* (also known as *Under the Skin*), Capcom Entertainment, 2004.

Voice of beast man, *Masters of the Universe: He–Man—Defender of Grayskull,* Midas Interactive Entertainment, 2005.

Voice of Koga, *Inuyasha: Ogi ranbu* (also known as *Inuyasha: Feudal Combat*), Bandai Games, 2005.

Voices of Chaplain Varnus, imperial guardsman, and member of Kasrkin squad, and sounds of imperial guard vehicles, *Warhammer 40,000: Dawn of War—Winter Assault,* THQ, 2005.

Voice, *Warhammer 40,000: Dawn of War—Dark Crusade,* THQ, 2006.

Voice of Sergeant Joe Galtosino, *The Godfather* (also known as *The Godfather: The Game*), Electronic Arts, 2006.

Voice of Sergeant Joe Galtosino, *The Godfather: The Don's Edition,* Electronic Arts, 2007.

McQUEEN, Armelia 1952–

PERSONAL

Born January 6, 1952, in North Carolina.

Career: Actress.

Awards, Honors: *Theatre World* Award, 1978, for *Ain't Misbehavin'.*

CREDITS

Stage Appearances:
Ain't Misbehavin' (musical revue), Longacre Theatre, New York City, 1978–79, Plymouth Theatre, New York City, 1979–81, and Belasco Theatre, New York City, 1981–82, revived with original cast, Ambassador Theatre, New York City, 1988–89.
5–6–7–8 … Dance!, Theatre at Radio City Music Hall, New York City, 1983.
Mrs. Annie Yeamons, *Harrigan 'n Hart* (musical), Longacre Theatre, 1985.
The Wonderful Ice Cream Suit, Pasadena Playhouse, Pasadena, CA, 1990.
Dorian Gray (musical; staged reading), Theatre at the Arcade, Culver City, CA, 1999.

Appeared in other productions, including benefits.

Major Tours:
Bloody Mary, *South Pacific* (musical), U.S. cities, 1997–98.

Film Appearances:
Ann, *Sparkle,* Warner Bros., 1976.
Nell (the night club singer), *Quartet,* New World Pictures, 1981.
Dee, *Action Jackson,* Twentieth Century–Fox, 1988.
Sadie, *No Holds Barred,* New Line Cinema, 1989.
Oda Mae's sister, *Ghost* (also known as *Duch, Duh, Fantasma, Ghost—Do outro lado da vida, Ghost, la sombra del amor, Ghost, mas alla del amor, Ghost—Nachricht vom Sam, Ghost—naekyma-etoen rakkaus, Ghost—New York no maboroshi, Mon fantome d'amour,* and *Uwierz w ducha*), Paramount, 1990.
Billie, *Waiting Game,* Nichol Moon Films, 1996.
Ruthie, *Bulworth* (also known as *Tribulations, Bulworth—Candidato em perigo, Bulworth—Il senatore, El senador Bulworth, Koko kansan Bulworth,* and *Politicamente incorreto*), Twentieth Century–Fox, 1998.
Mrs. Clay, *Life* (also known as *Ate que a fuga os separe, Condenados a fugarse, E a vida, La vie, Lebenslaenglich, Perpete,* and *Venner for livet*), Universal, 1999.
Mama Nia, *The Blessing Way,* Freehart Productions, 2000.
Nurse Wanda, *English as a Second Language,* 2005, Inferno Distribution, 2007.
Bertha Maxwell, *Cordially Invited,* Equalaris Productions, 2008.
Louise, *The Hustle,* 2008.

Broadway: Beyond the Golden Age (documentary; also known as *B.G.A. 2* and *Broadway: The Golden Age Two*), Second Act Productions, 2008.

Television Appearances; Series:
Red queen, *Adventures in Wonderland,* Disney Channel, c. 1991–95 (other sources cite 1992–95 or 1993–95).

Television Appearances; Movies:
Social worker, *Face of a Stranger,* CBS, 1991.

Television Appearances; Specials:
Ain't Misbehavin' (musical), NBC, 1982.
(Uncredited; in archive footage) Nell from *Quartet, The Wandering Company,* [Great Britain], 1984.
Mrs. Thompson, *Merry Christmas, George Bailey,* PBS, 1997.
"Broadway's Lost Treasures III: The Best of the Tony Awards," *Great Performances,* PBS, 2005.

Television Appearances; Episodic:
Fanny, "Dueling Voodoo," *Frank's Place,* CBS, 1988.
Gloria, "The Good Human Bar," *L.A. Law,* NBC, 1990.
Miss Hodgett, "Carmilla," *Nightmare Classics,* Showtime, 1990.
Judge, "Will Goes a Courtin'," *The Fresh Prince of Bel-Air,* NBC, 1993.
Mamma Jama, "In Search of … Martin," *Martin,* Fox, 1994.
Ms. Glidden, "Black History Month," *The Sinbad Show* (also known as *Sinbad* and *Ein Vater fuer zwei*), Fox, 1994.
Auntie Liz, "Not Quite Mr. Right," *Living Single* (also known as *My Girls*), Fox, 1996.
"Send Me an Angel," *VR.5* (also known as *Avenging Angel, Virtual Reality, VR,* and *VR5*), Sci-Fi Channel, 1997.
Carol Edwards, "A Prayer for the Lying," *L.A. Doctors* (also known as *L.A. Docs, Kliniken, Kohtaloni Los Angeles,* and *Medicos de Los Angeles*), CBS, 1998.
Shirley, "Love, Honor & Obey," *The Good News* (also known as *Good News*), UPN, 1998.
Maxine, "Go with the Flo," *All about the Andersons,* The WB, 2003.
Nurse, "Smoke on the Water," *The Mullets,* UPN, 2003.
Curvacia, "Close Encounters of the Nerd Kind," *That's So Raven* (also known as *Absolutely Psychic, That's So Raven!, Es tan Raven, Phenomene Raven,* and *Raven blickt durch*), Disney Channel, 2004.
April–Dawn McKee, "Unknown Soldier," *JAG,* CBS, 2005.

Appeared as Annie in "Face Your Demon, Semen," an unaired episode of *Inconceivable,* NBC; and appeared as Lou–Anne in "Donuts" and "Runaways," both unaired episodes of *Mr. Belvedere* (also known as *Mister Belvedere*), ABC.

Television Appearances; Pilots:
University registrar, "Moving out, Moving in, Moving on," *Related,* The WB, 2005.

Appeared as the university registrar in the unaired pilot for *Related,* The WB.

RECORDINGS

Albums; with Others:
Ain't Misbehavin' (original Broadway cast recording), RCA Victor Broadway, 1978.
Jerome Kern Revisited, Volume 4 (also known as *Ben Bagley's "Jerome Kern Revisited, Volume 4"*), Painted Smiles, 1983.
Mostly Mercer, Painted Smiles, 1986.
The 14th Annual S.T.A.G.E. Benefit, Varese Sarabande, 1998.

MR. AMERICA
See HOGAN, Hulk

MITCHELL, Kenneth 1974–
(Ken Mitchell)

PERSONAL

Full name, Kenneth Alexander Mitchell; born November 25, 1974, in Toronto, Ontario, Canada; married Susan May Pratt, May, 2006; children: Lilah Ruby. *Education:* University of Guelph, B.L.A.

Addresses: *Agent*—Innovative Artists, 1505 Tenth St., Santa Monica, CA 90401. *Manager*—The Hofflund Company, 9465 Wilshire Blvd., Suite 420, Beverly Hills, CA 90212.

Career: Actor. Appeared in television commercials, including Campbell Soup, AT&T, Adidas, 2000, Bell Mobility communications service, Hyundai automobiles, Heineken beer, Lay's Chips, Dentyne Ice gum, Canadian Club Whiskey, Clariton allergy products, Nokia communications service, Taco Bell, Honda automobiles, and Bud Light beer. Played soccer in college.

Awards, Honors: Canadian Society of Landscape Architecture Silver Medal.

CREDITS

Film Appearances:
(As Ken Mitchell) Soldier, *No Man's Land* (short), Cine-Clix Distribution, 2000.
Ric, *The Green* (short), 2001.
Chris, *Why Don't You Dance* (short), 2002.
(As Ken Mitchell) Alan, *The Recruit,* Buena Vista, 2003.
Ralph Cox, *Miracle,* Buena Vista, 2004.
Nick Allen, *Tennis, Anyone …?,* Fireside Releasing, 2005.
John Dykstra, *5–25–77,* 2007.
Keith Morrison, *Home of the Giants,* Conquistador Worldwide Media, 2007.

Television Appearances; Series:
(As Ken Mitchell) Spencer Matthew, *Leap Years,* Showtime, 2001.
Marc Taggart, *Odyssey 5,* Showtime, 2002.
Eric Green, *Jericho,* CBS, 2007—.

Television Appearances; Miniseries:
Edgar, *Iron Road,* CBC, 2008.

Television Appearances; Movies:
(As Ken Mitchell) Tom Hawkings III, *Charms for the Easy Life,* Showtime, 2002.

Television Appearances; Episodic:
Wade Solomon, "Break on Through," *Grey's Anatomy,* ABC, 2006.
Robert Gordon, "Deviant," *CSI: Miami,* CBS, 2006.
Keith Soto, "Exposure," *The Unit,* CBS, 2006.

MOLALE, Brandon 1971–

PERSONAL

Born November 24, 1971, in Pocatello, ID. *Education:* Fresno State University, B.A., advertising and marketing; studied improvisation with the Groundlings; studied acting with Larry Moss, Patsy Rodenburg, Richard Lawson, David Kagen, Alan Feinstein, Paul Tuerpe, Deke Anderson, Brian Reise, Al Guarino, and Gary Spatz. *Avocational Interests:* Playing guitar.

Addresses: *Agent*—House of Representatives, 400 South Beverly Dr., Suite 101, Beverly Hills, CA 90212.

Manager—DDC Entertainment, 7890 Vicksburg Ave., Los Angeles, CA 90045.

Career: Actor, stuntperson, and football coordinator. Acted as a football coordinator in television spots for *The King of Queens,* 2001, 2003; acted as stunt coordinator for commercial for Powerade, 2001 and Gatorade, 2005. Worked with numerous charities, including the Los Angeles Police Memorial Foundation, Children Affected by AIDS Foundation, and Project Angel Food. Played football at Fresno State University; previously worked as a radio disc jockey and sushi roller.

CREDITS

Film Appearances:
Big Boy, *Forbidden Highway,* Cameo Films, 1999.
(Uncredited) Neanderthal jail guard, *The Flintstones in Viva Rock Vegas,* MCA/Universal, 2000.
Officer worker number five, *Room 302* (short), 2001.
Play room bouncer, *Knight Club,* American World Pictures, 2001.
Police officer number one, *The Naked Run* (short), 2002.
Policeman, *Donut Holes* (short), 2002.
Kevin Ward, the N.Y. Jets, *Mr. Deeds,* Columbia, 2002.
Doorman, *The Master of Disguise,* Columbia, 2002.
Policeman number two, *Wrong Turn* (short), 2003.
(Uncredited) Goon, *The Rundown* (also known as *Welcome to the Jungle*), Universal, 2003.
Blazer, *Dodgeball: A True Underdog Story* (also known as *Dodgeball* and *Voll auf die nusse*), Twentieth Century–Fox, 2004.
Limo driver, *Collateral,* DreamWorks, 2004.
Kojak, *Outpost* (short), 2004.
Guard Malloy, *The Longest Yard,* Paramount, 2005.
(Uncredited) Torturer, *Mission: Impossible III* (also known as *M:i:III* and *Mission: Impossible III*), Paramount, 2006.
Navy guy, *The Guardian,* Buena Vista, 2006.
Kevlar guy, *Reno 911!: Miami* (also known as *"Reno 911!: Miami": The Movie*), 2007.
State trooper, *The Dead One,* 2007.
Piken, *Big Stan,* Metro–Goldwyn–Mayer, 2007.
Male courtesan number one, *Balls of Fury,* Rogue Pictures, 2007.
Coach, *Bar Starz,* 2007.
Mover, *Hotel California,* 2008.
Starship Dave, 2008.
The man, *The Farmhouse,* 2008.

Film Work:
(Uncredited) Football stunts, *The Waterboy,* 1998.
Utility stunts, *Whatever It Takes,* Columbia, 2000.
Stunt actor, *The Flintstones in Viva Rock Vegas,* MCA/Universal, 2000.

Utility stunts, *The One* (also known as *Jet Li's "The One"*), Columbia, 2001.
(Uncredited) Stunts, *Hulk,* Universal, 2003.
Stunt actor, *The Rundown* (also known as *Welcome to the Jungle*), Universal, 2003.
Stunt actor, *Cheaper by the Dozen,* Twentieth Century–Fox, 2003.
Stunts, *The Ladykillers,* Buena Vista, 2004.
Stunt actor, *The Guardian,* Buena Vista, 2006.

Television Appearances; Series:
Hank Collins, *Days of Our Lives* (also known as *DOOL* and *Days*), NBC, 1999–2003.
Various characters, *The Tonight Show with Jay Leno,* NBC, 1999—.
Various characters, *Jimmy Kimmel Live!,* ABC, 2003.
Moonlight, CBS, 2007.

Television Appearances; Movies:
Armed soldier, *Area 57,* 2007.

Television Appearances; Pilots:
Big cop, *The Sarah Connor Chronicles,* Fox, 2008.

Also appeared in *Twilight,* The WB; *Then Came Jones,* ABC.

Television Appearances; Pilots:
NFL deputy, *Then Came Jones* (movie), ABC, 2003.

Television Appearances; Episodic:
Hunk number one, *Sunset Beach,* NBC, 1999.
The man, "Love and Foster Kids Aren't Always Blind," *One World,* NBC, 1999.
Teammate number two, "Heroes," *The Jersey,* Disney Channel, 1999.
Rocco, "The Provider," *Boy Meets World,* ABC, 2000.
Marine pilot, "At Poverty Level," *Pensacola: Wings of Gold,* syndicated, 2000.
Football player number two, "When Opportunity Knocks," *Arli$$,* HBO, 2000.
Casino guard, "The Two Mrs. Thornsons: Part 1," *The Huntress,* USA Network, 2001.
Various roles, *Spy TV,* NBC, 2001.
Juggy boyfriend, "Juggy Water Park," *The Man Show,* Comedy Central, 2001.
Policeman, "Fifteen Candles," *One on One,* UPN, 2001.
Stone Cold Edie Austin, *Mad TV,* Fox, 2002.
Cop number one, "All That Bloopers—Ask Ashley," *All That,* Nickelodeon, 2002.
T. J., "Timothy Weber," *America's Most Wanted* (also known as *A.M.W.* and *America's Most Wanted: America Fights Back*), Fox, 2002.

T. J., "Timothy Weber Capture," *America's Most Wanted* (also known as *A.M.W.* and *America's Most Wanted: America Fights Back*), Fox, 2002.

Clark Bynum, "Hijacker Heroes," *It's a Miracle,* PAX, 2002.

Cop, *Doggy Fizzle Televizzle,* MTV, 2003.

Chad, "Object Lessons," *Coupling* (also known as *Coupling U.S.*), NBC, 2003.

Karate instructor, "Can't You Hear Me Knocking," *That '70s Show,* Fox, 2005.

Mike, "Til We Meat Again," *Boston Legal,* ABC, 2005.

Rookie Dupris, "Cop School," *Reno 911!,* Comedy Central, 2005.

Rocco, "Mr. & Mrs. Witch," *Charmed,* The WB, 2006.

Himself, "I Love a Party," *Tori & Dean: Inn Love,* 2007.

Army Special Agent Jack Reynolds, "Sharif Returns," *Navy NCIS: Naval Criminal Investigative Service* (also known as *NCIS* and *NCIS: Naval Criminal Investigative Service*), CBS, 2007.

Also appeared as Pima County jailor, "Hot Shot," *Arrest & Trial,* syndicated.

Television Work; Series:

Stunt actor, *America's Most Wanted* (also known as *A.M.W.* and *America's Most Wanted: America Fights Back*), Fox, 1988.

Stunts, *Arli$$,* HBO, 1996.

Stunt double for Junior Seau, *The Jersey,* Disney Channel, 1999.

Stunt double, *Angel* (also known as *Angel: The Series*), The WB, 1999.

Stunt actor, *That's Life,* CBS, 2000.

Stunt actor, *Gilmore Girls,* The WB, 2000.

Football coordinator (opening credits), *Everybody Loves Raymond* (also known as *Raymond*), CBS, 2001.

Football coordinator, *American Family* (also known as *American Family: Journey of Dreams*), PBS, 2002.

Football coordinator and stunt coordinator, *American Dreams* (also known as *Our Generation*), NBC, 2002.

Stunt actor, *She Spies,* NBC, 2002.

Stunt double, *Firefly* (also known as *Firefly: The Series*), 2002.

Television Work; Movies:

Hunter: Back in Force, NBC, 2003.

RECORDINGS

Video Games (as a Motion Capture Actor):

God of War, Son Computer Entertainment America, 2005.

OTHER SOURCES

Electronic:

Brandon Molale Website, http://www.brandonmolale. com, November 10, 2007.

MONROE, Kathleen
See MUNROE, Kathleen

MOORE, Joel 1977–
(Joel D. Moore, Joel David Moore)

PERSONAL

Full name, Joel David Moore; born September 25, 1977, in Portland, OR. *Education:* Southern Oregon University, B.F.A., 2001.

Addresses: *Agent*—Innovative Artists, 1505 10th St., Santa Monica, CA 90401. *Manager*—Ryan Management, 3107 Dona Marta Dr., Studio City, CA 91604.

Career: Actor. Oregon Shakespeare Festival, company player; appeared in numerous plays at the Dream Center of Los Angeles; appeared in numerous television commercials, including Cingular Wireless, 2003, Siemens products, 2003, Best Buy stores, McDonalds, Quaker State auto products, Kohls department stores, eBay, and the state of California.

Awards, Honors: MTV Movie Award nomination (with others), best on–screen team, 2005, for *Dodgeball: A True Underdog Story;* Gold Vision Award (with Adam Green), Santa Barbara International Film Festival, 2007, for *Spiral.*

CREDITS

Film Appearances:

First Greek, *Foxfire,* Samuel Goldwyn Company, 1996.

(As Joel David Moore) Charlie, *Lost* (short), 2003.

Rolf, *Raising Genius,* Allumination Filmworks, 2004.

(As Joel David Moore) Owen, *Dodgeball: A True Underdog Story* (also known as *Dodgeball* and *Voll auf die nusse*), Twentieth Century–Fox, 2004.

Actor and Joel, *Sledge: The Untold Story,* 2005.

Nick Walker, *Reel Guerillas* (short), 2005.

(As Joel David Moore) J. P., *Grandma's Boy,* Twentieth Century–Fox, 2006.

(As Joel David Moore) Bardo, *Art School Confidential,* Sony Pictures Classics, 2006.

(As Joel David Moore) Pound employee, *The Shaggy Dog,* Buena Vista, 2006.

Miles, *Miles from Home* (short), 2006.

Ben, *Hatchet,* Anchor Bay Entertainment, 2006.

Kenny, *The Elder Son,* 2006.

Mason, *Spiral,* 2007.

Joe, *Shanghai Kiss,* 2007.
Zak, *The Dead One,* Echo Bridge Home Entertainment, 2007.
Greg, *Wieners,* Screen Gems, 2007.
Himself, *Confessions of an Action Star,* Shoreline Entertainment, 2007.
(As Joel David Moore) Nate Cooper, *The Hottie and the Nootie,* Summit Entertainment, 2008.

Film Work:
Director, *Miles from Home* (short), 2006.
Director and executive producer, *Spiral,* 2007.
Executive producer, *Shadowheart,* Pure Flix Entertainment, 2008.

Television Appearances; Series:
Peter Steinem, *Deep Cover,* 2002.
Eddie Carson, *LAX,* NBC, 2004–2005.

Television Appearances; Movies:
Cooter, *The Dukes of Hazzard: The Beginning,* ABC Family, 2007.

Television Appearances; Episodic:
Hoover, "This Old Nerd," *City Guys,* NBC, 2001.
Hoover, "Al's in Toyland," *City Guys,* NBC, 2001.
Hartzell, "Chapter Seventeen," *Boston Public,* Fox, 2001.
Hartzell, "Chapter Thirty–Nine," *Boston Public,* Fox, 2002.
(As Joel D. Moore) Usher number two, "Insured by Smith & Wesson," *Boomtown,* NBC, 2002.
"The Eleventh Hour," *Providence,* NBC, 2002.
"Romance Looming," *Sabrina, the Teenage Witch* (also known as *Sabrina*), The WB, 2003.
(As Joel David Moore) Karl, Vamp henchman, "Salvage," *Angel* (also known as *Angel: The Series*), The WB, 2003.
(As Joel David Moore) Video clerk, "The Opening," *Six Feet Under,* HBO, 2003.
(As Joel D. Moore) Dan, "Bad Liver," *Strong Medicine,* Lifetime, 2003.
(As Joel David Moore) Malcolm Reeves, "Sparkle," *The Guardian,* CBS, 2004.
Brian Pines, "Declawed," *The Inside,* Fox, 2005.
(As Joel David Moore) Guy in the yellow hat, "Dog Eat Dog," *CSI: Crime Scene Investigation* (also known as *C.S.I.* and *Les Experts*), CBS, 2005.
(As Joel David Moore) Greg, NSA liaison, "Snatch and Grab," *E–Ring,* NBC, 2005.
(As Joel David Moore) Greg, NSA liaison, "Weekend Pass," *E–Ring,* NBC, 2005.
(Uncredited) Greg, NSA liaison, "The General," *E–Ring,* NBC, 2005.
(Uncredited) College student, "One Day, One Room," *House, M.D.* (also known as *House*), Fox, 2007.

(As Joel David Moore) Eddie, "Act Your Age," *House, M.D.* (also known as *House*), Fox, 2007.

Stage Appearances:
Tommy, *Stella by Starlight,* Laguna Playhouse, Laguna Beach, CA, 2002.

WRITINGS

Screenplays:
Spiral, 2007.

MUNROE, Kathleen
(Kathleen Monroe)

PERSONAL

Female.

Addresses: *Manager*—Magnolia Entertainment, 9595 Wilshire Blvd., Suite 601, Beverly Hills, AC 90212.

Career: Actress.

CREDITS

Television Appearances; Series:
Annabelle Banks, *Beautiful People,* ABC Family Channel, 2005–2006.
Nathalie Lacriox, *Durham County,* 2007.

Television Appearances; Pilots:
Elizabeth, *111 Gramercy Park,* ABC, 2003.
Gina, *Family Curse,* The WB, 2003.
Annabelle Banks, *Beautiful People,* ABC Family Channel, 2005.
Detective Mary Elizabeth Grosz, *Suspect,* ABC, 2007.

Television Appearances; Movies:
(Uncredited) *Dying to Dance,* NBC, 2001.
Scottie, *Last Call* (also known as *Fitzgerald*), Showtime, 2002.

Television Appearances; Specials:
Zia, *Ice Age Columbus: Who Were the First Americans,* Discovery Channel, 2005.

Television Appearances; Episodic:
Secretary, "Thin Air," *1–800–Missing* (also known as *Missing*), Lifetime, 2003.
Rachel, "Secrets and Lies," *Tarzan,* The WB, 2003.

(As Kathleen Monroe) Young Irene, "War & Peace," *Show Me Yours,* Oxygen, 2004.

Monica Salzburg, "Making the Grade," *Kevin Hill,* UPN, 2004.

Heather Bram, "Hair of the Dog," *The Dresden Files,* Sci–Fi Channel, 2007.

Katie's mom, "The Kids Are Alright," *Supernatural,* CW Network, 2007.

Tina Haggans, *Moonlight,* CBS, 2007.

Film Appearances:

Lexus, *Drummer Boy,* Drummerboy Film, 2002.

Connie, *Eternal* (also known as *Eternelle*), Regent Releasing, 2005.

Kim, *The White Dog Sacrifice,* Kaboom! Entertainment, 2005.

Aleil Camden, *Decoding Aleil* (short film), 2005.

Carly, *Perennial* (short film), Perennial Productions, 2006.

MURPHY, Ryan 1966–

PERSONAL

Born in 1966, in Indianapolis, IN; father, cofounder of a publishing company; mother, cofounder of a publishing company. *Education:* Studied journalism at Indiana University.

Addresses: *Agent*—Creative Artists Agency, 2000 Avenue of the Stars, Los Angeles, CA 90067.

Career: Writer, producer, and director. Began career as an entertainment and lifestyle journalist, contributing to publications such as *The Washington Post, Rolling Stone, Los Angeles Times,* and *Miami Herald.*

Awards, Honors: Emmy Award nomination, outstanding directing for a drama series, 2004, for *Nip/Tuck;* Hollywood Breakthrough Award, breakthrough directing, Hollywood Film Festival, 2006.

CREDITS

Film Work:

Director and producer, *Running with Scissors,* TriStar, 2006.

Television Work; Series:

Creator and executive producer, *Popular,* The WB, 1999–2001.

Creator, executive producer, and showrunner, *Nip/Tuck,* FX Channel, 2005—.

Television Work; Pilots:

Executive producer and director, *4 Oz.,* FX Channel, 2007.

Television Director; Episodic:

Nip/Tuck, FX Channel, 2003–2006.

Television Appearances; Episodic:

"Ryan Murphy," *Life After Film School,* 2006.

The Film Programme (also known as *Film 2007*), BBC, 2007.

WRITINGS

Screenplays:

The Furies, 1999.

Running with Scissors, TriStar, 2006.

Television Pilots:

4 Oz., FX Channel, 2007.

Television Episodes:

Popular, The WB, 1999–2001.

Nip/Tuck, FX Channel, 2003–2006.

MUSSO, Mitchel 1991–

PERSONAL

Full name, Michael Tate Musso; born July 9, 1991, in Garland, TX (some sources say Rockwall, TX); brother of Marc Musso (an actor).

Addresses: *Agent*—William Morris Agency, One William Morris Pl., Beverly Hills, CA 90212. *Manager*—Reel Talent/Reel Kids, 980 N. Bundy, Los Angeles, CA 90049.

Career: Actor. Appeared in television commercials, including Gogurt, 2004.

Awards, Honors: Young Artist Award nomination (with Marc Musso), best performance in a feature film—young actor age ten or younger, 2004, for *Secondhand Lions;* Saturn Award nomination, best performance by a younger actor, Academy of Science Fiction, Fantasy and Horror Films, 2007, for *Monster House.*

CREDITS

Film Appearances:

Cub scout, *The Keyman* (also known as *Finding Redemption*), Mainline Releasing, 2002.

Ritchie, *Am I Cursed?* (short), 2002.

Boy, *Secondhand Lions,* New Line Cinema, 2003.

Haley Joel Osment: An Actor Comes of Age (documentary short), New Line Home Video, 2004.

On the Set with "Secondhand Lions" (documentary short), New Line Home Video, 2004.

Voice of D. J., *Monster House* (animated; also known as *Neighbourhood Crimes & Peepers*), Columbia, 2006.

Television Appearances; Series:

Oliver Oken, *Hannah Montana,* Disney Channel, 2006—.

Jeremy, *Phineas and Ferb,* Disney Channel, 2007.

Television Appearances; Movies:

Raymond Figg, *Life Is Ruff,* Disney Channel, 2005.

Josh Whitley, *"Walker, Texas Ranger": Trial by Fire,* CBS, 2005.

Television Appearances; Specials:

The Disney Channel Games, Disney Channel, 2006, 2007.

Sing–Along Bowl–Athon, 2006.

Television Appearances; Pilots:

Alex Mandel, *Hidden Howie* (also known as *Hidden Howie: The Private Life of a Public Nuisance*), Bravo, 2003.

T. J. Savage, *Complete Savages,* ABC, 2004.

Owen Dewitt, *Stacked,* Fox, 2005.

Television Appearances; Episodic:

One Nad, "Soup to Nuts," *Oliver Beene,* Fox, 2004.

Voice of Aang, "Avatar Day," *Avatar: The Last Airbender* (animated), Nickelodeon, 2006.

"Round 5," *Dancing with the Stars,* ABC, 2007.

"Round 8," *Dancing with the Stars,* ABC, 2007.

Disney's Really Shorty Report, Disney Channel, 2007.

Kevin, "Mascot Prep," *Shorty McShorts' Shorts,* Disney Channel, 2007.

Voice of Curt, "The Powder Puff Boys," *King of the Hill* (animated), Fox, 2007.

Voice of surf kid, "Four Wave Intersection," *King of the Hill* (animated), Fox, 2007.

RECORDINGS

Video Games:

D. J., *Monster House,* THQ, 2006.

Music Videos:

"The Big Dismal," 2003.

N–O

NEELY, Blake 1969–

PERSONAL

Born April 28, 1969, in Paris, TX.

Addresses: *Agent*—The Gorfaine Schwartz Agency, 4111 West Alameda Ave., Suite 509, Burbank, CA 91505. *Manager*—Robert Urband and Associates, 8981 Sunset Blvd., Suite 311, West Hollywood, CA 90069.

Career: Composer, conductor, and orchestrator.

Awards, Honors: Emmy Award nomination, outstanding main title theme music, 2003, for *Everwood*.

CREDITS

Film Work:
Orchestrator, *The Iron Giant* (animated), Warner Bros., 1999.

Orchestrator, *Frequency,* New Line Cinema, 2000.

Conductor and orchestrator, *Vangelis: Mythodea—Music for the NASA Mission, 2001 Mars Odyssey,* 2001.

Conductor and orchestrator, *Crazy/Beautiful,* Buena Vista, 2001.

Music preparation, *The Shipment,* Promark Entertainment Group, 2001.

(Uncredited) Orchestrator, *Collateral Damage,* Warner Bros., 2002.

Additional orchestrations, *Blade II,* New Line Cinema, 2002.

Music preparation and orchestrator, *High Crimes,* Twentieth Century–Fox, 2002.

Additional music conductor and orchestrator, *K–19: The Widowmaker* (also known as *K*19: The Widowmaker, K–19—Showdon in der Tiefe,* and *K–19: Terreur sous la mer*), Paramount, 2002.

Conductor and orchestrator, *Blue Crush,* Universal, 2002.

Orchestrator, *The Recruit,* Buena Vista, 2003.

Orchestrator, *Ned Kelly* (also known as *Ned Kelly: Public Enemy No. 1*), Focus Features, 2003.

Conductor, *Pirates of the Caribbean: The Curse of the Black Pearl* (also known as *P.O.T.C.*), Buena Vista, 2003.

Additional orchestrator, *Open Range,* Buena Vista, 2003.

Conductor, score arranger, and score programmer, *The Last Samurai* (also known as *The Last Samurai: Bushidou*), Warner Bros., 2003.

Conductor, *Something's Gotta Give,* Columbia, 2003.

Orchestrator, *Against the Ropes* (also known as *Die Promoterin* and *The Promoter*), Paramount, 2004.

Additional conductor, *Secret Window,* Columbia, 2004.

Conductor, *The Day After Tomorrow,* Twentieth Century–Fox, 2004.

Conductor, *Suchimuboi* (animated; also known as *Steamboy*), Triumph Films, 2004.

Conductor, score synthesizer programmer, and synthesizer orchestra, *Catwoman,* 2004.

Conductor, music producer, and orchestrator, *First Daughter,* 2004.

Conductor, *Spanglish,* 2004.

Music conductor and orchestrations, *Dirty Dancing: Havana Nights,* Lionsgate, 2004.

Conductor, *The Island,* DreamWorks, 2005.

Music score producer and orchestrator, *King Kong* (also known as *Kong: The Eighth Wonder of the World* and *Peter Jackson's "King Kong"*), Universal, 2005.

Conductor, *Nacho Libre,* Paramount, 2006.

Score producer, *Starter for 10,* Picturehouse, 2006.

Music conductor, *Click,* Sony, 2006.

Conductor, *The Prestige,* Buena Vista, 2006.

Conductor, *Pirates of the Caribbean: At World's End* (also known as *P.O.T.C. 3* and *Pirates 3*), Buena Vista, 2007.

Conductor, *The Simpsons Movie* (animated), Twentieth Century–Fox, 2007.

Conductor, *Michael Clayton,* Warner Bros., 2007.
Orchestrator, *Enchanted,* Buena Vista, 2007.

Film Appearances:
Himself, *The Blood Pact: The Making of "Blade II"* (documentary), New Line Cinema, 2002.

Television Orchestrator; Miniseries:
(Uncredited) *Band of Brothers,* HBO, 2001.
Feast of All Saints (also known as *Anne Rice's "The Feast of All Saints"*), ABC, 2001.

Television Orchestrator; Specials:
S & M: Metallica with Michael Kamen Conducting the San Francisco Symphony Orchestra, 1999.

WRITINGS

Film Scores:
It's the Cheese (short), Choice Entertainment, 2003.
Oedipus (short; also known as *Oedipus: The Movie*), 2004.
Frog–g–g!, Vital Fluid, 2004.
First Daughter, Twentieth Century–Fox, 2004.
The Wedding Date, Universal, 2005.
Get Froggged!: Behind the Scenes of "Frog–g–g!" (documentary short), Go Kart Films, 2005.
Magnificent Desolation: Walking on the Moon 3D (animated short documentary), IMAX, 2005.
Starter for 10, Picturehouse Entertainment, 2006.
Sugar Boxx, 2006.
Elvis and Anabelle, Goldcrest Films International, 2007.

Film Additional Music:
Pirates of the Caribbean: The Curse of the Black Pearl (also known as *P.O.T.C.*), Buena Vista, 2003.
The Last Samurai (also known as *The Last Samurai: Bushidou*), Warner Bros., 2003.
Something's Gotta Give, Columbia, 2003.
King Arthur (also known as *King Arthur: Director's Cut*), Buena Vista, 2004.
Catwoman, Warner Bros., 2004.
The Island, DreamWorks, 2005.
King Kong (also known as *Kong: The Eighth Wonder of the World* and *Peter Jackson's "King Kong"*), Universal, 2005.
RV (also known as *RV: Runaway Vacation* and *Die chaoscamper RV*), Columbia, 2006.
(Uncredited) *The Da Vinci Code,* Sony, 2006.

Film Songs:
First Daughter, Twentieth Century–Fox, 2004.

Television Theme Music; Series:
Everwood, The WB, 2002–2006.
Jack & Bobby, The WB, 2004–2005.

Television Additional Music; Miniseries:
Revelations, Sci–Fi Channel, 2005.
(Uncredited) *Into the West,* TNT, 2005.

Television Scores; Movies:
The Samurai, 2003.
Kat Plus One, 2004.
Brothers & Sisters: A Family Matter, 2007.

Television Scores; Specials:
The True Story of Seabiscuit, Arts and Entertainment, 2003.

Television Scores; Pilots:
Related, The WB, 2006.
Pushing Daisies, ABC, 2007.
Dirty Sexy Money, ABC, 2007.
Eli Stone, ABC, 2007.
The Sarah Connor Chronicles, Fox, 2008.

Television Scores; Episodic:
Conquest, 2002.
Everwood, The WB, 2002–2006.
Wild West Tech, History Channel, 2003–2004.
Dr. Vegas, CBS, 2004.
Jack & Bobby, The WB, 2004–2005.
Related, The WB, 2005.
What About Brian, ABC, 2006–2007.
Brothers & Sisters, ABC, 2006–2007.
Notes from the Underbelly, ABC, 2006–2007.
Traveler, ABC, 2007.
Dirty Sexy Money, ABC, 2007.

Television Additional Music; Episodic:
Revelations, NBC, 2004–2005.

DVD Scores:
A Date with Debra: The Wedding DVD (documentary short), Universal Home Entertainment, 2005.

Books:
Wrote *Piano for Dummies.*

NOBLE, John 1948–
(John Nogle)

PERSONAL

Born August 20, 1948, in Port Pirie, South Australia; children: Samantha (an actress).

Addresses: *Agent*—Amber Raitz, Coast to Coast Talent, Inc., 3950 Barham Blvd., Los Angeles, CA 90068. *Manager*—Nicolas Bernheim, Seven Summits Pictures and Management, 8906 West Olympic Blvd., Ground Floor, Beverly Hills, CA 90211; Rolland Management, 205 Beattie St., P.O. Box 1510, Rozelle, New South Wales 2039, Australia.

Career: Actor, director, and educator. Stage Company of South Australia, artistic director, 1977–87; Brent Street School of the Arts, Sydney, Australia, head of drama department, 1997–2000; teacher at National Institute of Dramatic Arts, Flinders University, Carclew Youth Drama Camps, and elsewhere; operator of private training studio; voice teacher, and acting teacher. Australian Drama Festival, Adelaide, chair, 1982; Adelaide Festival Centre, trustee for nearly ten years.

Member: Association of Community Theatres (of Australia; founding member; past chair).

Awards, Honors: DVD Exclusive Award nomination (with others), best audio commentary for a DVD release, DVD Exclusive Awards, 2003, for *The Lord of the Rings: The Two Towers;* National Board of Review Award, 2003, Screen Actors Guild Award, 2004, Phoenix Film Critics Society Award nomination, 2004, and Critics Choice Award, Broadcast Film Critics Association, 2004, all best acting ensemble (with others), for *The Lord of the Rings: The Return of the King.*

CREDITS

Film Appearances:
Dr. Richards, *The Dreaming,* Platinum Disc, 1988.
Prime minister's minder, *A Sting in the Tale* (also known as *Scorpio*), Video Entertainment, 1990.
Sergeant, *They Call Me Mr. Brown,* Home Cinema Group, 1990.
General Booth, *The Nostradamus Kid,* Live Entertainment, 1993.
Mr. Morris, *The Monkey's Mask* (also known as *Cercle intime, La maschera di scimmia,* and *Poetry, Sex*), Strand Releasing, 2001.
Denethor (credited as John Nogle in extended edition), *The Lord of the Rings: The Two Towers* (also known as *The Two Towers, Der Herr der ringe: Die zwei tuerme,* and *Bechdebis mbrdzanebeli*), New Line Cinema, 2002.
Denethor, *The Lord of the Rings: The Return of the King* (also known as *The Return of the King* and *Der Herr der ringe: die rueckkehr des koenigs*), New Line Cinema, 2003.
Howard Peet, *Fracture,* Polyphony Entertainment/New Zealand Film Commission, 2004.

Himself, *Ringers: Lord of the Fans* (documentary), Sony Pictures Home Entertainment, 2005.
Ben, *Voodoo Lagoon,* Shoreline Entertainment, 2006.
Ivan Yugorsky, *Running Scared,* New Line Cinema, 2006.
Prince Admantha, *One Night with the King,* Rocky Mountain Pictures, 2006.
Eddie Thomas, *Risen,* Burn Hand Film Productions, 2007.

Television Appearances; Series:
Dr. John Madsen, *All Saints,* Seven Network, 1998–2004.
Dr. Helpman, *Home and Away,* Seven Network, 2006.
Blackbeard, *Pirate Islands: The Lost Treasure of Fiji,* 2007.

Television Appearances; Movies:
Sorrentino, *Airtight,* UPN, 1999.
Dad, *Virtual Nightmare,* UPN, 2000.
Paul Baylis, *Superfire* (also known as *Firefighter—Inferno in Oregon* and *Superfire—Inferno in Oregon*), ABC, 2002.
Fergus Hunter, *The Outsider,* Showtime, 2002.
Irving Pichel, *The Mystery of Natalie Wood,* ABC, 2004.

Television Appearances; Episodic:
Rigoletto, "The Mystery of the Spanish Chest," *Poirot* (also known as *Agatha Christie's "Poirot"*), PBS, 1991.
Sergeant, "Hostage," *Police Rescue,* AVC, 1991.
Mr. Michaels, "One on One," *Time Trax,* syndicated, 1993.
Graham James, "Future Past and Present," *Big Sky,* 1997.
Dr. Harry, "Epiphany," *Water Rats,* Nine Network, 1998.
Christian Ambrose, "Epiphany," *Tales of the South Seas,* Ten Network, 2000.
Commander Warren, "Beech on the Run," *The Bill,* ITV1, 2001.
Inspector Anderson, "The Knife," *The Lost World* (also known as *Sir Arthur Conan Doyle's "The Lost World"*), syndicated, 2001.
Michael Kranz, "Disgraceful Conduct," *Stingers,* Nine Network, 2002.
Adam Gallagher, "Fruit Market Underworld," *Young Lions,* 2002.
Adam Gallagher, China Town"," *Young Lions,* 2002.
Adam Gallagher, "The Navy: Part 2," *Young Lions,* 2002.
Adam Gallagher, "Serial Killer: Part 2," *Young Lions,* 2002.
Guest, *Filmland,* 2003.
Meurik, "Camelot," *Stargate SG–1* (also known as *La porte des etoiles*), Sci–Fi Channel, 2006.
Anatoly Markov, "Day 6: 5:00 p.m.–6:00 p.m.," *24,* Fox, 2007.

Anatoly Markov, "Day 6: 6:00 p.m.–7:00 p.m.," *24,* Fox, 2007.

The chief executive officer, "Pandemonium: Part 2," *The Unit,* CBS, 2007.

Appeared as Eddie Clark in *Above the Law.*

Television Appearances; Miniseries:
Appeared as Ben, *Hill's' End.*

Stage Appearances:
Dr. Reid, *The Arab's Mouth,* Smug Theatre Company, Sydney, Australia, 2003.

Edison, Johnson, Strauss, and Harvey, *Room 207: Nicolas Tesla,* X–Ray Theatre Company, 2003.

Also appeared as Pasha Salem, *The Abduction from the Seraglio,* State Opera of South Australia; multiple roles, *Errol Flynn's Great Big Adventure Book for Boys,* Stage Company of South Australia, and Edinburgh Festival, Edinburgh, Scotland; Robert Greene, *Cheapside,* and the brother, *The Christian Brothers,* Stage Company of South Australia; Prince Leopold, *Czarda's Princess,* State Opera of South Australia; Maxim Gorky, *Death of Danko,* Stage Company of South Australia, Adelaide Festival Trust; Reeves, *The Death of George Reeves,* and the man, *The Elocution of Benjamin Franklin,* Stage Company of South Australia; autocrat, *Give Us Time,* Adelaide Festival Theatre; Dirk, *Impropriety,* and Mordecai, *In Duty Bound,* C. Cummings Productions; Gloucester, *King Lear,* Stage Company of South Australia; Michel, *La Musica,* and Arthur, *On Tidy Endings,* Lookout Theatre Club, Sydney; Stuart Gunn, *The Perfectionist,* Stage Company of South Australia; Alonso, *The Tempest,* and Krasin, *Traitors,* State Theatre Company of South Australia; Hugh, *Translations,* and Chaim, *Two,* Stage Company of South Australia.

Stage Director:
Percy and Rose, Adelaide Festival of Arts, Adelaide, Australia, 1982, then national tour.

Sons of Cain, West End production, London, 1986.

Radio Appearances:
Performed in radio plays for Australian Broadcasting Corp.

RECORDINGS

Videos:
Voice of Denethor (in archive footage), *The Lord of the Rings: The Third Age* (video game), Electronic Arts, 2004.

NYMAN, Michael Robert 1965–
(Michael Nyman)

PERSONAL

Born April 20, 1965, in Long Beach, CA; married Michelle Pearlman, July 9, 2005.

Career: Actor. The Zeitgeist Theatre Company, member; First Stage Alert Theatre Company, cofounder.

CREDITS

Film Appearances:
Cop, *Shadow of the Dragon,* 1992.

(As Michael Nyman) Guard, *The Divine Enforcer* (also known as *Deadly Avenger*), Prism Pictures, 1992.

(As Michael Nyman) Frog, *Frogtown II* (also known as *Hell Comes to Frogtown II* and *Return to Frogtown*), York Entertainment, 1993.

(As Michael Nyman) Guard, *Desert Passion,* 1993.

(As Michael Nyman) Hawk, *Road to Revenge,* Grant Enterprises, 1993.

(Uncredited) Skinhead, *Skins* (also known as *Gang Boys*), Spectrum Films, 1994.

Bank robber driver, *Reverse Heaven,* 1994.

(Uncredited) New York uniform cop, *The Usual Suspects* (also known as *Die ublichen verdachtigen*), Gramercy Pictures, 1995.

(As Michael Nyman) Contact, *Hell's Paradox* (short), 1996.

Oscar, *Bottom Feeders,* 1997.

Cowboy, *The Blue Hotel* (short), Big Film Shorts, 1997.

Jerk number one, *Journey of Redemption,* 2002.

(As Michael Nyman) Officer Spiegel, *Maniacal,* Brain Damage Films, 2003.

Gilly, *Beneath the Mississippi,* 2005.

Eye twitch hitman, *The Trap,* Alpine Pictures, 2005.

Detective Richard Miles, *Camjackers,* 2006.

Larry, *Subdivision,* Synchronicity Independent, 2006.

Bishop, *The Last Bad Neighborhood,* 2006.

Father of babies, *Live Evil,* 2007.

Jeremiah, *Awaken the Dead,* Brain Damage Films, 2007.

Film Work; Other:
Executive producer, *Bottom Feeders,* 1997.

Associate producer and associate producer, *Beneath the Mississippi,* 2005.

Television Appearances; Movies:
(Uncredited) Rancher number two, *Full Body Massage,* Showtime, 1995.

Television Appearances; Specials:
(Uncredited) Television repair guy, *Fuse Fangoria Chainsaw Awards,* Fuse Network, 2006.

Television Appearances; Episodic:
Larry Lobato, "Kristin Lobato Case," *Guilty or Innocent?,* Discovery Channel, 2005.
Police officer, "Super Print," *LA Forensics,* 2006.
William Bliss, "Who Killed Superman," *North Mission Road,* 2006.

OGLESBY, Marsha

PERSONAL

Addresses: *Office*—Brooklyn Films, 11200 Chalon Rd., Los Angeles, CA 90049.

Career: Producer and development executive. Brooklyn Films, Los Angeles, CA, senior vice president (development and production).

CREDITS

Film Work:
Production assistant, *Hangfire,* Motion Picture Corporation of America, 1991.
Assistant production coordinator, *Driving Me Crazy,* Motion Picture Corporation of America, 1991.
Production coordinator, *Double Trouble,* Motion Picture Corporation of America, 1992.
Producer, *Tie–died: Rock 'n' Roll's Most Deadicated Fans* (documentary short), Fox Lorber, 1995.
Development executive, *Up Close & Personal,* Buena Vista, 1996.
Development executive, *D3: The Mighty Ducks,* Buena Vista, 1996.
Development executive, *Red Corner,* Metro–Goldwyn–Mayer, 1997.
Producer, *The Next Tenant,* 1998.
Producer, *Things You Can Tell Just By Looking at Her,* United Artists, 2000.
Executive producer, *The Rules of Attraction* (also known as *Die regein des spiels*), Lions Gate Films, 2002.
Producer, *Sky Captain and the World of Tomorrow,* Paramount, 2004.
Producer, *Brave New World* (documentary), Paramount, 2005.
Executive producer, *Land of the Blind,* Bauer Martinez Studios, 2006.
Coproducer, *88 Minutes,* TriStar, 2007.
Coproducer, *Righteous Kill,* Overture Films, 2008.

Film Appearances:
Herself, *Brave New World* (documentary), Paramount, 2005.

Television Work; Miniseries:
Post–production supervisor, *Mama Flora's Family,* CBS, 1998.
Coproducer, *Uprising,* NBC, 2001.
Producer, *The Starter Wife,* USA Network, 2007.

Television Work; Movies:
Associate producer, *Sixty Minute Man,* 2006.

Television Work; Pilots:
Associate producer, *Boomtown,* NBC, 2002.

OHTSJI, Kevan
(Kevin Ohstji, Kevin Ohtsji)

PERSONAL

Born in Vancouver, British Columbia, Canada.

Addresses: *Agent*—The Characters Talent Agency, 1200–1205 West 2nd Ave., Vancouver, BC V6H 3Y4 Canada.

Career: Actor.

CREDITS

Film Appearances:
(Professional debut) Takeshi Shimazaki, *Crying Freeman,* Warner Bros., 1995.
Dion Edwards, *American Dragons* (also known as *Double Edge*), Orion Home Video, 1998.
Tracking technician, *Dreamcatcher* (also known as *L'attrapeur de reves*), Warner Bros., 2003.
Doughboy, *Thralls* (also known as *Blood Angels*), Screen Media Films, 2004.
Anesthesiologist, *The Butterfly Effect,* New Line Cinema, 2004.
Roger, *Eighteen,* TLA Releasing, 2004.
Kamakura, *G.I. Joe: Valor vs. Venom* (animated), Paramount Home Video, 2004.
Tyrell, *Human Nature,* The Asylum, 2004.
Voice of Taro Kitano, *Acceleracers: Speed of Silence* (animated), Warner Home Video, 2005.
Roshi servant, *Elektra,* Twentieth Century–Fox, 2005.
Yakuza, *Everything's Gone Green* (short), Sundance Film Festival, 2005.
Francis, *Little Black Caddy* (short), 2005.

Akira Kudo, *The Shortest Dream* (short), 2005.
Mountain guard number one, *Spymate,* Miramax, 2006.
Miles, *Live Feed,* MTI Video, 2006.
Taro Kitano, *AcceleRacers: The Ultimate Race* (animated), Warner Home Video, 2006.
Ken, "Prey," *Hell Hath No Fury,* Brain Damage Films, 2006.

Television Appearances; Series:
Hot Wheels Highway 35 World Race, 2003.
Oshu, *Stargate SG–1* (also known as *La porte des etoiles*), Sci–Fi Channel, 2003–2005.

Television Appearances; Miniseries:
(As Kevin Ohtsji) Barman, *Traffic* (also known as *Traffic: The Miniseries*), USA Network, 2004.
Hiromi Okuda, *Race to Mars,* Discovery Channel Canada, 2007.

Television Appearances; Movies:
Team leader number one, *Jeremiah* (also known as *Die Bibel: Jeremia* and *Geremia il profeta*), PAX, 1998.
Auto executive, *The Goodbye Girl* (also known as *Neil Simon's "The Goodbye Girl"*), TNT, 2004.
Donnie, *Too Cool for Christmas* (also known as *A Very Cool Christmas*), Lifetime, 2004.
Voice of Taro Kitano, *AcceleRacers: Ignition* (animated), Cartoon Network, 2005.
Sniper number two, *FBI: Negotiator,* Lifetime, 2005.

Television Appearances; Pilots:
Cop, *A.M.P.E.D.,* Spike, 2007.

Television Appearances; Episodic:
"Hope," *Three,* The WB, 1998.
Hotel clerk, "Bardo Thodol," *Millennium,* Fox, 1999.
Akio Igawa, "Attack of the Teki–Ya," *Viper,* syndicated, 1999.
Technician, "The Trial of Joshua Bridges," *First Wave,* Sci–Fi Channel, 2000.
Gang leader, "Stairway to Heaven," *Seven Days* (also known as *Seven Days: The Series*), UPN, 2000.
Roommate, "Stranger in the Mirror," *Mysterious Ways,* PAX, 2000.
Toshiro, "Bond, Jimmy Bond," *The Lone Gunmen,* Fox, 2001.
Uniform, "Birds Have Been at Her," *Da Vinci's Inquest,* CBC, 2001.
Cho, "The Human Factor," *The Outer Limits* (also known as *The New Outer Limits*), Showtime and syndicated, 2002.
Danny Kwan, "Crush," *Smallville* (also known as *Smallville Beginnings* and *Smallville: Superman the Early Years*), The WB, 2002.
Ricky Tran, "Rachel Glass and the No Good, Very Bad Day," *Breaking News,* Bravo, 2002.
Tony, "Rewind," *The Twilight Zone,* UPN, 2003.

Frymire, "Point of the Spear," *Andromeda* (also known as *Gene Roddenberry's "Andromeda"*), Sci–Fi Channel, 2003.
"One More Day's Light," *Andromeda* (also known as *Gene Roddenberry's "Andromeda"*), Sci–Fi Channel, 2005.
"Chaos and the Stillness of It," *Andromeda* (also known as *Gene Roddenberry's "Andromeda"*), Sci–Fi Channel, 2005.
Paul, "The Tempting Spice," *Godiva's,* Bravo, 2006.
Gogo, "Triage," *Saved,* TNT, 2006.
F.B.I technician, "The Trader," *Traveler,* ABC, 2007.

Also appeared as Kenny Logan, "Muddy Footprints," *Beyond Belief: Fact or Fiction* (also known as *Beyond Belief*).

RECORDINGS

Video Games:
(As Kevin Ohstji) Toru, *Need for Speed: Most Wanted,* Electronic Arts, 2005.

OTHER SOURCES

Electronic:
Kevin Ohtsji Website, http://www.ohtsji.com, December 1, 2007.

OJEDA, Juan
See STORM, T. J.

OMAN, Chad

PERSONAL

Born in Wichita Falls, TX; married; children: four. *Education:* Southern Methodist University, undergraduate degree in finance; studied filmmaking at New York University; studied screen writing at University of California at Los Angeles.

Addresses: *Office*—Jerry Bruckheimer Films, 1631 Tenth St., Santa Monica, CA 90404.

Career: Producer and actor. Motion Picture Corporation of America, founding employee, then senior vice president of production, 1989–95; Jerry Bruckheimer Films, president of production, 1995—.

CREDITS

Film Work:
Coproducer, *Driving Me Crazy,* 1991.
Coproducer and second unit director, *Double Trouble,* 1992.
Coproducer, *Sketch Artist,* 1992.
Coproducer, *Love, Cheat and Steal,* 1993.
Coproducer, *The Desperate Trail,* 1994.
Associate producer, *Dumb & Dumber* (also known as *Dumb Happens* and *Dumb and Dumber*), New Line Cinema, 1994.
Co–executive producer, *The War at Home,* Buena Vista, 1996.
Executive producer, *Con Air,* Buena Vista, 1997.
Executive producer, *Armageddon,* Buena Vista, 1998.
Executive producer, *Enemy of the State,* Buena Vista, 1998.
Executive producer, *The Rock Star,* 1999.
Producer, *Remember the Titans,* Buena Vista, 2000.
Executive producer, *Gone in Sixty Seconds,* Buena Vista, 2000.
Executive producer, *Coyote Ugly,* Buena Vista, 2000.
Executive producer, *Pearl Harbor* (also known as *Pearl Harbour*), Buena Vista, 2001.
Executive producer, *Down and Under,* Warner Bros., 2001.
Executive producer and production executive, *Black Hawk Down,* 2001.
Executive producer, *Bad Company* (also known as *Ceska spojka*), Buena Vista, 2002.
Executive producer, *Kangaroo Jack,* Warner Bros., 2003.
Executive producer, *Pirates of the Caribbean: The Curse of the Black Pearl* (also known as *P.O.T.C.*), Buena Vista, 2003.
Executive producer, *Veronica Guerin,* Buena Vista, 2003.
Executive producer, *Bad Boys II* (also known as *Good Cops: Bad Boys II*), Columbia, 2003.
Executive producer, *King Arthur,* Buena Vista, 2004.
Executive producer, *National Treasure* (also known as *Sonomo*), Buena Vista, 2004.
Executive producer, *Glory Road,* Buena Vista, 2006.
Executive producer, *Pirates of the Caribbean: Dead Man's Chest* (also known as *P.O.T.C. 2* and *Pirates 2*), Buena Vista, 2006.
Executive producer, *Deja Vu,* Buena Vista, 2006.
Executive producer, *Pirates of the Caribbean: At World's End* (also known as *P.O.T.C. 3* and *Pirates 3*), Buena Vista, 2007.
Executive producer, *National Treasure: Book of Secrets,* Buena Vista, 2007.

Film Appearances:
G–Man number one, *Double Trouble,* 1992.
Ugly hunter, *Pumpkinhead II: Blood Wings* (also known as *Pumpkinhead 2: The Demon Returns*), 1994.
Jones, *Cover Me,* 1995.

Television Work; Series:
Production consultant, *Dangerous Minds,* 1996.
Consulting producer, *S.O.F. Special Ops Force,* 1997.

Television Work; Movies:
Coproducer, *Sketch Artist II: Hands That See* (also known as *A Feel for Murder* and *Sketch Artist II*), Showtime, 1995.
Producer, *Swing Vote* (also known as *The Ninth Justice*), ABC, 1999.

OPEL, Nancy

PERSONAL

Education: Graduated from The Juilliard School.

Career: Actress. Actors Company Theatre, member of company.

Awards, Honors: Antoinette Perry Award nomination, best actress in a musical, 2002, for *Urinetown the Musical;* Drama Desk Award nomination, outstanding featured actress in a play, 2003, for *Polish Joke.*

CREDITS

Stage Appearances:
Member of company and understudy for the role of Eva, *Evita,* Broadway Theatre, New York City, 1979–83.
Betty and Dee, *Sunday in the Park with George* (workshop production), Playwrights Horizons Theatre, New York City, 1983.
Young man on bank, Frieda, and Betty, *Sunday in the Park with George,* Booth Theatre, New York City, 1984–85.
Eleanor Roosevelt, *Teddy & Alice,* Minskoff Theatre, New York City, 1987–88.
Hope Harcourt, *Anything Goes,* Vivian Beaumont Theatre, New York City, 1987–89.
Frieda and Betty, *Sunday in the Park with George* (concert performance), St. James Theatre, New York City, 1994.
Kafka in "Words, Words, Words," Betty in "Sure Thing," and Trotsky's wife in "Variations on the Death of Trotsky," *All in the Timing* (series), John Houseman Theatre, New York City, 1994.
Dossie and understudy for the role of Pamela, *Getting Away with Murder,* Broadhurst Theatre, New York City, 1996.

"Fascinating Rhythms" (concert performance), *American Music Theatre Festival,* 1996–97.

Annie in "Foreplay," appeared in "Speed–the–Play," village crone in "Dr. Fritz or: The Forces of Light," and wife in "Degas, c'est moi," *Mere Mortals and Others* (series of one–acts), John Houseman Theatre, then Henry Miller's Theatre, New York City, both 1997.

Corine, *Triumph of Love,* Royale Theatre, New York City, 1997–98.

Angela, *Darlene* (double–bill with *The Guest Lecturer),* George Street Playhouse, New Brunswick, NJ, 1998.

Businesswoman in "Babel's in Arms," Sarah in "The Mystery at Twicknam Vicarage," Bebe I in "Enigma Variations," the machine in "Soap Opera," and Edna in "Lives of the Saints or: Polish Joke," *Lives of the Saints* (series of short comedies), Berkshire Theatre Festival, Philadelphia Theatre Company, then Stockbridge, MA, 1999.

Wise Guy (workshop production), New York Theatre Workshop, 1999.

Understudy Capulat, Isabelle's mother, and Lady India, *Ring Round the Moon,* Belasco Theatre, New York City, 1999.

Nurse, *Loot,* George Street Playhouse, 2000.

Nothing Like a Dame 2000 (benefit performances), Shubert Theatre, New York City, 1999, then Richard Rodgers Theatre, New York City, 2000.

Mrs. Hatch, "On a Clear Day You Can See Forever," in *Encores!,* City Center Theatre, New York City, 2000.

Multiple roles, including Queenie, *Honk!,* North Shore Music Theatre, 2000.

Storybook: The Lyrics of Nan Knighton (benefit performance), Dream Street Cabaret, New York City, 2000.

Penelope Pennywise, *Urinetown,* American Theatre of Actors, New York City, 2001–2004.

Hair, New Amsterdam Theatre, New York City, 2004.

Yente, *Fiddler on the Roof,* Minskoff Theatre, New York City, 2004–2006.

My Deah, Abingdon Theatre Company, New York City, 2006.

Also appeared in *Harmonies of the Boswell Sisters* (cabaret), Rainbow and Stars; *Rhythm on the Rainbow* (cabaret); *Don Juan in Chicago,* Off–Broadway production; *Hundreds of Hats,* Off–Broadway production; *Personals,* Off–Broadway production; *All in the Timing* and *Stay, Carl, Stay,* New Hope Performing Arts Festival; *Blue Window,* Santa Fe Festival Theatre, Santa Fe, NM; *Candide,* Alliance Theatre; *I Love a Piano,* TriArts Theatre; *Marry Me a Little,* Hartman Theatre; *Polish Joke.*

Major Tours:

The Drowsy Chaperone Tour, North American cities, 2007.

Film Appearances:

Sue, *The Ice Storm,* Twentieth Century–Fox, 1997.

Mom, *Second Skin,* 1998.

Reporter (Feld House), *Marci X,* Paramount, 2003.

(Uncredited) Ensemble, *The Producers,* Universal, 2005.

Television Appearances; Specials:

Frieda and Betty, "Sunday in the Park with George," *Broadway on Showtime,* Showtime, then *American Playhouse,* PBS, both 1986.

The 58th Annual Tony Awards (also known as *The 2004 Tony Awards),* CBS, 2004.

Television Appearances; Episodic:

Sybil, *Ryan's Hope,* ABC, 1975.

Henkel, "Encore," *Law & Order,* NBC, 1996.

Nina, "Suite Sorrow," *Law & Order: Criminal Intent* (also known as *Law & Order: CI),* NBC, 2003.

Teri Carthage, "Infected," *Law & Order: Special Victims Unit* (also known as *Law & Order: SVU* and *Special Victims Unit),* NBC, 2006.

Also appeared in *One Life to Live,* ABC.

RECORDINGS

Albums:

Sunday in the Park with George (original cast recording), RCA, 1990.

Evita, MCA, 1990.

Triumph of Love (original Broadway cast recording), Jay, 1998.

The Sidewalks of New York: Tin Pan Alley, Winter and Winter, 1999.

ORSER, Leland 1960–
  (Eric Orser, Lee Orser)

PERSONAL

Full name, Leland Jones Orser; born August 6, 1960, in San Francisco, CA; married Roma Downey (an actress), 1987 (divorced, 1989); married Jeanne Tripplehorn (an actress), October 14, 2000; children: (second marriage) August. *Education:* Attended drama school in London, England.

Addresses: *Agent*—The Gersh Agency, 232 North Canon Dr., Beverly Hills, CA 90210. *Manager*—Burstein Company, 15304 Sunset Blvd., Suite 208, Pacific Palisades, CA 90272.

Career: Actor.

Awards, Honors: Helen Hayes Theatre Award nomination, best supporting actor, Washington THeatre Awards Society, for *The Secret Rapture.*

CREDITS

Film Appearances:

Julian, *Cover Story,* Arrow Entertainment, 1993.

Crazed man in massage parlor, *Se7en,* New Line Cinema, 1995.

James, *Red Ribbon Blues,* Kushner–Locke Productions/Red Ribbon Productions, 1995.

Dr. Riley, *Phoenix,* Triad Studios, 1995.

Used car salesman, *Girl in the Cadillac,* Columbia TriStar Home Video, 1995.

Pellman, *Dead Badge,* 1995.

Benny Bakst, *Baby Face Nelson,* 1995.

Technician and first medical assistant, *Independence Day* (also known as *ID4*), Twentieth Century–Fox, 1996.

Test Tube, *Escape from L.A.* (also known as *John Carpenter's "Escape from L.A."*), Paramount, 1996.

Michael Perkett, *Invader* (also known as *Lifeform*), Live Entertainment, 1996.

James, *Red Ribbon Blues,* 1996.

Detective Barnaby, *Excess Baggage,* Columbia, 1997.

Purvis, *Alien: Resurrection* (also known as *Alien 4*), Twentieth Century–Fox, 1997.

Lieutenant DeWindt, *Saving Private Ryan,* Paramount, 1998.

Charles Moore, *Very Bad Things,* PolyGram Filmed Entertainment, 1998.

Detective Andrew Hollingworth, *Resurrection,* Columbia TriStar Home Video, 1999.

Richard Thompson, *The Bone Collector,* Universal, 1999.

Billy Idol, *Rebel Yell* (also known as *Rebel Yell: The Billy Idol Story*), 2001.

Major Jackson, *Pearl Harbor* (also known as *Pearl Harbour*), Buena Vista, 2001.

Lionel Dolby, *Confidence* (also known as *Confidence: After Dark* and *En toute confiance*), Lions Gate Films, 2003.

Wesley Owen Welch, *Daredevil* (also known as *Daredevil: A Daring New Vision*), Twentieth Century–Fox, 2003.

Lamb, *Runaway Jury,* Twentieth Century–Fox, 2003.

Himself, *One Step Beyond: The Making of "Alien: Resurrection"* (documentary), Twentieth Century–Fox Home Entertainment, 2003.

Edmund Cutler, *Twisted,* Paramount, 2004.

Bernie Teitel, *The Good German,* Warner Bros., 2006.

Sam, *Taken,* Twentieth Century–Fox, 2008.

Film Work:

Director, *Morning* (short), 2007.

Television Appearances; Series:

Dr. Lucien Dubenko, *ER,* NBC, 2004–2007.

Television Appearances; Movies:

Terry Wechsler, *Piranha* (also known as *Roger Corman Presents "Piranha"*), Showtime, 1995.

Wheelchair guy, *Back to Back* (also known as *Back to Back: American Yakuza 2*), HBO, 1996.

Lassiter, *To Love, Honor, and Deceive* (also known as *The Protected Wife*), ABC, 1997.

Travis, *My Brother's Keeper* (also known as *Brother's Keeper*), USA Network, 2002.

Television Appearances; Pilots:

Wendall Rickle, *Wonderland,* ABC, 2000.

Sol Binder, *Homeland Security* (movie), NBC, 2004.

Television Appearances; Specials:

The 100 Scariest Movie Moments, Bravo, 2004.

Television Appearances; Episodic:

Edward, "Belly of the Beast," *Gabriel's Fire,* 1991.

Waiter, "The Case of the Libertine Belle," *The Golden Girls,* NBC, 1991.

Don MacKenzie, "Windy," *Empty Nest,* NBC, 1991.

Chip Englund, "Graduation Day," *Reasonable Doubts,* NBC, 1991.

Assistant director, "Reality Takes a Holiday," *Eerie, Indiana,* 1992.

Mark, "Do No Forsake Me, O' My Postman," *Cheers,* NBC, 1992.

Lyle, "Memory Man," *Moon over Miami,* ABC, 1993.

Ralph, "My Funny Valentine," *Herman's Head,* Fox, 1993.

Richard Daggett, "That's Why the Lady Is a Stamp," *L.A. Law,* NBC, 1993.

Gai, "Sanctuary," *Star Trek: Deep Space Nine* (also known as *DS9, Deep Space Nine,* and *Star Trek: DS9*), syndicated, 1993.

Zeppo, "Zeppo Marks Brothers," *NYPD Blue,* ABC, 1994.

Jason Ludwig, "Firewalker," *The X–Files,* Fox, 1994.

Clerk, "The Washington Affair; Parts 1 & 2," *Dr. Quinn, Medicine Woman,* CBS, 1994.

Mark, "The Naked and the Dead, But Mostly the Naked," *Married ... with Children,* Fox, 1995.

Colonel Lovok, "The Die Is Cast," *Star Trek: Deep Space Nine* (also known as *DS9, Deep Space Nine,* and *Star Trek: DS9*), syndicated, 1995.

Myron Elkins, "Chapter Two," *Murder One,* 1995.

Phil, "Portrait of a Marriage," *Ned and Stacey,* Fox, 1995.

Director, "The Two That Got Away," *Married ... with Children,* Fox, 1995.

Leonard Blum, *High Incident,* 1995.

Professor Gittelson, "Get Back," *Mad About You,* NBC, 1996.

Lon, "Boyd Gets Shrunk," *Boston Common,* NBC, 1996.

Director, "Kiss of the Coffee Woman," *Married ... with Children,* Fox, 1996.

Les Street, "He's Not Guilty, He's My Brother," *NYPD Blue,* ABC, 1996.

Henry, "Good Grief," *Almost Perfect,* CBS, 1996.

John Highsmith, "A Draining Experience," *NYPD Blue,* ABC, 1997.

Dejaren, "Revulsion," *Star Trek: Voyager* (also known as *Voyager*), UPN, 1997.

Argyle, "Amnesia aka Unforgotten," *The Pretender,* NBC, 1998.

"Queens for a Day," *Brooklyn South,* CBS, 1998.

Argyle, "Unsinkable," *The Pretender,* NBC, 1999.

Dr. Arthur Zeller, "Descent," *The Outer Limits* (also known as *The New Outer Limits*), Showtime and syndicated, 1999.

Argyle, "Cold Dick," *The Pretender,* NBC, 2000.

Wendall Rickle, "20/20 Hindsight," *Wonderland,* ABC, 2000.

Morris Pearson, "Stalker," *CSI: Crime Scene Investigation* (also known as *C.S.I., CSI: Las Vegas,* and *Les Experts*), CBS, 2002.

Dinner for Five, Independent Film Channel, 2003.

Kevin Walker, "Coerced," *Law & Order: Special Victims Unit* (also known as *Law & Order: SVU* and *Special Victims Unit*), NBC, 2003.

Loomis, "Carpenter Street," *Enterprise* (also known as *Star Trek: Enterprise*), UPN, 2003.

Brent Gilroy, "Porn Free," *Shark,* CBS, 2007.

Also appeared as Fritz Scott, "Duty to Serve," *The Lyon's Den,* NBC.

Stage Appearances:

Appeared in *The Secret Rapture,* Olney Theatre, Olney, MD; performed in other stage productions at East Coast theatres.

WRITINGS

Screenplays:

Morning (short), 2007.

OSMENT, Emily 1992–

PERSONAL

Full name, Emily Jordan Osment; born March 10, 1992, in Los Angeles, CA; daughter of Eugene (an actor) and Theresa (a teacher) Osment; sister of Haley Joel Osment (an actor). *Religion:* Roman Catholic. *Avocational Interests:* Writing action novels, playing golf, drawing, knitting, singing, and playing soccer.

Addresses: *Agent*—Coast to Coast Talent, Inc., 3350 Barham Blvd., Los Angeles, CA 90068.

Career: Actress. Appeared in television commercials, including FTD floral, 1998, and McDonald's; appeared in radio commercials.

Awards, Honors: Young Artist Award nomination, best performance in a television movie or pilot—young actress age ten or under, 2000, for *Sarah, Plain and Tall: Winter's End;* Young Artist Award nomination, best performance in a feature film—young actress age ten or under, 2003, for *Spy Kids 2: Island of Lost Dreams;* Young Artist Award nomination (with others), best young ensemble in a feature film, 2004, for *Spy Kids 3–D: Game Over.*

CREDITS

Film Appearances:

Miranda Aiken, *The Secret Life of Girls* (also known as *Unglued*), 1999.

Herself, *Cast and Crew* (short), 1999.

Voice, *Edwurd Fudwupper Fibbed Big* (short), 2000.

Gerti Giggles, *Spy Kids 2: Island of Lost Dreams* (also known as *Spy Kids 2: The Island of Lost Dreams*), Miramax, 2002.

Gerti Giggles, *Spy Kids 3–D: Game Over* (also known as *Spy Kids 3: Game Over*), Dimension Films, 2003.

Additional voices, *Lilo & Stitch 2: Stitch Has a Glitch* (animated), Buena Vista Home Entertainment, 2005.

Voice of Trick, *Holidaze: The Christmas That Almost Didn't Happen* (animated), Walmart, 2006.

Cassie, *The Haunting Hour: Don't Think About It* (also known as *R. L. Stine's "The Haunting ZHour: Don't Think About It"*), Universal Studios Home Entertainment, 2007.

Television Appearances; Series:

Lilly Truscott, *Hannah Montana,* Disney Channel, 2006—.

Television Appearances; Movies:

Cassie Witting, *Sarah, Plain and Tall: Winter's End,* CBS, 1999.

Television Appearances; Specials:

The Disney Channel Games, Disney Channel, 2006, 2007.

Sing-Along Bowl-Athon, 2006.

Television Appearances; Episodic:

Dahlia, "Dick, Who's Coming to Dinner," *3rd Rock from the Sun* (also known as *3rd Rock* and *Life As We Know It*), NBC, 1999.

Alyssa, "With God as My Witness," *Touched by an Angel,* CBS, 2000.

Lelani Mayolanofavich, "The One With the Halloween Party," *Friends,* NBC, 2001.

Tall Skunk Girl, "Mascot Prep," *Shorty McShorts' Shorts,* Disney Channel, 2007.

Disney's Really Short Report, Disney Channel, 2007.

OXENBERG, Catherine 1961–

(Catherine, Princess Catherine Oxenberg, Princess, Catherine Van Dien, Princess Catherine Oxenberg Van Dien)

PERSONAL

Born September 22, 1961, in New York, NY; daughter of Howard Oxenberg (a businessman) and Princess Elizabeth of Yugoslavia; married Robert Evans (a producer), July 12, 1998 (annulled, July 21, 1998); married Casper Van Dien (an actor), May 8, 1999; children: India; (second marriage) Maya, Celeste. *Education:* Studied acting with Stanley Zaraff, Joanne Baron, and The Groundling's Theatre; studied psychology, philosophy and mythology at Columbia University; attended Harvard University.

Addresses: *Agent*—Darryl Marshak, Gold, Marshak, Liedtike and Associates, 3500 West Olive Ave., Suite 1400, Burbank, CA 91505.

Career: Actress. Previously worked as a professional model, appearing on the covers of *Cosmopolitan, Glamour,* and *Interview.*

Awards, Honors: *Soap Opera Digest* Awards, outstanding actress in a supporting role in a prime time serial and outstanding new actress in a prime time serial, 1985, both for *Dynasty;* Bambi Award, 1986; Grace Award, most inspirational television acting, MovieGuide Awards, 2002, for *The Miracle of the Cards.*

CREDITS

Film Appearances:

Eve Trent, *The Lair of the White Worm,* Vestron, 1988.

Herself, *Walking after Midnight,* Kay Film, 1988.

Kristen, *Overexposed,* Concorde, 1990.

(As Catherine) Herself, *The Global Forum,* 1990.

Kate, *Sexual Response* (also known as *Take My Body*), Columbia TriStar Home Video, 1992.

Voice of herself, *CyberFin Virtual Dolphin Swim,* 1994.

Patsy "Boom–Boom" Parker, *Boys Will Be Boys,* A–pix Entertainment, 1997.

Morgana, *Arthur's Quest,* A–pix Entertainment, 1999.

Sarah, *Time Served,* Trimark Pictures, 1999.

Bailey, *The Collectors,* New City Releasing, 1999.

Cassandra Barashe, *The Omega Code,* Providence Entertainment, 1999.

Susan Renart, *Sanctimony,* 2000.

Sasha, *Perilous,* 2000.

The Flying Dutchman, New City Releasing, 2000.

Marion Shergold, *The Miracle of the Cards,* 2001.

Always Greener, 2001.

Margaret, *The Vector File* (short), 2002.

Technician number one, *Starship Troopers: Marauder,* Stage 6 Films, 2007.

Television Appearances; Series:

Amanda Bedford Carrington, *Dynasty,* ABC, 1984–89.

Ashley Hunter–Coddington, *Acapulco H.E.A.T.,* syndicated, 1993–94.

Herself, *I Married a Princess,* Lifetime, 2005.

Leandra Thames, *Watch Over Me,* MyNetwork, 2006–2007.

Television Appearances; Miniseries:

Fiona Matthews McDonald, *Ring of Scorpio,* 1990.

Television Appearances; Movies:

(Television debut) Lady Diana Spencer, *The Royal Romance of Charles and Diana,* CBS, 1982.

Nancy Church, *Still Crazy Like a Fox* (also known as *Crazy Like a Fox: The Movie*), CBS, 1987.

Princess Alisa, *Roman Holiday,* CBS, 1987.

Jade Greene, *Swimsuit* (also known as *Swimsuit: The Movie*), NBC, 1989.

Lisa Duncan, *Trenchcoat in Paradise,* CBS, 1989.

Angela Hemmings, *Bony,* 1990.

Dr. Aja Turner, *K–9000,* Fox, 1991.

Princess Diana, *Charles and Diana: Unhappily Ever After* (also known as *Charles and Diana: A Palace Divided, Charles et Diana,* and *A Palace Divided*), ABC, 1992.

Jordy/Natalie Browning, *Rubdown,* USA Network, 1993.

Simone Hollister, *Treacherous Beauties* (also known as *Les armes de la passion*), CBS, 1994.

Sergeant Tina Walcott, *Catch Me If You Can* (also known as *Deadly Game* and *Hide and Seek*), Fox Family Channel, 1998.

(As Catherine Van Dien) Thrill Seekers spokesperson, *The Time Shifters* (also known as *Thrill Seekers*), 1999.

(As Catherine Van Dien) Forest Service woman, *A Friday Night Date* (also known as *La rage au volant* and *Road Rage*), 2000.

Lacy Anderson, *The Flying Dutchman* (also known as *Frozen in Fear*), 2001.

Marion Shergold, *The Miracle of the Cards* (also known as *Le miracle des cartes*), PAX, 2001.

Kate Barnes, *Premonition* (also known as *The Psychic*), 2004.

Television Appearances; Pilots:
Michelle Lloyd, *Cover Up,* CBS, 1984.

Television Appearances; Specials:
The 43rd Annual Golden Globe Awards, 1986.
That's What Friends Are For: AIDS Concert '88, Showtime, 1988.
Host, *This Island Earth,* Disney Channel, 1992.
Host, *Royals: Dynasty or Disaster,* Fox, 1993.
(As Princess Catherine Oxenberg Van Dien) *"Dynasty": The E! True Hollywood Story,* E! Entertainment Television, 2001.
TV's Most Memorable Weddings, NBC, 2003.
"Dynasty" Reunion: Catfights & Caviar, CBS, 2006.

Television Appearances; Episodic:
"My Mother, My Chaperone/The Present/The Death and Life of Sir Alfred Demerest/Welcome Aboard: Parts 1 & 2," *The Love Boat,* ABC, 1984.
(As Princess Catherine Oxenberg) Host, *Saturday Night Live* (also known as *SNL*), NBC, 1986.
"Egypt," *The Love Boat,* ABC, 1986.
(As Princess) *Primero izquierda,* 1991.
Simone Hollister, "Treacherous Beauties," *The Harlequin Romance Movies* (also known as *CBS Sunday Afternoon Showcase*), CBS, 1994.
Sydney Mercer, "Oy Vey, You're Gay," *The Nanny,* CBS, 1995.

(Uncredited) Sydney Mercer, "Where's Fran?" *The Nanny,* CBS, 1996.
Erika, "Bad Boyz," *Baywatch Hawaii,* syndicated, 2000.
The Tony Danza Show, syndicated, 2005.
Claudia Penchant, "Brothers Grim," *Out of Practice,* CBS, 2005.
Larry King Live, CNN, 2006.
Host, "Tea, Tennis, Croquet and Cricket," *American Princess,* NBC, 2007.
Host, "Art and Aristocracy," *American Princess,* NBC, 2007.

Television Work; Series:
Producer, *I Married a Princess,* Lifetime, 2005.

RECORDINGS

Video Games:
Female pilot, *Starship Troopers,* Empire Interactive, 2005.

OTHER SOURCES

Periodicals:
The Economist, September 30, 1989, p. 48.
Variety, July 13, 1998, p. 6.
People Weekly, July 7, 1997, p. 37; August 10, 1998, p. 118; May 16, 2005, p. 101.

Electronic:
Catherine Oxenberg Website, http://catherineoxenberg.com/.

P

PACKER, David 1962–

PERSONAL

Born August 25, 1962, in Passaic, NJ.

Addresses: *Agent*—Premiere Artists Agency, 8899 Beverly Blvd., Suite 510, Los Angeles, CA 90048.

Career: Actor.

Awards, Honors: Cable Ace Award, best actor in a dramatic series, 1994, for *Big Al.*

CREDITS

Film Appearances:
Emergency doctor, *RoboCop,* Orion, 1987.
Eddie, *You Can't Hurry Love* (also known as *Greetings from L.A.* and *Lovestruck*), Lightning, 1988.
Sam Brown, *Trust Me,* Cinecom, 1989.
Count Messner, *Valentino Returns,* Skouras, 1989.
Joey Curtis, *The Runnin' Kind,* 1989.
Mark Olander, *Crazy People,* Paramount, 1990.
Bill, *Cityscapes: Los Angeles,* 1994.
Lane, *Strange Days,* Twentieth Century–Fox, 1995.
Sergeant Collins, *True Crime* (also known as *Dangerous Kiss* and *True Detective*), Trimark Pictures, 1995.
Brad, *Bombshell,* Trimark Pictures, 1996.
Ben Lowenstein, *No Strings Attached* (also known as *The Last Obsession*), Redwood Communications, 1997.
Bidwell, *Almost Heroes,* Warner Bros., 1998.
Howard, *Beach Movie* (also known as *Board Heads* and *Boardheads*), 1998.
Al Barsini, *You're Killing Me …,* 1999.
George, *Intrepid* (also known as *Deep Water*), 2000.

Joel, *Hollywood Palms,* 2001.
Elliot, *Infested,* Columbia TriStar, 2002.

Television Appearances; Series:
Neil "Trout" Troutman, *The Best Times,* 1985.
Marty Dissler, *My Talk Show* (also known as *Second City Presents … My Talk Show*), syndicated, 1990–91.
Dr. Gil Zuchetti, *Birdland,* ABC, 1994.

Television Appearances; Miniseries:
Daniel Bernstein, *V* (also known as *V: The Original Mini Series*), NBC, 1983.
Daniel Bernstein, *V: The Final Battle,* NBC, 1984.

Television Appearances; Movies:
Danny, *High School U.S.A.,* NBC, 1983.
Brian, *First Steps,* CBS, 1985.
Glenn Bell, *Call Me Anna* (also known as *My Name Is Anna* and *Call Me Anna; The Patty Duke Story*), ABC, 1990.
Cliff Sloan, Brian, and Mark Gallaway, *Silent Motive,* Lifetime, 1991.
Tony DeGeorgio, *Day–O,* NBC, 1992.
Jack Morgan, *The Courtyard,* Showtime, 1995.
Johnny, *Heartless,* USA Network, 1997.
Brad, *Bombshell,* 1997.

Television Appearances; Specials:
Leo, *Big Al,* Showtime, 1993.

Television Appearances; Pilots:
Bobby, *Hotel,* 1982.
Jeff Hoffstetter, *What's Alan Watching?* (also known as *Outrageous*), CBS, 1989.

Television Appearances; Episodic:
Waiter, "Class Act," *Fame,* 1982.

Willie Andrews, "Legionnaires: Part 2," *St. Elsewhere,* 1982.

Falcon Crest, 1983.

Wounded soldier, "U.N., the Night and the Music," *M*A*S*H,* CBS, 1983.

"Houston: Duffy's Choice," *Lottery!,* 1983.

Man in bar, "Bitter Harvest," *Falcon Crest,* 1984.

Terry O'Neil, "In Re: The Marriage of Watson," *thirtysomething,* ABC, 1988.

Larry Haber, "Son of a Pilot," *Nurses,* 1991.

David Green, *Going to Extremes,* 1992.

Dave, *Phenom,* 1993.

Dr. Gil Zuchetti, *Birdland,* 1993.

Ethan Ballou, *Sweet Justice,* 1994.

Roddy, *The Home Court,* 1995.

Mr. Ledbetter, "The Match Game," *ER,* NBC, 1996.

Roddy, "Mike Solomon: Unplugged," *The Home Court,* NBC, 1996.

Sam Jessup, *High Incident,* 1996.

Jonathan, "Things Change," *Boy Meets World,* ABC, 1998.

The killer, "The Monster Within," *Profiler,* NBC, 1998.

Lanny Zeiter, "Fools Russian," *Brooklyn South,* 1998.

Jenson, "Lt. Hobson, U.S.N.," *Early Edition,* CBS, 1998.

V.I.P., 1998.

Emergency room shooter, "Blood Ties," *Diagnosis Murder,* CBS, 1999.

Jack & Jill, The WB, 1999.

Rick, "Jamie," *Grapevine,* CBS, 2000.

Rudy Metzer, "Shelby," *The Division* (also known as *Heart of the City*), Lifetime, 2002.

Hugo Karlin, "Random Acts of Violence," *CSI: Crime Scene Investigation* (also known as *C.S.I., CSI: Las Vegas,* and *Les Experts*), CBS, 2003.

Ken, "Shame," *The Guardian,* CBS, 2003.

Morty Sherman, "The Dove Commission," *CSI: NY* (also known as *CSI: New York*), CBS, 2005.

Also appeared as Peterson's lawyer, "Justice Delayed," *Courthouse.*

RECORDINGS

Video Games:
Jeff, *Double Switch,* 1993.

PAGE, Ken 1954–

PERSONAL

Born January 20, 1954, in St. Louis, MO.

Addresses: *Agent*—Buzz Halliday and Associates, 8899 Beverly Blvd., Suite 715, Los Angeles, CA 90048.

Career: Actor, director, and writer.

Awards, Honors: *Theatre World* Award, 1977, for *Guys and Dolls;* Drama Desk Award, best actor, 1978, for *Ain't Misbehavin';* Fennecus Awards, best actor in a limited role, 1988, for *Torch Song Trilogy,* best vocal performance, 1989, for *All Dogs Go to Heaven,* and 1993, for *The Nightmare before Christmas,* best song performance in studio, 1993, for "The Oogie Boogie Song" in *The Nightmare Before Christmas,* and best actor in a cameo role, 1994, for *I'll Do Anything.*

CREDITS

Film Appearances:
Kinney, *RoboCop,* Orion, 1987.

Murray, *Torch Song Trilogy,* New Line Cinema, 1988.

Andy, *Night Game,* Viacom, 1989.

Voice of King Gator, *All Dogs Go to Heaven* (animated), United Artists, 1989.

Voice of Oogie Boogie, *The Nightmare Before Christmas* (animated; also known as *Tim Burton's "Nightmare before Christmas"*), Buena Vista, 1993.

Hair person, *I'll Do Anything,* Columbia, 1994.

Cowardly Lion, *Oz: The American Fairyland* (documentary), Sirocco Productions, 1997.

Himself, *Geeks* (documentary), 2004.

Max Washington, *Dreamgirls,* Paramount, 2006.

Broadway: Beyond the Golden Age (documentary; also known as *B.G.A. 2* and *Broadway: The Golden Age Two*), 2008.

Television Appearances; Series:
Joe "Cheesecake" Tyson, *Sable,* ABC, 1987.

Chubby, *Teen Angel Returns,* 1990.

Dr. McHenry, *South Central,* Fox, 1994.

Florian, *State of Mind,* Lifetime, 2007.

Television Appearances; Movies:
Mayor Warren, *Polly,* NBC, 1989.

Dwight McCrea, *The Kid Who Loved Christmas,* syndicated, 1990.

Mayor Warren, *Polly: Comin' Home!,* 1990.

Old Deuteronomy, *Cats* (also known as *Andrew Lloyd Webber's "Cats"*), PBS, 1998.

Also appeared as the walrus, *Adventures in Wonderland,* Disney Channel.

Television Appearances; Specials:
Ken Page, *Ain't Misbehavin',* NBC, 1982.

Broadway Plays Washington on Kennedy Center Tonight, 1982.

Reno's Cabaret Reunion, Arts and Entertainment, 1989.

Television Appearances; Episodic:
Good Morning America, ABC, 1977.
Darnell Watkins, "The Big Reunion," *Family Matters,* ABC, 1990.
Mr. Topkins, *Rhythm & Blues,* 1992.
Reverend Kingsley, *The Sinbad Show,* 1993.
Voice, "American Dick," *Duckman* (animated), USA Network, 1994.
Ox, "There but for the Grace of God," *Touched by an Angel,* CBS, 1995.
Chef Andre, "Tickets," *Welcome to New York,* CBS, 2000.
Adair, "Crimes & Witch Demeanors," *Charmed,* The WB, 2004.
"Broadway's Lost Treasures III: The Best of the Tony Awards," *Great Performances,* PBS, 2005.

Stage Appearances:
Old Deuteronomy, *Cats,* Winter Garden Theatre, New York City, 1982.
Ain't Misbehavin', Ambassador Theatre, New York City, 1988–89.
God, *Faust,* La Jolla Playhouse, La Jolla, CA, 1995, then Goodman Theatre, Chicago, IL.
Jupiter, *Out of This World* (concert performance), City Center Theatre, New York City, 1995.
Senator Gallagher, *Call Me Madam* (concert performance), City Center Theatre, 1995.
Cowardly Lion/Zeke, *The Wizard of Oz,* Theatre at Madison Square Garden, New York City, 1997.
Ghost of Christmas past, *A Christmas Carol,* Theatre at Madison Square Garden, 1997.
Johnny Casino and Teen Angel, *Grease,* St. Louis, MO, 1999.
Narrator, "Candide" (concert performance), Festival 2000, Theatre at University of Florida, Gainesville, FL, 2000.
Roscoe, *Follies,* Wadsworth Theatre, Los Angeles, 2002.
Old Max, *How the Grinch Stole Christmas!,* Old Globe Theatre, San Diego, CA, 2003.

Also appeared in *American Songbook: Harold Arlen,* Lincoln Center Theatre, New York City; *Anyone Can Whistle* (concert performance), Theatre at Carnegie Hall, New York City; appeared in *Mr. Wonderful,* London; *Children of Eden,* London; *My One and Only* (concert performance), London; *The Wiz,* Broadway production; *It Ain't Nothing but the Blues;* as Nicely–Nicely Johnson, *Guys and Dolls.*

Major Tours:
Toured in *Ain't Misbehavin',* U.S. cities and Paris.

Stage Director:
Director of *Atom and Eve, Elegies for Angels, The Fantasticks, Nightlife* (revue), *Punks and Raging Queens,* and *To Sir with Love* (musical).

RECORDINGS

Albums:
Ain't Misbehavin' (original cast recording), BMG/RCA, 1978.
Cats (original Broadway cast recording), Uni/Mercury, 1982.
The Nightmare Before Christmas (soundtrack recording), Uni/Disney, 1993.
VA—Celebrate Broadway, Volume 2: *You Gotta Have a Gimmic,* BMC/RCA, 1994.
Out of This World (original cast recording), DRG, 1996.

Video Games:
(English version) Voice of Oogie Boogie, *Kingdom Hearts* (also known as *Kingdom Hearts: Final Mix* and *Kingudamu hatsu*), Square Electronic Arts, 2002.
Oogie Boogie, *The Nightmare Before Christmas: Oogie's Revenge,* Buena Vista Interactive, 2004.
Voice of Oogie Boogie, *Kingdom Hearts: Chain of Memories,* 2004.
(English version) Voice of Oogie Boogie, *Kingdom Hearts II* (also known as *Kingudamu hatsu II*), Square Enix, 2005.
Oogie Boogie, *Kingdom Hearts II: Final Mix+,* Square Enix Company, 2007.

WRITINGS

Stage:
Author of book for the musical *To Sir with Love;* also author of *Nightlife* (revue).

PALICKI, Adrianne 1983–
(Annie Palicki)

PERSONAL

Born May 6, 1983, in Toledo, OH.

Addresses: *Agent*—Jason Shapiro, United Talent Agency, 9560 Wilshire Blvd., Suite 500, Beverly Hills, CA 90212. *Manager*—Laura Cohn, Evolution Entertainment, 901 North Highland Ave., Los Angeles, CA 90038.

Career: Actress.

CREDITS

Television Appearances; Series:
Brianna, *South Beach,* UPN, 2006.
Tyra Collette, *Friday Night Lights,* NBC, 2006–2007.

Television Appearances; Pilots:
Judy Robinson, *The Robinsons: Lost in Space,* The WB, 2004.
Nadia/Siren, *Aquaman,* 2006.
Jessica Moore, *Supernatural,* The WB, 2005.
Tyra Collette, *Friday Night Lights,* NBC, 2006.

Television Appearances; Movies:
Whitney Addison, *Popstar,* 2005.

Television Appearances; Awards Presentations:
The 2007 Teen Choice Awards, Fox, 2007.

Television Appearances; Episodic:
Kara, "Covenant," *Smallville* (also known as *Smallville Beginnings* and *Smallville: Superman the Early Years*), The WB, 2004.
Jessica Geiger, "Love, Lies, and Lullabies," *Quintuplets,* Fox, 2004.
Miranda, "Formalities," *CSI: Crime Scene Investigation* (also known as *C.S.I., CSI: Las Vegas,* and *Les experts*), CBS, 2004.
Lisa Ruddnick, "The Ex–Games," *North Shore,* Fox, 2005.
Lisa Ruddnick, "The End," *North Shore,* Fox, 2005.
Jessica Moore, "Bloody Mary," *Supernatural,* The WB, 2005.
Last Call with Carson Daly, NBC, 2006.
Jessica Moore, "What Is and What Should Never Be," *Supernatural,* CW Network, 2007.
Voices of Princess Leia Organa, Rainbow Brite, and wife, "Moesha Poppins," *Robot Chicken* (animated), Cartoon Network, 2007.

Film Appearances:
(As Annie Palicki) The pretty girl, *Rewrite* (short film), Fly High Films/Golden Spittoon Productions, 2003.
(As Annie Palicki) Rachel, *Getting Rachel Back* (short film), Fly High Films/Golden Spittoon Productions, 2003.
Isabelle, *Seven Mummies,* American World Entertainment, 2006.

PAOLO, Connor 1990–
    (Conor Paolo)

PERSONAL

Born July 11, 1990, in New York, NY; father a writer; mother a musician. *Education:* Attended Lee Strasberg Theatre Institute; trained with Peggy Lewis.

Addresses: *Agent*—Abrams Artists Agency, 9200 Sunset Blvd., Suite 1130, Los Angeles, CA 90069.

Career: Actor. Appeared in commercials. Affiliated with the volunteer organization Kids for Kids.

Awards, Honors: Young Artist Award nomination, best supporting young actor in a feature film, 2007, for *World Trade Center.*

CREDITS

Film Appearances:
Young Sean Devine, *Mystic River,* Warner Bros., 2003.
Young Alexander, *Alexander* (also known as *Alexandre;* also released as *Alexander Revisited: The Final Cut;* censored version released as *Alexander: The Director's Cut*), Warner Bros., 2004.
Steven McLoughlin, *World Trade Center,* Paramount, 2006.
Warren Hardesky, *Snow Angels,* Warner Independent Pictures, 2007.
Ross, *Favorite Son,* Howard Libov Productions, 2007.
Jack, *Camp Hope,* Holedigger Films, 2008.

Television Appearances; Series:
Travis O'Connell, a recurring role, *One Life to Live,* ABC, 2004.
Eric van der Woodsen, *Gossip Girl,* The WB, 2007.

Television Appearances; Pilots:
Eric van der Woodsen, *Gossip Girl,* The WB, 2007.

Television Appearances; Episodic:
Zachary Connor, "Juvenile," *Law & Order: Special Victims Unit* (also known as *Law & Order: SVU* and *Special Victims Unit*), NBC, 2002.
Teddy Winnock, "Web," *Law & Order: Special Victims Unit* (also known as *Law & Order: SVU* and *Special Victims Unit*), NBC, 2006.

Stage Appearances:
Nathan Lukowski, *The Full Monty* (musical), Eugene O'Neill Theatre, New York City, 2003.
Duke of York, *Richard III,* Martinson Hall, Public Theatre, New York City, 2004.

Appeared as Dill in a production of *To Kill a Mockingbird,* Ford's Theatre, Washington, DC; also appeared in productions of *Brundibar* (children's opera) and *Gale Gates,* New York City.

RECORDINGS

Video Games:
(As Conor Paolo) Voice of Tom, *Bully* (also known as *Canis Canem Edit*), Rockstar Games, 2006.

PARKE, Evan 1968–
(Evan Dexter Parke)

PERSONAL

Full name, Evan Dexter O'Neal Parke; born January 2, 1968, in Kingston, Jamaica. *Education:* Cornell University, bachelor's degree in economics; Yale School of Drama, M.F.A., 1997; attended acting workshops at the Negro Ensemble Company and the American Theatre of Harlem; studied film producing at the New York Film Academy. *Avocational Interests:* Marital arts, equestrian, and reading.

Addresses: *Agent*—Agency for the Performing Arts, 405 South Beverly Dr., Beverly Hills, CA 90212. *Manager*—Essential Talent Management, 6565 Sunset Blvd., Suite 415, Los Angeles, CA 90028.

Career: Actor. Heartsong Entertainment Group (a production company), cofounder (with Neko Parham). Worked in corporate America for three years.

CREDITS

Film Appearances:
Voice, *The Amistad Revolt: All We Want Is Make Us Free* (documentary short), 1995.
(As Evan Dexter Parke) Jack, *The Cider House Rules,* Miramax, 1999.
(As Evan Dexter Parke) Malcolm La Mont, *The Replacements,* Warner Bros., 2000.
(As Evan Dexter Parke) Gunnar, *Planet of the Apes,* Twentieth Century–Fox, 2001.
(As Evan Dexter Parke) Lieutenant Mayberry, *Nightstalker,* Smooth Pictures, 2002.
Dexter Clinic guard, *Kiss Kiss Bang Bang,* Warner Bros., 2005.
Second homeless man, *Fellowship* (short), 2005.
Hayes, *King Kong* (also known as *Kong: The Eighth Wonder of the World* and *Peter Jackson's "King Kong"*), Universal, 2005.
"King Kong": Peter Jackson's Production Diaries (documentary), MCA/Universal Home Video, 2005.
Recreating the Eighth Wonder: The Making of "King Kong" (documentary), Universal Studios Home Video, 2006.
Danny, *The Air I Breathe,* ThinkFilm, 2007.
Basham, *All Roads Lead Home,* 2008.

Television Appearances; Series:
Rafe, *All My Children,* ABC, 1997–98.
Judge Blanchard, *As the World Turns,* CBS, 1999.
Charlie Bernard, *Alias,* ABC, 2001–2002.

Detective Raymond Cooper, *Dragnet* (also known as *L.A. Dragnet*), ABC, 2003–2004.

Television Appearances; Movies:
(As Evan Dexter Parke) Junior, *My Brother's Keeper* (also known as *Brother's Keeper*), USA Network, 2002.
(As Evan Dexter Parke) Mumms, *Second String,* TNT, 2002.

Television Appearances; Pilots:
(As Evan Dexter Parke) *All Souls,* UPN, 2001.
Shane, *Jake In Progress,* ABC, 2005.

Television Appearances; Episodic:
(As Evan Dexter Parke) Carl, "Daddy, I Don't Need an Edumacation," *One on One,* UPN, 2003.
Etobi, "Popdukes," *Fastlane,* Fox, 2003.
Shane, "Check Please," *Jake In Progress,* ABC, 2005.
Owen Butler, "In the Rough," *Medium,* NBC, 2005.
Kahn, "Something Wicca This Way Goes," *Charmed,* The WB, 2005.
Albert "Big Al" Grafton, "Manhattan Manhunt," *CSI: NY* (also known as *CSI: New York*), CBS, 2005.
"Five Pillars," *E–Ring,* NBC, 2006.
Michael, "Tapping the Squid," *Huff,* Showtime, 2006.
Gorro, "Country Crossover," *Law & Order: Criminal Intent* (also known as *Law & Order: CI*), NBC, 2006.
Frank Cole, "The Beginning," *Without a Trace* (also known as *W.A.T.*), CBS, 2007.

Stage Appearances:

Appeared as ensemble singer and understudy Scar and Mufasa, *The Lion King.*

RECORDINGS

Video Games:
Voice of Hayes, *"King Kong": The Official Game of the Movie* (also known as *Kong: The 8th Wonder of the World*), Ubi Soft Entertainment, 2005.

PASCAL, Adam 1970–

PERSONAL

Born October 25, 1970, in New York, NY; son of Wendy Seaman; married Cybele Chivian (a playwright), December 19, 1998; children: Lennon Jay, Montgomery

Lovell. *Education:* Attended University of Southern Florida; studied communications at New York Institute of Technology.

Addresses: *Agent*—Innovative Artists, 1505 10th St., Santa Monica, CA 90401. *Manager*—GEF Entertainment, 122 North Clark Dr., Suite 401, Los Angeles, CA 90048.

Career: Actor and producer. Taught "Working in the Theatre" seminars at City University of New York, c. 2000. Previously worked as rock musician, primarily with the band Mute, 1985–94. Also worked as a personal trainer.

Awards, Honors: *Theatre World* Award, outstanding new performer, Obie Award, best actor in a musical, *Village Voice,* Antoinette Perry Award nomination, and Drama Desk Award nomination, lead actor in a musical, 1996, Critics Choice Award nomination (with others), best song, Black Reel Award nomination (with others), best ensemble, 2006, all for *Rent.*

CREDITS

Stage Appearances:
Roger, *Rent,* New York Theatre Workshop, New York City, 1994, then off–Broadway production, then Nederlander Theatre, New York City, 1995–96, then Shaftsbury Theatre, London, 1998–99, the New York City, 2007.

My Favorite Broadway: The Love Songs, City Center, New York City, 2000.

This Is Your Song: Broadway Sings Elton John, New Amsterdam Theatre, New York City, 2000.

Radames, *Aida* (also known as *Elaborate Lives: The Story of Aida*), Chicago, then Palace Theatre, New York City, 2000, 2004.

Radames, *Chess,* New Amsterdam Theatre, 2003.

Emcee, *Cabaret,* Studio 54 Theatre, New York City, 2003–2004.

Claude Bukowski, *Hair!,* New Amsterdam Theatre, 2004.

Stage Work:
Coproducer, *Fully Committed,* Cherry Lane Theatre, New York City, 1999–2001.

Film Appearances:
Eddie, *SLC Punk!,* Sony Pictures Classics, 1999.

Theo, *The School of Rock* (also known as *School of Rock*), Paramount, 2003.

Nicholi, *Temptation,* 2004.

Roger Davis, *Rent,* Sony Pictures Releasing, 2005.

Himself, *No Day But Today: The Story of "Rent"* (documentary), Sony Pictures Home Entertainment, 2006.

Theo, *American Primitive,* 2007.

Bobby, *Goyband,* 2008.

Television Appearances; Specials:
The 50th Annual Tony Awards, CBS, 1996.

"My Favorite Broadway: The Love Songs," *Great Performances,* PBS, 2001.

Broadway's Best, Bravo, 2002.

Television Appearances; Episodic:
The Rosie O'Donnell Show, syndicated, 1996.

Today (also known as *The Today Show* and *NBC News Today*), NBC, 2000, 2005, 2006.

Trackers, Oxygen, 2000.

CNN Showbiz Today, Cable News Network, 2000.

Live with Regis and Kelly, syndicated, 2005.

Ellen: The Ellen DeGeneres Show, syndicated, 2005.

The View, ABC, 2005.

The Tony Danza Show, syndicated, 2005.

Dennis Hofferman, "Willkommen," *Cold Case,* CBS, 2006.

RECORDINGS

Albums:
Rent: Original Broadway Cast Recording, c. 2000.

Civilian, Sh–K–Boom Records, 2004.

OTHER SOURCES

Periodicals:
Interview, June, 1996, p. 105.

PENN, Arthur 1922–

PERSONAL

Full name, Arthur Hiller Penn; born September 27, 1922, in Philadelphia, PA; son of Harry (a watch repairer) and Sonia (a nurse; maiden name, Greenberg) Penn; brother of Irving Penn (a photographer); married Peggy Maurer (a therapist), January 27, 1955; children: Matthew (a director), Molly. *Education:* Attended Black Mountain College, Asheville, NC, 1947–48, and Universities of Perugia and Florence, Italy, 1949–50; studied at Actors Studio; trained for the stage with Michael Chekhov.

Addresses: *Contact*—Bell and Co., 535 Fifth Ave., 21st Floor, New York, NY 10017–3610.

Career: Director, producer, actor, and writer. Worked for a Philadelphia, PA, radio station in the 1940s; Soldiers Show Company, Paris, member of company, 1945; NBC–TV, New York City, worked as a floor manager for *Colgate Comedy Hour,* c. 1952; associated with Berkshire Theatre, Stockbridge, MA, 1966; Actors Studio, New York City, teacher, president, 1994–2000, president emeritus, 2000—. Black Mountain College, Asheville, NC, faculty member, 1947. *Military service:* U.S. Army, Infantry, 1943–45.

Awards, Honors: Grand Prize, Brussels Film Festival, 1958, for *The Left–Handed Gun;* Antoinette Perry Award nomination, best director, 1958, for *Two for the Seesaw;* Emmy Award nomination, best director of a television program of one hour or more, 1958, and Sylvania Award, television directing, 1959, both for "The Miracle Worker," *Playhouse 90;* Sylvania Award, television directing, 1959, for *Man on a Mountain Top;* Drama Critics Circle Award, best musical, 1959, for *Fiorello!;* Antoinette Perry Award, best director of a dramatic play, 1960, for *The Miracle Worker* (stage version); Drama Critics Circle Award, best director of a drama, 1960, *Toys in the Attic;* Antoinette Perry Award nomination, best director of a dramatic play, and Drama Critics Circle Award, both 1961, for *All the Way Home;* OCIC Award of International Catholic Organization for Cinema and Audiovisual, San Sebastian International Film Festival, 1962, Academy Award nomination, best director, 1963, and Directors Guild of America Award nomination, outstanding director of a motion picture, 1963, all for *The Miracle Worker* (film version); nomination for Golden Lion, Venice Film Festival, 1965, for *Mickey One;* Academy Award nomination, best director, Golden Globe Award nomination, best motion picture director, Directors Guild of America Award nomination, outstanding director of a motion picture, Bodil Award, best non–European film, Film Award nomination, best film from any source, British Academy of Film and Television Arts, Golden and Grand Jury Prize, Mar del Plata Film Festival, all 1968, and Kinema Junpo Awards, best foreign language film and best director of a foreign language film, 1969, all for *Bonnie and Clyde;* Academy Award nomination, best director, and Screen Award nomination (with Venable Herndon), best drama written directly for the screen, Writers Guild of America, both 1970, for *Alice's Restaurant;* nominations for Golden Laurel Award, best director, Producers Guild of America, 1970 and 1971; special mention for FIPRESCI Prize, Moscow International Film Festival, 1971, for *Little Big Man;* nomination for Golden Spike, Valladolid International Film Festival, 1996, for *Inside;* Akira Kurosawa Award, San Francisco International Film Festival, 1996; Emmy Award nomination (with others), outstanding drama series, 2001, for *Law & Order;* Career Achievement Award, Los Angeles Film Critics Association, 2002; Joseph L. Mankiewicz Excellence in Filmmaking Award, Director's View Film Festival, 2003; Savannah Film and Video Festival

Award, outstanding achievement in cinema, 2003; honorary Golden Berlin Bear, Berlin International Film Festival, 2007.

CREDITS

Film Director:
The Left–Handed Gun, Warner Bros., 1958.
The Miracle Worker, United Artists, 1962.
(Uncredited) *The Train* (also known as *John Frankenheimer's "The Train,"* *Le train,* and *Il treno*), 1964.
(And producer) *Mickey One,* Columbia, 1965.
The Chase, Columbia, 1966.
Bonnie and Clyde (also known as *Bonnie and Clyde ... Were Killers!*), Warner Bros., 1967.
Alice's Restaurant, United Artists, 1969.
Little Big Man, National General, 1970.
"The Highest," *Visions of Eight* (documentary; also known as *Olympic Visions, Muenchen 1972—8 beruehmte Regisseure sehen die Spiele der XX. Olympiade,* and *Olympiade Muenchen 1972*), 1973.
Night Moves, Warner Bros., 1975.
The Missouri Breaks, United Artists, 1976.
(And coproducer) *Four Friends* (also known as *Georgia's Friends*), Twentieth Century–Fox, 1981.
Target, Warner Bros., 1985.
Dead of Winter, Metro–Goldwyn–Mayer, 1987.
(And producer) *Penn & Teller Get Killed* (also known as *Dead Funny*), Warner Bros., 1989.
Lumiere et compagnie (documentary; also known as *Lumiere y compania* and *Lumiere and Company*), 1995.

Film Appearances:
Naked in New York (documentary), Fine Line, 1994.
Arthur Penn (documentary), 1995.
In the Shadow of Hollywood (documentary); also known as *A l'ombre d'Hollywood*), National Film Board of Canada, 2000.
Small man, *On a Shoestring* (short film), 2004.

Stage Director:
Blue Denim, Westport, CT, 1956.
The Lovers, Broadway production, 1957.
Two for the Seesaw, Haymarket Theatre, London, 1958, then Booth Theatre, New York City, 1958–59.
The Miracle Worker, Playhouse Theatre, New York City, 1959–61.
Toys in the Attic, Hudson Theatre, New York City, 1960–61.
An Evening with Mike Nichols and Elaine May, John Golden Theatre, New York City, 1960–61.
All the Way Home, Belasco Theatre, New York City, 1960–61.
In the Counting House, Biltmore Theatre, New York City, 1962.

My Mother, My Father, and Me, Broadway production, 1962–63.

Lorenzo, Plymouth Theatre, New York City, 1963.

Golden Boy (musical), Majestic Theatre, New York City, 1964–66.

Wait Until Dark, Ethel Barrymore Theatre, Shubert Theatre, George Abbott Theatre, and Music Box Theatre, all New York City, 1966.

Felix, Broadway production, 1972.

Sly Fox, Broadhurst Theatre, New York City, 1976–78.

Golda, Morosco Theatre, New York City, 1977–78.

Monday after the Miracle, Eugene O'Neill Theatre, New York City, 1982.

Hunting Cockroaches, Manhattan Theatre Club Stage I, New York City, 1987.

One of the Guys, New York Shakespeare Festival, Estelle R. Newman Theatre, Public Theatre, New York City, 1990.

Fortune's Fool, Music Box Theatre, New York City, then Truglia Theatre, Stamford Center for the Arts, Stamford, CT, both 2002.

Sly Fox, Ethel Barrymore Theatre, 2004.

Stage Work; Other:

Executive producer, *The Silent Partner,* Actors Studio, New York City, 1972.

Television Work; Series:

Director, *Playhouse 90,* CBS, multiple episodes (including "The Miracle Worker"), 1957–58.

Executive producer, *Law & Order,* NBC, 2000–2001.

Television Director; Movies:

(And producer) *Flesh and Blood,* NBC, 1968.

The Portrait (also known as *Painting Churches*), TNT, 1993.

Inside, 1996.

Television Director; Episodic:

"The Tears of My Sister," *Gulf Playhouse* (also known as *Gulf Playhouse: First Person*), NBC, 1953.

"The Lawn Party," *Goodyear Television Playhouse* (also known as *Goodyear Playhouse*), 1954.

"Adapt or Die," *Philco Television Playhouse* (also known as *Arena Theatre, The Philco–Goodyear Television Playhouse,* and *Repertory Theatre*), NBC, 1954.

"Beg, Borrow, or Steal," *Philco Television Playhouse* (also known as *Arena Theatre, The Philco–Goodyear Television Playhouse,* and *Repertory Theatre*), NBC, 1954.

"The Fix," *100 Centre Street,* Arts and Entertainment, 2001.

Television Appearances; Specials:

Arthur Penn, 1922–: Themes and Variants, 1970.

Hello Actors Studio, 1987.

A Personal Journey with Martin Scorsese through American Movies, 1995.

Rod Serling: Submitted for Your Approval, 1995.

Marlon Brando: The Wild One, AMC, 1996.

"Take Two: Mike Nichols and Elaine May" (also known as "Nichols and May: Take Two"), *American Masters,* PBS, 1996.

The Moviemakers: Arthur Penn, 1996.

Buckminster Fuller: Thinking Out Loud, 1996.

Searching for Arthur, 1998.

Sammy Davis Jr.: The E! True Hollywood Story, E! Entertainment Television, 2001.

(Uncredited) *Reel Radicals: The Sixties Revolution in Film,* AMC, 2002.

AFI's 100 Years … 100 Heroes & Villains (also known as *AFI's 100 Years, 100 Heroes & Villains: America's Greatest Screen Characters*), CBS, 2003.

"Patty Duke," *Biography,* Arts and Entertainment, 2003.

Edge of Outside, TCM, 2006.

Brando, TCM, 2007.

Television Appearances; Episodic:

Inside the Actors Studio, Bravo, 1994, 1999.

American Cinema, 1995.

Ketzwayo, "The Umpatra," *BeastMaster,* 1999.

Ketzwayo, "Circle of Life," *BeastMaster,* 1999.

"Today Is a Good Day: Remembering Chief Dan George," *Life and Times,* 1999.

"Gene Hackman," *Bravo Profiles,* Bravo, 2000.

"Brando," *Imagine,* BBC, 2004.

(In archive footage) *Cinema mil,* 2005.

WRITINGS

Screenplays:

(With William Gibson) *The Miracle Worker* (adapted from Gibson's television special), United Artists, 1962.

(With Venable Herndon) *Alice's Restaurant,* United Artists, 1969, published by Doubleday, 1970.

Television Episodes:

Philco Television Playhouse (also known as *Arena Theatre, The Philco–Goodyear Television Playhouse,* and *Repertory Theatre*), NBC, 1955—.

Plays:

Fiorello! (musical), 1959.

Other:

Contributor to periodicals.

OTHER SOURCES

Books:

Cawelti, John, editor, *Focus on Bonnie and Clyde,* Prentice-Hall, 1973.

Haustrate, Gaston, *Arthur Penn,* 1986.

International Dictionary of Films and Filmmakers, Volume 2: *Directors,* St. James Press, 1996.

Kolker, Robert, *A Cinema of Loneliness: Penn, Stone, Kubrick, Scorsese, Spielberg, Altman,* Oxford University Press, 2000.

Vernaglione, Paolo, *Arthur Penn,* 1988.

Wood, Robin, *Arthur Penn,* Studio Vista, 1967, Praeger, 1969.

Zuker, Joel Stewart, *Arthur Penn: A Guide to References and Resources,* G. K. Hall, 1980.

Periodicals:

American Film, December, 1981.

Los Angeles Times, February 9, 1985.

New York, December 8, 1980.

Playbill, April 30, 2002, pp. 16–17.

Other:

Arthur Penn, 1922–: Themes and Variants (television special), 1970.

Arthur Penn (documentary film), 1995.

The Moviemakers: Arthur Penn (television special), 1996.

Searching for Arthur (television special), 1998.

PETERS, Bernadette 1948–

PERSONAL

Original name, Bernadette Lazzara; born February 28, 1948, in Ozone Park, NY; daughter of Peter (a baker and truck driver) and Marguerite (a homemaker; maiden name, Maltese) Lazzara; married Michael Wittenberg (an investment advisor), July 20, 1996 (died, September 26, 2005). *Education:* Attended Quintana School for Young Professionals, New York City; studied acting with David Le Grant, tap dancing with Oliver McCool III, and singing with Jim Gregory.

Addresses: *Agent*—William Morris Agency, 1325 Avenue of the Americas, New York, NY 10019; One William Morris Pl., Beverly Hills, CA 90212.

Career: Actress, singer, and dancer. Performed in concert in Edmonton, Alberta, Canada, 1961; nightclub entertainer, beginning in the 1970s; appeared in television commercial for Breyer's Ice Cream, 1988.

Member: Actors' Equity Association, American Federation of Television and Radio Artists, Screen Actors Guild.

Awards, Honors: Drama Desk Award, outstanding performance, 1968, for *Dames at Sea; Theatre World* Award, 1968, for *George M!;* Antoinette Perry Award nomination, best supporting actress in a musical play, 1971, for *On the Town;* Antoinette Perry Award nomination, best actress in a Broadway musical, 1974, for *Mack and Mabel;* Emmy Award nomination, outstanding continuing or single performance by a supporting actress in a variety or music program, 1977, for *The Muppet Show;* Golden Globe Award nomination, best motion picture actress in a supporting role, 1977, for *Silent Movie;* Golden Globe Award nomination, best television actress—musical or comedy, 1977, for *All's Fair;* Best of Las Vegas Award, 1980; Golden Globe Award, best film actress in a musical or comedy, 1981, for *Pennies from Heaven;* Antoinette Perry Award nomination, best actress in a musical, 1984, for *Sunday in the Park with George;* Drama League Award, outstanding performance of the season, 1985, Antoinette Perry Award and Drama Desk Award, both best actress in a musical, 1986, all for *Song and Dance;* Distinguished Performance Award, Drama League of New York, 1986; CableACE Award, National Cable Television Association, 1986, for *Sunday in the Park with George;* Hasty Pudding Woman of the Year Award, Hasty Pudding Theatricals, Harvard University, 1987; Drama Desk Award nomination, 1987; Woman of the Year Award, 1993; Antoinette Perry Award nomination, 1993, and Sarah Siddons Award, actress of the year, 1994, both for *The Goodbye Girl;* President's Award, "Mr. Abbott" Awards Dinner, 1995; Theater Hall of Fame, inductee, 1996; Grammy Award nomination, 1996, for *I'll Be Your Baby Tonight;* Grammy Award nomination, 1997, for *Sondheim Etc: Bernadette Peters Live at Carnegie Hall;* Golden Satellite Award nomination, best performance by an actress, International Press Academy, 1998, for *Cinderella;* Outer Critics Circle Award, Drama Desk Award, and Antoinette Perry Award, all outstanding actress in a musical, 1999, for *Annie Get Your Gun;* Emmy Award nomination, outstanding guest actress in a comedy, 2001, for *Ally McBeal;* Daytime Emmy Award nomination, outstanding performer in a children's special, 2003, for *Bobbie's Girl;* Antoinette Perry Award nomination, best actress in a musical, Drama Desk Award, outstanding actress in a musical, 2003, both for *Gypsy;* Star on Hollywood Walk of Fame, Live Theatre; Hollywood Bowl Hall of Fame, inductee.

CREDITS

Stage Appearances:

Tessie, *The Most Happy Fella,* New York City Center Theatre, New York City, 1959.

Alice Burton, *This Is Goggle,* 1962.

Jenny, *Riverwind,* 1966.

Cinderella, *The Penny Friend,* Stage 73 Theatre, New York City, 1966–67.

(Broadway debut) *The Girl in the Freudian Slip,* Booth Theatre, New York City, 1967.

Bettina, *Johnny No–Trump,* Cort Theatre, New York City, 1967.

Alice, *Curley McDimple,* Wheeler Theatre, New York City, 1967–68.

Josie Cohan, *George M!,* Palace Theatre, New York City, 1968.

Ruby, *Dames at Sea,* Bowerie Lane Theatre, New York City, 1968–69.

Gelsomina, *La Strada,* Lunt–Fontanne Theatre, New York City, 1969.

Consuelo, *Nevertheless They Laugh,* Lambs Club Theatre, New York City, 1971.

Hildy, *On the Town,* Imperial Theatre, New York City, 1971–72.

Dorine, *Tartuffe,* Philadelphia Drama Guild Theatre, Philadelphia, PA, 1972–73.

Mabel Normand, *Mack and Mabel,* Majestic Theatre, New York City, 1974.

Sally, *Sally and Marsha,* Manhattan Theatre Club Downstage, New York City, 1982.

Dot, *Sunday in the Park with George,* Playwrights Horizons Theatre, New York City, 1983, then Booth Theatre, 1984–85.

Emma, *Song and Dance,* Royale Theatre, New York City, 1985–86.

Witch, *Into the Woods,* Martin Beck Theatre, New York City, 1987–89.

The Goodbye Girl, 1993.

Annie Oakley (title role), *Annie Get Your Gun,* Marquis Theatre, New York City, 1999.

Broadway Bears III, Hudson Theatre at Millennium Broadway, New York City, 2000.

Bernadette Peters, Bass Performance Hall, Fort Worth, TX, 2001.

Mama Rose, *Gypsy,* Shubert Theatre, New York City, 2003.

Major Tours:

Gypsy, U.S. cities, 1961–62.

Carolotta Monti, *W. C.,* U.S. cities, 1971.

Film Appearances:

Allison, *Ace Eli and Rodger of the Skies,* Twentieth Century–Fox, 1973.

Warden's secretary, *The Longest Yard* (also known as *The Mean Machine*), Paramount, 1974.

Vilma Kaplan, *Silent Movie,* Twentieth Century–Fox, 1976.

Little Dee, *Vigilante Force,* United Artists, 1976.

Melody, *W. C. Fields and Me,* Universal, 1976.

Marie Kimble Johnson, *The Jerk,* Universal, 1979.

Aqua, *Heartbeeps,* Universal, 1981.

Eileen, *Pennies from Heaven,* Metro–Goldwyn–Mayer, 1981.

Rutanya Wallace, *Tulips,* Avco Embassy, 1981.

Lily St. Regis, *Annie,* Columbia, 1982.

Eleanor, *Slaves of New York,* Tri–Star, 1989.

Lou Ann McGuinn, *Pink Cadillac,* Warner Brothers, 1989.

Muse, *Alice,* Orion, 1990.

Marie D'Agoult, *Impromptu,* Hemdale, 1991.

Peter Allen: The Boy from Oz, 1995.

Voice of Angelique, *Beauty and the Beast: The Enchanted Christmas* (animated; also known as *Beauty and the Beast 2*), 1997.

Voice of Sophie, *Anastasia* (animated), 1997.

Herself and voice of Sophie, *The Magical Journey of "Anastasia"* (documentary short), Twentieth Century Fox Home Entertainment, 1997.

Voice of Rita, *Wakko's Wish* (animated; also known as *Steven Spielberg Presents "Animaniacs: Wakko's Wish"*), 1999.

Elise Ellis, *Snow Days* (also known as *Let It Snow*), 1999.

(Uncredited) Herself, *The Making and Meaning of "We Are Family"* (documentary; also known as *We Are Family*), 2002.

Voice of Sue, *The Land Before Time X: The Great Longneck Migration* (animated), Universal, 2003.

Rebecca Gromberg, *It Runs in the Family* (also known as *Family Business*), Metro–Goldwyn–Mayer, 2003.

Herself, *The Making of "Anastasia"* (documentary), Twentieth Century Fox Home Entertainment, 2006.

Come le formiche (also known as *Wine and Kisses*), 2007.

Broadway: Beyond the Golden Age (documentary; also known as *B.G.A 2* and *Broadway: Beyond the Golden Age 2*), 2008.

Television Appearances; Series:

Charlotte (Charley) Drake, *All's Fair,* CBS, 1976–77.

Skit characters, *The Carol Burnett Show,* CBS, 1991.

Voice of Rita, *Animaniacs* (animated; also known as *Steven Spielberg Presents "Animaniacs"*), 1993.

Television Appearances; Miniseries:

Genevieve Selsor, *The Martian Chronicles,* 1980.

Circe, *The Odyssey* (also known as *Die Abenteuer des Odysseus, Homer's "Odyssey,"* and *Odysseia*), 1997.

Television Appearances; Movies:

Trudy Engles, *The Islander,* 1978.

Lily St. Regis, *Lights, Camera, Annie!,* 1982.

Rothenberg, *David,* ABC, 1988.

Jane Murray, *The Last Best Year of My Life,* ABC, 1990.

Tammy Faye Bakker, "Fall from Grace," *Sunday Night at the Movies,* NBC, 1990.

Cinderella's stepmother, *Cinderella* (also known as *Rodgers & Hammerstein "Cinderella"*), ABC, 1997.

Helen Ayers, *What the Deaf Man Heard,* NBC, 1997.

Faith Shawn, *Holiday in Your Heart,* ABC, 1997.

Margo/"Titania," *Prince Charming,* TNT, 2001.

Bailey Lewis, *Bobbie's Girl,* Showtime, 2002.

Television Appearances; Pilots:
Sarah Leaf, *Adopted*, ABC, 2005.

Television Appearances; Specials:
Josie Cohan, *George M!* (adaptation of the Broadway musical), NBC, 1970.
Bing Crosby—Cooling It, NBC, 1970.
Lady Larken, *Once Upon a Mattress*, CBS, 1972.
Burt and the Girls, NBC, 1973.
Bing Crosby—Cooling It, CBS, 1973.
Libby, *Paradise Lost*, 1974.
Cohost and presenter, *The 29th Annual Tony Awards*, ABC, 1975.
Josie Cohan, *George M!*, CBS, 1976.
Bing Crosby's White Christmas, CBS, 1976.
Performer, *The 48th Annual Academy Awards*, ABC, 1976.
Ringmaster, *Circus of the Stars*, CBS, 1977.
Bob Hope's All-Star Comedy Tribute to Vaudeville, NBC, 1977.
Uncle Tim Wants You, CBS, 1977.
The Beatles Forever, NBC, 1977.
They Said It With Music: Yankee Doodle to Ragtime, 1977.
Mac Davis' Christmas Odyssey: 2010, NBC, 1978.
The Magic of David Copperfield, 1978.
Perry Como's Springtime Special, ABC, 1979.
Ringmaster, *Circus of the Stars #3*, CBS, 1979.
Musical Comedy Tonight, PBS, 1979.
Sally, *Bob Hope Special: Bob Hope in the Star Makers*, NBC, 1980.
Presenter, *The 53rd Annual Academy Awards*, ABC, 1981.
Baryshnikov in Hollywood, CBS, 1982.
Bob Hope's "All-Star Birthday at Annapolis" (also known as *All-Star Birthday Party at Annapolis* and *Bob Hope Special: Bob Hope's All-Star Birthday in Annapolis*), NBC, 1982.
Texaco Star Theatre: Opening Night, NBC, 1982.
George Burns and Other Sex Symbols, NBC, 1982.
Bob Hope Special: Bob Hope's Pink Panther Thanksgiving Gala, NBC, 1982.
Women I Love: Beautiful But Funny (also known as *Bob Hope's "Women I Love: Beautiful But Funny"*), 1982.
George Burns Celebrates Eighty Years in Show Business, NBC, 1983.
Presenter and performer, *The 38th Annual Tony Awards*, CBS, 1984.
Bob Hope's Happy Birthday Homecoming, NBC, 1985.
The Night of 100 Stars II, ABC, 1985.
Dot and Marie, *Sunday in the Park with George*, Showtime, 1986.
Presenter and performer, *The 40th Annual Tony Awards*, CBS, 1986.
Presenter and performer, *The 41st Annual Tony Awards*, CBS, 1987.
Performer and presenter, *The 59th Annual Academy Awards Presentation*, ABC, 1987.

Happy 100th Birthday Hollywood (also known as *Happy Birthday, Hollywood*), ABC, 1987.
The Music Makers: An ASCAP Celebration of American Music at Wolf Trap, PBS, 1987.
A Star-Spangled Celebration, ABC, 1987.
Evening at Pops, PBS, 1987.
Ruby Lee Carter, *Diana Ross … Red Hot Rhythm and Blues*, ABC, 1987.
A Musical Toast: The Stars Shine on Public Television, 1987.
Presenter and performer, *The 42nd Annual Tony Awards*, CBS, 1988.
The 42nd Annual Tony Awards, CBS, 1988.
The Kennedy Center Honors: A Celebration of the Performing Arts, CBS, 1989.
A Broadway Christmas, Showtime, 1990.
Presenter, *The 44th Annual Tony Awards*, CBS, 1990.
The 33rd Annual Grammy Awards, CBS, 1991.
The Creative Spirit, 1992.
Performer, *The 47th Annual Tony Awards*, CBS, 1993.
The Kennedy Center Honors: A Celebration of the Performing Arts, 1993.
Performer, *The 66th Annual Academy Awards*, ABC, 1994.
Presenter, *The 48th Annual Tony Awards*, CBS, 1994.
Narrator, *Going, Going, Almost Gone!: Animals in Danger*, 1994.
Some Enchanted Evening: Celebrating Oscar Hammerstein II (also known as *Celebrating Oscar Hammerstein II*), PBS, 1995.
Salute to Steven Spielberg (also known as *The 23rd American Film Institute Life Achievement Award: A Salute to Steven Spielberg*), NBC, 1995.
A Tribute to Stephen Sondheim, 1995.
Presenter and performer, *The 50th Annual Tony Awards*, CBS, 1996.
The 53rd Presidential Inaugural Gala: An American Journey, 1997.
Presenter, *The 51st Annual Tony Awards*, CBS, 1997.
Bernadette Peters in Concert, PBS, 1998.
Hey Mr. Producer (also known as *Hey Mr. Producer!: The Musical World of Cameron Mackintosh*), PBS, 1998.
Quincy Jones—The First 50 Years, 1998.
Host, *Disney's Young Musicians Symphony Orchestra*, 1998.
Performer, *The 53rd Annual Tony Awards*, CBS, 1999.
Irving Berlin: An American Song, 1999.
"Saturday Night Live": 25th Anniversary Primetime Special, NBC, 1999.
AFI … 100 Years, 100 Laughs: America's Funniest Movies, CBS, 2000.
Presenter, *The 54th Annual Tony Awards*, CBS and PBS, 2000.
Presenter, *The 55th Annual Tony Awards*, CBS and PBS, 2001.
Richard Rodgers: The Sweetest Sounds, PBS, 2001.
Presenter, *The 2001 Creative Arts Emmy Awards*, E! Entertainment Television, 2001.

Host and performer, *The 56th Annual Tony Awards,* CBS, 2002.

Performer, *The 57th Annual Tony Awards,* CBS, 2003.

The 26th Annul Kennedy Center Honors: A Celebration of the Performing Arts, CBS, 2003.

Presenter, *The 58th Annual Tony Awards* (also known as *The 2004 Tony Awards*), CBS, 2004.

Performer and presenter, *The 59th Annual Tony Awards,* CBS, 2005.

Presenter, *The 61st Annual Tony Awards,* CBS, 2007.

Television Appearances; Episodic:

House Party, 1952.

Horn & Hardart Children's Hour, 1953.

Girl, "The Christmas Tree," *Hallmark Hall of Fame* (also known as *Hallmark Television Playhouse*), 1958.

"We Interrupt This Season," *NBC Experiment in Television,* NBC, 1967.

Carol Burnett Show, CBS, 1969, 1974.

The Mike Douglas Show, 1970.

The Tonight Show Starring Johnny Carson, NBC, 1970, 1971, 1978.

"Lost Paradise," *Theatre in America,* PBS, 1971.

Toast of the Town (also known as *The Ed Sullivan Show*), 1971.

Kathy Griffith, "The Split: Rumpus in the Rumpus Room," *Maude,* 1972.

The Carol Burnett Show (also known as *Carol Burnett and Friends*), 1972, 1975, 1977.

"Love and the Hoodwinked Honey," *Love, American Style,* ABC, 1973.

The Merv Griffin Show, 1974.

Linda Galloway, "Gloria Suspects Mike," *All in the Family,* CBS, 1975.

Showoffs, 1975.

You Don't Say, 1975.

"In Again, Out Again," *McCoy,* NBC, 1976.

Bebe Murchison, "The Day New York Turned Blue," *McCloud,* NBC, 1976.

Dinah! (also known as *Dinah and Friends*), 1976.

(Uncredited) *Saturday Night Live* (also known as *SNL*), NBC, 1976.

Herself and various characters, *The Sonny and Cher Show,* 1976.

Herself, *The Muppet Show,* 1977.

Host, *Saturday Night Live* (also known as *SNL*), NBC, 1981.

Sleeping Beauty and Princess Debbie, "Sleeping Beauty," *Faerie Tale Theater* (also known as *Shelley Duvall's "Faerie Tale Theater"*), Showtime, 1983.

"Trevor Farrell," *An American Portrait,* CBS, 1984.

Kate, "The Jingle Belles," *Carol & Company,* 1990.

Witch, "Into the Woods," *American Playhouse,* PBS, 1991.

The Howard Stern Show, 1991.

The soprano, "The Last Mile," *Great Performances,* PBS, 1992.

"Sondheim: A Celebration at Carnegie Hall," *Great Performances,* PBS, 1993.

Herself, "Montana," *The Larry Sanders Show,* HBO, 1994.

Remember WENN, 1996.

The Rosie O'Donnell Show, syndicated, 1997, 1999, 2002.

Victoria Sherwood, "Baby, It's Cold Outside," *The Closer,* CBS, 1998.

Hollywood Squares (also known as *H2* and *H2: Hollywood Squares*), 1998.

The Martin Short Show, 1999.

Voice of Fifi, "Fifi," *Teacher's Pet* (animated), ABC, 2000.

Inside the Actors Studio, Bravo, 2000.

Rachel, "Sliding Frasiers," *Frasier,* NBC, 2001.

Cassandra Lewis, "The Getaway," *Ally McBeal,* Fox, 2001.

Cassandra Lewis, "The Obstacle Course," *Ally McBeal,* Fox, 2001.

"30th Anniversary: A Celebration in Song," *Great Performances,* PBS, 2003.

The View, ABC, 2003.

Herself, "Rose," *Character Studies,* PBS, 2005.

The Early Show, CBS, 2005.

"Every Dog Had His Day," *The Apprentice: Martha Stewart,* NBC, 2005.

Live with Regis and Kelly, syndicated, 2005, 2007.

Gin, "Whatever Happened to Baby Gin?," *Will & Grace,* NBC, 2006.

Stella Danquiss, "Choreographed," *Law & Order: Special Victims Unit* (also known as *Law & Order: SVU* and *Special Victims Unit*), NBC, 2006.

This Week, BBC, 2006.

Judge Mariana Folger, "Guantanomo by the Bay," *Boston Legal,* ABC, 2007.

Also appeared in *Juvenile Jury; Name That Tune; They Said It with Music; Lonely Man; House of Numbers; Ten Seconds to Hell; Warriors Five;* as host, *Rich, Thin, and Beautiful.*

Television Appearances; Pilots:

Doris, *The Owl and the Pussycat,* NBC, 1975.

Marie Trudy Engels, *The Islander,* CBS, 1978.

Television Appearances; Miniseries:

Genevieve Seltzer, *The Martian Chronicles,* NBC, 1980.

Circe, *The Odyssey* (also known as *Die Abenteuer ver des Odysseus, Homer Odyssey,* and *Odissea*), NBC, 1997.

RECORDINGS

Albums:

Bernadette Peters, MCA, 1980.

Now Playing, MCA, 1981.

Sondheim: Sunday in the Park with George, RCA, 1985.

A Collector's Sondheim, 1985.
Bernadette Peters in "Song and Dance": The Songs, 1986.
I'll Be Your Baby Tonight, Angel, 1996.
Sondheim Etc., Angel, 1997.
Bernadette Peters Loves Rodgers and Hammerstein, Angel, 2002.

OTHER SOURCES

Books:
Contemporary Musicians, Vol. 27, Gale Group, 2000.

Periodicals:
Opera News, August, 2002, p. 60.
Parade Magazine, April 14, 2002, p. 22.
People Weekly, March 29, 1982, p. 70.
Playbill, May 31, 2003, pp. 4, 12.

PHILLIPS, Chynna 1968–

PERSONAL

Full name, Gilliam Chynna Phillips; born February 12, 1968, in Los Angeles, CA; daughter of John (a singer and recording artist) and Michelle (a singer and recording artist) Phillips; half–sister of Bijou Phillips (am actress, singer, and model) and Mackenzie Phillips (an actress); married William "Billy" Baldwin (an actor), September 9, 1995; children: Jamison (daughter), Vance Alexander, Brooke Michelle.

Addresses: *Agent*—(voice work), Special Artists Agency, 9465 Wilshire Blvd., Suite 890, Beverly Hills, CA 90212.

Career: Actress, singer, and songwriter. Wilson Phillips (music group), singer, songwriter, and recording artist, 1990–93, 2004.

Awards, Honors: Awards with Wilson Phillips include Grammy Award nomination, album of the year, National Academy of Recordings Arts and Sciences, 1990, for *Wilson Phillips;* Grammy Award nomination, song of the year, and American Music Award nomination, favorite pop–rock single, and *Billboard* Music Award, hot 100 single of the year, all 1990, for "Hold On;" Grammy Award nominations, best new artist and best pop duo or group, both 1990; American Music Award nomination, favorite new pop–rock artist, 1990; Grammy Award nomination, best pop vocal performance by a duo or group, 1991, for "You're in Love."

CREDITS

Television Appearances; Movies:
Megan Lawrence, *Moving Target,* NBC, 1988.
Alma, *Goodbye, Miss 4th of July* (also known as *Farewell, Miss Freedom*), Disney Channel, 1988.
Jessica, *The Comeback,* CBS, 1989.
Mona Voight, *Traveling Man,* HBO, 1989.
Roxanne Pulitzer (title role), *Roxanne: The Prize Pulitzer* (also known as *The Prize Pulitzer*), NBC, 1989.
Kim MacAfee, *Bye Bye Birdie,* ABC, 1995.

Television Appearances; Episodic:
Howard Stern, E! Entertainment Television, 1995, 2004.
"Carnie Wilson," *Revealed with Jules Asner,* E! Entertainment Television, 2002.
"The 80s III," *VH–1 Where Are They Now?,* VH1, 2002.
Live with Regis and Kelly, syndicated, 2004.
Primetime Live (also known as *ABC Primetime* and *Primetime*), ABC, 2004.
Celebrity Blackjack, Game Show Network, 2004.
The Tony Danza Show, syndicated, 2004.
Voice of Kitty, "13," *Danny Phantom* (animated), Nickelodeon, 2004.
Voice of Kitty, "Lucky in Love," *Danny Phantom* (animated), Nickelodeon, 2005.
Voice of Kitty, "Girl's Night Out," *Danny Phantom* (animated), Nickelodeon, 2007.

Television Appearances; Specials:
Lifetime Salutes Mom, Lifetime, 1987.
Videosyncrasy: The Generations Special, The Family Channel, 1991.
Back to School '92, CBS, 1992.
Lifetime Applauds: The Fight Against Breast Cancer, Lifetime, 1995.
Intimate Portrait: Mackenzie Phillips, Lifetime, 2000.
"Carnie Wilson," *Biography,* Arts and Entertainment, 2001.
An All–Star tribute to Brian Wilson, TNT, 2001.
Intimate Portrait: Michelle Phillips, Lifetime, 2002.
Women Rock!, Lifetime, 2004.
I Love the '90s, VH1, 2004.
Livin' It: Unusual Suspects, 2005.

Television Appearances; Awards Presentations:
The 1990 MTV Video Music Awards, MTV and syndicated, 1990.
The 1990 Billboard Music Awards, Fox, 1990.
The American Music Awards, ABC, 1991.
The 33rd Annual Grammy Awards, CBS, 1991.
MTV Video Music Awards 1992 (also known as *The 1992 MTV Video Music Awards*), MTV, 1992.
Presenter, *The 1992 Billboard Music Awards,* Fox, 1992.
The 1995 Billboard Music Awards, Fox, 1995.

Television Appearances; Miniseries:

(With Wilson Phillips) *I Love the '90s: Part Deux,* VH1, 2005.

Film Appearances:

Little Boy Blue, 1975.
Mia, *Some Kind of Wonderful,* Paramount, 1987.
Cindy Moore, *The Invisible Kid,* Taurus Films, 1988.
Mary Frances "Miffy" Young, *Caddyshack II,* Warner Bros., 1988.
Mimi, *Say Anything ...,* Twentieth Century–Fox, 1989.

Film Work; Song Performer:

"I Live for You," *Striptease,* Columbia, 1996.
"Dance, Dance, Dance," *The Princess Diaries 2: Royal Engagement,* Buena Vista, 2004.

RECORDINGS

Albums with Wilson Phillips:

Wilson Phillips, SBK Records, 1990.
Shadows and Light, SBK Records, 1992.
The Best of Wilson Phillips, Excelsior, 1998.
Greatest Hits, SBK Records, 2000.
Pacific Coast Highway, 2004.
California, Columbia, 2004.
The Best of Wilson Phillips, Capitol, 2005.

Also recorded the singles, "Hold On," Capitol, 1990; "Impulsive," Capitol, 1990; "You're in Love," Capitol, 1991; "Otro Amor," Capitol, 1991; "The Dream Is Still," CBK Records, 1992; "You Won't See My Cry," SBK Records, 1992; "Give It Up," SBK Records, 1992; "Flesh & Blood," SBK Records, 1993; and "Go Your Own Way"/"Already Gone," Columbia, 2004.

Solo Albums:

Naked and Sacred, EMI, 1995.

Videos:

Wilson Phillips: The Videos, 1990.
Shadows and Light: From a Different View, 1992.

Appeared in the Wilson Phillips music videos "Wilson Phillips," Capitol, 1991; "Shadows & Light," Capitol, 1992; and "The Making of Shadows and Light," 1992; also appeared in the music video "Into the Great Wide Open" by Tom Petty and the Heartbreakers.

WRITINGS

Songs Featured in Films:

"I Live for You," *Striptease,* Columbia, 1996.

"Hold On," *Harold & Kumar Go to White Castle* (also known as *Harold & Kumar Get the Munchies* and *Harold et Kumar chassent le burger*), New Line Cinema, 2004.

OTHER SOURCES

Periodicals:

Billboard, September 30, 1995, p. 18.
People Weekly, May 31, 2004; October 15, 2007, p. 128.

PINNEY, Clay
(Clayton Pinney, Clayton W. Pinney)

PERSONAL

Addresses: *Contact*—Clay Pinney Special Effects, 3540 Hayden Ave., Culver City, CA.

Career: Special effects supervisor, special effects coordinator, and special effects foreman.

Awards, Honors: Academy Award nomination, best effects—visual effects, and Film Award nomination (with others), best visual effects, British Academy of Film and Television Arts, 1992, both for *Backdraft;* Universe Reader's Choice Award (with others), best special effects in a genre motion picture, *Sci–Fi Universe Magazine,* 1996, Academy Award (with others), best effects—visual effects, Saturn Award (with others), best special effects, Academy of Science Fiction, Fantasy and Horror Films, Film Award nomination (with others), best achievement in special visual effects, British Academy of Film and Television Arts, 1997, all for *Independence Day;* Saturn Award (with others), best special effects, 1999, for *Godzilla.*

CREDITS

Film Special Effects:

The Man with Two Brains, Warner Bros., 1983.
D.C. Cab (also known as *Mr. T and Company* and *Street Fleet*), 1983.
Fear City, 1984.
(As Clayton Pinney) *Fright Night,* Columbia, 1985.
Brewster's Millions, Universal, 1985.
Star Trek IV: The Voyage Home (also known as *The Voyage Home: Star Trek IV*), Paramount, 1986.
The Witches of Eastwick, Warner Bros., 1987.
Moon Over Parador, 1988.
Moving, 1988.

Fatal Instinct, 1993.
Blown Away, Metro–Goldwyn–Mayer, 1994.
Theodore Rex, 1995.
Soldier, Warner Bros., 1998.
Meet the Fockers, Universal, 2004.
The Standard v. 15 (short), Oracle Films, 2004.
Flightplan, Buena Vista, 2005.

Film Special Effects Foreman:

Poltergeist II: The Other Side, 1986.
(As Clayton Pinney) *Who Framed Roger Rabbit,* 1988.
Avalon, 1990.
Backdraft, Universal, 1991.

Film Special Effects Coordinator:

She's Out of Control, Columbia, 1989.
(As Clayton Pinney) *Cold Dog Soup,* Anchor Bay Entertainment, Inc., 1990.
(As Clayton Pinney) *Toys,* Twentieth Century–Fox, 1992.
Blown Away, Metro–Goldwyn–Mayer, 1994.
The Specialist (also known as *El Especialista*), Warner Bros., 1994.
Volcano, Twentieth Century–Fox, 1997.
Imposter, Miramax, 2001.

Film Special Effects Supervisor:

Bugsy, TriStar, 1991.
The American President, Universal, 1995.
Blue Streak (also known as *Der Diamanten–Cop*), Columbia/Sony Pictures Entertainment, 1999.
The Cell, New Line Cinema, 2000.
Lost Souls, New Line Cinema, 2000.
Anger Management, Columbia, 2003.
(U.S.) *The Matrix Reloaded,* Warner Bros., 2003.
Peter Pan, Universal, 2003.
Meet the Fockers, Universal, 2004.
Charlotte's Web (also known as *Schweinchen Wilbur und seine freunde*), Paramount, 2006.
My Super Ex–Girlfriend, Twentieth Century–Fox, 2006.
Next, Paramount, 2007.
Rush Hour 3, New Line Cinema, 2007.

Film Work; Other:

Film special mechanical effects, *My Science Project,* 1985.
Film special prop construction, *Lorenzo's Oil,* 1992.
(As Clayton W. Pinney) Film special effects crew member, *Fire Birds,* 1990.
Mechanical effects supervisor, *Independence Day* (also known as *ID4*), Twentieth Century–Fox, 1996.
Mechanical effects coordinator, *Volcano,* Twentieth Century–Fox, 1997.
Mechanical effects supervisor, *Godzilla,* TriStar, 1998.
(As Clayton Pinney) Special effects consultant: additional photography, *Flightplan,* Buena Vista, 2005.

Film Appearances:

Himself, *Crash Course* (documentary short; also known as *The Freeway Chase* and *The Matrix Reloaded: The Freeway Chase*), Warner Home Video, 2003.
Himself, *The Burly Man Chronicles* (documentary), Warner Home Video, 2004.

PORYES, Michael

PERSONAL

Addresses: *Agent*—Paradigm, 360 North Crescent Dr., North Bldg., Beverly Hills, CA 90210.

Career: Writer and producer. Previously worked as a waiter.

Awards, Honors: Humanitas Prize nomination (with others), thirty–minute category, 1992, for *Roseanne;* Emmy Award nomination (with others), outstanding children's program, 2007, for *Hannah Montana.*

CREDITS

Television Work; Series:

Story editor, *Good Morning, Miss Bliss* (also known as *Saved by the Bell: The Junior High Years*), Disney Channel, 1987.
Creator and producer, *Relatively Speaking,* syndicated, 1988.
Story editor and story consultant, *Saved by the Bell,* NBC, 1989.
Coproducer, *Joe's Life,* ABC, 1993.
Produce and coproducer, *Me and the Boys,* ABC, 1994.
Producer, *Maybe This Time,* ABC, 1995.
Executive producer, *Veronica's Closet,* NBC, 1997.
Supervising producer, *Cybill,* CBS, 1997.
Co–executive producer, *Cybill,* CBS, 1997–98.
Consulting producer and co–executive producer, *Veronica's Closet,* NBC, 1998–99.
Consulting producer, *The Hughleys,* UPN, 2000–2001.
Creator and executive producer, *That's So Raven* (also known as *That's So Raven!*), Disney Channel, 2002–2006.
Creator and consultant, *That's So Raven* (also known as *That's So Raven!*), Disney Channel, 2003–2005.
Executive producer and creator, *Hannah Montana,* Disney Channel, 2005–2007.

WRITINGS

Television Episodes:

Alice, CBS, 1976.
The Facts of Life, NBC, 1979.
The Fall Guy, ABC, 1981.

Small Wonder, syndicated, 1985.

"Keeping Up with Marci," *Who's the Boss?,* ABC, 1985.

"Educating Tony," *Who's the Boss?,* ABC, 1986.

Good Morning, Miss Bliss (also known as *Saved by the Bell: The Junior High Years*), Disney Channel, 1987.

Saved by the Bell, NBC, 1989.

"Driver's Education," *Saved by the Bell,* NBC, 1990.

Dear John, NBC, 1991–92.

(Story only) "This Old House," *Roseanne,* ABC, 1993.

Joe's Life, ABC, 1993.

Me and the Boys, ABC, 1994.

The Blue Brothers Animated Series, UPN, 1997.

"From Boca, with Love," *Cybill,* CBS, 1997.

"Mother's Day," *Cybill,* CBS, 1997.

(Story only) "Where's a Harpoon When You Need One?," *Cybill,* CBS, 1997.

Chicago Sons, NBC, 1997.

Veronica's Closet, NBC, 1998–99.

That's So Raven (also known as *That's So Raven!*), Disney Channel, 2002–2003.

"Grandmas Don't Let Your Babies Grow up to Play Favorites," *Hannah Montana,* Disney Channel, 2006.

"Oops! I Meddled Again," *Hannah Montana,* Disney Channel, 2006.

PRINCESS
    See OXENBERG, Catherine

PROCTOR, Phil 1940–
    (Vinnie Gumba, Philip Proctor, Phillip Proctor, Firesign Theatre)

PERSONAL

Born July 28, 1940, in Goshen, IN; raised in New York, NY; married Barbro Semmingsen (a television producer; marriage ended); married another time (marriage ended); married Melinda Peterson (an actress); some sources cite other marriages; children: Kristin (an actress). *Education:* Yale University, graduated, 1962.

Addresses: *Agent*—Cunningham, Escott & Dipene, 10635 Santa Monica Blvd., Suite 130, Los Angeles, CA 90025.

Career: Actor, voice performer, comedian, and writer. Firesign Theatre (comedy troupe), member of company, beginning in the 1960s. Antaeus Theatre Company, North Hollywood, CA, performer and director. Pyro Playhouse and More Sugar, founder. Also involved in the production of advertisements and industrial films. Host of awards presentations. Also known as Phillip Proctor.

Member: Actors' Equity Association.

Awards, Honors: *Theatre World* Award, 1964, for *The Amorous Flea;* Grammy Award nomination (with the Firesign Theatre), best comedy album, National Academy of Recording Arts and Sciences, c. 1985, for *Three Faces of Al;* Grammy Award nomination (with the Firesign Theatre), best comedy album, 1999, for *Give Me Immortality or Give Me Death; LA Weekly* Award (with others), c. 2001, for *The Man Who Had All the Luck;* Grammy Award nomination (with the Firesign Theatre), best comedy album, c. 2002, for *The Bride of Firesign;* Gold World Medal (with the Firesign Theatre), best regularly scheduled comedy program, New York International Radio Festival, New York Festivals, 2002, for *XM Comedy/Firesign Theatre Presents: Fools in Space;* named best actor by the *Los Angeles Free Press;* 33rd Annual Minicon Science Fiction Convention, named the guest of honor; with the Firesign Theatre, honored guest at other events.

CREDITS

Film Appearances:

Turret gunner, *The Thousand Plane Raid,* United Artists, 1969.

Fred, *A Safe Place,* Columbia, 1971.

(As the Firesign Theatre) *Martian Space Party* (also known as *The Firesign Theatre's "Martian Space Party"* and *The Martian Space Party*), Asso Film, 1972.

Limb Ashauler, Martian voices, Sam Evans, Beaulah Bell, Nino the mindboggler, Bunny Crumbhunger, General Curtis Goatheart, and colonel, *Everything You Know Is Wrong* (also known as *Firesign Theatre Sez "Everything You Know Is Wrong"*), 1975.

Sonic Boom (short film), 1975.

Christian A. Broder, *Tunnel Vision* (also known as *Tunnelvision*), New Line Cinema, 1976.

Walter Concrete, *Cracking Up,* American International Pictures, 1977.

J–man Barton, *J–Men Forever,* International Harmony, 1979.

Prosecutor's voice, *Human Experiments* (also known as *Beyond the Gate*), 1980.

Voice, *Below the Belt,* Atlantic Releasing, 1980.

Voices of Rocky Rococo, Ma Yolk, and Dr. Dogg, *Nick Danger in the Case of the Missing Yolk,* LodesTone Media/More Sugar, 1983.

Art Fisher, *Sam's Son,* Invictus Entertainment, 1984.

Television voice, *Stoogemania* (also known as *Party Stooge*), Atlantic Releasing, 1985.

Mike, "Silly Pate," *Amazon Women on the Moon* (also known as *Cheeseburger Film Sandwich*), Universal, 1987.

Newscaster, *Hostile Witness*, 1988.

Hypnotist, *Desired Effect*, 1989.

Police chief, *Robo–Chic* (also known as *Cyber–Chic* and *Robo–C.H.I.C.*), Action International Pictures, 1989.

Randolph Whitlock, *Night Life* (also known as *Campus Spirits* and *Grave Misdemeanours*), RCA/Columbia, 1989.

Lou, *Lobster Man from Mars*, 1989, Electric Pictures, 1990.

Voice of French mouse, *The Rescuers Down Under* (animated), Buena Vista, 1990.

Voices of king and prince, *Petronella* (animated short film), Filmfair Communications, 1990.

Original Spin, 1993.

Voices, *The Visitors*, c. 1994.

Dubbed voices for Pavel and Mr. Marshal for English version, *Un indien dans la ville* (also known as *An Indian in Paris*, *An Indian in the City*, and *Little Indian, Big City*), Buena Vista, 1996, originally released by Canal+, 1994.

Axl, *Bio–Dome*, Metro–Goldwyn–Mayer, 1996.

Voices of guards and citizens of Paris, *The Hunchback of Notre Dame* (animated), Buena Vista, 1996.

Voices, *Fair Game*, 1996.

Voices, *Space Jam* (live action and animated), Warner Bros., 1996.

Voice of Howard "Howie" DeVille, *A Rugrats Vacation* (animated), Paramount, 1997.

Voices of boat captain and Snowball the cat, *Hercules* (animated), Buena Vista, 1997.

Voices, *Amistad*, DreamWorks, 1997.

Voices, *Wag the Dog* (also known as *Bite the Bullet*), New Line Cinema, 1997.

Voice of drunk monkey, *Doctor Dolittle* (also known as *Dr. Dolittle*), Twentieth Century–Fox, 1998.

Voices of ants, grasshoppers, and a fly, *A Bug's Life* (animated), Buena Vista, 1998.

Voices of Howard "Howie" DeVille and Igor, *The Rugrats Movie* (animated; also known as *Ipanat*, *Les razmoket*, *Les razmoket, le film*, *Ratjetoe, de rugrats film*, *Rollinger*, *Rugrats, aventuras en panales*, *Rugrats—Der Film*, *Rugrats—Il film*, *Rugrats: La pelicula—Aventuras en panales*, *Rugrats mozi—Fecsegoe tipegoek*, and *Rugrats: O filme*), Paramount, 1998.

Voices of people of Atlantis and explorers, *Atlantis* (animated; also known as *Atlantis: The Lost Empire*), Buena Vista, 1998.

(As the Firesign Theatre) *God's Clowns* (short film), c. 1998.

Voices of soldiers, *The Iron Giant* (animated), Warner Bros., 1999.

Rob's father, *The Independent*, New City Releasing, 2000.

RBTV floor director, *The Adventures of Rocky & Bullwinkle* (also known as *Die Abenteuer von Rocky und Bullwinkle*), Universal, 2000.

Voice of Howard "Howie" DeVille, *Rugrats in Paris: The Movie* (animated; also known as *Rugrats in Paris: The Movie—Rugrats II* and *Rugrats in Paris—Der Film*), Paramount, 2000.

Voice of Charlie, *Monsters, Inc.* (animated), Buena Vista, 2001.

Voice of chef for English version, *Sen to Chihiro no kamikakushi* (anime; also known as *Miyazaki's "Spirited Away," Sen*, *Sen and the Mysterious Disappearance of Chihiro*, *Spirited Away*, and *The Spiriting Away of Sen and Chihiro*), Buena Vista, 2001.

Voice of drunk monkey, *Dr. Dolittle 2* (also known as *Doctor Dolittle 2*, *DR2*, *DR.2*, *Docteur Dolittle 2*, *Elaeintohtori 2*, and *Il Dottor Dolittle 2*), Twentieth Century–Fox, 2001.

Voices of second golfer and second scientist, *Recess: School's Out* (animated; also known as *Recess: The Ultimate Summer Vacation* and *Summer Vacation: The Ultimate Recess*), Buena Vista/Walt Disney Pictures, 2001.

Voice of Bob the seahorse, *Finding Nemo* (animated), Buena Vista, 2003.

Voice of Howard "Howie" DeVille, *Rugrats Go Wild* (animated; also known as *Rescue Me*, *The Rugrats Meet the Wild Thornberrys*, *The Rugrats Movie III*, *Rugrats 3: Rescue Me*, *Les razmoket rencontrent les Delajungle*, *Los rugrats: Vacaciones salvajes*, *Os rugrats e os Thornberrys vao aprontar*, and *Ratjetoe en de Thornberrys—Bij de beesten af*), Paramount, 2003.

Voices of Inuits and others, *Brother Bear* (animated; also known as *Tierra de osos*), Buena Vista, 2003.

Voice of Wolfgang von Goethe, *Proteus* (animated documentary; also known as *Proteus: A Nineteenth Century Vision*), First Run Features/Icarus Films, 2004.

Judge, *I'm Not Gay* (short film), Big Film Shorts, 2005.

Voice of rebel, *Thru the Moebius Strip* (animated), Fantastic Films International, 2005.

Voices, *I Build the Tower* (documentary; also known as *I Build the Tower: The Life and Work of Sam Rodia*), 2005.

Voice of Gary the baker, *Bongee Bear and the Kingdom of Rhythm* (animated), Yankee Films, 2006.

Voices of drunk monkey and stray dog, *Dr. Dolittle 3*, Twentieth Century–Fox Home Entertainment, 2006.

Voice of first amigo, *Happily N'Ever After* (animated), Lions Gate Films, 2007.

Film Additional Voices:

Beauty and the Beast (animated), Buena Vista, 1991, longer edition released as *Beauty and the Beast: Special Edition*.

Aladdin (animated), Buena Vista, 1992.

Kurenai no buta (anime; also known as *Crimson Pig, Porco rosso, Porco rosso—O ultimo heroi romantico,* and *Punainen sika*), Studio Ghibli/Tokuma Shoten, 1992, Manga Films, 1994, dubbed version released by Buena Vista Home Video.

The Lion King (animated; also known as *El rey leon*), Buena Vista, 1994.

Toy Story (animated), Buena Vista, 1995.

Hercules (animated), Buena Vista, 1997.

Pocahontas II: Journey to a New World (animated; also known as *Disney's "Pocahontas II: Journey to a New World"* and *Pocahontas: Journey to a New World*), Buena Vista Home Video, 1998.

Doug's First Movie (animated; also known as *The First Doug Movie Ever*), Buena Vista, 1999.

Tarzan (animated; also known as *Disney's "Tarzan"*), Buena Vista/Walt Disney Pictures, 1999.

Toy Story 2 (animated), Buena Vista, 1999.

Tarzan & Jane (animated), Buena Vista Home Video, 2002.

Treasure Planet (animated), Buena Vista, 2002.

Brother Bear (animated; also known as *Tierra de osos*), Buena Vista, 2003.

My Name Is Modesty: A Modesty Blaise Adventure (also known as *Modesty Blaise: The Beginning* and *My Name Is Modesty*), Buena Vista Home Video, c. 2003.

Home on the Range (animated), Buena Vista, 2004.

Racing Stripes, Warner Bros., 2005.

(As Philip Proctor) *Barnyard* (animated; also known as *Barnyard: The Original Party Animals* and *Der Tierisch verrueckte Bauernhof*), Paramount, 2006.

Film Automated Dialogue Replacement Voices or Group Member:

Full Moon High, Orion, 1981.

Endangered Species, Metro–Goldwyn–Mayer, 1982.

Revenge of the Ninja (also known as *Ninja II* and *Way of the Ninja*), Cannon, 1983.

The Adventures of Buckaroo Banzai: Across the Eighth Dimension, Columbia, 1984.

Ninja III: The Domination (also known as *Ninja III, Ninja 3: The Domination,* and *Trancers*), Cannon, 1984.

Lifeforce, TriStar, 1985.

Vision Quest (also known as *Crazy for You*), Warner Bros., 1985.

Three Amigos! (also known as *Three Amigos, The Three Caballeros, De kom, de saa—de lob!, Drei Amigos!, I tre amigos!, Kolme kaverusta, Shlosha Amigos, Tre amigos, Tres amigos, Tres amigos!,* and *Trois amigos!*), Orion, 1986.

Russkies, New Century Vista Film Company, 1987.

The Secret of My Success (also known as *The Secret of My Succe$s*), Universal, 1987.

Shy People, Cannon, 1987.

Police Academy 5: Assignment Miami Beach, Warner Bros., 1988.

Rambo III (also known as *Rambo 3* and *Rambo 3.*), TriStar, 1988.

Cohen and Tate, Bon Bon Films, 1989.

Police Academy 6: City under Siege, Warner Bros., 1989.

Scenes from the Class Struggle in Beverly Hills, Universal, 1989.

When Harry Met Sally, Columbia, 1989.

Corporate Affairs, Concorde Pictures, 1990.

Die Hard 2 (also known as *Die Hard 2: Die Harder*), Twentieth Century–Fox, 1990.

Gremlins 2: The New Batch (also known as *Gremlins 2* and *Monolith*), Warner Bros., 1990.

The Hunt for Red October (also known as *A la poursuite d'Octobre Rouge, Caca ao Outubro Vermelho, Cacada ao Outubro Vermelho, Caccia a Ottobre Rosso, Jagd auf "Roter Oktober," Jagten paa Rode Oktober, Jakten paa Roed Oktober, La caza del Octubre Rojo, Polowanie na Czerwony Pazdziernik, Punaisen Lokakuun metsaestys,* and *Vadaszat a Voeroes Oktoberre*), Paramount, 1990.

Opportunity Knocks, Universal, 1990.

Pretty Woman (also known as *$3000*), Buena Vista, 1990.

The Rookie, Warner Bros., 1990.

Waiting for the Light, Triumph Releasing, 1990.

Young Guns II (also known as *Hell Bent for Leather* and *Young Guns II: Blaze of Glory*), Twentieth Century–Fox, 1990.

City Slickers (also known as *Live, Love and Cows, A vida, o amor e as vacas, Amigos, sempre amigos, City Slickers—Die Grosstadt–Helden, City slickers—jakten paa det foersvunna leeendet, Cowboys de ciudad, Jakten paa det foersvunna leendet, Kaupunkicowboyt, La vie, l'amour, les vaches, La vie, l'amour ... les vaches, Scappo dalla citta—la vita, l'amore e le vacche, Stadszwervers,* and *Ti ekanes baba stin agria dysi*), Columbia, 1991.

The Doctor (also known as *A doktor, Der Doktor—Ein gewoehnlicher Patient, El doctor, Katkera rohto, Lakaren—han som aelskade livet, Le docteur,* and *Un medico, un uomo*), Buena Vista, 1991.

Hook, TriStar, 1991.

The Marrying Man (also known as *Too Hot to Handle*), Buena Vista, 1991.

Oscar (also known as *A mala das trapalhadas, L'embrouille est dans le sac, Oscar czyli 60 klopotow na minute, Oscar—Minha filha quer casar, Oscar, quita las manos, Oscar—un fidanzato per due figlie,* and *Oscar—Vom Regen in die Traufe*), Buena Vista, 1991.

The Rocketeer, Buena Vista, 1991.

Freejack, Warner Bros., 1992.

Lenny, 1992.

Mistress (also known as *Hollywood Mistress*), Rainbow Releasing, 1992.

Newsies (musical; also known as *Extra! Extra!, The News Boys,* and *Newsboys*), Buena Vista, 1992.

The Flintstones (also known as *The Flintstones: The Live–Action Movie*), Universal, 1994.

Maverick, Warner Bros., 1994.

Miracle on 34th Street, Twentieth Century–Fox, 1994.

The Specialist, Twentieth Century–Fox, 1994.

Die Hard: With a Vengeance (also known as *Die Hard—Mega Hard, Die Hard New York, Die Hard 3, Glass Trap 3,* and *Simon Says*), Twentieth Century–Fox, 1995.

Free Willy 2: The Adventure Home (also known as *Free Willy 2*), Warner Bros., 1995.

The Stars Fell on Henrietta, Warner Bros., 1995.

Stuart Saves His Family (also known as *Como salvar sua familia, Rescate familiar, Sekopaeiden seurakunta, Stuart sauve sa famille,* and *Stuart Stupid—Eine Familie zum Kotzen*), Paramount, 1995.

Theodore Rex (also known as *T. Rex*), New Line Cinema, 1995.

Village of the Damned (also known as *John Carpenter's "Village of the Damned"*), Universal, 1995.

Up Close and Personal (also known as *Golden Girl*), Buena Vista, 1996.

That Old Feeling, Universal, 1997.

Saving Private Ryan (also known as *Private Ryan*), DreamWorks, 1998.

Sphere, Warner Bros., 1998.

Wonder Boys (also known as *Die Wonder Boys* and *Wonderboys—Lauter Wunderknaben*), Paramount, 2000.

Sinbad: Legend of the Seven Seas (animated), DreamWorks, 2003.

Meet the Fockers (also known as *Meet the Fokkers, Meet the Parents 2, Entrando numa fria maior ainda, Familjen aer vaerre, Kohtumine Fockeritega, L'autre belle–famille, La familia de mi esposo, Los Fockers, Los Fockers: La familia de mi esposo, Los padres de el, Meine Frau, ihre Schwiegereltern und ich, Mi presenti i tuoi?, Mon beau–pere, mes parents et moi, Painajainen perheessae, Svigers er aller verst,* and *Uns compadres do pior*), Universal, 2004.

Shark Tale (animated; also known as *Sharkslayer*), DreamWorks, 2004.

Flightplan (also known as *Flight plan* and *High jinx at thirty thousand feet*), Buena Vista, 2005.

Film Looper or Loop Group Member:

Custom looper, *Scenes from the Class Struggle in Beverly Hills,* Universal, 1989.

Member of automated dialogue replacement loop group, *Cabin Boy,* Buena Vista, 1994.

Member of automated dialogue replacement loop group, *101 Dalmatians,* Buena Vista, 1996.

Member of automated dialogue replacement loop group, *The Trigger Effect,* Gramercy Pictures, 1996.

Member of automated dialogue replacement loop group, *Susan's Plan* (also known as *Die Again, Dying to Get Rich, Delitto imperfetto, El pla de la Susan, El plan de Susan, Petollinen suunnitelma,* and *Susan a un plan*), Kusher–Locke, 1998.

Member of loop group, *The Story of Us* (also known as *The Story of Love*), Universal, 1999.

Member of loop group, *Mickey's Twice upon a Christmas* (animated), Buena Vista, 2004.

Member of automated dialogue replacement loop group, *Borat: Cultural Learnings of America for Make Benefit Glorious Nation of Kazakhstan* (also known as *Borat* and *Borat!*), Twentieth Century–Fox, 2006.

Film Director and Producer:

(As the Firesign Theatre) *Martian Space Party* (also known as *The Firesign Theatre's "Martian Space Party"* and *The Martian Space Party*), Asso Film, 1972.

Everything You Know Is Wrong (also known as *Firesign Theatre Sez "Everything You Know Is Wrong"*), 1975.

Film Work; Other:

(As the Firesign Theatre) Editor, *Martian Space Party* (also known as *The Firesign Theatre's "Martian Space Party"* and *The Martian Space Party*), Asso Film, 1972.

(As the Firesign Theatre) Character creator, *Nick Danger in the Case of the Missing Yolk,* LodesTone Media/More Sugar, 1983.

Special effects technician, *One Missed Call* (also known as *Don't Pick Up the Cell Phone!*), Warner Bros., 2008.

Television Appearances; Series:

Tobie Kurtz, *The Edge of Night,* CBS, 1962–63.

Regular performer, *The Starland Vocal Band Show,* CBS, 1977.

Voice of King Gerard, *The Smurfs* (animated; also known as *Smurfs' Adventures*), NBC, c. 1981–85 (some sources cite c. 1984–88.

The National Snoop, NBC, beginning c. 1983.

Voice of King Gerard, *Johann and Peewee* (animated), c. 1985.

Narrator, *Against the Odds,* Nickelodeon, c. 1986–89.

Announcer, *The Will Shriner Show,* beginning 1987.

Father Frankie, *13 East,* NBC, 1990.

Voice of wizard, *Story Book Theatre,* early 1990s.

Voice of Bruno, *The Pirates of Dark Water* (animated; also known as *Dark Water*), ABC, 1991–92.

Voices of Willie Wombat and Chief Bushrat, *Taz–Mania* (animated), Fox, 1991–93.

Voices of Howard "Howie" DeVille, Allen Murphy, and others, *Rugrats* (animated; also known as *Adventures in Diapers, Aventuras en panales, Ipanat, Las diabluras de Tommy, Les razmoket,* and *Rollinger*), Nickelodeon, 1991–2003.

Voice of Brainboy's father, *The Tick* (animated), Fox, 1994–96.

Multiple voices, including Tim Burr, *Where on Earth Is Carmen Sandiego?* (animated), Fox, 1994–96, Fox Family Channel, 1998–99, also broadcast on PAX TV.

Announcer, *Ink,* CBS, 1996–97.

Voice of Forgo, *Over the Top,* ABC, 1997.

Announcer, *America's Greatest Pets,* UPN, 1998–99.

Announcer, *Big Brother* (also known as *Big Brother 3*), CBS, 2002.

Announcer, *Big Brother* (also known as *Big Brother 4: The X Factor*), CBS, 2003.

Voices of Howard "Howie" DeVille and others, *All Grown Up* (animated; also known as *Rugrats All Grown Up, Les razbitume, Los nuevos rugrats,* and *Rugratazo*), Nickelodeon, beginning 2003.

Announcer, *Big Brother* (also known as *Big Brother 5*), CBS, 2004.

Announcer, *Big Brother* (also known as *Big Brother 6*), CBS, 2005.

Television Appearances; Movies:

Generation, ABC, 1985.

Terrorist on Trial: The United States vs. Salim Ajami (also known as *Hostile Witness, In the Hands of the Enemy,* and *Terrorist on Trial*), ABC, 1989.

Norman Decker, *Bad Attitudes,* Fox, 1991.

Bruno, *Based on an Untrue Story,* Fox, 1993.

Voice of Jeremy Creek's father, *The Town That Santa Forgot* (animated), Cartoon Network, 1993.

The inspector, *Menno's Mind* (also known as *The Matrix 2* and *Power.com*), Showtime, 1996.

Rail official, *Witch Hunt,* Lifetime, Channel 5 (England), Network Ten (Australia), and Radiotelevisione Italiana (RAI, Italy), 1999.

Oregon delegate, *Running Mates* (also known as *Washington Slept Here*), TNT, 2000.

Television Appearances; Specials:

John Ritter: Being of Sound Mind and Body (also known as *The John Ritter Special*), ABC, 1980.

Steve Martin's "Twilight Theater" (also known as *Twilight Theater*), NBC, 1982.

(As the Firesign Theatre) Harryl Hee, Ed Snifter, and Wino Brothers wine announcer, *Fireside Theatre: Eat or Be Eaten* (also known as *Eat or Be Eaten*), Cinemax, 1985.

Voices of frog servant, fox soldier, and rat soldier, "The Kingdom Chums: Little David's Adventure" (animated), *ABC Weekend Specials,* ABC, 1986.

Voice, "Liberty and the Littles" (animated), *ABC Weekend Specials,* ABC, 1986.

(As the Firesign Theatre) *Comic Relief,* HBO, 1986.

Barker, *Harry Anderson's Sideshow,* NBC, 1987.

Voice, *Sport Goofy in Soccermania* (animated; also known as *Soccermania* and *Sport Goofy Soccer*), NBC, 1987.

(As the Firesign Theatre) *Firesign Theatre: Weirdly Cool* (also known as *Weirdly Cool*), PBS, 2001.

Television Appearances; Episodic:

Uncle Danny Reads the Funnies (also known as *Uncle Dan the Funny Paper Man*), WPIX (New York City), c. 1949.

Bobo, "Sara–Jane, You Never Whispered Again," *Run for Your Life,* NBC, 1968.

Bernard (young French king), "Noblesse Oblige," *Daniel Boone,* NBC, 1970.

Wendell, "The Insurance Is Canceled," *All in the Family* (also known as *Justice for All* and *Those Were the Days*), CBS, 1971.

The Ralph Story Show, CBS, c. 1972.

Chad Bennett, "A Farewell Tree from Marly," *The Rookies,* ABC, 1973.

Mr. Vincent, "The Lady Comes Across," *Diana,* NBC, 1973.

The Hollywood Squares, NBC and syndicated, c. 1976.

(As the Firesign Theatre) *An Evening at the Improv,* syndicated, c. 1981.

Al, *No Soap, Radio,* ABC, 1982.

Andre (a producer), "Pros and Cons," *The A Team,* NBC, 1983.

Benny, "D.J. D.O.A.," *Simon & Simon,* CBS, 1983.

Harry Fortune, "Room 3502," *Simon & Simon,* CBS, 1983.

Phil, "Catch a Falling Star," *Highway to Heaven,* NBC, 1984.

Anything for Money, syndicated, 1984.

The New Hollywood Squares, 1984.

Bloopers and Practical Jokes, NBC, c. 1984.

Blaylock, "Amazing Face," *St. Elsewhere,* NBC, 1985.

Man, "Power," *Cagney & Lacey,* CBS, 1985.

"Examination Day/A Message from Charity," *The Twilight Zone* (also known as *The New Twilight Zone*), CBS, 1985.

(As the Firesign Theatre) *Comedy Tonight,* syndicated, 1985.

St. Elsewhere, NBC, several episodes, 1985–88.

Clown, "The Landlords," *Webster,* ABC, 1986.

"Sinbad Goes to Mars," *The A Team,* NBC, c. 1986.

Brothers, Showtime, c. 1986.

Newscaster, *Hard Knocks,* Showtime, c. 1987.

Gallery owner, "A Class Act," *Cagney & Lacey,* CBS, 1988.

"Baby on Board," *Hooperman,* ABC, 1988.

Cat burglar, *Webster,* syndicated, c. 1988.

The Judge, syndicated, c. 1988.

Deyoung, "Crossroads: Parts 1 & 2," *Night Court,* NBC, 1990.

Donald Crowley, "What You Don't Know Can Kill You," *Freddy's Nightmares* (also known as *Freddy's Nightmares: A Nightmare on Elm Street: The Series, Freddy, le cauchemar de vos nuits, Freddyn painajaiset, Las pesadillas de Freddy,* and *Les cauchemars de Freddy*), syndicated, 1990.

Radio talk show producer, *His & Hers,* CBS, 1990.

Pierre, "Babes in Boyland," *Babes,* Fox, 1991.

Fred Deville, "Undressed for Success," *Night Court,* NBC, 1992.

Ron, "Goodbye, Mr. Gordon," *The Golden Girls* (also known as *Golden Girls, Miami Nice, Bnot Zahav, Cuori senza eta, Las chicas de oro, Les craquantes, Los anos dorados, Oereglanyok, Pantertanter,* and *Tyttoekullat*), NBC, 1992.

Vincent Vale, "Just a Gigolo," *The Golden Palace,* CBS, 1992.

Auctioneer, "Will Steps Out," *The Fresh Prince of Bel–Air,* NBC, 1994.

Danny Brash, "Can We Talk?," *The Sinbad Show,* Fox, 1994.

Television voice, "The B–Team of Life," *Boy Meets World* (also known as *Cory si restul lumii, Crescere che fatica, Das Leben und ich, De wereld om de hoek, Du store verden!, Et gutteliv, Incorigible Cory, Isojen poikien leikit, O mundo e dos jovens, O rapaz e o mundo,* and *Yo y el mundo*), ABC, 1994.

Marv Brickleman, *General Hospital* (also known as *Hopital central* and *Hospital general*), ABC, 1994 (multiple episodes).

Bob Wilkins, *The Young and the Restless* (also known as *Y&R, The Innocent Years, Atithasa niata, Les feux de l'amour, Schatten der Leidenschaft,* and *Tunteita ja tuoksuja*), CBS, 1995.

Robot salesperson, *Futurequest* (also known as *Future Quest*), PBS, c. 1995.

Art dealer, "Party Girl," *Brotherly Love,* NBC, 1997.

Cliff St. John, "Dave Barry, Call Your Agent," *Dave's World,* CBS, 1997.

Voices of Red Skull and Rhienholdt Kragor, "Six Forgotten Warriors Chapter 2: Unclaimed Legacy," *Spider–Man* (animated; also known as *New Spiderman* and *Spiderman*), Fox, 1997.

Voices of Red Skull and Rhienholdt Kragor, "Six Forgotten Warriors Chapter 3: Secrets of the Six," *Spider–Man* (animated; also known as *New Spiderman* and *Spiderman*), Fox, 1997.

Voices of Red Skull and Rhienholdt Kragor, "Six Forgotten Warriors Chapter 4: The Six Fight Again," *Spider–Man* (animated; also known as *New Spiderman* and *Spiderman*), Fox, 1997.

Voices of Red Skull, Rhienholdt Kragor, and Electro, "Six Forgotten Warriors Chapter 5: The Price of Heroism," *Spider–Man* (animated; also known as *New Spiderman* and *Spiderman*), Fox, 1997.

Voice, "Citizenship," *Adventures from the Book of Virtues* (animated; also known as *The Book of Virtues*), PBS, 1997.

Voices of Rabbi Kloner and others, *Nothing Sacred* (also known as *Priesthood*), ABC, c. 1998.

Armored car driver, "Ten Feet Tall and Bullet Proof," *Stingers,* Nine Network (Australia), 1999.

Prison warden, "Lunatic Fringe: Part 1," *Stingers,* Nine Network (Australia), 1999.

Feofanov, "Legacy: Part 2," *JAG,* CBS, 2000.

Voices of game host and body builder, "A Tiger by the Tail," *The Wild Thornberrys* (animated; also known as *The Thornberrys*), Nickelodeon, 2000.

Voice of Miracon, "Reflections of Evil," *Power Rangers Time Force,* Fox, 2001.

Voice of first humanoid, "War World: Part 1," *Justice League* (animated; also known as *JL, JLA, Justice League of America,* and *Justice League Unlimited*), Cartoon Network, 2002.

"Hello Goodbye," *State of Grace,* ABC Family Channel, 2002.

(As Philip Proctor) Voices of Dr. Cornea and ogre, "Nursery Crimes/My Peeps," *Grim & Evil* (animated; also known as *The Grim Adventures of Billy & Mandy*), Cartoon Network, 2004.

Reverend Bob Patterson, "Notapusy," *Arrested Development* (also known as *AD, Arrested development—Les nouveaux pauvres, Firma Ruffel & Baag, Firma Ruffel & Bygg, Sukuvika,* and *Ti presento i miei*), Fox, 2005.

Snorri Magnusson, "Windows," *The Loop,* Fox, 2007.

Voice of music teacher, "The Headband," *Avatar: The Last Airbender* (animated; also known as *Avatar—Der Herr der Elemente*), Nickelodeon, 2007.

Appeared in other programs. Contributed the voice of a patent agent to "The People's Party," an episode of the unaired series *The Blues Brothers Animated Series* (animated; also known as *The Blues Brothers*), UPN.

Television Appearances; Pilots:
(As Philip Proctor) Cliff, *Packin' It In,* 1983.

The National Snoop, NBC, c. 1983.

Mr. Wilson, *Me and Mrs. C.,* NBC, 1984.

Voices, *Nutty News Reels,* HBO, 1984.

Pop Quiz, Disney Channel, 1985.

Voice, *Say What?,* CBS, 1992.

Crabby passenger, "The New Pilot, Literally," *The Crew* (also known as *Cabin Pressure*), NBC, 1995.

Television Additional Voices; Series:
The Jetsons (animated; later known as *The New Jetsons*), multiple networks, beginning c. 1962, including syndicated, 1985 and 1987.

Scooby and Scrappy–Doo (animated), ABC, 1979–80.

Heathcliff (animated), ABC, 1980–81.

Richie Rich (animated), ABC, 1980–82, CBS, 1986, some sources cite beginning c. 1996.

Heathcliff and Marmaduke (animated), ABC, 1981–82.

The Smurfs (animated; also known as *Smurfs' Adventures*), NBC, 1981–90.

Flintstones Funnies (animated), NBC, 1982–84.

Shirt Tales (animated), NBC, 1982–84, CBS, 1984–85.

Alvin and the Chipmunks (animated; also known as *The Chipmunks* and *Chipmunks Go to the Movies*), NBC, 1983–91.

Flintstones Kids (animated), ABC, 1986–88 and 1990.

Bill and Ted's Excellent Adventures (animated), CBS, 1990–91, Fox, 1991–92.

The Pirates of Dark Water (animated; also known as *Dark Water*), ABC, 1991–92.

Babylon 5 (also known as *B5, Babylon 5.,* and *Spacecenter Babylon 5*), syndicated, 1993–99.

The Tick (animated), Fox, 1994–96.

Television Automated Dialogue Replacement Voices; Series:
Robotman (animated), beginning c. 1984.

Pound Puppies (animated), ABC, 1986–88.

Midnight Caller, NBC, c. 1988–91.

Parker Lewis Can't Lose (also known as *Parker Lewis*), Fox, 1990–93.

The Mommies (also known as *Mommies*), NBC, 1993–95.

Time Trax, syndicated, 1993–95.

The Cosby Mysteries, NBC, 1994–95.

Lois & Clark: The New Adventures of Superman (also known as *Lois & Clark* and *The New Adventures of Superman*), ABC, c. 1994–95.

One West Waikiki, CBS, 1994, syndicated, 1995–96.

Honey, I Shrunk the Kids: The TV Show (also known as *Disney's "Honey, I Shrunk the Kids: The TV Show"* and *Honey, I Shrunk the Kids*), syndicated, 1997–2000.

Television Work; Automated Dialogue Replacement Voices; Miniseries:

Gambler V: Playing for Keeps (also known as *The Gambler 5*), CBS, 1994.

Television Automated Dialogue Replacement Voices; Movies:

Love Is Forever (also known as *Comeback*), CBS, c. 1983.

Generation, ABC, 1985.

Thirteen at Dinner (also known as *Agatha Christie's "Thirteen at Dinner"*), CBS, 1985.

Thompson's Last Run, CBS, 1986.

Body of Evidence, CBS, 1988.

Brotherhood of the Rose, CBS, 1989.

Danielle Steel's "Family Album" (also known as *Family Album*), NBC, 1994.

Sleep, Baby, Sleep, NBC, 1994.

Television Member of Automated Dialogue Replacement Loop Group; Movies:

Menno's Mind (also known as *The Matrix 2* and *Power.com*), Showtime, 1996.

(As Philip Proctor) "The Challenge," *The Wonderful World of Disney,* ABC, 2003.

Television Automated Dialogue Replacement Voices; Specials:

Salute to America's Pets, ABC, 1992.

Television Automated Dialogue Replacement Voices; Pilots:

ER (also known as *Emergency Room*), NBC, 1994.

Television Work; Automated Dialogue Replacement Voices; Other:

The Punisher, CBS, 1992.

Stage Appearances:

Algernon, *Ernest in Love,* Denison Summer Theatre, 1960.

Raif Rackstraw, *HMS Pinafore* (opera), Denison Summer Theatre, 1960.

Title role, *Tom Jones* (musical), Yale University, New Haven, CT, 1960.

Take Me Along, Denison Summer Theatre, 1960.

You Never Can Tell, Denison Summer Theatre, 1960.

Edwin Booth, *Booth Is Back in Town* (musical), Yale University, 1961.

Alan Seymour, *Picnic,* Ross Common Playhouse, c. 1962.

Arthur, *Suddenly Last Summer,* Ross Common Playhouse, c. 1962.

Horatio, *Kiss Me Kate,* Ross Common Playhouse, c. 1962.

The husband, *Dial M for Murder,* Ross Common Playhouse, c. 1962.

The Barroom Monks, Martinique Theatre, New York City, 1962.

Portrait of the Artist as a Young Man, Martinique Theatre, 1962.

Post office clerk and understudy for the role of Trofimov, *The Cherry Orchard,* Theatre Four, New York City, 1962–63.

Jack, *Thistle in My Bed,* Gramercy Arts Theatre, New York City, 1963.

Understudy for the role of Rolfe, *The Sound of Music* (musical), Mark Hellinger Theatre, New York City, c. 1963.

Horace, *The Amorous Flea* (musical), East 78th Street Playhouse, New York City, beginning 1964, Las Palmas Theatre, Los Angeles, 1966.

Abundantly Yours, Paramus Playhouse, Paramus, NJ, between 1964 and 1966.

The Snowball Tree, Actors Studio East, New York City, 1965.

Understudy for the role of Evan Morgan, *A Time for Singing* (musical), Boston, MA, then Broadway Theatre, New York City, both 1966.

Understudy, *A Race of Hairy Men,* Henry Miller Theatre, New York City, 1966.

(With Firesign Theatre) *Freak for a Week* (benefit performance), Santa Monica Civic Auditorium, Santa Monica, CA, 1967.

(With Firesign Theatre) *Waiting for the Electrician,* Experimental Arts Festival, University of California, Los Angeles, 1967.

Jack Argue (the playwright), *Museeka,* Center Theatre Group, Los Angeles, 1969.

War of the Worlds (also known as *War of the Worlds 50th Anniversary Production*), c. 1988.

Ladies of the Camellias, West End Playhouse, Van Nuys, CA, 1988, 1990.

Boris, *Nude Radio,* Actors Studio West, 1989.

Trend Armor, Lee Strasberg Institute, 1992.

(With the Firesign Theatre) *Back from the Shadows—The Firesign Theatre's 25th Anniversary Reunion Show* (also known as *The Firesign Theatre: Back from the Shadows, 25th Anniversary Concert,* and *25th Anniversary Reunion: Back from the Shadows*), Paramount Theatre, Seattle, WA, 1993.

Church, Bang! Studio, Hollywood, CA, 1996.

New England, South Coast Repertory Theatre, Costa Mesa, CA, 1996.

State of the Union, L.A. Theatre Works, Theatre at Doubletree Guest Quarters, Santa Monica, CA, 1996.

Zoika's Apartment (staged reading), Mark Taper Theatre, Los Angeles, 1996.

Lieutenant the duke of Dunstable, *Patience* (opera), Antaeus Theatre Company, NoHo Theatre and Arts Festival, North Hollywood, CA, then John Anson Ford Ampitheatre, [Inside] The Ford, Los Angeles, both 1998.

Rabelais and member of the Erotica Quartet, *Over the Rainbow* (tribute to Yip Harburg), Salon at the Taper, Mark Taper Theatre, c. 1999.

(As Philip Proctor) Patterson "Pat" Beeves, *The Man Who Had All the Luck,* Antaeus Theatre Company, Ivy Substation, Culver City, CA, 2000.

Tristan, *The Liar, or the Truth Can't Be Trusted* (also known as *The Liar*), Antaeus Theatre Company, Secret Rose Theatre, North Hollywood, CA, then Chamizal International Siglos de Oro Festival, El Paso, TX, both 2000.

Appeared in other productions with the Antaeus Theatre Company, North Hollywood, CA. Appeared in various productions at Yale University, including appearances as Abdullah in *Camino Real;* as Richard (the duke of Gloucester) in *Henry the VI, Part 3;* and as Tim Briscoe in *Man Better Man* (musical); also in Yale University productions of *Notes form the Underground* (one–act play), *A Sleep of Prisoners,* and *Thieves' Carnival.* With the Firesign Theatre, wrote and performed other material for the stage. Performer at other venues and performer with the Yale Russian Chorus in the former Soviet Union.

Major Tours:

Horace, *The Amorous Flea* (musical), U.S. cities, beginning c. 1964.

Charlie Dalrymple, *Brigadoon* (musical), U.S. cities, between 1964 and 1966.

Nicky, *Bell, Book, and Candle,* U.S. cities, between 1964 and 1966.

Og, *Finian's Rainbow* (musical), U.S. cities, between 1964 and 1966.

Ken Powell (editor), *Generation,* Florida cities, 1966–67.

Toured U.S. cities with Peter Bergman, c. 1976–77; toured with the Firesign Theatre, Western U.S. cities, 2005, and on other tours.

Stage Director:

"Go," *I Know You Better Than I Do Myself,* Court Theatre, Los Angeles, 1997.

Truth Be Told: An Evening of Urban Encounters (solo show; also known as *Truth Be Told*), Ventura Court Theatre, Studio City, CA, 1998.

(With Melinda Peterson) *Robin, Polished by Love,* Antaeus Theatre Company, NoHo Theatre and Arts Festival, North Hollywood, CA, 1999.

The Plot to Overthrow Christmas (benefit), Antaeus Classical Company, North Hollywood, CA, c. 2004.

Radio Appearances; as the Firesign Theatre:

Radio Free Oz (series), KPFK, beginning 1966, later KRLA (Los Angeles).

The Les Crane Show (episodic), c. 1968.

Live from the Magic Mushroom (series; also known as *Magic Mushroom*), KRLA, c. 1968.

Early Sunday Morning Oz (series), KMET (Los Angeles), 1968–69.

The Firesign Theatre Radio Hour, KPPC (Pasadena, CA), 1970.

Dear Friends! (series), KPKF, 1970–71, also syndicated.

About a Week, 1971.

Election commentator, *Morning Edition,* National Public Radio, 1980.

Host, *Firesign Festival* (special), KCRW and other stations, 1990.

Back from the Shadows—The Firesign Theatre's 25th Anniversary Reunion Show (also known as *The Firesign Theatre: Back from the Shadows* and *25th Anniversary Reunion: Back from the Shadows*), PBS Radio, c. 1994.

Performer and host, *XM Comedy/Firesign Theatre Presents: Fools in Space* (also known as *Fools in Space*), XM Satellite Radio, Channel 150, 2001–2002.

(As the Firesign Theatre) *All Things Considered* (series), National Public Radio, 2002 and 2003.

Appeared in other radio programs with the Firesign Theatre, including *Earplay* and *Radio Hour Hour.* Also wrote and performed other material for the radio, including other material for National Public Radio.

War of the Worlds (special; also known as *War of the Worlds 50th Anniversary Production*), c. 1988.

Voice of Murphy, "Many Friends," *The Apotheosis Saga,* c. 1995.

The Phoenix (play), National Public Radio, 1995.

The Water Faucet Vision (play), National Public Radio, 1995.

State of the Union (play), L.A. Theatre Works, KCRW, 1996.

The Secretariat (play), National Public Radio, 1997.

Voices of Harry Gantz and the king, *Buddy Shell, Metaphysical Private Investigator* (episodic), KCLU, 1998.

Appeared in other radio programs.

Radio Work; with Others:
(As the Firesign Theatre) Director, *XM Comedy/Firesign Theatre Presents: Fools in Space* (also known as *Fools in Space*), XM Satellite Radio, Channel 150, 2001–2002.

Editor of radio interviews, Yale University, c. 1958–62. With the Firesign Theatre, created other pieces for radio, including parodies of advertisements.

RECORDINGS

Albums; with the Firesign Theatre:
Waiting for the Electrician or Someone Like Him, Columbia, 1968.
How Can You Be in Two Places at Once When You're Not Anywhere at All?, Columbia, 1969.
Don't Crush That Dwarf, Hand Me the Pliers, Columbia, 1970.
I Think We're All Bozos on This Bus, Columbia, 1971.
Dear Friends, Columbia, 1972.
Not Insane, Columbia, 1972.
Firesign Theatre Live: Westbury Music Fair, 1974.
The Tale of the Giant Rat of Sumatra, Columbia, 1974.
In the Next World You're on Your Own, Columbia, 1975.
Questions & Answers: Firesign Live, 1975.
Forward into the Past (also known as *Forward into the Past—An Anthology*), Columbia, 1976.
Firesign World, Wizardo Records/Dog and Cat, 1977.
Just Folks … A Firesign Chat, 1977.
Nick Danger: The Case of the Missing Shoe (EP), Rhino, 1979.
Lawyer's Hospital, Rhino, 1982.
Three Faces of Al, Rhino, 1984.
Fighting Clowns—A Musical Cabaret (also known as *Fighting Clowns*), Mobile Fidelity, 1993.
Shoes for Industry! (also known as *Shoes for Industry! The Best of the Firesign Theatre*), Sony, 1993.
Back from the Shadows—The Firesign Theatre's 25th Anniversary Reunion Show (also known as *The Firesign Theatre: Back from the Shadows* and *25th Anniversary Reunion: Back from the Shadows*), Mobile Fidelity, 1994.
The Pink Hotel Burns Down (also known as *The Pink Hotel Burns Down: A Collection of Rare & Unreleased Material*), LodesTone Media, 1996.
Radio Now, c. 1998.
Give Me Immortality or Give Me Death, Rhino, 1999.
In the Firezone: Firesign Theatre Live in Seattle, 1999.
Nick Danger: The Daily Feed Tapes, LodesTone Media, 2000.
Anythynge You Want To (also known as *Anything You Want To* and *Anythynge You Want To: Shakespeare's Lost Comedie*), LodesTone Media/Whirlwind Media, 2001.
The Bride of Firesign, Rhino/Wea, 2001.
All Things Firesign, Artemis Records, 2003.

Also recorded other albums and other works with the Firesign Theatre.

Albums; with Peter Bergman:
A Firesign Chat with Papoon, Columbia, 1972.
Papoon for President, C. 1972.
TV or Not TV, Columbia, 1973.
What This Country Needs, Columbia, 1975.
Give Us a Break (also known as *The Comedy of Proctor and Bergman/Give Us a Break*), Mercury, 1978.

Other recordings with Bergman include *The (Sort of) History of Proctor and Bergman: On the Road.*

Albums; with Others:
(Announcer) *National Lampoon Sex, Drugs, Rock 'n' Roll, and the End of the World* (also known as *Sex, Drugs, Rock 'n' Roll, and the End of the World*), Passport, 1982.
(With David Ossman) *Not Another Talk Show/The Cabinet of Dr. Marconi,* LodesTone Media, 1997.

Affiliated with the album *Visit to Planet Proctor.* Appeared in other recordings.

Albums; Cast Recordings:
Tom Jones, Carillon, 1960.
Booth Is Back in Town, Carillon, 1961.
A Time for Singing, Warner Bros., 1966.

Singles:
(As the Firesign Theatre) Station break/"Forward into the Past," 1969–70.
(As the Firesign Theatre) "Fighting Clowns" (consists of side 1: "Hey Reagan," and side 2, "Hey Carter"), 1980.
(As Vinnie Gumba) "Rappa This" (also known as "Rappadis: Vinnie Gumba"), Laurie, c. 1990.

Videos; as the Firesign Theatre:
The Madhouse of Dr. Fear, c. 1979.
Hot Shorts, Sony Pictures Home Entertainment, 1989.
Boom Dot Bust, Rhino, 2000.

Appeared in other videos.

Music Videos:
The Foreman, "Ain't a Liberal No More," 1995.

Video Games:
Voice, *The Magic Jukebox,* Philips Interactive, 1995.
Voice, *Sandy's Circus,* Philips Interactive, 1995.

Voice, *Where in the U.S.A. Is Carmen Sandiego?*, Broderbund, 1995.

Voice of Dr. Jeremiah Crick, *The Lighthouse*, Sierra, 1996.

Multiple voices, *Normalcy*, 1996.

Voice, *Pyst*, Palladium, c. 1996.

Voice, *Battlezone*, 1998.

Voices of Soviet military police personnel, *Indiana Jones and the Infernal Machine*, LucasArts Entertainment, 1999.

Voices of Thomas Azzameen, imperial officers, and rebel pilot, *Star Wars: X–Wing Alliance*, LucasArts Entertainment, 1999.

Voices of attack tank driver, second rebel trooper, and stormtrooper sergeant, *Star Wars: Force Commander*, 2000.

Voices of Monty the jambalaya tourist and three–headed monkey, *Escape from Monkey Island*, LucasArts Entertainment, 2000.

(As Philip Proctor) Voices of Parkington, Al, Semyon, and Ramon, *Freedom: First Resistance*, 2000.

Voices of Tako, Commander Roq, and civil war helm officer, *Star Trek: Klingon Academy*, 2000.

Voice of Desolator, *Command & Conquer: Red Alert 2* (also known as *Command & Conquer: Red Alert 2—Yuri's Revenge*), 2001.

Voices of Viceroy Nute Gunray, Jedi master, and empire cruiser captain, *Star Wars: Galactic Battlegrounds*, 2001.

Voice, *Command & Conquer: Yuri's Revenge* (also known as *Red Alert 2 Expansion Pack: Yuri's Revenge*), 2001.

Voice of Father Salade, *La Pucelle* (also known as *La Pucelle: Tactics*), Mastiff, 2002.

Voice of Flotsam, *Dark Chronicle* (also known as *Dark Cloud 2*), Sony Computer Entertainment America, 2002.

Voices of architect Roberto Bianchi and bishop, *Eternal Darkness: Sanity's Requiem* (also known as *Eternal Darkness*), Nintendo of America, 2002.

Voices of Faustus and others, *Blood Omen II: Legacy of Kain*, Eidos Interactive, 2002.

Voices, *Soldier of Fortune II: Double Helix*, Activision, 2002.

Voice of second Soviet, *Secret Weapons over Normandy*, LucasArts Entertainment Company, 2003.

Voices of Arjan Manjani and others, *SOCOM II: U.S. Navy SEALs*, Sony Computer Entertainment America, 2003.

Voices of Bayra and Donga for English version, *Final Fantasy X–2* (also known as *Fainaru fantajii X–2*), Square Enix, 2003.

Voices of captain, monk, and old peasant, *Armed & Dangerous*, LucasArts Entertainment Company, 2003.

Voices of German public address system announcer and ivory hunters, *Indiana Jones and the Emperor's Tomb*, LucasArts Entertainment Company, 2003.

Voices of men, *Legacy of Kain: Defiance* (also known as *Legacy of Kain: Soul Reaver III*), Eidos Interactive, 2003.

Voice, *Lionheart: Legacy of the Crusader* (also known as *Lionheart*), Black Isle Studios, 2003.

Voice of King Theoden of Rohan, *The Lord of the Rings: The Battle for Middle–Earth*, 2004.

Voice of Ukki White, *Piposaru academia: Dossari! Sarugee daizenshuu* (also known as *Ape Academy* and *Ape Escape Academy*), Sony Computer Entertainment, 2004.

Voices of Proust, Pulikovsky, Samaev, a soldier, and others, *Syphon Filter: The Omega Strain* (also known as *Syphon Filter 4*), Sony Computer Entertainment America, 2004.

Voice, *Champions of Norrath: Realms of EverQuest*, Sony Online Entertainment, 2004.

Voices, *Doom 3* (also known as *Doom III*), Vicarious Visions, 2004.

Voice of Mr. White, *Area 51*, Midway Manufacturing Corporation, 2005.

Voice of professor, *Saru gecchu P* (also known as *Ape Escape: On the Loose*), Sony Computer Entertainment, 2005.

Voice of Q, *James Bond 007: From Russia with Love*, EA Games, 2005.

Voices of the professor and Monkey White, *Saru gecchu 3* (also known as *Ape Escape 3*), Sony Computer Entertainment, 2005.

(As Philip Proctor) Voice, *Call of Duty 2*, Activision, 2005.

Voice, *Call of Duty 2: Big Red One*, Activision, 2005.

(As Philip Proctor) Voice, *Dungeons & Dragons: DragonsHard*, Infogrames, 2005.

(As Philip Proctor) Voice, *Rainbow Six: Lockdown*, Ubisoft, 2005.

Voices, *Gun*, Activision, 2005.

Voice of Chaigidiel for English version, *Metal Gear Ac!d 2*, Konami, c. 2005.

(As Philip Proctor) Voice of King Theoden of Rohan, *The Lord of the Rings: The Battle for Middle–Earth II*, Electronic Arts, 2006.

Voice of King Theoden of Rohan, *Lord of the Rings: Battle for Middle Earth II—Rise of the Witch King*, EA Games, 2006.

Voice of Russell Barnaby, *Dead Rising*, Capcom, 2006.

Voices of Baron Mordo and Edwin Jarvis, *Marvel: Ultimate Alliance*, Activision, 2006.

(As Philip Proctor) Voice, *Company of Heroes*, THQ, 2006.

Voice, *Night Watch*, Nival Interactive/Novia Disk Company, 2006.

Voice, *SOCOM: U.S. Navy SEALS—Combined Assault*, Sony Computer Entertainment America, 2006.

Voice, *SOCOM: U.S. Navy SEALS: Fireteam Bravo 2*, Sony Computer Entertainment America, 2006.

Voice, *Syphon Filter: Dark Mirror*, Sony Computer Entertainment America, 2006.

Voices for English version, *Fainaru fantaji XII* (also known as *Final Fantasy XII*), Square Enix, 2006.

(As Philip Proctor) Voices for English version, *Gothic 3*, JoWood Productions Software, 2006.

Voice for English version, *Shin Onimusha: Dawn of Dreams* (also known as *Onimusha: Dawn of Dreams*), Capcom, 2006.

(As Philip Proctor) Voice, *Supreme Commander*, THQ, 2007.

(As Philip Proctor) Voice, *Titan Quest: Immortal Throne*, THQ, 2007.

(As Philip Proctor) Voice, *World in Conflict*, Massive Entertainment, 2007.

Video Game Work:
Cocreator, *Pyst*, Palladium, c. 1996.

Audiobooks:
Steve Solomon, *Favorite Son*, Bantam Books on Tape, 1988.

Bruce Feirstein, *Real Men Don't Bond*, Simon & Schuster, 1993.

WRITINGS

Screenplays:
(As Philip Proctor) *Zachariah*, Cinerama Releasing, 1971.

(As the Firesign Theatre) *Martian Space Party* (also known as *The Firesign Theatre's "Martian Space Party"* and *The Martian Space Party*), Asso Film, 1972.

Everything You Know Is Wrong (also known as *Firesign Theatre Sez "Everything You Know Is Wrong"*), 1975.

Cracking Up, American International Pictures, 1977.

(As Philip Proctor; with Peter Bergman) *Americathon* (based on a play by Proctor and Bergman; also known as *Americathon 1998* and *Amerika 1998*), United Artists, 1979.

(As Philip Proctor) *J–Men Forever*, International Harmony, 1979.

Nick Danger in the Case of the Missing Yolk, LodesTone Media/More Sugar, 1983.

(As the Firesign Theatre) *God's Clowns* (short film), c. 1998.

Teleplays; as the Firesign Theatre; Specials:
Fireside Theatre: Eat or Be Eaten (also known as *Eat or Be Eaten*), Cinemax, 1985.

(And with others) *Comic Relief*, HBO, 1986.

Firesign Theatre: Weirdly Cool (also known as *Weirdly Cool*), PBS, 2001.

Author of material that has appeared in various programs.

Teleplays; with Others; Episodic:
The Starland Vocal Band Show, CBS, 1977.

Writings for the Stage; as the Firesign Theatre:
Freak for a Week (benefit performance), Santa Monica Civic Auditorium, Santa Monica, CA, 1967.

Waiting for the Electrician, Experimental Arts Festival, University of California, Los Angeles, 1967.

Back from the Shadows—The Firesign Theatre's 25th Anniversary Reunion Show (also known as *The Firesign Theatre: Back from the Shadows, 25th Anniversary Concert*, and *25th Anniversary Reunion: Back from the Shadows*), Paramount Theatre, Seattle, WA, 1993.

With the Firesign Theatre, writer and performer in a tour of Western U.S. cities, 2005, and on other tours. (With Peter Bergman) *Americathon*, c. 1976–77.

With Bergman, writer and performer in a tour of U.S. cities, c. 1976–77. Wrote and performed other material with others.

Writings for Radio; as the Firesign Theatre:
Radio Free Oz (series), KPFK, beginning 1966, later KRLA (Los Angeles).

The Les Crane Show (episodic), c. 1968.

Live from the Magic Mushroom (series; also known as *Magic Mushroom*), KRLA, c. 1968.

Early Sunday Morning Oz (series), KMET (Los Angeles), 1968–69.

The Firesign Theatre Radio Hour, KPPC (Pasadena, CA), 1970.

Dear Friends! (series), KPKF, 1970–71, also syndicated.

About a Week, 1971.

Morning Edition, National Public Radio, 1980.

Firesign Festival (special), KCRW and other stations, 1990.

Back from the Shadows—The Firesign Theatre's 25th Anniversary Reunion Show (also known as *The Firesign Theatre: Back from the Shadows* and *25th Anniversary Reunion: Back from the Shadows*), PBS Radio, c. 1994.

XM Comedy/Firesign Theatre Presents: Fools in Space (also known as *Fools in Space*), XM Satellite Radio, Channel 150, 2001–2002.

(As the Firesign Theatre) *All Things Considered* (series), National Public Radio, 2002 and 2003.

Contributed to radio programs with the Firesign Theatre, including *Earplay* and *Radio Hour Hour*. With the Firesign Theatre, wrote and performed other material for the radio, including parodies of advertisements.

Albums; with the Firesign Theatre:
Waiting for the Electrician or Someone Like Him, Columbia, 1968.

How Can You Be in Two Places at Once When You're Not Anywhere at All?, Columbia, 1969.

Don't Crush That Dwarf, Hand Me the Pliers, Columbia, 1970.

I Think We're All Bozos on This Bus, Columbia, 1971.

Dear Friends, Columbia, 1972.

Not Insane, Columbia, 1972.

Firesign Theatre Live: Westbury Music Fair, 1974.

The Tale of the Giant Rat of Sumatra, Columbia, 1974.

In the Next World You're on Your Own, Columbia, 1975.

Questions & Answers: Firesign Live, 1975.

Forward into the Past (also known as *Forward into the Past—An Anthology*), Columbia, 1976.

Firesign World, Wizardo Records/Dog and Cat, 1977.

Just Folks ... A Firesign Chat, 1977.

Nick Danger: The Case of the Missing Shoe (EP), Rhino, 1979.

Lawyer's Hospital, Rhino, 1982.

Three Faces of Al, Rhino, 1984.

Fighting Clowns—A Musical Cabaret (also known as *Fighting Clowns*), Mobile Fidelity, 1993.

Shoes for Industry! (also known as *Shoes for Industry! The Best of the Firesign Theatre*), Sony, 1993.

Back from the Shadows—The Firesign Theatre's 25th Anniversary Reunion Show (also known as *The Firesign Theatre: Back from the Shadows* and *25th Anniversary Reunion: Back from the Shadows*), Mobile Fidelity, 1994.

The Pink Hotel Burns Down (also known as *The Pink Hotel Burns Down: A Collection of Rare & Unreleased Material*), LodesTone Media, 1996.

Radio Now, c. 1998.

Give Me Immortality or Give Me Death, Rhino, 1999.

In the Firezone: Firesign Theatre Live in Seattle, 1999.

Nick Danger: The Daily Feed Tapes, LodesTone Media, 2000.

Anythynge You Want To (also known as *Anything You Want To* and *Anythynge You Want To: Shakespeare's Lost Comedie*), LodesTone Media/Whirlwind Media, 2001.

The Bride of Firesign, Rhino/Wea, 2001.

All Things Firesign, Artemis Records, 2003.

Also recorded other albums and other works with the Firesign Theatre.

Albums; with Peter Bergman:

A Firesign Chat with Papoon, Columbia, 1972.

Papoon for President, C. 1972.

TV or Not TV, Columbia, 1973.

What This Country Needs, Columbia, 1975.

Give Us a Break (also known as *The Comedy of Proctor and Bergman/Give Us a Break*), Mercury, 1978.

Other recordings with Bergman include *The (Sort of) History of Proctor and Bergman: On the Road.*

Albums; with Others:

National Lampoon Sex, Drugs, Rock 'n' Roll, and the End of the World (also known as *Sex, Drugs, Rock 'n' Roll, and the End of the World*), Passport, 1982.

(With David Ossman) *Not Another Talk Show/The Cabinet of Dr. Marconi,* LodesTone Media, 1997.

Affiliated with the album *Visit to Planet Proctor.* Appeared in other recordings.

Singles:

(As the Firesign Theatre) Station break/"Forward into the Past," 1969–70.

(As the Firesign Theatre) "Fighting Clowns" (consists of side 1: "Hey Reagan," and side 2, "Hey Carter"), 1980.

(As Vinnie Gumba) "Rappa This" (also known as "Rappadis: Vinnie Gumba"), Laurie, c. 1990.

Videos; as the Firesign Theatre:

The Madhouse of Dr. Fear, c. 1979.

Hot Shorts, Sony Pictures Home Entertainment, 1989.

Boom Dot Bust, Rhino, 2000.

Contributed material that appears in other videos.

Humorous Writings; with the Firesign Theatre:

The Firesign Theatre's "Big Book of Plays" (also known as *Big Book of Plays*), Straight Arrow Books, 1972.

The Firesign Theatre's "Big Mystery Joke Book" (also known as *Big Mystery Joke Book*), Simon & Schuster, 1974.

Bozobook: Or, Clam Calendar & Book of Ours: Excerpts form the Notebooks of the Firesign Theatre, Volume '71, Turkey Press, 1981.

Author of the introduction for the book *Cool Cats.* Contributor to periodicals, including *East Village Other.*

ADAPTATIONS

The Firesign Theatre's character of Nick Danger has appeared in stories appearing in periodicals and books.

OTHER SOURCES

Periodicals:

TV Guide, August 9, 2003, p. 7.

Electronic:

Planet Proctor, http://www.planetproctor.com, September 8, 2007.

Q–R

RAFFIN, Deborah 1953–
(Debra Raffin)

PERSONAL

Full name, Deborah Iona Raffin; born March 13, 1953, in Los Angeles, CA; daughter of Trudy Marshall (an actress); married Michael Viner (a producer, writer, actor, musical director, and manager), August 4, 1974 (divorced, 2005). *Education:* Attended Valley College; studied under Kate Fleming at London's National Theatre; studied acting with Milton Katselas.

Addresses: *Manager*—Benedetti Management, 13400 Moorpark St., Studio City, CA, 91602.

Career: Actress and producer. Dove Audio (later Dove Entertainment), (with Michael Viner) cofounder and co-owner, 1985–97, executive vice president and head of spoken–word audio division,?–1997; New Millennium Entertainment, (with Viner) cofounder and co–owner, c. 1998—. Previously worked as a model.

Member: Screen Actors Guild, Actors Equity Association, American Federation of Television and Radio Artists.

Awards, Honors: Emmy Award nomination, best actress, 1977, for *Nightmare in Badham County;* Golden Globe nomination, best motion picture actress—drama, 1981, Bronze Halo Award, Southern California Motion Picture Council, Gold Horse Award, Golden Horse Film Festival and Awards, and Christopher Award, all for *Touched by Love.*

CREDITS

Film Appearances:
(Film debut) Trina Stanley, *40 Carats,* Columbia, 1973.
Patti Ratteree, *The Dove,* Paramount, 1974.
January Wayne, *Once Is Not Enough* (also known as *Jacqueline Susann's "Once Is Not Enough"*), Paramount, 1975.
Casey Forster, *God Told Me To* (also known as *Demon*), New World, 1976.
Jennifer, *The Sentinel,* Universal, 1977.
Cindy Simmons, *Ransom* (also known as *Assault on Paradise, Maniac,* and *The Town That Cried Terror*), New World, 1977.
Hanging on a Star, 1978.
Lena Canada, *Touched by Love* (also known as *To Elvis, with Love*), Columbia, 1979.
Dr. Evelyn Howard, *Dance of the Dwarfs* (also known as *Dance of the Dwarves* and *Jungle Heat*), Panache, 1983.
Kathryn Davis, *Death Wish III,* Filmways, 1985.
Ranger's girlfriend, *Predator: The Concert,* 1987.
Title role, *Claudia* (also known as *Claudia' Story*), 1989.
Julie Vale, *Scanners II: The New Order,* Media Home Entertainment, 1992.
Elly Dinsmore, *Morning Glory,* Academy Entertainment, 1993.
Herself, *Superman Screen Tests* (documentary short), 2001.

Also appeared in *The Predator.*

Film Executive Producer:
Wilde (also known as *Oscar Wilde*), Dove International, 1997.

Television Appearances; Series:
Gloria Munday, *Foul Play*, ABC, 1981.
Julie Camden Hastings, *7th Heaven* (also known as *Seventh Heaven*), The WB, 1996–2005.

Television Appearances; Miniseries:
Chris Farris, *The Last Convertible*, NBC, 1979.
Casey Tcholok, *Noble House* (also known as *James Clavell's "Noble House"*), NBC, 1988.

Television Appearances; Movies:
The American Sportsman, ABC, 1965.
Cathy Phillips, *Nightmare in Badham County* (also known as *Nightmare*), ABC, 1976.
Lee Larson, *Ski Lift to Death* (also known as *Snowblind*), CBS, 1978.
Cynthia Miller, *How to Pick Up Girls!*, ABC, 1978.
Willa Barnes (title role), *Willa*, CBS, 1979.
Suzy, *Mind over Murder* (also known as *Deadly Vision*), CBS, 1979.
Brooke Hayward, *Haywire*, CBS, 1980.
Barbara Gibbons, *For the Love of It*, ABC, 1980.
Anna Medley, *Killing at Hell's Gate*, CBS, 1981.
Lilah Ward, *For Lovers Only*, ABC, 1982.
Iris Murdoch, *Sparkling Cyanide* (also known as *Agatha Christie's "Sparkling Cyanide,"* CBS, 1983.
Elisabeth St. Claire, *Running Out*, CBS, 1983.
Barbara Jones, *Threesome*, CBS, 1984.
Last Video and Testament (also known as *Hammer House of Mystery and Suspense: "Last Video and Testament"*), 1984.
Judy Hale, *Lace II*, ABC, 1985.
Attitudes, Lifetime, 1989.
Sara, *Night of the Fox* (also known as *Le complot du renard*), syndicated, 1990.
Sister Megan, *The Sands of Time* (also known as *Sidney Sheldon's "The Sands of Time"*), syndicated, 1992.
Emily Allison, *A Perry Mason Mystery: "The Case of the Grimacing Governor,"* NBC, 1994.
Monica Arins, *Home Song* (also known as *LaVyrle Spencer's "Home Song,"* CBS, 1996.
Amelia Hartland, *Book of Days*, PAX, 2003.

Television Appearances; Pilots:
Margie, "Margie Passes," *Of Men, Of Women*, ABC, 1973.

Television Appearances; Specials:
Presenter, *The 47th Annual Academy Awards*, NBC, 1975.
Performer, *Circus of the Stars*, CBS, 1977.
The 38th Annual Golden Globe Awards, CBS, 1981.
Night of 100 Stars II, 1985.
Hollywood Women, 1994.
The Golden Globe's 50th Anniversary Celebration, NBC, 1994.
Intimate Portrait: Diane Lane, Lifetime, 2002.

Look, Up in the Sky: The Amazing Story of Superman, Arts and Entertainment, 2006.

Television Appearances; Episodic:
Gloria Munday, *Foul Play*, 1981.
Sharon Miles, "Something in the Walls," *The Twilight Zone*, syndicated, 1988.
Carolann "Punky" Dunhurst, "Carolann," *B. L. Stryker*, ABC, 1989.
Maia Graves, "Clock," *Law & Order: Special Victims Unit* (also known as *Law & Order: SVU* and *Special Victims Unit*), NBC, 2006.

Also appeared in *Dinner Date*.

Television Work; Miniseries:
Coproducer, *Windmills of the Gods*, CBS, 1988.

Television Work; Movies:
Producer and director, *Family Blessings* (also known as *LaVyrle Spencer's "Family Blessings,"* CBS, 1996.
Producer, *Home Song* (also known as *LaVyrle Spencer's "Home Song,"* CBS, 1996.
Producer, *Unwed Father*, ABC, 1997.
Executive producer, *Futuresport*, ABC, 1998.

Television Director; Episodic:
"The Kid Is Out of the Picture," *7th Heaven* (also known as *Seventh Heaven*), The WB, 2003.
"The Anniversary," *7th Heaven* (also known as *Seventh Heaven*), The WB, 2004.

Stage Appearances:
Appeared as Ophelia, *Hamlet*, National Theatre of Great Britain, London; in *Bus Stop* and *Taken in Marriage*, both produced by the Burt Reynolds Dinner Theatre, Jupiter, FL; *Cat on a Hot Tin Roof; Come Blow Your Horn; Social Security; Beau Jest.*

RECORDINGS

Taped Readings:
Forever, Dove Entertainment, 1986.
Morning Glory, Dove Audio, 1989, New Millennium Audio, 2003.
(With others) *American Rhapsody*, New Millennium, 2000.
Shrink Rap, Recorded Books, 2003.

Also read other audio books including *The Adventures of Tom Sawyer.*

WRITINGS

Screenplays:
(With Charles Jarrott) *Morning Glory*, Academy Entertainment, 1993.

Nonfiction:

(And editor) *Sharing Christmas: Cherished Memories from 100 Celebrated Men and Women All Over the World,* Warner Books, 1990.

Sharing Christmas, Volume 2, 1992.

(Editor) *A Gift of Sharing: A Celebration of Christmas and Chanukah,* Dove Books, 1996.

OTHER SOURCES

Periodicals:

Hollywood Reporter, February 22, 1988.

Publishers Weekly, June 16, 1997, p. 10; November 8, 1999, p. 19; April 17, 2000, p. 18.

RALPH, Michael
(Mike Ralph)

PERSONAL

Brother of Sheryl Lee Ralph (an actress).

Addresses: *Agent*—(voice work) TGMD Talent Agency, 6767 Forest Lawn Dr., Suite 101, Los Angeles, CA 90068. *Manager*—Sherry Marsh, Marsh Entertainment, 12444 Ventura Blvd., Suite 203, Studio City, CA 91604.

Career: Actor. Appeared in commercial for Cingular Wireless telecommunications.

CREDITS

Television Appearances; Series:

Spencer Boyer, a recurring role, *A Different World,* NBC, between 1990 and 1993.

Tyrell, *Cleghorne!,* The WB, 1995.

Kelly, *The Bernie Mac Show,* Fox, between 2001 and 2006.

Television Appearances; Miniseries:

Car thief, *To Serve and Protect,* NBC, 1999.

Voice of Shaq number eight, *Out of Order,* Showtime, 2003.

Television Appearances; Movies:

Dion, *Rebound: The Legend of Earl "The Goat" Manigault* (also known as *Rebound*), HBO, 1996.

Lusher, *Black Cat Run,* HBO, 1998.

Little Richard, NBC, 2000.

Falco, *The Right Temptation,* HBO, 2000.

Drake & Josh Go Hollywood, Nickelodeon, 2006.

Television Appearances; Specials:

Voices of officer, trumpeter, and first peach–fuzz, *The Princess and the Pauper: An Animated Special from the "Happily Ever After: Fairy Tales for Every Child" Series* (animated), HBO, 2000.

Speaker, "The Old Settler," *PBS Hollywood Presents,* PBS, 2001.

Soul Decisions, Showtime, c. 2003.

Julius, *Dense,* Showtime, 2004.

Television Appearances; Pilots:

Odd Jobs, NBC, 1997.

Television Appearances; Episodic:

"Windy City Blues," *Renegade,* USA Network and syndicated, 1993.

Leon, "Mr. Science Show," *The Sinbad Show* (also known as *Sinbad*), Fox, 1994.

Leon, "The Telethon," *The Sinbad Show* (also known as *Sinbad*), Fox, 1994.

Issac Caldwell, "Born in the USA," *The Commish,* ABC, 1994.

Promoter, "Get a Job," *Martin,* Fox, 1994.

Mr. Hayes, "A Matter of Principal," *Hangin' with Mr. Cooper,* ABC, 1995.

Mr. Alexander, "A Shift in the Night," *ER,* NBC, 1996.

Calvin Campbell, "Hakeem's Birthday," *Moesha,* UPN, 1997.

Bernie, *Players,* NBC, 1997.

Gene Rush, *Hitz,* UPN, 1997.

Lonnie Cochran, "Heir Today, Gone Tomorrow," *The Parkers,* UPN, 2000.

Paralegal, "All I Want for Christmas Is My Dead Uncle's Cash," *Yes, Dear,* CBS, 2000.

John, "Surprise, Surprise: Part 2," *All of Us,* UPN/CW Network, 2004.

Sam Finney, "Brutus," *Numb3rs* (also known as *Num3ers*), CBS, 2006.

Film Appearances:

Monkey, *Marked for Death,* Twentieth Century–Fox, 1990.

Member of crowd, *Malcolm X* (also known as *X*), Warner Bros., 1992.

Mules, *Scenes from the New World,* 1994.

Trevor, *Drop Squad,* Gramercy, 1994.

Rastafarian flasher, *Last Resort* (also known as *National Lampoon's "Last Resort"* and *National Lampoon's "Scuba School"*), Rose & Ruby Productions, 1994.

Romaine, *Woo,* New Line Cinema, 1998.

(As Mike Ralph) Second inmate, *Blow,* New Line Cinema, 2001.

Bumba Clot, *The Rules of Attraction* (also known as *Die Regeln des spiels*), Lions Gate Films, 2002.

Debater Steve, *Totally Baker: A Pot–u–mentary,* Laughter Heals, 2007.

Mr. Sanchez, *The Adventures of Teddy P. Brains: Journey into the Rain Forest,* Clarendon Entertainment, 2007.

RECORDINGS

Video Games:

Voices of steadfast driver and torpedo launcher driver, *Star Wars: Galactic Battlegrounds,* LucasArts Entertainment, 2001.

Voice of fifth rebel wing man, *Star Wars: Rogue Squadron II—Rogue Leader* (also known as *Rogue Leader* and *Star Wars: Rogue Squadron II*), LucasArts Entertainment, 2001.

Voices, *Star Wars: Knights of the Old Republic* (also known as *Star Wars: KOTOR*), LucasArts Entertainment, 2003.

Voices of Abu Bakr, Craps, and Motorhead, *The Chronicles of Riddick: Escape from Butcher Bay,* Vivendi Universal Games, 2004.

Voice of gangster, *Grand Theft Auto: San Andreas* (also known as *GTA: San Andreas* and *San Andreas*), Rockstar Games, 2004.

Voices of SWAT Officer Allen "Python" Jackson and Jean Trouffant, *S.W.A.T. 4,* Vivendi Universal Games, 2005.

Voice from Division Energy, *The Incredible Hulk: Ultimate Destruction,* Vivendi Universal Games, 2005.

Voice of masked assailant, *50 Cent: Bulletproof,* Vivendi Universal Games, 2005.

Voice of SWAT Officer Allen, *SWAT 4: The Stetchkov Syndicate,* Irrational Games, 2006.

Voice, *World in Conflict,* Massive Entertainment, 2007.

RALPH, Sheryl Lee 1956(?)–

PERSONAL

Born December 30, 1956 (some sources say 1955), in Waterbury, CT; daughter of Stanley (a college administrator) and Ivy (a fashion designer) Ralph; sister of Michael Ralph (an actor); married Eric George Maurice (an art collector), December, 1990 (divorced, 2001); married Vincent Hughes (a state senator), July 30, 2005; children: (first marriage) Etienne George–Nelson, Ivy–Victoria Julia. *Education:* Rutgers University, B.A., English literature and theatre arts; trained for the stage with the Negro Ensemble Company, New York City.

Addresses: *Agent*—William Morris Agency, One William Morris Pl., Beverly Hills, CA 90212.

Career: Actress, singer, director, producer, and writer. Elsinore's Atlantic Casino Hotel, Atlantic City, NJ, singer, 1985; Island Girl Productions, founder and owner, beginning 1990; International Jamaican Film and Music Festival, affiliated with "Cinema Inna Yard." Designer of Le Petit Etienne, a line of children's clothing; codirector of annual Los Angeles Children's Toy Drive.

Member: Screen Actors Guild, Actors' Equity Association, American Federation of Television and Radio Artists, Delta Sigma Theta (honorary member).

Awards, Honors: Antoinette Perry Award nomination, best actress in a musical, Drama Desk Award nomination, outstanding actress in a musical, 1982, for *Dreamgirls;* Independent Spirit Award, best supporting female, Independent Features Project West, 1991, for *To Sleep with Anger;* Image Award nominations, outstanding supporting actress in a comedy series, National Association for the Advancement of Colored People, 1998, 1999, 2000, 2001, 2002, all for *Moesha.*

CREDITS

Film Appearances:

Barbara Hanley, *A Piece of the Action,* Warner Bros., 1977.

Lola, *Finding Maubee,* Metro–Goldwyn–Mayer/United Artists, 1988.

Voice of Rita, *Oliver & Company* (animated), Buena Vista, 1988.

Lola Quinn, *The Mighty Quinn,* Metro–Goldwyn–Mayer/United Artists, 1989.

Receptionist, *Skin Deep* (also known as *Blake Edward's "Skin Deep"*), Twentieth Century–Fox, 1989.

Linda, *To Sleep with Anger,* Samuel Goldwyn, 1990.

Miss Loretta, *The Distinguished Gentleman,* Buena Vista, 1992.

Beverly Dumont, *Mistress* (also known as *Hollywood Mistress*), Tribeca, 1992.

Florence Watson, *Sister Act 2: Back in the Habit,* Buena Vista, 1993.

Miss Pyrite, *The Flintstones,* Universal, 1994.

Roberta, *White Man's Burden* (also known as *White Man*), 1995.

Charlotte, *Lover's Knot,* Republic, 1996.

Ruth Clark, *Bogus,* Warner Bros., 1996.

Sylvia Jones, *Jamaica Beat,* 1997.

Secrets, 1998.

Chantal, *Personals* (also known as *Hook'd Up*), Unapix Entertainment, 1998.

Voice, *The Easter Story Keepers,* 1998.

Gayle Redford, *Deterrence,* 1999.

Linda Cray, *Unconditional Love,* Home Entertainment, 1999.

Nurse, *Lost in the Pershing Point Hotel,* Pershing Point Productions/Pierrepont Productions, 2000.

Mamie, *Baby of the Family,* DownSouth Filmworks, 2001.

Mama, *Frankie D,* 2007.

Herself, *Angels Can't Help But Laugh* (documentary), 2007.

Broadway: Beyond the Golden Age (documentary; also known as *B.G.A. 2* and *Broadway: The Golden Age Two*), 2008.

Film Work:
Director, *Race Card,* 2000.

Television Appearances; Series:
Laura "Mac" McCarthy, *Search for Tomorrow,* CBS, 1983–84.

Maggie Bryan, *Code Name: Foxfire,* NBC, 1985.

Ginger St. James, *It's a Living,* syndicated, 1986–89.

Vicki St. James, *New Attitude,* 1990.

Etienne Toussant–Bouvier, *Designing Women,* CBS, 1992–93.

Maggie Foster, *George,* ABC, 1993.

Dee Mitchell, *Moesha,* UPN, 1996–2001.

Lieutenant Dee Banks, *The District,* CBS, 2000–2001.

Reverend Ruby, *Exes & Oh's,* 2006.

Television Appearances; Miniseries:
Miss Rosalee, *The Gambler Returns: Luck of the Draw,* NBC, 1991.

Television Appearances; Movies:
Doris Campbell, *The Neighborhood* (also known as *Breslin's "Neighborhood"*), NBC, 1982.

Corelle, *Sister Margaret and the Saturday Night Ladies,* CBS, 1986.

Marjorie Duncan, *No Child of Mine* (also known as *The Fight for Baby Jesse* and *The Fight for Jesse*), CBS, 1993.

Hypolita Kropotkin, *Witch Hunt,* HBO, 1994.

Dr. Pamela Prentiss, *The Jennie Project,* Disney Channel, 2001.

Aunt Amy, *Odicie,* Black Entertainment Television, 2007.

Television Appearances; Specials:
The 7th Annual Black Achievement Awards, 1986.

Presenter, *The 19th Annual NAACP Image Awards,* NBC, 1987.

Happy 100th Birthday, Hollywood! (also known as *Happy Birthday, Hollywood!*), ABC, 1987.

Performer, *The 42nd Annual Tony Awards,* CBS, 1988.

The 16th Annual Black Filmmakers Hall of Fame, syndicated, 1989.

Host, *The 11th Annual American Black Achievement Awards,* syndicated, 1989.

The 22nd Annual NAACP Image Awards, NBC, 1990.

Host, *Story of a People: The Black Road to Hollywood,* 1990.

Voices That Care, Fox, 1991.

Host, *Story of a People: The Black Road to Hollywood,* syndicated, 1991.

The 24th Annual NAACP Image Awards, NBC, 1992.

Children of Africa, 1993.

Presenter, *The 7th Annual Soul Train Music Awards,* syndicated, 1993.

Judge, *The 1994 Miss USA Pageant,* CBS, 1994.

It's Hot in Here: UPN Fall Preview, UPN, 1996.

"Secrets," *Showtime Black Filmmaker Showcase,* Showtime, 1997.

Acapulco Black Film Festival, 2000.

Judge, *The 80th Annual Miss America Pageant,* ABC, 2000.

The 42nd Annual L.A. County Arts Commission Holiday Celebration, 2001.

10 Biggest Celebrity Oops, E! Entertainment Television, 2004.

E! 101 Most Starlicious Makeovers, E! Entertainment Television, 2004.

101 Most Unforgettable SNL Moments, E! Entertainment Television, 2004.

E! 101 Most Awesome Moments in Entertainment, E! Entertainment Television, 2004.

Novelette, *Kink in My Hair,* 2004.

I Love the '90s: Part Deux, VH1, 2005.

Bring That Year Back 2006: Laugh Now, Cry Later, Black Entertainment Television, 2006.

Television Appearances; Pilots:
The Krofft Komedy Hour, ABC, 1978.

Maggie Bryan, *Code Name: Foxfire* (also known as *Slay It Again, Sam*), NBC, 1985.

Roberta, *Pros and Cons,* ABC, 1986.

Vicki St. James, *New Attitude,* ABC, 1990.

Television Appearances; Episodic:
Nurse, "Shut Down," *A.E.S. Hudson Street,* 1978.

"A Little Bit of England," *Baa Baa Black Sheep* (also known as *Black Sheep Squadron*), 1978.

Vanessa, "J. J. and the Plumber's Helper," *Good Times,* 1978.

Joelle, "Murray Gets Sacked and Paula Gets Hired," *Husbands, Wives, and Lovers,* CBS, 1978.

Bobbie, "The Spaceships Are Coming," *Wonder Woman* (also known as *The New Adventures of Wonder Woman* and *The New Original Wonder Woman*), CBS, 1979.

Jeanie, "Louise's Convention," *The Jeffersons,* 1979.

Glenna, "The Overlord," *V* (also known as *V: The Series*), 1984.

Maggie Bryan, "La Paloma," *Code Name: Foxfire* (also known as *Slay It Again, Sam*), NBC, 1985.

"Love and the English Teacher," *New Love American Style,* ABC, 1986.

Josie Clifford, "The Return of Typhoon Thompson," *Hunter,* NBC, 1986.

"Love Is a Kick," *New Love American Style,* ABC, 1986.

Renee Quintana, "Beef Jerky," *L.A. Law,* NBC, 1987.

Show singer, "Gershwin's Trunk," *Amazing Stories* (also known as *Steven Spielberg's "Amazing Stories"*), 1987.

Body by Jake, syndicated, 1988.

Mooshy Tucker, "Dark Streets," *Falcon Crest,* 1990.

Mooshy Tucker, "Crimes of the Past," *Falcon Crest,* 1990.

Host, *Soul Train,* 1996.

The Rosie O'Donnell Show, syndicated, 1996, 1998.

Oddville, MTV, 1997.

Voice of second lioness, "Flood Warning," *The Wild Thornberrys* (animated), Nickelodeon, 1998.

Zsa Zsa Goowhiggie, "What Price Harvey?" *Sabrina, the Teenage Witch* (also known as *Sabrina*), ABC, 1999.

Dee Mitchell, "Daddy's Girl," *The Parkers,* ABC, 1999.

Hollywood Squares (also known as *H2* and *H2: Hollywood Squares*), 1999, 2001.

Voice of Mrs. Lasalle, "Me Know No," *Recess* (also known as *Disney's "Recess"*), Disney Channel, 2000.

The Roseanne Show, 2000.

Dee Banks, *The District,* CBS, 2000.

Voice of Aunt Dee, "Romeo Must Wed," *The Proud Family* (animated), Disney Channel, 2002.

Voice of Trina Jessup, "Pop's Girlfriend," *Static Shock* (animated), The WB, 2002.

Voice of Cheetah, "Injustice for All: Parts 1 & 2," *Justice League* (animated; also known as *JL* and *Justice League Unlimited*), Cartoon Network, 2002.

Voice of Trina Jessup, "Consequences," *Static Shock* (animated), The WB, 2003.

Florence, "She Ain't Heavy, She's My Partner," *Whoopi,* NBC, 2003.

Janet Ellis, "Luck Be a Lady," *Las Vegas,* NBC, 2003.

The Wayne Brady Show, syndicated, 2003.

Voice of Cheetah, "Kid Stuff," *Justice League* (animated; also known as *JL* and *Justice League Unlimited*), Cartoon Network, 2004.

Claire, "Madonna Is a Ho," *Barbershop,* Showtime, 2005.

Claire, "What's Good for the Cos" *Barbershop,* Showtime, 2005.

Claire, "A Black Man Invented the Stop Light," *Barbershop,* Showtime, 2005.

Claire, "Debates and Dead People," *Barbershop,* Showtime, 2005.

Entertainment Tonight (also known as *E.T.*), syndicated, 2005, 2007.

In the Mix (also known as *In the Cutz*), Urban America, 2006.

Nurse, "And Baby Makes Three," *7th Heaven* (also known as *Seventh Heaven*), The WB, 2006.

Gloria Gallant, "Strange Bedfellows," *ER,* NBC, 2006.

Gloria Gallant, "21 Guns," *ER,* NBC, 2006.

Also appeared in *Search for Tomorrow;* as herself, "Wild on Jamaica," *Wild On.*

Television Work; Specials:

Producer and director, "Secrets," *Showtime Black Filmmaker Showcase,* Showtime, 1999.

Television Director; Episodic:

"Single Black Female," *The Parkers,* UPN, 2001.

Stage Appearances:

Faith, *Reggae,* Biltmore Theatre, New York City, 1980.

Deena Jones, *Dreamgirls,* Imperial Theatre, New York City, 1981.

Jill Undergrowth, *Identical Twins from Baltimore,* Tiffany Theatre, Los Angeles, 1987.

Muzzy van Hossmere, *Thoroughly Modern Millie,* Marquis Theatre, New York City, 2002.

Margo Channing, *Applause,* Freud Playhouse, Westwood, CA, 2005.

Stage Producer:

Divas: Simply Singing (benefit concerts), beginning 1991.

RECORDINGS

Albums:

In the Evening, Sid Bernstein's New York Music Company, 1984.

Also recorded "Here Comes the Rain."

Videos:

Coproducer, codirector, and host, *Sheryl Lee Ralph's Beauty Basics,* Lorimar Home Video, 1987.

Music Videos:

Appeared in "Voices That Care."

Taped Readings:

The Hand I Fan With, 1997.

WRITINGS

Screenplays:

Race Card, 2000.

Television Specials:

"Secrets," *Showtime Black Filmmaker Showcase,* Showtime, 1999.

Other:

(Coauthor) *Sheryl Lee Ralph's Beauty Basics* (instructional video), Lorimar Home Video, 1987.

Coauthor (with Ralph Farquhar) of the script *Red Rum and Coke.*

OTHER SOURCES

Books:
Contemporary Black Biography, Volume 18, Gale, 1998.

Periodicals:
Black Enterprise, February, 2007, p. 148.
Ebony, March, 2003, p. 82.
Essence, December, 1993, p. 62.
Jet, August 22, 2005, p. 30.

RAPHAEL, Sally Jessy 1943–

PERSONAL

Original name, Sally Lowenthal; born February 25, 1943, in Easton, PA; daughter of Jesse (a business executive) and Dede Lowry (a painter; maiden name, Raphael) Lowenthal; married Andrew Vladimir (an advertising executive and professor of hotel management), c. 1959 (divorced, 1964); married Karl Soderlund (a radio station manager and actor), c. 1964; children: (first marriage) Allison Vladimir Romanoff (deceased), Andrea; (second marriage) Jason ("J. J."; adopted), two stepdaughters, and three foster children, including Monica Franciscus. *Education:* Attended Carnegie–Mellon University; Columbia University, B.F.A.; University of Puerto Rico, M.F.A.; studied at Actors Studio, New York City. *Avocational Interests:* Collecting Ozark twig furniture and antique dolls.

Career: Talk show host and producer. WPIX–TV, New York City, television news anchor; WHOA–Radio, San Juan, PR, reporter; Associated Press, correspondent from the Caribbean; WAPA–TV, San Juan, host of a cooking program, 1965–67, and a talk show; radio and television broadcaster in Miami, FL, and Fort Lauderdale, FL, 1969–74; WMCA–Radio, New York City, cohost of a morning talk show, 1976–81; NBC Talknet, New York City, talk show host, 1982–88; ABC Talkradio, New York City, talk show host, 1988–91; hosts weekday talk show on www.sallyjr.com, 2004. Appeared in television commercials including, Lipton Sizzle and Stir, 2001. Owner of a perfume factory, 1964–68, an art gallery, 1964–69, and The Wine Press (wine bar), New York City, 1979–83; also operated a bed–and–breakfast business in Bucks County, PA. Active with charitable organizations, including UNICEF and DARE America.

Awards, Honors: Bronze Medal, International Film and Television Festival of New York, 1985; Daytime Emmy Award nominations, 1988, 1990, 1991, 1992, outstanding talk show host, Daytime Emmy Award, outstanding talk show host, 1989, all for *Sally Jessy Raphael;* named Talk Show Host of the Year, National Association of Radio Talk Show Hosts, 1992.

CREDITS

Television Appearances; Series:
Host, *Sally Jessy Raphael* (also known as *In Touch with Sally Jessy Raphael, Sally,* and *The Sally Show*), syndicated, 1983–2002.
Herself, *Another World* (also known as *Another World: Bay City*), 1993.
Herself, *The Surreal Life,* VH1, 2004–2005.

Television Appearances; Movies:
Herself, *Kojak: Fatal Flaw,* ABC, 1989.
Judge, *No One Would Tell,* NBC, 1996.

Television Appearances; Specials:
The 16th Annual Daytime Emmy Awards, NBC, 1989.
MDA Jerry Lewis Telethon, syndicated, 1990.
Happy Birthday, Bugs: 50 Looney Years (also known as *Hollywood Celebrates Bugs Bunny's 50th Anniversary*), CBS, 1990.
Cohost, *Why Bother Voting?,* PBS, 1992.
Donahue: The 25th Anniversary, NBC, 1992.
Host, *Di: Prisoner in the Palace* (documentary), Fox, 1992.
In a New Light '93, 1993.
Adoption Vigilantes, 1994.
Intimate Portrait: Sally Jessy Raphael, Lifetime, 1997.
Sally Jessy Raphael: Behind the Real Glasses, 1999.
It's Only Talk: The Real Story of America's Talk Show, 1999.
The Barbi Twins: The E! True Hollywood Story, E! Entertainment Television, 2001.
Comedy Central Presents: The N.Y. Friars Club Roast of Chevy Chase, Comedy Central, 2002.

Also appeared as host, *The Surreal Reunion: Season 4,* VH1.

Television Appearances; Episodic:
"The Making of a Martyr," *The Equalizer,* CBS, 1989.
The Jerry Springer Show, 1991.
The Howard Stern Show, 1991.
Where in the World is Carmen Sandiego?, PBS, 1991.
"All the Life That's Fit to Print," *Murphy Brown,* CBS, 1993.
Herself, "The Strike," *The Nanny,* CBS, 1994.
Herself, "The Last Auction Hero," *Dave's World,* CBS, 1994.

Dr. Gina Lawson, "Love Is Murder," *Diagnosis Murder,* CBS, 1996.

Mrs. Angeli, "Flesh and Blood," *Touched by an Angel,* CBS, 1996.

Herself, "A Halloween Story," *Sabrina, the Teenage Witch* (also known as *Sabrina*), ABC, 1996.

Gourmet Getaways with Robin Leach, 1996.

The Rosie O'Donnell Show, syndicated, 1997, 1999.

On the Inside, 1997.

"TLC," *Behind the Music* (also known as *VH1's "Behind the Music"*), VH1, 1999.

At Home With … 1999.

Da Ali G Show, 2000.

"Mexicans Day," *TV Funhouse,* Comedy Central, 2000.

"Jenny's 10th Anniversary Show," *Jenny Jones,* 2001.

Hollywood Squares (also known as *H2* and *H2: Hollywood Squares*), syndicated, 2003.

Chappelle's Show, Comedy Central, 2004.

(Uncredited) *Howard Stern,* E! Entertainment Television, 2005.

"Chat Shows," *The Story of Light Entertainment,* BBC2, 2006.

Herself, "Operation: Seduce Simone," *The Knights of Prosperity,* ABC, 2007.

Also appeared in *Conspiracy of Silence; The John Larroquette Show; Nightline; The Tonight Show,* NBC.

Television Executive Producer; Miniseries:

The Third Twin (also known as *Ken Follett's "The Third Twin"*), CBS, 1997.

Television Executive Producer; Movies:

The Stalking of Laurie Show (also known as *Rivales*), USA Network, 2000.

A Mother's Testimony, 2001.

Film Appearances:

Herself, *She–Devil,* 1989.

Talk show host, *Resident Alien* (also known as *Resident Alien: Quentin Crisp in America*), 1990.

Herself, *The Addams Family,* 1991.

Herself, *The Associate,* Buena Vista, 1996.

Herself, *Meet Wally Sparks,* Trimark Pictures, 1997.

Herself, *Double Whammy,* 2001.

Herself, *The Guru* (also known as *Le gourou et les femmes*), Universal, 2002.

Herself, *Unconditional Love,* New Line Cinema, 2002.

Herself, *Pauly Shore Is Dead,* CKrush Entertainment, 2003.

Stage Appearances:

Narrator, *The Rocky Horror Show,* Circle in the Square Theatre, New York City, 2001.

WRITINGS

Books:

(With M. J. Abadie) *Finding Love: A Practical Guide for Men and Women,* Arbor House (New York City), 1984.

(With Pam Proctor) *Sally: Unconventional Success* (autobiography), 1990.

OTHER SOURCES

Books:

Newsmakers 1992, Gale, 1992.

Periodicals:

Ladies Home Journal, February, 1992, p. 120.

People Weekly, October 20, 1986, p. 91; September 19, 1988, p. 61; February 3, 1992, p. 58; February 17, 1992, p. 57; March 31, 1997, p. 50; January 31, 1998, p. 14.

Electronic:

Sally Jessy Raphael Website, http://www.sallyjr.com, October 10, 2007.

RASCHE, David 1944–

PERSONAL

Born August 7, 1944, in St. Louis, MO; father, a minister and farmer; married Heather Lupton (an acting teacher), c. 1976; children: three. *Education:* Graduated from Elmhurst College; University of Chicago, M.A., divinity; trained at Second City Workshop, Chicago, IL; studied acting with Sanford Meisner.

Addresses: *Agent*—Innovative Artists, 1505 10th St., Santa Monica, CA 90401. *Manager*—Liebman Entertainment, 235 Park Ave. South, 10th Floor, New York, NY 10003.

Career: Actor and writer. Second City (comedy group), Chicago, IL, member of company; Victory Gardens Theatre, Chicago, founding member, 1974.

Awards, Honors: DramaLogue Award, best play, 1994, for *Jackie.*

CREDITS

Film Appearances:

(Uncredited) *An Unmarried Woman,* Twentieth Century–Fox, 1978.

Gregory Paynes–Whitney–Smith, *Manhattan*, United Artists, 1979.

David Ritchie, *Something Short of Paradise* (also known as *Perfect Love*), American International Pictures, 1979.

Stopwatch producer, *Just Tell Me What You Want*, Warner Bros., 1980.

Eddie White, *Honky Tonk Freeway*, Universal, 1981.

Michael Taylor, *Fighting Back* (also known as *Death Vengeance*), Paramount, 1982.

Jeff the "KGB" agent, *Best Defense* (also known as *Best Defence*), Paramount, 1984.

Dan, *Cobra*, Warner Bros., 1986.

Buckley, *Native Son*, American Playhouse, 1986.

Cal McGinnis, *Ray's Male Heterosexual Dance Hall*, Chanticleer, 1987.

Donald Sumner, *Made in Heaven*, Warner Bros. Home Video, 1987.

Steve, *Wicked Stepmother*, Metro–Goldwyn–Mayer, 1989.

Detective Mike Parnell, *An Innocent Man* (also known as *A Hard Rain*), Buena Vista, 1989.

Sloane Vaughn, *Wedding Band*, IRS Media, 1990.

Buddy Wheeler, *Masters of Menace*, 1990, New Line Cinema, 1991.

Dr. Paul Kirkwood and Dennis, *Delirious*, Metro–Goldwyn–Mayer, 1991.

Hal Devlin, *Bingo!*, TriStar, 1991.

Baker, *Twenty Bucks*, Triton Pictures, 1993.

Jeff, *A Million to Juan* (also known as *A Million to One*), Samuel Goldwyn Company, 1994.

Chaz Frederick, *Bigfoot: The Unforgettable Encounter*, Republic, 1994.

Phillip, the fourth patient, *Magic in the Water* (also known as *Glenorky* and *Le lac magique*), TriStar, 1995.

Master of ceremonies at luau, *Lieberman in Love*, Chanticleer, 1995.

Amy's dad, *Pie in the Sky*, Fine Line, 1996.

Alan, *That Old Feeling*, Universal, 1997.

Richard, *Friends and Lovers* (also known as *Friends & Lovers*), Lions Gate Films, 1999.

Stig Ludwigssen, *The Big Tease*, Warner Bros., 1999.

Denny, *The Settlement*, Bedford Entertainment, 1999.

Jack Stanford, *Pros and Cons*, New Line Home Video, 1999.

Martin Shutte, *Off the Lip*, Abandon Pictures, 2000.

Elliot Chevron, *Teddy Bears' Picnic*, Magnolia Pictures, 2002.

Taylor Abbott, *Divine Secrets of the Ya–Ya Sisterhood*, Warner Bros., 2002.

Mr. Dan McNerney, *Just Married* (also known as *Voll verheiratet*), Twentieth Century–Fox, 2003.

Warren Ward, *Exposed*, Mainline Releasing, 2003.

Dr. Martin Shutte, *Off the Lip*, Hannover House, 2004.

Himself, *Sledge Hammer: Go Ahead, Make Me Laugh* (documentary short), IDT Entertainment, 2004.

Himself, *Gun Crazy: Memorable Moments with the Cast of "Sledge Hammer!"* (documentary short), 2005.

Phil, *Perception*, Empire Pictures, 2005.

General, *Final Approach*, Green Communications, 2006.

President Ballentine, *The Sentinel*, Twentieth Century–Fox, 2006.

Donald Freeman Greene, *United 93* (also known as *Vol 93*), Universal, 2006.

Senator, *Flags of Our Fathers*, DreamWorks Distribution, 2006.

Doug, *The Girl in the Park*, 2007.

Thomas Sparrow, *The Spy and the Sparrow*, 2008.

Television Appearances; Series:

Wes Leonard, *Ryan's Hope*, ABC, 1976.

Sam Rawlings, *Code Name: Foxfire* (also known as *Slay It Again, Sam*), NBC, 1985.

Stewart Webber, *Sara*, 1985.

Title role, *Sledge Hammer!* (also known as *Sledge Hammer: The Early Years*), ABC, 1986.

Jack Trenton, *Nurses*, NBC, 1992–94.

Peter, *High Society*, CBS, 1995.

Voices, *Santo Bugato* (animated), CBS, 1995.

President Whitman, *DAG*, NBC, 2000.

Also appeared in *The Trials of Rosie O'Neill*.

Television Appearances; Miniseries:

Brother Nahum, *Signs and Wonders*, PBS, 1995.

Television Appearances; Movies:

Jack Collins, *Sanctuary of Fear* (also known as *Father Brown, Detective, Girl in the Park,* and *Sanctuary of Death*), NBC, 1979.

Dr. David McKeeson, *Special Bulletin*, NBC, 1983.

Donald Catton, *The Lost Honor of Kathryn Beck* (also known as *Act of Passion*), CBS, 1984.

Sandy, *Secret Witness*, CBS, 1988.

Sheriff Lauder, *Silhouette*, 1990.

Ted Forstmann, *Barbarians at the Gate*, HBO, 1993.

Alfred Rayne, *"Hart to Hart": Old Friends Never Die*, 1994.

Don Polson, *Out There*, Showtime and syndicated, 1995.

Ben Landry, *A Perry Mason Mystery: The Case of the Jealous Jokester*, NBC, 1995.

Payne, *Dead Weekend*, Showtime, 1995.

Patrick Kinsley, *Columbo: A Trace of Murder*, 1997.

Dr. Derek Early, *Tourist Trap*, ABC, 1998.

Robert Sinclair, *Hard Time: Hostage Hotel*, TNT, 1999.

Eddie Moran, *"The Mob Scene," The Lot*, American Movie Classics, 2001.

Television Appearances; Specials:

Reverend Howard Woode, *Hellfire*, syndicated, 1985.

Grave squad lawyer, *Partners*, Showtime, 1994.

Voice, *Empires: The Roman Empire in the First Century*, PBS, 2001.

Television Appearances; Pilots:
Sam Rawlings, *Code Name: Foxfire* (also known as *Slay It Again, Sam*), NBC, 1985.
President Whitman, *DAG*, NBC, 2000.

Television Appearances; Episodic:
"Death in a Toy Balloon," *The Andros Target*, 1977.
William Gardner, "Falling Star," *Mrs. Columbo* (also known as *Kate Columbo, Kate Loves a Mystery,* and *Kate the Detective*), 1979.
Robert Wellesly, "Melonvote," *SCTV Network 90* (also known as *SCTV Comedy Network* and *SCTV Network*), 1982.
Surf, "Bushido," *Miami Vice*, NBC, 1985.
Richard Lubin, "Thank You, Shirley," *Kate & Allie*, CBS, 1986.
David McCoy, "Beauty and the Breast," *L.A. Law*, NBC, 1992.
David McCoy, "Double Breasted Suit," *L.A. Law*, NBC, 1992.
Jack Trenton, "Love and Marriage," *Empty Nest*, 1993.
"Who Killed the Legal Eagle?" *Burke's Law*, CBS, 1994.
Voice of Baron Von Dillweed, "Married Alive," *Duckman* (animated), USA Network, 1995.
Peter, "Finnigan's Rainbow," *High Society*, 1995.
Michael, "War and Sleaze," *Just Shoot Me!*, NBC, 1998.
Carl, "The State Dinner," *The West Wing*, NBC, 1999.
Kenny Daniels, "Family Circus," *Grown Ups*, 1999.
Evan, "Susan and the Professor," *Suddenly Susan*, NBC, 2000.
Evan, "The Reversal," *Suddenly Susan*, NBC, 2000.
Evan, "Finale: Parts 1 & 2," *Suddenly Susan*, NBC, 2000.
Dr. Bruckner, "The Birth Day," *For Your Love*, The WB, 2001.
Doc Croc, "The Wedding Planner," *Providence*, NBC, 2002.
Mr. Baranski, "Reversal of Fortune," *MDs*, ABC, 2002.
Lawyer, "Grandma Sues," *Malcolm in the Middle*, Fox, 2003.
Norton Andrews, "While You Were Out," *She Spies*, NBC, 2003.
Lee, "Hellbound Train," *Robbery Homicide Division* (also known as *R.H.D./LA: Robbery Homicide Division/Los Angeles*), CBS, 2003.
Coach Patterson, "Mr. Monk Goes Back to School," *Monk*, USA Network, 2003.
Tim Valentine, "Die Fast, Die Furious," *Las Vegas*, NBC, 2004.
Donald Warwick, "Acceptance," *The Book of Daniel*, NBC, 2006.

Stage Appearances:
Sexual Perversity in Chicago, Chicago, IL, 1974.
John, Off–Broadway production, 1976.
Mark, *The Shadow Box*, Morosco Theatre, New York City, 1977.

Ivan Miroski, German entrepreneur, and Lenin, *Isadora Duncan Sleeps with the Russian Navy*, American Place Theatre, New York City, 1977.
Peter, *Lunch Hour*, Ethel Barrymore Theatre, New York City, 1980.
Jacques and His Master, Los Angeles production, 1980.
Eugene Winter, *Geniuses*, Playwrights Horizons Theatre, New York City, 1982–83.
David, *To Gillian on Her 37th Birthday*, Circle in the Square Downtown, New York City, 1984.
The Custom of the Country, McGinn–Cazale Theatre, New York City, 1985.
Bobby Gould, *Speed–the–Plow*, Royale Theatre, New York City, 1988.
Fred, *A Christmas Carol*, Hudson Theatre, New York City, 1990.
Frank Elgin, *The Country Girl*, Roundabout Theatre, New York City, 1991.
Edmond, Atlantic Theatre, New York City, 1996.
Richard O'Neill, *Getting and Spending*, Helen Hayes Theatre, New York City, 1998.
Randall, *Last Dance*, Manhattan Theatre Club Stage II, New York City, 2003.
Josie Cartwright, Lawrence, and Two, *Five by Tenn*, Manhattan Theatre Club Stage II, New York City, 2004.
Victor Fleming, *Moonlight and Magnolias*, Manhattan Theatre Club, New York City, 2005.
Joey Francis Lesley, *Elvis and Juilet*, Abingdon Theatre Company, New York City, 2006.
Jack McCullough, *Regrets Only*, Manhattan Theatre Club Stage I, New York City, 2006–2007.

Also appeared in *Beyond Therapy; Loose Ends*, Broadway production; *The Taming of the Shrew*.

Radio Appearances; Series:
Appeared as Piett, *Star Wars: The Empire Strikes Back*, National Public Radio.

WRITINGS

Stage Plays:
Jackie, Los Angeles, 1994.

RAY, De
    See DAVIS, DeRay

RAYCOLE, Jazz 1988–
    (Jazzmine Dillingham)

PERSONAL

Full name, Jazzmine Raycole Dillingham; born February 11, 1988, in Stockton, CA. *Avocational Interests:* Shopping and cooking.

Career: Actress. Trained as a dancer.

Awards, Honors: Young Artist Award nomination, best performance in a television series (comedy or drama)—young actress age ten or younger, 2006, for *My Wife and Kids.*

CREDITS

Film Appearances:
(As Jazzmine Dillingham) Puppy, *Babe* (also known as *Babe, the Gallant Pig*), Universal, 1995.
Onika Harris, *Waiting to Exhale,* Twentieth Century–Fox, 1995.

Television Appearances; Series:
Claire Kyle, *My Wife and Kids,* ABC, 2001.
Allison Hawkins, *Jericho,* CBS, 2006—.

Television Appearances; Miniseries:
Lead dancer, *From the Earth to the Moon,* HBO, 1998.

Television Appearances; Pilots:
Vicky, *Clubhouse,* CBS, 2004.

Television Appearances; Episodic:
Sierra, "Nick the Player," *The Parent 'Hood,* The WB, 1996.
Angela, "Ellen: A Hollywood Tribute: Part 2," *Ellen* (also known as *These Friends of Mine*), ABC, 1998.
Vanessa, "Henderson House Party," *Smart Guy,* The WB, 1998.
Kayla, "We Got No Game," *The Jamie Foxx Show,* The WB, 1998.
Guest dancer, *Fox Kids Fun,* 1999.
Geneva, "Daddio," *Malcolm & Eddie,* UPN, 1999.
Megan, "Careless," *Law & Order: Special Victims Unit* (also known as *Law & Order: SVU* and *Special Victims Unit*), NBC, 2004.
Lisa, "Everybody Hates Halloween," *Everybody Hates Chris,* UPN, 2005.
Lisa, "Everybody Hates Drew," *Everybody Hates Chris,* UPN, 2006.
Kimberly, "Mr. Monk and the Big Game," *Monk,* USA Network, 2006.
Melissa Hudson, "Take Your Daughter to Work Day," *The Office* (also known as *The Office: US Version*), NBC, 2006.
Melissa Hudson, "Cocktails," *The Office* (also known as *The Office: US Version*), NBC, 2007.
Sharon, "Flashpoint," *Lincoln Heights,* ABC Family, 2007.

REARDON, Daniel
    See RIORDAN, Daniel

REDFORD, Amy 1970–
    (Amy Hart Redford)

PERSONAL

Born October 22, 1970; daughter of Robert (an actor, producer, and director) and Lola (maiden name, Van Wagenen) Redford; sister of James Redford (a writer). *Education:* Attended University of Colorado; trained for the theatre in London and in San Francisco, CA.

Addresses: *Manager*—Jennifer Wiley, Framework Entertainment, 9057 Nemo St., Suite C, West Hollywood, CA 90069.

Career: Actress, producer, and director.

CREDITS

Film Appearances:
Elizabeth Brenner, *Giving It Up* (also known as *Casanova Falling*), Lions Gate Films, 1999.
Times editor, *Mergers & Acquisitions,* 2001, Go Kart Films, 2006.
Reporter, *Maid in Manhattan* (also known as *Made in New York*), Columbia, 2002.
Ally, *Cry Funny Happy,* 7th Floor/Spot Creative, 2003.
Andie, *Last Man Running,* 2003.
Chloe Harden, *This Revolution,* Screen Media Films, 2005.
Sylvia McCord, *Strike the Tent* (also known as *The Last Confederate: The Story of Robert Adams*), 2005, ThinkFilm, 2007.
Annie Dresden, *The Music Inside,* Montana Motion Picture Corp., 2005.
Jenny, *When I Find the Ocean,* Cypress Moon Productions, 2006.
Cynthia, *First Person Singular,* Spot Creative, 2007.
Sister Victoria, *The Drum Beats Twice,* Justice for All Productions, 2008.
Sunshine Cleaning, Back Lot Pictures/Big Beach Films, 2008.
Helen, *The Understudy,* Mansion Pictures, 2008.

Film Work:
Producer and director, *The Guitar,* Carolco, 2007.

Television Appearances; Episodic:
(As Amy Hart Redford) Emergency room doctor, "House Arrest," *The Sopranos,* HBO, 2000.
(As Amy Hart Redford) Susan Welch, "Closure: Part 2," *Law & Order: Special Victims Unit* (also known as *Law & Order: SVU* and *Special Victims Unit*), NBC, 2000.

Amy Fincher, "Drama Queens," *Sex and the City,* HBO, 2000.

Open Mike with Mike Bullard (also known as *The Mike Bullard Show* and *Open Mike*), Global, 2002.

Maureen Garros, "View from Up Here," *Law & Order: Criminal Intent* (also known as *Law & Order: CI*), NBC, 2005.

Television Producer; Series:

Aperture, 2007.

Stage Appearances:

The Messenger, Rattlestick Theatre, New York City, 2000.

Catherine Bronson, *Golden Ladder,* Players Theatre, New York City, 2002.

Sara, *Bhutan,* New York Stage and Film, Cherry Lane Theatre, New York City, 2006.

RECORDINGS

Videos:

Once Upon a Time in the South: Behind "The Last Confederate," ThinkFilm, 2007.

OTHER SOURCES

Periodicals:

New York Times, October 31, 2006.

People Weekly, May 22, 2000, p. 111.

REDFORD, Robert 1937–

PERSONAL

Full name, Charles Robert Redford, Jr.; born August 18, 1937, in Santa Monica, CA; son of Charles Robert (an accountant) and Martha (maiden name, Hart) Redford; married Lola Van Wangeman, September 12, 1958 (divorced, 1985); children: Scott (deceased), Shauna, David James ("Jamie"; a writer and producer), Amy Hart (an actress). *Education:* Attended University of Colorado, 1955, and Pratt Institute, 1958; studied painting in Europe; attended American Academy of Dramatic Arts, New York City.

Addresses: *Office*—c/o Sundance Institute, 8530 Wilshire Blvd., 3rd Floor, Beverly Hills, CA 90211; Wildwood Enterprises Inc./South Fork Pictures, 725 Arizona Ave., Suite 306, Santa Monica, CA 90401.

Agent—Creative Artists Agency, 2000 Avenue of the Stars, Los Angeles, CA 90067. *Publicist*—PMK/HBH Public Relations, 700 San Vicente Blvd., Suite G910, West Hollywood, CA 90069.

Career: Actor, director, and producer. Wildwood International (production company; later Wildwood Enterprises), founder, 1969; Sundance Resort, Provo, UT, owner; Sundance Institute (for independent filmmakers), Salt Lake City, UT, founder and president, beginning 1981; host of Sundance Film Festival and co–creator of Sundance Film Channel (cable television network), 1995—; South Fork Films, founder, 1983. Institute for Resource Management, founder, 1983, and fundraiser for various interests and causes. Formerly active with Natural Resources Defense Council and Environmental Defense Fund. Previously worked for International Business Machines and Standard Oil in the 1950s, and as a carpenter and shop assistant.

Member: Kappa Sigma.

Awards, Honors: *Theatre World* Award, 1961, for *Sunday in New York;* Emmy Award nomination, best supporting actor, 1962, for *Alcoa Premiere;* Golden Globe Award, most promising male newcomer of the year, 1966, for *Inside Daisy Clover;* Hasty Pudding Man of the Year Award, Hasty Pudding Theatricals, Harvard University, 1970; Film Award, best actor, British Academy of Film and Television Arts, 1971, for *Butch Cassidy and the Sundance Kid, Downhill Racer,* and *Tell Them Willie Boy Is Here;* Golden Apple Award, male star of the year, Hollywood Women's Press Club, 1973; Academy Award nomination, best actor, 1974, for *The Sting;* Golden Globe awards, male world film favorite, 1975, 1977, and 1978; National Board of Review Award, best director, 1980, Academy Award, best director, Golden Globe Award, and Directors Guild of America Award (with others), outstanding directorial achievement for feature films, all 1981, for *Ordinary People;* Dartmouth Film Society award, 1990; Golden Globe Award nomination, best director, 1993, for *A River Runs Through It;* Cecil B. DeMille Award, Hollywood Foreign Press Association, 1994; Academy Award nomination and Golden Globe Award nomination, both best director, Academy Award nomination (with others), New York Film Critics Award, and Film Award, British Academy of Film and Television Arts, all best picture, 1995, for *Quiz Show;* Life Achievement Award, Screen Actors Guild, 1996; Golden Globe Award nomination, best director of a motion picture, and Blockbuster Entertainment Award nomination, favorite actor in a drama or romance, both 1999, for *The Horse Whisperer.* Honorary L.H.D., University of Colorado, 1987; Audubon Medal, National Audubon Society, 1989, for "lifetime campaign for environmental protection"; honorary D.Univ., University of Massachusetts, 1990; National Medal of Freedom, National Endowment for the Arts, 1996; Freedom in Film Award,

Nashville Film Festival, 2001; Honorary Academy Award, 2002; honorary doctorate of humane letters, Bard College, 2004; Kennedy Center Honors, 2005; Special Prize for Outstanding Contribution to World Cinema, Karlovy Vary International Film Festival, 2005; named an Officer of the French Ordre des Arts et des Lettres.

CREDITS

Film Appearances:

(Uncredited) Basketball player, *Tall Story,* 1960.

Private Ray Loomis, *War Hunt,* T–D Enterprises/United Artists, 1962.

Captain Hank Wilson, *Situation Hopeless … But Not Serious,* Paramount, 1965.

Wade Lewis, *Inside Daisy Clover,* Warner Bros., 1966.

Eubber Reeves, *The Chase,* Columbia, 1966.

Owen Legate, *This Property Is Condemned,* Paramount, 1966.

Paul Bratter, *Barefoot in the Park,* Paramount, 1967.

David Chappellet, *Downhill Racer,* Paramount, 1967.

Harry Longbaugh, the Sundance Kid, *Butch Cassidy and the Sundance Kid,* Twentieth Century–Fox, 1969.

Christopher Cooper, *Tell Them Willie Boy Is Here* (also known as *Willie Boy*), Universal, 1970.

"Big Halsey" Knox, *Little Fauss and Big Halsey,* Paramount, 1970.

The Making of "Butch Cassidy and the Sundance Kid," 1970.

Title role, *Jeremiah Johnson,* Warner Bros., 1972.

Himself, *The Saga of Jeremiah Johnson,* 1972.

John Archibald Dortmunder, *The Hot Rock* (also known as *How to Steal a Diamond in Four Uneasy Lessons*), Twentieth Century–Fox, 1972.

Bill McKay, *The Candidate,* Warner Bros., 1972.

Hubbell Gardner, *The Way We Were,* Columbia, 1973.

Johnny Hooker, *The Sting,* Universal, 1973.

Jay Gatsby, *The Great Gatsby,* Paramount, 1974.

Title role, *The Great Waldo Pepper,* Universal, 1974.

Narrator, *Following the Tundra Wolf,* 1974.

Joe Turner, *Three Days of the Condor* (also known as *3 Days of the Condor*), Paramount, 1975.

Major Julian Cook, *A Bridge Too Far,* United Artists, 1975.

Narrator, *Broken Treaty at Battle Mountain* (documentary), 1975.

Bob Woodward, *All the President's Men,* Warner Bros., 1976.

Himself, *Pressure and the Press: The Making of "All the President's Men,"* 1976.

Norman "Sonny" Steele, *The Electric Horseman,* Columbia, 1979.

Henry Brubaker, *Brubaker,* Twentieth Century–Fox, 1980.

Roy Hobbs, *The Natural,* TriStar, 1984.

Denys Finch Hatton, *Out of Africa,* Universal, 1985.

Tom Logan, *Legal Eagles,* Universal, 1986.

Narrator, *To Protect Mother Earth* (also known as *Broken Treaty II;* documentary), 1989.

Narrator, *Changing Steps,* 1989.

Narrator, *Yosemite: The Fate of Heaven,* 1989.

Jack Weil, *Havana,* Universal, 1990.

Himself, *Our Biosphere: The Earth in Our Hands,* 1991.

(Uncredited) Narrator, *A River Runs Through It,* Columbia, 1992.

Martin Bishop/Martin Brice, *Sneakers,* Universal, 1992.

Narrator, *Incident at Oglala* (also known as *Leonard Peltier: A True Story*), Miramax, 1992.

John Gage, *Indecent Proposal,* Paramount, 1993.

Warren Justice, *Up Close and Personal,* Buena Vista, 1996.

Himself, *Wild Bill, Hollywood Maverick: The Life and Times of William A. Wellman* (documentary; also known as *Wild Bill, Hollywood Maverick*), Turner Pictures, 1996.

Himself, *Anthem* (documentary), Zeitgeist Films, 1997.

Tom Booker, *The Horse Whisperer,* Buena Vista, 1998.

Himself, *Endredando sombras* (documentary; also known as *Entangling Shadows*), Producciones Amaranta, 1998.

Forever Hollywood (documentary), Eastman Kodak Co., 1999.

Himself, *New York in the 50's,* Avatar Films, 2001.

Nathan Muir, *The Spy Game,* Universal, 2001.

Lieutenant General Eugene Irwin, *The Last Castle,* DreamWorks Distribution, 2001.

Himself, *The Making of "Spy Game"* (documentary short), Universal Home Entertainment, 2001.

Himself, *More About the Condor* (documentary short), Studio Canal, 2001.

Himself, *The Making of "Sneakers"* (documentary short), Universal Studios Home Video, 2001.

Himself, *Sundance 20* (documentary), Sundance Channel, 2002.

Himself, *Abby Singer* (also known as *Abby Singer 2007*), 2003.

Wayne Hayes, *The Clearing* (also known as *Anatomie einer entfuhrung*), Fox Searchlight Pictures, 2004.

Narrator, *Sacred Planet* (documentary short), Buena Vista, 2004.

Himself, *Film Trix 2004* (documentary short), 2004.

Einar Gilkyson, *An Unfinished Life* (also known as *Ein Ungezahmtes leben*), Miramax, 2005.

Himself, *Trudell* (documentary), Balcony Releasing, 2005.

Himself, *The Art of "The Sting"* (documentary), Universal Studios Home Video, 2005.

Voice of Ike the Horse, *Charlotte's Web* (also known as *Schweinchen Wilbur und seine freunde*), Paramount, 2006.

Narrator, *Cosmic Collisions* (documentary short), 2006.

Himself, *All That Follows Is True: The Making of "Butch Cassidy and the Sundance Kid"* (documentary short), Fox Home Video, 2006.

Himself, *Woodward and Bernstein: Lighting the Fire* (documentary short), Warner Home Video, 2006.

Himself, *Telling the Truth About Lies: The Making of "All the President's Men"* (documentary short), Warner Home Video, 2006.

Dr. Stephen Malley, *Lions for Lambs,* Metro–Goldwyn–Mayer, 2007.

Himself, *The Unforeseen* (documentary), Cinema Guild, 2007.

Broadway: Beyond the Golden Age (documentary; also known as *B.G.A.2* and *Broadway: The Golden Age Two*), 2008.

Also appeared in *The Crow Killer.*

Film Work:

Coproducer, *Downhill Racer,* Paramount, 1967.

Coproducer, *All the President's Men,* Warner Bros., 1976.

Director, *Ordinary People,* Paramount, 1980.

Executive producer, *The Solar Film,* 1981.

Producer, *The Natural,* TriStar, 1984.

Executive producer, *Promised Land* (also known as *Young Hearts*), Vestron, 1987.

Executive producer, *Some Girls* (also known as *Sisters*), Metro–Goldwyn–Mayer/United Artists, 1988.

Director and producer, *The Milagro Beanfield War,* Universal, 1988.

Executive producer, *The Dark Wind,* 1991.

Executive producer, *Incident at Oglala* (also known as *Leonard Peltier: A True Story*), Miramax, 1992.

Director and producer, *A River Runs Through It,* New Line Cinema, 1992.

Executive producer, *King of the Hill,* 1993.

Director and producer, *Quiz Show,* 1994.

Coproducer, *The American President,* 1995.

Executive producer, *She's the One,* Twentieth Century–Fox, 1996.

Executive producer, *No Looking Back,* Gramercy, 1998.

Executive producer, *Slums of Beverly Hills,* Twentieth Century–Fox, 1998.

Producer, *A Civil Action,* Buena Vista, 1998.

Director and producer, *The Horse Whisperer,* Buena Vista, 1998.

Director and producer, *The Legend of Bagger Vance,* DreamWorks Distribution, 2000.

Executive producer, *How to Kill Your Neighbor's Dog* (also known as *Mad Dogs and Englishman*), Millennium Films, 2000.

Executive producer, *People I Know* (also known as *Im inneren kreis* and *Der innere kreis*), Myriad Pictures/South Fork Pictures, Miramax, 2001.

Executive producer, *Love in the Time of Money,* THINKFilm, 2002.

Executive producer, *The Motorcycle Diaries* (also known as *Diarios de motocicleta, Carnets de voyage, Die reise des jungen,* and *Voyage a motocyclette*), Focus Features, 2004.

Executive producer, *The Unforeseen* (documentary), 2007.

Director and producer, *Lions for Lambs,* Metro–Goldwyn–Mayer, 2007.

Television Appearances; Specials:

"Captain Brassbound's Conversion," *Hallmark Hall of Fame,* NBC, 1960.

The 53rd Annual Academy Awards, ABC, 1981.

Narrator, "Condor," *National Audubon Society Specials,* PBS, 1986.

The Golden Eagle Awards, syndicated, 1987.

Narrator, *Living Dangerously,* Arts and Entertainment, 1987.

Bill Moyer's World of Ideas, PBS, 1988.

Narrator, "Grizzly and Man: Uneasy Truce," *National Audubon Society Specials,* PBS, 1988.

People Magazine on TV, CBS, 1989.

Robert Redford and Sydney Pollack: The Men and Their Movies (also known as *Robert Redford: The Man, the Movies, and the Myth*), NBC, 1990.

The New Hollywood, NBC, 1990.

The Challenge to Wildlife: A Public Television Special Report, PBS, 1990.

Narrator, *Three Flags over Everest,* PBS, 1990.

Host and narrator, "Wolves," *National Audubon Society Specials,* PBS, 1990.

Here's Looking at You, Warner Bros., 1991.

Naked Hollywood, 1991.

The Kennedy Center Honors: A Celebration of the Performing Arts, 1992.

Hollywood and Politics, 1992.

Stars in the Making, 1995.

Paul Newman: Hollywood's Charming Rebel, 1995.

Inside the Academy Awards, 1995.

Honoree, *The Second Annual Screen Actors Guild,* NBC, 1996.

Narrator, *Wallace Stegner: A Writer's Life,* 1997.

Independents Day, Sundance Channel, 1998.

Host, *Visions of Grace: Robert Redford and "The Horse Whisperer,"* 1998.

Forever Hollywood, 1999.

Bill Bradley: In the Game, 1999.

Narrator, *The Mystery of Chaco Canyon,* 2000.

Robert Redford: Hollywood Outlaw, 2000.

Paul Newman, 2001.

"Butch Cassidy and the Sundance Kid: Outlaws of Time," *History v. Hollywood,* History Channel, 2001.

The 74th Annual Academy Awards, ABC, 2002.

OL Salt Lake City 2002, 2002.

Robert Redford, Bravo, 2002.

Once Upon a Time in Utah, Sundance, BBC, 2003.

Host, *National Anthem: Inside the Vote for Change Concert Tour,* Sundance, 2004.

Presenter, *AFI Life Achievement Award: A Tribute to Meryl Streep,* USA Network, 2004.

A "Dr. Phil" Primetime Special: Family First, CBS, 2004.

The Making of "The Motorcycle Diaries," 2004.

Biography Special: The Fondas, Arts and Entertainment, 2004.

Something About Sydney Pollack, 2004.
The 62nd Annual Golden Globe Awards, NBC, 2005.
The Secret Man, NBC, 2005.
Honoree, *The 28th Annual Kennedy Center Honors: A Celebration of the Performing Arts,* CBS, 2005.
The Mark Twain Prize: Neil Simon, 2006.
The Kennedy Center Presents: The 2006 Mark Twain Prize, PBS, 2006.

Also appeared in *Hollywood and Politics,* CNN.

Television Appearances; Pilots:
Tanner on Tanner, Sundance, 2004.

Television Appearances; Episodic:
"The Case of the Treacherous Toupee," *Perry Mason,* CBS, 1958.
Jimmy Coleman, "Iron Hand," *Maverick,* ABC, 1960.
Bill Johnson, "The Last Gunfight," *The Deputy,* NBC, 1960.
Lieutenant Lott, "In the Presence of Mine Enemies," *Playhouse 90,* CBS, 1960.
John Torsett, "The Bounty Hunter," *Tate,* NBC, 1960.
"The Golden Deed," *Moment of Fear,* NBC, 1960.
"Comanche Scalps," *Tate,* NBC, 1960.
Don Parritt, "The Iceman Cometh," *Play of the Week,* syndicated, 1960.
"Born a Giant," *Our American Heritage,* NBC, 1960.
Danny Tilford, "Breakdown," *Rescue 8,* 1960.
Dick Hart, "The Case of the Treacherous Toupee," *Perry Mason,* 1960.
Blue Jacket, "Captain Brassbound's Conversion," *Hallmark Hall of Fame* (also known as *Hallmark Television Playhouse*), 1960.
"Black Monday," *Play of the Week,* syndicated, 1961.
Baldwin, "Tombstone for a Derelict," *Naked City,* ABC, 1961.
George Harrod, "The Coward," *Americans,* NBC, 1961.
Johnny Gates, "The Grudge," *Whispering Smith,* NBC, 1961.
Janosh, "First Class Mouliak," *Route 66,* CBS, 1961.
Art Ellison, "The Covering Darkness," *Bus Stop,* ABC, 1961.
Hitchhiker, "Lady Killer," *The New Breed,* ABC, 1961.
Charlie Marx, "The Right Kind of Medicine," *Alfred Hitchcock Presents,* NBC, 1961.
Chuck Marsden, "A Piece of the Action," *The Alfred Hitchcock Hour,* CBS, 1962.
Mark Hadley, "The Burning Sky," *Dr. Kildare,* NBC, 1962.
George Laurents, "The Voice of Charlie Pont," *Alcoa Premiere,* ABC, 1962.
Harold Beldon, "Nothing in the Dark," *The Twilight Zone* (also known as *Twilight Zone*), 1962.
Jackson Emmit Parker, "Snowball," *The Untouchables,* ABC, 1963.
David Chesterman, "A Tangled Web," *The Alfred Hitchcock Hour,* CBS, 1963.

Nick Oakland, "The Last of the Big Spenders," *The Dick Powell Show* (also known as *The Dick Powell Theatre*), NBC, 1963.
Roger Morton, "Bird and Snake," *Breaking Point,* ABC, 1963.
Matthew Cordell, "The Evil That Men Do," *The Virginian* (also known as *The Men from Shiloh*), NBC, 1963.
Gary Degan, "The Siege," *The Defenders,* CBS, 1964.
V.I.P.—Schaukel, 1980.
Narrator, "Do You Mean There Are Still Real Cowboys?," *The American Experience,* PBS, 1988.
Narrator, *The Mystery of Chaco Canyon,* PBS, 1989.
Narrator, "Yosemite: The Fate of Heaven," *The American Experience,* PBS, 1989.
The Kennedy Center Honors: A Celebration of the Performing Arts, 1992.
"Waldo Salt: A Screenwriter's Journey," *American Masters,* PBS, 1992.
"Rod Serling: Submitted for Your Approval," *American Masters,* PBS, 1995.
"Paul Newman: Hollywood's Charming Rebel," *Biography,* Arts and Entertainment, 1995.
The Rosie O'Donnell Show, syndicated, 1998.
"Robert Redford: Hollywood Outlaw," *Biography,* Arts and Entertainment, 2000.
"The Legend of Bagger Vance," *HBO First Look,* HBO, 2000.
"Inside the Walls of 'The Last Castle,'" *HBO First Look,* HBO, 2001.
"Robert Redford," *Bravo Profiles,* Bravo, 2001.
The Ray Martin Show, 2001.
Independent Day, 2002.
Leute heute, 2002.
Festival Pass with Chris Gore, Starz, 2002.
Carl Schurz, "What Is Freedom?," *Freedom: A History of Us,* PBS, 2003.
Captain M. M. Miller, "A War to End Slavery," *Freedom: A History of Us,* PBS, 2003.
"Dustin Hoffman," *The Hollywood Greats* (also known as *Hollywood Greats*), BBC1, 2004.
"The Clearing," *Anatomy of a Scene,* Sundance, 2004.
Ahora, 2004.
Tanner on Tanner, Sundance, 2004.
"Robert Redford & Paul Newman," *Iconoclasts,* Sundance, 2005.
Host, "The Power of Knowledge," *The New Heroes,* 2005.
Host, "Technology of Freedom," *The New Heroes,* 2005.
Host, "Power of Enterprise," *The New Heroes,* 2005.
Host, "Dreams of Sanctuary," *The New Heroes,* 2005.
"Robert Redford," *HARDtalk Extra,* BBC, 2005.
Inside the Actors Studio, Bravo, 2005.
Hardball with Chris Matthews, CNBC, 2005.
The Al Franken Show, Sundance, 2005.
Magazine, 2005.
20/20 (also known as *ABC News 20/20*), ABC, 2005.
Narrator, "America's Underwater Treasures: Part I & II," *Jean–Michel Cousteau: Ocean Adventures,* 2006.

"The Unforeseen," *Now with Bill Moyers* (also known as *Now*), PBS, 2007.
Corazon de ..., 2006.

Also appeared in an episode of *Sesame Street.*

Television Work; Series:
Executive producer, *Iconoclasts,* Sundance, 2005–2006.
Executive producer, *Big Ideas for a Small Planet,* Sundance, 2007.

Television Work; Movies:
Executive producer, *Grand Avenue,* HBO, 1996.
Executive producer, *Skinwalkers,* PBS, 2002.
Executive producer, *Coyote Waits,* PBS, 2003.
Executive producer, *A Thief of Time,* PBS, 2004.

Television Work; Specials:
Creative advisor, *The Native Americans,* 1994.
Executive producer, *Visions of Grace: Robert Redford and "The Horse Whisperer,"* 1998.

Television Work; Episodic:
Executive producer, "Yosemite: The Fate of Heaven," *The American Experience,* PBS, 1989.

Stage Appearances:
Tall Story, Broadway production, 1959.
The Highest Tree, Longacre Theatre, New York City, 1960.
Little Moon of Alban, 1960.
Sunday in New York, Broadway production, 1961–62.
Paul Bratter, *Barefoot in the Park,* Broadway production, 1963–64.

RECORDINGS

Videos:
Film–Fest DVD: Issue 1—Sundance, 1999.

Also associated with the video *California Condor.*

WRITINGS

Screenplays:
The Solar Film, 1981.

Television Episodes:
"Yosemite: The Fate of Heaven," *The American Experience,* PBS, 1989.

Other Writings:
The Outlaw Trail (memoir), Grosset (New York, NY), 1978.

Contributor of articles to periodicals, including *American Film, Film Comment,* and *National Geographic.*

OTHER SOURCES

Books:
Contemporary Authors, Volume 107, Gale, 1983.
Crowther, Bruce, *Robert Redford,* Spellmount, 1985.
Downing, David, *Robert Redford,* W. H. Allen & Co., 1982.
Encyclopedia of World Biography Supplement, Volume 18, Gale, 1998.
International Dictionary of Films and Filmmakers, Volume 3: *Actors and Actresses,* St. James Press, 1996.
Reed, D. A., *Robert Redford,* Sherbourne, 1975.
Schoell, William, *The Sundance Kid: A Biography of Robert Redford,* Taylor Trade Publishing, 2006.
Spada, James, *The Films of Robert Redford,* Citadell Press, 1977.

Periodicals:
American Film, March, 1988, p. 26.
Entertainment Weekly, fall, 1996; September 5, 1997; November 1, 1999, p. 91.
Film Comment, January/February, 1988, p. 32.
Interview, September, 1994; January, 1997.
Newsweek, May 28, 1984, p. 75.
New York, December 10, 1990, p. 34.
People Weekly, February 18, 1980, p. 96; June 8, 1998, p. 86.
Premiere, February, 1991, p. 88; June, 1998, p. 37.
Rolling Stone, October 6, 1994.
Sports Illustrated, May 7, 1984, p. 92.
USA Today, May, 1999, p. 62.

RINKER, Scott
(Scott Allen Rinker)

PERSONAL

Married Cathleen Kaelyn, December 19, 1998.

Career: Actor. Appeared in television commercials, including Snapple Teas.

CREDITS

Film Appearances:
Lover (photo), *Safe Journey* (short), 1999.

Tom Ford, *Tomorrow By Midnight* (also known as *Midnight 5*), Capitol Films, 1999.

Carl, *Horror 101*, Taurus Entertainment Company, 2000.

Shane Torian, *They Crawl* (also known as *Crawlers*), Lions Gate Films Home Entertainment, 2001.

Ben Steinman, *Shoot or Be Shot* (also known as *Shooting Stars*), Iron Entertainment, 2002.

Mason Kemeny, *Storm Watch* (also known as *Code Hunter* and *Virtual Storm*), Velocity Home Entertainment, 2002.

(As Scott Allen Rinker) Ben, *Stress, Orgasms, and Salvation*, 2005.

Cop, *Pulled Over* (short), 2005.

(As Scott Allen Rinker) Paul, *Gamers*, Sideshow Productions, 2006.

Spencer, *Falling*, 2007.

Television Appearances; Movies:

John George Nicolay, *The Day Lincoln Was Shot*, TNT, 1998.

(As Scott Allen Rinker) Jimmy, *Jane Doe: The Wrong Face*, Hallmark Channel, 2005.

Television Appearances; Episodic:

Mr. Williamson, "Ballad of Maggie Day," *Maggie*, Lifetime, 1998.

Tommy Newman, "Drew Dates a Senior," *The Drew Carey Show*, ABC, 1998.

Guy, "Let's Eat Cake," *Beverly Hills, 90210*, Fox, 1999.

Resident advisor, "The Freshman," *Buffy the Vampire Slayer* (also known as *BtVS, Buffy,* and *Buffy the Vampire Slayer: The Series*), The WB, 1999.

Dan, "Strong Sexual Content," *Action*, syndicated, 1999.

Waiter, "Abstinence Makes the Heart Grow Fonder," *Rude Awakening*, Showtime, 1999.

Tim, "Ambulance Chaser," *G vs E* (also known as *Good vs Evil*), Sci–Fi Channel, 2000.

Doug, "The Time She Made a Temporary Decision," *Time of Your Life*, Fox, 2000.

Doug, "The Time They Found a Solution," *Time of Your Life*, Fox, 2000.

Barry Weiland, "Smartest Guy in the World," *The Huntress*, USA Network, 2001.

Antique store customer, "The Wraps," *Special Unit 2* (also known as *SU2*), UPN, 2001.

Jason, "Chapter Thirty–Eight," *Boston Public*, Fox, 2002.

(As Scott Allen Rinker) Curtis, "Coming Home," *Without a Trace* (also known as *W.A.T.*), CBS, 2003.

(As Scott Allen Rinker) Gareb, "United," *Enterprise* (also known as *Star Trek: Enterprise*), UPN, 2005.

(As Scott Allen Rinker) Gareb, "The Aenar," *Enterprise* (also known as *Star Trek: Enterprise*), UPN, 2005.

(As Scott Allen Rinker) Noel Abbott, "You Really Got Me," *Crossing Jordan*, NBC, 2005.

(As Scott Allen Rinker) Host, "The Slutty Pumpkin," *How I Met Your Mother*, CBS, 2005.

(As Scott Allen Rinker) Solial, "Battle of the Hexes," *Charmed*, The WB, 2005.

(Scenes deleted) Dr. Wexler, "First Responders," *The Unit*, CBS, 2006.

(As Scott Allen Rinker) Bobby, "Fools for Love," *House M.D.* (also known as *House*), Fox, 2006.

(As Scott Allen Rinker) Reggie, "Demon Child," *Ghost Whisperer*, CBS, 2006.

(As Scott Allen Rinker) Reggie, "The Vanishing," *Ghost Whisperer*, CBS, 2006.

(As Scott Allen Rinker) Reggie, "The One," *Ghost Whisperer*, CBS, 2006.

(As Scott Allen Rinker) Reggie, "The Collector," *Ghost Whisperer*, CBS, 2006.

(As Scott Allen Rinker) Luke Hamilton, "Open Season," *Criminal Minds*, CBS, 2007.

(As Scott Allen Rinker) Dr. Klein, "Depth Perception," *Greek*, ABC Family, 2007.

(As Scott Allen Rinker) Matt Burris, "Student Body," *Shark*, CBS, 2007.

Dr. Evan Klimkew, "Intern in the Incinerator," *Bones*, Fox, 2007.

RIORDAN, Daniel
(Daniel Reardon, Dan Riordan, Daniel Riordian)

PERSONAL

Career: Actor.

CREDITS

Film Appearances:

Surveyor, *Breakin' 2: Electric Boogaloo* (also known as *Breakin' 2 is Electric Boogaloo*), Cannon Pictures, 1984.

Removal man, *My Blue Heaven*, Warner Bros., 1990.

Mercedes man, *The Walter Ego* (short), 1991.

Rhinehardt, *Pentathlon*, Live Entertainment, 1994.

Pilot/strapping young man, *Ed Wood*, Buena Vista, 1994.

Turbo Man, *Jingle All the Way*, Twentieth Century–Fox, 1996.

Northmour, *The Pavilion*, Bleiberg Entertainment, 1999.

Dan, *The Waiting Game*, Seventh Art Releasing, 1999.

Jack Starr, *Suspended Animation* (also known as *Mayhem*), First Run Features, 2001.

Charney, *Last Mountain*, 2005.

L.A. deejay, *Dreamgirls*, Paramount, 2006.

Film Work:

Video reference cast, *Pocahontas* (animated), Buena Vista, 1995.

Television Appearances; Series:

Megatron, Galvatron, and Omega Prime, *Transformers: Robots in Disguise,* Fox, 2001.

Television Appearances; Movies:

Harry, *The B.R.A.T. Patrol,* ABC, 1986.
Husband, "Parole Board," *Prison Stories: Women on the Inside,* HBO, 1991.
Ty Farrel/Captain Zoom, *The Adventures of Captain Zoom in Outer Space,* Starz, 1995.
(As Dan Riordan) Paulie, *Where There's a Will,* Hallmark Channel, 2006.

Television Appearances; Pilots:

The announcer, *Bob Patterson,* ABC, 2001.

Television Appearances; Episodic:

Stanley, "FoxTrot," *Mr. Belvedere,* ABC, 1988.
Rondon, "Coming of Age," *Star Trek: The Next Generation* (also known as *Stark Trek: TNG*), syndicated, 1988.
First guard, "Progress," *Star Trek: Deep Space Nine* (also known as *DS9, Deep Space Nine,* and *Star Trek: DS9*), syndicated, 1993.
Mover number two, "Out of the Ashes," *Sisters,* NBC, 1993.
Gilbert Langley, "The Party's Over," *Silk Stalkings,* USA Network, 1993.
Rex Walker, "Charlie," *Renegade,* USA Network and syndicated, 1994.
Stan, "Boxing Helena," *The Fresh Prince of Bel–Air,* NBC, 1996.
Cyborg Sam, "Cyborg Sam I Am," *Weird Science,* USA Network, 1996.
Voice of narrator, "The Heart of the Elephant: Parts 1 & 2," *Conan* (also known as *Conan the Adventurer*), syndicated, 1997.
"Judd"/Reid Northmoor, "Chocktaw L–9," *Team Knight Rider,* syndicated, 1997.
Dr. Gregory Othon, "Blood Will Out," *Diagnosis Murder,* CBS, 1998.
Duras, "Judgment," *Enterprise* (also known as *Star Trek: Enterprise*), UPN, 2003.
Duras, "The Expanse," *Enterprise* (also known as *Star Trek: Enterprise*), UPN, 2003.
Younger thug, "Cheyenne, WY," *Carnivale,* HBO, 2005.
Bartender, "Mr. Monk and Little Monk," *Monk,* USA Network, 2005.
Voice of General Mung, "The Painted Lady," *Avatar: The Last Airbender* (animated), Nickelodeon, 2007.

RECORDINGS

Video Games:

(As Daniel Riordian) Corvus, the Celestial Watcher, Morcalavin, *Heretic II,* Activision, 1998.

(Uncredited) Voice of Nathan Zachary, *Crimson Skies,* Microsoft, 2000.
Voice of Arkantas/Kastor, *Age of Mythology,* 2002.
(As Dan Riordan) Voice of Brother Zoltan, *Armed & Dangerous,* LucasArts Entertainment Company, 2003.
Voice of Rannek, *Forgotten Realms: Demon Stone,* Atari, 2004.
(As Dan Riordan) Various characters, *EverQuest II,* Sony Online Entertainment, 2004.
Voice, *Hitman: Blood Money,* Eidos Interactive, 2005.
(English version) Voice of Decius Brutus, Vipsanius, and additional voices, *Shadow of Rome,* Capcom Entertainment, 2005.
Voice of Samson, *"The Incredible Hulk": Ultimate Destruction,* Vivendi Universal Games, 2005.
(As Dan Riordan) Mister Sinister, Stryfe, *X–Men Legends II: Rise of Apocalypse,* Activision, 2005.
Voice of Pierre Beaumont and Colonel George Washington, *Age of Empires III,* 2005.
Voice of additional USA VO, *"24": The Game,* 2K Games, 2006.
Voice of Martian Manhunter, *Justice League Heroes* (also known as *"Justice League Heroes": The Flash*), Warner Bros. Interactive Media, 2006.
(As Daniel Reardon) Voice of Xerxes, Hydarnes, and additional voices, *300: March to Glory,* 2007.
Voice of Bonecrusher and Decepticons, *Transformers: The Game,* Activision, 2007.

WRITINGS

Screenplays:
The Pavilion, 1999.

ROBBINS, Steve

PERSONAL

Addresses: *Office*—Vision View Entertainment, 561 Broadway, 12B, New York, NY 10012.

Career: Producer.

Awards, Honors: Daytime Emmy Award (with others), outstanding children/youth/family special, 2004, for *The Incredible Mrs. Ritchie.*

CREDITS

Film Executive Producer:
Quicksand (also known as *Un tueur aux trousses*), Starmedia Home Entertainment, 2001.
Crocodile Dundee in Los Angeles, Paramount, 2001.

Partners in Action, DEJ Productions, 2002.
Absolon, Hannibal Pictures, 2003.
Crime Spree (also known as *Wanted*), DEJ Productions, 2003.
Bright Young Things, ThinkFilm, 2003.
In My Father's Den, Tartan USA, 2004.
Beyond the Sea, Lions Gate Films, 2004.
Man About Dog, Redbus Film Distribution, 2004.
The Wedding Date, Universal, 2005.

Film Work; Other:
Prop maker, *The Adventures of Ford Fairlane,* Twentieth Century–Fox, 1990.
Associate producer and first assistant director, *Intrique,* Sin City Video, 1999.

Television Executive Producer; Specials:
The Incredible Mrs. Ritchie (also known as *L'incroyable Mme Richie*), Showtime, 2003.

ROBERTSON, Kathleen 1973–

PERSONAL

Born July 8, 1973, in Hamilton, Ontario, Canada. *Education:* Studied dance in Hamilton, Ontario, Canada.

Addresses: *Agent*—Innovative Artists, 1505 10th St., Santa Monica, CA 90401. *Manager*—Untitled Entertainment, 1801 Century Park East, Suite 700, Los Angeles, CA 90067. *Publicist*—Pinnacle Public Relations, 8265 Sunset Blvd., Suite 201, Los Angeles, CA 90046.

Career: Actress and producer.

Awards, Honors: Young Artist Award nominations, best young actress costarring in an off–primetime or cable series, 1991, 1992, both for *Maniac Mansion;* Gemini Award nomination, best performance by an actress in a leading role in a dramatic program or miniseries, Academy of Canadian Cinema and Television, 2002, for *Torso: The Evelyn Dick Story;* Canadian Comedy Award nomination, film—pretty funny female performance, 2002, for *Scary Movie 2;* Gemini Award nomination, best performance by an actress in a leading role in a dramatic program or miniseries, 2007, for *Last Exit;* Gemini Award nomination (with others), best ensemble in a comedy program or series, 2007, for *The Business.*

CREDITS

Film Appearances:
Left Out, 1985.
Darla, *Blown Away,* 1992.

"Patrick"/Melody, *Lapse of Memory* (also known as *Memoire traquee*), Gerard Mital Productions/Max Films Productions, 1992.
Lucifer, *Nowhere,* Fine Line, 1997.
Ticket girl, *I Wore Up Early the Day I Died* (also known as *Ed Wood's "I Woke Up Early the Day I Died"* and *I Awoke Early the Day I Died*), 1998.
Cheryl, *Dog Park* (also known as *Reserve aux chiens*), New Line Cinema, 1998.
Veronica, *Splendor,* Samuel Goldwyn Company, 1999.
G.Q. photo–shoot model, *Runaway Bride,* Paramount, 1999.
Rhonda, *Psycho Beach Party,* Strand Releasing, 2000.
Wanda Love (Miss Tennessee), *Beautiful,* Destination Films, 2000.
Theo, *Scary Movie 2* (also known as *Scarier Movie*), Dimension, 2001.
Evelyn Dick, *Torso,* Shaftesbury Films, 2001.
Grace, *Speaking of Sex,* Omnibus, 2001.
Big Boy waitress, *I Am Sam,* 2001.
Thea, *XX/XY,* IFC Films, 2002.
Swoop journalist, *I Love Your Work,* THINKFilm, 2003.
Donna, *Mail Cop,* 2004.
Elizabeth, *Until the Night,* American World Pictures, 2004.
Eden Ross, *Control,* Lions Gate Films, 2004.
Carol Van Ronkel, *Hollywoodland,* Focus Features, 2006.
Ali, *Player 5150,* 2007.
Amy, *The Hill,* 2008.

Television Appearances; Series:
Tina Edison, *Maniac Mansion,* Family Channel, 1990.
Clare Arnold, *Beverly Hills, 90210,* Fox, 1994–97.
Jeannie Falls, *Girls Club,* Fox, 2002.
Julia Sullivan, *The Business,* Independent Film Channel, 2006–2007.

Television Appearances; Miniseries:
Azkadellia, *Tin Man,* Sci–Fi Channel, 2007.

Television Appearances; Movies:
Sara Dobbs, *Quiet Killer* (also known as *Black Death* and *New York, alerte a la peste*), CBS and CTV, 1992.
Bobby Swaggart, *Liar's Edge* (also known as *Intimate Delusions*), Showtime, 1992.
Darla, *Blown Away,* HBO, 1993.
Julie, *Survive the Night* (also known as *Night Hunt*), USA Network, 1993.
Susan Williams, *In the Line of Duty: The Price of Vengeance,* NBC, 1994.
Evelyn Dick, *Torso: The Evelyn Dick Story* (also known as *Le Torse* and *Torso*), CTV, 2002.
Rachel Speller, *In the Dark,* 2003.
Beth Welland, *Last Exit,* CTV, 2006.

Television Appearances; Episodic:
"Grounded," *My Secret Identity,* syndicated, 1988.
Cynthia Bundy, "The Prom," *C.B.C.'s Magic Hour,* 1990.
Daria, *E.N.G.,* Lifetime, 1990.
Anne Morrison, "Passages," *The Hidden Room,* 1993.
"Upstairs, Upstairs," *Heaven Help Us,* 1994.
Tracy Bird, "Who Killed the World's Greatest Chef?" *Burke's Law,* CBS, 1995.
Darla Pearson, "View from Up Here," *Law & Order: Criminal Intent* (also known as *Law & Order: CI*), NBC, 2005.
Kathy/Diana Marvin, "Ghost in the Machine," *Medium,* NBC, 2006.

Television Executive Producer; Series:
The Business, Independent Film Channel, 2007.

OTHER SOURCES

Periodicals:
Parade, June 10, 2001, p. 18.

Electronic:
Kathleen Robertson Website, http://www.kathleen-robertson.com, December 7, 2007.

RUE, Sara 1978(?)–

PERSONAL

Original name, Sara Schlackman; born January 26, 1978 (some sources say 1979), in New York, NY; daughter of Marc (a stage manager) and Joan (a municipal employee and former actress; maiden name, Rue) Schlackman; married Mischa Livingstone, 2001. *Education:* Attended Professional Children's School, New York City. *Avocational Interests:* Collecting and playing vintage guitars, playing poker.

Addresses: *Agent*—Endeavor, 9601 Wilshire Blvd., 3rd Floor, Beverly Hills, CA 90210. *Manager*—Alan David Management, 8840 Wilshire Blvd., Beverly Hills, CA 90211.

Career: Actress. Songwriter and performer at coffee houses in and around Los Angeles.

Awards, Honors: Special Jury Prize (with Lili Taylor), performance, Indianapolis International Film Festival, 2004, for *A Slipping-Down Life.*

CREDITS

Television Appearances; Series:
Edda Pasetti, *Grand,* NBC, 1990.
Monica, *Phenom,* ABC, 1993–94.
Darby Gladstone, *Minor Adjustments,* NBC, 1995, UPN, 1996.
Breeny Kennedy, *Zoe, Duncan, Jack & Jane* (also known as *Zoe*), The WB, 1999.
Carmen Ferrara, *Popular,* The WB, 1999–2001.
Claude Casey, *Less Than Perfect,* ABC, 2002–2006.

Television Appearances; Movies:
Jacquelyn, *Family Reunion: A Relative Nightmare,* ABC, 1995.
Kimberly Jones, *For My Daughter's Honor* (also known as *Indecent Seduction*), CBS, 1996.
Silent Hearts (also known as *Nowhere to Go*), Lifetime, 1998.
Gabby, *This Time Around,* ABC Family Channel, 2003.

Television Appearances; Pilots:
Melanie, *The Simple Life,* CBS, 1998.
Play Nice, CBS, 2006.
Nurses (also known as *Philadelphia General*), Fox, 2007.

Television Appearances; Specials:
The 2000 Teen Choice Awards, Fox, 2000.
ABC's Christmas in Aspen, ABC, 2002.
VH1 Big in 2002 Awards, VH1, 2002.
VH1 Big in '03, VH1, 2003.
A Life of Laughter: Remembering John Ritter, ABC, 2003.
Comedy Central Presents: The Commies, Comedy Central, 2003.
A Merry Mickey Celebration, ABC, 2003.
The Disco Ball, ABC, 2003.
Presenter, *The Commies,* Comedy Central, 2003.
Presenter, *The 31st Annual American Music Awards,* ABC, 2003.
Presenter, *Lifetime's 4th Annual Women Rock! Songs from the Movies,* Lifetime, 2003.
The 7th Annual Prism Awards, FX Channel, 2003.
VH1 Big in '04, VH1, 2004.
Host, *ABC Extreme Bloopers,* ABC, 2004.

Television Appearances; Episodic:
Roseanne as a teenager, "Halloween IV," *Roseanne,* ABC, 1992.
Angie, "Mating Rituals," *Blossom,* NBC, 1995.
Angie, "Hi Diddly Dee," *Blossom,* NBC, 1995.
"Don't Ask, Don't Tell," *ER,* NBC, 1996.
Bertha Sugs, "Ticket to Ride," *Pearl,* CBS, 1996.
Amy, "Prom Night," *Ned and Stacey,* Fox, 1997.
Rhonda Fritz, "The Ties That Bind," *Chicago Hope,* CBS, 1998.

Melanie, "Sara's Ex," *The Simple Life*, CBS, 1998.

Melanie, "The Luke and Sara Show," *The Simple Life*, CBS, 1998.

Joyce Adler, "Lows in the Mid–Eighties," *Will & Grace*, NBC, 2000.

Amanda McCafferty, "Hide and Seek," *The Division* (also known as *Heart of the City*), Lifetime, 2002.

Amanda McCafferty, "Remembrance," *The Division* (also known as *Heart of the City*), Lifetime, 2002.

Amanda McCafferty, "Acts of Betrayal," *The Division* (also known as *Heart of the City*), Lifetime, 2003.

The babysitter, *Mad TV*, Fox, 2003.

"Los Angeles: Elm Street," *Trading Spaces*, The Learning Channel, 2003.

Late Night with Conan O'Brien, NBC, 2003.

The Late Late Show with Craig Kilborn (also known as *The Late Late Show*), CBS, 2003, 2004.

Live with Regis and Kelly, syndicated, 2004.

The Tony Danza Show, syndicated, 2004.

The Jane Pauley Show, NBC, 2004.

Life & Style, 2004.

Good Day Live, syndicated, 2004.

Celebrity Blackjack, Game Show Network, 2004.

Celebrity Poker Showdown, Bravo, 2004, 2005.

Jimmy Kimmel Live, ABC, 2004, 2005.

Ellen: The Ellen DeGeneres Show, syndicated, 2004, 2005.

The View, ABC, 2005.

"From A to D," *Kathy Griffin: My Life on the D–List*, Bravo, 2005.

E! Hollywood Hold 'Em, E! Entertainment Television, 2005.

The Late Late Show with Craig Ferguson, CBS, 2005, 2006.

Naomi, "Repeated Blows to His Unformed Head," *Two and a Half Men*, CBS, 2006.

Naomi, "Castrating Sheep in Montana," *Two and a Half Men*, CBS, 2007.

Film Appearances:

Jessica Hanson, *Rocket Gibraltar*, Columbia, 1988.

Megan Scanlan, *Passed Away*, Buena Vista, 1992.

Earth girl, *Can't Hardly Wait*, Columbia, 1998.

Nowhere to Go (also known as *Silent Hearts*), 1998.

Violet, *A Slipping Down Life*, DVC Entertainment, 1999.

Debbie, *A Map of the World* (also known as *Unschuldig verfolgt*), USA Films, 1999.

Nurse Martha, *Pearl Harbor* (also known as *Pearl Harbour*), Buena Vista, 2001.

Gypsy, *Gypsy 83*, 2001.

Babysitter, *The Ring*, DreamWorks, 2002.

Title role, *Barbara Jean* (short), 2005.

Charlotte Louis, *Danny Roane: First Time Director*, Lionsgate, 2006.

(Uncredited) Attorney General, *Idiocracy*, Twentieth Century–Fox, 2006.

Candy, *For Christ's Sake*, 2007.

Torry, *Man Maid*, 2007.

Doogs, *The Hill*, 2008.

Film Work:

Producer, *Barbara Jean* (short), 2005.

Executive producer, *A Little Night Fright* (short), 2007.

Stage Appearances:

Crystal, *The Water Children*, Matrix Theatre, Los Angeles, 1998.

Also appeared in *Seventh Word, Four Syllables* and *The Shallow End*, both Ensemble Studio Theatre, New York City.

RUSSELL, Kurt 1951–

PERSONAL

Full name, Kurt Vogel Russell; born March 17, 1951, in Springfield, MA; son of Bing Oliver (a professional baseball player and actor) and Louise Julia (maiden name, Crone) Russell; married Season Hubley (an actress), March 17, 1979 (divorced, 1984); companion of Goldie Hawn (an actress, producer, and director), beginning 1983; children: (with Hubley) Boston; (with Hawn) Wyatt. *Politics:* Libertarian. *Avocational Interests:* Auto racing (world class modified stock), flying (licensed pilot), skiing.

Addresses: *Agent*—Creative Artists Agency, 2000 Avenue of the Stars, Los Angeles, CA 90067.

Career: Actor. Appeared in television commercial for Zero–M Toys, 1966; Cosmic Entertainment, cofounder, 2003. Minor league baseball player, including stints with the Rainbows, Bend, OR, and Sun Kings, El Paso, TX, 1971–73. *Military service:* California Air National Guard.

Member: Screen Actors Guild, American Federation of Television and Radio Artists, Professional Baseball Players Association, and Stuntman's Association.

Awards, Honors: Emmy Award nomination, best actor in a limited series or special, 1979, for *Elvis;* Golden Globe Award nomination, best supporting actor in a motion picture, 1984, for *Silkwood;* Blockbuster Entertainment Award, favorite actor in an adventure or drama, 1997, for *Executive Decision;* The Disney Legends Award, 1998; DVD Premiere Award nomination (with others), best audio commentary, library release, 2003, for *Used Cars;* Life Career Award,

Academy of Science Fiction, Fantasy and Horror Films, 2003. Has also received ten baseball awards, one golf championship trophy, and several auto racing trophies.

CREDITS

Film Appearances:

The Absent–Minded Professor, Buena Vista, 1961.

(Uncredited) Boy who kicked Mike, *It Happened at the Worlds Fair,* 1963.

Jamie McPheeters, *Guns of Diablo,* 1964.

Whitey, *Follow Me, Boys!,* Buena Vista, 1966.

Willie Prentiss, *Mosby's Marauders* (also known as *Willie and the Yank*), 1966.

Ronnie Gardner, *The Horse in the Grey Flannel Suit,* Buena Vista, 1968.

Sidney Bower, *The One and Only Genuine Original Family Band* (also known as *The Family Band*), 1968.

Rich, *Guns in the Heather* (also known as *Spy–Busters* and *The Secret of Boyne Castle*), 1969.

Dexter Riley, *The Computer Wore Tennis Shoes,* Buena Vista, 1970.

Narrator, *Dad, Can I Borrow the Car?,* 1970.

Steven Post, *The Barefoot Executive,* Buena Vista, 1971.

Johnny Jesus, *Fools' Parade* (also known as *Dynamite Man from Glory Jail*), Columbia, 1971.

Dexter Riley, *Now You See Him, Now You Don't,* Buena Vista, 1972.

Ray Ferris, *Charley and the Angel,* Buena Vista, 1972.

Bart, *Superdad,* Buena Vista, 1974.

Dexter Riley, *The Strongest Man in the World,* Buena Vista, 1975.

Morgan "Two Persons" Bodeen, *The Captive* (also known as *Captive: The Longest Drive 2* and *The Longest Drive*), 1976.

Rudy Russo, *Used Cars,* Columbia, 1980.

Snake Plissken, *Escape from New York* (also known as *John Carpenter's "Escape from New York"*), Avco Embassy, 1981.

Voice of adult Copper, *The Fox and the Hound* (animated), Buena Vista, 1981.

MacReady, *The Thing* (also known as *John Carpenter's "The Thing"*), Universal, 1982.

Drew Stephens, *Silkwood,* Twentieth Century–Fox, 1983.

Mike "Lucky" Lockhart, *Swing Shift,* Warner Bros., 1984.

Malcolm Anderson, *The Mean Season,* Orion, 1985.

Reno Hightower, *The Best of Times,* Universal, 1986.

Jack Burton, *Big Trouble in Little China* (also known as *John Carpenter's "Big Trouble in Little China"*), Twentieth Century–Fox, 1986.

Dean Proffitt, *Overboard,* Metro–Goldwyn–Mayer/United Artists, 1987.

Wayland Jackson, *Winter People,* Columbia, 1988.

Lieutenant Nick Frescia, *Tequila Sunrise,* Warner Bros., 1988.

Gabriel "Gabe" Cash, *Tango and Cash,* Warner Bros., 1989.

Lieutenant Stephen "Bull" McCaffrey and Dad McCaffrey, *Backdraft,* Universal, 1990.

Michael Carr, *Unlawful Entry,* Twentieth Century–Fox, 1992.

Title role, *Captain Ron,* Buena Vista, 1992.

Wyatt Earp, *Tombstone,* Buena Vista, 1993.

(Uncredited) Voice of Elvis Presley, *Forrest Gump,* 1994.

Colonel Jonathan "Jack" O'Neil, *Stargate* (also known as *Stargate, la porte des etoiles*), Metro–Goldwyn–Mayer, 1994.

Dr. David Grant, *Executive Decision* (also known as *Critical Decision*), Warner Bros., 1996.

Snake Plissken, *Escape from L.A.* (also known as *John Carpenter's "Escape from L.A."*), Paramount, 1996.

Jeff Taylor, *Breakdown,* Paramount, 1997.

Sergeant Todd, *Soldier,* Warner Bros., 1998.

Himself, *"The Thing:" Terror Takes Shape* (documentary; also known as *John Carpenter's "The Thing: Terror Takes Shape"*), Universal, 1998.

Michael Zane, *3000 Miles to Graceland,* Warner Bros., 2001.

Dr. Curtis McCabe, *Vanilla Sky,* Paramount/DreamWorks Distribution, 2001.

Interstate 60 (also known as *I–60* and *Interstate 60: Episodes of the Road*), Redeemable Features, Samuel Goldwyn, 2001.

Himself, *The Making of "Tombstone"* (documentary short), 2002.

Eldon Perry, *Dark Blue,* Metro–Goldwyn–Mayer, 2002.

Himself, *Prelude to a Dream* (documentary short), Paramount Home Video, 2002.

Himself, *Blue Code* (documentary short), Metro–Goldwyn–Mayer Home Entertainment, 2003.

Himself, *Return to "Escape from New York"* (documentary short), Metro–Goldwyn–Mayer Home Entertainment, 2003.

Herb Brooks, *Miracle,* Buena Vista, 2004.

Himself, *First Impressions: Herb Brooks with Kurt Russell & the Filmmakers,* 2004.

Himself, *The Making of "Miracle"* (documentary short), 2004.

Himself, *Jiminy Glick in Lalawood,* Metro–Goldwyn–Mayer, 2004.

Steve Stronghold/The Commander, *Sky High,* Buena Vista, 2005.

Ben Crane, *Dreamer: Inspired by a True Story* (also known as *Dreamer*), DreamWorks, 2005.

Robert Ramsey, *Poseidon,* Warner Bros., 2006.

Himself, *"Poseidon": A Ship on a Soundstage* (short), Warner Home Video, 2006.

Stuntman Mike, *"Death Proof," Grindhouse* (also known as *Quentin Tarantino's "Death Proof"*), Dimension Films, 2007.

Film Work:

Stunt performer, *Backdraft,* Universal, 1990.

Producer, *Escape from L.A.* (also known as *John Carpenter's Escape from L.A.*), Paramount, 1996.

Television Appearances; Series:
Jaimie McPheeters, *The Travels of Jaimie McPheeters,* ABC, 1963–64.
Various roles, *Daniel Boone,* NBC, 1965–69.
Bo Larsen, *The New Land,* ABC, 1974.
Morgan Beaudine, *The Quest,* NBC, 1976.

Television Appearances; Movies:
Jamie McPheeters, *Guns of Diablo,* 1964.
Charles Joseph Whitman, *The Deadly Tower* (also known as *Sniper*), NBC, 1975.
Shan Mullins, *Search for the Gods,* ABC, 1975.
Morgan "Two Persons" Beaudine, *The Quest* (also known as *The Longest Drive* and *The Quest: The Longest Drive*), NBC, 1976.
Johnny, *Christmas Miracle in Caulfield, USA* (also known as *The Christmas Coal Mine Miracle*), CBS, 1977.
Elvis Presley, *Elvis* (also known as *Elvis the Movie*), ABC, 1979.
Laurence Kendall, *Amber Waves,* ABC, 1980.

Television Appearances; Specials:
Super Comedy Bowl 2, 1972.
NBC team, *Battle of the Network Stars,* ABC, 1977.
The Making of "The Mean Season," 1985.
Premiere Presents: Christmas Movies '89, Fox, 1989.
The 61st Annual Academy Awards Presentation, ABC, 1989.
Voices That Care, Fox, 1991.
First Person with Maria Shriver, NBC, 1991.
An American Saturday Night, ABC, 1991.
100 Years of the Hollywood Western, 1994.
Presenter, *The Blockbuster Entertainment Awards,* CBS, 1995.
The American Film Institute Salute to Steven Spielberg, 1995.
The 2nd Annual Screen Actors Guild Awards, NBC, 1996.
Presenter, *The 68th Annual Academy Awards,* ABC, 1996.
Blockbuster Entertainment Awards, UPN, 1997.
Intimate Portrait: Halle Berry, Lifetime, 1998.
Masters of Fantasy: John Carpenter, 1998.
The 73rd Annual Academy Awards, ABC, 2001.
America: A Tribute to Heroes, 2001.
Dobe and a Company of Heroes, 2002.
AFI Tribute to Meryl Streep (also known as *AFI Life Achievement Award: A Tribute to Meryl Streep*), USA Network, 2004.
Moving Image Salutes Ron Howard, Bravo, 2006.

Television Appearances; Episodic:
Sugarfoot (also known as *Tenderfoot*), 1957.
Our Man Higgins, c. 1962.

Knute, "Seventeen Gypsies and a Sinner Named Charlie," *Sam Benedict,* 1963.
Peter Hall, "Everybody Knows You Left Me," *The Eleventh Hour,* 1963.
Bobby, "Delinquent for a Day," *Our Man Higgins,* 1963.
Packy Kerlin, "Blue Heaven," *Gunsmoke* (also known as *Gun Law* and *Marshal Dillon*), CBS, 1964.
Philip Gerard, Jr., "Nemesis," *The Fugitive,* ABC, 1964.
Toby Shea, "A Father for Toby," *The Virginian,* NBC, 1964.
Christopher Larson, "The Finny Foot Affair," *The Man from U.N.C.L.E.,* NBC, 1964.
Jungle boy, "Gilligan Meets Jungle Boy," *Gilligan's Island,* CBS, 1965.
Amdu Denning, "The Brothers," *The Virginian,* NBC, 1965.
Elick Hart, "The Colt," *The Legend of Jesse James,* ABC, 1966.
Grey Smoke, "Meanwhile, Back at the Reservation," *Laredo,* NBC, 1966.
Quano, "The Challenge," *Lost in Space,* CBS, 1966.
Dan Winslow, "The Tormenters," *The FBI,* ABC, 1966.
Eddie, "In a Plain Paper Wrapper," *The Fugitive,* ABC, 1966.
"Willie and the Yank," *The World of Disney,* NBC, 1967.
"The Mosby Raiders," *The World of Disney,* NBC, 1967.
"The Matchmaker," *The World of Disney,* NBC, 1967.
"Terror on the Trail," *The World of Disney,* NBC, 1967.
Jay Baker, "Charade of Justice," *The Road West,* 1967.
Rich, "The Secret of Boyne Castle" (also known as "Guns in the Weather" and "Spy Busters"), *The World of Disney,* NBC, 1969.
"Blue Heaven," *Gunsmoke,* CBS, 1969.
"Target Boone," *Daniel Boone,* NBC, 1969.
William P. Lovering, "The Spitball Kid," *Then Came Bronson,* NBC, 1969.
Dan Rondo, "The Guns of Johnny Rondo," *High Chaparral,* NBC, 1970.
"Disneyland Showtime," *Disneyland* (also known as *Disney's Wonderful World, The Disney Sunday Movie, The Magical World of Disney, The Wonderful World of Disney, Walt Disney, Walt Disney Presents,* and *Walt Disney's Wonderful World of Color*), 1970.
"Love and the First Nighters," *Love, American Style,* ABC, 1970.
Jerry Patman, "This Is Jerry. See Jerry Run? Run, Jerry, Run, Run, Run, Run," *Storefront Lawyers* (also known as *Men at Law*), CBS, 1970.
"Paul Revere Rides Again," *Room 222,* ABC, 1971.
"Beginner's Luck," *Love Story,* NBC, 1973.
J. D. Crawford, "Country Boy," *Police Story,* NBC, 1974.
Buck Henry, "Trail of Bloodshed," *Gunsmoke* (also known as *Gun Law* and *Marshal Dillon*), CBS, 1974.
Kane, "Scar Tissue," *Hec Ramsey,* NBC, 1974.
Todd Conway, "Double Jeopardy," *Harry O,* ABC, 1975.
Officer David Singer, "Empty Weapon," *Police Story,* NBC, 1975.

Peter Valcher, "Deadly Doubles," *Hawaii Five–O* (also known as *McGarrett*), CBS, 1977.

The Arsenio Hall Show, syndicated, 1989.

Wogan (also known as *The Wogan Years*), 1991.

Late Show with David Letterman (also known as *The Late Show*), NBC, 1994, 2006.

The Rosie O'Donnell Show, syndicated, 1996, 1997, 1998.

The Entertainment Business, 1998.

"Kurt Russell: Hollywood's Heavy Hitter," *Biography,* Arts and Entertainment, 1999.

Late Night with Conan O'Brien, NBC, 2003.

The Heaven and Earth Show (also known as *Heaven and Earth with Gloria Hunniford*), BBC, 2004.

The O'Reilly Factor, Fox News, 2004.

The Oprah Winfrey Show (also known as *Oprah*), syndicated, 2004.

The Tonight Show with Jay Leno, NBC, 2004, 2005, 2006, 2007.

Die Johannes B. Kerner Show (also known as *JBK*), 2005.

60 Minutes, CBS, 2005.

Today (also known as *NBC News Today* and *The Today Show*), NBC, 2005.

"The Making of 'Poseidon,'" *HBO First Look,* HBO, 2006.

Corazon de ..., 2006.

Entertainment Tonight (also known as *E.T.*), syndicated, 2007.

Jimmy Kimmel Live, ABC, 2007.

Last Call with Carson Daly, NBC, 2007.

Ellen: The Ellen DeGeneres Show, syndicated, 2007.

"Festivalen I Cannes Death Proof," *Nyhetsmorgon,* 2007.

Television Work; Movies:
Executive producer, *14 Hours,* TNT, 2005.

Stage Appearances:
The Hasty Heart, Ahmanson Theatre, Los Angeles, 1982.

RECORDINGS

Videos:
Appeared in the music video "Voices That Care."

WRITINGS

Screenplays:
(With others) *Escape from L.A.* (also known as *John Carpenter's "Escape from L.A."*), Paramount, 1996.

OTHER SOURCES

Books:
Newsmakers, Issue 4, Gale Group, 2007.

Periodicals:
Starlog, February, 1995; November, 1996; January, 1999.

S

SABARA, Evan 1992–

PERSONAL

Full name, Evan Michael Sabara; born June 14, 1992, in Torrance, CA; twin brother of Daryl Sabara (an actor).

Addresses: *Manager*—Lynda Goodfriend Artists Management, 338 S. Beachwood Dr., Burbank, CA 91506.

Career: Actor.

Awards, Honors: Special Award (with others), outstanding young ensemble in a new medium, Young Artist Awards, 2005, for *The Polar Express.*

CREDITS

Film Appearances:
Additional voices, *Dinosaur* (animated), 2000.
Intruder spy kid, *Spy Kids,* Miramax, 2001.
Creepy kid, *Spy Kids 3–D: Game Over* (also known as *Spy Kids 3: Game Over*), Dimension, 2003.
Additional voices, *Finding Nemo* (animated), Buena Vista, 2003.
Additional voice, *Home on the Range* (animated), Buena Vista, 2004.
Oliver Portman, *Raising Helen,* Buena Vista, 2004.
Young boy, *The Polar Express,* Warner Bros., 2004.
(English version) Voice of boy and additional voices, *Tonari no Totoro* (animated; also known as *My Neighbor Totoro* and *My Neighbour Totoro*), Walt Disney Pictures, 2005.
Kid, *Her Best Move,* Summertime Films, 2007.
Kip, *Welcome to Paradise,* First Look International, 2007.

Film Stunts:
Spy Kids 2: Island of Lost Dreams (also known as *Spy Kids 2: The Island of Lost Dreams*), Miramax, 2002.

Television Appearances; Series:
Voice of Robin/Dick Grayson, *The Batman* (animated), The WB, 2006–2007.

Television Appearances; Movies:
J. T. Thompson, *A Season for Miracles* (also known as *Hallmark Hall of Fame: "A Season for Miracles"*), CBS, 1999.
Edward Tally at age 10, *Murder Without Conviction,* Hallmark Channel, 2004.

Television Appearances; Episodic:
Jared Leary, "Masquerade," *ER,* NBC, 1998.
Avery Siegel, "The Wrong Man," *Judging Amy,* CBS, 2003.
Denial Mitello, "Flirtin' with Disaster," *10–8: Officers on Duty* (also known as *10–8*), ABC, 2004.
Roger, "Malcolm Visits College," *Malcolm in the Middle,* Fox, 2004.
Zach, "The Perfect Person: Part 2," *Committed,* NBC, 2005.
Kid in locker, "Morp," *Malcolm in the Middle,* Fox, 2006.

SARIN, Victor 1945–
(Vic Sarin)

PERSONAL

Born 1945, in Kashmir, India; father, a diplomat.

Addresses: *Agent*—Pacific Arts Management, 685–1285 West Broadway, Vancouver, British Columbia V6H 3X8 Canada.

Career: Cinematographer and director.

Member: Canadian Society of Cinematographers.

Awards, Honors: Genie Award nomination, best achievement in cinematography, Academy of Canadian Cinema and Television, 1982, for *Heartaches;* Gemini Award nomination, best photography in a dramatic program or series, Academy of Canadian Cinema and Television, 1986, for *The Suicide Murders;* Gemini Award nomination, best photography in a dramatic program or series, 1987, for *The Last Season;* Gemini Award nominations, best direction in a dramatic program or miniseries and best photography in a comedy, variety, or performing arts program or series, 1988, for *Family Reunion;* Gemini Award nomination, best photography in a dramatic program or series, 1990, for *Divided Loyalties;* Gemini Award, best photography in a dramatic program or series, 1990, for *Love and Hate: The Story of Colin and Joanne Thatcher;* Emmy Award (with Michael Boland), outstanding individual achievement in informational programming—cinematography, 1992, for *Millennium: Tribal Wisdom and the Modern World;* Australian Film Institute Award nomination, best achievement in cinematography, 1993, for *On My Own;* Genie Award nomination, best achievement in cinematography, 1996, for *Margaret's Museum;* award for best theatrical feature, Canadian Society of Cinematographers, 1996; Daytime Emmy Award nomination, outstanding directing in a children's special, 1998, for *In His Father's Shoes;* Emmy Award nomination, outstanding directing in a children's special, 2000, for *Sea People;* Video Premiere Award nomination, best directing, 2001, for *Left Behind;* Leo Award nomination, best direction in a feature length drama, Motion Picture Arts and Sciences Foundation of British Columbia, 2006, for *Murder Unveiled;* Leo Award nominations, best screenwriting in a feature length drama (with Patricia Finn), best cinematography in a feature length drama, and best direction in a feature length drama, all 2007, for *Partition;* also received two CableACE Awards, eight Prix Anik Awards, and a Canadian Film and Television Production Association achievement award.

CREDITS

Film Cinematographer:
The Naked Peacock (documentary), Danton Films, 1975.
Bix (documentary; also known as *Bix: Ain't None of Them Play Like Him Yet*), Bridge Film Productions, 1981.
Heartaches, Motion Picture Marketing, 1982.
Hugh MacLennan: Portrait of a Writer, 1982.
Going to War, 1985.
The Canadian Observer: An Introduction to Hugh MacLennan, 1985.

The Last Season, Canadian Broadcasting Corp., 1986.
Dancing in the Dark (also known as *Danse a contre–jour*), New World Pictures, 1986.
Loyalties (also known as *Double allegeance*), Cinema Group, 1987.
Nowhere to Hide, New Century Vista, 1987.
(As Vic Sarin) *Norman's Awesome Experience* (also known as *A Switch in Time*), Hemdale Home Video/Southgate Video, 1988.
Family Reunion, 1988.
Namumkin, 1988.
The Long Road Home (also known as *Le retour de l'exil*), 1989.
Divided Loyalties, Glen–Warren Productions, 1989.
Solitary Journey, 1989.
Cold Comfort, 1989, Republic, 1990.
Bye Bye Blues, 1989, Circle Films, 1990.
On My Own (also known as *Il colore dei suoi occhi*), Alliance Communications Corp./Rosa Colosimo Films, 1992.
Cold Sweat, 1993.
(As Vic Sarin) *The Burning Season,* Primedia Pictures/Sirens Films, 1993.
Tapoori, 1993.
God's Dominion: Shepherds to the Flock, 1993.
(And camera operator) *Whale Music,* 1994.
(As Vic Sarin) *Margaret's Museum* (also known as *Le musee de Margaret*), 1995.
Urban Safari, Warwick Pictures, 1996.
Salt Water Moose, Hallmark Home Entertainment, 1996.
The Hidden Dimension, Imax Corp., 1997.
Love on the Side (also known as *Deluxe Combo Platter* and *Love on the Side*), Zennpix, 2004.
Partition, Seville Pictures, 2007.
A Shine of the Rainbows, Seville Pictures, 2008.

Film Director:
So Many Miracles (documentary), 1987.
Solitary Journey, 1989.
Cold Comfort, 1989.
(As Vic Sarin) *The Legend of Gator Face,* Hallmark Home Entertainment, 1996.
Left Behind (also known as *Left Behind: The Movie*), Cloud Ten Pictures, 2001.
Love on the Side (also known as *Deluxe Combo Platter* and *Love on the Side*), Zennpix, 2004.
Partition, Seville Pictures, 2007.
A Shine of Rainbows, Seville Pictures, 2008.

Film Work; Other:
Second unit camera operator, *Spasms,* Blossom Pictures, 1982.
Camera operator, *Whale Music,* 1994.
Executive producer, *Love on the Side* (also known as *Deluxe Combo Platter* and *Love on the Side*), 2004.
Executive producer, *Civic Duty,* Freestyle Releasing, 2006.

Producer, *Journey of the Heart: The Making of "Partition"* (documentary), Seville Pictures, 2007.

Film Appearances:

Himself, *The Making of "Left Behind: The Movie"* (documentary short), 2000.

Television Cinematographer; Miniseries:

Love and Hate: The Story of Colin and Joanne Thatcher (also known as *Love and Hate: A Marriage Made in Hell*), NBC, 1989.

Television Cinematographer; Movies:

The Insurance Man from Ingersoll, 1975.
The Fighting Men (also known as *Men of Steel*), 1977.
Someday Soon, 1977.
Crossbar, 1979.
The Wordsmith, 1979.
War Brides, 1980.
Rumours of Glory, 1983.
Charlie Grant's War, 1984.
The Suicide Murders, 1985.
Turning to Stone (also known as *Concrete Hell*), 1985.
A Moving Picture, 1989.
The David Milgaard Story, 1992.
Artesmia, 1992.
Spenser: Ceremony, 1993.
Spenser: Pale Kings and Princes, Lifetime, 1994.
Not Our Son, CBS, 1994.
Spenser: A Savage Place, 1995.
Wounded Heart, 1995.
(As Vic Sarin) *Hearts Adrift,* 1996.
(As Vic Sarin) *The Waiting Game* (also known as *Clair comme le cristal* and *Harlequin's "The Waiting Game"*), Showtime, 1998.
(As Vic Sarin) *Sea People,* Showtime, 1999.
Recipe for Murder (also known as *Murray Maguire M.E.*), PAX, 2001.

Television Director; Movies:

Passengers, 1980.
The Other Kingdom, 1984.
The David Milgaard Story, 1992.
Spenser: Ceremony, 1993.
(As Vic Sarin) *Trial at Fortitude Bay,* CBC, 1994.
Spenser: Pale Kings and Princes, 1994.
Wounded Heart, 1995.
Hearts Adrift, 1996.
The Waiting Game (also known as *Clair comme le cristal* and *Harlequin's "The Waiting Game"*), Showtime, 1998.
Hard to Forget (also known as *Amoureux d'une ombre* and *Harlequin's "Hard to Forget"*), The Movie Channel, 1998.
(As Vic Sarin) *Sea People,* Showtime, 1999.
Recipe for Murder (also known as *Murray, M.E.*), 2001.
Murder Unveiled, CBC, 2005.

Television Cinematographer; Specials:

David Thomas: The Incredible Time Travels of Henry Osgood, 1986.

Television Director; Specials:

Riel (documentary), CBC, 1979.
In His Father's Shoes (also known as *Les chaussures de mon pere*), 1997.

Television Cinematographer; Episodic:

"A Woman of Appetites," *Telescope,* 1971.
Seeing Things, 1983.
"VCR–Very Careful Rape," *Alfred Hitchcock Presents,* NBC, 1988.
"Animal Lovers," *Alfred Hitchcock Presents,* NBC, 1988.
"Prism," *Alfred Hitchcock Presents,* NBC, 1988.
"Houdini on Channel 4," *Alfred Hitchcock Presents,* NBC, 1988.
Millennium: Tribal Wisdom and the Modern World, 1992.

Television Director; Episodic:

Spenser: For Hire, ABC, 1985.
"Hippocratic Oath," *Alfred Hitchcock Presents,* NBC, 1988.
"Hacker," *Neon Rider,* syndicated, 1990.
Millennium: Tribal Wisdom and the Modern World, 1992.
"The Agony Column," *Wind at My Back,* 1997.
Hope Island, PAX, 1999.
Flatland, 2002.

WRITINGS

Screenplays:

Partition, 2007.
A Shine of Rainbows, 2008.

SCARDINO, Don 1949–
(Chelo Scardino)

PERSONAL

Full name, Donald Joseph Scardino; born February 17, 1949, in New York, NY; son of jazz musicians; married Pamela Blair (an actress), 1984 (divorced, 1991); married Dana L. Williams, 1995; children: (second marriage) one. *Education:* Attended City College of the City University of New York.

Addresses: *Agent*—Endeavor, 9601 Wilshire Blvd., 3rd Floor, Beverly Hills, CA 90210.

Career: Actor, director, and producer. Playwrights Horizons Theatre, New York City, artistic director, 1991–96. Made stage debut in summer stock. Also composer and recording artist.

Member: Directors Guild of America, American Federation of Television and Radio Artists, Society of Stage Directors and Choreographers, Actors' Equity Association, Screen Actors Guild.

Awards, Honors: Daytime Emmy Award nomination, outstanding younger leading man in a drama series, 1986, for *Another World;* Emmy Award nomination, outstanding individual achievement in directing in a variety or music program, 1994, for *Tracey Takes On New York;* Obie Award, best director, *Village Voice,* 1995, for *A Cheever Evening;* Emmy Award nomination, outstanding directing for a variety or music program, 1998, for "Smoking," *Tracey Takes On …;* Directors Guild of America Award nomination, outstanding directorial achievement in a musical or variety program, 1998, for "Tracey Takes On … Vegas," *Tracey Takes On …;* Film Showcase Jury Award, U.S. Comedy Arts Festival, best feature, 2000, for *Advice from a Caterpillar;* Annual Cable Excellence (ACE) Award, National Cable Television Association, for *Tracey Takes On ….*

CREDITS

Stage Appearances:
Understudy for the roles of Christopher, Eric, and Charlot, *The Playroom,* Brooks Atkinson Theatre, New York City, 1965.

Dom, *The Loves of Cass McGuire,* Helen Hayes Theatre, New York City, 1966.

Robert Conklin, *The Rimers of Eldritch,* Cherry Lane Theatre, New York City, 1967.

John Edwards, *Johnny No–Trump,* Cort Theatre, New York City, 1967.

35914, *The Unknown Soldier and His Wife,* Vivian Beaumont Theatre, Lincoln Center, New York City, 1967.

Jimmy Gordon, *My Daughter, Your Son,* Booth Theatre, New York City, 1969.

Young man, *Park* (musical), John Golden Theatre, New York City, 1970.

Godspell (musical), Cherry Lane Theatre, then Promenade Theatre, New York City, 1971, later Royal Alexandra Theatre, Toronto, Ontario, Canada, then Playhouse Theatre, New York City, 1972–73, then Broadhurst Theatre, Plymouth Theatre, and Ambassador Theatre, all New York City, 1976–77.

Bob Rettie, *Moonchildren,* Theatre de Lys, New York City, 1974.

Matthew and crusader, *The Glorious Age* (musical), Theatre Four, New York City, 1975.

Zinko, *Kid Champion,* New York Shakespeare Festival, Anspacher Theatre, Public Theatre, New York City, 1975.

Antipholus, *The Comedy of Errors,* New York Shakespeare Festival, Delacorte Theatre, Public Theatre, New York City, 1975.

Wilfred Varney, *Secret Service,* Playhouse Theatre, 1976.

Rodney Bevan, *Boy Meets Girl,* Playhouse Theatre, 1976.

David, *Scribes,* Marymount Manhattan Theatre, New York City, 1977.

Jake, *I'm Getting My Act Together and Taking It on the Road* (musical), Anspacher Theatre, Public Theatre, 1978.

Private Johnny Perkins, *King of Hearts* (musical), Minskoff Theatre, New York City, 1978.

Eugene Gant, *Angel* (musical), Minskoff Theatre, 1978.

Rich Forrester, *Holeville* (musical), Theatre at Brooklyn Academy of Music, Brooklyn, NY, 1979.

A Christmas Garland, Manhattan Theatre Club, New York City, 1979.

Reporter, *How I Got That Story,* Folger Theatre Group, Washington, DC, 1980–1981, then Westside Arts Theatre, New York City, 1982.

Double Feature (musical), Theatre of St. Peters Church, New York City, 1981.

Demetrius, *A Midsummer Night's Dream,* Theatre at Brooklyn Academy of Music, 1981.

Thomas Appletree, *The Recruiting Officer,* Theatre at Brooklyn Academy of Music, 1981.

George Garga, *Jungle of Cities,* Playhouse Theatre, 1981.

Hang on to the Good Times (musical), Manhattan Theatre Club, 1985.

Major Tours:
Bob Rettie, *Moonchildren,* U.S. cities, 1974.

Stage Director:
How I Got That Story, Canadian production, 1982.

A Kiss Is Just a Kiss, Theatre at Manhattan Punch Line, New York City, 1983.

Kid Purple, Theatre at Manhattan Punch Line, Susan Bloch Theatre, New York City, 1984.

"Field Day," *Young Playwrights Festival,* Playwrights Horizons Theatre, New York City, 1985.

"Life under Water," *Marathon 85,* 1985.

The Hit Parade, Theatre at Manhattan Punch Line, 1986.

The Further Adventures of Kathy and Mo, Second Stage, New York City, 1986.

Highest Standard of Living, Playwrights Horizons Theatre, 1986.

"Women and Wallace," *Young Playwrights Festival,* Playwrights Horizons Theatre, 1988.

Godspell (musical), Lamb's Theatre, New York City, 1988.

A Few Good Men, Music Box Theatre, New York City, and John F. Kennedy Center for the Performing Arts, Washington, DC, 1989–91.

Making Movies, Promenade Theatre, New York City, 1990.

On the Bum, or the Next Train Through, Playwrights Horizons Theatre, 1992.

Later Life, Playwrights Horizons Theatre, 1993.

An Imaginary Life, Playwrights Horizons, 1993–94.

A Cheever Evening, Playwrights Horizons, 1994–95.

Sacrilege, Belasco Theatre, New York City, 1995.

Oldest Living Confederate Widow Tells All, Old Globe Theatre, San Diego, CA 2003.

Lennon, Broadhurst Theatre, New York City, 2005.

Also directed productions of *I'm Getting My Act Together and Taking It on the Road.*

Stage Director; Major Tours:
A Few Good Men, U.S. cities, c. 1991.

Stage Producer:
Flaubert's Latest, Playwrights Horizons Theatre, New York City, 1992.

Film Appearances:
(As Chelo Scardino) Homer Edwards, *Homer,* National General, 1970.

Sandy Hoffman, *The People Next Door,* Avco Embassy, 1970.

Michael, *Rip–off* (also known as *Virgin Territory* and *Rever en couleur*), Phoenix, 1971.

Mick, *Squirm,* American International Pictures, 1976.

Ted Bailey, *Cruising* (also known as *William Freidkin's "Cruising"*), United Artists, 1980.

Marvin, *He Knows You're Alone* (also known as *Blood Wedding*), Metro–Goldwyn–Mayer, 1980.

Film Director:
Me and Veronica, True Pictures, 1992.
The Deal, 1998.
Advice from a Caterpillar, 1999.

Television Appearances; Series:
Dr. John "Johnny" Fletcher, Jr., *The Guiding Light* (also known as *Guiding Light*), CBS, 1965–67.

Andy Hurley, *Love Is a Many–Splendored Thing,* 1968.

Marty Egan, *As the World Turns,* CBS, 1969–70.

Ernest 11, *The Whiteoaks of Jaina,* CBC, 1972.

Frank Ryan, *Ryan's Hope,* ABC, 1981.

Gregory "Greg" Nelson, *All My Children,* 1984.

Chris Chapin, *Another World* (also known as *Another World: Bay City*), NBC, 1985–86.

Television Appearances; Movies:
Wilfred Varney, *Secret Service,* 1977.
Charlie Cotchipee, *Purlie,* 1981.

Television Appearances; Specials:
Wilfred, *Secret Service,* PBS, 1977.

Quiet on the Set! Behind the Scenes at "Molly Dodd," Lifetime, 1990.

Friends of Gilda, 1993.

Television Appearances; Pilots:
Curley Treadway, *The Flim–Flam Man,* NBC, 1969.
Rick, *Hereafter,* NBC, 1975.
Billy Joe Pearson, *Side by Side,* CBS, 1976.
Mooney, *The Rubber Gun Squad,* NBC, 1977.

Television Appearances; Episodic:
The Patty Duke Show, ABC, 1964.

"Stones," *N.Y.P.D.,* ABC, 1968.

Sandy Hoffmann, "The People Next Door," *CBS Playhouse,* CBS, 1968.

Dr. Ferguson, "The Medicine Ball," *The Ghost & Mrs. Muir,* 1969.

Chris Payden, "The Glory Shouter," *Name of the Game,* NBC, 1970.

"Death in a Toy Balloon," *The Andros Targets,* 1977.

"Here's Why You Order from the Spanish Side of the Menu," *The Days and Nights of Molly Dodd,* Lifetime, 1989.

Television Work; Series:
Supervising producer, *The Days and Nights of Molly Dodd,* NBC, 1987 and 1988, then Lifetime, 1989–91.

Co–executive producer, *Deadline,* NBC, 2000.

Co–executive producer, *The Education of Max Bickford,* CBS, 2001–2002.

Producer, *30 Rock,* NBC, 2007—.

Television Director; Movies:
Chestnut Hill, 2001.

Television Director; Pilots:
The Human Factor, CBS, 1992.
Likely Suspects, Fox, 1992.

Television Director; Specials:
Tracey Ullmann Takes On New York, 1993.

Television Director; Episodic:
Another World (also known as *Another World: Bay City*), NBC, 1986–87.

Nick and Hillary, NBC, 1989.

The Days and Nights of Molly Dodd, NBC, 1987 and 1988, then Lifetime, 1989–91.

"Women and Wallace," *American Playhouse,* PBS, 1990.

"Twenty–seven Wagons Full of Cotton," *American Playwrights Theatre: The One Acts,* Arts and Entertainment, 1990.

Against the Law, Fox, 1991.

Likely Suspects, 1992.

Law & Order, NBC, 1991–2006.

Central Park West (also known as *C.P.W.*), CBS, 1995.

"Fire: Part 1," *Homicide: Life on the Street,* NBC, 1995.

Under Fire, 1995.

"Christmas Daze," *Pearl,* CBS, 1996.

"Smoking," *Tracy Takes On ...,* HBO, 1996.

Public Morals, CBS, 1996.

"Tracy Takes On ... Vegas," *Tracy Takes On ...,* HBO, 1996.

Soul Man, ABC, 1997.

Cosby, CBS, 1998–2000.

Deadline, NBC, 2000.

"April Is the Cruelest Month," *Sports Night,* ABC, 2000.

"Bells and a Siren," *Sports Night,* ABC, 2000.

"Lies, Damn Lies and Statistics," *The West Wing,* NBC, 2000.

DAG, NBC, 2000.

"Love Stories," *100 Centre Street,* Arts and Entertainment, 2001.

"Queenie's Running," *100 Centre Street,* Arts and Entertainment, 2001.

The Education of Max Bickford, CBS, 2001–2002.

"End of the Month," *100 Centre Street,* Arts and Entertainment, 2002.

"Hurricane Paul," *100 Centre Street,* Arts and Entertainment, 2002.

"Tomorrow," *Law & Order: Criminal Intent* (also known as *Law & Order: CI*), NBC, 2002.

Ed, NBC, 2002–2003.

"Blink," *Law & Order: Criminal Intent* (also known as *Law & Order: CI*), NBC, 2003.

"Zoonotic," *Law & Order: Criminal Intent* (also known as *Law & Order: CI*), NBC, 2003.

"Wrecking Ball," *George Lopez,* ABC, 2004.

Hope & Faith, ABC, 2004–2006.

"Managers," *My Boys,* TBS, 2006.

30 Rock, NBC, 2006—.

"The Emergency," *The Singles Table,* NBC, 2007.

"Operation: Seduce Simone," *Knights of Prosperity,* ABC, 2007.

"Operation: Fighting Shape," *Knights of Prosperity,* ABC, 2007.

"Operation: Panic Room," *Knights of Prosperity,* ABC, 2007.

"Operation: Oswald Montecristo," *Knights of Prosperity,* ABC, 2007.

"Balance," *Rescue Me* (also known as *Rescue Me: FDNY*), FX Channel, 2007.

"Seven," *Rescue Me* (also known as *Rescue Me: FDNY*), FX Channel, 2007.

Also directed *One Life to Live,* ABC.

Television Work; Pilots:

Theme song performer, *The Film–Flam Man,* NBC, 1969.

WRITINGS

Stage Scores:

Lennon, Broadhurst Theatre, New York City, 2005.

Film Music:

(As Chelo Scardino) *Homer,* National General, 1970.

Television Music; Pilots:

The Flim–Flam Man, NBC, 1969.

OTHER SOURCES

Periodicals:

New York Times, August 25, 1991, pp. H5, H18.

Variety, June 10, 1991, p. 70.

SCHEER, Paul 1976–

PERSONAL

Born January 31, 1976, in New Hyde Park, NY. *Education:* Attended New York University; studied with the Atlantic Theater Company, the Upright Citizens Brigade, and the Chicago City Limits Training Program.

Addresses: *Agent*—Agency for the Performing Arts, 405 South Beverly Dr., Beverly Hills, CA 90212; Endeavor, 9601 Wilshire Blvd., 3rd Floor, Beverly Hills, CA 90210. *Manager*—3 Arts Entertainment, 9460 Wilshire Blvd., 7th Floor, Beverly Hills, CA 90212.

Career: Actor and writer. Chicago City Limits (comedy troupe), New York City, member; Upright Citizens Brigade Theater, New York City, performer; performed the MySpace Improv Show, Upright Citizen's Brigade Theater, Los Angeles, CA; appeared in television commercials for GameRiot, 2004.

CREDITS

Film Appearances:

Lenny Pear, *Blackballed: The Bobby Dukes Story* (also known as *Blackballed*), The 7th Floor, 2004.

Little Pete, *School for Scoundrels,* Weinstein Company, 2006.

Junior, *Trainwreck: My Life as an Idiot,* Chicago Pictures Distribution, 2007.

Annoying customer, *Watching the Detectives,* Peace Arch Films, 2007.

Tucker Taylor, *Slice* (short), 2007.
Starship Dave, Twentieth Century–Fox, 2008.

Television Appearances; Series:
Various, *Late Night with Conan O'Brien*, NBC, 1993.
Various characters, *Upright Citizens Brigade*, Comedy Central, 1998–2000.
Regular, *Burly TV*, 2001.
Best Week Ever, VH1, 2003–2006.
Additional characters, *Crossballs: The Debate Show* (also known as *Crossballs*), Comedy Central, 2004.
Sketch characters, *McEnroe*, CNBC, 2004.
Various characters, *Human Giant*, MTV, 2007.

Television Appearances; Pilots:
Voice of Ashton Kutcher, *Starveillance*, E! Entertainment Network, 2007.
Motel clerk, *Raines*, NBC, 2007.

Television Appearances; Specials:
Best Summer Ever, VH1, 2004.
Best Year Ever, VH1, 2004–2006.

Television Appearances; Episodic:
Guest panelist, *American Morning*, CNN, 2004, 2005.
Weekends at the DL, Comedy Central, 2005.
Today (also known as *NBC News Today* and *The Today Show*), NBC, 2005, 2006.
Panelist, "Cruise Control," *Dateline NBC* (also known as *Dateline*), NBC, 2006.
"MySpace," *Good Morning America*, ABC, 2006.
Late Show with David Letterman (also known as *The Late Show*), CBS, 2007.
Last Call with Carson Daly, NBC, 2007.
Guest host, *KTLA Morning News* (also known as *KTLA Morning Show*), 2007.
10 Items or Less, TBS, 2007.

Television Executive Producer; Series:
Human Giant, MTV, 2007.

WRITINGS

Television Episodes:
Burly TV, 2001.
Crossballs: The Debate Show (also known as *Crossballs*), Comedy Central, 2004.

OTHER SOURCES

Electronic:
Paul Scheer Website, http://www.paulscheer.com, October 20, 2007.

SCHMIDT, Kevin 1988–
(Kevin G. Schmidt)

PERSONAL

Born August 16, 1988, in Andover, KS; brother of Kenneth Schmidt (an actor) and Kendall Schmidt (an actor).

Addresses: *Agent*—Coast to Coast Talent, Inc., 3350 Barham Blvd., Los Angeles, CA 90068.

Career: Actor. Appeared in television commercials.

Awards, Honors: Young Artist Award nomination, best performance in a television comedy series—guest starring young actor, 2002, for *Grounded for Life*; Young Artist Award (with others), best young ensemble in a feature film, 2004, for *Cheaper by the Dozen*; Young Artist Award nomination (with others), best performance in a feature film—young ensemble cast, 2006, for *Cheaper by the Dozen 2*.

CREDITS

Film Appearances:
Young Michael Reid, *Mind Rage* (also known as *Mind Lies*), Mainline Releasing, 2000.
(As Kevin G. Schmidt) Henry Baker, *Cheaper by the Dozen*, Twentieth Century–Fox, 2003.
(As Kevin G. Schmidt) Lenny at age thirteen, *The Butterfly Effect*, New Line Cinema, 2004.
(As Kevin G. Schmidt) Skip, *Catch That Kid* (also known as *Mission Without Permission* and *Mission: Possible—Diese kids sind nicht zu fassen!*), Twentieth Century–Fox, 2004.
(As Kevin G. Schmidt) Henry Baker, *Cheaper by the Dozen 2*, Twentieth Century–Fox, 2005.
Jeff Pryce, *Resurrection Mary*, 2007.

Television Appearances; Series:
(As Kevin G. Schmidt) Brad Saminski, *Clubhouse*, CBS, 2004.

Television Appearances; Miniseries:
Tom Clarke as child, "Jacob and Jesse," *Taken* (also known as *Steven Spielberg Presents "Taken"*), Sci–Fi Channel, 2002.

Television Appearances; Pilots:
Brad Saminski, *Clubhouse*, CBS, 2004.

Television Appearances; Episodic:
Kyle, "Jimmy Was Kung–Fu Fighting," *Grounded for Life*, Fox, 2001.

Timmy, *The Downer Channel*, NBC, 2001.
Thor kid number two, "Thor," *Curb Your Enthusiasm*, HBO, 2001.
Leiws, "Rights of Passage," *Judging Amy*, CBS, 2001.
(As Kevin G. Schmidt) Kid at dance, "The Good Fight," *Providence*, NBC, 2002.
Skitch, "Shrink Wrap," *The King of Queens*, CBS, 2002.
Gerald, "Small Packages," *The District*, CBS, 2002.
Subscriber number two/teen, *The Division*, Lifetime, 2002.
Kevin, "Dummy and Dummier," *The Pitts*, Fox, 2003.
(As Kevin G. Schmidt) Billy, "Ice Queen," *JAG*, CBS, 2003.
"Grudge Match," *The Mullets*, UPN, 2003.
Oliver Beene, Fox, 2003.
Joey, *Come to Papa*, NBC, 2004.
Ted Huberty, "Legacy," *The Guardian*, CBS 2004.
Leo, "Mr. Monk and Little Monk," *Monk*, USA Network, 2005.
Steven Wexford, *Numb3rs*, CBS, 2007.

SCHOLTE, Tom

PERSONAL

Career: Actor and producer.

Awards, Honors: Genie Award nomination, best supporting actor, Academy of Canadian Cinema and Television, 2002, for *Last Wedding;* Gemini Award, best guest actor in a dramatic series, Academy of Canadian Cinema and Television, 2002, for *Da Vinci's Inquest.*

CREDITS

Film Appearances:
Trevor MacIntosh, *Live Bait*, Cypher Productions, 1995.
Arnold the gas guy, *Drive, She Said*, Beyond Films, 1997.
David, *Dirty*, Telefilm Canada, 1998.
Harold, *Babette's Feet* (short film), 1999.
Reporter, *Snow Falling on Cedars*, MCA/Universal, 1999.
Michael, *Untitled* (short film), Crazy 8s Film, 1999.
Peter, *No More Monkeys Jumpin' on the Bed*, Jumpin' on the Bed Productions, 2000.
Writer, *What Else Have You Got?* (short film), Inter-Muses Productions/Green Room Film, 2000.
Tom, *Lunch with Charles* (also known as *Yu Chalisi wu can*), Long Shong Entertainment Group, 2001.
Peter, *Last Wedding*, ThinkFilm, 2001.
For My Father (short film), 2002.
Peter, *Exposures* (short film), 2003.
Acker, *The Core*, Paramount, 2003.

Mover, *Moving Malcolm*, Mongrel Media, 2003.
Father James, *See Grace Fly*, Domino Film & Television International, 2003.
Len Birnbaum, *Jinnah—On Crime: White Knight, Black Widow*, Canadian Broadcasting Corp., 2003.
Attorney Merle Crowe, *Walking Tall*, Metro–Goldwyn–Mayer, 2004.
Danny Fitterson, *Lies Like Truth*, Brightlight Pictures, 2004.
Edward Lynch, *The Thing Below* (also known as *Ghost Rig 2: The Legend of the Sea Ghost* (also known as *Sea Ghost*), DEJ Productions, 2004.
Gerard Mackelwain, *Marie Tyrell* (short film), Vtape, 2004.
Roger, *Everyone*, TLA Releasing, 2005.
Paul, *The Hamster Cage*, 2005.
Voice of Slim, *Hastings Street* (short film), Larry Kent Productions, 2007.

Film Work:
Coproducer, *The Hamster Cage*, 2005.

Television Appearances; Movies:
Deputy Hutchins, *Dead Ahead*, USA Network, 1996.
Monte Marks, *Goldrush: A Real Life Alaskan Adventure* (also known as *Gold Rush!*), ABC, 1998.

Television Appearances; Episodic:
Howie Samek, "The Infestation/Human Apportation," *PSI Factor: Chronicles of the Paranormal*, syndicated, 1996.
Young Johanson, "Piper Maru," *The X–Files*, Fox, 1996.
Michael Sloan, "Detour," *The X–Files*, Fox, 1997.
Deputy Cooper, "Fortune Teller," *Dead Man's Gun*, Showtime, 1997.
David, "Oppenheimer Park," *Da Vinci's Inquest*, CBC, 2001.
Sports nut, "Unreasonable Doubt," *The Dead Zone* (also known as *Stephen King's "The Dead Zone"*), USA Network, 2002.
First writer, "Gabe's Story," *The Twilight Zone*, UPN, 2002.
Chazen, "Prophecy," *Stargate SG–1* (also known as *La porte des etoiles*), Sci–Fi Channel, 2003.
Lee Styles, "C'mon I Tip Waitresses," *Cold Squad*, CTV, 2005.

SCHULTZ, Michael A. 1938–
(Michael Schultz)

PERSONAL

Born November 10, 1938, in Milwaukee, WI; son of Leo (an insurance salesman) and Katherine Frances (a factory worker; maiden name, Leslie) Schultz; married

Gloria Jean Jones (an actress), December 6, 1965; children: Brandon (an actor), additional child. *Education:* Marquette University, B.F.A., theatre; also attended University of Wisconsin.

Addresses: *Agent*—International Creative Management, 10250 Constellation Way, 9th Floor, Los Angeles, CA 90067.

Career: Director and producer.

Member: African–American Steering Committee.

Awards, Honors: Obie Award, best direction, *Village Voice,* 1968, for *Song of the Lusitanian Bogey;* Antoinette Perry Award nomination, best director of a dramatic play, and Drama Desk Award, outstanding director, 1969, both for *Does a Tiger Wear a Necktie?;* Technical Grand Prize and Golden Palm Award nomination, Cannes Film Festival, 1977, both for *Car Wash;* honorary Ph.D., Emerson University, 1984; inductee, Black Filmmakers Hall of Fame, 1991; Oscar Micheaux Award, 1991; Lifetime Achievement Award, Miami International Coproduction Film Conference, 1992; Best American Film, Santa Barbara International Film Festival, American Black Film Festival Award, best film, 2004, Black Reel Award, best director—independent film, 2005, all for *Woman Thou Art Loosed;* Christopher Award, for *Ceremonies of Dark Old Men.*

CREDITS

Stage Director:
Waiting for Godot, McCarter Theatre, Princeton, NJ, 1966.
Song of the Lusitanian Bogey, Negro Ensemble Company, St. Marks Playhouse, New York City, then London, both 1968.
Kongis Harvest, Negro Ensemble Company, St. Marks Playhouse, 1968.
God Is a (Guess What?), Negro Ensemble Company, St. Marks Playhouse, 1968–1969.
Does a Tiger Wear a Necktie?, Eugene O'Neill Memorial Theatre, Waterford, CT, then Belasco Theatre, New York City, both 1969.
The Reckoning, St. Marks Playhouse, 1969.
Every Night When the Sun Goes Down, Eugene O'Neill Memorial Theatre, 1969.
The Dream on Monkey Mountain, Eugene O'Neill Memorial Theatre, 1969, then Mark Taper Forum, Los Angeles, 1970, later St. Marks Playhouse, 1971.
Operation Sidewinder, Vivian Beaumont Theatre, New York City, then Mark Taper Forum, both 1970.
Sambo, Mobile Theatre, 1970.
Woyzeck, St. Marks Playhouse, 1970.

The Three Sisters, Westport Country Playhouse, Westport, CT, 1973.
Thoughts, Westport Country Playhouse, then Theatre De Lys, New York City, both 1973.
The Poison Tree, Westport Country Playhouse, 1973.
The Cherry Orchard, Anspacher Theatre, New York City, 1973.
What the Winesellers Buy, Mark Taper Forum, Los Angeles, then Vivian Beaumont Theatre, later New Theatre for Now, Los Angeles, all 1974.
Mulebone, Helen Hayes Public Theatre, Lincoln Center, New York City, 1991.

Stage Work; Other:
Stage manager, *The Old Glory,* American Place Theatre, 1964, then Theatre De Lys, both New York City, 1965.
Stage manager, *Command Performance,* Maidman Playhouse, New York City, 1966.
Lighting director, *Daddy Goodness,* Negro Ensemble Company, St. Marks Playhouse, New York City, 1968.

Stage Appearances:
Francesco, "Benito Cereno," *The Old Glory,* American Place Theatre, 1964, then Theatre De Lys, both New York City, 1965.

Film Director:
Together for Days (also known as *Black Cream*), Olas, 1972.
Honeybaby, Honeybaby (also known as *Honey Baby* and *Three Days in Beirut*), Kelly/Jordan, 1974.
Cooley High, American International, 1975.
Car Wash, Universal, 1976.
Greased Lightning, Warner Bros., 1977.
Which Way Is Up?, Universal, 1977.
Sgt. Pepper's Lonely Hearts Club Band (also known as *Banda de los corazones*), Universal, 1978.
Scavenger Hunt, Twentieth Century–Fox, 1979.
Carbon Copy, Avco Embassy, 1981.
(Uncredited) *Bustin' Loose,* Universal, 1983.
The Last Dragon (also known as *Berry Gordy's "The Last Dragon"*), Tri–Star, 1985.
Krush Groove, Warner Bros., 1985.
Disorderlies, Warner Bros., 1987.
Livin' Large (also known as *The Tapes of Dexter Jackson*), Samuel Goldwyn/Night Life, 1991.
Woman Thou Art Loosed, Magnolia Pictures, 2004.

Film Work; Other:
Producer (with Doug McHenry), *Krush Groove,* Warner Bros., 1985.
Producer (with George Jackson), *Disorderlies,* Warner Bros., 1987.
Editor, *The Show,* 1995.

Executive producer, *Phat Beach,* 1996.
Editor, *Ritual,* 1999.

Television Work; Series:
Producer, *Everwood* (also known as *Our New Life in Everwood*), The WB, 2002.

Television Director; Movies:
Carbon Copy, 1981.
Benny's Place, ABC, 1982.
The Jerk, Too, 1984.
Timestalkers, CBS, 1986.
The Spirit, ABC, 1987.
Rock 'n Roll Mom, ABC, 1988.
Tarzan in Manhattan, CBS, 1989.
Jury Duty: The Comedy (also known as *The Great American Sex Scandal*), ABC, 1990.
Day–O (also known as *Dayo*), NBC, 1992.
Young Indiana Jones and the Hollywood Follies, Family Channel, 1994.
Young Indiana Jones: Travels with Father, Family Channel and ABC, 1996.
Killers in the House, USA Network, 1998.
My Last Love (also known as *To Live For*), ABC, 1999.
L.A. Law: The Movie, NBC, 2002.

Television Work; Specials:
Director, *To Be Young, Gifted, and Black,* PBS, 1972.
Director, *Ceremonies in Dark Old Men,* 1975.
Director and producer, *Earth, Wind and Fire in Concert,* HBO, 1982.
Director, *For Us the Living: The Medgar Evers Story* (also known as *For Us the Living*), 1983.
Editor, *112th & South Central: Through the Eyes of the Children,* 1993.

Also directed *Fade Out—The Erosion of Black Images in the Media* (documentary).

Television Director; Pilots:
Change at 125th Street, CBS, 1974.
The Jerk, Too, NBC, 1984.
Hammer, Slammer, and Slade, ABC, 1990.
Shock Treatment, 1995.
Eli Stone, ABC, 2007.

Television Director; Episodic:
"The Madam," *Toma,* ABC, 1974.
Movin On, NBC, 1974.
"The Dark and Bloody Ground," *The Rockford Files* (also known as *Jim Rockford, Private Investigator*), NBC, 1974.
Baretta, ABC, 1975.
What's Happening!, 1976.
Starsky & Hutch, ABC, 1977.
"Sacred Hearts," *Picket Fences,* CBS, 1992.

"Frog Men," *Picket Fences,* CBS, 1993.
"Where There's a Will," *L.A. Law,* 1993.
Route 66, 1993.
The Adventures of Brisco County Jr. (also known as *Brisco County Jr.*), 1993.
Chicago Hope, CBS, 1994.
Sisters, NBC, 1994–96.
"Call Me Incontestable," *Diagnosis Murder,* CBS, 1995.
Promised Land (also known as *Home of the Brave*), CBS, 1996.
Buffy the Vampire Slayer (also known as *Buffy the Vampire Slayer: The Series* and *Buffy*), The WB, 1997.
Michael Hayes, CBS, 1997.
"The Guardian," *JAG,* CBS, 1997.
The Practice, ABC, 1997–2001.
Ally McBeal, Fox, 1997–2001.
Charmed, The WB, 1998.
Ally, Fox, 1999.
"Empty Pockets," *Wasteland,* 1999.
"Assassins," *Felicity,* The WB, 1999.
"The Depths," *Felicity,* The WB, 1999.
"Four Drops of Blood," *Family Law,* CBS, 1999.
"Cry Me a Liver," *City of Angels,* NBC, 2000.
"Chapter Seven," *Boston Public,* Fox, 2000.
"The Tutor," *That's Life,* CBS, 2000.
"Chick Flick," *Charmed,* The WB, 2000.
"Charmed Again: Part 1," *Charmed,* The WB, 2001.
Philly, ABC, 2001.
"To Walk on Wings," *JAG,* CBS, 2001.
"The Killer," *JAG,* CBS, 2001.
Everwood (also known as *Our New Life in Everwood*), The WB, 2002–2005.
"Today I Am a Man," *Jack & Bobby,* The WB, 2004.
Method & Red, Fox, 2004.
"Legacy," *Jack & Bobby,* The WB, 2005.
"Frank's Best," *Cold Case,* CBS, 2005.
"Celebrity Twin Could Hang: Film at Eleven," *Pepper Dennis,* The WB, 2006.
"The Great Stink," *Gilmore Girls,* The WB, 2006.
"Freedom," *Eli Stone,* ABC, 2007.
"The My Two Dads," *The O.C.,* Fox, 2007.
"Valentine's Day Massacre," *Brothers & Sisters,* ABC, 2007.
"Baby Doe," *Lincoln Heights,* ABC Family, 2007.
"Secrets and Guys," *October Road,* ABC, 2007.

Television Appearances; Specials:
Acapulco Black Film Festival, 2000.

RECORDINGS

Videos:
Focused Digizine #1, Focused Productions, 2004.

SEALE, John 1942–

PERSONAL

Full name, John Clement Seale; born October 5, 1942, in Warwick, Queensland, Australia; son of Eric Clement and Marjorie Lyndon (maiden name, Pool) Seale; married Louise Lee Mutton, September 23, 1967; children: Brianna Lee, Derin, Anthony. *Education:* Attended high school in Sydney, New South Wales, Australia. *Avocational Interests:* Building boats, sailing.

Career: Cinematographer, director of photography, photographer for films, and camera operator. Australian Broadcasting Corporation, camera assistant in film department, 1962–68.

Member: Australian Cinematographers Society, American Society of Cinematographers.

Awards, Honors: Australian Film Institute Award nomination, best achievement in cinematography, 1981, for *The Survivor;* Milli Award, cinematographer of the year, and Golden Tripod Award, both Australian Cinematographers Society, 1983, for *Goodbye Paradise;* Australian Film Institute Award, best achievement in cinematography, 1984, for *Careful, He Might Hear You;* Australian Film Institute Award nomination, best achievement in cinematography, 1984, for *Silver City;* Milli Award, cinematographer of the year, and Golden Tripod Award, both c. 1985, British Society of Cinematographers Award nomination, 1985, Academy Award nomination and Film Award nomination, British Academy of Film and Television Arts, both 1986, all best cinematography, for *Witness;* Golden Tripod Award, c. 1986, for *Children of a Lesser God;* Academy Award nomination and American Society of Cinematographers Award nomination, both best cinematography, 1989, for *Rain Man;* British Society of Cinematographers Award nomination, best cinematography, 1989, for *Dead Poets Society;* named cinematographer of the year, *Premiere* magazine, 1989, and Film Award nomination (with Alan Root), British Academy of Film and Television Arts, best cinematography, 1990, for *Gorillas in the Mist;* tribute from the Film Critics Circle of Australia, 1990; Los Angeles Film Critics Association Award and Boston Society of Film Critics Award, both 1996, Academy Award, American Society of Cinematographers Award, Film Award, British Academy of Film and Television Arts, Chicago Film Critics Association Award, European Film Award, Golden Satellite Award, International Press Academy, Florida Film Critics Award, and British Society of Cinematographers Award nomination, all best cinematography, 1997, for *The English Patient;* Excellence in Cinematography Award, Hawaii International Film Festival, 1997; inducted into the Australian Cinematographers Society Hall of Fame, 1997; Chauvel Award, Brisbane International Film Festival, 1997; Kodak Vision Award, 1997; honorary doctorate, Griffith University, 1997; Film Award nomination, British Academy of Film and Television Arts, Chicago Film Critics Association Award nomination, Golden Satellite Award nomination, and Sierra Award nomination, Las Vegas Film Critics Society, all best cinematography, 2000, for *The Talented Mr. Ripley;* American Society of Cinematographers Award nomination, outstanding achievement in cinematography in theatrical releases, 2001, for *The Perfect Storm;* Australia Day Honour, for work in the arts, 2002; Academy Award nomination, Phoenix Film Critics Society Award nomination, Film Award nomination, British Academy of Film and Television Arts, and American Society of Cinematographers Award nomination, all best cinematography, 2004, for *Cold Mountain;* Order of Australia Medal (OAM), Medal in the General Division.

CREDITS

Film Cinematographer:

Alvin Purple (also known as *Ahkera Alvin, seksikauppias, O devasso renitente,* and *O poniros Alvin kai ta koritsia tou*), Roadshow Entertainment/Warner Bros., 1973.

Deathcheaters (also known as *Death Cheaters*), Roadshow Entertainment, 1976.

Cries from a Cold Aquarium (short film), 1978.

Heart, Head & Hand (short documentary film), 1979.

The Dangerous Summer (short documentary film), 1980.

Fatty Finn, Hoyts Distribution, 1980.

Doctors and Nurses, 1981.

Goose Flesh, c. 1981.

Ginger Meggs, 1982.

Goodbye Paradise, 1982.

BMX Bandits (also known as *Short Wave*), Nilsen Premiere, 1983.

Fighting Back (also known as *Death Vengeance* and *Fighting Free*), Enterprise, 1983.

Careful, He Might Hear You (also known as *Ostroznie, moga cie uslyszec* and *P.S.—kahden tulen vaelissae*), Hoyts Distribution, 1983, Twentieth Century–Fox, 1984.

Silver City, Samuel Goldwyn, 1984.

The Empty Beach (also known as *Cliff Hardy—yksityisetsivae, Ein Toter weiss zuviel,* and *Pusta plaza*), Jethro, 1985.

Witness (also known as *Called Home, A tanu, A testemunha, Der Einzige Zeuge, Ha–Ed, Peter Weirin todistaja, Swiadek, Temoin sous surveillance, Testigo en peligro, Todistaja, Unico testigo, Vidnet, Vittne till morde, Witness—il testimone,* and *Witness: Temoin sous surveillance*), Paramount, 1985.

Children of a Lesser God (also known as *Bortom alla ord, Dzieci gorszego Boga, Egy kisebb isten gyermekei, Figli di un dio minore, Filhos do silencio, Gottes vergessene Kinder, Hijos de un dios menor, Les enfants du silence, Paidia enos katoterou theou, Sanaton rakkaus, Te amare en silencio,* and *Yeladim Horgim L'Yeladim*), Paramount, 1986.

The Hitcher (also known as *Hitcher, A morte pede carona, Autostopowicz, Carretera al infierno, Ha–Trempist, Hitcher, der Highway Killer, The hitcher—La lunga strada della paura, L'autostoppeur, Liftaren, Liftari,* and *Terror na autoestrada*), TriStar, 1986.

The Mosquito Coast (also known as *Mosquito Coast, A costa do mosquito, La costa de los mosquitos, Moskiittorannikko,* and *Moskitkusten*), Warner Bros., 1986.

Stakeout (also known as *Debaixo de olho, Die Nacht hat viele Augen, Etroite surveillance, Kyttaeyskeikka, Ojne i natten, Procedimeiento ilegal, Sorveglianza ... speciale, Spanarna, Stakeout—Die Nacht hat viele Augen,* and *Tocaia*), Buena Vista, 1987.

(With Alan Root) *Gorillas in the Mist* (also known as *Gorillas in the Mist: The Story of Dian Fossey, De dimhoeljda bergens gorillor, Gorilas en la niebla, Gorilas na bruma, Gorilla nella nebbia, Gorillak a koedben, Gorillas im Nebel, Gorilles dans la brume, Gorilot B'Arafell, Gorily v mlze, Goryle we mgle, Nas montanhas dos gorilas, Nas montanhas dos gorilas—A aventura de Dian Fossey,* and *Sumuisten vuorten gorillat*), Universal, 1988.

Rain Man (also known as *Cuando dos hermanos se encuentran, Encontro de irmaos, Esoeember, Ish Ha–Geshem, Kisni covek, Rainman, Rain man—l'uomo della pioggia, Sademies,* and *Yagmur adam*), Metro–Goldwyn–Mayer/United Artists, 1988.

Dead Poets Society (also known as *Der Club der toten Dichter, Dode poeters klub, Doeda poeters saellskap, El club de los poetas muertos, Holt koeltoek tarsasaga, Kuolleiden runoilijoiden seura, L'attimo fuggente, La sociedad de los poetas muertos, La societe des poetes disparus, Le cercle des poetes disparus, O clube dos poetas mortos, O kyklos ton hamenon poiiton, Sociedade dos poetas mortos,* and *Stowarzyszenie umarlych poetow*), Buena Vista, 1989.

The Doctor (also known as *A doktor, Der Doktor—Ein gewoehnlicher Patient, El doctor, Katkera rohto, Lakaren—han som aelskade livet, Le docteur,* and *Un medico, un uomo*), Buena Vista, 1991.

Lorenzo's Oil (also known as *Lorenzo, Acto de amor, L'huile de Lorenzo, L'olio di Lorenzo, Lorenzo olaja, Lorenzon oeljy, Lorenzos Oel, Lorenzos olja, Lorenzo's oil: el aceite de la vida, O oleo de Lorenzo, Olej Lorenzo,* and *Un milagro para Lorenzo*), Universal, 1992.

The Firm (also known as *A Ceg, A firma, Die Firma, Fachada, Firma, Firmaets mand, Firman, Il socio, La firme,* and *La tapadera*), Paramount, 1993.

The Paper (also known as *Cronisti d'assalto, El periodico, Etusivu, For deadline, Ha–Eeton, Le journal, O jornal, The paper: detras de la noticia, The Paper—Primeira pagina, Press–stopp!, Schlagzeilen, Schlagzeilen—Je haerter, desto besser,* and *To protosselido*), Universal, 1994.

The American President (also known as *Hallo, Mr. President, Perfect Couple, Amerikan baskani, Amerikan presidentti, Ameriski predsednik, Amerykanski prezydent, Den amerikanske presidenten, El presidente y Miss Wade, Il presidente–Una storia d'amore, Le president et Miss Wade, Meu querido presidente, Mi querido presidente, Milosc w Bialym Domu, O erotas tou proedrou, Presidenten och Miss Wade, Szerelem a feher hazban, Uma noite com o presidente,* and *Un president americain*), Columbia, 1995.

Beyond Rangoon (also known as *Rangoon, A Szabadsag oesvenyein, Burma'da goezyaslari, Ha–Briha M'Rangoon, Mas alla de Rangun, Mas alla del Rangun, Nainen Burmassa, Oltre Rangoon, Pera apo ti Rangoon, Rangoon—Im Herzen des Sturms,* and *Skugga oever Rangoon*), Columbia, 1995.

City of Angels (also known as *A cidade dos anjos, Aenglarnas stad, Englenes by, Enkelten kaupunki, I poli ton angelon, Ingerul pazitor, La cite des anges, La citta degli angeli, Melekler sehri, Mesto angelov, Miasto aniolow, Stadt der Engel,* and *Un angel enamorado*), Warner Bros., 1998.

Static (short film), 1998.

At First Sight (also known as *Sight Unseen, A premiere vue, A prima vista, A primeira vista, A primera vista, Auf den ersten Blick, Dotyk milosci, Elsoe latasra, Ensi silmaeyksellae, Ilk goerueste ask, Me tin proti matia, Premier regard,* and *Vid foersta oegonkastet*), Metro–Goldwyn–Mayer, 1999.

The Talented Mr. Ripley (also known as *The Mysterious Yearning Secretive Sad Lonely Troubled Confused Loving Musical Gifted Intelligent Beautiful Tender Sensitive Haunted Passionate Talented Mr. Ripley*), Paramount, 1999.

The Perfect Storm (also known as *Perfect Storm, Den perfekta stormen, Der Sturm, En pleine tempete, Furtuna perfecta, Gniew oceanu, La tempesta perfetta, La tempete, La tormenta perfecta, Mar em furia, Meren raivo, Tempestade, Tormenta perfecta,* and *Una tormenta perfecta*), Warner Bros., 2000.

Harry Potter and the Sorcerer's Stone (also known as *Harry Potter, Harry Potter and the Philosopher's Stone, Harry Potter a kamen mudrcu, Harry Potter a l'ecole des sorciers, Harry Potter e a pedra filosofal, Harry Potter e la pietra filosofale, Harry Potter en de steen der wijzen, Harry Potter es a boelcsek koeve, Harry Potter i kamien filozoficzny, Harry Potter i la pedra filosofal, Harry Potter ja viisasten kivi, Harry Potter och de vises sten, Harry Potter og de vises stein, Harry Potter og de vises sten, Harry Potter og viskusteinninn, Harry Potter und der Stein der Weisen,* and *Harry Potter y la piedra filosofal*), Warner Bros., 2001.

Cold Mountain (also known as *Aeter till Cold Mountain, Behazra L'Cold Mountain, Epistrofi sto Cold Mountain, Kuemale maeele, Paeaemaeaeraenae Cold Mountain, Regresso a Cold Mountain, Retour a Cold Mountain, Ritorno a Cold Mountain, Tilbage til Cold Mountain,* and *Unterwegs nach Cold Mountain*), Miramax, 2003.

Dreamcatcher (also known as *Dreamcatcher, l'attrape–reves, Droemfaangare, El cazador de suenos, L'acchiappasogni, L'attrapeur de reves, O apanhador de sonhos, O cacador de sonhos, Unenae-opueuedja,* and *Unensieppaaja*), Warner Bros., 2003.

Spanglish (also known as *Espangles, Espanglish, Naesten helt perfekt—Spanglish, Spanglish—J'en perds mon latin!, Spanglish—kaeaennoeskukkasia,* and *Spanglish—kielikukkasia*), Columbia, 2004.

Poseidon (also known as *The Poseidon Adventure, Le Poseidon,* and *Poseidon'dan kacis*), Warner Bros., 2006.

Cinematographer for the unfinished film *Horror Movie.*

Film Director of Photography:
The Survivor (also known as *El superviviente* and *Le survivant d'un monde parallele*), Greater Union Organisation (GUO), 1981.

The English Patient (also known as *Angielski pacient, Angielski pacjent, Az angol beteg, Den engelske patient, Den engelske patienten, Der englische Patient, El pacient angles, El paciente ingles, Englantilainen potilas, Il paziente inglese, Ingiliz hasta, Le patient anglais,* and *O paciente ingles*), Miramax, 1996.

Ghosts of Mississippi (also known as *Ghosts from the Past, Das Attentat, Fantasmas del pasado, Fantasmas do pasado, Fantomes du Mississippi, Gecmisten ruhlar, Ha–Ruhot Shel Mississipi, L'agguato—Ghosts from the Past, Les fantomes du passe, Menneisyyden aaveet,* and *Skuggor fraan det foerflutna*), Columbia, 1996.

Film Camera Operator:
Nickel Queen (also known as *Ghost Town Millionairess* and *The Nickel Queen*), Z, c. 1971.

Alvin Purple (also known as *Ahkera Alvin, seksikauppias, O devasso renitente,* and *O poniros Alvin kai ta koritsia tou*), Roadshow Entertainment/Warner Bros., 1973.

Assistant camera operator, *The Man from Hong Kong* (also known as *The Dragon Files* and *Zhi dao huang long*), 1975.

(Uncredited) *Picnic at Hanging Rock,* 1975.

Break of Day, 1976.

Caddie, 1976.

Mad Dog Morgan (also known as *Mad Dog*), 1976.

The Last Wave (also known as *Black Rain*), 1977.

Blue Fin, 1978.

The Irishman, 1978.

Money Movers, 1978.

Second unit camera operator, *Stunt Rock* (also known as *Sorcery* and *Stuntrock*), Corona Film, 1978.

Weekend of Shadows, 1978.

Dawn!, 1979.

The Odd Angry Shot, 1979.

The Earthling, Filmways Pictures, 1980.

Fatty Finn, Hoyts Distribution, 1980.

Gallipoli (also known as *Galipolje, Gallipoli—An die Hoelle verraten,* and *Gli anni spezzati*), Paramount, 1981.

First camera crew camera operator, *The Mosquito Coast* (also known as *Mosquito Coast, A costa do mosquito, La costa de los mosquitos, Moskiittoranni-kko,* and *Moskitkusten*), Warner Bros., 1986.

Second unit camera operator, *Impolite,* The Asylum, c. 1992.

Beyond Rangoon (also known as *Rangoon, A Szabadsag oesvenyein, Burma'da goezyaslari, Ha–Briha M'Rangoon, Mas alla de Rangun, Mas alla del Rangun, Nainen Burmassa, Oltre Rangoon, Pera apo ti Rangoon, Rangoon—Im Herzen des Sturms,* and *Skugga oever Rangoon*), Columbia, 1995.

The English Patient (also known as *Angielski pacient, Angielski pacjent, Az angol beteg, Den engelske patient, Den engelske patienten, Der englische Patient, El pacient angles, El paciente ingles, Englantilainen potilas, Il paziente inglese, Ingiliz hasta, Le patient anglais,* and *O paciente ingles*), Miramax, 1996.

The Talented Mr. Ripley (also known as *The Mysterious Yearning Secretive Sad Lonely Troubled Confused Loving Musical Gifted Intelligent Beautiful Tender Sensitive Haunted Passionate Talented Mr. Ripley*), Paramount, 1999.

Assistant camera operator for second unit, *Trapped* (also known as *Call, 24 Hours, Acorralada, Ansassa, Atrapada, Encurralada, Loksus, Mauvais piege, Pieges, 24 ore,* and *24 Stunden Angst*), Columbia, 2002.

Film Work; Other:
Second unit photographer, *The Year of Living Dangerously* (also known as *A Veszelyes elet eve, Braennpunkt Djakarta, Ein Jahr in der Hoelle, El ano que vivimos en peligro, El ano que vivimos peligrosamente, L'annee de tous les dangers, O ano de todos os perigos, O ano em que vivemos em perigo, O ano que vivemos em perigo, Rakkaus veitsenteraellae,* and *Un anno vissuto pericolosamente*), Metro–Goldwyn–Mayer, 1982.

Director, *Till There Was You* (also known as *Doch dann kam sie, Doelig hemlighet, L'ultimo carico d'oro,* and *Vaarallista kultaa*), Sovereign Pictures, c. 1991.

First assistant photographer for second unit, *Rat Race* (also known as *No Brain Race, Course folle, Der Nackte Wahnsinn, El mundo esta loco loco, Esta tudo louco!, Rat Race—Der nackte Wahnsinn, Rat*

Race—*Sk(r)attjakten, Ratas a la carrera, Rottaralli, Sk(r)attjakten, Ta todo mundo louco! Uma corrida por milhoe$,* and *Ueldoezesi mania*), Paramount, 2001.

First assistant photographer for second unit, *The Core* (also known as *Core, Fusion—The Core, A Mag, Au coeur de la terre, The Core—Der innere Kern, Detonacao, Die Terranauten, El nucleo, Jedro, Jezgra, Kor, O nucleo—Missao ao centro da Terra, O pyrinas: Apostoli sto kentro tis Gis,* and *Ytimessae*), Paramount, 2003.

Film Appearances; Documentaries:

Run Nickel Run/Nickel Queen: The Making of a Movie, c. 1971.

Visions of Light: The Art of Cinematography, 1991.

Himself, *Cinematographer Style,* T–Stop Production, 2006.

Himself, *Not Quite Hollywood,* Film Finance Corporation, 2008.

Television Camera Operator; Series:

Second assistant camera operator, *The Odyssey,* beginning c. 1996.

Television Director of Photography; Miniseries:

Worked on the series *The Law,* 1980.

Television Camera Operator; Movies:

Harness Fever (also known as *Born to Run*), 1977, broadcast on *WonderWorks,* PBS.

Second assistant camera operator, *Sky High* (also known as *Jovens voadores* and *Yloes taivaalle*), NBC, 1990.

Second assistant camera operator, *City Boy* (also known as *Chico de ciudad* and *City Boy—Allein durch die Wildnis*), c. 1992, broadcast on *WonderWorks,* PBS.

First assistant b camera operator, *Killers in the House* (also known as *Captivity*), USA Network, 1998.

First assistant b camera operator, *Shadow Warriors II: Hunt for the Death Merchant* (also known as *Assault on Death Mountain, Shadow Warriors 2, A montanha do diabo, Attack mot Death Mountain, Il guerreiros das sombras II,* and *Les guerriers de l'ombre*), TNT, 1999.

Television Director of Photography; Specials:

New South Wales Images (documentary), [Australia], 1979.

Television Director of Photography; Episodic:

"Boney Buys a Woman," *Boney* (also known as *Bonaparte*), Amalgated Global Television, 1972, Independent Television (England), c. 1975.

"Top Kid," *Winners* (also known as *Campeones*), [Australia], c. 1985, broadcast as an episode of *Wonderworks,* PBS, 1987.

"Drive, She Said," *Trying Times,* PBS, 1987.

"Get a Job," *Trying Times,* PBS, 1987.

Television Camera Operator; Episodic:

Worked on *Harness Fever* (also known as *Born to Run*), 1977, broadcast on *WonderWorks,* PBS; and on *City Boy* (also known as *Chico de ciudad* and *City Boy—Allein durch die Wildnis*), c. 1992, also broadcast on *WonderWorks,* PBS.

Television Appearances; Awards Presentations:

The 69th Annual Academy Awards, ABC, 1997.

(In archive footage) *The 76th Annual Academy Awards,* ABC, 2004.

Television Appearances; Episodic:

Himself, "Creating 'The Perfect Storm,'" *HBO First Look,* HBO, 2000.

RECORDINGS

Videos:

Himself, *Making Angels,* 1998.

Himself, *The Hitcher—How Do These Movies Get Made?,* Kinowelt Home Entertainment, 2003.

Himself, *Climbing "Cold Mountain,"* Miramax Home Entertainment, 2004.

Himself, *Between Two Worlds: The Making of "Witness,"* Paramount Home Video, 2005.

Himself, *Entrenched: The Making of "Gallipoli,"* Paramount Home Video, 2005.

Himself, *Poseidon: A Ship on a Soundstage,* Warner Home Video, 2005.

Appeared in *ACS Video Series,* Australian Cinematographers Society.

SEGAN, Noah 1983–
(Noah G. Segan)

PERSONAL

Born October 5, 1983, in New York, NY. *Avocational Interests:* Boxing and playing guitar.

Addresses: *Agent*—Talentworks, 3500 West Olive Ave., Suite 1400, Burbank, CA 91505. *Manager*—Untitled Entertainment, 331 North Maple Dr., 3rd Floor, Beverly Hills, CA 90210.

Career: Actor. Appeared on the book covers of Alex Sanchez's *Rainbow Boys* and *Rainbow High*.

Awards, Honors: Copper Wing Award (with others), best ensemble, Phoenix Film Festival, 2006, for *Self Medicated*.

CREDITS

Film Appearances:
Hank, *Myron's Movie,* 2004.
Dode, *Brick,* Focus Features, 2005.
Donovan, *Waterborne,* MTI Home Video, 2005.
Twink, *Adam & Steve,* TLA Releasing, 2005.
Trevor, *Self Medicated,* THINKFilm, 2005.
Basil Hallward, *The Picture of Dorian Gray,* 2006.
Michael Elliot, *The Visitation,* Twentieth Century–Fox, 2006.
Don Bolles, *What We Do Is Secret,* Vision Films, 2007.
Sean, *Still Green,* 2007.
J. T., *Deadgirl,* 2007.
The Duke, *The Brothers Bloom,* Weinstein Company, 2008.
John, *Cabin Fever 2: Spring Fever,* Lions Gate Films Home Entertainment, 2008.
Boba Fett number two, *Fanboys,* Weinstein Company, 2008.
The Box Collector, 2008.

Film Assistant to Director of Photography:
The Singing Detective, Paramount Classics, 2003.
Nobody's Perfect, 2004.

Television Appearances; Series:
John Roger "J. J." Forbes, *Loving,* ABC, 1991.
Voice of Henry, *Kablam!* (also known as *KaBlam!*), Nickelodeon, 1996.
(As Noah G. Segan) Conner Lockhart, *Days of Our Lives* (also known as *Days* and *DOOL*), NBC, 2007.

Television Appearances; Pilots:
Quentin Kelly, *Grace Under Fire,* ABC, 1993.

Television Appearances; Episodic:
Robby, "The Undergraduate," *Married ... with Children,* Fox, 1995.
George, "Castaways," *Dawson's Creek,* The WB, 2003.
Kelly James, "Homebodies," *CSI: Crime Scene Investigation* (also known as *C.S.I.* and *Les Experts*), CBS, 2003.
Kyle Hendricks, "One Shot, One Kill," *Navy NCIS: Naval Criminal Investigative Service* (also known as *NCIS* and *NCIS: Naval Criminal Investigative Service*), CBS, 2004.

RECORDINGS

Music Videos:
Appeared in The Foo Fighters' "The One."

SEMLER, Dean 1943–
   (Dean Sempler)

PERSONAL

Born 1943, in Renmark, South Australia; married Annie (an actress); children: Ingrid (also known as Tilly).

Addresses: *Agent*—Crayton Smith Agency, 11271 Ventura Blvd., Suite 423, Studio City, CA 91604.

Career: Cinematographer, director of photography, director, and camera operator. Australian Broadcasting Corporation (ABC), worked as studio camera operator and floor manager for ABC–TV; Australian Commonwealth Film Unit/Film Australia, documentary filmmaker of several government–sponsored films, 1971–81; photographer for other documentary films, anthropological films, and television news broadcasts. Australian Film and Television School, presenter of lighting workshops.

Member: Australian Cinematographers Society, American Society of Cinematographers, Directors Guild of America.

Awards, Honors: Bronze Medallion, Kodak Awards for Cinematography, Australian Film Institute, 1975, for *A Steam Train Passes;* Australian Film Institute Award nominations, best cinematography, 1982, for *Mad Max 2,* and 1983, for *Undercover;* named cinematographer of the year, Australian Cinematographers Society, and Australian Film Institute Award, best cinematography, both 1984, for *Razorback;* Australian Film Institute Award nominations, best cinematography, 1985, for *The Coca–Cola Kid,* and 1988, for *The Lighthorsemen;* Australian Film Institute Award and Australian Film Critics Circle Award, both best cinematography, 1989, for *Dead Calm;* Academy Award, American Society of Cinematographers Award, British Society of Cinematographers Award nomination, and Chicago Film Critics Association Award, all 1991, and Film Award nomination, British Academy of Film and Television Arts, 1992, all best cinematography, for *Dances with Wolves;* inducted into the Australian Cinematographers Society Hall of Fame, 1997; Australia Day Honour, 2002; Hawaii International Film Festival Award, excellence in cinematography, 2003; Dallas–Fort Worth Film Critics

Association Award and Phoenix Film Critics Society Award, both 2006, Central Ohio Film Critics Association Award, American Society of Cinematographers Award nomination, and Online Film Critics Society Award nomination, all 2007, all best cinematography, for *Apocalypto;* Order of Australia Medal (OAM), Medal in the General Division.

CREDITS

Film Cinematographer:

The Choice (short film), 1971.

Hector and Milly Save Uncle Tom, 1971.

(With others) *Where Dead Men Lie* (short film), 1971.

I Need More Staff (short film), 1973.

Dancing (short film), Australian Film and Television School, 1980.

The Earthling, Filmways Pictures, 1980.

Hoodwink, New South Wales Films, 1981.

Mad Max 2 (also known as *Mad Max II, Mad Max 2: The Road Warrior, The Road Warrior, Asfalttisoturi, Interceptor, il guerriero della strada, Le defi, Mad Max 2: A cacada continua, Mad Max II—Der Vollstrecker, Mad Max 2, el guerriero della strada, Mad Max 2: Le defi, Mad Max 2: Maanteesodalane,* and *Mad Max 2: O guerriero da strada*), Warner Bros., 1982.

Kitty and the Bagman, Quartet, 1983.

Undercover, Roadshow Entertainment, 1983.

Razorback (also known as *Doedens kaftar, Harjaniska, Hirmukarju, O corte da navalha, Razorback—Kampfkoloss der Hoelle, Razorback—O javali assassino,* and *Razorback: oltre l'urlo del demonio*), Warner Bros., 1984.

The Coca–Cola Kid (also known as *Coca–Cola Kid, Coca–Cola kid, Coca Cola Kid,* and *Coca cola kid*), Cinecom Pictures/Film Gallery, 1985.

Mad Max beyond Thunderdome (also known as *Mad Max 3, Mad Max III, Mad Max alem da cupula do trovao, Mad Max: au–dela du dome du tonnerre, Mad Max bortom Thunderdome, Mad Max i la cupula del tro, Mad Max i tordenkuplen, Mad Max—Jenseits der Donnerkuppel, Mad Max, mas alla de la cupula del trueno, Mad Max oltre la sfera del tuono, Mad Max—ukkosmyrsky,* and *Mad Max 3.—Az Igazsag csarnokan innen es tul*), Warner Bros., 1985.

Bullseye, Cinema Group Entertainment, 1986.

Going Sane, Sea Change–New South Wales Films, 1986.

The Lighthorsemen, Cinecom International, 1988.

Farewell to the King (also known as *Addio al re, Adios al rey, Der Dschungelkonig von Borneo, Farewell to the King—Sie nannten ihn Leroy, Huvudjaegarnas konung, Jaeaehyvaeiset kuninkaalle,* and *L'adieu au roi*), Orion, 1989.

Impulse (also known as *Doppia identita, Double jeu, Impulse—Von gefaehrlichen Gefuehlen, Impulso,*

Impulso para matar, Odruch, Pelottava houkutus, and *Tentacao perigosa*), Warner Bros., 1990.

Young Guns II (also known as *Hell Bent for Leather* and *Young Guns II: Blaze of Glory*), Twentieth Century–Fox, 1990.

City Slickers (also known as *Live, Love and Cows, A vida, o amor e as vacas, Amigos, sempre amigos, City Slickers—Die Grosstadt–Helden, City slickers—jakten paa det foersvunna leeendet, Cowboys de ciudad, Jakten paa det foersvunna leendet, Kaupunkicowboyt, La vie, l'amour, les vaches, La vie, l'amour … les vaches, Scappo dalla citta–la vita, l'amore e le vacche, Stadszwervers,* and *Ti ekanes baba stin agria dysi*), Columbia, 1991.

The Power of One (also known as *Au bout de soi, Egyedul a ringben, Ensam aer stark, Im Glanz der Sonne, La forza del singolo, La fuerza de uno, La puissance de l'ange, O poder de um jovem,* and *Yksin kaikkia vastaan*), Warner Bros., 1992.

Last Action Hero (also known as *Extremely Violent, Az Utolso akciohoes, Den siste actionhjaelten, Der Letzte Action Held, El ultimo gran heroe, El ultimo heroe en accion, L'ultim gran heroi, Last Action Hero—l'ultimo grande eroe, Le dernier des heros, O ultimo grande heroi,* and *Zadnja velika pustolovscina*), Columbia, 1993.

Super Mario Bros. (also known as *Super Mario, Super Mario Brothers,* and *Super Mario Brothers: The Movie*), Buena Vista, 1993.

The Three Musketeers (also known as *The Musketeers, A Harom testoer, De tre musketerer, De tre musketoererna, Die Drei Musketiere, I tre moschettieri, Kolme muskettisoturia, Les trois mousquetaires, Los tres mosqueteros, Os tres mosqueteiros,* and *Trije musketirji*), Buena Vista, 1993.

The Cowboy Way (also known as *Cowboy Way, Deux cow–boys a New York, Dyo cowboy sti N. Yorki, Machen wir's wie Cowboys, Sexy Cowboys schiessen schaerfer, Sonny & Pepper. Due irresistibili cowboy,* and *Vaqueros de Nueva York*), Universal, 1994.

Waterworld (also known as *O'lum Ha–Mayim, Potopljeni svet, Su duenyasi, Un monde sans terre, Vatnaveroeld, Vizivilag,* and *Waterworld—O segredo das aguas*), Universal, 1995.

Gone Fishin' (also known as *Gone Fishing, A grande pescaria, Anem a pescar, Chi pesca trova, Der $100.000 Fisch, Der 100.000 $ Fisch—Zwei Freunde gehen baden, Dos chiflados en remojo, Kahjo kalareissu,* and *Peche party*), Buena Vista, 1997.

Trojan War (also known as *Rescue Me*), Warner Bros., 1997.

Nutty Professor II: The Klumps (also known as *Klumps, The Klumps, The Nutty Professor II, Nutty II: The Klumps, Boelcsek koevere 2—A Klump csalad, Den galna professorn 2—Klumps, El professor chiflado II, El professor chiflado II: La familia Klump, Familie Klumps und der verrueckte Professor, La famiglia del professore matto, La famille foldingue, Nigaud de professeur II: Les Klumps, Nutty Professor II:*

Familien Kump, O professor aloprado 2—A familia Klump, O professor chanfrado 2, and Paehkaehullu professori 2: Klumpit), Universal, 2000.

Heartbreakers (also known as *Breakers, The Breakers, heartBREAKeRS, Beautes empoisonnees, Doce trapaca, Heartbreakers—Achtung: Scharfe Kurven, HeartBreakers—vizio di famiglia, Las estafadoras, Las seducoras, Les enjoleuses, Matadoras, Sydaentenmurskaajat,* and *Wielki podryw*), Metro–Goldwyn–Mayer, 2001.

We Were Soldiers (also known as *The Lost Patrol, We Were Soldiers Once ... and Young, Am fost cindva soldati ... si tineri, Bili smo vojnici, Bylismy zolnierzami, Cuando eramos soldados, Fomos herois, Fuimos heroes, Fuimos soldados, Katonak voltunk, Nous etions soldats, Olimme sotilaita,* and *Wir waren Helden*), Paramount, 2001.

D–Tox (also known as *Detox, Eye See You, The Outpost, Compte a rebours mortel, D–Tox—Compte a rebours mortel, D–Tox—Im Auge der Angst, D–Tox: Ojo asesino, Detoks, Detoksikatsia,* and *Im Auge der Angst*), Universal, 2002.

Dragonfly (also known as *Apparitions, Calling, Dragonfly: La sombra de la libelula, El misterio de la libelula, Il segno della libellula—Dragonfly, Im Zeichen der Libelle, Libellule, Minyma siopis, Misterul libelulei, O misterio da libelula, O poder dos sentidos, Sudenkorento,* and *Szitakoetoe*), Universal, 2002.

xXx (also known as *Agent XXX, Triple X, XXX, xXx—Triple X,* and *Triplo X*), Columbia, 2002.

Bruce Almighty (also known as *A Minden6o, Aman tanrim!, Bruce Allmaechtig, Bruce den allsmaektige, Bruce den almaegtige, Bruce Ha–Gadol M'Kulam, Bruce le tout–puissant, Bruce—taivaanlahja, Bruce tout–puissant, Como Dios, Koikvoimas Bruce, Thoes gia mia evdomada, Todo poderoso, Todopoderoso, Todopodroso,* and *Una settimana da Dio*), Universal, 2003.

The Alamo (also known as *Alamo, Bowie, Alamo—Der Traum, das Schicksal, die Legende, Alamo—Gli ultimi eroi, El Alamo, El Alamo. La leyenda,* and *O Alamo*), Buena Vista, 2004.

The Longest Yard (also known as *Benknaeckargaenget, El clan de los rompehuesos, Golpe baixo, Golpe bajo—El juego final, L'altra sporca ultima meta, Le dernier essai, Luunmurskaajat, Mi–temps au mitard,* and *Spiel ohne Regeln*), Paramount, 2005.

Stealth (also known as *Ameaca invisivel—Stealth, Furtif, La amenaza invisible—Stealth, Mahitiko stealth—I aorati apeili, Niewidzialny, Stealth—Arma suprema, Stealth—Det osynliga hotet,* and *Stealth—Unter dem Radar*), Columbia, 2005.

Apocalypto (also known as *Mel Gibson's "Apocalypto"* and *Apokalipto*), Buena Vista, 2006.

Click (also known as *Cambia la tua vita con un click, Clic, Click, i zoi se fast forward, Click—perdiendo el control, Click—telecommandez votre vie, Klick,* and *Klik!*), Sony Pictures Releasing, 2006.

Just My Luck (also known as *Lady Luck, Lucky, Lucky Girl, Baciati dalla sfortuna, C'est bien ma chance!,* Devuelveme mi suerte, Erotas stin tyhi, Golpe de suerte, Sorte no amor,* and *Zum Glueck gekuesst*), Twentieth Century–Fox, 2006.

I Now Pronounce You Chuck and Larry (also known as *Chuck und Larry—Wie Feuer und Flamme, Damadi oepebilirsin, Declaro–vos marido e ... marido, Ferj es ferj, Gasilca pred oltarjem, Haermed foerklarar jag er Chuck og Larry, Io vi dichiaro marito e marito, Je vous declare Chuck et Larry, Jeg erklaerer jer nu for Chuck og Larry, Kdyz si Chuck bral Larryho, Kui Chuck abiellub Larryga, O kyrios tou kyriou, Os declaro marido y marido, Quand Chuck recontre Larry, Voitte suudella sulhasta,* and *Yo los declaro marido y ... Larry*), Universal, 2007.

Film Cinematographer; Documentaries:

Dundiwuy's House Opening, c. 1970.

Pain for This Land (also known as *Pain for This Land: Footage from the Early Years*), c. 1970.

At the Canoe Camp, 1971.

One Man's Response (also known as *One Man's Response—A Film about Narritjin Maymuru at Yirrkala in 1971*), 1971.

Purification Ceremony (also known as *Purification Ceremony for a Woman Injured at Yirrkala* and *Purification Ceremony: Caledon Bay*), 1971.

This Is My Thinking, 1971.

"Water for a City," *Australian Geography,* 1971.

In Memory of Malawan, 1971, also 1983.

Dhapi Ceremony at Yirrkala–1972, 1972.

The Gathering Flame, 1972.

Golf the Australian Way, 1972.

President Suharto in Australia, 1972.

The Fifth Facade, 1973.

"Kilkenny Primary School, South Australia," *Through My Eyes,* 1973.

The Koala: Phascolarctos cinereus, 1973.

"The Vintage," *Australian Colour Diary,* 1973.

And Their Ghosts May be Heard, 1974.

The Care behind the Smile, 1974.

From a Long Time Ago: Hollow Log Painting, 1974.

Marrakulu Funeral (also known as *Marrakulu Funeral: Yirrkala 1974*), 1974.

"Monarch of the Rails: N.S.W. Railways," *Cinesound Review,* 1974.

Moving On, 1974.

A Race of Horses, 1974.

Singing in the Rain (also known as *Singing in the Rain Yirrkala in 1974*), 1974.

State Visit to Australia by Their Imperial Majesties the Shahanshah Aryamehr and the Shahbanou of Iran (also known as *The Shah of Iran's Visit to Australia*), 1974.

A Steam Train Passes, 1974.

"Landscape: A Pattern of Change," *Australian Geography,* 1975.

Hard Time Now ... For the Children, c. 1976.

"The Bamboo Bends and Does Not Break," *Asian Insight,* 1976.

"Hong Kong, Singapore—Fragrant Harbour, Lion City," *Asian Insight*, 1976.

"Indonesia—Unity in Diversity," *Asian Insight*, 1976.

"Malaysia—Sparrow with Sparrow, Raven with Raven," *Asian Insight*, 1976.

"Philippines—The Furthest Cross," *Asian Insight*, 1976.

"Thailand: Do Good Receive Good, Do Evil Receive Evil," *Asian Insight*, 1976.

Dungguwan at Gurka'wuy (series), 1976.

Madarrpa Funeral at Gurka'wuy, 1976.

Reading for Meaning: The Goodman Model, 1976.

Why Can't They Be Like We Were? (series), 1976.

All in the Same Boat, 1977.

Granville, 1977.

Hassles, 1977.

Helpem Mifala: Aid for Solomon Islands, 1977.

"Outback Supply," *Frontiers Down Under*, 1977.

Thirst, 1977.

"Kerry," *Growing Up*, 1977.

"Wendy," *Growing Up*, 1977.

Co–ops at Work in Solomon Islands, 1978.

Five Bells (also known as *Five Bells: Sights and Sounds of Sydney Harbour*), 1978.

Iu Mi Nao–Solomon Islands Regains Independence, 1978.

Narritjin in Canberra, 1978.

People of the Sea—Changing Traditions in the Solomon Islands, 1978.

Chase That Dream: The Pursuit of Home Ownership in Australia, 1979.

Please Don't Leave Me, 1979.

Saturday, 1979.

"Totora and Siwa," *Solomon Islands*, 1979.

"War without Weapons," *Aspects of Australia*, 1979.

"Farming," *Soviet Style* (also known as *Farming: Soviet Style*), 1979.

"People of Influence," *Soviet Style* (also known as *People of Influence: Soviet Style*), 1979.

"The People's Music," *Soviet Style* (also known as *The People's Music: Soviet Style*), 1979.

"Politics," *Soviet Style* (also known as *Politics: Soviet Style*), 1979.

"School's In," *Soviet Style* (also known as *School's In: Soviet Style*), 1979.

"Working," *Soviet Style* (also known as *Working: Soviet Style*), 1979.

Baruya Muka Archival (series), 1979, released in 1991.

"Araha Ana Romo," *Solomon Islands*, 1980.

"Moro: Melanesian Bigman," *Solomon Islands*, 1980.

"Nambo," *Solomon Islands*, 1980.

My Country, Djarrakpi, 1980.

Narritjin Maymuru, 1980.

Stepping Out: The Debolts Grow Up, 1980.

Stepping Out: The Birth of a Theatre of the Mentally Handicapped, 1980.

Conversations with Dundiwuy Wanambi, 1982.

"Ha'a alahanga ni ulawa," *Solomon Islands*, 1982.

"People of Niupani," *Solomon Islands*, 1982.

"Taem Bifo Long Lauru: Choiseul Customs," *Solomon Islands*, 1982.

"Volo momoru: The Turtle Net," *Solomon Islands*, 1982.

"Wogasia," *Solomon Islands*, 1982.

The Human Face of Russia, 1984.

Film Director of Photography:

Let the Balloon Go (also known as *Anna pallon lentaeae*), released as a feature film by Inter Planetary Productions Corporation, 1977, originally broadcast on Australian television, 1976.

Second unit director of photography, *The Earthling*, Filmways Pictures, 1980.

Cocktail (also known as *Koktejl* and *Koktel*), Buena Vista, 1988.

(As Dean Sempler) *Dead Calm* (also known as *Dead Calm: A Voyage into Fear, Calma de morte, Calma total, Calme blanc, Krouaziera stin akri tou tromou, Lungnt vatten, Martw cisza, Ore 10: Calma piatta, Rasvatyyni, Rasvatyyni—matka pelkoon, Terror a bordo*, and *Todesstille*), Warner Bros., 1988.

Young Guns (also known as *A Vadnyugat fiai, Arma joven, Mlode strzelby, Nuoret sankarit, Os jovens pistoleiros, Unga hjaeltar, Young guns—giovani pistole*, and *Young Guns—Sie fuerchten weder Tod noch Teufuel*), Twentieth Century–Fox, 1988.

K–9 (also known as *Canino (K–NINO), Chien de flic, En snut paa hugget, K–9—Um policial bom pra cachorro, K–nino, Kyttaekaksikko, Mein Partner mit der kalten Schnauze, Nume de cod: K–9, Poliziotto a 4 zampe, Poliziotto a quattro zampe*, and *Superagent K–9*), Universal, 1990.

Dances with Wolves (also known as *Bailando con lobos, Balla coi lupi, Ballant amb llops, Danca com lobos, Dancas com lobos, Dansar med vargar, Danse avec les loups, Danser med ulve, Danser med ulver, Danza con lobos, Der mit dem Wolf tanzt, Farkasokkal tancolo, Horevontas me tous lykous, Il danse avec les loups, Kurtlarla dans, Plese z volkovi, Roked Im Ze'evim, Tanczacy z wilkami*, and *Tanssii susien kanssa*), Orion, 1991.

The Bone Collector (also known as *Bone Collector, A Csontember, Colectionarul de oase, Der Knochenjaeger, Die Assistentin, El coleccionista de huesos, El col.leccionista d'ossos, I samlarens spaar, Il collezionista di ossa, Le desosseur, Luunkeraeaejae, O coleccionador de ossos, O colecionador de ossos, Sberatel kosti*, and *Syllektis oston*), Universal, 1999.

Second unit director of photography, *The Adventures of Pluto Nash* (also known as *Pluto Nash, Las aventuras de Pluto Nash, Les aventures de Pluto Nash*, and *Pluto Nash—Im Kampf gegen die Mondmafia*), Warner Bros., 2002.

Get Smart, Warner Bros., 2008.

Film Director:

Five Bells (documentary; also known as *Five Bells: Sights and Sounds of Sydney Harbour*), 1978.

Saturday (documentary), 1979.

(Uncredited) And second unit director, *Super Mario Bros.* (also known as *Super Mario, Super Mario Brothers,* and *Super Mario Brothers: The Movie*), Buena Vista, 1993.

Firestorm (also known as *Firestorm—Brennendes Inferno, Liekkien vangit, Onda de fogo, Orage de feu, Tempesta di fuoco, Tormenta de fogo, Tormenta de fuego,* and *Tuezvihar*), Twentieth Century–Fox, 1998.

The Patriot (also known as *El ultimo patriota, Le patriote, Patriootti, The Patriot: Estado de guerra, Patriota, Patrioten,* and *Piege a haut risque*), Buena Vista, 1998.

Worked on the unfinished film *The Kangaroo Kid.*

Film Camera Operator:
The Lighthorsemen, Cinecom International, 1988.

Film Appearances:
Himself, *Cinematographer Style* (documentary), T–Stop Production, 2006.

Television Director of Photography; Miniseries:
The Dismissal, Network Ten (Australia), 1983.

Bodyline (also known as *It's Not Just Cricket*), Network Ten, 1984.

Return to Eden (also known as *Paluu Eden, Ritorno a Eden,* and *Tillbaka till Eden*), syndicated, 1984.

Melba, Seven Network (Australia), 1987.

Television Director; Miniseries:
Art of Film: About Television (documentary), 1968.

Second unit director, *Lonesome Dove* (also known as *Den laanga faerden, Der Ruf des Adlers, O ceu como horizonte, Os pistoleiros do oeste, Paloma solitaria, Vaarojen maa,* and *Weg in die Wildnis*), CBS, 1989.

Second unit director, *Son of the Morning Star* (also known as *Aamutaehden poika* and *General Custers letzte Schlacht*), ABC, 1991.

Television Cinematographer; Miniseries:
Lonesome Dove (also known as *Den laanga faerden, Der Ruf des Adlers, O ceu como horizonte, Os pistoleiros do oeste, Paloma solitaria, Vaarojen maa,* and *Weg in die Wildnis*), CBS, 1989.

Television Director of Photography; Movies:
Do I Have to Kill My Child?, [Australia], 1976.

Let the Balloon Go (also known as *Anna pallon lentaeae*), [Australia], 1976, released as a feature film by Inter Planetary Productions Corporation, 1977.

Second unit director of photography, *Cass,* Nine Network (Australia), 1978.

A Good Thing Going, Nine Network, 1978.

Passion Flower (also known as *Come l'orchidea, Kuuma kausi, Moerderische Gefuehle,* and *Passion Flower—Leidenschaft und Ehrgeiz*), CBS, 1986.

The Clean Machine (also known as *Poliisiryhmae*), Network Ten (Australia), 1988.

Television Director of Photography; Specials:
After the Flood (documentary), 1984.

Television Floor Manager; Specials:
The Valley of Water, 1962.

Television Appearances; Awards Presentations:
The 63rd Annual Academy Awards, ABC, 1991.

Television Appearances; Episodic:
Himself, "Firestorm," *HBO First Look,* HBO, 1998.

RECORDINGS

Videos:
Himself, *We Were Soldiers: Getting It Right* (short), Paramount, 2002.

Himself, *Dances with Wolves: The Creation of an Epic,* Metro–Goldwyn–Mayer Home Entertainment, 2003.

Himself, *xXx: A Filmmaker's Diary* (short), Columbia, 2003.

Himself, *Return of the Legend: The Making of "The Alamo"* (short), Touchstone Home Video, 2004.

Himself, *Harnessing Speed,* Sony Pictures Home Entertainment, 2005.

Music Video Photography Director:
Rammstein, "Feuer frei!," c. 2002.

WRITINGS

Screenplays:
Saturday (documentary), 1979.

Teleplays; Miniseries:
Art of Film: About Television (documentary), 1968.

SERPICO, Terry

PERSONAL

Education: State University of New York at Purchase, B.F.A.

Career: Actor and stunts.

CREDITS

Film Actor:
Montgomery Valentine, *Cyber Vengeance,* Amsell Entertainment, 1995.
Strip club owner, *Donnie Brasco,* TriStar, 1997.
Tony, *Cop Land,* Miramax, 1997.
Sniper number one, *The Peacemaker,* DreamWorks, 1997.
Evidence technician, *Random Hearts,* Columbia, 1999.
Cop number one, *Bringing Out the Dead,* Paramount, 1999.
Con Ed worker number one, *Frequency,* 2000.
Officer Bolton, *Hannibal,* Metro–Goldwyn–Mayer, 2001.
Laguna, Fries Film Group, 2001.
Sergeant Dunning, *Company K,* 2004.
FBI Agent Lewis, *The Interpreter* (also known as *L'Interprete*), Universal, 2005.
Michael Kerry, *Find Me Guilty* (also known as *Find Me Guilty: The Jackie Dee Story*), Yari Film Group Releasing, 2006.
Detective number three, *The Departed,* Warner Bros., 2006.
Mr. Iker, *Michael Clayton,* Warner Bros., 2007.
Louie Kennick, *Fast Company,* 2007.

Film Stunts:
Daredevil (also known as *Daredevil: A Daring New Vision*), Twentieth Century–Fox, 2003.
New York Minute, Warner Bros., 2004.
(Vane Bros. victim) *Ladder 49,* Buena Vista, 2004.
Alfie, Paramount, 2004.
Stay, Twentieth Century–Fox, 2005.
My Super Ex–Girlfriend, Twentieth Century–Fox, 2006.
The Bourne Ultimatum, Universal, 2007.

Television Appearances; Series:
100 Centre Street, Arts and Entertainment, 2001–2002.
Frank Sherwood, *Army Wives,* Lifetime, 2007.

Television Appearances; Miniseries:
Pulaski, *The Path to 9/11,* ABC, 2006.
The Bronx Is Burning, ESPN, 2006.

Television Appearances; Movies:
Station attendant, *Earthly Possessions,* HBO, 1999.
Karl Miller, *Homicide: The Movie,* NBC, 2000.
Jake Cunningham, *Amy and Isabelle* (also known as *Oprah Winfrey Presents: "Amy and Isabelle"*), ABC, 2001.

Television Appearances; Pilots:
Leo, *Jonny Zero,* Fox, 2005.

Television Appearances; Episodic:
Redabow's client, "A Game of Checkers," *Oz,* HBO, 1997.
Freakie, "Losing Your Appeal," *Oz,* HBO, 1998.
Lofton, "This Band of Brothers," *Third Watch,* NBC, 2000.
Ron Johnson, "Closure," *Law & Order: Special Victims Unit* (also known as *Law & Order: SVU* and *Special Victims Unit*), NBC, 2000.
Jay Brannigan, "Dissonance," *Law & Order,* NBC, 2001.
Leslie Roche, "The Extra Man," *Law & Order: Criminal Intent* (also known as *Law & Order: CI*), NBC, 2001.
Frank Miller, "Patriot," *Law & Order,* NBC, 2002.
Earl Carnicki, "But Not Forgotten," *Law & Order: Criminal Intent* (also known as *Law & Order: CI*), NBC, 2003.
Les Cooper, "Rotten," *Law & Order: Special Victims Unit* (also known as *Law & Order: SVU* and *Special Victims Unit*), NBC, 2003.
Clyde Bowen, "Eminence Front: Parts 1 & 2," *Line of Fire,* ABC, 2004.
Deacon Brinn, "Quarry," *Law & Order: Special Victims Unit* (also known as *Law & Order: SVU* and *Special Victims Unit*), NBC, 2005.
Cousin Eddie, "Voicemail," *Rescue Me* (also known as *Rescue Me: FDNY*), FX Channel, 2005.
Cousin Eddie, "Devil," *Rescue Me* (also known as *Rescue Me: FDNY*), FX Channel, 2006.
All American agent, *Traveler,* ABC, 2006.
Kidnapped, NBC, 2006.

Television Stunts; Episodic:
"Wu's on First?," *Homicide: Life on the Street* (also known as *Homicide*), NBC, 1997.

Stage Appearances:
Franzy, *Edith Stein,* Jewish Repertory Theatre, New York City, 1994.

SHANKMAN, Adam 1964–
(Adam M. Shankman)

PERSONAL

Full name, Adam Michael Shankman; born November 27, 1964, in Los Angeles, CA. *Education:* Studied dance at Juilliard School.

Addresses: *Agent*—United Talent Agency, 9560 Wilshire Blvd., Suite 500, Beverly Hills, CA 90212. *Publicist*—I/D Public Relations, 8409 Santa Monica Blvd., West Hollywood, CA 90069.

Career: Choreographer, actor, and director. Choreographer for television commercials. Worked as an actor and dancer in New York City and in regional productions.

Awards, Honors: Bob Fosse Award nomination, 1994, for *The Flintstones;* Best Stage Concept Award, *Performance* magazine, 1995, for choreography of a Barry White tour; DramaLogue Awards, best choreography, for *Tight Quarters* and *West Side Story;* Bob Fosse Award, best choreography, for a software commercial for SAP–Office America.

CREDITS

Film Choreographer:
The Gun in Betty Lou's Handbag, Buena Vista, 1992.
Weekend at Bernie's II, TriStar, 1993.
(Camp Chippewa) *Addams Family Values,* Paramount, 1993.
Milk Money, Paramount, 1994.
The Flintstones, Universal, 1994.
Miami Rhapsody, Buena Vista, 1995.
Tank Girl, United Artists, 1995.
Don Juan DeMarco, New Line Cinema, 1995.
Casper, Universal, 1995.
Frankenstein Sings, 1995.
Congo, 1995.
Mrs. Winterbourne, TriStar, 1996.
The Relic (also known as *Das Relikt* and *Relikt—Das museum der angst*), Paramount, 1997.
Traveller, October Films, 1997.
George of the Jungle, Buena Vista, 1997.
Boogie Nights, New Line Cinema, 1997.
A Life Less Ordinary, Twentieth Century–Fox, 1997.
Scream 2, Dimension/Miramax, 1997.
(As Adam M. Shankman) *Anastasia,* Twentieth Century–Fox, 1997.
Antz, 1998.
Almost Heroes, 1998.
Forces of Nature, 1999.
Deuce Bigalow: Male Gigolo, Buena Vista, 1999.
Blast from the Past, New Line Cinema, 1999.
She's All That, Miramax, 1999.
The Out–of–Towners, Paramount, 1999.
Dudley Do–Right, Universal, 1999.
Isn't She Great (also known as *Ist sie nicht groBartig?*), Universal, 2000.
(As Adam M. Shankman) *Mission to Mars* (also known as *M2M*), Buena Vista, 2000.
The Wedding Planner (also known as *Wedding Plannet—verliebt, verlobt, verplant*), Columbia, 2001.
(Spaff animation and cartoon animation) *Monkeybone,* 2001.
Stuck on You, Twentieth Century–Fox, 2003.
Hairspray, New Line Cinema, 2007.

Also choreographed *Meet the Deedles.*

Film Director:
Cosmo's Tale (short), 1998.
The Wedding Planner (also known as *Wedding Planet—verliebt, verlobt, verplant*), Columbia, 2001.
A Walk to Remember, Warner Bros., 2002.
Bringing Down the House, Buena Vista, 2003.
The Pacifier (also known as *Gnome* and *La pacifacteur*), Buena Vista, 2005.
Cheaper by the Dozen 2, Twentieth Century–Fox, 2005.
Hairspray, New Line Cinema, 2007.
Topper, Walt Disney Company, 2008.

Film Executive Producer:
The Pacifier (also known as *Gnome* and *La pacifacteur*), Buena Vista, 2005.
Cheaper by the Dozen 2, Twentieth Century–Fox, 2005.
Hairspray, New Line Cinema, 2007.
Bedtime Stories, Buena Vista, 2008.

Film Producer:
Step Up, Buena Vista, 2006.
Premonition, Sony, 2007.
Step Up 2 the Streets, Metro–Goldwyn–Mayer, 2008.

Film Work; Other:
Animation ghost references, *Casper,* 1995.
Live action reference (Los Angeles Dancers), *Anastasia,* Twentieth Century–Fox, 1997.
Physical comedy consultant, *Inspector Gadget,* Buena Vista/Walt Disney Pictures, 1999.
(Uncredited) Executive soundtrack producer, *A Walk to Remember,* 2002.
Dance consultant, *Catch Me If You Can,* DreamWorks, 2002.

Film Appearances:
Driver, *Rockula,* Cannon, 1990.
Waiter, *Midnight Cabaret,* Warner Bros., 1990.
Timid man, *The Gun in Betty Lou's Handbag,* Buena Vista, 1992.
Wolfie, *Monster Mash: The Movie* (also known as *Frankenstein Sings*), Prism Pictures, 1995.
Ghost dancer, *Scream 2,* Dimension/Miramax, 1997.
(Uncredited) Medical assistant, *A Walk to Remember,* Warner Bros., 2002.
Choreographer and waiter, *Stuck on You,* Twentieth Century–Fox, 2003.
(Uncredited) Driving instructor, *The Pacifier* (also known as *Gnome* and *Le Pacificateur*), Buena Vista, 2005.
Clam bake chef, *Cheaper by the Dozen 2,* Twentieth Century–Fox, 2005.
Nightclub dancer, *Step Up,* Buena Vista, 2006.

Talent agent number one, *Hairspray,* New Line Cinema, 2007.
Himself, *Portrait of a Choreographer* (short), 2007.

Television Choreographer; Specials:
The 1995 Billboard Music Awards, Fox, 1995.

Also choreographed broadcasts of the Soul Train Awards.

Television Director; Specials:
(Steve Martin's opening film segment) *The 75th Annual Academy Awards,* ABC, 2003.

Television Choreographer; Episodic:
(Dance sequences) *Down the Shore,* 1991.
Roundhouse, 1992.
Ellen, ABC, 1994.
Friends, NBC, 1996.
"Once More, With Feeling," *Buffy the Vampire Slayer* (also known as *BtVS, Buffy,* and *Buffy the Vampire Slayer: The Series*), UPN, 2001.

Also choreographed for *Caroline in the City.*

Television Director; Episodic:
Directed *Monk,* USA Network; *Worst Week of My Life,* Fox.

Television Appearances; Movies:
Shoe shop customers, *The Red Shoes,* 1983.
Washerwoman, *The Wind in the Willows,* 1983.

Television Appearances; Specials:
Reel Comedy: Bringing Down the House, Comedy Central, 2003.
Paul Abdul: The E! True Hollywood Story, E! Entertainment Television, 2003.
The 2006 MTV Movie Awards, MTV, 2006.
"Welcome to the '60s: On the Set of 'Hairspray'," *HBO First Look,* HBO, 2007.
The Oprah Winfrey Show (also known as *Oprah*), syndicated, 2007.

Dancer for Academy Awards presentation, 1989.

Television Appearances; Episodic:
"Steve Martin," *Biography,* Arts and Entertainment, 2006.

Stage Choreographer:
Choreographer for productions of *Commitment to Life,* Parts VII, VIII, and IX; *Eating Raoul; Patti Lupone on Broadway; Promises, Promises; Tight Quarters,* Tiffany Theatre, Los Angeles; and *West Side Story,* Los Angeles.

Radio Appearances; Episodic:
Fresh Air with Terry Gross, National Public Radio, 2007.

RECORDINGS

Music Videos:
Choreographer for "I'm Your Baby Tonight," by Whitney Houston; also Aaron Neville, the B52s, Johnny Gill, Stevie Wonder, and Barry White. Dancer in music videos for Paula Abdul and Janet Jackson.

SHER, Antony 1949–
(Anthony Sher, Sir Antony Sher)

PERSONAL

Born June 14, 1949, in Cape Town, South Africa; immigrated to England, 1968, naturalized citizen, 1979; son of Emmanuel (in business) and Margery Sher; companion of Gregory Doran (a director). *Education:* Attended Webber–Douglas Academy of Dramatic Art, London, 1969–71. *Religion:* Jewish. *Avocational Interests:* Painting, writing, classical music.

Addresses: *Agent*—ICM, Oxford House, 76 Oxford St., London W1D 1BS.

Career: Actor, artist, and writer. Royal Shakespeare Company, Stratford–on–Avon, England, associated artist, beginning 1982. Artist, with work exhibited at Barbican Theatre and National Theatre, London. *Military service:* Completed compulsory military service in South Africa.

Awards, Honors: London Critics' Circle Award, best actor, 1984, *Drama* Magazine Award, best actor, *Evening Standard* Theatre Award, best actor, Laurence Olivier Award and actor of the year, Society of West End Theatre, 1985, all for *Richard III;* Laurence Olivier Award, best actor, 1985, for *Torch Song Trilogy;* Laurence Olivier Award, best actor, *Theatre World* Award, Antoinette Perry Award nomination, best actor in a play, 1997, all for *Stanley;* Peter Sellers Award for Comedy, *Evening Standard* British Film Awards, 1997, for *Mrs. Brown;* Chlotrudis Award nomination, best supporting actor, 1998, for *Indian Summer* and *Mrs. Brown;* honorary doctorate of letters, Liverpool University, 1998; Screen Actors Guild Award (with others), outstanding performance by a cast, 1999, for *Shakespeare in Love;* decorated Knight Commander of the Order of the British Empire, 2000; honorary degree, University of Exeter, 2004; Drama Desk Award, outstanding solo performance, 2006, for *Primo.*

CREDITS

Stage Appearances:

Teeth 'n' Smiles, Royal Court Theatre, London, 1975.

Muhammad, *Goose–Pimples,* Hampstead Theatre Club, London, 1981.

Austin, *True West,* National Theatre, London, 1981–90.

Fool, *King Lear,* Royal Shakespeare Theatre, Stratford–on–Avon, England, then Barbican Theatre, London, 1982–83.

Moliere, Other Place Theatre, Stratford–on Avon, then Pit Theatre, London, 1983.

Title role, *Tartuffe,* Pit Theatre, 1983.

Martin Glass, *Maydays,* Barbican Theatre, 1983.

Marcel Fiote, *Red Noses,* Barbican Theatre, 1985.

Title role, *Richard III,* Barbican Theatre, 1985.

Arnold Backoff, *Torch Song Trilogy,* Albery Theatre, London, 1985.

Vindice, *The Revenger's Tragedy,* Swan Theatre, Stratford–on–Avon, then Pit Theatre, 1987–88.

Shylock, *The Merchant of Venice,* Royal Shakespeare Company, Stratford–on–Avon, then Barbican Theatre, 1988.

Johnny Smit, *Hello and Goodbye,* Almeida Theatre, London, 1988.

Peter Singer, *Singer,* Royal Shakespeare Company, Barbican Theatre, then Pit Theatre, 1990.

Joseph K., *The Trial,* Lyttelton Theatre, London, 1991.

Arturo Ui, *The Resistible Rise of Arturo Ui,* Olivier Theatre, London, 1991–92.

Mikhail Lvovich Astrov, *Uncle Vanya,* National Theatre, 1992.

Title role, *Tamburlaine the Great,* Royal Shakespeare Company, Barbican Theatre, 1994.

Sir Stanley Spencer, *Stanley,* Royal National Theatre, London, 1996, then Circle in the Square, New York City, 1997.

Leontes, *The Winter's Tale,* Royal Shakespeare Company, Royal Shakespeare Theatre, London, 1999.

Title role, *Macbeth,* Royal Shakespeare Company, Swan Theatre, then Young Vic Theatre, London, 1999–2000, later Long Wharf Theatre, New Haven, CT, 2000.

Gustav Mahler, *Mahler's Conversion,* 2001.

Domitian Caesar, *The Roman Actor,* 2002.

Malevole, *The Malcontent,* 2002.

Tsafendas, *ID,* Almeida Theatre, 2003.

Iago, *Othello,* 2004.

Title role *Primo,* National Theatre, London, 2004, then Cape Town, South Africa and Music Box Theatre, New York City, 2005.

Primo Levi, *Primo,* Heritage Theatre, 2005.

Also appeared in *Cloud Nine,* Royal Court Theatre, London; *The Glad Hand,* London production; *John, Paul, George, Ringo, and Bert,* Lyric Theatre, London; *Prayer for My Daughter,* London production; *Titus Andronicus,* National Theatre Company; and *Travesties,* Royal Shakespeare Company; *Astonish Me; The Cherry Orchard; A Flea in Her Ear; The Good Woman of Setzuan; The Government Inspector; Knickers; Teeth and Smiles; Twelfth Night; Ziggomania; Travesties; True West.*

Major Tours:

Title role, *Macbeth,* Japanese cities, c. 2000.

Stage Director:

Directed *Breakfast with Mugabe,* Royal Shakespeare Company, London.

Film Appearances:

Soldier at cinema, *Yanks* (also known as *Yanks— Gestern waren wir noch freunde*), Universal, 1979.

Bellboy, *Superman II,* Warner Bros., 1980.

Mark Gertler: Fragments of a Biography, 1981.

Oliver Shadey, *Shadey,* Film Four International, 1984.

Loki, *Eric the Viking* (also known as *Erik viking*), Orion, 1990.

Moliere, 1990.

Tartuffe, 1990.

Dr. Ernest Zeigler, *The Young Poisoner's Handbook* (also known as *Das Handbuch des jungen giftmischers*), 1995, Cineplex Film Properties, 1996.

Chief weasel, *The Wind in the Willows* (also known as *Mr. Toad's Wild Ride*), 1996, Columbia, 1997.

Jack, *Indian Summer* (also known as *Alive and Kicking*), First Look Pictures Releasing, 1996.

Benjamin Disraeli, *Mrs. Brown* (also known as *Her Majesty, Mrs. Brown* and *Mrs. Brown*), Miramax, 1997.

Dr. Moth, *Shakespeare in Love,* Miramax, 1998.

Ben Azra, *The Miracle Maker,* 2000.

Hitler, *Churchill: The Hollywood Years,* Pathe, 2004.

Chef, *A Higher Agency* (short), 2005.

Primo Levi, *Primo,* HBO Films, 2007.

Television Appearances; Miniserie:

The Don, *Look at the States We're In!,* BBC, 1995.

Gerald Lewis Q.C., *The Jury,* ITV1 and PBS, 2002.

Erza Ben Ezra (The Rabbi), *The Company,* TNT, 2007.

Television Appearances; Movies:

Tasic, *Collision Course,* Granada, 1979.

Mr. Alpert, *One Fine Day* (also known as *Six Plays by Alan Bennett: "One Fine Day"*), ITV, 1979.

Howard Kirk, *The History Man* (also known as *Malcolm Bradbury's "The History Man"*), BBC, 1981.

Tartuffe, *Tartuffe, or The Imposter,* BBC and PBS, 1983.

David Samuels, *The Land of Dreams,* BBC, 1990.

Changing Step, BBC, 1990.

Title role, *Genghis Cohn,* BBC and Arts and Entertainment, 1993.

Sergeant Cuff, *The Moonstone,* BBC and PBS, 1996.

Moncoutant, *Hornblower: The Frogs and the Lobsters* (also known as *Horatio Hornblower: The Wrong War*), ITV and Arts and Entertainment, 1999.
Voice of Ben Azra, *The Miracle Maker*, ABC, 2000.

Television Appearances; Specials:
Himself, *Camp Christmas*, 1993.
King Richard III, HBO, 1996.
(As Anthony Sher) Leontes, King of Sicilia, *The Winter's Tale*, 1999.
Title role, *Macbeth*, 2001.
Gerald Ballantyne, *Home*, BBC4, 2003.
The "Evening Standard" Theatre Awards 2003, ITV, 2003.
Primo, HBO, 2007.

Television Appearances; Episodic:
"The Sheik of Pickersgill," *Pickersgill People*, BBC, 1978.
Morris, "Cold Harbour," *ITV Playhouse*, ITV, 1978.
"The Out of Town Boys," *Play for Today*, BBC1, 1979.
The Dame Edna Experience, ITV, 1989.
Scum editor, "The Crying Game," *The Comic Strip Presents*, BBC2 and MTV, 1992.
Voice of Richard, "King Richard III," *Shakespeare: The Animated Tales* (animated), BBC2 and HBO, 1994.
Mr. Prothrow, "Re–arranging the Dust," *One Foot in the Grave*, BBC1, 1995.
The don, "The Organisation," *Look at the State We're In!*, BBC, 1995.
Macbeth, "A Time of Revolution," *In Search of Shakespeare*, PBS, 2004.
Macbeth, "The Lost Years," *In Search of Shakespeare*, PBS, 2004.
Macbeth, "The Duty of Poets," *In Search of Shakespeare*, PBS, 2004.
Macbeth, "For All Time," *In Search of Shakespeare*, PBS, 2004.
(As Sir Antony Sher) Himself, "Othello," *The South Bank Show*, ITV, 2004.
Frank Jeremy, "Jack's Back," *Murphy's Law*, BBC and BBC America, 2004.

WRITINGS

Screenplays:
(With others) *Mark Gertler: Fragments of a Biography*, 1981.
Primo, Heritage Theatre, 2005.

Television Movies:
Changing Step, BBC1, 1990.

Television Specials:
Primo, HBO, 2007.

Stage Plays:
ID, Almeida Theatre, London, 2003.
Primo, National Theatre, London, 2004.

Books:
The Year of the King (nonfiction), Chatto & Windus, 1985.
Middlepost (novel), Knopf (New York City), 1988.
Characters (paintings and sketches), 1989.
The Indoor Boy (novel), Viking (New York City), 1992.
Cheap Lives (novel), Little, Brown (Boston, MA), 1995.
(With Gregory Doran) *Woza Shakespeare!: "Titus Andronicus" in South Africa* (nonfiction), 1997.
The Feast (novel), Little, Brown, 1998.
Beside Myself: An Autobiography, Hutchinson, 2001.

OTHER SOURCES

Periodicals:
Daily Telegraph, January 5, 2001.
New Statesman, May 10, 1985; January 15, 1999, p. 38.
New York, March 17, 1997.
New York Times, February 2, 1997.

SHERMAN, Richard M. 1928–
(Dick Sherman, Richard Sherman)

PERSONAL

Full name, Richard Morton Sherman; born June 12, 1928, in New York, NY; son of Al (a composer) and Rosa (maiden name, Dancis) Sherman; brother of Robert B. Sherman (a composer, lyricist, and screenwriter); married Ursula Elizabeth Gluck, July 6, 1957; children: Linda Sue, Gregory Vincent, Victoria Lynn. *Education:* Attended University of Southern California, 1945; Bard College, B.A., 1949.

Career: Composer, lyricist, and screenwriter. Formed Music World Publications; Walt Disney Productions, Burbank, CA, songwriter and composer, 1960–71; songwriter and composer, 1971—; formed Redstring Productions (with David Aniel and Robert J. Sherman), 1997. *Military service:* U.S. Army, stationed in Korea, 1953–55.

Member: Academy of Motion Picture Arts and Sciences, Broadcast Music, Inc., National Academy of Recording Arts and Sciences, Composers and Lyricists Guild, Writers Guild of America.

Awards, Honors: (All with brother, Robert B. Sherman): Academy Award, best score, Grammy Award, best score, 1964, Golden Globe Award nomination, best original score, 1965, all for *Mary Poppins;* Academy Award, best song, Golden Laurel Award, best song, Producers Guild of America, 1964, both for "Chim Chim Cheree"; Christopher Medal, 1965; Academy Award nomination, best song, 1968, for "Chitty Chitty Bang Bang"; Golden Globe Award nomination, best original score, 1969, for *Chitty Chitty Bang Bang;* Academy Award nomination, best song score, 1971, for *Bedknobs and Broomsticks;* Academy Award nomination, best song, 1971, for "The Age of Not Believing," from *Bedknobs and Broomsticks;* Academy Award nomination, best song score, and Moscow Film Festival First Prize, best song score, 1973, Golden Globe Award nomination, best original score, 1974, all for *Tom Sawyer;* star on Hollywood Walk of Fame, 1976; Golden Globe Award nomination, best original score, and Academy Award nomination, best song score, Anthony Asquith Award for Film Music, British Academy of Film and Television Arts, all 1977, for *The Slipper and the Rose: The Story of Cinderella;* Academy Award nomination, best song, 1977, for "The Slipper and the Rose Waltz"; Academy Award nomination, best song, 1978, for "When You're Loved," from *The Magic of Lassie;* Annie Award nomination, outstanding individual achievement for music, International Animated Film Society, 2000, for *The Tigger Movie;* Songwriters Hall of Fame, inductee, 2005. One diamond, four platinum, and sixteen gold records between 1965 and 1983.

CREDITS

Film Appearances:
Guard, *Bacchanale,* 1970.
(Scenes deleted) Wonderworld bandleader, *Beverly Hills Cop III,* 1994.
Himself, *Walt Disney's "The Jungle Book": The Making of a Musical Masterpiece* (documentary short), Walt Disney Home Video, 1997.
Himself, *Mary Poppins Practically Perfect in Every Way: The Magic Behind the Masterpiece* (documentary short; also known as *Walt Disney's "Mary Poppins Practically Perfect in Every Way: The Magic Behind the Masterpiece"*), Walt Disney Home Video, 1997.
(As Richard Sherman) Himself, *The "Fantasia" Legacy: The Concert Feature* (documentary; also known as *The Making of "Fantasia"*), Buena Vista Home Entertainment, 2000.
(As Richard Sherman) Himself, *Muse Magic: The Sherman Brothers—"The Sword in the Stone"* (documentary short), Buena Vista Home Entertainment, 2001.
Himself, *Muse Magic: The Sherman Brothers—"Bedknobs and Broomsticks"* (documentary short), Buena Vista Home Entertainment, 2001.
Himself, *Songs of the Silly Symphonies* (documentary short; also known as *The Song of the Silly Symphonies*), Buena Vista Home Entertainment, 2001.

Himself, *"The Parent Trap": Caught in the Act,* Buena Vista Home Entertainment, 2002.
Himself, *The Many Adventures of Winnie the Pooh: The Story Behind the Masterpiece* (documentary short), Buena Vista Home Entertainment, 2002.
Himself, *Making of the Sherman Brothers* (documentary short), Buena Vista Home Video, 2003.
Himself, *The Musical Legacy of Paul Smith* (documentary short), Buena Vista Home Entertainment, 2003.
Himself, *"Mary Poppins": A Musical Journey with Richard Sherman* (documentary short), Buena Vista Home Entertainment, 2004.
Himself, *Supercalifragilisticexpialidocious: The Making of "Mary Poppins,"* 2004.
Himself, *Silly Symphonies Rediscovered* (documentary short), Buena Vista Home Entertainment, 2006.

Television Work; Specials:
Producer, *Goldilocks,* 1971.

Television Appearances; Specials:
The 37th Annual Academy Awards, ABC, 1965.
(As Richard Sherman) *Cubby Broccoli: The Man Behind Bond,* 2000.
(As Richard Sherman) *Walt: The Man Behind the Myth,* 2001.
(As Richard Sherman) *I Love Christmas,* 2001.
(As Richard Sherman) *The 100 Greatest Musicals,* Channel 4, 2003.
Best Ever Family Films, 2005.
(As Richard Sherman) *The 100 Greatest Family Films,* Channel 4, 2005.

Television Appearances; Episodic:
The Disney Family Album, 1984.

RECORDINGS

Albums:
Recorded the comedy album *Smash Flops.*

Video Games:
My Interactive Pooh, Mattel Media, 1998.

WRITINGS

Film Scores:
Symposium of Popular Songs, 1962.
Mary Poppins, Buena Vista, 1964.
The One and Only Genuine Original Family Band (also known as *The Family Band*), Buena Vista, 1968.
Chitty Chitty Bang Bang (also known as *Ian Fleming's "Chitty Chitty Bang Bang"*), United Artists, 1968.
Snoopy, Come Home! (animated), National General, 1972.

Charlotte's Web (animated; also known as *E. B. White's "Charlotte's Web"*), Paramount, 1973.

The Magic of Lassie, International Picture Show, 1978.

Learn Along with Me: DVD1 (animated short), Tiny Oaks Montessori School, 2006.

The Boys (documentary), 2007.

Film Music and Lyrics (with Robert B. Sherman):
20,000 Leagues Under the Sea, Buena Vista, 1954.

The Absent–Minded Professor, Buena Vista, 1961.

The Parent Trap, Buena Vista, 1961.

Big Red, Buena Vista, 1962.

Bon Voyage, Buena Vista, 1962.

Moon Pilot, Buena Vista, 1962.

Legend of Lobo, 1962.

The Castaways (also known as *In Search of Castaways*), Buena Vista, 1962.

Symposium of Popular Songs, 1962.

The Golden Horseshoe Revue, 1962.

Miracle of the White Stallions (also known as *The Flight of the White Stallions*), Buena Vista, 1963.

Summer Magic, Buena Vista, 1963.

The Sword in the Stone (animated), Buena Vista, 1963.

Mary Poppins, Buena Vista, 1964.

Those Calloways, Buena Vista, 1964.

The Misadventures of Merlin Jones, Buena Vista, 1964.

My Fair Lady, 1964.

The Monkey's Uncle, Buena Vista, 1965.

That Darn Cat!, Buena Vista, 1965.

Winnie the Pooh, 1965.

Follow Me, Boys!, Buena Vista, 1966.

The Happiest Millionaire, Buena Vista, 1967.

The Jungle Book (animated), Buena Vista, 1967.

A Boy Called Nuthin', 1967.

The Adventures of Bullwhip Griffin, 1967.

Monkeys, Go Home, 1967.

The Gnome–Mobile, 1967.

Chitty Chitty Bang Bang (also known as *Ian Fleming's "Chitty Chitty Bang Bang"*), United Artists, 1968.

The One and Only Genuine Original Family Band (also known as *The Family Band*), Buena Vista, 1968.

Winnie the Pooh and the Blustery Day, 1968.

(And with Terry Gilkyson, Floyd Huddleston, and Al Rinker) *The Aristocats* (animated), Buena Vista, 1970.

Bedknobs and Broomsticks, Buena Vista, 1971.

Snoopy, Come Home! (animated), National General, 1972.

Charlotte's Web (animated; also known as *E. B. White's "Charlotte's Web"*), Paramount, 1973.

Tom Sawyer, United Artists, 1973.

Huckleberry Finn, United Artists, 1974.

The Slipper and the Rose (also known as *The Story of Cinderella*), Universal, 1976.

The Many Adventures of Winnie the Pooh, 1977.

The Magic of Lassie, International Picture Show, 1978.

Magic Journeys, 1982.

Gung Ho, 1986.

Little Nemo: Adventures in Slumberland (animated), Hemdale Releasing, 1990.

Beverly Hills Cop III, Paramount, 1994.

Winnie the Pooh: Seasons of Giving (also known as *Disney's Winnie the Pooh: Seasons of Giving*), Buena Vista Home Video, 1999.

The Tigger Movie (animated), Buena Vista, 2000.

Film Songs:
(As Dick Sherman) *"What's Your Sad Story?" Nightmare,* United Artists, 1956.

Screenplays (with Robert B. Sherman):
Tom Sawyer (also known as *A Musical Adaptation of Mark Twain's "Tom Sawyer"*), United Artists, 1973.

Huckleberry Finn (also known as *Mark Twain's "Huckleberry Finn": A Musical Adaptation*), United Artists, 1974.

(And with Bryan Forbes) *The Slipper and the Rose: The Story of Cinderella* (also known as *The Slipper and the Rose*), Universal, 1976.

(And with Jean Holloway) *The Magic of Lassie,* International Picture Show, 1978.

Television Music; Series (with Robert B. Sherman):
Walt Disney's Wonderful World of Color, NBC, 1961.

Also composer for *Bell Telephone Hour,* NBC; *Welcome to Pooh Corner;* and *The Enchanted Musical Playhouse.*

Television Music; Movies:
The Horsemasters, 1961.

Petronella, 1986.

Sick: The Life and Death of Bob Flanagan, Super Masochist, 1996.

Television Music; Specials:
Michelle Kwan Skates to Disney's Greatest Hits, ABC, 1999.

Stage Music and Lyrics:
(With Robert B. Sherman) *Over Here!,* Shubert Theatre, New York City, 1974.

(With Milton Larsen) *New Faces of 1980,* Bonfils Theatre, Denver, CO, c. 1980.

(With Robert B. Sherman) *Chitty Chitty Bang Bang: The Stage Musical,* London Palladium, London, 2002, Hilton Theatre, New York City, 2005.

(With Robert B. Sherman) *Mary Poppins,* New Amsterdam Theatre, New York City, 2006—.

Books:
(With Robert B. Sherman) *Walt's Time: From Before to Beyond,* Camphor Tree, 1998.

OTHER SOURCES

Electronic:

Richard M. Sherman Website, http://www. shermanmusic.com, October 20, 2007.

SHORE, Howard 1946–
　　(Howard Shore and His Band of Angels, Howard Shore and His All Nurse Band, Howard Shore and His Bobby Blue Band, Howard "Bud" Shore)

PERSONAL

Full name, Howard Leslie Shore; born October 18, 1946, in Toronto, Ontario, Canada; son of Mac (a journalist) and Bernice (a dancer; maiden name, Ash) Shore; uncle of Ryan Shore (a composer); married Elizabeth Ann Cotnoir, August 3, 1990; children: May. *Education:* Attended the Berklee College of Music, 1965–67.

Addresses: *Manager*—Columbia Artists Management, 1790 Broadway, New York, NY 10019–1412. *Publicist*—Chasen and Company, 8899 Beverly Blvd., Suite 408, Los Angeles, CA 90048.

Career: Composer, musical director, music producer, arranger, and conductor. Lighthouse (Canadian musical band), founding member, 1969–72; also performed with Howard Shore and His Band of Angels, Howard Shore and His All Nurse Band, and Howard Shore and His Bobby Blue Band; guest conductor of symphony orchestras; also a concert performer. Canadian Broadcasting Corporation (CBC), worked as a composer and songwriter; also helped create the musical group the Blues Brothers.

Member: American Society of Composers, Authors and Publishers.

Awards, Honors: Juno awards (with Lighthouse), best group, Canadian Academy of Recording Arts and Sciences, 1972, 1973, and 1974; Juno Award nomination (with Lighthouse), best group, 1975; Genie Award nomination, best music score, Academy of Canadian Cinema and Television, 1980, for *The Brood;* Saturn Award nomination, best music, Academy of Science Fiction, Fantasy, and Horror Films, 1987, for *The Fly;* ASCAP Film and Television Music Award, top box office film, American Society of Composers, Authors and Publishers, 1989, for *Big;* Genie Award, best music score, 1989, and Saturn Award nomination, best music, 1990, both for *Dead Ringers;* ASCAP Film and Televi-

sion Music Award, top box office film, Film Award nomination, best original music, British Academy of Film and Television Arts, and Saturn Award nomination, best music, all 1992, for *The Silence of the Lambs;* Genie Award nomination, best music score, 1992, for *Naked Lunch;* ASCAP Film and Television Music Award, top box office film, 1994, for *Mrs. Doubtfire;* Gotham Composer Award, Independent Features Project, 1994; Los Angeles Film Critics Association Award, best music, 1994, Saturn Award, best music, 1995, and Grammy Award nomination, best instrumental composition written for a motion picture or for television, National Academy of Recording Arts and Sciences, 1996, all for *Ed Wood;* two ASCAP Film and Television Music awards, top box office film, 1995, for *Philadelphia* and for *The Client;* ASCAP Film and Television Music Award, top box office film, and Saturn Award nomination, best music, both 1996, for *Se7en;* ASCAP Film and Television Music Award, top box office film, 2000, for *Analyze This;* ASCAP Film and Television Music awards, most performed theme, 2000, 2001, 2002, 2003, 2004, and 2005; Los Angeles Film Critics Association Award, best music score, World Soundtrack awards, best original orchestral soundtrack of the year and public choice award, and World Soundtrack Award nomination, soundtrack composer of the year, all 2001, Academy Award, best music, original score, Critics Choice Award, best composer, Broadcast Film Critics Association, Chicago Film Critics Association Award, best original score, Sierra Award, best score, Las Vegas Film Critics Society, Phoenix Film Critics Society Award, best original score, ASCAP Film and Television Music Award, top box office film, Golden Globe Award nomination, best original score for a motion picture, nomination for Anthony Asquith Award for Film Music, British Academy of Film and Television Arts, American Film Institute Award nomination, composer of the year, Saturn Award nomination, best music, and Online Film Critics Society Award nomination, best original score, all 2002, and Grammy Award, best score soundtrack album for a motion picture, television, or other visual media, 2003, all for *The Lord of the Rings: The Fellowship of the Ring;* Georges Delerue Prize, Flanders International Film Festival, 2002, for *Spider;* Phoenix Film Critics Society Award, best original song, and World Soundtrack Award nomination, best original song written for a film, both with others, 2003, for "Gollum's Song," *The Lord of the Rings: The Two Towers;* ASCAP Film and Television Music Award, top box office film, 2003, for *Panic Room;* nomination for Anthony Asquith Award for Film Music, and World Soundtrack Award nominations, best original soundtrack of the year and soundtrack composer of the year, all 2003, for *Gangs of New York;* Hollywood Film Award, outstanding achievement in music in film, Hollywood Film Festival, 2003; ASCAP Film and Television Music Award, top box office film, Critics Choice Award nomination, best composer, Broadcast Film Critics Association, Saturn Award nomination, best music, Chicago Film Critics Association Award nomination, best original score, Phoenix

Film Critics Society Award nomination, best original score, and Online Film Critics Society Award nomination, best original score, all 2003, and Grammy Award, best score soundtrack album for a motion picture, television, or other visual media, 2004, all for *The Lord of the Rings: The Two Towers;* Henry Mancini Award, American Society of Composers, Authors and Publishers, 2004; Academy Award, best music, original score, Golden Globe Award, best original score for a motion picture, Critics Choice Award, best composer, Broadcast Film Critics Association, Saturn Award, best music, Chicago Film Critics Association Award, best original score, Sierra Award, best score, Las Vegas Film Critics Society, Phoenix Film Critics Society Award, best original score, ASCAP Film and Television Music Award, top box office film, Online Film Critics Society Award, best original score, nomination for Anthony Asquith Award for Film Music, and Golden Satellite Award nomination, best original score, International Press Academy, all 2004, Grammy Award, best score soundtrack album for a motion picture, television, or other visual media, 2005, and designation as the best film soundtrack of all time, Classic FM (radio station in Great Britain), all for *The Lord of the Rings: The Return of the King;* Academy Award, best original song, Golden Globe Award, best original song for a motion picture, and World Soundtrack Award nomination, best original song written for a film, all 2004, and Grammy Award, best song written for a motion picture, television, or other visual media, 2005, all with others, all for "Into the West," *The Lord of the Rings: The Return of the King;* Chicago Film Critics Association Award, best original score, and Seattle Film Critics Award, best music, both 2004, Golden Globe Award, best original score for a motion picture, Critics Choice Award, best composer, Broadcast Film Critics Association, Golden Satellite Award nomination, best original score, nomination for Anthony Asquith Award for Film Music, World Soundtrack Award nominations, best original soundtrack of the year and soundtrack composer of the year, and Online Film Critics Society Award nomination, best original score, all 2005, and Grammy Award nomination, best score soundtrack album for a motion picture, television, or other visual media, 2006, all for *The Aviator;* National Board of Review Award, career achievement, 2005; Critics Choice Award nomination, best composer, Broadcast Film Critics Association, 2007, for *The Departed;* honorary doctorate of letters, York University, Canada, 2007.

CREDITS

Film Work; Conductor and Orchestrator:
M. Butterfly, Warner Bros., 1993.

Sliver (also known as *Sliver—Gier der Augen*), Paramount, 1993.

The Client (also known as *Az Uegyfel, Der Klient, El cliente, Il cliente, Klient, Klienten, Le client, O cliente, O pelatis,* and *Paeaemies*), Warner Bros., 1994.

Nobody's Fool, Paramount, 1994.

Moonlight and Valentino, Gramercy Pictures, 1995.

White Man's Burden (also known as *White Man*), Twentieth Century–Fox, 1995.

Before and After, Buena Vista, 1996.

Crash, Fine Line Features, 1996.

The Truth about Cats & Dogs, Twentieth Century–Fox, 1996.

Cop Land, Miramax, 1997.

The Game, Polygram Filmed Entertainment, 1997.

Dogma (also known as *Bearclaw, God,* and *Dogme*), Miramax, 1998.

eXistenZ, Dimension Films, 1999.

The Cell, New Line Cinema, 2000.

Esther Kahn (also known as *eSTheR KaHN*), Bac Films, 2000.

The Yards, Miramax, 2000.

The Lord of the Rings: The Fellowship of the Ring (also known as *The Fellowship of the Ring, The Lord of the Rings: The Fellowship of the Ring: The Motion Picture, A Gyrueruek ura: A gyuerue szoevetsege, Der Herr der Ringe: Die Gefaehrten, El senor de los anillos: La comunidad del anillo, El senyor dels anells: La comunitat de l'anell, El senyor dels anells: La germandat de l'anell, Hringadrottinssaga: Foeruneyti hringsins, Il signore degli anelli—La compagnia dell'anello, Le seigneur des anneaux—La communaute de l'anneau, O senhor dos aneis—A irmandade do anel, O senhor dos aneis: A sociedade do anel, Pan prstenu: Spolecenstvo prstenu, Ringenes herre: Eventyret om ringen, Ringenes herre: Ringens brorskap, Sagan om ringen: Haerskarringen, Sormuste isand: Sormuse vennaskond, Stapinul inelelor: Fratia inelului, Tara sormusten herrasta—Sormuksen ritarit,* and *Wladca pierscieni: Druzyna pierscienia*), New Line Cinema, 2001.

The Score, Paramount, 2001.

The Lord of the Rings: The Two Towers (also known as *The Two Towers, Banjieui jewang du jaeeui tam, Bechdebis mbrdzanebeli, Der Herr der Ringe: Die zwei Tuerme, El senor de los anillos: Las dos torres, El senyor dels anells: Les dues torres, Hringadrottinssaga: Tveggja turna tal, Il signore degli anelli—Le due torri, Le seigneur des anneaux—Les deux tours, O senhor dos aneis: As duas torres, Ringenes herre: De to taarne, Ringenes herre: To taarn, Sagan om ringen: Sagan om de tvaa tornen, Sormuste isand: Kaks kantsi, Stapanul inelelor: Cele doua turnuri, Tara sormusten herrasta—Kaksi tornia,* and *Wladca pierscieni: Dwie wieze*), New Line Cinema, 2002.

Spider, Sony Pictures Classics, 2002.

The Lord of the Rings: The Return of the King (also known as *The Return of the King, A Gyrueruek ura: A kiraly viszater, Der Herr der Ringe: Die Rueckkehr des Koenigs, El senor de los anillos: El retorno del rey, El senyor dels anells: El retorn del rei, Gospodar prstanov: Vrnitev kralja, Hringadrottinssaga: Hilmir snyr heim, Il signore degli anelli—Il ritorno*

del re, *Le seigneur des anneaux—Le retour du roi, O senhor dos aneis: O retorno do rei, Pan prstenu: Navrat krale, Ringenes herre: Atter en konge, Ringenes herre: Kongen vender tilbage, Sagan om ringen: Sagan om konungens aaterkomst, Sormuste isand: Kuninga tagsitulek, Tara sormusten herrasta—Kuninkaan paluu,* and *Wladca pierscieni: Powrot krola*), New Line Cinema, 2003.
The Aviator, Miramax/Warner Bros., 2004.
A History of Violence, New Line Cinema, 2005.
The Last Mimzy, New Line Cinema, 2007.

Music Conductor:
Dead Ringers (also known as *Alter ego*), Twentieth Century–Fox, 1988.
She–Devil, Orion, 1990.
A Kiss before Dying, Universal, 1991.
Naked Lunch (also known as *Le festin nu*), Twentieth Century–Fox, 1991.
Prelude to a Kiss, Twentieth Century–Fox, 1992.
Philadelphia, TriStar, 1993.
Looking for Richard, Twentieth Century–Fox, 1996.
Striptease, Columbia, 1996.
That Thing You Do!, Twentieth Century–Fox, 1996.
High Fidelity, Buena Vista, 2000.

Film Music Orchestrator:
Quick Change, Warner Bros., 1991.
Mrs. Doubtfire (also known as *Gospa Doubtfire—ocka v krilu, Gveret Doubtfire, Madame Doubtfire, Mme. Doubtfire, Mrs. Doubtfire—Das stachelige Hausmaedchen, Mrs. Doubtfire—Das stachelige Kindermaedchen, Mrs. Doubtfire—isae sisaekkoenae, Mrs. Doubtfire—Mammo per sempre, Pani Doubtfire, Papa para sempre, Para por siempre, Senora Doubtfire, papa de por vida, Sra. Doubtfire, papa de por vida, Uma baba quase perfeita,* and *Vaelkommen mrs. Doubtfire*), Twentieth Century–Fox, 1993.
Ed Wood, Buena Vista, 1994.

Film Music Arranger:
High Fidelity, Buena Vista, 2000.
The Aviator, Miramax/Warner Bros., 2004.

Film Music Producer:
Gilda Live, Warner Bros., 1980.
Additional music producer, *Places in the Heart,* TriStar, 1984.
Belizaire the Cajun, Skouras Pictures, 1985.
Moonlight and Valentino, Gramercy Pictures, 1995.
Song producer, *The Score,* Paramount, 2001.
The Aviator, Miramax/Warner Bros., 2004.
The Last Mimzy, New Line Cinema, 2007.

Film Work; Other:
Music coordinator, *Silkwood,* Twentieth Century–Fox, 1983.

Music supervisor, *Postcards from the Edge,* Columbia, 1991.
Music mixer, *Dogma* (also known as *Bearclaw, God,* and *Dogme*), Miramax, 1998.
Music consultant, *Shadow Magic* (also known as *Xi yang jing*), Sony Pictures Classics, 2000.

Film Appearances:
Himself, *Gilda Live,* Warner Bros., 1980.
Lucio Crisco, *Unspeakable,* Troma Entertainment, 2000.
(Uncredited) Orchestra pit conductor, *King Kong* (also known as *King Kong: The Eighth Wonder of the World* and *Peter Jackson's "King Kong"*), Universal, 2005.

Television Appearances; Series:
(Sometimes credited as Howard "Bud" Shore, Howard Shore and His All Nurse Band, Howard Shore and His Band of Angels, or Howard Shore and His Bobby Blue Band) Himself and various characters, *Saturday Night Live* (also known as *NBC's "Saturday Night," Saturday Night, Saturday Night Live '80, SNL,* and *SNL 25*), NBC, 1975–80.

Television Appearances; Specials:
(Uncredited; in archive footage) Beekeeper bandleader, *Saturday Night Live: 15th Anniversary,* NBC, 1989.
(Uncredited) Audience member, *Saturday Night Live: 25th Anniversary* (also known as *Saturday Night Live: 25th Anniversary Primetime Special*), NBC, 1999.
(Uncredited; in archive footage) Beekeeper bandleader, *Saturday Night Live: The Best of John Belushi,* NBC, 2005.
Himself, *Live from New York: The First Five Years of Saturday Night Live* (also known as *SNL: The First Five Years*), NBC, 2005.

Television Appearances; Awards Presentations:
The 74th Annual Academy Awards, ABC, 2002.
The 76th Annual Academy Awards, ABC, 2004.
The 62nd Annual Golden Globe Awards, NBC, 2005.

Television Appearances; Episodic:
Himself, *Lo + plus,* 1996.
Himself, "David Lynch Special," *Tracks,* 2007.

Television Work; Series:
(Sometimes credited as Howard "Bud" Shore, Howard Shore and His All Nurse Band, Howard Shore and His Band of Angels, or Howard Shore and His Bobby Blue Band) Musical director, musician, and sometimes conductor, *Saturday Night Live* (also known as *NBC's "Saturday Night," Saturday Night, Saturday Night Live '80, SNL,* and *SNL 25*), NBC, 1975–80.

Television Musical Director; Specials:
The Hart & Lorne Terrific Hour (series of specials), CBC, beginning c. 1971.
Coca–Cola Presents Live: The Hard Rock (also known as *Live: The Hard Rock*), NBC, 1988.

Stage Music Producer:
Gilda Radner—Live from New York, Winter Garden Theatre, New York City, 1979.

Worked on amateur theatre productions.

Stage Appearances:
Member of the Candy Slice Group, *Gilda Radner—Live from New York,* Winter Garden Theatre, New York City, 1979.

RECORDINGS

Albums; with Lighthouse:
Lighthouse, RCA Victor, 1969.
Peacing It All Together, RCA Victor, 1970.
Suite Feeling, RCA Victor, 1970.
One Fine Morning, Evolution, 1971.
Lighthouse Live!, Evolution, 1972.
One Fine Light, RCA Victor, 1972.
Sunny Days, Edsel, 1972.
Thoughts of Movin' On, Evolution, 1972.
Can You Feel It, Polydor, 1974.
Good Day, Polydor, 1974.
Sunny Days Again: The Best of Lighthouse, MCA, 1999.

Album Work:
Producer, *Live from New York* (also known as *Gilda Radner—Live from New York*), Warner Bros./Wea, c. 1979.

Worked on other albums.

Videos:
Himself, *Inside the Labyrinth: The Making of "The Silence of the Lambs,"* Metro–Goldwyn–Mayer/United Artists Home Entertainment, 2001.
Himself, *The Making of "The Lord of the Rings,"* 2002.
Himself, *People Like Us: Making "Philadelphia,"* Columbia/TriStar Home Video, 2003.
Himself, *Creating the Lord of the Rings Symphony: A Composer's Journey through Middle–Earth,* Aurum Producciones, 2004.
Himself, *Acts of Violence,* New Line Cinema, 2006.
Himself, *Scoring the Silence* (short), Twentieth Century–Fox Home Entertainment/Metro–Goldwyn–Mayer Home Entertainment, 2006.

Video Musical Director:
The Best of John Belushi, 1985.
The Best of Dan Aykroyd, 1986.
Saturday Night Live Christmas (also known as *Saturday Night Live Christmas Past*), 1999.

Video Games:
Voice of Rohan guard, *The Lord of the Rings: The Return of the King,* EA Games, 2003.

WRITINGS

Film Music:
I Miss You, Hugs and Kisses (also known as *Drop Dead, Dearest* and *Left for Dead*), Astral, 1978.
The Brood (also known as *Chromosome, David Cronenberg's "The Brood,"* and *La clinique de la terreur*), New World Pictures, 1979.
Scanners (also known as *Telepathy 2000*), Avco–Embassy Pictures, 1981.
Videodrome (also known as *Zonekiller*), Universal, 1983.
(Including title song) *Nothing Lasts Forever,* 1984.
Places in the Heart, TriStar, 1984.
After Hours, Geffen/Warner Bros., 1985.
Fire with Fire (also known as *Captive Hearts*), Paramount, 1986.
The Fly (also known as *La mouche*), Twentieth Century–Fox, 1986.
Heaven, Island Pictures, 1987.
Nadine, TriStar, 1987.
Big, Twentieth Century–Fox, 1988.
Dead Ringers (also known as *Alter ego*), Twentieth Century–Fox, 1988.
Moving, Warner Bros., 1988.
The Local Stigmatic, 1989.
Signs of Life (also known as *One for Sorrow, Two for Joy*), Avenue Entertainment, 1989.
An Innocent Man, Buena Vista, 1990.
The Lemon Sisters (also known as *Lemon Sisters, Ha–Ahayot Limon, Mulheres, amigas e irmas,* and *Os meus problemas com os homens*), Miramax, 1990.
Made in Milan (short documentary), 1990.
(Including title song) *She–Devil,* Orion, 1990.
A Kiss before Dying, Universal, 1991.
Naked Lunch (also known as *Le festin nu*), Twentieth Century–Fox, 1991.
Additional music, *Quick Change,* Warner Bros., 1991.
The Silence of the Lambs, Orion, 1991.
Prelude to a Kiss, Twentieth Century–Fox, 1992.
Single White Female (also known as *Drusha Shutafa Ravaka, Enlig pige soger, Ensam ung kvinna soeker ..., Inserzione pericolosa, J. F. partagerait appartement, Jeune femme chercher colocataire, Jovem procura companheira, Mujer blanca soltera busca ..., Mujer soltera busca, Mulher solteira procura ..., Nuori naimaton nainen, Sublokatorka,* and *Weiblich, ledig, jung sucht ...*), Columbia, 1992.

Guilty as Sin, Buena Vista, 1993.

M. Butterfly, Warner Bros., 1993.

Mrs. Doubtfire (also known as *Gospa Doubtfire—ocka v krilu, Gveret Doubtfire, Madame Doubtfire, Mme. Doubtfire, Mrs. Doubtfire—Das stachelige Hausmaedchen, Mrs. Doubtfire—Das stachelige Kindermaedchen, Mrs. Doubtfire—isae sisaekkoenae, Mrs. Doubtfire—Mammo per sempre, Pani Doubtfire, Papa para sempre, Para por siempre, Senora Doubtfire, papa de por vida, Sra. Doubtfire, papa de por vida, Uma baba quase perfeita,* and *Vaelkommen mrs. Doubtfire*), Twentieth Century–Fox, 1993.

Philadelphia, TriStar, 1993.

Sliver (also known as *Sliver—Gier der Augen*), Paramount, 1993.

The Client (also known as *Az Uegyfel, Der Klient, El cliente, Il cliente, Klient, Klienten, Le client, O cliente, O pelatis,* and *Paeaemies*), Warner Bros., 1994.

Ed Wood, Buena Vista, 1994.

Nobody's Fool, Paramount, 1994.

Moonlight and Valentino, Gramercy Pictures, 1995.

Se7en (also known as *Seven, The Seven Deadly Sins, Hetedik, Los siete pecados capitales, Pecados capitales, 7 pecados mortais, Sedam, Sedem, Sieben, Siedem, Sietsemaen, Sep7, Sept, Sete pecados mortais, Seven—Os sete crimes capitais, Seven—Os sete pecados capitais,* and *Yedi*), New Line Cinema, 1995.

(Including song "Drive–By") *White Man's Burden* (also known as *White Man*), Twentieth Century–Fox, 1995.

Before and After, Buena Vista, 1996.

Crash, Fine Line Features, 1996.

Looking for Richard, Twentieth Century–Fox, 1996.

(Unused score) *Ransom,* Buena Vista, 1996.

Striptease, Columbia, 1996.

That Thing You Do!, Twentieth Century–Fox, 1996.

The Truth about Cats & Dogs, Twentieth Century–Fox, 1996.

Cop Land, Miramax, 1997.

(Including song "Room 277") *The Game,* Polygram Filmed Entertainment, 1997.

Dogma (also known as *Bearclaw, God,* and *Dogme*), Miramax, 1998.

Silver, 1998.

Analyze This (also known as *Analyze Me, Mafia blues, Analizame, Analyse–moi ca, Analyse to, Analysera mera!, Depresja gangstera, Familieterapi, Mafia no diva, Reine Nervensache, Terapia e pallottole, Terapian tarpeessa, Uma questao de nervos, Una terapia peligrosa,* and *Una terapia peligrosa (Analyze this)*), Warner Bros., 1999.

eXistenZ, Dimension Films, 1999.

Gloria, Columbia, 1999.

Camera (short film), 2000.

The Cell, New Line Cinema, 2000.

Esther Kahn (also known as *eSTHeR KaHN*), Bac Films, 2000.

High Fidelity, Buena Vista, 2000.

(Including song "Saturn") *The Yards,* Miramax, 2000.

(Including song "In Dreams") *The Lord of the Rings: The Fellowship of the Ring* (also known as *The Fellowship of the Ring, The Lord of the Rings: The Fellowship of the Ring: The Motion Picture, A Gyrueruek ura: A gyuerue szoevetsege, Der Herr der Ringe: Die Gefaehrten, El senor de los anillos: La comunidad del anillo, El senyor dels anells: La comunitat de l'anell, Hringadrottinssaga: Foeruneyti hringsins, Il signore degli anelli—La compagnia dell'anello, Le seigneur des anneaux–La communaute de l'anneau, O senhor dos aneis—A irmandade do anel, O senhor dos aneis: A sociedade do anel, Pan prstenu: Spolecenstvo prstenu, Ringenes herre: Eventyret om ringen, Ringenes herre: Ringens brorskap, Sagan om ringen: Haerskarringen, Sormuste isand: Sormuse vennaskond, Stapinul inelelor: Fratia inelului, Tara sormusten herrasta—Sormuksen ritarit,* and *Wladca piercsieni: Druzyna piercsienia*), New Line Cinema, 2001.

The Score, Paramount, 2001.

(Including song "Brooklyn Heights") *Gangs of New York,* Miramax, 2002.

(Including songs such as "Gollum's Song") *The Lord of the Rings: The Two Towers* (also known as *The Two Towers, Banjieui jewang du jaeeui tam, Bechdebis mbrdzanebeli, Der Herr der Ringe: Die zwei Tuerme, El senor de los anillos: Las dos torres, El senyor dels anells: Les dues torres, Hringadrottinssaga: Tveggja turna tal, Il signore degli anelli—Le due torri, Le seigneur des anneaux–Les deux tours, O senhor dos aneis: As duas torres, Ringenes herre: De to taarne, Ringenes herre: To taarn, Sagan om ringen: Sagan om de tvaa tornen, Sormuste isand: Kaks kantsi, Stapanul inelelor: Cele doua turnuri, Tara sormusten herrasta—Kaksi tornia,* and *Wladca piercsieni: Dwie wieze*), New Line Cinema, 2002.

Panic Room, Columbia/TriStar, 2002.

Spider, Sony Pictures Classics, 2002.

(Including songs such as "Into the West") *The Lord of the Rings: The Return of the King* (also known as *The Return of the King, A Gyrueruek ura: A kiraly viszater, Der Herr der Ringe: Die Rueckkehr des Koenigs, El senor de los anillos: El retorno del rey, El senyor dels anells: El retorn del rei, Gospodar prstanov: Vrnitev kralja, Hringadrottinssaga: Hilmir snyr heim, Il signore degli anelli—Il ritorno del re, Le seigneur des anneaux–Le retour du roi, O senhor dos aneis: O retorno do rei, Pan prstenu: Navrat krale, Ringenes herre: Atter en konge, Ringenes herre: Kongen vender tilbage, Sagan om ringen: Sagan om konungens aaterkomst, Sormuste isand: Kuninga tagsitulek, Tara sormusten herrasta—Kuninkaan paluu,* and *Wladca piercsieni: Powrot krola*), New Line Cinema, 2003.

The Aviator, Miramax/Warner Bros., 2004.

A History of Violence, New Line Cinema, 2005.

(Unused score) *King Kong* (also known as *King Kong: The Eighth Wonder of the World* and *Peter Jackson's "King Kong"*), Universal, 2005.

La opresion (short film), 2005.

The Departed (also known as *Departed, Infernal Affairs, A tegla, Agents troubles, Departed—Unter Feinden, The Departed—Entre inimigos, The departed—Il bene e il male, Dipateddo, Dvostruka igra, Ha–Shtoolim, Infiltracja, Kahe tule vahel, Koestebek, Les infiltres, Los infiltrados, O pliroforiodotis, Os infiltrados,* and *Parakit hoad faengtua koan chao-pho*), Warner Bros., 2006.

Too Commercial for Cannes (short film), New Line Home Video, 2006.

Eastern Promises (also known as *Epikindynes yposh-eseis, Keleti igeretek, Les promesses de l'ombre, Promesas del este, Promesses de l'ombre,* and *Toedliche Versprechen*), Alliance Atlantis Motion Picture Distribution/Focus Features, 2007.

(Including song "Hello (I Love You)") *The Last Mimzy,* New Line Cinema, 2007.

Film Music; Songs:

"Blood on White Shoes," *Frogs for Snakes,* 1998.

"Piano Four," *Last Night* (also known as *Minuit*), 1998.

"Mooby Theme Song," *Jay and Silent Bob Strike Back* (also known as *VA5* and *View Askew 5*), Miramax/Dimension Films, 2001.

Main title music, *Beat the Devil* (short film; also known as "Beat the Devil," *The Hire* and *The Hire: Beat the Devil*), BMW Films, 2002.

Television Music; Series:

(With others) *Saturday Night Live* (also known as *NBC's "Saturday Night," Saturday Night, Saturday Night Live '80, SNL,* and *SNL 25*), NBC, 1975–80.

Theme music, *Saturday Night Live* (also known as *NBC's "Saturday Night," Saturday Night, Saturday Night Live '80, SNL,* and *SNL 25*), NBC, beginning 1975.

Main title music and finale, *Antonella,* Artear (Argentina) and Channel 3 (Israel), beginning 1991.

Main title theme, *Late Night with Conan O'Brien,* NBC, 1993—.

Television Music; Specials:

Steve Martin's Best Show Ever, NBC, 1981.

The New Show, NBC, 1984.

Big Shots in America, NBC, 1985.

Additional music, *Coma,* 1997.

The Making of "Panic Room," 2002.

Late Night with Conan O'Brien: 10th Anniversary Special, NBC, 2003.

Lord of the Brush, Bravo, 2005.

Television Music; Episodic:

"Regina vs. Horvath," *Scales of Justice,* [Canada], 1990.

"Regina vs. Logan," *Scales of Justice,* [Canada], 1990.

Stage Music:

The Fly (opera; libretto by David Henry Hwang), Theatre du Chatelet, Paris, 2008, and LA Opera, Dorothy Chandler Pavilion, Los Angeles, beginning 2008.

Other Music:

Composed pieces for orchestras, concert bands, marching bands, other groups, and various instruments, including *The Lord of the Rings Symphony.*

Albums; with Lighthouse:

Lighthouse, RCA Victor, 1969.

Peacing It All Together, RCA Victor, 1970.

Suite Feeling, RCA Victor, 1970.

One Fine Morning, Evolution, 1971.

Lighthouse Live!, Evolution, 1972.

One Fine Light, RCA Victor, 1972.

Sunny Days, Edsel, 1972.

Thoughts of Movin' On, Evolution, 1972.

Can You Feel It, Polydor, 1974.

Good Day, Polydor, 1974.

Sunny Days Again: The Best of Lighthouse, MCA, 1999.

Albums Featuring Shore's Compositions:

Live from New York (also known as *Gilda Radner–Live from New York*), Warner Bros./Wea, c. 1979.

The Fly, Varese Sarabande, 1986.

Belizaire the Cajun, Arhoolie Productions, 1987.

Big, 1988, Varese Sarabande, 2002.

The Silence of the Lambs, MCA Records, 1991.

Dead Ringers: Music from the Films of David Cronenberg, Silva Screen Records, 1992.

Naked Lunch, Milan/BMG, 1992.

Prelude to a Kiss, RCA/Milan/BMG, 1992.

M. Butterfly, Varese Sarabande, 1993.

Mrs. Doubtfire, Fox Records, 1993.

The Client, Elektra Records, 1994.

Ed Wood, Hollywood Records, 1994.

Philadelphia: Original Score, Epic Records/BMG, 1994.

Philadelphia: Original Soundtrack, Epic Records/BMG, 1994.

Nobody's Fool, Milan/BMG, 1995.

Se7en, TVT Records, 1995.

White Man's Burden, Tag Recordings, 1995.

Before and After, Hollywood Records, 1996.

Crash, Milan/BMG, 1996.

Looking for Richard, Angel Records, 1996.

The Truth about Cats and Dogs, A&M Records, 1996.

Cop Land, Milan/BMG, 1997.

The Game, London Records, 1997.

Videodrome, Varese Sarabande, 1998.

Dogma, Maverick, 1999.

eXistenZ, RCA Victor/BMG, 1999.

Analyze This, Varese Sarabande, 2000.

The Cell, New Line Records, 2000.

Esther Kahn, Naive, 2000.

(With others) Various artists, *Reel Life: The Private Music of Film Composers, Vol. 1,* Arabesque Recordings, 2000.

The Yards, Sony/BMG, 2000.

The Lord of the Rings: The Fellowship of the Ring, Reprise Records, 2001.

The Score, Varese Sarabande, 2001.

Gangs of New York, Interscope Records, 2002.

The Lord of the Rings: The Two Towers, Reprise Records, 2002.

Panic Room, Varese Sarabande, 2002.

Spider, Virgin Records, 2002.

The Lord of the Rings: The Return of the King, Reprise Records, 2003.

The Aviator, Decca Records, 2005.

The Fly/Fly II, Varese Sarabande, 2005.

A History of Violence, New Line Records, 2005.

Naked Lunch—Silver Screen Edition, Milan/BMG, 2005.

The Departed: Original Score, New Line Records, 2006.

The Departed: Original Soundtrack, Warner Sunset, 2006.

The Last Mimzy, New Line Records, 2007.

Many of Shore's songs, scores, and other compositions have been featured in films, television programs, videos, albums, and other media and have been published in various formats.

Compilation Albums Featuring Shore's Compositions:

The Lord of the Rings: The Motion Picture Trilogy, Reprise, 2003.

The Lord of the Rings: Fellowship of the Ring—The Complete Recordings, Reprise, 2005.

Video Music:

Inside the Labyrinth: The Making of "The Silence of the Lambs," Metro–Goldwyn–Mayer/United Artists Home Entertainment, 2001.

Big–atures, New Line Home Video, 2002.

Costume Design (short), New Line Home Video, 2002.

A Day in the Life of a Hobbit (short), New Line Home Video, 2002.

Designing Middle–Earth (short), New Line Home Video, 2002.

Digital Grading (short), New Line Home Video, 2002.

Editorial: Assembling an Epic (short), New Line Home Video, 2002.

The Fellowship of the Cast (short), New Line Home Video, 2002.

From Book to Script (short), New Line Home Video, 2002.

J. R. R. Tolkien: Creator of Middle–Earth (short), New Line Home Video, 2002.

The Making of "The Lord of the Rings," 2002.

New Zealand as Middle–Earth (short), New Line Home Video, 2002.

The Road Goes Ever On … (short), New Line Home Video, 2002.

Scale, New Line Home Video, 2002.

The Soundscapes of Middle–Earth (short), New Line Home Video, 2002.

Storyboards and Pre–viz: Making Words into Images (short), New Line Home Video, 2002.

The Battle for Helm's Deep Is Over … (short), New Line Home Video, 2003.

Cameras in Middle–Earth, New Line Home Video, 2003.

Designing Middle–Earth (short), New Line Home Video, 2003.

Editorial: Refining the Story, New Line Home Video, 2003.

From Book to Script: Finding the Story (short), New Line Home Video, 2003.

J. R. R. Tolkien: Origins of Middle–Earth (short), New Line Home Video, 2003.

Music for Middle–Earth (short), New Line Home Video, 2003.

People Like Us: Making "Philadelphia," Columbia/ TriStar Home Video, 2003.

The Taming of Smeagol (short), New Line Home Video, 2003.

Warriors of the Third Age (short), New Line Home Video, 2003.

Weta Digital (short), New Line Home Video, 2003.

Weta Workshop (short), New Line Home Video, 2003.

Creating the Lord of the Rings Symphony: A Composer's Journey through Middle–Earth, Aurum Producciones, 2004.

Filming for Your Life: Making "After Hours" (short), Warner Home Video, 2004.

Acts of Violence, New Line Cinema, 2006.

Scoring the Silence (short), Twentieth Century–Fox Home Entertainment/Metro–Goldwyn–Mayer Home Entertainment, 2006.

Video Game Music:

The Lord of the Rings: The Two Towers (also known as *O senhor dos aneis: As duas torres*), Electronic Arts, 2002.

The Lord of the Rings: The Return of the King (also known as *O senhor dos aneis: O regresso do rei*), EA Games, 2003.

The Lord of the Rings: The Battle for Middle–Earth, 2004.

Lord of the Rings: Battle for Middle–Earth II—Rise of the Witch King, EA Games, 2006.

OTHER SOURCES

Books:

Contemporary Musicians, Volume 48, Gale, 2004.

Periodicals:

Entertainment Weekly, May 17, 2004, p. 50.

Playback, June, 2004, pp. 18–19.

Electronic:
Howard Shore, http://www.howardshore.com, August 26, 2007.

SHORE, Ryan 1974–

PERSONAL

Full name, Ryan Powell Shore; born December 29, 1974, in Toronto, Ontario, Canada; nephew of Howard Shore (a composer); married Melissa Giattino, 2005. *Education:* Berklee College of Music, graduated.

Addresses: *Agent*—Vasi Vangelos, First Artists Management, 16000 Ventura Blvd., Suite 605, Encino, CA 91436.

Career: Composer, musician, orchestrator, music producer, and music arranger. Matchbox Twenty (rock group), saxophonist; also performs as clarinetist and flutist; orchestrator, music arranger and producer, conductor, and music performer for stage benefit performances in New York City. Arts and Entertainment Network, composer of "musical identity" for *Biography* magazine and *History Channel* magazine.

Member: American Society of Composers, Authors, and Publishers.

Awards, Honors: Elmer Bernstein Scoring Award, Woodstock Film Festival, and Best Score Award, New York First Run Film Festival, both 2001, for *Cadaverous;* Clive Davis Award, best score, New York First Fun Film Festival, 2002, for *Shadowplay;* Grand Prize, best film score, Rhode Island International Film Festival, and Best Score Award, New York First Run Film Festival, both 2004, for *Rex Steele: Nazi Smasher;* nomination for Film and Television Music Awards, best score for an independent feature film, 2007, for *Numb.*

CREDITS

Film Work:
Music arranger, *Pep Squad* (also known as *I've Been Watching You 2: Prom Night*), Asylum/Thunderhead Films, 1998.
Music orchestrator, *Analyze This,* Warner Bros., 1999.
Orchestrator, *Dogma,* Lions Gate Films, 1999.
Orchestrator and conductor, *Vulgar,* Lions Gate Films, 2000.
Orchestrator, *Shadowplay* (animated short film), New York University, 2002.

Music conductor, music producer, and music performer, *Prime,* Universal, 2005.
Saxophone soloist, *Kettle of Fish,* Blue Sky Media, 2006.
Music conductor, *Jack Brooks: Monster Slayer,* Brookstreet Pictures, 2007.

Film Appearances:
(Uncredited) Violinist in string trio, *Fur: An Imaginary Portrait of Diane Arbus,* Picturehouse Entertainment, 2006.

Television Appearances; Episodic:
Musical guest, *Late Show with David Letterman* (also known as *The Late Show* and *Late Show Backstage*), CBS, 2000.

Stage Appearances:
Music performer for *Hasty Pudding: Romancing the Throne,* Harvard University, Cambridge, MA; actor and singer in *2001 Gypsy of the Year,* Palace Theatre.

Stage Work:
Worked as orchestrator, music arranger, and/or music director for various stage presentations, including *Christmas Interruptus,* Producer's Club and High Spirits Room, New York City; *Christmas with the Jollies,* Danny's Skylight Room, New York City; *Frank Skillern Show; God Bless You, Senator D'Amato,* Surf Reality Theatre, New York City; *The Land of Fake Believe,* Caroline's Comedy Club, New York City; *The Unintended Video,* Samuel Beckett Theatre, New York City; *The Vanity of Jack Kerouac,* Boston Conservatory Studio Theatre, Boston, MA; and *Wall to Wall: Frank Loesser,* Symphony Space.

RECORDINGS

Albums:
Albums from stage concerts and benefits for which Shore was orchestrator, music arranger and producer, conductor, and music performer include *Barbra Duets Album* by Steven Brinberg; *Finishing the Act* by Craig Rubano; *Now's the Time to Fall in Love* by Stephanie Pope; *Sounds of Love* by Kristopher McDowell; and *What's a Nic Girl Like You ...* by Darrin Baker.

WRITINGS

Film Music:
Earthlight, DVD International, 1998.
A Letter from the Western Front (animated short film), Ex Mortis Films, 1999.
Scout's Honor (short film), 1999.
Cadaverous (short film), 2000.

Vulgar, Lions Gate Films, 2000.

Harvard Man, Lions Gate Films, 2001.

Inherent Darkness and Enlightenment (short film), Moderncine, 2002.

Apology to Josh Fleischman (short film), 2002.

Shadowplay (animated short film), New York University, 2002.

Coney Island Baby, Frontlot Productions/double A Films, 2003.

Summer of the Serpent (short film), 2004.

Rex Steele: Nazi Smasher (animated film), Woohoo! Pictures, 2004.

212, Blue Fish Productions, 2005.

Confession, Artist View Entertainment, 2005.

Prime, Universal, 2005.

Composer of jazz songs, *Kettle of Fish,* Blue Sky Media, 2006.

Headspace, Freestyle Releasing, 2006.

Fur: An Imaginary Portrait of Diane Arbus, Picturehouse Entertainment, 2006.

Numb, Scanbox Entertainment, 2007.

The Girl Next Door (also known as *Jack Ketchum's "The Girl Next Door"*), Moderncine/Modern Girl Productions, 2007.

Senki (also known as *Shadowz*), Bavaria Film International, 2007.

Jack Brooks: Monster Slayer, Brookstreet Pictures, 2007.

Made for Each Other, Moderncine/Off Shoot Productions, 2008.

Television Music; Movies:

Song "Testin' the Waters," *Powerplay,* HBO, 1999.

Lift, Showtime, 2001.

Call Me: The Rise and Fall of Heidi Fleiss, USA Network, 2004.

Ladies Night, USA Network, 2005.

Television Music; Specials:

The Investigators: Heartshot—A Novel Idea for a Murder, Court TV, 2004.

Also provided music for *The Investigators: Made Scientist,* Court TV.

Television Music; Episodic:

"A Deadly Campaign," *Power, Privilege & Justice,* Court TV, 2004.

Television Music; Other:

Provided music for the pilot, *Desperate Housewives,* ABC; for *The Danny and Melissa Show,* Nickelodeon; and for *Twas the Night,* HBO.

Stage Music:

Composer of music for *God Bless You, Senator D'Amato,* Surf Reality Theatre, New York City; *The Van-*

ity of Jack Kerouac, Boston Conservatory Studio Theatre, Boston, MA; and *The Unintended Video,* Samuel Beckett Theatre, New York City.

OTHER SOURCES

Periodicals:

Boca Raton, May–June, 2000, pp. 73, 220.

Film Score Monthly, August, 2001, pp. 17, 48.

Hollywood Reporter, January, 2000, pp. 19, 41.

Electronic:

Ryan Shore Official Site, http://www.ryanshore.com, November 15, 2007.

SIGLER, Jamie–Lynn 1981–
(Jamie–Lynn DiScala, Jamie–Lynn Siegler)

PERSONAL

Boron May 15, 1981, in Jericho, NY; daughter of Steve (an amateur baseball player) and Consuela "Connie" (a homemaker) Sigler; married A. J. DiScala (a talent manager), July 11, 2003 (divorced, 2006). *Education:* Briefly attended New York University, c. 1999.

Addresses: *Agent*—United Talent Agency, 9560 Wilshire Blvd., Suite 500, Beverly Hills, CA 90212.

Career: Actress and singer. Appeared in stage musicals as a child; voice for commercials; appeared in print ads; spokesperson for National Eating Disorders Association and Anorexia Bulimia Association. Also worked as drama teacher and songwriter. Credited as Jamie–Lynn DiScala for the duration of her marriage, 2003–05.

Awards, Honors: YoungStar Awards, best young actress in a television drama series, *Hollywood Reporter,* 1999, 2000, Screen Actors Guild Award (with others), outstanding ensemble in a drama series, 2000, Young Artist Award nominations, best young supporting actress in a television drama series, 2000, 2001, ALMA Award nominations, outstanding actress in a television series, American Latin Media Arts Awards, 2001, 2002, and Screen Actors Guild Award nominations (with others), outstanding ensemble in a drama series, 2001, 2002, 2003, 2005, and 2007, all for *The Sopranos.*

CREDITS

Television Appearances; Series:

Meadow Soprano, *The Sopranos,* HBO, 1999–2007.

Television Appearances; Movies:

Title role, *Call Me: The Rise and Fall of Heidi Fleiss,* USA Network, 2004.

Alexis Manetti, *Lovewrecked,* ABC Family Channel, 2005.

Television Appearances; Miniseries:

I Love the '90s: Part Deux, VH1, 2005.

Maggy Rule, *The Gathering,* Lifetime, 2007.

Television Appearances; Specials:

Host, *Fake ID Club 2001,* MTV, 2001.

Intimate Portrait: Young Hollywood, Lifetime, 2002.

Broadway's Best, Bravo, 2002.

100% NYC: A Concert Celebrating the Tribeca Film Festival, MTV and VH1, 2003.

VH1 Divas, VH1, 2003.

InStyle Greatest Celebrity Weddings, VH1, 2004.

Celebrity Weddings: In Style (also known as *In Style: Celebrity Weddings*), ABC, 2004.

Presenter, *Fashion Rocks,* Fox, 2004.

The Sopranos: A Sitdown, HBO, 2007.

Television Appearances; Awards Presentations:

The 51st Annual Primetime Emmy Awards, Fox, 1999.

Presenter, *The 4th Annual Latin Grammy Awards,* CBS, 2003.

Presenter, *The 45th Annual Grammy Awards,* CBS, 2003.

Presenter, *The 60th Annual Tony Awards,* CBS, 2006.

The BRICK Awards, CW Network, 2007.

Presenter, *The 2007 ESPY Awards,* ESPN, 2007.

Television Appearances; Pilots:

Meadow Soprano, *The Sopranos,* HBO, 1999.

Television Appearances; Episodic:

Total Request Live (also known as *Total Request with Carson Daly* and *TRL*), MTV, 2001.

Celebrity Blackjack, Game Show Network, 2004.

Ro, "Queens for a Day: Parts 1 & 2," *Will & Grace,* NBC, 2004.

Ms. Fern, "Say What?/Higgly Harmonies," *Higglytown Heroes,* Disney Channel, 2005.

Herself, "The Orange Bowl," *Newlyweds: Nick & Jessica,* MTV, 2005.

Punk'd, MTV, 2005.

"Hot to Tot," *Kathy Griffin: My Life on the D-List,* Bravo, 2005.

(Uncredited) "Em Algum Lugar do Futuro," *Cidade dos Homens,* 2005.

In the Mix (also known as *In the Cutz*), Urban America Network, 2006.

(As Jamie-Lynn Siegler) "Life After ...," *20/20* (also known as *ABC News 20/20*), ABC, 2006.

Ms. Fern, "The Big Pink Elephant Sale," *Higglytown Heroes,* Disney Channel, 2007.

Entertainment Tonight (also known as *Entertainment This Week, E.T., ET Weekend,* and *This Week in Entertainment*), syndicated, 2007.

Television Guest Appearances; Episodic:

The Oprah Winfrey Show (also known as *Oprah*), syndicated, 2000.

Good Morning America, ABC, 2000, 2002.

The View, ABC, 2000, 2001, 2002.

The Rosie O'Donnell Show, syndicated, 2001.

Politically Incorrect (also known as *P.I.*), ABC, 2001.

The Tonight Show with Jay Leno, NBC, 2001.

Today (also known as *NBC News Today* and *The Today Show*), NBC, 2001.

The Big Breakfast, Channel 4, 2001.

Face to Face with Connie Chung, 2002.

The Early Show, CBS, 2002.

Last Call with Carson Daly, NBC, 2002.

The Caroline Rhea Show, syndicated, 2002.

Late Night with Conan O'Brien, NBC, 2002, 2004, 2006.

The Sharon Osbourne Show (also known as *Sharon*), syndicated, 2003.

Late Show with David Letterman (also known as *The Late Show* and *Late Show Backstage*), CBS, 2003, 2004.

Ellen: The Ellen DeGeneres Show, syndicated, 2004.

On-Air with Ryan Seacrest, syndicated, 2004.

Jimmy Kimmel Live, ABC, 2004, 2006.

Paula Zahn Now, Cable News Network, 2005.

Showbiz Tonight, Cable News Network, 2005.

Guest cohost, *The View,* ABC, 2007.

Film Appearances:

Young Angie, *A Brooklyn State of Mind,* Miramax, 1997.

Natalie, *Campfire Stories,* Velocity Home Entertainment, 2001.

Third sexy woman, *Death of a Dynasty,* TLA Releasing, 2003.

Amy Baker, *Extreme Dating,* Franchise Pictures, 2004.

Alli Butterman, *Homie Spumoni,* R-Caro Productions, 2006.

Cathy, *Dark Ride,* Lions Gate Films, 2005.

Alexa, *Blinders* (short film), Dying Art Productions, 2006.

Lynn, *New York City Serenade,* Archer Entertainment, 2007.

Stage Appearances:

Belle, *The Beauty and the Beast* (musical), Lunt-Fontanne Theatre, New York City, 2002–2003.

Appeared in productions of *Anne Frank, Annie* (musical), and *The Sound of Music* (musical).

Major Tours:
It's a Wonderful Life, U.S. cities, 1993.
Title role, *Cinderella,* U.S. cities, 2001.

RECORDINGS

Videos:
Released the music video "Cry Baby," Edel America, 1998; also appeared in the music video "Through the Rain" by Mariah Carey.

Albums:
Here to Heaven, Edel America, 2001.

WRITINGS

Autobiography:
(With Sheryl Berk) *Wise Girl: What I've Learned about Life, Love, and Loss,* Pocket Books, 2002.

OTHER SOURCES

Books:
Sigler, Jamie–Lynn, and Sheryl Berk, *Wise Girl: What I've Learned about Life, Love, and Loss,* Pocket Books, 2002.

Periodicals:
Cosmopolitan, October, 2002, p. 118.
People Weekly, April 16, 2001, p. 137; March 16, 2006, p. 81.
Teen People, September, 2002, pp. 152–154.
TV Guide, December 8, 2001, pp. 36–38; March 27, 2004, pp. 38–39; October 8, 2007, p. 70.

Electronic:
Jamie–Lynn Sigler Official Site, http://www.jamielynnsigler.com, November 15, 2007.

SINGLETON, Isaac C., Jr.
 (Isaac Singleton; Isaac C. Singleton; Isac Singleton; Isaac Singleton, Jr.)

PERSONAL

Born in Melbourne, FL; son of Isaac C. Singleton, Sr.

Addresses: *Manager*—Richard Schwartz Management, 2934 ½ Beverly Glen Circle, Suite 107, Bel Air, CA 90077.

Career: Actor. Appeared in television commercial for Bud Light, 2005.

CREDITS

Film Appearances:
(As Isac Singleton) Samson, *McCinsey's Island,* Big Island Productions, 1998.
Black pirate, *Pirates: 3D Show* (short; also known as *Pirates 4D*), 1999.
Mo Cooper, *Ready, Willing & Able,* Showcase Entertainment, 1999.
Sarris' guard, *Galaxy Quest,* DreamWorks, 1999.
Kidnapper, *Charlie's Angels* (also known as *3 Engel fur Charlie*), Columbia, 2000.
Guard number one, *Fish* (short), 2001.
Thug in alley, *The Falkland Man* (also known as *Final Assault* and *Los Bravos*), Creative Light Entertainment, 2001.
Limbo's second handler and first ape soldier, *Planet of the Apes,* Twentieth Century–Fox, 2001.
(As Isaac Singleton, Jr.) Air marshal, *Anger Management,* 2003.
Bo'sun, *Pirates of the Caribbean: The Curse of the Black Pearl* (also known as *P.O.T.C.*), Buena Vista, 2003.
Attendant Rufus, *Breaking Dawn,* Lions Gate Films Home Entertainment, 2004.
Doctor, *Wit's End,* 2005.
The butcher, *2001 Maniacs,* Lions Gate Films, 2005.
Xerox, *Hooked* (short), 2006.
A. J., *Duel of Legends,* 2007.
Gregor, *The Perfect Sleep,* Destiny Entertainment Productions, 2007.

Film Stunts:
Rosewood, Warner Bros., 1997.

Television Appearances; Series:
Incognito, *Herushingu* (also known as *Hellsing*), 2001.
In the corner with Brian Vermeire's announcer, *Open Call,* 2004.

Television Appearances; Movies:
Kelly Richaurd, *Polly and Marie,* 2007.

Television Appearances; Specials:
Planet of the Apes: Rule the Planet, Fox, 2001.

Television Appearances; Pilots:
Tarzan's Return, syndicated, 1996.

Television Appearances; Episodic:
First roughneck, "Triangle," *The X–Files,* Fox, 1998.

(As Isaac Singleton, Jr.) Bouncer, "Sabrina and the Pirates," *Sabrina, the Teenage Witch* (also known as *Sabrina*), ABC, 1999.

(As Isaac C. Singleton) Maggio, "My Man Sammo," *Martial Law,* CBS, 1999.

(As Isaac Singleton) "Revenge of the Jirds," *Sheena,* syndicated, 2000.

Rudy Coombs, "Blue Christmas," *Crossing Jordan,* NBC, 2001.

Karsh, *Wanted,* TNT, 2004.

RECORDINGS

Video Games:

Voice of Lurtz, *The Lord of the Rings: The Battle for Middle-Earth,* 2004.

(As Isaac Singleton, Jr.) *Dungeons & Dragons: Dragonshard,* Infogames UK Ltd., 2005.

Voice, *The Incredibles: Rise of the Underminer,* 2005.

(As Isaac Singleton, Jr.) Lurtz, *The Lord of the Rings: The Battle for Middle-Earth II,* Electronic Arts, 2006.

Voice of Lurtz, *Lord of the Rings: Battle for Middle Earth II—Rise of the Witch King,* EA Games, 2006.

(As Isaac Singleton) Voice, *Supreme Commander,* THQ, 2007.

SMITH, Maggie 1934–

PERSONAL

Full name, Margaret Natalie Smith; born December 28, 1934, in Ilford, Essex, England; daughter of Nathaniel (a public health pathologist) and Margaret (a secretary; maiden name, Hutton) Smith; married Robert Stephens (an actor and producer), June 29, 1967 (divorced, May, 1974 or February, 1975); married Beverley Cross (a playwright and screenwriter), June 23, 1975 (died March 20, 1998); children: (first marriage) Chris Larkin (an actor), Toby (an actor). *Education:* Trained for the stage at Oxford Playhouse School, Oxford, England.

Addresses: *Agent*—Toni Howard, International Creative Management, 10250 Constellation Way, Ninth Floor, Los Angeles, CA 90067; ICM London, Oxford House, 76 Oxford St., London W1D 1BS, England.

Career: Actress. Old Vic Theatre Company, London, member of company, 1959–63; National Theatre Company, London, charter member of company, 1963–70; Stratford Festival of Canada, Stratford, Ontario, Canada, member of company, 1976–80. Appeared in advertisements. Chichester Cinema at New Park, vice president.

Member: British Academy of Film and Television Arts (fellow), United British Artists (director, beginning 1982), Academy of Motion Pictures Arts and Sciences.

Awards, Honors: Film Award nomination, most promising newcomer, British Academy of Film and Television Arts, 1959, for *Nowhere to Go; Evening Standard* Award, best actress, 1962, for *The Private Ear* and *The Public Eye;* Variety Club Award, best actress, 1963, for *Mary, Mary;* Golden Globe Award nomination, most promising newcomer—female, 1964, for *The V.I.P.s;* Academy Award nomination, best actress in a supporting role, and Golden Globe Award nomination, best motion picture actress—drama, both 1966, for *Othello;* Film Award nomination, best British actress, British Academy of Film and Television Arts, 1966, for *Young Cassidy;* nomination for Golden Laurel Award, outstanding female new face, Producers Guild of America, 1966; Society of Film and Television Arts Award, 1969, Academy Award, best actress in a leading role, Film Award, best actress, British Academy of Film and Television Arts, Golden Globe Award nomination, best motion picture actress—drama, and nomination for Golden Laurel Award, best female dramatic performance, all 1970, for *The Prime of Miss Jean Brodie; Evening Standard* Award, best actress, 1970, for *Hedda Gabler;* Los Angeles Drama Critics Circle Award, performance, 1970, for *The Three Sisters;* decorated commander, Order of the British Empire, 1970 (some sources cite 1969), decorated dame commander, 1990; honorary D.Litt., University of St. Andrews, 1971, and Cambridge University, 1994 (some sources cite 1995); Variety Club Award, best actress, 1972, Outer Critics Circle Award, distinguished performance, Antoinette Perry Award nomination, best actress in a play, and Drama Desk Award nomination, outstanding actress in a play, all 1975, all for *Private Lives;* Academy Award nomination, best actress, and Golden Globe Award nomination, best motion picture actress—musical/comedy, both 1973, for *Travels with My Aunt;* Film Award nomination, best supporting actress, British Academy of Film and Television Arts, 1979, for *Death on the Nile;* Academy Award and Kansas City Film Critics Circle Award, best supporting actress, and Golden Globe Award, best motion picture actress—musical/comedy, all 1979, *Evening Standard* British Film Award, best actress, 1980, and Film Award nomination, best supporting actress, British Academy of Film and Television Arts, 1980, all for *California Suite;* Antoinette Perry Award nomination, best actress in a play, 1980, and Outer Critics Circle Award, distinguished performance, both for *Night and Day; Evening Standard* Award, best actress, 1981, for *Virginia; Evening Standard* British Film Award and Film Award nomination, British Academy of Film and Television Arts, both best actress, 1982, for *Quartet;* Saturn Award nomination, best supporting actress, Academy of Science Fiction, Fantasy, and Horror Films, 1982, for *Clash of the Titans;* Television Award nomination, best actress, British Academy of Film and Television Arts, 1983, for *Mrs. Silly;* Film

Award, best actress, British Academy of Film and Television Arts, 1985, for *A Private Function; Evening Standard* Award, best actress, 1985, for *The Way of the World;* Taormina Gold Award, 1985; Kansas City Film Critics Circle Award, Academy Award nomination, and Film Award nomination, British Academy of Film and Television Arts, all best supporting actress, and Golden Globe Award, best performance by an actress in a supporting role in a motion picture, all 1987, for *A Room with a View;* Film Award, British Academy of Film and Television Arts, and *Evening Standard* British Film Award, both best actress, 1989, for *The Lonely Passion of Judith Hearne;* Royal Television Society Award, best actor—female, and Television Award nomination, best actress, British Academy of Film and Television Arts, both 1989, for "Bed among the Lentils," *Talking Heads;* Antoinette Perry Award and Outer Critics Circle Award, both best actress in a play, 1990, for *Lettice and Lovage;* Hanbury Shakespeare Prize, FVS Foundation, 1991; fellow, British Film Institute, 1992; Emmy Award nomination, best actress in a miniseries or special, 1993, for *Suddenly, Last Summer;* Television Award nomination, best actress, British Academy of Film and Television Arts, 1993, for *Memento Mori;* Special Lifetime Achievement Award, British Academy of Film and Television Arts, 1993; Film Award nomination, best supporting actress, British Academy of Film and Television Arts, 1994, for *The Secret Garden;* inducted into the Theatre Hall of Fame, 1994; *Evening Standard* Award, best actress, 1996, for *Three Tall Women;* National Board of Review Award (with others), best ensemble cast, 1996, for *The First Wives Club;* Laurence Olivier Award nomination, best actress, Society of West End Theatre, 1998, for *A Delicate Balance;* Chlotrudis Award nomination, best supporting actress, 1998, for *Washington Square;* William Shakespeare Award for Classical Theatre, Shakespeare Theatre, Washington, DC, 1999; Film Award, best performance by an actress in a supporting role, British Academy of Film and Television Arts, 2000, for *Tea with Mussolini;* Emmy Award nomination, outstanding supporting actress in a miniseries or movie, and Television Award nomination, best actress, British Academy of Film and Television Arts, both 2000, for *David Copperfield;* Laurence Olivier Award nomination, best actress, 2000, for *The Lady in the Van;* named one of the greatest British film actresses, Orange Film Survey, 2001; Southeastern Film Critics Association Award, best supporting actress, 2001, Golden Satellite Award, International Press Academy, Kansas City Film Critics Circle Award, Academy Award nomination, Film Award nomination, British Academy of Film and Television Arts, Chicago Film Critics Association Award nomination, Phoenix Film Critics Society Award nomination, and Online Film Critics Society Award nomination, all best supporting actress, Golden Globe Award nomination, best performance by an actress in a supporting role in a motion picture, and Audience Award nomination, best actress, European Film awards, all 2002, for *Gosford Park;* Screen Actors Guild Award, Critics Choice Award, Broadcast Film Critics Association, Florida Film Critics

Circle Award, Special Achievement Award from the Golden Satellite awards, International Press Academy, Online Film Critics Society Award, and Phoenix Film Critics Society Award nomination, all best ensemble cast, all with others, 2002, for *Gosford Park;* Saturn Award nomination, best supporting actress, 2002, for *Harry Potter and the Sorcerer's Stone;* Phoenix Film Critics Society Award nomination (with others), best ensemble cast, 2003, for *Harry Potter and the Chamber of Secrets;* Emmy Award, outstanding lead actress in a miniseries or movie, 2003, and Golden Globe Award nomination and Golden Satellite Award nomination, both best performance by an actress in a miniseries or a motion picture made for television, both 2004, all for *My House in Umbria;* Audience Award nomination (with Judi Dench), best actress, European Film awards, 2005, for *Ladies in Lavender;* honored with a star on Great Britain's Avenue of Stars.

CREDITS

Film Appearances:

(Uncredited) Party guest, *Child in the House,* 1956.

Bridget Howard, *Nowhere to Go,* 1958.

Chantal, *Go to Blazes,* 1962.

Miss Mead, *The V.I.P.s* (also known as *International Hotel*), Metro–Goldwyn–Mayer, 1963.

Philpott, *The Pumpkin Eater* (also known as *Bitter frugt, Frenesia del piacere, Le mangeur de citrouilles, Neljas avioliittoni,* and *Siempre estoy sola*), Columbia/Royal Films International, 1964.

Desdemona, *Othello,* Warner Bros., 1965.

Herself, *Sean O'Casey: The Spirit of Ireland* (short film; also known as *Sean O'Casey: El espiritu de Irlanda*), 1965.

Nora, *Young Cassidy* (also known as *Cassidy, der Rebell, El sonador rebelde, Il magnifico irlandese, Le jeune Cassidy, Nuori Cassidy—kapinanlietsoja, O rebelde sonhador, Oproreren,* and *Uppviglaren*), Metro–Goldwyn–Mayer, 1965.

Sarah Watkins, *The Honey Pot* (also known as *Anyone for Venice?, It Comes Up Murder,* and *Mr. Fox of Venice*), United Artists, 1967.

Patty Terwilliger Smith, *Hot Millions,* Metro–Goldwyn–Mayer, 1968.

Jean Brodie, *The Prime of Miss Jean Brodie,* Twentieth Century–Fox, 1969.

Music hall star, *Oh! What a Lovely War,* Paramount, 1969.

Aunt Augusta Bertram, *Travels with My Aunt,* Metro–Goldwyn–Mayer, 1972.

Lila Fisher, *Love and Pain (and the Whole Damn Thing)* (also known as *Love and Pain and the Whole Damn Thing* and *Love, Pain and the Whole Damn Thing*), Columbia, 1973.

Dora Charleston, *Murder by Death* (also known as *Assassinato por morte, Eine Leiche zum Dessert, Invito a cena con delitto, Middag med mord, Mord med doden til folge, Murha, murha, paeaestae-kaeae etsivaet irti!, Slaepp deckarna loss, det aer mord, Un cadaver a los postres,* and *Un cadavre au dessert),* Columbia, 1976.

Diana Barrie, *California Suite* (also known as *Neil Simon's "California Suite"),* Columbia, 1978.

Miss Bowers, *Death on the Nile* (also known as *Agatha Christie's "Death on the Nile," Assassinio sul Nilo, Doden paa Nilen, Doeden paa Nilen, Eglima sto Neilo, Kuolema Niilillae, Morte no Nilo, Morte sobre o Nilo, Mort sur le Nil, Smierc Nilu,* and *Tod auf dem Nil),* Paramount, 1978.

Lois Heidler, *Quartet,* New World Pictures, 1981.

Thetis, *Clash of the Titans,* United Artists, 1981.

Daphne Castle, *Evil under the Sun* (also known as *Agatha Christie's "Evil under the Sun"* and *Maldad bajo el sol),* Universal, 1982.

Lady Isabel Ames, *The Missionary,* Columbia, 1982.

Miss Anderson, *Better Late Than Never* (also known as *Whose Little Girl Are You?),* Galaxy, 1983.

Joyce Chilvers, *A Private Function,* New Yorker Films/Island Alive, 1985.

Lily Wynn, *Lily in Love* (also known as *Playing for Keeps* and *Jatszani kell),* New Line Cinema, 1985.

Charlotte Bartlett, *A Room with a View,* Cinecom International, 1986.

Judith Hearne, *The Lonely Passion of Judith Hearne,* Island Pictures, 1987.

Voice of Rozaline, *Romeo–Juliet,* 1990.

Granny Wendy Moira Angel Darling, *Hook,* TriStar, 1992.

Mother Superior, *Sister Act* (also known as *Apaca show, Cambio de habito, Do cabare para o convento, En vaersting till syster, Halloj i klosteret, Mudanca de habito, Nune pojejo, Nunnia ja konnia, Rock 'n' nonne, Sister Act—Eine himmlische Karriere, Sister Act: una monja de cuidado, Sister Act—una svitata in abito da suora,* and *Una monja de cuidado),* Buena Vista, 1992.

Mrs. Medlock, *The Secret Garden,* Warner Bros., 1993.

Mother Superior, *Sister Act 2: Back in the Habit* (also known as *Apaca–show 2., Cambio de habito 2, Cambio de habito 2: Mas locuras en el convento, Do cabare para o convento 2, En vaersting till syster II, En vaersting till syster 2—Redo att synda igen, Halloj i klosteret 2—Nonnernes hus, Mudanca de habito 2: Mais confusoes no convento, Mudanca de habito 2: Mais loucuras no convento, Nune pojejo 2, Nunnia ja konnia 2: Lisaeae saepinaeae, Rock 'n' nonne 2: De retour au couvent, Sister Act, acte 2, Sister Act 2: de vuelta al convento, Sister Act 2—In goettlicher Mission,* and *Sister act 2—piu svitata che mai),* Buena Vista, 1993.

Duchess of York, *Richard III,* Metro–Goldwyn–Mayer, 1995.

Gunilla Garson Goldberg, *The First Wives Club* (also known as *Der Club der Teufelinnen, El club de las divorciadas, El club de las primeras esposas, El club de las primeres esposes, Elvalt noek klubja, Foere detta fruars klubb, Forstekoneklubben, Hylaettyjen vaimojen kerho, Il club delle prime mogli, Ilk esler kuluebue, Klub vrazjih babnic, Le club des ex, O clube das desquitadas, O clube das divorciadas,* and *Zmowa pierwszych zon),* Paramount, 1996.

Aunt Lavinia Penniman, *Washington Square,* Buena Vista, 1997.

Lady Hester Random, *Tea with Mussolini* (also known as *Un te con Mussolini),* G2 Films, 1999.

Lady Myra Naylor, *The Last September,* Trimark Pictures, 1999.

Constance (Countess of Trentham), *Gosford Park,* USA Films, 2001.

Professor Minerva McGonagall, *Harry Potter and the Sorcerer's Stone* (also known as *Harry Potter, Harry Potter and the Philosopher's Stone, Harry Potter a kamen mudrcu, Harry Potter a l'ecole des sorciers, Harry Potter e a pedra filosofal, Harry Potter e la pietra filosofale, Harry Potter en de steen der wijzen, Harry Potter es a boelcsek koeve, Harry Potter i kamien filozoficzny, Harry Potter i la pedra filosofal, Harry Potter ja viisasten kivi, Harry Potter och de vises sten, Harry Potter og de vises stein, Harry Potter og de vises sten, Harry Potter og viskusteinninn, Harry Potter und der Stein der Weisen,* and *Harry Potter y la piedra filosofal),* Warner Bros., 2001.

Caro Eliza Bennett, *Divine Secrets of the Ya–Ya Sisterhood* (also known as *Clan Ya–Ya, The Secrets of Ya–Ya, Die Goettlichen Geheimnisse der Ya–Ya–Schwestern, Divinos secretos, Divinos segredos, Exomologiseis gynaikon, I sublimi segreti delle Ya–Ya Sisters, Jumalaiset Ja Ja siskot, Jumalaiset ja-jasiskot, Les divins secrets, Les divins secrets des petites Ya–Ya, Ya–Ya flickornas gudomliga hemligheter, Ya–Ya–flickornas gudomliga hemligheter,* and *Ya–ya–sostrenes guddommelige hemmeligheder),* Warner Bros., 2002.

Professor Minerva McGonagall, *Harry Potter and the Chamber of Secrets* (also known as *Incident on 57th Street, Harry Potter a tajemna komnata, Harry Potter e a camara dos segredos, Harry Potter e a secreta, Harry Potter e la camera dei segreti, Harry Potter en de geheime kamer, Harry Potter es a titkok kamraja, Harry Potter et la chambre des secrets, Harry Potter i la cambra secreta, Harry Potter ja salaisuuksien kammio, Harry Potter och hemlighet-ernas kammare, Harry Potter og hemmelighedernes kammer, Harry Potter og leyniklefinn, Harry Potter og mysteriekammeret, Harry Potter si camera secretelor, Harry Potter und die Kammer des Schreckens, Harry Potter y la camara de los secretos,* and *Harry Potter y la camara secreta),* Warner Bros., 2002.

Professor Minerva McGonagall, *Harry Potter and the Prisoner of Azkaban* (also known as *Harry Potter e il prigioniero di Azkaban, Harry Potter en de gevangene van Azkaban, Harry Potter e o prisioneiro de Azkaban, Harry Potter et le prisonnier d'Azkaban, Harry Potter i el pres d'Azkaban, Harry Potter ja Azkabanin vanki, Harry Potter och faan-*

gen fraan Azkaban, *Harry Potter og fangen fra Az-kaban, Harry Potter og fanginn fra Azkaban, Harry Potter und der Gefangene von Askaban,* and *Harry Potter y el prisionero de Azkaban*), Warner Bros., 2004, IMAX version released as *Harry Potter and the Prisoner of Azkaban: The IMAX Experience.*

Grace Hawkins, *Keeping Mum,* ThinkFilm, 2005.

Janet Widdington, *Ladies in Lavender,* Roadside Attractions, 2005.

Professor Minerva McGonagall, *Harry Potter and the Goblet of Fire* (also known as *Harry Potter e il calice di fuoco, Harry Potter en de vuurbeker, Harry Potter e o calice de fogo, Harry Potter et la coupe de feu, Harry Potter i el calze de foc, Harry Potter ja liekehtivae pikari, Harry Potter och den flammande baegaren, Harry Potter og eldbikarinn, Harry Potter og flammernes pokal, Harry Potter og ildbegeret, Harry Potter und der Feuerkelch, Harry Potter y el caliz de fuego,* and *O Harry Potter kai to kypelo tis fotias*), Warner Bros., 2005, IMAX version released as Harry Potter and the *Goblet of Fire: The IMAX Experience.*

Lady Gresham, *Becoming Jane,* Miramax, 2007.

Professor Minerva McGonagall, *Harry Potter and the Order of the Phoenix* (also known as *Tip Top, Hari Poter i Red Feniksa, Harry Potter e a Ordem da Fenix, Harry Potter e l'ordine della Fenice, Harry Potter en de orde van de feniks, Harry Potter es a Foenix Rendje, Harry Potter et l'ordre du phenix, Harry Potter i l'orde del Fenix, Harry Potter ja feeniksin kilta, Harry Potter och fenixordern, Harry Potter og foniksordenen, Harry Potter und der Orden des Phoenix,* and *Harry Potter y la orden del Fenix*), Warner Bros., 2007.

Stage Appearances:

Viola, *Twelfth Night* (also known as *Twelfth Night, or What You Will*), Oxford Dramatic Society, Oxford Playhouse, Oxford, England, 1952.

Performer, *New Faces 56 Revue* (musical revue; also known as *New Faces of 1956* and *New Faces of '56*), Ethel Barrymore Theatre, New York City, 1956.

Performer, *Share My Lettuce,* Lyric Theatre Hammersmith, then Comedy Theatre, both London, 1957.

Vera Dane, *The Stepmother,* St. Martin's Theatre, London, 1958.

Celia, *As You Like It,* Old Vic Theatre, London, 1959–60.

Lady Plyant, *The Double Dealer,* Old Vic Theatre, 1959–60.

Maggie Wylie, *What Every Woman Knows,* Old Vic Theatre, 1959–60.

Mistress Ford, *The Merry Wives of Windsor,* Old Vic Theatre, 1959–60.

The queen, *Richard II,* Old Vic Theatre, 1959–60.

Daisy, *Rhinoceros,* Strand Theatre, London, 1960.

Lucile, *The Rehearsal,* Royal Theatre, then Bristol Old Vic Theatre, Globe Theatre (now Gielgud Theatre),

London, Queen's Theatre, London, and Apollo Theatre, London, 1961.

Doreen, *The Private Ear,* and Belinda, *The Public Eye* (double–bill), Globe Theatre (now Gielgud Theatre), 1962.

Narrator, *Pictures in the Hallway* (dramatic reading), Mermaid Theatre, London, 1962.

Mary (title role), *Mary, Mary,* Queen's Theatre, 1963.

Silvia, *The Recruiting Officer,* National Theatre Company, Old Vic Theatre, 1963.

Beatrice, *Much Ado about Nothing,* National Theatre Company, Old Vic Theatre, 1964.

Desdemona, *Othello,* National Theatre Company, Old Vic Theatre, then Chichester Festival Theatre, Chichester, England, 1964.

Hilda Wangel, *The Master Builder,* National Theatre Company, Old Vic Theatre, 1964.

Myra, *Hay Fever,* National Theatre Company, Old Vic Theatre, 1964.

Clea, *Black Comedy,* National Theatre Company, Old Vic Theatre, 1965.

Title role, *Miss Julie,* National Theatre Company, Old Vic Theatre, 1965–66.

Marcela, *A Bond Honoured,* National Theatre Company, Old Vic Theatre, 1966.

Margery Pinchwife, *The Country Wife,* National Theatre Company, Old Vic Theatre, 1969.

Title role, *Hedda Gabler,* National Theatre Company, Old Vic Theatre, 1970.

Masha, *The Three Sisters,* National Theatre Company, Old Vic Theatre, then Center Theatre Group, Mark Taper Forum, Los Angeles, 1970.

Mrs. Sullen, *The Beaux' Stratagem,* National Theatre Company, Old Vic Theatre, 1970.

Amanda Prynne, *Private Lives,* Queen's Theatre, 1972.

Title role, *Peter Pan,* Theatre at the Coliseum, London, 1973, then Los Angeles production, 1974, later Forty–Sixth Street Theatre, New York City, 1975.

Connie Hudson, *Snap,* Vaudeville Theatre, London, 1974.

Amanda Prynne, *Private Lives,* Forty–Sixth Street Theatre, 1975.

Cleopatra, *Antony and Cleopatra,* Stratford Festival of Canada, Avon Theatre, Stratford, Ontario, Canada, 1976.

Masha, *The Three Sisters,* Stratford Festival of Canada, Avon Theatre, 1976.

Millamant, *The Way of the World,* Stratford Festival of Canada, Avon Theatre, 1976.

The actress, *The Guardsman,* Ahmanson Theatre, Los Angeles, 1976, then Stratford Festival of Canada, 1977–78.

Lady Macbeth, *Macbeth,* Stratford Festival of Canada, Avon Theatre, 1976, 1977–78.

Amanda Prynne, *Private Lives,* Stratford Festival of Canada, Avon Theatre, 1977–78.

Judith Bliss, *Hay Fever,* Stratford Festival of Canada, Avon Theatre, 1977–78.

The queen, *Richard II,* Stratford Festival of Canada, Avon Theatre, 1977–78.

Rosalind, *As You Like It,* Stratford Festival of Canada, Avon Theatre, 1977–78.

Titania and Hippolyta, *A Midsummer Night's Dream,* Stratford Festival of Canada, Avon Theatre, 1977–78.

Ruth Carson, *Night and Day,* Phoenix Theatre, London, then John F. Kennedy Center for the Performing Arts, Washington, DC, and American National Theatre and Academy (ANTA) Playhouse, New York City, 1979–80.

Beatrice, *Much Ado about Nothing,* Stratford Festival of Canada, Avon Theatre, 1980.

Masha, *The Seagull,* Stratford Festival of Canada, Avon Theatre, 1980.

Virginia Woolf (title role), *Virginia,* Stratford Festival of Canada, Avon Theatre, 1980, then West End production, 1981.

Millamant, *The Way of the World,* Chichester Festival Theatre, 1984–85.

Jocasta, *The Infernal Machine,* Lyric Theatre Hammersmith, 1986.

Nadia, *Interpreters,* Queen's Theatre, 1986.

Halina, *Coming into Land,* National Theatre, Lyttelton Theatre, London, 1987.

Lettice Douffet, *Lettice and Lovage,* Globe Theatre (now Gielgud Theatre), 1987–90, then Ethel Barrymore Theatre, 1990.

Lady Bracknell, *The Importance of Being Earnest,* London, 1993.

Three Tall Women, Wyndham's Theatre, London, 1994–95.

Susan, *Bed among the Lentils* (also known as "Bed among the Lentils," *Talking Heads*), Chichester Festival Theatre, Minerva Theatre, 1996.

Claire, *A Delicate Balance,* Theatre Royal Haymarket, London, 1997, 1998.

Miss Shepherd, *The Lady in the Van,* Queen's Theatre, 1999–2000.

Madeleine Palmer, *The Breath of Life,* Theatre Royal Haymarket, 2002–2003.

Elizabeth, *The Lady from Dubuque,* Theatre Royal Haymarket, 2007.

Some sources cite appearances in other productions, including *The War Plays.*

Major Tours:

Kathy, *Strip the Willow,* 1960.

Susan, *Bed among the Lentils* (also known as "Bed among the Lentils," *Talking Heads*), cities in Australia and New Zealand, 2004.

Toured with *On the Fringe* (revue), Scottish cities, then London.

Stage Work:

Worked as an assistant stage manager, Oxford Playhouse, Oxford, England.

Television Appearances; Miniseries:

Aunt Betsey Trotwood, *David Copperfield,* BBC, 1999, broadcast on *Masterpiece Theatre* (also known as *ExxonMobil Masterpiece Theatre* and *Mobil Masterpiece Theatre*), PBS, 2000.

Herself, *Francesco's Italy: Top to Toe,* BBC, 2006.

Television Appearances; Movies:

Title role, *Mrs. Silly,* Granada Television, 1983.

Mrs. Mabel Pettigrew, *Memento Mori,* BBC, 1992, broadcast on *Masterpiece Theatre* (also known as *ExxonMobil Masterpiece Theatre* and *Mobil Masterpiece Theatre*), PBS, c. 1992.

Lily Marlowe, *Curtain Call,* Starz!, 1999.

Queen Alexandra, *All the King's Men* (also known as *Todos os homens do rei*), BBC, 1999, broadcast on *Masterpiece Theatre* (also known as *ExxonMobil Masterpiece Theatre* and *Mobil Masterpiece Theatre*), PBS, 2000.

Mrs. Emily Delahunty, *My House in Umbria* (also known as *La mia casa in Umbria, Ma maison en Ombre, Mein Haus in Umbrien, Mi casa en Umbria,* and *Ta mystiria tou paradeisou*), HBO, 2003.

Mary, *Capturing Mary,* BBC, 2007.

Television Appearances; Specials:

Dixie Evans, "The Big Knife," *ITV Play of the Week* (also known as *Play of the Week*), Independent Television (England), 1958.

"Hay Fever," *ITV Play of the Week* (also known as *Play of the Week*), Independent Television, 1960.

Beatrice, *Much Ado about Nothing,* BBC, 1967, syndicated, 1971.

Ann Whitefield, "Man and Superman," *Play of the Month,* BBC, 1968.

Irina Arkadina, "The Seagull," *Play of the Month,* BBC, 1968.

Epifania, "The Millionairess," *Play of the Month,* BBC, 1972.

Portia, "The Merchant of Venice," *Play of the Month,* BBC, 1972.

(In archive footage) Miss Bowers, *Death on the Nile: Making of Featurette,* 1978.

Herself and Daphne Castle, *The Making of Agatha Christie's "Evil under the Sun,"* 1982.

(Uncredited; in archive footage) Actress in *Quartet, The Wandering Company,* 1984.

Mrs. Violet Venable, *Suddenly, Last Summer,* BBC–2, 1993, broadcast on *Great Performances,* PBS, 1993.

(In archive footage) *50 Years of Funny Females* (also known as *Fifty Years of Funny Females*), ABC, 1995.

Herself, *Agnieszka Holland on the Set,* 1997.

Herself, *On the Set of "Washington Square,"* [Poland], 1997.

(In archive footage) Professor Minerva McGonagall, *J. K. Rowling: Harry Potter and Me,* BBC, 2002.

Herself, *Inside "Harry Potter and the Goblet of Fire,"* 2005.

Appeared in other television programs.

Television Appearances; Awards Presentations:
Presenter, *The 24th Annual Tony Awards,* NBC, 1970.
Presenter, *The 43rd Annual Academy Awards,* NBC, 1971.
Presenter, *The 50th Annual Academy Awards,* ABC, 1978.
Presenter, *The 51st Annual Academy Awards,* ABC, 1979.
(Uncredited; in archive footage) Charlotte Bartlett, *The 59th Annual Academy Awards,* ABC, 1987.
The 44th Annual Tony Awards, CBS, 1990.
The Orange British Academy Film Awards, 2000, 2001.
Presenter, *The 74th Annual Academy Awards,* ABC, 2002.
Judi Dench: A BAFTA Tribute, BBC, 2002.
Ronnie Barker: A BAFTA Tribute, BBC, 2004.

Television Appearances; Episodic:
"Family Business," *The Makepeace Story,* BBC, 1955.
"Night of the Plague," *Kraft Theatre* (also known as *Kraft Mystery Theatre* and *Kraft Television Theatre*), NBC, 1957.
"The Widower," *Armchair Theatre,* Associated British Picture Corporation (England), 1958.
Herself, *Parkinson,* BBC, 1973.
Herself, *The Carol Burnett Show* (also known as *Carol Burnett and Friends*), CBS, 1974, 1975 (multiple episodes).
Herself, *Dinah!* (also known as *Dinah* and *Dinah and Friends*), syndicated, 1977.
Susan, "Bed among the Lentils," *Talking Heads* (also known as *Talking Heads: Bed among the Lentils*), BBC, 1988, broadcast on *Masterpiece Theatre* (also known as *ExxonMobil Masterpiece Theatre* and *Mobil Masterpiece Theatre*), PBS, 1989.
Herself, *The Rosie O'Donnell Show,* syndicated, 2001.
Herself, *When I Was a Girl,* WE (Women's Entertainment Television), 2002.
Herself, "Harry Potter and the Prisoner of Azkaban," *HBO First Look,* HBO, 2004.
(In archive footage) Herself, "Actresses," *Britain's Finest,* Channel 5 (England) and History Channel (Great Britain), 2005.
Herself, "Planet Potter," *Planet Voice,* 2005.
(In archive footage) Herself, "Sobre 'Maldad bajo el sol,'" *Ciclo Agatha Christie,* 2005.
Herself, *The Charlie Rose Show* (also known as *Charlie Rose*), PBS, 2005.
Herself, *Today* (also known as *NBC News Today* and *The Today Show*), NBC, 2005.

Television Appearances; Other:
Some sources cite appearances in *Boy Meets Girl, Home and Beauty, On Approval, A Phoenix Too Frequent,* and *Services Rendered.*

RECORDINGS

Videos:
(In archive footage) Herself, *Oscar's Greatest Moments,* 1992.
Herself, *Interviews with Professors & More,* 2003.
(Uncredited; in archive footage) Professor Minerva McGonagall, *Interviews with Students,* 2003.
(Uncredited; in archive footage) Professor Minerva McGonagall, *Creating the Vision,* 2004.
Herself, *Preparing for the Yule Ball* (short), 2006.
(In archive footage) The millionairess, *Changing Time,* 2006.
(Uncredited; in archive footage) Professor Minerva McGonagall, *Harry vs. the Horntail: The First Task,* 2006.
(In archive footage) Epifania, *Are Friends Electric,* 2007.

OTHER SOURCES

Books:
Burton, Hal, editor, *Acting in the Sixties,* BBC, 1970.
Coveney, Michael, *Maggie Smith: A Bright Particular Star,* Gollancz, 1992.
International Dictionary of Films and Filmmakers, Volume 3: *Actors and Actresses,* St. James Press, fourth edition, 2000.
International Dictionary of Theatre, Volume 3: *Actors, Directors, and Designers,* St. James Press, 1996.

Periodicals:
Economist, November 16, 2002, pp. 84–85.
Entertainment Weekly, February 22, 2002, p. 56; March 15, 2002, pp. 32–34.
New York Times, January 7, 1989; March 18, 1990.
New York Times Magazine, March 18, 1990.
Observer (London), November 18, 1982.
People Weekly, April 28, 1986, p. 47.
Premiere, April, 2002, p. 92.
Radio Times, September 26, 1992.
Show, November, 1972.
Telegraph, November 12, 1994, pp. 40–41, 43.
Times (London), July 14, 1990.

SMITH, Stephen
    See McHATTIE, Stephen

SNAKE, Abe
    See LOCKE, Peter

SNYDER, David L. 1944–
(David Snyder)

PERSONAL

Born September 22, 1944, in Buffalo, NY; son of Albert R. and Louise M. (maiden name, Passero) Snyder; married Terry Finn (an actress), August 1, 1990; children: David Michael (in corporate sales), Amy Lynne Snyder–Taylor (a makeup artist), Finn Henry (an actor). *Politics:* Democrat. *Avocational Interests:* Film history.

Addresses: *Agent*—Innovative Artists Talent and Literary Agency, 1505 10th St., Santa Monica, CA 90401.

Career: Production designer, art director, visual consultant, concept director, producer, second unit director, and set director. Long Wharf Theatre, New Haven, CT, technical director, 1971–72; Snyder Bros. Productions, Inc., Hollywood, Los Angeles, president. Speaker at film festivals and universities, including the Tokyo International Film Festival, American Film Institute, University of California, Los Angeles, University of California, San Diego, and Ryerson Polytechnic University. Free Thinkers (rock band), drummer and vocalist; worked as architectural designer and toy designer.

Member: Academy of Motion Picture Arts and Sciences, National Academy of Television Arts and Sciences, Motion Picture Art Directors Guild, Directors Guild of America.

Awards, Honors: Film Award, best production design, British Academy of Film and Television Arts, London Critics Circle Film Award, special achievement, and Academy Award nomination, best art direction–set decoration, all with others, 1983, for *Blade Runner.*

CREDITS

Film Production Designer:

Strange Brew (also known as *The Adventures of Bob & Doug McKenzie* and *The Adventures of Bob & Doug McKenzie: Strange Brew*), Metro–Goldwyn–Mayer/United Artists, 1983.
Racing with the Moon, Paramount, 1984.
The Woman in Red, Orion, 1984.
My Science Project, Buena Vista, 1985.
Pee–wee's Big Adventure (also known as *Pee–wee Big Adventure, A grande aventura de Pee Wee, Ha–Harptka Ha–Gdola Shel Pee Wee Herman, La gran aventura de Pee–wee, Pee–ween suuri seikkailu, Pee–wees irre Abenteuer,* and *Pee–Wees stora aventyr*), Warner Bros., 1985.
Armed and Dangerous, Columbia, 1986.
Back to School, Orion, 1986.
Summer School, Paramount, 1987.
Moving, Warner Bros., 1988.
She's Out of Control, Columbia, 1989.
Cold Dog Soup (also known as *Cold Dog—Zur Hoelle mit dem Himmelhund, En jycke i soppan, Enterrando o cachorro da sogra!, Kylmaeae koirakeittoa, Sopa de cao a moda da casa, Una notte un cane un sogno,* and *Una notte, un cane, un sogno*), HandMade Films, 1990.
Bill & Ted's Bogus Journey, Orion, 1991.
Sharkskin (short film), 1991.
Class Act, Warner Bros., 1992.
Demolition Man, Warner Bros., 1993.
Super Mario Bros. (also known as *Super Mario, Super Mario Brothers,* and *Super Mario Brothers: The Movie*), Buena Vista, 1993.
Terminal Velocity (also known as *Caida libre, Fritt fall, Hiz siniri, Queda livre, Terminal velocity—vapaa pudotus, Toedliche Geschwindigkeit, Ultima sansa, Vegsebesseg, Velocidad terminal,* and *Velocidade terminal*), Buena Vista, 1994.
An Alan Smithee Film: Burn Hollywood Burn (also known as *Burn, Hollywood, Burn*), Buena Vista, 1997.
Vegas Vacation (also known as *National Lampoon's "Vegas Vacation"*), Warner Bros., 1997.
Soldier (also known as *Star Force Soldier, A Katona, Le soldat, Sodur, Soldado implacavel,* and *Soldatul*), Warner Bros., 1998.
The Whole Nine Yards (also known as *Bergyilkos a szomszedom, Falsas aparencias, Falsas apariencias, FBI: Protezione testimoni, Full pakke, Keine halben Sachen, Koko potti, Le nouveau voisin, Meu vizinho mafioso, Mi vecino, el asesino, Mon voisin le tueur, Ni fod under, Oss torpeder emellan,* and *Ubica mekog srca*), Warner Bros., 2000.
The One (also known as *Jet Li's "The One," Confrontation, Az Egyetlen, El unico, Le seul, O confronto,* and *Tylko jeden*), Columbia, 2001.
Deuces Wild (also known as *Deuces Wild—Wild in den Strassen, Gaenget fraan Brooklyn, Jovenes salvajes, Jovens selvagens,* and *Ruas selvagens*), Metro–Goldwyn–Mayer, 2002.
Redline, Chicago Releasing, 2007.
Days of Wrath, Foxy Films, 2008.

Production designer for other films.

Film Art Director:

The Idolmaker (also known as *Rock machine*), United Artists, 1980.
In God We Tru$t (also known as *Gimme That Prime Time Religion*), Universal, 1980.

(As David Snyder) *Blade Runner* (also known as *Blade Runner—Metropolis 2020, Blade Runner—O cacador de androides, Blade Runner—Omades exontoseos, Der Blade Runner, El cazador implacable, Iztrebljevalec, Lowca androidow, Perigo iminente, Szarnyas fejvadasz,* and *Vanatorul de recompense*), Warner Bros., 1982.

Brainstorm (also known as *Agyhalal, Brainstorm—aivomyrsky, Brainstorm generazione elettronica, Burza mozgow, Mozdana oluja, Projecto Brainstorm, Projekt Brainstorm, Projeto Brainstorm, Proyecto Brainstorm,* and *Thyella ston egefalo*), Metro–Goldwyn–Mayer, 1983.

Film Producer:

Associate producer, *Cold Dog Soup* (also known as *Cold Dog—Zur Hoelle mit dem Himmelhund, En jycke i soppan, Enterrando o cachorro da sogra!, Kylmaeae koirakeittoa, Sopa de cao a moda da casa, Una notte un cane un sogno,* and *Una notte, un cane, un sogno*), HandMade Films, 1990.

Executive producer, *Rainbow* (also known as *Les voyageurs de l'arc–en–ciel*), Allegro/Vine International, 1995.

(With others) *Days of Wrath,* Foxy Films, 2008.

Film Second Unit Director:

Super Mario Bros. (also known as *Super Mario, Super Mario Brothers,* and *Super Mario Brothers: The Movie*), Buena Vista, 1993.

Rainbow (also known as *Les voyageurs de l'arc–en–ciel*), Allegro/Vine International, 1995.

The Whole Nine Yards (also known as *Bergyilkos a szomszedom, Falsas aparencias, Falsas apariencias, FBI: Protezione testimoni, Full pakke, Keine halben Sachen, Koko potti, Le nouveau voisin, Meu vizinho mafioso, Mi vecino, el asesino, Mon voisin le tueur, Ni fod under, Oss torpeder emellan,* and *Ubica mekog srca*), Warner Bros., 2000.

Film Original Concept Designer:

Zoot Suit (musical), Universal, 1981.

Miracle Mile (also known as *A setenta minutos do fim, Appel d'urgence, Cudowna mila, Die Nacht der Entscheidung, Miracle Mile—pelon maili, Nacht der Entscheidung–Miracle Mile,* and *Soluzione finale*), Twentieth Century–Fox/Columbia, 1988.

(Uncredited) *Deep Blue Sea* (also known as *Deep Blue, Alerta en lo profundo, Blu profondo, Duboko modro more, Duboko plavo more, Perigo no oceano, Peur bleue, Terreur sous la mer,* and *Vathia agria thalassa*), Warner Bros., 1999.

Film Visual Consultant:

Session Man (short film), Chanticleer Films, 1991.

Rainbow (also known as *Les voyageurs de l'arc–en–ciel*), Allegro/Vine International, 1995.

The Decadent Visitor (short film), 1999.

Den of Lions, Millennium Films, 2003.

The Safe Side (short film), Aigner Clark Creative, 2005.

Dark Streets, Capture Film International/LA Dark Streets, 2007.

Television Production Designer; Series:

When the Whistle Blows, ABC, 1980.

(And visual consultant) *The Casino,* Fox, 2004.

The Contender, NBC and ESPN, beginning 2005.

Meet Mister Mom, NBC, beginning 2005.

Miracle Workers, ABC, beginning 2006.

Television Art Director; Series:

Rock Concert (also known as *Don Kirschner's "Rock Concert"*), syndicated, c. 1973–82.

Assistant art director, *The Incredible Hulk* (also known as *De Hulk, Den otrolige Hulken, El hombre increible, El increible Hulk, Hulken, L'incredible Hulk,* and *L'incroyable Hulk*), CBS, 1978–82.

Assistant art director, *Taxi,* ABC, 1978–82, NBC, 1982–83.

Buck Rogers in the 25th Century (also known as *Buck Rogers*), NBC, 1979–81.

Galactica 1980 (also known as *Battlestar Galactica*), ABC, 1980.

Television Production Designer; Movies:

Captain America, CBS, 1979.

Starflight: The Plane that Couldn't Land (also known as *Airport 85* and *Starflight One*), ABC, 1983.

Sins of the Past (also known as *Forbidden Secrets*), ABC, 1984.

(And second unit director) *Race against Time* (also known as *Gabriel's Run, Allein gegen den Tod, Contrarreloj, Correndo contra o tempo, Corsa contro il tempo, L'homme traque,* and *La revolte d'un homme traque*), TNT, 2000.

Television Work; Specials:

Assistant art director, *Olivia,* ABC, 1978.

Television Work; Awards Presentations:

Assistant art director, *The 50th Annual Academy Awards,* ABC, 1978.

Television Work; Episodic:

Scenic designer, *Showbiz Today,* Cable News Network, 1990.

(Uncredited) Visual consultant, "You Can't Always Get What You Want," *Rock Star: INXS,* CBS, 2005.

Television Appearances; Specials:

(As David Snyder) Himself, *On the Edge of "Blade Runner,"* Channel 4 (England), 2000.

Television Appearances; Episodic:
Himself, *Showbiz Today,* Cable News Network, 1986.

Stage Designer:
Assistant set designer, *A Midnight Moon at the Greasy Spoon,* Los Angeles Actors Theatre, Hollywood, Los Angeles, 1974.
Assistant set designer, *Summer Voices,* Circle Theatre, Hollywood, Los Angeles, 1974.
Set designer, *The Venus of Menschen Falls,* Los Angeles Actors Theatre, 1976.
Assistant set designer, *Streamers,* Westwood Playhouse, Los Angeles, 1977.
Production designer, *Zen Boogie* (musical), Solari Theatre, Beverly Hills, CA, 1978.

Stage Technical Director:
The Contractor, Long Wharf Theatre, New Haven, CT, 1971–72.
Hamlet, Long Wharf Theatre, 1971–72.
The Iceman Cometh, Long Wharf Theatre, 1971–72.
Patrick's Day, Long Wharf Theatre, 1971–72.
A Streetcar Named Desire, Long Wharf Theatre, 1971–72.
Troika: An Evening of Russian Comedy (consists of *The Wedding, The Country Woman,* and *A Swan Song*), Long Wharf Theatre, 1971–72.
The Way of the World, Long Wharf Theatre, 1971–72.
You Can't Take It with You, Long Wharf Theatre, 1971–72.

RECORDINGS

Videos:
Himself, *Dangerous Days: Making Blade Runner* (also known as *Dangerous Days*), Warner Home Video, 2007.

Music Video Art Director:
Jessica Simpson, "Sweetest Sin," 2003.

Singles:
Recorded singles with the Free Thinkers, beginning 1965.

OTHER SOURCES

Periodicals:
Cinefantastique, November, 1998, pp. 10–15.
Entertainment Weekly, October 16, 1998, p. 16.
Los Angeles, February 1, 2007, pp. 2, 88–93, 185–90.
Premiere, November, 1998, p. 108.
Starlog, August, 1993, pp. 75–81; August, 1998, pp. 30–35.

Electronic:
David L. Snyder Motion Picture Design, http://www.davidlsnyderfilm.com, August 27, 2007.

SOLARI, Camille

PERSONAL

Career: Actress. Billboard model for Dickies Jeans.

CREDITS

Film Appearances:
Agent Star, *Toad Warrior* (also known as *Hell Comes to Frogtown II*), 1996.
Scan nurse, *Bombshell,* Trimark Pictures, 1996.
Agent Banner, *Max Hell Comes to Frogtown* (also known as *Max Hell Frog Warrior*), Tag Entertainment, 2002.
Monica, *Saved by the Rules,* 2003.
Mimi, *Intoxicating,* Rogue Arts, 2003.
Lisa, *Baggage,* 2003.
Concubine, *Galaxy Hunter,* 2004.
Melinda, *Hold Up* (short), Apollo Cinema, 2004.
Starshyp, *Hookers Inc.,* ITN Distribution, 2006.
Lucy, *True True Lie,* Verve Pictures, 2006.
Phaedra Hill, *The Bliss* (also known as *Rocker*), 2006.
(Uncredited) Girl, *Factory Girl,* Metro–Goldwyn–Mayer, 2006.
Agent Morgan, *Money to Burn,* 2007.
Herself, *Life on the Road with Mr. and Mrs. Brown* (documentary), 2007.

Film Work:
Producer, *Hookers Inc.,* ITN Distribution, 2006.
Co–executive producer, *True True Lie,* Verve Pictures, 2006.
Producer, *The Bliss* (also known as *Rocker*), 2006.
Executive producer, *Money to Burn,* 2007.
Director and producer, *Life on the Road with Mr. and Mrs. Brown* (documentary), 2007.

Television Appearances; Movies:
Bombshell, Sci–Fi Channel, 1997.

Television Appearances; Episodic:
Lisa, "Dick Soup for the Soul," *3rd Rock from the Sun* (also known as *3rd Rock* and *Life As We Know It*), NBC, 2001.
"Ed Hardy and Z Boys Party at Viper Room," *Videofashion! News,* 2006.
"Svetka Erotica: Ludacris Event," *The Black Carpet,* 2006.

"James Brown Documentary," *ABC Evening News* (also known as *ABC WorldNews Tonight*), ABC, 2006.
"James Brown Documentary: Life on the Road with Mr. and Mrs. Brown," *NBC Nightly News,* NBC, 2006.
Love is in the Heir, 2006.
"Waist Deep Premiere," *BET Nightly News,* Black Entertainment Television, 2007.
"Svetca Erotica Ludacris Charity Event," *BET Nightly News,* Black Entertainment Television, 2007.

Television Work; Movies:
Casting assistant, *Bombshell,* Sci–Fi Channel, 1997.

WRITINGS

Screenplays:
Hookers, Inc., ITN Distribution, 2006.
True True Lie, Verve Pictures, 2006.
The Bliss (also known as *Rocker*), 2006.
Life on the Road with Mr. and Mrs. Brown (documentary), 2007.

SPELVIN, George, Jr.
 See DOUGLAS, Kirk

SPINNEY, Carroll 1933–
 (Ed Spinney)

PERSONAL

Born December 26, 1933, in Waltham, MA; married first wife (divorced, 1971); married Debra Jean Gilroy, 1979; children: (first marriage) Jessica, Melissa Brooke, Benjamin. *Education:* Attended art school in Boston. *Avocational Interests:* Drawing, painting.

Addresses: *Contact*—c/o Children's Television Workshop, One Lincoln Place, New York, NY 10023; Greater Talent Network, 437 Fifth Ave., New York, NY 10016.

Career: Actor.

Awards, Honors: Daytime Emmy awards (with others), outstanding individual achievement in children's programming, 1974, 1976, 1979, Daytime Emmy Award, special classification of outstanding individual achievement—performers, 1984, Daytime Emmy Award nomination, outstanding performer in a children's series, 1999, Daytime Emmy Award (with Kevin Clash), best performer in a children's series, 2007, all for *Sesame Street;* Star on the Hollywood Walk of Fame, 1994; received honorary Doctorate of Humane Letters, Eastern Connecticut State University, 2000; named a Living Legend, Library of Congress, 2000; Lifetime Achievement Award, Daytime Emmy Awards, 2006.

CREDITS

Film Appearances:
Voice of Big Bird, *The Muppet Movie,* Columbia TriStar Home Video, 1979.
Voice of Oscar the Grouch, *The Great Muppet Caper,* Universal, 1981.
(As Caroll Spinney) Voice of Big Bird, Oscar the Grouch, and Bruno, *Sesame Street Presents Follow That Bird* (also known as *Follow That Bird*), Warner Bros., 1985.
(As Caroll Spinney) Voice of Big Bird and Oscar the Grouch, *The Adventures of Elmo in Grouchland,* Columbia, 1999.

Film Work:
Muppet performer, *The Great Muppet Caper,* 1981.

Television Appearances; Series:
Mr. Lion, *Bozo's Big Top,* 1966.
Big Bird, Oscar the Grouch, and Bruno, *Sesame Street* (also known as *Canadian Sesame Street*), PBS, 1969—.
Voice of Oscar the Grouch, *Shalom Sesame,* 1987.
Big Bird, *Elmo's Musical Adventure,* 2000.
(Uncredited) Voice of Oscar, *Play with Me Sesame,* Noggin, 2002.

Television Appearances; Movies:
Big Bird and Oscar the Grouch (uncredited), *Big Bird Brings Spring to Sesame Street,* 1987.
Big Bird and Oscar the Grouch, *A Muppet Family Christmas,* 1987.
Big Bird and Oscar the Grouch (uncredited), *The Adventures of Super Grover,* 1987.
Big Bird and Oscar the Grouch, *Elmo Saves Christmas,* Children's Television Workshop, 1996.
Big Bird, *Cinderelmo,* Fox, 1999.

Television Appearances; Specials:
Voice of Big Bird and Oscar, *Julie on Sesame Street,* 1973.
Voice, *Out to Lunch,* 1974.
Voice of Big Bird, *NBC Salutes the 25th Anniversary of the Wonderful World of Disney,* NBC, 1978.
Voice of Big Bird and Oscar, *Christmas Eve on Sesame Street,* 1978.

Voice of Big Bird and Oscar the Grouch, *A Sesame Street Christmas*, 1978.

Voice of Big Bird and Oscar the Grouch, *A Walking Tour of Sesame Street*, 1979.

Voice of Big Bird, *Bob Hope on the Road of China*, 1979.

The 22nd Annual TV Week Logie Awards, Nine Network, 1980.

Voice of Big Bird and Oscar, *Big Bird in China*, 1983.

Voice of Big Bird and Oscar the Grouch, *Don't Eat the Pictures: Sesame Street at the Metropolitan Museum of Art*, 1983.

Performer, *Henson's Place*, 1984.

Big Bird, *Night of 100 Stars II*, 1985.

Voice of Big Bird, Oscar the Grouch, and Bruno, *The Muppets: A Celebration of 30 Years*, 1986.

Voice of Big Bird and Oscar the Grouch, *A Muppet Family Christmas*, 1987.

(Uncredited) Voice of Big Bird and Oscar, *The Adventures of Super Grover*, 1987.

(Uncredited) Voice of Big Bird and Oscar the Grouch, *Big Bird Brings Spring to Sesame Street*, 1987.

(As Caroll Spinney) Big Bird, *Kids Like These*, 1987.

Big Bird, *Big Bird in Japan*, 1988.

Big Bird, Oscar the Grouch, and Bruno, *Sesame Street Special* (also known as *Put Down the Duckie, Put Down the Duckie: A Sesame Street Special, Sesame Street: Put Down the Duckie—An All–Star Music Special,* and *The Sesame Street Special*), PBS, 1988.

Voice of Big Bird and Oscar the Grouch, *Sesame Street: 20 and Counting*, 1989.

Voice of Big Bird and Oscar, *The Muppets Celebrated Jim Henson*, 1990.

Voice of Big Bird, *Big Bird's Birthday or Let Me Eat Cake*, 1991.

Voice of Big Bird and Oscar, *Sesame Street Stays Up Late!* (also known as *Sesame Street Stays Up Late! A Monster New Year's Eve Party*), 1993.

Voice of Muppet performer, *The World of Jim Henson*, 1994.

Voice of Big Bird and Oscar the Grouch, *Sesame Street Jam: A Musical Celebration*, 1994.

Voice of Big Bird and Oscar, *Sesame Street's All–Star 25th Birthday: Stars and Streets Forever!*, 1994.

Big Bird, *Elmo Saves Christmas*, 1996.

Voice of Big Bird and Oscar, *Elmopalooza*, 1998.

Himself, *Sesame Street Unpaved*, 1999.

Voice of Big Bird, *Cinderelmo*, 1999.

Voice of Big Bird and Oscar, *Sesame Street*, 2000.

Sesame Street, 2001.

Big Bird, *50 Greatest TV Animals*, Animal Planet, 2003.

Big Bird and Oscar the Grouch, *The 31st Annual Daytime Emmy Awards*, NBC, 2004.

Voice of Big Bird and Oscar the Grouch, *Sesame Street Presents: The Street We Live On* (also known as *Sesame Street: Elmo's World—The Street We Live*), 2004.

Big Bird and Oscar the Grouch, *The 32nd Annual Daytime Emmy Awards*, ABC, 2006.

Big Bird and Oscar the Grouch, *Elmo's Christmas Countdown*, ABC, 2007.

Television Appearances; Episodic:

Big Bird, *The Flip Wilson Show*, 1970.

Voice of Big Bird, "A Special Program with Arthur Fiedler and Friends from Sesame Street," *Evening at Pops*, PBS, 1971.

Big Bird, "131," *The Electric Company*, PBS, 1972.

Oscar the Grouch, "453," *The Electric Company*, PBS, 1975.

Big Bird, *The Muppet Show*, 1978.

Big Bird, "Competition," *Mister Rogers' Neighborhood*, PBS, 1981.

Big Bird, "The Stan Plan," *Soul Man*, 1998.

"Tweet! Tweet! Tweet!," *Between the Lions*, 2000.

"Close–Up: Sesame Street," *Biography*, Arts and Entertainment, 2001.

(As Big Bird) *Hollywood Squares* (also known as *H2* and *H2: Hollywood Squares*), syndicated, 2001.

(As Oscar the Grouch) *Hollywood Squares* (also known as *H2* and *H2: Hollywood Squares*), syndicated, 2001.

(Uncredited) Voice of Big Bird, *Rove Live*, Ten Network, 2003.

Big Bird, "Eppur Si Muove," *The West Wing*, NBC, 2004.

Television Work; Series:

Creator, *Rascal Rabbit*, 1955.

Also worked as a puppeteer, *The Judy and Goggle Show*.

Television Puppeteer; Specials:

A Muppet Family Christmas, 1987.

Sesame Street, 2000.

RECORDINGS

Videos:

Voice of Big Bird, *Learning About Numbers*, 1986.

Voice of Big Bird and Oscar the Grouch, *Learning About Letters*, 1986.

Voice of Big Bird, *The Best of Ernie and Bert*, 1988.

Voice of Big Bird and Oscar the Grouch, *Count It Higher: Great Music Videos from Sesame Street*, 1988.

Picklepuss, Pop, *Wow, You're a Cartoonist!*, 1988.

Oscar the Grouch and Big Bird, *Sesame Songs: Rock & Roll*, 1990.

Oscar the Grouch, *Sesame Songs: Monster Hits!*, 1990.

Voice of Oscar the Grouch and Big Bird, *Sesame Songs: Sing–Along Earth Songs*, 1993.

Big Bird, *It's Not Easy Being Green*, 1994.

Voice of Big Bird and Oscar, *Elmo Saves Christmas,* 1996.

Elmopalooza, Children's Television Workshop, 1999.

Zoe's Dance Moves, Sony Wonder, 2003.

(As Caroll Spinney) Voice of Big Bird, *Sesame Street: Three Bears and a New Baby,* Sony Wonder, 2003.

Big Bird, *What's the Name of That Song,* Sony Wonder, 2004.

Big Bird, *Sesame Street: Friends to the Rescue,* Genius Products, 2005.

Big Bird, *Elmo Visits the Doctor,* Sony Wonder, 2005.

Big Bird and Oscar, *Guess That Shape and Color* (short), 2006.

Oscar and Big Bird, *A Sesame Street Christmas Carol,* Genius Products, 2006.

Elmo's World: What Makes You Happy?, Genius Products, 2007.

CDs:

Elmopalooza!, Sony Wonder, 1999.

Also recorded music CDs: *Sesame Street: Big Bird Leads the Band; Sesame Street: Bert's Blockbusters; Sesame Street: Kid's Favorite Songs; Sesame Street: Best of Elmo;* and *Sesame Street: Sing Along Travel Songs.*

WRITINGS

Television Specials:
(Uncredited) *Big Bird in China,* 1983.

Books:
(With J Milligan) *The Wisdom of Big Bird (And the Dark Genius of Oscar the Grouch): Lessons from a Life in Feathers,* Villard, 2003.

OTHER SOURCES

Periodicals:
Parade Magazine, February 18, 2001, p. 22.
People, December 4, 2000, pp. 115–16.
Publishers Weekly, March 24, 2003, p. 68.

Electronic:
Carroll Spinney Website, http://www.carollspinney. com, October 20, 2007.

STARK, Jim

PERSONAL

Addresses: *Office*—Stark Sales, 366 Broadway, Suite 2A, New York, NY 10013.

Career: Producer, actor, and screenwriter. Stark Sales, New York, NY, producer.

Awards, Honors: Independent Spirit Award nomination, best feature, Independent Features Project West, 1990, for *Mystery Train.*

CREDITS

Film Producer:
Coffee and Cigarettes (short), Electric Pictures, 1986.
Coffee and Cigarettes II (short; also known as *Coffee and Cigarettes II: Memphis Version*), 1989.
Mystery Train, Orion, 1989.
In the Soup (also known as *In the Soup—Alles Kino* and *In the soup—un mare di guai*), Triton Pictures, 1992.
Cold Fever (also known as *A koldum klaka*), Artistic License, 1995.
I'll Take You There, DEJ Productions, 1999.
The Missing, Roadshow Entertainment, 1999.
"Twins" and "Strange to Meet You," *Coffee and Cigarettes,* United Artists, 2003.
Factotum (also known as *Factotum: A Man Who Performs Many Jobs*), IFC Films, 2005.
Love, Frontier Films, 2005.

Film Coproducer:
Down by Law (also known as *Down by Law—Alles im Griff*), Island Pictures, 1986.
The Living End, Strand Releasing, 1992.
Color of a Brisk and Leaping Day, Artistic License, 1996.
The Quickie, Monarch Home Video, 2001.
Country Wedding, 2008.

Film Executive Producer:
Night on Earth (also known as *Une nuit sur terre*), Fine Line, 1991.
Homework, 2004.

Film Associate Producer:
The Doom Generation (also known as *Doom Generation*), Trimark, 1995.
Marco Polo: Haperek Ha'aharon (also known as *Marco Polo: The Missing Chapter*), Flashstar, 1996.

Film Production Consultant:
Synthetic Pleasures, Samba Entertainment, 1995.

Film Appearances:
Detective, *Sleepwalk,* First Run Features, 1986.
Pall bearer at airport, *Mystery Train,* Orion, 1989.
Keep It for Yourself (short), 1991.
American Cinema, PBS, 1995.

Betting producer, *Cannes Man* (also known as *Canne$ Man* and *Con Man*), 1996.

How Do You Like Iceland? (documentary), 2005.

WRITINGS

Screenplays:

Cold Fever (also known as *A koldum klaka*), Artistic License, 1995.

Factotum (also known as *Factotum: A Man Who Performs Many Jobs*), IFC Films, 2005.

STOJKA, Andre
(Andre Stojika)

PERSONAL

Addresses: *Agent*—International Creative Management, 10250 Constellation Way, Ninth Floor, Los Angeles, CA 90067; Danis, Panero & Nist, 9201 West Olympic Blvd., Beverly Hills, CA 90212.

Career: Actor and voice artist. Provided work for advertisements, television promotional spots, and film trailers.

Member: Historical Society of Southern California.

CREDITS

Film Appearances:

ESS voice, *Wolfen* (also known as *Lobos humanos* and *Wolfen, la belva immortale*), Orion/Warner Bros., 1981.

Animated Film Appearances:

Voices of Starlite, wizard, and Spectran, *Rainbow Brite and the Star Stealer,* Warner Bros., 1985.

Voice of Owl, *Pooh's Grand Adventure: The Search for Christopher Robin* (also known as *Winnie the Pooh's Most Grand Adventure*), Buena Vista Home Video, 1997.

Voice of Owl, *Winnie the Pooh: Seasons of Giving* (also known as *Disney's "Winnie the Pooh: Seasons of Giving"*), Buena Vista Home Video, 1999.

Voice of Owl, *The Tigger Movie* (also known as *Tigger: The Movie*), Buena Vista, 2000.

Voice of king, *Cinderella II: Dreams Come True* (also known as *Cendrillon 2: une vie de princesse, Cenicienta II: Un suneo hecho realidad,* and *Cinderella 2—Traeume werden wahr*), Buena Vista Home Video, 2002.

Voice of Owl, *Piglet's Big Movie* (also known as *Ferkels grosses Abenteuer, Grislings store eventyr, Knorretjes grote film, La gran pelicula de Piglet, Le grand film de Porcinet, Leitao—O filme, Nasses stora film, Nasun suuri elokuva,* and *Pimpi, piccolo grande eroe*), Buena Vista, 2003.

Voice of Osho for dubbed version, *Heisei tanuki gassen pompoko* (anime; also known as *The Raccoon War* and *Pom poko*), 2004.

Voice of king, *Cinderella III: A Twist in Time* (also known as *Askungen—Det magiska trollspoeet, Assepoester—Terug in de tijd, Assepoester 3, Cinderella—Wahre Liebe siegt, Le sortilege de Cendrillon,* and *Stahtopouta—Strofi sto hrono*), Buena Vista, 2007.

Film Additional Voices:

The Emperor's New Groove (animated; also known as *Disney's "Keizer Kuzco," Kingdom in the Sun, Kingdom of the Sun, A nova onda do imperador, Careva nova aeud, Ein Koenigreich fuer ein Lama, El emperador y sus locuras, Eszeveszett birodalom, Keisarin uudet kuviot, Keizer kuzco, Kejsarens nya stil, Kejserens nye flip, Kuzco, l'empereur megalo, Las locuras del emperador, Le follie dell'imperatore, Pacha e o imperador,* and *Un empereur nouveau genre*), Buena Vista, 2000.

Television Appearances; Series:

Voice, *Spider–Man* (animated; also known as *Spider–Man and His Amazing Friends* and *Spiderman 2000*), NBC, 1981–82, 1984–86.

Voice, *The All–New Scooby and Scrappy–Doo Show* (animated), ABC, 1983–84.

Voice of Starlite, *Rainbow Brite* (animated; also known as *Blondine au pays de l'arc–en–ciel* and *Maho shojo rainbow Brite*), syndicated, c. 1984–85.

Voice, *The New Jetsons* (animated), syndicated, 1985.

Voice of Owl, *The Book of Pooh* (puppet series; also known as *El libro de Pooh*), Disney Channel, 2001–2002.

Voices of Archimedes and Owl, *House of Mouse* (animated; also known as *Disney's "House of Mouse," Mickey's Club,* and *Musehus*), ABC, 2001–2002.

Television Appearances; Animated Specials:

Voices of first victim, elder Og, mother, and Og father, "The Secret World of Og," *ABC Weekend Specials,* ABC, 1983.

Voices of Grim Creeper and Mummy Daddy, *Scooby–Doo and the Ghoul School* (also known as *Scooby–Doo et l'ecole des diablesses*), Cartoon Network, 1988.

Voice of Owl, *Boo! to You, Winnie-the-Pooh,* CBS, 1996.

Voice of Owl, *A Winnie the Pooh Thanksgiving,* ABC, 1998.

Voice of Owl, *Winnie the Pooh: A Valentine for You,* ABC, 1999.

Television Appearances; Animated Episodes:

Voice of the Penguin, "The Case of the Stolen Powers," *The Super Powers Team: Galactic Guardians* (also known as *SuperFriends VI*), ABC, 1985.

Voice of Professor Sprock, "Riddle in the Middle of the Earth," *Yogi's Treasure Hunt* (also known as *The Funtastic World of Hanna–Barbera*), syndicated, 1985.

Voice of Dr. Dexter, "A Gummi a Day Keeps the Doctor Away," *The Gummi Bears* (also known as *Disney's "Adventures of the Gummi Bears"*), NBC, 1989.

Voice of company boss, "Comic Book Capers," *Darkwing Duck* (also known as *Darkwing Duck—Der Schrecken der Bosewichte, El pato Darkwing, Myster Mask,* and *Varjoankka*), ABC and syndicated, 1991.

Voice of Dr. Ohm, "SWAT Kats Unplugged," *Swat Kats: The Radical Squadron,* syndicated, 1994.

Voices of first announcer and doctor, "The Bad News Plastic Surgeons/Exchange Student/I. M. Weasel: I. R. In the Wrong Cartoon," *Cow and Chicken,* Cartoon Network, 1998.

Voices of Basil Tarragon, second bear, and Owl, "The Wrongest Yard/Druid, Where's My Car?," *The Grim Adventures of Billy & Mandy* (also known as *Grim & Evil*), Cartoon Network, 2006.

Television Additional Voices; Animated Series:

The Adventures of Jonny Quest (also known as *Jonny Quest*), ABC, 1964–65, CBS, 1967–70, ABC, 1970–72, NBC, 1979–72, and 1980–81, syndicated, 1986.

The Jetsons, CBS, c. 1969–71, NBC, 1971–76, 1979–81, 1982–83.

Scooby and Scrappy–Doo, ABC, c. 1979–80.

The Smurfs (also known as *Smurfs' Adventures*), NBC, 1981–90.

Scooby & Scrappy–Doo/The Puppy's New Adventures (also known as *The Scooby and Scrappy–Doo Puppy Hour* and *The Scooby–Doo Puppy Hour*), ABC, 1982–83.

The Shirt Tales, NBC, 1982–84, CBS, 1984–85.

Challenge of the GoBots, syndicated, 1984–85.

Fantastic Max (also known as *The Funtastic World of Hanna–Barbera* and *El fantastico Max*), syndicated, 1988–90.

The Pirates of Dark Water (also known as *Dark Water*), ABC, 1991–93.

RECORDINGS

Animated Videos:

Voice, *David and Goliath* (also known as *Greatest Adventure Stories from the Bible: David and Goliath*), 1985.

Voice, *Noah's Ark,* 1986.

Voice of Owl, *Winnie the Pooh Playtime: Cowboy Pooh,* 1994.

Voice of Owl, *Winnie the Pooh Playtime: Detective Tigger,* 1994.

Voice of Owl, *Winnie the Pooh Playtime: Pooh Party,* 1994.

Voice of Owl, *Winnie the Pooh Un–Valentine's Day,* 1995.

Voice of Owl, *Winnie the Pooh Learning: Growing Up,* 1996.

Voice of Owl, *Winnie the Pooh Learning: Helping Others,* 1997.

Voice of Owl, *Winnie the Pooh Learning: Making Friends,* 1998.

Voice of Owl, *Winnie the Pooh Learning: Sharing & Caring,* 1998.

Voice of Owl, *Winnie the Pooh Playtime: Fun 'n Games,* 1998.

Voice of Owl, *Winnie the Pooh Playtime: Happy Pooh Day,* 1998.

Voice of Owl, *Winnie the Pooh Friendship: Clever Little Piglet,* 1999.

Voice of Owl, *Winnie the Pooh Friendship: Pooh Wishes,* 1999.

Voice of Owl, *Winnie the Pooh Franken Pooh,* 1999.

Voice of Owl, *Winnie the Pooh: Imagine That, Christopher Robin,* 1999.

Voice of Owl, *Winnie the Pooh Learning: Working Together,* 1999.

Voice of Owl, *Winnie the Pooh Spookable Pooh,* 2000.

Voice of Owl, *Winnie the Pooh: Shapes & Sizes,* Buena Vista Home Entertainment, 2006.

Voice of Owl, *Winnie the Pooh: Wonderful Word Adventure,* Buena Vista Home Entertainment, 2006.

Video Games:

Voice of Mauruku, *The Mark of Kri,* Sony Computer Entertainment America, 2002.

Voice of Owl for English version, *Kingdom Hearts II* (also known as *Kingudamu hatsu II*), Square Enix, 2005.

(As Andre Stojika) Voice for English version, *Shin Onimusha: Dawn of Dreams* (also known as *Onimusha: Dawn of Dreams*), Capcom Entertainment, 2006.

STORM, T. J.
(Juan Ojeda)

PERSONAL

Original name, Juan Ojeda; born February 14, in IN; raised in Hawaii. *Education:* Trained at the Joanne Barron/D. W. Brown Acting Academy; studied several martial arts disciplines, dance, and music.

Addresses: *Office*—Eye of the Storm Entertainment, 13547 Ventura Blvd., Box 270, Sherman Oaks, CA 91423. *Agent*—Hervey/Grimes Talent Agency, 10561 Missouri Ave., Suite 2, Los Angeles, CA 90025.

Career: Actor. Martial artist with belts in arashi–ryu karate, tae kwon do, ninjitsu, jujitsu, and northern shaolin kung fu. Eye of the Storm Entertainment (production company), Sherman Oaks, CA, partner. Optimum Fitness Organization, personal trainer. Volunteer for various organizations, including the American Cancer Society, Big Brothers Big Sisters of America, Children Uniting Nations, Ronald McDonald House, Stars for Charity, United Way, Dragonfest, and animal charities.

Member: Screen Actors Guild.

Awards, Honors: Inducted into the Masters Hall of Fame (martial arts hall of fame), 2000.

CREDITS

Film Appearances:
(As Juan Ojeda) Mickey, *Breathing Fire,* 1991.
Fullock, *Dragon Fury,* 1995.
(Uncredited) Guest fighter, *Mortal Kombat* (also known as *Combate mortal, Kombat mortel, Mortal Kombat: La pelicula, Oeluemcuel savas,* and *Smrtonosni spopad*), New Line Cinema, 1995.
Enter the Blood Ring, Armed for Action, c. 1995.
Abdul Sabbah, *Kick of Death,* 1997.
Person from rival tribe, *Once upon a Time in China and America* (also known as *Once upon a Time in China VI, Huang Fei Hong: Zhi xi yu xiong shi,* and *Wong Fei Hung: Chi sai wik hung shut*), 1997.
Second villain, *La quebradita,* 1997.
Cinque, *Corrupt,* Sterling Home Entertainment, 1999.
Josef, *The Wrecking Crew,* Sterling Home Entertainment, 1999.
King, *Urban Menace,* Sterling Home Entertainment, 1999.
Montgomery Pettigrew, *Doomsdayer* (also known as *Il giorno del giudizio*), ABS–CBN Entertainment/ Quantum Entertainment, 1999.
Officer, *Epoch of Lotus,* 2000.
J. C., *The Organization,* Cool Room Entertainment/ Storm Factory, 2001.
Jamaican taxi driver, *A Month of Sundays* (also known as *Meu avo, meu amigo*), PorchLight Entertainment, 2001.
Repo man, *Big Shots,* Greed & Avarice Productions, 2001.
Rick, *The Ultimate Game,* Amsell Entertainment, 2001.
Jax, *Law of the Fist* (short film), 2003.
Melique, *Redemption,* Artisan Entertainment, 2003.

Officer Dence (some sources spell name Officer Dense), *Miss Cast Away* (also known as *Miss Castaway and the Island Girls*), Showcase Entertainment, 2004.
Ninja, *Death to the Supermodels* (also known as *Operacion Bikini*), Metro–Goldwyn–Mayer Home Entertainment, 2005.
Strong man and third Kagan vampire guard, *BloodRayne* (also known as *BloodRayne, dipsa gia ekdikisi*), 2005, Romar Entertainment, 2006.
Muslim champion, *Soldier of God,* Anthem Pictures, 2006.
Sepuko, *Vagabond,* Tiberia Pictures, 2006.
Maginty, *The Punisher: War Zone* (also known as *The Punisher 2, The Punisher: Welcome Back, Frank,* and *The Untitled Punisher Sequel*), Lionsgate, 2008.

Some sources cite an appearance in *Diamonds from the Bantus,* Polydoor Pictures, 2002.

Film Fight Choreographer:
The Ultimate Game, Amsell Entertainment, 2001.
(And stunt coordinator) *FBI Guys* (short film), 2006.
The Tides (short film), Subvert, 2007.

Television Appearances; Series:
Doom master, *V.R. Troopers* (also known as *Cybertron* and *Saban's "V.R. Troopers"*), 1995–96.
Bayu, *Conan* (also known as *Conan the Adventurer* and *Conan: The Adventurer*), syndicated, 1997–98.

Television Appearances; Episodic:
Lenkoff, "In the Dark," *Martial Law* (also known as *Le flic de Shanghai, Ley marcial,* and *Piu forte ragazzi*), CBS, 2000.

RECORDINGS

Videos:
Himself, *Cardio Kung Fu* (also known as *Cardio Kung Fu—The Spiritual Workout*), c. 2000.

Video Developer:
(With Van Ayasit) *Cardio Kung Fu* (also known as *Cardio Kung Fu—The Spiritual Workout*), c. 2000.

Video Games:
Voice of Brad Garrison, *Dead Rising,* Capcom Entertainment, 2006.

Provided voices for various video games.

Video Game Work:
Motion capture actor, *Dead Rising,* Capcom Entertainment, 2006.

Provided motion capture work for various video games.

WRITINGS

Videos:

Cardio Kung Fu (also known as *Cardio Kung Fu—The Spiritual Workout*), c. 2000.

OTHER SOURCES

Periodicals:

Martial Arts and Combat Sports, November, 1999, pp. 60–66.

Martial Arts Illustrated, November, 1998, pp. 85–86.

STORMS, Kirsten 1984–

PERSONAL

Full name, Kirsten Renee Storms; born April 8, 1984, in Orlando, FL; daughter of Mike (a sportscaster) and Karen Storms; sister of Gretchen Storms (an actress).

Addresses: *Agent*—Paradigm, 360 North Crescent Dr., North Bldg., Beverly Hills, CA 90210. *Manager*—Elements Entertainment, 1635 North Cahuenga Blvd., 5th Floor, Los Angeles, CA 90028. *Publicist*—Nicole Nassar Public Relations, 1111 Tenth St., Suite 104, Santa Monica, CA 90403.

Career: Actress. Appeared in commercials, including "Talk with Me Barbie" doll, Tyco toys, Sea World amusement park, and Galoob Baby Doll.

Awards, Honors: Young Artist Award nomination, best performance by a leading young actress in a television movie or pilot, 2000, for *Zenon: Girl of the 21st Century;* Young Artist Award nomination, best performance by a young actress in a daytime television series, Soap Chat Awards, outstanding younger actress and favorite friendship (with others), Soap Chat Internet Web Site, *Soap Opera Digest* Award, outstanding child actor, 2001, Young Artist Award, best performance in a television drama series—leading young actress, 2002, *Soap Opera Digest* Award nomination, outstanding younger lead actress, 2003, *Soap Opera Digest* Award nomination (with others), favorite triangle, 2005, all for *Days of Our Lives.*

CREDITS

Film Appearances:

Venus, *Crayola Kids Adventures: The Trojan Horse,* 1997.

Belle's Tales of Friendship, 1999.

Voice of Bonnie Rockwaller, *"Kim Possible": The Secret Files* (animated), Walt Disney Home Entertainment, 2003.

Also appeared in *Have You Seen Lucky?; Something in the Kiss; Three's a Crowd.*

Television Appearances; Series:

Isabella "Belle" Black, *Days of Our Lives* (also known as *Days* and *DOOL*), NBC, 1999–2004.

Voice of Bonnie Rockwaller, *Kim Possible* (animated; also known as *Disney's "Kim Possible"*), Disney, 2002–2007.

Betsy Young, *Clubhouse,* CBS, 2004.

Maria Maximilliana "Maxie" Jones, *General Hospital,* ABC, 2005—.

Maria Maximilliana "Maxie" Jones, *General Hospital: Night Shift,* Soap Net, 2007.

Television Appearances; Movies:

Teenaged Melissa, *Love Letters,* ABC, 1999.

Emily, *Johnny Tsunami,* Disney Channel, 1999.

Zenon Kar, *Zenon: Girl of the 21st Century,* Disney Channel, 1999.

Laurie, raped girl, *"The Rockford Files": If It Bleeds ... It Leads,* 1999.

Zenon Kar, *Zenon: The Zequel,* Disney Channel, 2001.

Zenon Kar, *Zenon: Z3* (also known as *Zenon: Zee Three*), Disney Channel, 2004.

Voice of Bonnie Rockwaller, *"Kim Possible": So the Drama* (also known as *Disney's "Kim Possible Movie: So the Drama"*), Disney Channel, 2005.

Television Appearances; Specials:

Aphrodite, *The Crayola Kids Adventures: The Trojan Horse,* 1997.

Isabella "Belle" Black, *Days of Our Lives' 35th Anniversary,* NBC, 2000.

Herself and Isabella "Belle" Black, *"Days of Our Lives" Christmas,* NBC, 2001.

Voice of Bonnie Rockwaller, *"Kim Possible": A Stitch in Time* (also known as *Disney's "Kim Possible: A Stitch in Time"*), Disney Channel, 2003.

Presenter, *The 30th Annual Daytime Emmy Awards,* ABC, 2003.

The 31st Annual Daytime Emmy Awards, NBC, 2004.

The 32nd Annual Daytime Emmy Awards, CBS, 2005.

SOAPnet Reveals ABC Soap Secrets, Soap Net and ABC, 2005.

I Love the '80s 3-D, VH1, 2005.

Television Appearances; Pilots:

Second kid, *The Cape,* syndicated, 1996.

Betsy Young, *Clubhouse,* CBS, 2004.

Television Appearances; Episodic:

Ashley, "Julio Is My Dad," *Second Noah,* ABC, 1996.

Ashley, "A Dog's Life," *Second Noah,* ABC, 1996.

Betsy, "All in the Family Room," *You Wish,* ABC, 1998.

Lydia, "It's Called Depression," *Any Day Now,* Lifetime, 1998.

Laura Cummings, "It Takes Two, Baby," *7th Heaven* (also known as *Seventh Heaven*), The WB, 1998.

Melanie, *One World,* NBC, 1999.

Sing Me a Story with Belle (also known as *Disney's Sing a Me a Story: With Belle*), Disney Channel, 1999.

Mandy Silverman, "Like Father, like Son," *Movie Stars,* The WB, 1999.

Laura Cummings, "One Hundred," *7th Heaven* (also known as *Seventh Heaven*), The WB, 2001.

Nicki Peterson, "The Parties," *That's So Raven* (also known as *That's So Raven!*), Disney Channel, 2003.

Jackie Collins Presents, E! Entertainment Television, 2004.

Miss Marshall, "Cop Killer," *CSI: Miami,* CBS, 2005.

"Birthday Boy," *There & Back: Ashley Parker Angel,* MTV, 2006.

SoapTalk, Soap Net, 2006.

Jessica Gordon, "Sundown," *Skater Boys,* 2006.

Jessica Gordon, "Band of Gold," *Skater Boys,* 2006.

Also appeared in *All That.*

Stage Appearances:

Appeared in productions of *The Barney Show; Caroling Company; Kids of America; A Midsummer Night's Dream; The Show Goes On; The Sound of Music.*

OTHER SOURCES

Periodicals:

Soap World, May, 2000, p. 36.

SUMNER, John 1951–

PERSONAL

Born October 14, 1951, in Blackpool, Lancashire, England; married; children: one daughter, two stepsons.

Career: Actor. Performed at nightclubs in Auckland, New Zealand. RCA Records, worked in sales in New Zealand, 1976, then in artist and repertory and in marketing, Sydney, Australia; worked for a home video distributor in New Zealand until 1985; Guide Tools (training company), principal; database marketing specialist and trainer.

CREDITS

Television Appearances; Movies:

Inn owner, *Hercules: The Legendary Journeys— Hercules and the Lost Kingdom,* syndicated, 1994.

Senator Bob Belding, *Every Woman's Dream,* CBS, 1996.

Supervisor Pete, *Ready to Run,* Disney Channel, 2000.

Neville, *Atomic Twister,* TBS, 2002.

Jackson O'Connor, *Murder in Greenwich* (also known as *Dominick Dunne Presents: "Murder in Greenwich"*), USA Network, 2002.

Coach, *You Wish!,* Disney Channel, 2003.

Captain Ed Tessler, *Maiden Voyage,* 2004.

Television Appearances; Miniseries:

Mr. Arberg, *The Tommyknockers* (also known as *Stephen King's "The Tommyknockers"*), ABC, 1993.

Suzie's dad, *The Amazing Mrs. Pritchard,* PBS, 2006.

Television Appearances; Series:

Giles O'Connor, *Spin Doctors,* TV New Zealand, 2001.

Morrie Brownlee, *Shortland Street,* TV New Zealand, 2002.

Television Appearances; Episodic:

Mr. Stuyvesant, "The Handler," *The Rad Bradbury Theatre,* (also known as *The Bradbury Trilogy, Mystery Theatre, The Ray Bradbury Theatre, Le monde fantastique de Ray Bradbury,* and *Ray Bradbury presente*), USA Network, 1992.

Broteas, "The Road to Calydon," *Hercules: The Legendary Journeys,* syndicated, 1995.

Domesticles, "Once a Hero," *Hercules: The Legendary Journeys,* syndicated, 1996.

Domesticles, "The Wedding of Alcmene, *Hercules: The Legendary Journeys,* syndicated, 1996.

Lord Clairon, "Here She Comes, Miss Amphipolis," *Xena: Warrior Princess,* syndicated, 1997.

Spencius, "Hercules on Trial," *Hercules: The Legendary Journeys,* syndicated, 1998.

Dr. Benjamin Franklin, "The Floundering Father," *Jack of All Trades,* syndicated, 2000.

Walter Goldburn, "The Play's the Thing," *Revelations,* Sci–Fi Channel, 2003.

Television Appearances; Other:

Dr. Bell, *The Chosen,* 1998.

Film Appearances:

Judge, *The Rainbow Warrior* (also known as *The Sinking of the Rainbow Warrior*), Bonny Dore Productions, 1992.

Mailman, *Alex* (also known as *Alex: The Spirit of a Champion*), Roadshow Entertainment Video, 1993.

Deputy, *The Frighteners* (also known as *Robert Zemeckis Presents: "The Frighteners"*), MCA/Universal, 1996.

President Stone, *The Other Side of Heaven,* Excel Entertainment, 2001.

Obstetrician, *Whale Rider* (also known as *Geliebte Giganten—Wale* and *Te kaieke tohora*), Newmarket Films, 2003.

Herb, *King Kong* (also known as *Kong: The Eighth Wonder of the World* and *Peter Jackson's "King Kong"*), Universal, 2005.

Howard Anderson, *Perfect Creature,* Twentieth Century–Fox, 2005.

Stage Appearances:

Appeared as Emory in a production of *The Boys in the Band;* and in title role, *You're a Good Man, Charlie Brown.*

RECORDINGS

Videos:

King Kong: Peter Jackson's Production Diaries, MCA/Universal Home Video, 2005.

Recreating the Eighth Wonder: The Making of "King Kong," Universal Studios Home Video, 2006.

T

TENNANT, Victoria 1950(?)–

PERSONAL

Born September 30, 1950 (some sources say 1953), in London, England; daughter of Cecil (a talent agent and producer) and Irina (a prima ballerina; maiden name, Baronova) Tennant; married Peppo Vanini (a nightclub owner), 1969 (divorced, 1976); married Matthew Chapman (a writer and director), 1978 (divorced, 1982); married Steve Martin (an actor and comedian), November 20, 1986 (divorced, 1994); married Kirk Stambler (a lawyer), March 4, 1996; children: (fourth marriage) Katya Irina. *Education:* Studied ballet at the Elmhurst Ballet School; trained for the stage at the Central School of Speech and Drama, London.

Addresses: *Agent*—Don Buchwald and Associates, 6500 Wilshire Blvd., Suite 2200, Los Angeles, CA 90048.

Career: Actress. Involved with Search for Common Ground.

Member: Screen Actors Guild, British Actors' Equity.

Awards, Honors: Golden Globe Award nomination, best performance by actress in a supporting role in a series, miniseries, or motion picture made for television, 1984, for *The Winds of War.*

CREDITS

Film Appearances:
(Film debut) Doris Randall, *The Ragman's Daughter,* Twentieth Century–Fox, 1972.

Annette Dorberg, *Ich bin dein killer* (also known as *Nullpunkt*), 1979.
Dinner party guest, *The Dogs of War,* 1980.
Barbra, *Horror Planet* (also known as *Inseminoid* and *Horrorplanet*), 1980.
Lady Carnarvon, *Sphinx,* 1981.
Carol Redding and Betty, *A Stranger's Kiss,* Orion, 1983.
Terry Hoskins, *All of Me,* Universal, 1984.
Helden von Tiebolt/Helden Tennyson, *The Holcroft Covenant,* Thorn–EMI, 1985.
Corinne, *Flowers in the Attic,* Fries Entertainment, 1987.
Roberta Gillian, *Best Seller,* Orion, 1987.
Alice Gordon, *Zugzwang,* (also known as *Fool's Mate*), ZDF, 1989.
Hilary Thomas, *Whispers* (also known as *Dean R. Koontz's "Whispers"*), ITC Entertainment, 1990.
Aunt Lydia, *The Handmaid's Tale* (also known as *Die geschichte der dienerin*), Cinecom, 1990.
Sara McDowel, *L.A. Story,* TriStar, 1991.
Alicia Rieux, *La Peste* (also known as *The Plague*), 1992.
Blonde with dog, *Edie & Pen* (also known as *Desert Gamble*), 23rd Street Productions, 1997.
Mary, *Legend of the Mummy* (also known as *Bram Stoker's "Legend of the Mummy"* and *Bram Stoker's "The Mummy"*), New City Releasing/Goldbar International, 1997.
Herself, *We Married Margo,* 2000.
Herself, *The Making of "War and Remembrance"* (short), MPI Home Video, 2004.
Herself, *"War & Remembrance": Behind the Scenes* (short), MPI Home Video, 2004.
Eleanor, *Irene In Time,* Rainbow Film Company, 2007.

Television Appearances; Series:
Anita Hargraves, *Snowy River: The McGregor Saga,* Family Channel, 1993–94.

Television Appearances; Miniseries:
Pamela Tudsbury, *The Winds of War,* ABC, 1983.

Trish Lee, *Chiefs* (also known as *Once Upon a Murder*), CBS, 1983.
Pamela Tudsbury, *War and Remembrance,* ABC, 1988.
Francesca Cunningham Avery, *Voice of the Heart,* 1990.

Television Appearances; Movies:
Helen Curtiss, *La guerre des insectes,* 1981.
Estelle Taylor, *Dempsey,* CBS, 1983.
Gloria Garry, *Under Siege,* NBC, 1986.
Victoria Portman, *Maigret* (also known as *Inspector Maigret*), syndicated, 1988.
Audra, *Act of Will,* 1989.
Bitter divorcee, *Sister Mary Explains It All,* 2001.

Television Appearances; Specials:
Welcome Home, America!—A USO Salute to America's Sons and Daughters, ABC, 1991.
Intimate Portrait: Barbara Taylor Bradford, Lifetime, 1999.

Television Appearances; Episodic:
Bernice, "Who's Got the Lady?," *Tales of the Unexpected,* 1982.
"The Funniest Guy in the World," *George Burns Comedy Week,* CBS, 1985.
Valentina, "Red Snow," *Twilight Zone* (also known as *The New Twilight Zone*), CBS, 1986.
Bride, "Deadly Honeymoon," *Alfred Hitchcock Presents,* NBC, 1986.
Showbiz Today, 1990.
Victoria Larkin, "Deadly Games," *Diagnosis Murder,* CBS, 1997.
Dr. Toynton, "Blind Faith," *Providence,* NBC, 1999.
Irene, "Dancin'," *The Chris Isaak Show,* 2001.
Marta Sperling, "The Man on the Bridge," *JAG,* CBS, 2004.
"Steve Martin," *Biography,* Arts and Entertainment, 2006.
Maggie Kent, "My Scrubs," *Scrubs,* NBC, 2007.

Also appeared as Julia Stoner, "The Case of the Speckled Band," *Sherlock Holmes and Doctor Watson.*

Television Work; Movies:
Executive producer, *Sister Mary Explains It All,* 2001.

Stage Appearances:
Lesbia, *Getting Married,* Circle in the Square, New York City, 1991.

Also appeared in *Love Letters,* Steppenwolf Theatre, Chicago, IL.

WRITINGS

Screenplays:
Edie & Pen (also known as *Desert Gamble*), 23rd Street Productions, 1997.

Film Song Lyrics:
Hussy, 1979.

THOMAS, Sian 1953–
(Sian Polhill Thomas)

PERSONAL

Born September 20, 1953, in Stratford–on–Avon, Warwickshire, England. *Education:* Trained at Central School of Speech and Drama.

Addresses: *Agent*—Conway Van Gelder, Ltd., 18–21 Jermyn St., 3rd Floor, London SW1 6HP United Kingdom.

Career: Actress.

Awards, Honors: Martini Award, best supporting actress, TMA Theatre and Management Awards, for *Uncle Vanya;* Laurence Olivier Award nomination, best performance in a supporting role, Society of London Theatre, 2003, for *Up for Grabs.*

CREDITS

Stage Appearances:
Duchess de Cristoval, *Vautrin,* Glasgow Citizens Company, Scotland, 1977.
Suzanne Fellini, *Semi–Monde,* Glasgow Citizens Company, 1977.
Loot, Glasgow Citizens Company, 1977.
Jenny Diver, *Threepenny Opera,* Glasgow Citizens Company, 1978.
Floria, *Painter's Palace of Pleasure,* Glasgow Citizens Company, 1978.
Felicita, *Good Humored Ladies,* Glasgow Citizens Company, 1979.
Tamara, *Chinchilla,* Glasgow Citizens Company, 1979.
Anna, *Don Juan,* Glasgow Citizens Company, 1980.
Grusha Vachnadze, *The Caucasian Chalk Circle,* Glasgow Citizens Company, 1980.
Lisetta, *The Battlefield,* Glasgow Citizens Company, 1980.
Madame La Duchesse de Guermantes, *A Waste of Time,* Glasgow Citizens Company, 1980.
Melantha/Octavia, *Marriage a la Mode,* Glasgow Citizens Company, 1981.
Monimia, *The Orphan,* Greenwich Theatre, London, 1986.
The Way of the World, Royal National Theatre, London, 1995.
Julia, *A Delicate Balance,* Theatre Royal, London, 1997.

Queen Elizabeth, *Richard III,* Royal Shakespeare Company, Savoy Theatre, London, 1999.

Julie, *Sleep with Me,* Royal National Theatre, 1999.

Goneril, *King Lear,* Royal Shakespeare Company, Barbican Theatre, London, 1999.

Joanna, *Garden,* Royal National Theatre, Olivier Theatre, and *House,* Royal National Theatre, Lyttelton Theatre (performed simultaneously in separate theatres), 2000.

Liz, *Feelgood,* Hampstead Theatre, London, 2001.

Dawn, *Up for Grabs,* Wyndham's Theatre, London, 2002.

Also appeared in *The Winter Guest,* Almeida Theatre, London, then Leeds Playhouse, Leeds, England; *The Lover* and *The Stronger,* both Battersea Arts Theatre, London; *China, The Cutting,* and *A View of Kabul,* all Bush Theatre, London; *Ezra* and *The Worlds,* both Half Moon Theatre, London; title role in *Hedda Gabler,* Leicester Haymarket Theatre; as Desdemona, *Othello,* Lyric Theatre—Hammersmith, London, and Renaissance Theatre; *Private Lives,* Royal Exchange Theatre, Manchester, England; *Kaisers of Carnuntum,* Northern Broadsides Theatre; *The Illusion,* Old Vic Theatre, London; *Uncle Vanya,* Renaissance Theatre; *Bloody Poetry,* Royal Court Theatre, London; *Countrymania, The Misanthrope, The Mountain Giants, Square Rounds,* and *The Wandering Jew,* all Royal National Theatre, London; *Happy End* and as Katharina, *The Taming of the Shrew,* both Royal Shakespeare Company, Stratford–upon–Avon, England; *Pamela* and *Too True to be Good,* both Shared Experience Theatre; *A Passion in Six Days* and as Ophelia, *Hamlet,* both Sheffield Crucible Theatre, Sheffield, England; *Kindertransport,* Vaudeville Theatre, London; *Rainsnakes,* Young Vic Theatre, London.

Film Appearances:

Marilyn Oston, *Prick Up Your Ears,* 1987.

Thorhild the Sarcastic, *Erik the Viking* (also known as *Erik viking*), Orion, 1989.

Aileen Armitage, *Wide–Eyed and Legless* (also known as *The Wedding Gift*), 1994.

Rose Red, 1994.

Woman, *Crossings* (short), 2002.

The aunt, *Srendi Vashtar* (short), 2003.

Lady Darlington, *Vanity Fair,* Focus Features, 2004.

Madame Gaillard, *Perfume: The Story of a Murderer* (also known as *Das parfum—Die geschichte eines morders, Le parfum—histoire d'un meurtrier, perfume, El perfume–historia de un asesino,* and *Das Parfum—Die geschichte eines Morders*), DreamWorks, 2006.

Ameila Bones, *Harry Potter and the Order of the Phoenix,* Warner Bros., 2007.

Television Appearances; Series:

Lesley, *Maybury,* BBC, 1981.

Susan, *Tears Before Bedtime,* BBC, 1995.

(As Sian Polhill Thomas) Wife, *Hotel Babylon,* BBC America, 2006.

Television Appearances; Miniseries:

Lindsey Lucas, *Stanley and the Women,* ITV, 1991.

Miss Nelly, *Celia* (also known as *El Mundo de Celia*), 1992.

Lady Steyne, *Vanity Fair,* Arts and Entertainment and BBC, 1999.

Television Appearances; Movies:

Judith Cole, *Frankenstein Baby,* BBC, 1990.

Aileen Armitage, *Wide–Eyed and Legless* (also known as *The Wedding Gift*), BBC, 1993.

Queen Isobel, *Richard II,* 1997.

Mrs. Rees, *The Ruby in the Smoke,* PBS, 2006.

Television Appearances; Specials:

Doctor Saxon, *A Mind to Murder,* PBS, 1996.

Voice of Desdemona, *Othello,* PBS, 1996.

Television Appearances; Episodic:

Carol Sharp, "The Last Enemy," *Inspector Morse,* PBS, 1989.

Girl on farm, "Val De Ree (Ha Ha Ha Ha Ha)," *Victoria Wood* (also known as *Victoria Wood Presents ...,* BBC, 1989.

Mrs. Johnson, "What Care? What Compensation?," *No Job for a Lady,* 1992.

Martine Evans, "Ring of Deceit," *Taggart,* ITV, 1992.

Voice of Desdemona, "Othello," *Shakespeare: The Animated Tales* (animated), BBC2 and HBO, 1994.

Stella Powell, "Old Flames," *Doctor Finlay,* ITV and PBS, 1995.

Julie McAnearney, "Strap Me Vitals," *Blind Men,* ITV, 1997.

Nicola, "Monday," *The Worst Week of My Life,* BBC America, 2005.

Nicola, "Tuesday," *The Worst Week of My Life,* BBC America, 2005.

Nicola, "Wednesday," *The Worst Week of My Life,* BBC America, 2005.

Nicola, "Friday," *The Worst Week of My Life,* BBC America, 2005.

Elaine Gibb, "413," *The Bill,* ITV1, 2006.

Peggy Aynscombe, "Four Funerals and a Wedding," *Midsomer Murders,* ITV and Arts and Entertainment, 2006.

Helen Miller, *Vincent,* ITV, 2006.

Zoe Martin, "One for My Baby," *Holby City* (also known as *Holby*), BBC, 2006.

Ingrid Nielson, "Whom the Gods Would Destroy," *Lewis,* ITV, 2007.

Annie, "Dangerous Liaisons," *The Last Detective,* ITV, 2007.

Other Television Appearances:
Also appeared in *After the Party; The Bill; Billy Blues; Fallen Sons; Jury; Nancy Astor; Prick Up Your Ears; Rose Red; Shadow of the Noose.*

RECORDINGS

Taped Readings:
Lord Byron Poems, HighBridge Company, 2000.

Also read for recording of *Scandalous Risks,* Chivers.

THORPE, Alexis 1980–

PERSONAL

Full name, Alexis Ann Thorpe; born April 19, 1980, in Newport Beach, CA.

Career: Actress. Also worked as a model.

CREDITS

Film Appearances:
Supermodel, *The Adventures of Rocky & Bullwinkle* (also known as *Die Abenteuer von Rocky und Bullwinkle*), Universal, 2000.
Tiffany Granger, *Pretty Cool,* MTI Home Video, 2001.
Teddy, *The Forsaken* (also known as *The Forsaken: Desert Vampires*), Screen Gems, 2001.
Jennifer, *American Wedding* (also known as *American Pie: The Wedding* and *American Pie—Jetzt wird geheiratet*), Universal, 2003.
Morgan, *Pledge This!* (also known as *National Lampoon's "Pledge This"*), Vivendi Visual Entertainment, 2006.
Kyla Bradley, *Nightmare City 2035,* New Concorde Home Entertainment, 2007.
Jennifer, *The Unlikely's,* NGM Enterprises, 2007.
Linda, *The Man from Earth* (also known as *Jerome Bixby's "The Man from Earth"*), Shoreline Entertainment, 2007.

Television Appearances; Series:
Cassie DiMera/Cassie Brady, *Days of Our Lives* (also known as *Days* and *DOOL*), NBC, between 2002 and 2007.

Television Appearances; Episodic:
The Test, FX Channel, 2001.
Rianna Miner, *The Young and the Restless,* CBS, 2001.

Herself, "The One with the Soap Opera Party," *Friends,* NBC, 2003.
Mindy, "Occam's Razor," *House M.D.* (also known as *House*), Fox, 2004.
Amber, "Derek, Alex, and Gary," *Nip/Tuck,* FX Channel, 2005.

Television Appearances; Other:
Kelly Greer, *Dark Shadows,* 2004.

RECORDINGS

Videos:
Tiffany, *Emmanuelle 2000: Emmanuelle Pie,* Cine Plus, 2003.

TODD, Jennifer 1970–

PERSONAL

Born in 1970, in CA; sister of Suzanne Todd (a producer). *Education:* Attended the University of Southern California Film School.

Addresses: *Office*—Team Todd, 2900 West Olympic Blvd., Santa Monica, CA 90404. *Agent*—Creative Artists Agency, 2000 Avenue of the Stars, Los Angeles, CA 90067.

Career: Producer and assistant. Team Todd (a production company), cofounder and partner (with Suzanne Todd).

Awards, Honors: Lucy Award (with others), Women in Film, 2000; Emmy Award nomination (with others), outstanding made for television movie, 2000, for *If These Walls Could Talk 2;* Independent Spirit Award nomination (with others), best first feature, Independent Features Project West, 2001, for *Boiler Room;* Independent Spirit Award (with Suzanne Todd), best feature, American Film Institute (AFI) Film Award nomination (with Suzanne Todd), AFI movie of the year, 2002, both for *Memento.*

CREDITS

Film Assistant (to Joel Silver):
Lethal Weapon 2, Warner Bros., 1989.
Die Hard 2 (also known as *Die Hard 2: Die Harder*), Twentieth Century–Fox, 1990.

The Adventures of Ford Fairlane, Twentieth Century–Fox, 1990.

Predator 2, Twentieth Century–Fox, 1990.

Film Executive Producer:

Now and Then, New Line Cinema, 1995.

Ira & Abby, Magnolia Pictures, 2006.

Film Producer:

Austin Powers: International Man of Mystery (also known as *Austin Powers—Das Scharfste, was ihre majestat zu bieten hat*), New Line Cinema, 1997.

Idle Hands, Columbia, 1999.

Austin Powers: The Spy Who Shagged Me (also known as *Austin Powers 2: The Spy Who Shagged Me*), New Line Cinema, 1999.

Boiler Room, New Line Cinema, 2000.

Memento, Newmarket Films, 2000.

Austin Powers in Goldmember (also known as *Austin Powers: Goldmember*), New Line Cinema, 2002.

Must Love Dogs, Warner Bros., 2005.

Prime, Focus Features, 2005.

Zoom (also known as *Zoom: Academy for Superheroes*), Columbia, 2006.

Across the Universe, Columbia, 2007.

The Accidental Husband, Yari Film Group Releasing, 2007.

Television Assistant (to Joel Silver); Series:

Tales from the Crypt, HBO, 1989–92.

Television Executive Producer; Movies:

If These Walls Could Talk 2, HBO, 2000.

Television Assistant (to Joel Silver); Pilots:

Two–Fisted Tales, Fox, 1992.

Television Appearances; Episodic:

Also appeared as herself, "Memento," *Anatomy of a Scene,* Sundance.

TORRES, Liz 1947–

 (Queen of house music)

PERSONAL

Full name, Elizabeth Larrieu Torres; born September 27, 1947, in the Bronx, New York, NY (some sources cite Puerto Rico); married Peter Locke (a producer, director, writer, and actor). *Avocational Interests:* Collecting.

Addresses: *Agent*—Jerome Siegel & Associates, 1680 North Vine St., Hollywood, CA 90028.

Career: Actress, comedienne, and singer. Performed as a singer and comedienne, first at nightclubs, bathhouses, and other venues in New York City, then throughout the United States and the world, including a command performance for King Hassan III of Morocco, 1972, and at the White House for National Hispanic Heritage Week, during the administration of president Jimmy Carter, 1977. Appeared in advertisements. Write Act Repertory, Hollywood, CA, member of the board of directors. Active in charitable causes, including public television, the education of minorities, and organizations fighting AIDS. Also known the queen of house music.

Member: National Hispanic Foundation for the Arts.

Awards, Honors: Emmy Award nomination, outstanding guest actress in a comedy series, 1990, for *The Famous Teddy Z;* Lifetime Achievement Award, National Hispanic Academy of Media Arts and Sciences, 1994; Emmy Award nominations, outstanding supporting actress in a comedy series, 1994 and 1995, Golden Globe Award nomination, best performance by an actress in a supporting role in a series, miniseries, or motion picture made for television, 1995, NCLR Bravo Award, outstanding individual performance in a comedy series, National Council of La Raza, 1996, American Comedy Award nomination, funniest supporting female performer in a television series, 1996, NCLR Bravo Award, outstanding individual performance in a comedy series, 1997, and Nosotros Golden Eagle Award, outstanding actress in a television series, 1997, all for *The John Larroquette Show;* NCLR Bravo Award nomination, outstanding performance by a female in a variety or music series/special, 1996, for *Latino Laugh Festival;* El Angel Award, 1997, for contributions to Hispanic art in America; ALMA Award nomination, outstanding actress in a made–for–television movie or miniseries, American Latin Media Arts awards, 1999, for *Storm Chasers: Revenge of the Twister;* Alma Award nomination, outstanding actress in a new television series, 2001, and ALMA Award nomination, outstanding supporting actress in a television series, 2006, both for *Gilmore Girls;* DVD Premiere Award nomination, best supporting actress, DVD Exclusive awards, 2003, for *King Rikki.*

CREDITS

Television Appearances; Series:

Regular performer, *The Melba Moore–Clifton Davis Show,* CBS, 1972.

Regular performer, *Ben Vereen ... Comin' at Ya,* NBC, 1975.

Julie Erskine, *Phyllis,* CBS, 1975–76.

Teresa Betancourt, *All in the Family* (also known as *Justice for All* and *Those Were the Days*), CBS, 1976–77.

Miranda DeAngelo (Milt's wife), *Stockard Channing in Just Friends* (also known as *Just Friends*), CBS, 1979.

Elena Beltran, *Checking In,* CBS, 1981.

Maria, *The New Odd Couple,* ABC, 1982–83.

Gail, *Days of Our Lives* (also known as *Cruise of Deception: Days of Our Lives, Days, DOOL, Des jours et des vies, Horton–sagaen, I gode og onde dager, Los dias de nuestras vidas, Meres agapis, Paeivien viemaeae, Vaara baesta aar, Zeit der Sehnsucht,* and *Zile din viata noastra*), NBC, 1987.

Anna Maria Batista, *City,* CBS, 1990.

Mahalia Sanchez, *The John Larroquette Show* (also known as *Larroquette*), NBC, 1993–96.

Rosa, *Over the Top,* ABC, 1997.

Maria, *Los Beltran,* Telemundo, 1999–2001.

Miss Patty, *Gilmore Girls* (also known as *Gilmore Girls: Beginnings* and *The Gilmore Way*), The WB, 2000–2006, The CW, 2006–2007.

Rosa, *American Family* (also known as *American Family: Journey of Dreams*), PBS, 2002.

Television Appearances; Movies:

Juanita, *More Wild Wild West,* CBS, 1980.

Serafina Palumbo, *Murder Can Hurt You* (also known as *Nojack & Co*), 1980.

Susie, *Her Life as a Man,* NBC, 1984.

Miss Morales, *Father of Hell Town* (also known as *Hell Town*), NBC, 1985.

Laura, *Kate's Secret,* NBC, 1986.

Big Erma, *Poker Alice,* CBS, 1987.

Bernice, *Addicted to His Love* (also known as *Sisterhood*), ABC, 1988.

Isabella D'Agostino, *Miracle at Beekman's Place,* NBC, 1988.

Fortune teller, *Opposites Attract,* NBC, 1990.

Lucy, *Maid for Each Other,* NBC, 1992.

Lenora's mother, *Attack of the 5'2" Women* (also known as *National Lampoon's "Attack of the 5 Ft 2 Woman," Donne all'attacco!,* and *Mujeres al ataque*), Showtime, 1994.

Wallace Houston, *Storm Chasers: Revenge of the Twister* (also known as *Tornado, A revanche do tornado, Cacadores de tempestades, Le souffle de l'enfer, Souffle d'enfer, Storm Chasers—Im Auge des Sturms,* and *Twister—La venganza*), Family Channel, 1998.

Minerva's mother, *The Princess and the Barrio Boy* (also known as *She's in Love*), Showtime, 2000.

The Tooth Fairy, *Once upon a Christmas,* 2000.

The Tooth Fairy, *Twice upon a Christmas* (also known as *Crazy Christmas, Rudolfa's Revenge, La fille du Pere Noel,* and *Natal em perigo*), PAX TV, 2001.

Eugenie Underwood, *McBride: Anybody Here Murder Marty?,* The Hallmark Channel, 2005.

Television Appearances; Specials:

Cat, *Pinocchio* (musical), CBS, 1976.

Macy's Thanksgiving Day Parade, NBC, 1994.

Macy's Thanksgiving Day Parade, NBC, 1996.

The 107th Tournament of Roses Parade, NBC, 1996.

Latino Laugh Festival, Showtime, 1996.

The Second Annual Latino Laugh Festival (also known as *Latino Laugh Festival*), c. 1997.

Herself, *Gilmore Girls Backstage Special,* ABC Family Channel, 2004.

Television Appearances; Awards Presentations:

Presenter, *The VIDA Awards,* NBC, 1995.

1995 NCLR Bravo Awards, Fox, 1995.

1996 NCLR Bravo Awards, Fox, 1996.

Presenter, *The 12th Annual Hispanic Heritage Awards,* NBC, 1998.

Presenter, *Fifth Annual ALMA Awards,* ABC, 2000.

Presenter, *Hispanic Heritage Awards,* NBC, 2000.

Presenter, *2001 ALMA Awards,* ABC, 2001.

Television Appearances; Episodic:

Herself, *The David Frost Show,* syndicated, 1971.

Herself, *The Tonight Show Starring Johnny Carson* (also known as *The Best of Carson*), NBC, multiple episodes, 1971–76.

"Love and the Cryptic Gift/Love and Family Hour/Love and the Legend/Love and Sexpert," *Love, American Style,* ABC, 1972.

Herself, *Bandstand* (also known as *AB, American Bandstand, American Bandstand 1965, New American Bandstand 1966,* and *VH1's Best of "American Bandstand"*), ABC, 1976.

Herself, *Break the Bank,* ABC, 1976.

Herself, *Easy Does It … Starring Frankie Avalon* (also known as *Easy Does It*), CBS, 1976.

Herself, *$20,000 Pyramid,* ABC, 1976.

Anita, "The Game," *Starsky and Hutch,* ABC, 1978.

Anita, "Huggy Can't Go Home (a.k.a. Huggy Can't Go Back)," *Starsky and Hutch,* ABC, 1979.

Elena Beltran, "Florence's New Job: Parts 1 & 2," *The Jeffersons,* CBS, 1981, pilot for the series *Checking In.*

Secretary, "The Return of the Doo–Wop Girls," *Gimme a Break!,* NBC, 1983.

Second nurse, "Rodeo," *Gimme a Break!,* NBC, 1984.

Suprette owner, "Blues for Mr. Green," *Hill Street Blues,* NBC, 1984.

Suprette owner, "Mayo, Hold the Pickle," *Hill Street Blues,* NBC, 1984.

"The Long Flight," *Blue Thunder,* ABC, 1984.

Maria Fuentes, "Overnight Sensation," *Hunter,* NBC, 1986.

Susie, "Enid Quits," *You Again?,* NBC, 1986.

Judge Linda Ruiz–Quinones, "December Bribe," *L.A. Law,* NBC, 1987.

Mrs. Doyle, "I Never Played for My Father," *Duet,* Fox, 1987.

Mrs. Gambino, "Christmas," *The Wonder Years,* ABC, 1988.

Angie, "Teddy Gets a House Guest," *The Famous Teddy Z,* CBS, 1989.

Angie, "Teddy Goes to Malibu," *The Famous Teddy Z,* CBS, 1989.

Dr. Tamayo, "Fountain of Youth," *Alien Nation* (also known as *Spacecop L.A., Alien nacion,* and *Alien nation—ciudadanos del espacio*), Fox, 1989.

Employee, "Down Came the Rain and Washed the Spider Out: Part 1," *Knots Landing,* CBS, 1989.

Madame Rita, "Psycho Pheno–Mama," *Mama's Family,* NBC, 1989.

Gloria Diaz, "Sweet 15," *WonderWorks,* PBS, 1990.

Judge, "The Neighborhood," *Gabriel's Fire,* ABC, 1990.

Mrs. Torres, "The Importance of Being Alex," *Head of the Class,* ABC, 1990.

Judge Trevino, "Belly of the Beast," *Gabriel's Fire,* ABC, 1991.

Angelita Carmen Guadalupe Cecelia Jiminez, "It's a Wonderful Leap—May 10, 1958," *Quantum Leap,* NBC, 1992.

Sixth nanny, "Midnight Plane to Paris," *Murphy Brown,* CBS, 1992.

"Brooklyn and the Beast," *Tequila and Bonetti,* CBS, 1992.

"Tale of the Dragon," *Tequila and Bonetti,* CBS, 1992.

Hazel, "Hazel's of Belmar," *Down the Shore,* Fox, 1993.

Madame LePard, "The All–American Boy—Not!," *Empty Nest,* NBC, 1993.

Various voices, *Happily Ever After: Fairy Tales for Every Child* (animated), HBO, multiple episodes, beginning c. 1995.

Angela, "The Whistle Blower," *Moesha,* UPN, 1996.

Principal Maldonado, "Below the Rim," *Smart Guy,* The WB, 1997.

Mayor White, "A Day at the Races," *The Adventures of A.R.K.* (also known as *The Adventures of A.R.K. (Animal Rescue Kids)*), The Discovery Channel, c. 1997.

Consuela, "Immaculate Concepcion," *The Nanny,* CBS, 1998.

Elizabeth, "Caroline and the Bullfighter: Part 2," *Caroline in the City* (also known as *Caroline*), NBC, 1998.

Hannah Goldstein, "Theme of Life," *Ally McBeal,* Fox, 1998.

Art's lawyer, "Life Insurance," *Safe Harbor,* The WB, 1999.

Liz, "Books," *Tracey Takes On ...,* HBO, 1999.

Phyllis, "America," *Tracey Takes On ...,* HBO, 1999.

Phyllis, "Lies," *Tracey Takes On ...,* HBO, 1999.

Phyllis, "Scandal," *Tracey Takes On ...,* HBO, 1999.

Rosa Vazquez, "The Parent Trap," *Jesse,* NBC, 1999.

Mama, "Thinking of You; Mama's Soup Pot; The Letter," *Chicken Soup for the Soul,* PAX TV, 2000.

Ramona Ramirez, "I'm Okay, You're Crazy," *The Fighting Fitzgeralds,* NBC, 2001.

Ramona Ramirez, "One Angry Man (a.k.a. The Angry Man)," *The Fighting Fitzgeralds,* NBC, 2001.

Tia Gaby, "Cold Turkey," *The Brothers Garcia,* Nickelodeon, 2001.

Laverne, *TV411,* PBS, multiple episodes, beginning c. 2001.

Janet Crowley, "Court Date," *First Monday,* CBS, 2002.

Janet Crowley, "Crime and Punishment," *First Monday,* CBS, 2002.

Janet Crowley, "The Price of Liberty," *First Monday,* CBS, 2002.

"The Big Show," *Taina,* Nickelodeon, 2002.

Sarah Wilson, "A Little Help from My Friends," *ER* (also known as *Emergency Room*), NBC, 2003.

Sarah Wilson, "A Saint in the City," *ER* (also known as *Emergency Room*), NBC, 2003.

Herself, "Character You Love to Hate," *TV Land's Top Ten,* TV Land, 2005.

Herself, "Greatest TV Romances," *TV Land's Top Ten,* TV Land, 2005.

Esperanza, "Teach Your Children Well," *The New Adventures of Old Christine* (also known as *Old Christine*), CBS, 2006.

Evelyn, "Brothers," *Ugly Betty* (also known as *Betty in the USA, Betty the Ugly, Alles Betty!, Betty en los Estados Unidos, Cimlapsztori, Fula Betty,* and *Ruma Betty*), ABC, 2007.

Appeared as Juanita, *Good Advice,* CBS. Appeared in other programs, including *Almost Grown,* CBS; *Murder, She Wrote,* CBS; *Nurses,* NBC; and *Storytime,* PBS.

Television Appearances; Pilots:

Lupe (Abraham's friend), *Popi,* CBS, 1975.

Trini Santos, *Willow B: Women in Prison* (also known as *Cages*), ABC, 1980.

Elena Beltran, "Florence's New Job: Parts 1 & 2," *Checking In,* CBS, 1981, broadcast as an episode of *The Jeffersons.*

Airport official, *Not in Front of the Kids,* ABC, 1984.

Lola, *Taking It Home,* NBC, 1986.

Miss Camez, "B Men," *CBS Summer Playhouse,* CBS, c. 1989.

Helena Hernandez, *Greyhounds,* CBS, 1994.

Miss Patty, *Gilmore Girls* (also known as *Gilmore Girls: Beginnings* and *The Gilmore Way*), The WB, 2000.

Janet Crowley, *First Monday,* CBS, 2002.

Appeared as Miss Patty in the unaired pilot of *Gilmore Girls* (also known as *Gilmore Girls: Beginnings* and *The Gilmore Way*), The WB.

Film Appearances:

Park prostitute, *Utterly without Redeeming Social Value* (also known as *Baring It All*), Private Screenings, 1969.

Singer, *You've Got to Walk It Like You Talk It or You'll Lose That Beat,* JER Pictures, 1971.

Lady Zero, *Scavenger Hunt,* Twentieth Century–Fox, 1979.

Dolores Frantico, *America* (also known as *Moonbeam*), ASA Communications, 1986.

Miss Cortez, *Ordinary Heroes,* Juniper Releasing, 1986.

Bea, *Hot to Trot,* Warner Bros., 1988.

Rosa, *Sunset* (also known as *Catalina, Asesinato en Beverly Hills, Assassinato em Hollywood, Intrigo a hollywood, Meurtre a Hollywood,* and *Sunset— Daemmerung in Hollywood*), TriStar, 1988.

Big Rosa, *Thieves of Fortune* (also known as *Chameleon* and *May the Best Man Win*), Skouras Pictures, 1990.

Cab driver's wife, *Lena's Holiday,* Crown International Pictures, 1991.

Lieutenant Garcia, *Bloodfist IV: Die Trying* (also known as *Bloodfist 4—Deadly Dragon* and *Die Trying*), 1992.

Carney, *Rescue Me* (also known as *Street Hunter*), Cannon, 1993.

Judge Fernandez, *Body Shot,* EDKO Film, 1993.

Girl Talk, Frameline, 1993.

Mrs. Delgado, *A Million to Juan* (also known as *A Million to One*), Samuel Goldwyn Company, 1994.

Delores Rodriguez, *Just Cause,* Warner Bros., 1995.

Dita, *Permanent Midnight,* Artisan Entertainment, 1998.

Maria, *The Odd Couple II* (also known as *Neil Simon's "The Odd Couple II"*), Paramount, 1998.

Ruby Escadrillo, *The Wonderful Ice Cream Suit,* Buena Vista/Walt Disney Pictures, 1998.

Judge Sanchez, *Luminarias,* Artist View Entertainment, 1999.

Beauty college woman, *Joe Dirt* (also known as *The Adventures of Joe Dirt* and *Joe Dreck*), Columbia, 2001.

Julia, *Gabriela,* Power Point Films, 2001.

Mata Ortega, *King Rikki* (also known as *Rikki the Pig* and *The Street King*), Mistral Pictures/Dream Rock/ Moonstone Entertainment, 2002.

Nonna BonGiovanni, *Volare* (short film), Sky King Productions/Kings View Productions, 2004.

Teri Richards, *Taylor,* AIC/York Entertainment, 2005.

Mother, *West of Brooklyn,* 68 Cent Features, 2007.

Juanita, *Expecting Love,* CrossCut Films, 2008.

Some sources cite an appearance in *It Happened in Hollywood,* Screw Film, c. 1972.

Film Song Performer:

"Kitty Can't Help It," *The Carhops* (also known as *California Drive–In Girls* and *Kitty Can't Help It*), N.M.D. Film Distributing Company, 1975, International Film Distributors, 1976.

"Loca," *Dancin' thru the Dark,* Miramax, 1990.

Perfomer of songs that have appeared in films and television programs.

Stage Appearances:

Bunny, *House of Blue Leaves,* Coconut Grove Playhouse, Miami, FL, 1988.

Divas: Simply Singing (benefit concert), Los Angeles, 1995.

Stella Deems, *Follies* (musical), "Broadway's Best" series, Reprise!, Wadsworth Theatre, Los Angeles, 2002.

Appeared as Aldonza, *Man of La Mancha* (musical), Burt Reynolds Dinner Theater, Jupiter, FL; and as Googie Gomez, *The Ritz.* Appeared in *The Beautiful Mariposa, A Funny Thing Happened on the Way to the Forum* (musical), *A Girl Could Get Lucky, Kiss Me Kate* (musical), *Ladies, Murder at the Howard Johnson, The Musical Comedy Murders of 1940, She That One He the Other,* and *3 Broads 3.* Also appeared in a solo show and in other productions, including a tribute to Rita Moreno.

Major Tours:

Toured as Rosie in *Bye Bye, Birdie* (musical), and as Gittel Mosca in *Seesaw* (musical).

RECORDINGS

Albums:

Can't Get Enough (featuring Master C & J), Jack Trax, 1987.

The Queen Is in the House, Jive and Zomba Records, 1990.

Albums; with Others:

Master C & J, *Can't Get Enough (The Classics and More)* (featuring Liz Torres), Trax/RSK/Arvato Services, 2005.

Also appeared in recordings by other artists and in compilations.

Singles:

"What You Make Me Feel" (featuring Kenny "Jammin" Jason), Underground, 1986 and 1988.

"Can't Get Enough" (featuring Edward Crosby), State Street Records and ZYX Records, 1987.

"Can't Get Enough" (featuring Master C & J), Jack Trax, 1987.

"Mama's Boy," State Street Records and ZYX Records, 1987.

"No More Mind Games"/"Can't Get Enough," Jack Trax, 1987.

"Out of My Life"/"Don't Fuck with Me," Streetside Records, 1987.

"Out of My Life," Streetside Records, 1988.

"Touch of Love," BCM Records and Black Market, 1988.

(With the Crosby and the Get Down Gang) "You Belong to Me" (You Belong to Me bitch mix), c. 1988.

"I Don't Want You to Stop," Streetside Records, 1989.

"Payback Is a Bitch (What Goes Around Comes Around)," Jive, 1989.

"Queen B****," Streetside Records, 1989.

"If U Keep It Up," Jive, Mercury, Torso, and Black Market International, 1990.

"Set Urself Free," Radikal, 1995.

"Set Urself Free" (remix), Radikal, 1995.

"Set Yourself Free" (remix), Underground Music Department, 1996.

Performer in other recordings, including "Don't Let Love Pass U By," Streetside Records; and "Face It"/"Can't Get Enough" and "What You Make Me Feel"/"No More Mind Games," both Jack Trax.

Music Videos:

"If U Keep It Up," 1990.

WRITINGS

Writings for the Stage:

Affiliated with a solo show.

Albums:

(With Jessie Jones) *Can't Get Enough* (featuring Master C & J), Jack Trax, 1987.

The Queen Is in the House, Jive and Zomba Records, 1990.

Albums; with Others:

Master C & J, *Can't Get Enough (The Classics and More)* (featuring Liz Torres), Trax/RSK/Arvato Services, 2005.

Also contributed to recordings by other artists and to compilations.

Singles:

(Lyrics) "What You Make Me Feel" (featuring Kenny "Jammin" Jason), Underground, 1986 and 1988.

(With Edward Crosby and Jessie Jones) "Can't Get Enough" (featuring Crosby), State Street Records and ZYX Records, 1987.

"Can't Get Enough" (featuring Master C & J), Jack Trax, 1987.

"Mama's Boy," State Street Records and ZYX Records, 1987.

"No More Mind Games"/"Can't Get Enough," Jack Trax, 1987.

"Out of My Life"/"Don't Fuck with Me," Streetside Records, 1987.

"Out of My Life," Streetside Records, 1988.

(With Jones) "Touch of Love," BCM Records and Black Market, 1988.

(With the Crosby and the Get Down Gang) "You Belong to Me" (You Belong to Me bitch mix), c. 1988.

(With Jones) "I Don't Want You to Stop," Streetside Records, 1989.

"Payback Is a Bitch (What Goes Around Comes Around)," Jive, 1989.

"Queen B****," Streetside Records, 1989.

"If U Keep It Up," Jive, Mercury, Torso, and Black Market International, 1990.

"Set Urself Free," Radikal, 1995.

"Set Urself Free" (remix), Radikal, 1995.

"Set Yourself Free" (remix), Underground Music Department, 1996.

Wrote other recordings, including "Don't Let Love Pass U By," Streetside Records; and "Face It"/"Can't Get Enough" and "What You Make Me Feel"/"No More Mind Games," both Jack Trax.

OTHER SOURCES

Books:

Notable Hispanic American Women, Book 2, Gale, 1998.

TUDYK, Alan 1971–

PERSONAL

Full name, Alan Wray Tudyk; born March 16, 1971, in El Paso, TX; companion of Amy Sedaris (an actress and comic). *Education:* Studied drama at Lon Morris Junior College, 1990–91, and The Juilliard School, 1993–96.

Addresses: *Agent*—Endeavor, 9601 Wilshire Blvd., 3rd Floor, Beverly Hills, CA 90210. *Manager*—GEF Entertainment, 122 North Clark Dr., Suite 401, Los Angeles, CA 90048.

Career: Actor. Court Jesters Improv Troupe, New York, NY, founder; Rubber Chicken Standup Improv Troupe, Dallas, TX, founder.

Awards, Honors: Academic Excellence Award for Drama, Lon Morris Junior College, 1991; *Theatre World Award*, 1997, for *Bunny Bunny—Golda Radner: A Sort of Romantic Comedy;* MTV Movie Award nomination (with others), best on–screen team, 2005, for *Dodgeball: A True Underdog Story.*

CREDITS

Film Appearances:

Trevor, *35 Miles from Normal,* 1997.

Everton, *Patch Adams,* Universal, 1998.

Gerdhart, *28 Days,* Columbia, 2000.

Sam Traxler, *Wonder Boys* (also known as *Die Wonder Boys* and *Wonderboys—Lauter wunderknaben*), Paramount, 2000.

Wat Falhurst, *A Knight's Tale,* Columbia, 2001.

Himself, *Tournaments: A Cross Between Pro Football and Stock Car Racing* (documentary short), Columbia TriStar, 2001.

Himself, *The Rock Scene in 1370* (documentary short), Columbia TriStar, 2001.

Himself, *School of Hard Rocks* (documentary short), Columbia TriStar, 2001.

Monte man, *Hearts in Atlantis,* Warner Bros., 2001.

Voice of Oscar and Dab the Dodo, *Ice Age* (animated), Twentieth Century–Fox, 2002.

Himself, *Serenity: The 10th Character* (documentary short), 2003.

Himself, *Here's How It Was: The Making of "Firefly"* (documentary short), Twentieth Century Fox Home Entertainment, 2003.

Steve, *Dodgeball: A True Underdog Story* (also known as *Dodgeball* and *Voll auf die nusse*), Twentieth Century–Fox, 2004.

Sonny, *I, Robot,* Twentieth Century–Fox, 2004.

Himself, *Day Out of Days: The "I, Robot" Production Diaries* (documentary), Twentieth Century–Fox, 2004.

Wash, *Serenity,* Universal, 2005.

Pepe, *Rx* (also known as *Simple Lies*), Screen Media Ventures, 2005.

Himself, *Re–Lighting the Firefly* (documentary short), 2005.

Voice of Cholly, *Ice Age: The Meltdown* (animated; also known as *Ice Age 2* and *Ice Age: The Meltdown*), Twentieth Century–Fox, 2006.

Jack, *Knocked Up,* Universal, 2006.

Himself, *A Filmmaker's Journey,* 2006.

Himself, *Done the Impossible: The Fans' Tale of "Firefly" and "Serenity"* (documentary), 2006.

Danny, *Meet Market,* Seedsman Group, 2007.

Simon, *Death at a Funeral* (also known as *Sterben fur anfanger*), Metro–Goldwyn–Mayer, 2007.

Doc Potter, *3:10 to Yuma,* Lions Gate Films, 2007.

Television Appearances; Series:

Hoban "Wash" Washburne, *Firefly,* Fox, 2002–2003.

Television Appearances; Miniseries:

Nathan Wheeler, *Into the West,* TNT, 2005.

Television Appearances; Pilots:

Walker Eliot, *Capitol Law,* 2006.

Television Appearances; Specials:

The Making of "A Knight's Tale," HBO, 2001.

Sci Fi Inside: "Serenity," Sci–Fi Channel, 2005.

Television Appearances; Episodic:

Father, "Blank Stare: Parts 1 & 2," *Strangers with Candy,* Comedy Central, 2000.

Todd Peterson, "The Great Cane Robbery," *Frasier,* NBC, 2000.

"28 Days," *HBO First Look,* HBO, 2000.

"The Making of 'A Knight's Tale,'" *HBO First Look,* HBO, 2001.

"I, Robot," *HBO First Look,* HBO, 2004.

Best Week Ever, VH1, 2005.

Pastor Veal, "Meat the Veals," *Arrested Development,* Fox, 2005.

Carl Fisher, "Burn Out," *CSI: Crime Scene Investigation* (also known as *C.S.I.* and *Les Experts*), CBS, 2006.

Stage Appearances:

Supporting characters, *Bunny Bunny—Golda Radner: A Sort of Romantic Comedy* (also known as *Bunny Bunny*), Philadelphia, PA, then Lucille Lortel Theatre, New York City, 1996–97.

Candida, Yale Repertory Theatre, New Haven, CT, 1997.

Bently Summerhays, *Misalliance,* Laura Pels Theatre, New York City, 1997.

Etocles and Creon, *Oedipus,* Classic Stage Company, New York City, 1998.

Adam, *The Most Fabulous Story Ever Told,* New York Theatre Workshop, New York City, 1998–99.

Benny Bennet, *Epic Proportions,* Helen Hayes Theatre, New York City, 1999.

Kip Harris, *Wonder of the World,* Manhattan Theatre Club Stage I, New York City, 2001–2002.

Marlon, *The 24 Hour Plays 2004,* American Airlines Theatre, New York City, 2004.

Sir Lancelot, French Taunter, and other characters, *Monty Python's "Spamalot,"* Shubert Theatre, New York City, 2005.

Stewie, *The 24 Hour Plays 2005,* American Airlines Theatre, New York City, 2005.

Peter, *Prelude to a Kiss,* American Airlines Theatre, New York City, 2007.

RECORDINGS

Video Games:

Voice of Cholly, *Ice Age 2: The Meltdown,* Vivendi Universal Games, 2006.

TYSON, Richard 1961–
   (Richard M. Tyson)

PERSONAL

Full name, Richard Martin Tyson; born February 13, 1961, in Mobile, AL; married Tracy Kristofferson (an actress); children: one. *Education:* Cornell University, master of theatre arts. *Avocational Interests:* Fishing.

Addresses: *Manager*—Levine Management, 9028 Sunset Blvd., Penthouse 1, Los Angeles, CA 90069.

Career: Actor. Appeared in television commercial for ESPN, 1999; appeared in radio commercial for Fonesca Cigars, 2006.

CREDITS

Film Appearances:

Buddy Revell, *Three O'Clock High,* Universal, 1987.

Perry, *Two Moon Junction,* Lorimar Film Entertainment, 1988.

Cullen Crisp, Sr., *Kindergarten Cop,* Universal, 1990.

Guy Bush, *The Babe,* Universal, 1992.

Dak, *Dark Tide,* 1993.

Rodie, *Pharaoh's Army,* Orion Home Entertainment, 1995.

Owner of Stiffy's, *Kingpin,* Metro–Goldwyn–Mayer, 1996.

Koda, *Time Under Fire* (also known as *Beneath the Bermuda Triangle*), Royal Oaks Entertainment, 1996.

Paul Yeager, *The Glass Cage,* 1996.

Jack, *Liar's Poker,* North Branch Entertainment, 1997.

Bill Stenwick, *The Pandora Project,* Cinetel Films/New City Releasing, 1998.

(As Richard M. Tyson) Detective Krevoy, *There's Something About Mary* (also known as *There's Something More About Mary*), Twentieth Century–Fox, 1998.

Kenneth Blake, *Monsoon,* 1998.

Carl, *Implicated,* Columbia TriStar, 1998.

Streets, *Desert Thunder,* New Horizons Home Video, 1998.

Title role, *Genghis Khan,* 1998.

Robert the Fox, *Battlefield Earth* (also known as *Battlefield Earth: A Saga for the Year 3000*), Warner Bros., 2000.

Gun shop owner, *Me, Myself, and Irene,* Twentieth Century–Fox, 2000.

Busch, *Black Hawk Down,* Revolution Studios, 2001.

Paul Brody, *Firetrap,* PM Entertainment Group, 2001.

Dying on the Edge, 2001.

Gaspar Dias and Kenneth Blake, *Monsoon* (also known as *Tales of the Kama Sutra 2: Monsoon*), 2001.

Carruth, *Cottonmouth* (also known as *Lethal Force* and *Silent Justice*), Madison Home Video, 2002.

David, *Psychic Murders,* 2002.

Dan, *Last Flight Out,* World Wide Pictures Home Video, 2004.

Nikolay Klimov, *Moscow Heat,* Lightening Entertainment, 2004.

Jake, *Yesterday's Dream,* 2005.

Husband, *Lonesome Matador* (short), 2005.

Lancer Higgins, *Naked Run,* 2006.

Sheriff Brett Henchie, *The Visitation,* Twentieth Century–Fox, 2006.

Dean, *When I Find the Ocean,* 2006.

Mitchell Toblat, *Big Bad Wolf,* Screen Media Ventures, 2006.

Paul Judd, *Flight of the Living Dead: Outbreak on a Plane* (also known as *Flight of the Living Dead*), New Line Home Video, 2007.

Ralph, *The Dukes,* 2007.

Mr. VIP, *Stripper Academy,* Omega Entertainment, 2007.

Teddy, *Fear Chamber,* 2007.

Black Morgan Gandil, *Shoot First and Pray You Live (Because Luck Has Nothing to Do With It),* 2007.

Federal Marshall Tyree, *Sin–Jin Smyth,* Sunn Classic Pictures, 2007.

Johnny Dunn, *Jake's Corner,* Emerging Pictures, 2008.

Duke of Clarence, *Richard III,* 2008.

Television Appearances; Series:

Joe "Kaz" Kaczierowski, *Hardball,* NBC, 1989.

Dwayne Serlin, *Winnetka Road,* 1994.

Television Appearances; Movies:

Lute Newhouser, *Davy Crockett: Rainbow in the Thunder,* 1988.

Smoke, *Lakota Moon,* 1992.

Bud, *Red Shoe Diaries 3: Another Woman's Lipstick,* Showtime, 1993.

587: The Great Train Robbery, 1999.

Carl, *Implicated,* 1999.

Riggins, *Operation Sandman* (also known as *Operation Sandman: Warriors in Hell*), UPN, 2000.

Brechner, *Crusader*, 2004.
Gerald Rutledge, *The Trail to Hope Rose*, Hallmark Channel, 2004.

Television Appearances; Specials:
The Hollywood Christmas Parade, 1990.

Television Appearances; Episodic:
Daniel, "The Man Who Cried Wife," *Moonlighting*, ABC, 1986.
Corporal Whitlow, "Promised Land," *China Beach*, ABC, 1989.
Bud, "Talk to Me Baby," *Red Shoe Diaries*, 1992.
Cali, "Hotel California," *Dead at 21*, 1994.

Billy Long, "The Sweetest Gift," *Christy* (also known as *Catherine Marshall's "Christy"*), 1994.
Frank Rafferty, "Poachers," *The Sentinel*, UPN, 1997.
Art London, "Ain't That a Kick in the Head," *Buddy Faro*, CBS, 1998.
"Honor Among Strangers," *Martial Law*, CBS, 2000.
Mr. Brady, *Black Sash*, The WB, 2002.
Frank Needham, "Wannabe," *Boomtown*, NBC, 2003.
Frank Russo, "And Here's to You, Mrs. Azrael," *CSI: NY* (also known as *CSI: New York*), CBS, 2006.

Stage Appearances:
Chance Wayne, *Sweet Bird of Youth*, Theatricum Botanicum, Los Angeles, 1997.

V–Z

VAJNA, Andrew 1944–
(Andrew G. Vajna, Andrew George Vajna, Andy Vajna)

PERSONAL

Born August 1, 1944, in Budapest, Hungary. *Education:* Attended University of California, Los Angeles.

Addresses: *Office*—Cinergi Pictures Entertainment, 2308 Broadway St., Santa Monica, CA 90404.

Career: Producer. Began career as owner of motion picture theaters in Far East; Panasia Film Ltd. (a distribution, acquisition, and film representation company), Hong Kong, founder, c. early 1970s; Carolco Service, Inc. (financing and distribution company), founding partner with Mario Kassar and producer, 1976–89; American Film Marketers Association, founder and president, 1982; Cinergi Productions, Inc. (independent production company), Santa Monica, CA, founder, chairman, and CEO, 1990–97; Intercom (a distribution and production company), founder, 1997–?; C–2 Pictures, founder, 2003–06; revived Cinergi as Cinergi Pictures Entertainment, Santa Monica, CA, 2006.

Awards, Honors: Golden Satellite Award (with Alan Parker and Robert Stigwood), best motion picture—comedy or musical, International Press Academy, Golden Globe Award (with Parker and Stigwood), best motion picture—musical or comedy, 1996, both for *Evita.*

CREDITS

Film Producer:
Hei lu (also known as *The Deadly China Doll, Hak lui,* and *The Opium Trail*), Metro–Goldwyn–Mayer, 1973.

(With Mario Kassar, Joel Michaels, and Garth Drabinsky) *The Silent Partner,* 1978.
(As Andrew G. Vajna; with Donna Dubrow) *Medicine Man* (also known as *The Last Days of Eden*), Buena Vista, 1992.
Renaissance Man (also known as *Army Intelligence* and *By the Book*), Buena Vista, 1994.
(As Andrew G. Vajna) *The Scarlet Letter,* Buena Vista, 1995.
(As Andrew G. Vajna) *Nixon,* Buena Vista, 1995.
Amanda, Sony Pictures Entertainment, 1996.
Evita, Buena Vista, 1996.
A Miniszter felrelep (also known as *Out of Order*), InterCom, 1997.
I Spy (also known as *I–Spy*), Columbia, 2002.
Terminator 3: Rise of the Machines (also known as *T3* and *Terminator 3—Rebellion der maschinen*), 2003.
Basic Instinct 2 (also known as *Basic Instinct—Neues Spiel fur Catherine Tramell*), Metro–Goldwyn–Mayer, 2006.
Szabadsag, szerelem (also known as *Children of Glory*), 2006.

Also produced *Suzanne; Your Ticket Is No Longer Valid; Carbon Copy.*

Film Executive Producer (with Mario Kassar):
(And with Joel Michaels and Garth Drabinsky) *The Changeling,* 1979.
The Amateur, Twentieth Century–Fox, 1981.
First Blood (also known as *Rambo: First Blood*), Orion, 1982.
Superstition (also known as *The Witch*), Almi Pictures, 1982.
Rambo: First Blood Part II, TriStar, 1985.
Angel Heart (also known as *Aux portes de l'enfer*), TriStar, 1987.
Red Heat, TriStar, 1988.
Iron Eagle II, 1988.
Rambo III, TriStar, 1988.

DeepStar Six (also known as *Deep Star Six*), TriStar, 1989.

Johnny Handsome, TriStar, 1989.

Air America, TriStar, 1990.

Total Recall, TriStar, 1990.

Narrow Margin, TriStar, 1990.

Jacob's Ladder (also known as *Dante's Inferno*), TriStar, 1990.

Mountains of the Moon, TriStar, 1990.

Film Executive Producer:

The Victory (also known as *Escape to Victory*), 1981.

(As Andrew G. Vajna) *Tombstone,* Buena Vista, 1993.

(As Andrew G. Vajna) *Color of Night,* Buena Vista, 1994.

(As Andrew G. Vajna) *Die Hard: With a Vengeance* (also known as *Die Hard 3*), Twentieth Century–Fox, 1995.

Judge Dredd, Buena Vista, 1995.

Shadow Conspiracy, Buena Vista, 1997.

An Alan Smithee Film: Burn Hollywood Burn (also known as *Burn, Hollywood, Burn*), Buena Vista, 1997.

The 13th Warrior (also known as *The Thirteenth Warrior*), Buena Vista, 1999.

A Holocaust Szemei (documentary; also known as *Eyes of the Holocaust*), InterCom, 2000.

An American Rhapsody (also known as *Amerikai rapszodia*), Paramount Classics, 2001.

Freedom's Fury (documentary), 2006.

Film Presenter:

(As Andrew Vajna) *First Blood* (also known as *Rambo: First Blood*), Orion, 1982.

(As Andrew Vajna) *Extreme Prejudice,* TriStar, 1987.

(As Andrew Vajna) *Rambo III,* TriStar, 1988.

(As Andrew Vajna) *Red Heat,* TriStar, 1988.

(As Andrew Vajna) *DeepStar Six* (also known as *Deep Star Six*), TriStar, 1989.

(As Andrew Vajna) *Johnny Handsome,* TriStar, 1989.

(As Andrew Vajna) *Total Recall,* TriStar, 1990.

(As Andrew Vajna) *Narrow Margin,* TriStar, 1990.

Medicine Man (also known as *The Last Days of Eden*), Buena Vista, 1992.

Renaissance Man (also known as *Army Intelligence* and *By the Book*), Buena Vista, 1994.

Color of Night, Buena Vista, 1994.

Evita, Buena Vista, 1996.

Shadow Conspiracy, Buena Vista, 1997.

An Alan Smithee Film: Burn Hollywood Burn (also known as *Burn, Hollywood, Burn*), Buena Vista, 1997.

Terminator 3: Rise of the Machines (also known as *T3* and *Terminator 3—Rebellion der Maschinen*), 2003.

Presenter, *Basic Instinct 2* (also known as *Basic Instinct—Neues Spiel fur Catherine Tramell*), 2006.

Film Appearances:

Himself, *Guts and Glory* (short; also known as *Guts & Glory*) Artisan Entertainment, 2002.

Himself, *Afghanistan: Land in Crisis* (documentary short), Artisan Entertainment, 2002.

Himself, *We Get To Win This Time* (documentary short), Artisan Entertainment, 2002.

Himself, *Drawing First Blood* (documentary short; also known as *Drawing First Blood: 20 Years Later* and *Making of "First Blood"*), Artisan Entertainment, 2002.

Himself, *A Stuntman for All Seasons: A Tribute to Bennie Dobbins* (documentary short), Lions Gate Films, 2004.

Himself, *East Meets West: "Red Heat" and the Kings of Carolco* (documentary short), Lions Gate Films, 2004.

Television Work; Pilots:

Executive producer and co–producer, *The Sarah Connor Chronicles,* Fox, 2008.

Television Appearances; Specials:

Masters of Fantasy: Paul Verhoeven, 1997.

Inside "Terminator 3: Rise of the Machines," 2003.

Television Appearances; Episodic:

"Behind the Scenes: 'Die Hard: With a Vengeance,'" *HBO First Look,* HBO, 1995.

"Inside 'Terminator 3: Rise of the Machines,'" *HBO First Look,* HBO, 2003.

OTHER SOURCES

Periodicals:

Variety, May 6, 1991, p. C2.

Van DIEN, Catherine
    See OXENBERG, Catherine

van HEERDEN, Andre 1971(?)–

PERSONAL

Born c. 1971, in Lusaka, Zambia; immigrated to Canada, 1975; married, wife's name Carolyn; children: Ava (an actress), Elise. *Education:* Carleton University, Ottawa, Ontario, Canada, graduated (with high honors). *Religion:* Christian.

Career: Producer, director, writer, actor, and film editor. Also worked as production supervisor, online editor, and assistant camera operator; affiliated with the documentary project Startling Proofs, 1995.

CREDITS

Film Director:
Vanished, Cloud Ten Pictures, 1998.
Revelation (also known as *Apocalypse II: Revelation*), Providence Entertainment, 1999.
Tribulation, Artist View Entertainment/Cloud Ten Pictures, 2000.
Judgment (also known as *Apocalypse IV: Judgment* and *O.N.E.: One Nation Earth*), Cloud Ten Pictures, 2001.
Deceived, Shoreline Entertainment, 2002.

Film Producer:
Coproducer, *Left Behind* (also known as *Left Behind: The Movie*), Cloud Ten Pictures, 2000.
Producer, *Left Behind: World at War,* Columbia, 2005.

Film Appearances:
Bill Rowsome, *Revelation* (also known as *Apocalypse II: Revelation*), Providence Entertainment, 1999.
Man in New York studio, *Left Behind* (also known as *Left Behind: The Movie*), Cloud Ten Pictures, 2000.

Television Appearances; Specials:
The Passion: Films, Faith & Fury, Channel 4, 2006.

RECORDINGS

Videos:
The Making of "Left Behind: The Movie," 2000.
The Making of "Left Behind II: Tribulation Force," Cloud Ten Pictures, 2002.

WRITINGS

Screenplays:
Vanished, Cloud Ten Pictures, 1998.
Judgment (also known as *Apocalypse IV: Judgment* and *O.N.E.: One Nation Earth*), Cloud Ten Pictures, 2001.
Left Behind: World at War, Columbia, 2005.

OTHER SOURCES

Electronic:
Entertainment Zone, http://www.ez-entertainment.net, November 16, 2007.

Pulp Movies, http://www.pulpmovies.com, February 18, 2003.

Van PELT, Luke 1985–

PERSONAL

Born October 17, 1985, in Renton, WA.

Career: Actor.

CREDITS

Film Appearances:
Excited fan, *The Iron Man,* 2006.
Young astronaut, *Fractalus,* 2006.
Bruce, *Street Dreams,* 2007.
Ballplayer, *American Asian,* 2008.
Jack, *Finding Amanda,* 2008.
David, *AmerAsian,* 2008.

Television Appearances; Series:
Room 401, 2008.

Television Appearances; Episodic:
Noah Svenson, "Mario Tennis," *Gamers* (also known as *National Lampoon's "Gamers"*), 2005.
Himself, "The Veronicas: 4ever," *Making the Video,* MTV, 2005.
(Uncredited) Young husband, "Wrongful Death," *Justice,* Fox, 2006.
Paul Pontell, "For Whom the Bell Tolls," *The Wedding Bells,* Fox, 2007.
Himself, "Pink Is the New Black," *The Apprentice* (also known as *The Apprentice USA*), NBC, 2007.
Himself, "Day Seven," *Hell's Kitchen,* Fox, 2007.

WAGNER, Robin 1933–

PERSONAL

Full name, Robin Samuel Anton Wagner; born August 31, 1933, in San Francisco, CA; son of Jens Otto and Phyllis Edna Catherine (maiden name, Smith–Spurgeon) Wagner; married Paula (a producer; divorced); children: Kurt, Leslie, Christie. *Education:* Attended California School of Fine Arts, 1952–54. *Religion:* Roman Catholic.

Addresses: *Office*—Robin Wagner Studio, 890 Broadway, 6th Floor, New York, NY 10003–1211.

Career: Set designer. Scarab Productions, president, 1975; Columbia University, New York, NY, professor of theatre arts, 1988; The Design Edge, senior vice president, 1989. Has designed sets for operas, ballets, and other theatre productions around the world as well as for performers, including the Fifth Dimension, the Jo Jo Dancers, and the Rolling Stones. National Corporate Theatre Fund, advisory board member; League of Professional Theatre Training Programs, steering committee member; Broadway Theatre Institute, advisory committee member; Theatre Advisory Council for City of New York, advisory board member; New York Shakespeare Festival, trustee; New York International Festival of the Arts, member of the art advisory committee.

Member: United Scenic Artists.

Awards, Honors: Drama Desk Award, set design, 1971, for *Lenny;* Antoinette Perry Award nomination, best scenic designer, 1972, for *Jesus Christ Superstar;* Joseph Maharam Award, 1973; Boston Critics Award, 1974; Lumen Award, 1975; *Theatre World* Award, 1975; Joseph Maharam Award, 1975; Antoinette Perry Award nomination, best scenic designer, 1975, for *Mack and Mabel;* Antoinette Perry Award, best scenic designer, Drama Desk Award, set design, 1978, both for *On the Twentieth Century;* Outer Circle Critics Award, 1978; Dramalogue Award, 1980; Antoinette Perry Award nomination, best scenic designer, Drama Desk Award nomination, outstanding special effects, 1982, both for *Dreamgirls;* Joseph Maharam Award, 1982; Antoinette Perry Award, best scenic design, Drama Desk Award, set design, Outer Circle Critics Award, design, 1990, all for *City of Angels;* award for excellence in theatre, Ensemble Studio Theatre, 1990; Drama Desk Award nomination, outstanding set design, Outer Critics Circle Award, design, 1992, both for *Crazy for You;* Antoinette Perry Award nomination, best scenic design, 1992, for *Jelly's Last Jam;* Boston Critics Award, 1992; Laurence Olivier Award nomination, scenic design, Society of West End Theatre, 1993, for London production of *Crazy for You;* Antoinette Perry Award nomination, best scenic design, 1993, for *Angels in America: Millennium Approaches;* Dora Mayer Moore Award, Toronto Alliance for the Performing Arts, 1995; Lifetime Achievement Award, New England Theatre Conference, 1996; En Garde Arts honoree, 1996; Drama Desk Award nomination, outstanding set design for a musical, 1996, for *Victor/Victoria;* Drama Desk Award nomination, outstanding set design of a musical, 1997, for *Big;* Theatre Hall of Fame, inductee, 1999; Outer Critics Circle Award, outstanding scenic design, Antoinette Perry Award nomination, best scenic designer, Drama Desk Award, outstanding set design of a musical, 2000, all for *Kiss Me Kate;* Antoinette Perry Award, best scenic designer, Drama Desk Award, outstanding

set design of a musical, Outer Critics Circle Award, outstanding scenic design, 2001, all for *The Producers;* Laurence Olivier Theatre Award nomination, best set designer, Society of London Theatre, 2002, for *Kiss Me Kate;* two New York Critics Circle awards.

CREDITS

Stage Set Designer:
Don Pasquale, Golden Gate Opera Workshop, San Francisco, CA, 1953.
Amahl and the Night Visitors, Golden Gate Opera Workshop, 1953.
Zanetto, Golden Gate Opera Workshop, 1953.
Tea and Sympathy, Theatre Arts Colony, 1954.
Waiting for Godot, Actors Workshop, San Francisco, CA, 1957.
The Miser, Actors Workshop, 1958.
The Ticklish Acrobat, Actors Workshop, 1958.
The Filling Station, San Francisco Ballet Company, San Francisco, CA, 1958.
The Guardsman, Sacramento Civic Ballet, Sacramento, CA, 1958.
The Plaster Bambino, Actors Workshop, 1959.
And the Wind Blows, St. Marks Playhouse, New York City, 1959.
The Prodigal, Downtown Theatre, New York City, 1960.
Between Two Thieves, York Playhouse, New York City, 1960.
Borak, Martinique Theatre, New York City, 1960–61.
A Worm in Horseradish, Maidman Playhouse, New York City, 1961.
Entertain a Ghost, Irish Players, Actors Playhouse, New York City, 1962.
The Days and Nights of Beebee Fenstermaker, Irish Players, Sheridan Square Playhouse, New York City, 1962–63.
The Playboy of the Western World, Irish Players, 1962.
Cages, New York City, 1963.
In White America, Sheridan Square Playhouse, New York City, 1963.
The Burning, New York City, 1963.
The White Rose and the Red, New York City, 1964.
Dark of the Moon, Arena Stage, Washington, DC, 1964.
Galileo, Arena Stage, 1964.
In White America, Players Theatre, New York City, 1965.
A View from the Bridge, Sheridan Square Playhouse, 1965–66.
An Evening's Frost, Theatre de Lys, New York City, 1965–66.
The Condemned of Altona, Vivian Beaumont Theatre, New York City, 1966.
Oh What a Lovely War, Arena Stage, 1966.
Macbeth, Arena Stage, 1966.
Wind in the Willows, Arena Stage, 1966.
The Magistrate, Arena Stage, 1966–67.

The Crucible, Arena Stage, 1967.

Love Match, Los Angeles, 1967.

The Inspector General, Arena Stage, 1967.

Look Back in Anger, Arena Stage, 1967.

The Andersonville Trial, Arena Stage, 1967.

Galileo, Vivian Beaumont Theatre, 1967.

The Trial of Lee Harvey Oswald, American National Theatre and Academy, New York City, 1967.

A Certain Young Man, Stage 73, New York City, 1967.

Major Barbara, Arena Stage, c. 1967.

Poor Bitos, Arena Stage, c. 1967.

The Tenth Man, Arena Stage, c. 1968.

Room Service, Arena Stage, c. 1968.

The Iceman Cometh, Arena Stage, c. 1968.

The Blood Knot, Arena Stage, c. 1968.

Wind in the Willows, Arena Stage, c. 1968.

The Great White Hope, Arena Stage, 1968.

Hair, Biltmore Theatre, New York City, 1968–72.

Lovers and Other Strangers, Brooks Atkinson Theatre, New York City, 1968.

The Cuban Thing, Henry Millers Theatre, New York City, 1968.

The Great White Hope, Alvin Theatre, New York City, 1968–69.

Promises, Promises, Shubert Theatre, New York City, 1968–71.

Hair, Shaftesbury Theatre, London, 1968.

Jacques Brel Is Alive and Well and Living in Paris, Arena Stage, c. 1969.

The Cage, Arena Stage, c. 1969.

Edith Stein, Arena Stage, c. 1969.

You Can't Take It with You, Arena Stage, c. 1969.

The Watering Place, Music Box Theatre, New York City, 1969.

My Daughter, Your Son, Booth Theatre, New York City, 1969.

Promises, Promises, London, 1969.

The Cherry Orchard, Arena Stage, c. 1970.

The Chemmy Circle, Arena Stage, c. 1970.

Enchanted Night, Arena Stage, c. 1970.

The Police, Arena Stage, c. 1970.

Dance of Death, Arena Stage, c. 1970.

No Place to Be Somebody, Arena Stage, c. 1970.

Gantry, George Abbott Theatre, New York City, 1970.

The Rise and the Fall of the City of Mahagonny (also known as *Mahagonny*), Anderson Theatre, New York City, 1970.

The Engagement Baby, Helen Hayes Theatre, New York City, 1970.

Lenny, Brooks Atkinson Theatre, 1971–72.

Jesus Christ Superstar, Mark Hellinger Theatre, New York City, 1971–73.

Inner City, Ethel Barrymore Theatre, New York City, 1971–72.

Sugar, Majestic Theatre, New York City, 1972–73.

Lysistrata, Brooks Atkinson Theatre, 1972.

Julius Caesar, American Shakespeare Festival, Stratford, CT, 1972.

Antony and Cleopatra, American Shakespeare Festival, 1972.

Major Barbara, American Shakespeare Festival, 1972.

Seesaw, Uris Theatre, New York City, 1973.

Full Circle, American National Theatre and Academy, 1973.

Rachael Lily Rosenbloom and Don't You Ever Forget It!, Broadhurst Theatre, New York City, 1973.

Mack and Mabel, Majestic Theatre, 1974.

The Fifth Dimension with Jo Jo's Dance Factory, Uris Theatre, New York City, 1974.

Sergeant Peppers Lonely Hearts Club Band on the Road, Beacon Theatre, New York City, 1974–75.

A Chorus Line, Shubert Theatre, Boston, MA, 1975–90.

The Red Devil Battery Sign, Shubert Theatre, 1975.

Les Troyens, Vienna State Opera, Vienna, Austria, 1976.

Hamlet Connotations, American Ballet Theatre, New York City, 1976.

A Chorus Line, London, 1977.

West Side Story, Hamburg State Opera, Hamburg, Germany, 1977.

Julius Caesar, Stratford, CT, 1978.

On the Twentieth Century, St. James Theatre, New York City, 1978.

Ballroom, Majestic Theatre, 1978–79.

Comin Uptown, Winter Garden Theatre, New York City, 1979.

Swing, New York City, 1980.

42nd Street, Winter Garden Theatre, 1980–81, then Majestic Theatre, 1981–87, later St. James Theatre, 1987–89.

One Night Stand, Nederlander Theatre, New York City, 1980.

Semmelweiss, New York City, 1981.

Dreamgirls, Imperial Theatre, New York City, 1981–85.

Barber of Seville, Metropolitan Opera, New York City, 1982.

Mahalia, Hartford Theatre Company, Stamford, CT, 1981, then Hartman Theatre, Stamford, CT, 1982.

Merlin, Mark Hellinger Theatre, 1983.

Three Dances, Eliot Field Ballet, New York City, 1983.

Jewels, New York City Ballet, 1983.

Measure for Measure, New York Shakespeare Festival, Delacort Theatre, Central Park, New York City, 1985.

Song and Dance, Royale Theatre, New York City, 1985–86.

Chess, London, 1987.

Dreamgirls, Ambassador Theatre, New York City, 1987.

Teddy and Alice, Minskoff Theatre, New York City, 1987–88.

Chess, Imperial Theatre, New York City, 1988.

Jerome Robbins Broadway, Imperial Theatre, 1989–90.

City of Angels, Virginia Theatre, New York City, 1989–92.

Hamlet, Anspacher Theatre, Public Theatre, New York City, 1990.

William Tell, Royal Opera House, Covent Garden Theatre, London, 1991.

Crazy for You, Shubert Theatre, 1992–96.

Jelly's Last Jam, Virginia Theatre, 1992–93.

Crazy for You, London, 1993.

City of Angels, London, 1993.

Putting It Together, City Center Theatre, Stage I, then Manhattan Theatre Club, both New York City, 1993.

Angels in America: Millennium Approaches, Walter Kerr Theatre, New York City, 1993–94.

Angels in America: Perestroika, Walter Kerr Theatre, 1993–94.

Victor/Victoria, Marquis Theatre, New York City, 1995–97.

Death Defying Acts, Variety Arts Theatre, New York City, 1995–96.

Big, Schubert Theatre, 1996.

Dreamgirls, Providence Performing Arts Center, Providence, RI, 1997.

The Life, Ethel Barrymore Theatre, 1997–98.

Side Show, Richard Rodgers Theatre, New York City, 1997–98.

Saturday Night Fever, Palladium Theatre, London, 1998, then Minskoff Theatre, 1999–2000.

Kiss Me Kate, Martin Beck Theatre, New York City, 1999–2001, then Victoria Palace, London, 2001.

The Wild Party, Virginia Theatre, 2000.

The Producers, St. James Theatre, 2001–2007.

Flower Drum Song, Virginia Theatre, New York City, 2002–2003.

Never Gonna Dance, Broadhurst Theatre, 2003–2004.

The Boy from Oz, Imperial Theatre, 2003–2004.

Resurrection Blues, Old Vic Theatre, London, 2006.

A Chorus Line, Gerald Schoenfeld Theatre, New York City, 2006.

Young Frankenstein, Hilton Theatre, New York City, 2007—.

Also worked as set designer for *The Immortalist,* Encore Theatre, San Francisco, CA; *Dark Side of the Moon,* Encore Theatre; Tokyo productions of *A Chorus Line,* *Dreamgirls,* *42nd Street,* *City of Angels,* and *Crazy for You.*

Major Tours (as Set Designer):

Dreamgirls, North American cities, 1985–87.

Forty–second Street, U.S. cities, 1989.

The Producers, U.S. cities, c. 2002.

Also designed sets for *Hair; Promises, Promises; Swing.*

Stage Work; Other:

Lighting designer, *Borak,* Martinique Theatre, New York City, 1960–61.

Assistant to Mr. Edwards, *Big Fish, Little Fish,* American National Theatre and Academy, New York City, 1961.

Assistant to Mr. Edwards, *The Aspern Papers,* Playhouse Theatre, New York City, 1962.

Assistant to Mr. Edwards, *Harold,* Cort Theatre, New York City, 1962.

Lightening designer, *The Days and Nights of Beebee Fenstermaker,* Irish Players, Sheridan Square Playhouse, New York City, 1962–63.

Assistant to Mr. Smith, *110 in the Shade,* Broadhurst Theatre, New York City, 1963–64.

Assistant to Mr. Smith, *Hello, Dolly!,* St. James Theatre, New York City, 1964–70.

Assistant to Oliver Smith, *Luv,* Booth Theatre, New York City, 1966, then Broadhurst Theatre, New York City, 1966–67, then Helen Hayes Theatre, New York City, 1966–67.

Producer, *Million Dollar Musical,* Coconut Grove Playhouse, Coconut Grove, FL, 1987.

Film Production Designer:

My Old Man's Place (also known as *Glory Boy*), Cinerama, 1970.

Chess, 2003.

Film Art Direction:

My Old Man's Place (also known as *Glory Boy*), Cinerama, 1970.

Television Set Designer; Series:

NBC News, NBC, 1971.

Television Production Designer; Movies:

Hamlet, 1990.

Television Set Designer; Specials:

Il Barbiere di Siviglia, PBS, 1989.

"Jammin: Jelly Roll Morton on Broadway," *Great Performances,* PBS, 1992.

"Victor/Victoria," *Julie Andrews: Back on Broadway,* 1995.

Crazy for You (also known as *The Gershwins' "Crazy for You"*), PBS, 1999.

Kiss Me Kate, PBS, 2003.

Television Appearances; Specials:

The 44th Annual Tony Awards, CBS, 1990.

OTHER SOURCES

Books:

Contemporary Designers, 3rd edition, St. James Press, 1997.

WAITT, Norm 1955(?)–
(Norm Waitt, Jr.)

PERSONAL

Born c. 1955.

Addresses: *Office*—Gold Circle Films, 2000 Avenue of the Stars, Suite 600–N, Los Angeles, CA 90067.

Career: Producer. Gateway Computers, cofounder; Gold Circle Films, Los Angeles, CA, founder; Waitt Media, founder.

CREDITS

Film Executive Producer:
Strange Hearts (also known as *Rat in the Can* and *Roads to Riches*), Gold Circle Films, 2001.
Double Whammy, Lions Gate Films, 2001.
Tempted (also known as *Seduction fatale*), Gold Circle Films, 2001.
The Man from Elysian Fields, Samuel Goldwyn Films, 2001.
Bad Boy (also known as *Dawg*), Wartex International, 2002.
My Big Fat Greek Wedding (also known as *Mariage a la grecque* and *Le mariage grec*), IFC Films, 2002.
Wishcraft, Wishcraft LLC, 2002.
Poolhall Junkies, Samuel Goldwyn Films, 2002.
Sonny, Samuel Goldwyn Films, 2002.
The Badge, Gold Circle Films, 2002.
Thirteen Moons, Lot 47 Films, 2002.
DysFunKtional Films, Miramax, 2003.
Jiminy Glick in Lalawood, Metro–Goldwyn–Mayer, 2004.
The Wedding Date, Gold Circle Films, 2005.
White Noise, Universal, 2005.
The Long Weekend, Gold Circle Releasing, 2005.
Slither, Universal, 2006.
Because I Said So, Universal, 2007.
Whisper, Universal, 2007.
My Sassy Girl, Gold Circle Films, 2007.
How I Met My Boyfriend's Dead Fiance, Universal, 2007.
Town Creek, Gold Circle Films, 2008.

Film Producer:
Over My Dead Body, Universal, 2007.

Television Executive Producer; Movies:
Rolling Kansas, Comedy Central, 2004.
Griffin & Phoenix, Lifetime, 2006.

Television Executive Producer; Specials:
(As Norm Waitt, Jr.) *Stand and Be Counted,* The Learning Channel, 2000.

WALDEN, W. G. 1950–
(Snuff Walden)

PERSONAL

Full name, William Garrett Walden; born January 1, 1950, in Louisiana; raised in Texas. *Education:* Attended college in Houston, TX.

Addresses: *Agent*—Gorfaine/Schwartz Agency, 4111 West Alameda Ave., Suite 509, Burbank, CA 91505.

Career: Composer and musician. Stray Dog (musical trio), founder, 1968, and featured artist; nightclub performer; musical director, touring musician, or studio musician for numerous performers including Laura Branigan, Eric Burden, Rita Coolidge, Chaka Khan, Greg Lake, Carl Palmer, Donna Summers, and Stevie Wonder.

Awards, Honors: Shared Emmy Award nomination (with Stewart Levin), best main title theme music, 1988, for *thirtysomething;* BMI Television Music Award (with John Lennon and Paul McCartney), Broadcast Music Inc., 1988, 1989, 1990, for *The Wonder Years;* Emmy Award nomination, best main title theme music, 1992, for *I'll Fly Away;* BMI Television Music Award, 1993, for *The Jackie Thomas Show;* Emmy Award nomination, best dramatic underscore for a miniseries or special, 1994, for *The Stand;* BMI Television Music Award, 1994, 1995, for *Ellen;* BMI Television Music Award, 1994, 1995, 1996, for *Roseanne;* Emmy Award nomination, best main title theme music, 1995, for *My So–Called Life;* Emmy Award nomination, best dramatic underscore for a series, 1997, for "The Choice," *Early Edition;* Emmy Award nomination, best main title theme music, 1997, for *Early Edition;* BMI Television Music Award, 1997 (with Allen Reynolds), 1998, 1999, 2000, 2001, for *The Drew Carey Show;* BMI Television Music Award, 1999, for *The Norm Show;* BMI Television Music Award, 1999 (with Bennett Salvay, John Lennon, and Paul McCartney), 2000, 2002, 2003, for *Providence;* Emmy Award nomination (with Daniel Pelfrey), best dramatic underscore for a series, 2000, for "Help for the Lovelorn," *Felicity;* Emmy Award, best main title theme music, 2000, BMI Television Music Award, 2000, 2001, 2002, 2003, 2004, 2005, for *The West Wing;* Emmy Award nomination, outstanding dramatic underscore, 2001, for "In the Shadow of Two Gunmen," *The West Wing;* Richard Kirk Career Achievement

Award, Broadcast Music Inc., 2001; Emmy Award nomination (with Joseph Williams), outstanding main title theme music, 2003, for *Miracles;* Emmy Award nomination, outstanding main title theme music, 2005, for *Huff;* Emmy Award nomination, outstanding dramatic underscore for a series, 2007, for *Kidnapped.*

CREDITS

Television Music Director; Series:
thirtysomething, ABC, 1987–92.
The Wonder Years, ABC, 1987–93.

Television Work; Episodic:
Song arranger, "The Christmas Show," *Studio 60 on the Sunset Strip* (also known as *Studio 60*), NBC, 2006.

Also music arranger for *Roseanne,* ABC.

Television Appearances; Episodic:
Member of the Squigtones, "Shotz Talent Show IV," *Laverne & Shirley* (also known as *Laverne & Shirley & Company* and *Laverne & Company & Friends*), 1979.
Announcer, *Laurie Hill,* Disney Channel, 1992.

Film Work:
Guitarist, *Staying Alive,* 1983.
Song performer, "Tequila," *Aloha Summer,* 1988.

Film Appearances:
(As Snuff Walden; with Brother Dwayne and the Dwayneaires) *UFOria,* Universal, 1985.

RECORDINGS

Albums:
thirtysomething (soundtrack), Geffen Records, 1991.
Babylon Minstrels, Hollywood Records, 1992.
The Stand, ABC Circle Music, 1994.
Music by ... W. G. Snuffy Walden, Windham Hill Records, 2001.

Albums; Contributor:
My So–Called Life (soundtrack), Atlantic Records, 1995.
A Winter's Solstice VI, Windham Hill Records, 1997.
Celtic Christmas III, Windham Hill Records, 1997.
The Carols of Christmas II, Windham Hill Records, 1997.
Summer Solstice 2, Windham Hill Records, 1998.
Sounds of Wood & Steel, Windham Hill Records, 1998.
Celtic Christmas IV, Windham Hill Records, 1998.
Touch—Windham Hill 25 Years of Guitar, Windham Hill Records, 2001.

A Winter's Solstice, Vol. 1: Silver Anniversary Edition, Windham Hill Records, 2001.
A Windham Hill Christmas, Windham Hill Records, 2002.
Windham Hill Chill: Ambient Acoustic, Windham Hill Records, 2003.
Windham Hill Chill 2, Windham Hill Records, 2003.

Musician for recordings *Stray Dog* and *While You're Down There,* both by Stray Dog, released by Manticore; *Heartbreaker* by Free, A&M; *Second Street* by Back Street Crawler, Atlantic; and for recordings by Rabbit.

WRITINGS

Television Music; Pilots and Series:
(With Stewart Levin), *thirtysomething,* ABC, 1987.
The Wonder Years, ABC, 1987.
The Outsiders, Fox, 1990.
Working Girl, NBC, 1990.
Sisters, NBC, 1991.
I'll Fly Away, NBC, 1991–92.
Crossroads, ABC, 1992.
Laurie Hill, Disney Channel, 1992.
The Jackie Thomas Show, ABC, 1992.
Relativity, ABC, between 1993 and 1996.
Tom, ABC, 1994.
My So–Called Life, ABC, 1994.
Sweet Justice, NBC, 1994–95.
Ellen (also known as *These Friends of Mine*), ABC, between 1994 and 1996.
Roseanne, ABC, between 1994 and 1997.
The Monroes, ABC, 1995.
The Drew Carey Show, ABC, 1995–2004.
Early Edition, CBS, 1996.
Ink, CBS, 1996–97.
The Tom Show, 1997.
413 Hope St., 1997–98.
Cupid, ABC, 1998–99.
Maggie Winters, CBS, 1998–99.
(With Daniel Pelfrey) Dramatic underscore, "Help for the Lovelorn," *Felicity,* The WB, 1998–2000.
Sports Night, ABC, 1998–2000.
(Including song "Too Bad,") *The Norm Show* (also known as *Norm*), ABC, 1999–2001.
It's Like, You Know ..., ABC, 1999–2000.
Once and Again, ABC, 1999–2002.
Roswell (also known as *Roswell High*), UPN, 1999–2002.
The West Wing, NBC, 1999–2006.
Providence, NBC, 2000.
The $treet, Fox, 2000–2001.
Three Sisters, NBC, 2001.
Miracles, ABC, 2003.
Surface, NBC, 2005.
The War at Home, Fox, 2005–2007.
The Jake Effect (also known as *It's Not About Me*), NBC, 2005.

Studio 60 on the Sunset Strip (also known as *Studio 60*), NBC, 2006–2007.
Friday Night Lights, NBC, 2006–2007.
In Plain Sight, NBC, 2007.

Television Music; Series Only:
The Jackie Thomas Show, 1992.
First Years, NBC, 2001.
Hidden Hills, NBC, 2002.
Boomtown, NBC, 2002.
Mister Sterling, NBC, 2003.
The Brotherhood of Poland, New Hampshire, CBS, 2003.
Kidnapped, NBC, 2006–2007.

Television Music; Pilots:
Morning Glory, CBS, 1993.
Dellaventura, CBS, 1997.
Sherman's March, 2000.
The Third Coast, 2000.
George Lopez, ABC, 2002.
Georgetown, 2002.
Everwood, The WB, 2002.
The Lyon's Den, NBC, 2003.
Second Nature, 2003.
Joint Custody, 2004.
DeMarco Affairs, 2004.
The L Word, NBC, 2004.
1/4life, ABC, 2005.
The New Adventures of the Old Christine, The WB, 2006.
Heartland, TNT, 2007.
Lipstick Jungle, NBC, 2007.

Television Music; Movies:
Winnie, NBC, 1988.
(Including song "I Won't Let Go") *Roe vs. Wade,* NBC, 1989.
Burning Bridges, ABC, 1990.
Guess Who's Coming for Christmas? (also known as *UFO Cafe*), NBC, 1990.
The Chase, NBC, 1991.
Shoot First: A Cop's Vengeance, NBC, 1991.
The Good Fight, Lifetime, 1992.
Wild Card, USA Network, 1992.
A Place to Be Loved (also known as *Shattered Family*), CBS, 1993.
I'll Fly Away: Then and Now, 1993.
Rise and Walk: The Dennis Byrd Story, Fox, 1994.
Homecoming, Showtime, 1996.
A Friend's Betrayal (also known as *Stolen Youth*), NBC, 1996.

Television Music; Episodic:
Song "Hot Times in the City Streets," "Indian Summer," *Fame,* 1984.
The Van Dyke Show, CBS, 1988.

Song "Red," "Why Jordan Can't Read," *My So–Called Life,* ABC, 1994.
"Blood," *The Lyon's Den,* NBC, 2003.
"Temptation," *The Book of Daniel,* NBC, 2006.
"Tapping the Squid," *Huff,* Showtime, 2006.
"I Make Myself into Something New," *Heartland,* TNT, 2007.

Television Music; Other:
Dramatic underscore and incidental music, *The Stand* (miniseries; also known as *Stephen King's "The Stand"*), ABC, 1994.
Drew's Dance Party Special, 1998.

Film Music:
Song, "Breakaway," *The Flamingo Kid,* Twentieth Century–Fox, 1984.
Song "Please Mr. Postman," *Look Who's Talking Too,* 1990.
Leaving Normal, Universal, 1992.
Homage, Arrow Releasing, 1996.

OTHER SOURCES

Periodicals:
Guitar Player, March, 1990, pp. 42–48.

Electronic:
W. G. Snuffy Walden Official Site, http://www.wgsnuffywalden.com, August 11, 2007.

WALLS, Nancy 1966–

PERSONAL

Full name, Nancy Ellen Walls; born July 19, 1966, in Cohasset, MA; married Steve Carell (an actor and comedian), 1995; children: Elisabeth Anne, John. *Education:* Graduated from Boston College.

Career: Actress. Performed with the Second City Improv Company; appeared in television commercials for Ameritech Cellular Phones.

CREDITS

Film Appearances:
Flight attendant, *Anger Management,* Columbia, 2003.
Health clinic counselor, *The 40 Year Old Virgin* (also known as *The 40 Year–Old Virgin* and *The 40–Year–Old Virgin*), Universal, 2005.

Television Appearances; Series:

Various characters, *Saturday Night Live* (also known as *SNL*), NBC, 1995–96.

The Daily Show (also known as *Jon Stewart, The Daily Show with Jon Stewart,* and *The Daily Show with Jon Stewart Global Edition*), Comedy Central, 1999 2002.

Carol Stills, *The Office* (also known as *The Office: US Version*), NBC, 2005–2006.

Television Appearances; Specials:

Saturday Night Live: 25th Anniversary Primetime Special, NBC, 1999.

The Daily Show with Jon Stewart "Indecision 2000" Election Night Special, Comedy Central, 2000.

I Love the '70s, VH1, 2003.

Comedy Central Laughs for Life Telethon 2003, Comedy Central, 2003.

Live from the Red Carpet: The 2007 Golden Globe Awards, 2007.

Television Appearances; Episodic:

Jill, "Pearce's New Buddy," *LateLine,* NBC, 1998.

Various, *Random Play,* VH1, 1999.

Marcia, "T–Bones TV," *The Naked Trucker and T–Bones Show,* Comedy Central, 2007.

WARD, David S. 1945(?)–
(David Ward)

PERSONAL

Full name, David Schad Ward; born October 24, 1945 (some sources say 1947), in Providence, RI; son of Robert McCollum and Miriam (maiden name, Schad) Ward; married Rosana Desoto (an actress), September 20, 1980 (divorced); married Christine; children: (first marriage) Joaquin Atwood, Sylvana Bonifacia Desoto. *Education:* Pomona College, B.A., 1967; University of California at Los Angeles, M.F.A., 1970.

Addresses: *Agent*—International Creative Management, 10250 Constellation Way, 9th Floor, Los Angeles, CA 90067. *Manager*—Echo Lake Entertainment, 421 South Beverly Dr., 8th Floor, Beverly Hills, CA 90212.

Career: Screenwriter and director. Taught writing courses at Chapman University, Orange, CA, 2005.

Member: Academy of Motion Picture Arts and Sciences, Directors Guild, Writers Guild.

Awards, Honors: Academy Award, best original screenplay, Golden Globe Award nomination, best screenplay—motion picture, WGA Screen Award nomination, best drama written directly for the screen, Writers Guild of America, and Edgar Allan Poe Award nomination, best motion picture, Mystery Writers of America, 1974, all for *The Sting;* Academy Award nomination (with Nora Ephron and Jeff Arch), best screenplay written directly for the screen, Film Award nomination (with Nora Ephron and Jeff Arch), best original screenplay, British Academy of Film and Television Arts, and WGA Screen Award nomination (with Nora Ephron and Jeff Arch), best screenplay written directly for the screen, 1994, all for *Sleepless in Seattle;* Copper Wing Tribute Award, Phoenix Film Foundation, 2006.

CREDITS

Film Director:

Cannery Row (also known as *John Steinbeck's "Cannery Row"*), Metro–Goldwyn–Mayer/United Artists, 1982.

Major League, Paramount, 1989.

King Ralph, Universal, 1991.

The Program, Buena Vista, 1993.

Major League II, Warner Bros., 1994.

Down Periscope, Twentieth Century–Fox, 1996.

The Best Man, October Films/Polygram/Universal, 1999.

Film Producer:

Major League II, Warner Bros., 1994.

Film Appearances:

(As David Ward) Himself, *The Haunted World of Edward D. Wood, Jr.,* 1995.

Himself, *The Art of "The Sting"* (documentary), Universal Studios Home Video, 2005.

Himself, *Pass! Screenwriters on Surviving Hollywood Rejection* (documentary), 2008.

WRITINGS

Screenplays:

Steelyard Blues (also known as *The Final Crash*), Warner Bros., 1973.

The Sting, Universal, 1973.

Cannery Row (also known as *John Steinbeck's "Cannery Row"*; based on Steinbeck's novel of the same name), Metro–Goldwyn–Mayer/United Artists, 1982.

The Sting II, 1983.

(Uncredited; with Richard Kramer) *Saving Grace* (based on the novel by Celia Gittelson), Embassy, 1986.

(As David Ward; with John Nichols) *The Milagro Beanfield War* (based on the novel by Nichols), Universal, 1988.

(As David Ward) *Major League,* Paramount, 1989.

King Ralph, Universal, 1991.

(With Nora Ephron and Jeff Arch) *Sleepless in Seattle,* TriStar, 1993.
(With Aaron Latham) *The Program,* Buena Vista, 1993.
The Best Man, October Films/Polygram/Universal, 1999.
(Uncredited) *Sahara,* Paramount, 2005.
Flyboys, Metro–Goldwyn–Mayer, 2006.
Lucifer (short), 2007.

Also wrote *Dial Tone; San Joaquin; Handling Sin;* (with others) *The Mask of Zorro.*

WEINSTEIN, Paula 1945–

PERSONAL

Born November 19, 1945, in New York, NY; daughter of Isadore Meyerson and Hannah (maiden name, Dorner) Weinstein (a producer); married Mark Rosenberg, 1984 (died, November 6, 1992); children: Hannah Mark. *Education:* Attended Columbia University. *Politics:* Democrat. *Religion:* Jewish.

Addresses: *Office*—Spring Creek Pictures, 4000 Warner Blvd., Bldg. 144, Suite 100B, Burbank, CA 91522

Career: Producer. Began career as an assistant film editor, New York City; New York City Mayor's office, special events director, through 1973; worked as an agent at William Morris Agency and International Creative Management, Los Angeles, CA, 1973–76; Warner Bros., Burbank, CA, vice president of production, 1976–78; Twentieth Century–Fox, Los Angeles, CA, senior vice president, 1978–80; Ladd Company, vice president and partner, 1980–81; United Artists, president, 1981–82; Columbia Pictures, Burbank, CA, independent producer and consultant, 1983–84; WW Productions, cofounder, 1984–87; Metro–Goldwyn–Mayer's Worldwide Division, executive consultant, 1987–90; Spring Creek Productions, cofounder, 1990–98; Baltimore/Spring Creek Productions, cofounder, 1998–2002; Spring Creek Pictures, Burbank, CA, president, 2003—. Hollywood Women's Political Committee, founding member.

Awards, Honors: Bill of Rights Award (with Mark Rosenberg), Southern California Chapter of the American Civil Liberties Union, 1989; CableACE Award, best movie or miniseries, National Cable Television Association, Emmy Award nomination (with others), outstanding made for television movie, 1993, both for *Citizen Cohn;* CableACE Award, best movie or miniseries, Emmy Award (with others), outstanding made for television movie, Television Producer of the Year in Longform (with others), Producers Guild of America, 1996, all for *Truman;* Crystal Award, Women in Film, 1999.

CREDITS

Film Producer:
American Flyers, Warner Bros., 1985.
A Dry White Season, Metro–Goldwyn–Mayer, 1989.
The Fabulous Baker Boys, Twentieth Century–Fox, 1989.
Fearless, Warner Bros., 1993.
Flesh and Bone, Paramount, 1993.
With Honors, Warner Bros., 1994.
Something to Talk About (also known as *Grace Under Pressure*), Warner Bros., 1995.
Analyze This, Warner Bros., 1999.
Liberty Heights, Warner Bros., 1999.
The Perfect Storm (also known as *Der Sturm*), Warner Bros., 2000.
An Everlasting Piece, Columbia, 2000.
Bandits, Metro–Goldwyn–Mayer, 2001.
Possession, USA Films, 2002.
Analyze That, Warner Bros., 2002.
Looney Tunes: Back in Action (animated; also known as *Looney Tunes Back in Action: The Movie*), Warner Bros., 2003.
Envy, Columbia, 2004.
Monster–In–Law (also known as *Das Schwiegermoster*), New Line Cinema, 2005.
Rumor Has It … (also known as *Rumour Has It … *), Warner Bros., 2005.
The Astronaut Farmer, Warner Bros., 2006.
Blood Diamond, Warner Bros., 2006.
Pride and Glory, New Line Cinema, 2008.

Film Executive Producer:
The House of the Spirits (also known as *Andernes hus, A Casa dos espiritos,* and *Das Geisterhaus*), Miramax, 1993.
Deliver Us from Eva, Warner Bros., 2003.

Film Appearances:
Herself, *Inside "Bandits"* (documentary), 2001.

Television Co–Executive Producer; Miniseries:
Salem Witch Trials, CBS, 2002.

Television Executive Producer; Movies:
The Rose and the Jackal, TNT, 1990.
Bejeweled, Disney Channel, 1991.
Citizen Cohen, HBO, 1992.
Because Mommy Works, NBC, 1994.
Truman, HBO, 1995.
The Cherokee Kid, HBO, 1996.
First Time Felon, HBO, 1997.
Cloned, NBC, 1997.
Giving Up the Ghost, Lifetime, 1998.
If You Believe, Lifetime, 1999.
Crossed Over (also known as *Destins croises*), CBS, 2002.
Iron Jawed Angles, HBO, 2004.

Television Appearances; Specials:
Unauthorized Biography: Jane Fonda, syndicated, 1988.

Television Appearances; Episodic:
"Looney Tunes: Back in Action," *HBO First Look,* HBO, 2003.
Sunday Morning Shootout, AMC, 2004.
"Monster–In–Law," *HBO First Look,* HBO, 2005.
"Blood Diamond," *HBO First Look,* HBO, 2006.

WELSH, Kenneth 1942–
    (Ken Welsh)

PERSONAL

Born March 30, 1942, in Edmonton, Alberta, Canada; father, a railway worker; married Donna Haley (an actress; divorced); children: Devon. *Education:* Attended University of Alberta, Edmonton, Alberta, Canada.

Addresses: *Agent*—Marilyn Szatmary, Silver, Massetti, and Associates, 8730 Sunset Blvd., Suite 440, Los Angeles, CA 90069.

Career: Actor. O'Neill Playwrights Conference, Waterford, CT, actor for six summers.

Awards, Honors: Joseph Jefferson Award, 1975, for *Arturo Ui;* award from Association of Canadian Television and Radio Artists (now Alliance of Canadian Cinema, Television, and Radio Artists), 1984, for *Empire, Inc;* Genie Award nomination, best supporting actor, Academy of Canadian Cinema and Television, 1984, for *Tell Me that You Love Me;* Genie Award nomination, best supporting actor, 1985, for *Reno and the Doc;* Genie Award nomination, best supporting actor, 1987, for *Loyalties;* Gemini award, best actor in a dramatic program or miniseries, Academy of Canadian Cinema and Television, 1988, for *And Then You Die;* Gemini Award, best actor in a dramatic program or miniseries, 1990, for *Love and Hate: The Story of Colin and Joanne Thatcher;* Gemini award, best supporting actor, 1992, for *Deadly Betrayal: The Bruce Curtis Story;* Gemini Award nomination, best supporting actor, 1993, for *Grand Larceny;* Genie Award, best supporting actor, 1996, for *Margaret's Museum;* Gemini Award, best actor, 1998, for *Hiroshima;* Earl Grey Award, Academy of Canadian Cinema and Television, 1998; Daytime Emmy Award nomination, outstanding performer in a children's special, 1999, for *Edison: The Wizard of Light;* Gemini Award nomination, best supporting actor in a dramatic program or miniseries, 1999, for *Scandalous Me: The Jacqueline Susann Story;* honorary doctor-

ate, University of Alberta, 1999; Gemini Award nomination, best supporting actor in a dramatic program or miniseries, 2000, for *External Affairs;* decorated member, Order of Canada, 2004.

CREDITS

Television Appearances; Miniseries:
Sir James Munro, *Empire, Inc.,* 1984.
Luther Rosser, *The Murder of Mary Phagan,* NBC, 1988.
John Whistlow, *Champagne Charlie,* syndicated, 1989.
Colin Thatcher, *Love and Hate: The Story of Colin and Joanne Thatcher* (also known as *Love and Hate: A Marriage Made in Hell*), 1989.
Tom Stanfield, *Love, Lies and Murder,* NBC, 1991.
Michael Schottland, *Deadly Betrayal: The Bruce Curtis Story* (also known as *Journey into Darkness: The Bruce Curtis Story*), NBC, 1991.
Don Eisenberg, *Woman on the Run: The Lawrencia Bembenek Story* (also known as *Woman on Trial: The Lawrencia Bembenek Story*), NBC, 1993.
President Harry S. Truman, *Hiroshima,* Showtime, 1995.
Preston Barck, *The Third Twin* (also known as *Ken Follett's "The Third Twin"*), CBS, 1997.
Senator Shelby, *Thanks of a Grateful Nation* (also known as *The Gulf War*), Showtime, 1998.
John Hawke, *Revenge of the Land,* CBC, 1999.
Harry Truman, *Haven,* CBS, 2001.
Randall Spear, *H2O* (also known as *H2O: The Last Prime Minister*), CBC, 2004.
Chief of Staff Alan Horst, *Category 7: The End of the World,* CBS, 2005.
General Keilburger, *Covert One: The Hades Factor,* CBS, 2006.
Lord Beaverbrook, *Above and Beyond,* CBC, 2006.
Justice Beale, *St. Urbain's Horseman,* CBC, 2007.
Randall Spear, *The Trojan Horse,* CBC, 2007.

Television Appearances; Movies:
Ralph, *Brethren,* 1977.
Thomas E. Dewey, *F.D.R.: The Last Year,* 1980.
Love & Larceny, CBC, 1983.
Reno, *Reno and the Doc,* 1984.
Harry, *The Cuckoo Bird,* 1985.
Elder Seth, *Screwball Academy* (also known as *Divine Light* and *Loose Ends*), 1986.
Richard Miller, *A Stranger Waits,* CBS, 1987.
John Jacobs, *Liberace: Behind the Music,* CBS, 1988.
Harry Teller, *Blood Sport* (also known as *Dick Francis: Blood Sport*), CBS, 1989.
Jerry Wallace, *The Last Best Year,* ABC, 1990.
Ruggieri, *Murder in Black and White,* 1990.
Atkinson, *The Widowmaker,* 1990.
Nick Ruggieri, *Murder Times Seven* (also known as *Murder x 7*), 1990.
Ray McPhail, "High Country," *CBC's Magic Hour,* CBC, 1991.
Grand Larceny, CBC, 1991.

David Atwood, *Christmas on Division Street,* CBS, 1991.

Dr. Hammel, *Straight Line,* Disney Channel, 1991.

(As Ken Welsh) Attorney Wade Smith, *Cruel Doubt,* 1992.

Narrator, *Kurt Browning: Life on the Edge,* 1992.

Sam Skinner, *Dead Ahead: The Exxon Valdez Disaster* (also known as *Disaster at Valdez*), HBO, 1992.

Dick Chandler, *The Good Fight,* Lifetime, 1992.

Paul Michel, *A Mother's Right: The Elizabeth Morgan Story* (also known as *Shattered Silence*), ABC, 1992.

Guy Nast, *Adrift,* CBS, 1993.

Judge, *Bonds of Love,* CBS, 1993.

Judge Norton, *Shattered Trust: The Shari Karney Story* (also known as *Shattered Trust*), NBC, 1993.

Major General Harry Crerar, *Dieppe,* CBC, 1993.

Larry, *The Diary of Evelyn Lau,* CBC, 1993.

David Burns, *And Then There Was One,* Lifetime, 1994.

Dr. Ken Holcross, *Another Woman,* CBS, 1994.

Charles Bennett, *Getting Gotti,* CBS, 1994.

Irwin Stroud, *The Spider and the Fly,* Showtime, 1994.

Mr. Higgins, *Choices of the Heart: The Margaret Sanger Story,* Lifetime, 1995.

Dr. Bell, *Dancing in the Dark,* Lifetime, 1995.

Bill Palmer, *Vanished* (also known as *Danielle Steel's "Vanished"*), NBC, 1995.

James "Scotty" Reston, *Kissinger and Nixon,* TNT, 1995.

Sheriff Lenny Budd, *Dead Silence* (also known as *Silence de mort*), Fox, 1996.

Owen Jessop, *Escape Clause,* Showtime, 1996.

Coach Marlowe, *Habitat,* Sci-Fi Channel, 1997.

George Steinbrenner, *Joe Torre: Curveballs Along the Way,* Showtime, 1997.

Chase Woodward, *Dead Husbands* (also known as *Last Man on the List*), USA Network, 1998.

Armstrong, *Thunder Point* (also known as *Jack Higgins' "Thunder Point"*), Showtime, 1998.

Robert Susann, *Scandalous Me: The Jacqueline Susann Story* (also known as *Jacqueline Susann, la scandaleuse*), USA Network, 1998.

Caz Holowitz, *The Taking of Pelham One Two Three,* ABC, 1998.

Tower Mannette, *Mind Prey* (also known as *John Sandford's "Mind Prey"*), ABC, 1999.

Dr. James Franken, *Matthew Blackheart: Monster Smasher* (also known as *Blackheart*), syndicated, 1999.

Mayor Joe Shakespeare, *Vendetta,* HBO, 1999.

William Kunstler, *Who Killed Atlanta's Children?* (also known as *Echo of Murder*), Showtime, 2000.

Isaak Levin, *Love and Murder* (also known as *Criminal Instincts: Love and Murder* and *Crimes et passion*), Lifetime, 2000.

Peder Lund, *Deliberate Intent,* FX Network, 2000.

Dr. John Watson, *The Hound of the Baskervilles* (also known as *Le chien des Baskerville*), Odyssey Network, 2000.

Dr. John H. Watson, *The Royal Scandal* (also known as *Scandal in Bohemia* and *Le chant des sirenes*), Hallmark Channel, 2001.

Dr. Watson, *The Sign of Four* (also known as *Le signe des quatre*), Odyssey Network, 2001.

Sam Hathaway, *Sanctuary* (also known as *Nora Roberts' "Sanctuary"*), CBS, 2001.

James Baker, *The Day Reagan Was Shot,* Showtime, 2001.

Dr. Watson, *The Case of the Whitechapel Vampire,* Hallmark Channel, 2002.

The Man Who Saved Christmas, CBS, 2002.

John McNaughon, *The Pentagon Papers,* FX Network, 2003.

Sir Wilkes, *Eloise at the Plaza,* ABC, 2003.

Dr. Ben Murdoch, *Ice Bound* (also known as *Ice Bound: A Woman's Survival at the South Pole* and *Prison de glace*), CBS, 2003.

Sir Wilkes, *Eloise at Christmastime,* ABC, 2003.

Professor Wojcik, *Karol, un uomo diventato Papa* (also known as *Karol: A Man Who Became Pope* and *Karol. Czlowiek, ktory zostal papiezem*), Hallmark Channel, 2005.

Bishop Murphy, *Our Fathers,* 2005.

Television Appearances; Series:
Windom Earle, *Twin Peaks,* 1990–91.
Seymour Annisman, a recurring role, *Tilt,* ESPN, 2004.

Television Appearances; Specials:
Charles Surface, "The School for Scandal," *Great Performances,* PBS, 1975.
McWilliams, *Riel,* CBC, 1979.
Georges, *Piaf,* Entertainment Channel, 1982.
Narrator, *Kurt Browning: Life on the Edge,* 1992.
Thomas Edison, *Edison: The Wizard of Light,* HBO, 1998.
Narrator, *Madness of King Richard,* 2003.
Narrator, *Ferry Command: The Forgotten Flyers of WWII,* 2006.

Television Appearances; Pilots:
Chief Scott, *Dark Eyes,* ABC, 1995.
Neil, *D.C.,* The WB, 2000.
Joe Siri, *Witchblade,* TNT, 2000.
The Guardian, CBS. 2001.
Dr. James Franken, *Matthew Blackheart: Monster Smasher* (also known as *Blackheart*), syndicated, 2002.

Television Appearances; Episodic:
"1832," *The Newcomers,* CBC, 1977.
Crane, "Marionettes, Inc.," *The Ray Bradbury Theatre* (also known as *The Bradbury Trilogy, Mystery Theatre, Le monde fantastique de Ray Bradbury,* and *Rad Bradbury presente*), USA Network, 1985.
Sutherland, "The Walls Have Eyes," *Seeing Things,* CBC, 1986.

Lieutenant Webster Bloom, "Sleepless Dream," *Spenser: For Hire,* 1987.

Lieutenant Nicholas Webster, "The Heart of the Matter," *Spenser: For Hire,* 1987.

Jack Simonson, "Acts of Terror," *The Twilight Zone,* syndicated, 1988.

Father Brian Halloran, "By the Waters of Babylon," *Gideon Oliver* (also known as *By the Rivers of Babylon*), 1989.

Captain Wilder, "And the Moon Be Still as Bright," *The Ray Bradbury Theatre* (also known as *The Bradbury Trilogy, Mystery Theatre, Le monde fantastique de Ray Bradbury,* and *Rad Bradbury presente*), USA Network, 1990.

George Wilson, "Standard of Care," *Street Legal,* CBC, 1990.

Joe Revere, "The Doppelgaenger," *Beyond Reality,* 1991.

Vance Cavanaugh, "Temple," *Kung Fu: The Legend Continues,* 1994.

The colonel, "Duty Bound," *Lonesome Dove: The Series,* 1994.

Simon Gates, "Revelations," *The X–Files,* Fox, 1995.

Randal K. Bolt, "All the Queen's Horses," *Due South* (also known as *Direction: Sud*), CBS, 1996.

Randal K. Bolt, "Red, White, or Blue," *Due South* (also known as *Direction: Sud*), CBS, 1996.

Dr. Vasquez, "Tempests," *The Outer Limits* (also known as *The New Outer Limits*), 1997.

Hugo Lawery, "The Secret Shih Tan," *The Hunger,* 1997.

Buck Corona III, "The Jackalope," *Eerie, Indiana: The Other Dimension,* 1998.

Dean Marley, "The Gambler," *Dead Man's Gun,* Showtime, 1998.

Ben O'Dell, "Disappeared," *Law & Order,* 1998.

Cyrus Bolt, "Call of the Wild: Part 2," *Due South* (also known as *Un tandem du choc*), CTV (Canada), 1999.

Neil, "Truth," *D.C.,* The WB, 2000.

Neil, "Blame," *D.C.,* The WB, 2000.

(As Ken Welsh) James Florie, "Done to Death," *Murder Call,* Nine Network, 2000.

Mr. Surdjic, "Shinto Death Cults," *Twitch City,* Bravo, 2000.

Mr. Surdjic, "Angels All Week," *Twitch City,* Bravo, 2000.

District Attorney Saltzman, "Paying the Piper," *Falcone,* CBS, 2000.

Captain Joe Siri, "Parallax," *Witchblade,* TNT, 2001.

Captain Joe Siri, "Apprehension," *Witchblade,* TNT, 2001.

"Reunion," *The Guardian,* CBS, 2001.

Dr. Jackson Pruit, "In Transition," *Soul Food,* Showtime, 2002.

Dr. Jackson Pruit, "This Must Be Love," *Soul Food,* Showtime, 2002.

Judge M. Harrod, "We the People," *The Practice,* ABC, 2003.

Judge M. Harrod, "The Heat of Passion," *The Practice,* ABC, 2003.

Judge M. Harrod, "The Lonely People," *The Practice,* ABC, 2003.

Dr. Shelby Sloane, "Spare Parts," *ReGenesis,* The Movie Network, 2004.

Dr. Shelby Sloane, "Baby Bomb," *ReGenesis,* The Movie Network, 2004.

Dr. Shelby Sloane, "The Face of God," *ReGenesis,* The Movie Network, 2004.

This Is Wonderland, CBC, 2005.

Drunk Santa, "Lexmas," *Smallville* (also known as *Smallville Beginnings* and *Smallville: Superman the Early Years*), The WB, 2005.

Jamus, "The Ark," *Stargate: Atlantis* (also known as *La porte d'Atlantis*), Sci–Fi Channel, 2007.

Television Appearances; Other:

D'Artagnan, *The Three Musketeers,* 1969.

Piaf (also known as *Piaf: The Early Years*), 1974.

The evangelist, *Murder Sees the Light,* 1986.

King, *The Snow Queen,* 2005.

Film Appearances:

The Overfamiliar Subordinate (also known as *Un subalterne trop familier*), 1965.

Dr. Kilifter (some sources cite Dr. Webber), *Double Negative* (also known as *Deadly Companion*), Quadrant, 1980.

Sergeant Wheeler, *Phobia,* Paramount, 1980.

James Hall, *Of Unknown Origin,* Warner Bros., 1983.

David, *Tell Me that You Love Me* (also known as *Miri*), 1983.

Parker, *Hot Money* (also known as *Getting Centred, Going for Broke, The Great Madison County Robbery, Never Trust an Honest Thief,* and *Zen Business*), 1983.

Harrison, *Covergirl* (also known as *Dreamworld*), New World, 1984.

Doctor, *Falling in Love,* Paramount, 1984.

Covergirls, 1985.

Joe McKenzie, *Perfect,* Columbia, 1985.

Stephen Berecky, *The War Boy,* 1985.

Walter Frauenberger, *The Climb,* Grey Matter Entertainment, 1986.

Dr. Appel, *Heartburn,* Paramount, 1986.

Jim, *Lost!,* Norstar, 1986.

David Sutton, *Loyalties* (also known as *Double allegeance*), Norstar, 1986.

Radio voice, *Radio Days,* Metro–Goldwyn–Mayer, 1987.

Eddie Griffin, *And Then You Die,* 1987.

Inspector Brannigan, "Crocodile" *Dundee II,* Paramount, 1988.

Donald, *Another Woman,* Orion, 1988.

(As Ken Welsh) Hackett, *The House on Carroll Street,* 1988.

Harry Norton, *Physical Evidence,* Sony Pictures Releasing, 1989.

Roger Culver, *The January Man,* 1989.

Charlie Glesby, *Perfectly Normal,* Four Seasons Entertainment, 1990.

Dwight Armstrong, *The Freshman,* TriStar, 1990.

Lieutenant Bernard, *The Big Slice,* 1991.

Narrator, *Heart of Tibet,* 1991.

Uncle Yakub, *Eli's Lesson,* 1992.

Tim, *Boozecan,* 1994.

Kenneth Sexston, *Whale Music,* Seventh Art Releasing, 1994.

Senator Utley, *Timecop,* Universal, 1994.

Sheriff Tynert, *Legends of the Fall,* TriStar, 1994.

Lieutenant Mickey King, *Death Wish V: The Face of Death* (also known as *Death Wish: The Face of Death*), Trimark Pictures, 1994.

Detective Breech, *Hideaway,* TriStar, 1995.

Angus MacNeil, *Margaret's Museum* (also known as *Le musee de Margaret*), Cinepix Film Properties, 1995.

Father, *Turning April,* 1996.

Harry Parker, *Rowing Through,* 1996.

Jim Miller, *Portraits of a Killer* (also known as *Portraits of Innocence* and *Portraits de l'innocence*), Live Entertainment, 1996.

(As Ken Welsh) Sandy Lord, *Absolute Power,* Columbia, 1997.

Mr. Nagel, *The Wrong Guy,* Buena Vista, 1998.

Narrator, *The Man Who Might Have Been: An Inquiry Into the Life and Death of Herbert Norman* (documentary), National Film Board of Canada, 1998.

Michael Riordan, *External Affairs,* Alliance Atlantis, 1999.

Ira Rosen, *Love Come Down* (also known as *Cris du coeur*), Unapix Entertainment, 2000.

Chief Inspector Brodsky, *Bad Faith* (also known as *Cold Blooded* and *Le delateur*), 2000.

Father Crighton, *Focus,* Paramount, 2001.

Doc Nagobads, *Miracle,* Buena Vista, 2004.

Andy, *The Wild Guys,* MVP Entertainment, 2004.

Vice President Becker, *The Day after Tomorrow,* Twentieth Century–Fox, 2004.

Dr. Hepburn, *The Aviator,* Miramax/Warner Bros., 2004.

Mouse Delaney, *Bailey's Billion$,* Echo Bridge Entertainment, 2005.

Robert Bradford, *Four Brothers,* Paramount, 2005.

(As Ken Welsh) Dr. Mueller, *The Exorcism of Emily Rose,* Screen Gems, 2005.

Tom Malone, *The Fog,* Columbia, 2005.

Provost Higgins, *The Covenant,* Screen Gems, 2006.

Anderson, *One Way,* Universal, 2006.

Dr. Jeff Wagner, *Fantastic Four: Rise of the Silver Surfer* (also known as *4: Rise of the Silver Surfer*), Twentieth Century–Fox, 2007.

Silk (also known as *Seta* and *Sole*), Picturehouse Entertainment, 2007.

Interviewee, *Hamlet (Solo)* (documentary), S&S Productions, 2007.

Some sources also cite appearance in a movie titled *Hot Money,* 1989.

Stage Appearances:

Sir Thomas Grey, citizen, and attendant, *Henry V,* Stratford Festival, Stratford, Ontario, Canada, 1966.

First murderer and captain to Talbot, *Henry VI,* Stratford Festival, 1966.

Guard and courtier, *Twelfth Night,* Stratford Festival, 1966.

Lord Hastings, *Richard III,* Stratford Festival, 1967.

Fenton, *The Merry Wives of Windsor,* Stratford Festival, 1967.

Octavius Caesar, *Antony and Cleopatra,* Stratford Festival, 1967.

Hamlet, Stratford Festival, 1969.

Much Ado About Nothing, Stratford Festival, 1971.

MacDuff, *Macbeth,* Stratford Festival, 1971.

Sir Oliver Martext, *As You Like It,* Stratford Festival, 1972.

Edgar, *King Lear,* Stratford Festival, 1972.

Alessandro de Medici, *Lorenzaccio,* Stratford Festival, 1972.

Arturo Ui, Chicago, IL, 1975.

Orlando, *As You Like It,* American Shakespeare Theatre, Stratford, CT, 1976.

Dave, *Treats,* Hudson Guild Theatre, New York City, 1977.

Charlie Evans, *One Crack Out,* Marymount Manhattan Theatre, New York City, 1978.

Taylor, *Curse of the Starving Class,* New York Shakespeare Festival, Estelle R. Newman Theatre, Public Theatre, New York City, 1978.

Ivan Kusmich Shpyokin, *The Inspector General,* Circle in the Square, New York City, 1978.

Philip Hill, *Whose Life Is It, Anyway?,* Trafalgar Theatre, New York City, 1979.

Title role, *Cyrano de Bergerac,* Goodman Theatre, Chicago, IL, 1980.

Mary Barnes, Long Wharf Theatre, New Haven, CT, 1980.

Police inspector, Georges, the physiotherapist, and Angelo, *Piaf,* Plymouth Theatre, New York City, 1981.

Max, *The Real Thing,* Plymouth Theatre, 1984–85.

Virginia's father and Leonard Woolf, *Virginia,* New York Shakespeare Festival, Estelle R. Newman Theatre, Public Theatre, 1985.

Martin Heyman, *Social Security,* Ethel Barrymore Theatre, New York City, 1986–87.

Johnny, *Frankie and Johnny in the Clair de Lune,* Manhattan Theatre Club Stage I, New York City, 1986, then Westside Theatre Upstairs, New York City, 1987–89.

John Honeyman, *A Walk in the Woods,* Yale Repertory Theatre, New Haven, CT, 1987.

Standup Shakespeare, Theatre 890, New York City, 1987.

Horace Giddens, *The Little Foxes,* Vivian Beaumont Theatre, Lincoln Center, New York City, 1997.

Stage Work:

Creator, *Standup Shakespeare,* Theatre 890, New York City, 1987.

Directed *Under Milkwood,* Tyrone Guthrie Theatre, Minneapolis, MN.

WRITINGS

Plays:
(With Ray Leslee) *Standup Shakespeare,* Theatre 890, New York City, 1987.

WHITESELL, John
(John P. Whitesell, John P. Whitesell, II)

PERSONAL

Married Jolie, July, 1999.

Addresses: *Agent*—Creative Artists Agency, 2000 Avenue of the Stars, Los Angeles, CA 90067. *Manager*—The Collective, 9100 Wilshire Blvd., Suite 700 West, Beverly Hills, CA 90212.

Career: Director and producer.

Awards, Honors: Emmy Award (with others), outstanding direction for a drama series, Emmy Award nomination (with others), outstanding daytime drama series, 1985, both for *The Guiding Light;* Emmy Award nomination, outstanding individual achievement in directing in a comedy series, 1994, for *The John Larroquette Show.*

CREDITS

Film Director:
Calendar Girl (also known as *Me and Monroe*), Columbia, 1993.
See Spot Run, Warner Bros., 2001.
Malibu's Most Wanted, Warner Bros., 2003.
Big Momma's House 2, Twentieth Century–Fox, 2006.
Deck the Halls, Twentieth Century–Fox, 2006.

Film Producer:
Deck the Halls, Twentieth Century–Fox, 2006.

Television Work; Series:
Executive producer, *Another World* (also known as *Another World: Bay City*), 1986–88.
Consulting producer, *Cosby,* CBS, 1997–98.
Co–executive producer, *Damon,* Fox, 1998.
Producer, *Men, Women & Dogs,* 2001.

Television Director; Movies:
Clarissa (also known as *Clarissa, Now*), 1995.
Humor Me, 2004.

Television Director; Pilots:
Raising Miranda (also known as *Close to Home* and *My Life Story*), CBS, 1988.
The Bob and Larry Show, syndicated, 1990.
EOB, CBS, 1990.
The John Larroquette Show (also known as *Crossroads* and *Larroquette*), NBC, 1993.

Television Director; Episodic:
Another World (also known as *Another World: Bay City*), c. 1970.
Texas, NBC, 1980–82.
The Guiding Light, CBS, 1984–85.
Tattingers, NBC, 1988.
Nick and Hillary, NBC, 1988.
A Different World, NBC, 1989.
Baby Boom, NBC, 1989.
Doctor, Doctor, CBS, 1989.
One of the Boys, NBC, 1989.
(As John P. Whitesell II) *Coach,* ABC, 1989–90.
"Prescription for Death," *Law and Order,* NBC, 1990.
Roseanne, ABC, 1990–91.
"The Troubles," *Law and Order,* NBC, 1991.
"Out of Control," *Law and Order,* NBC, 1991.
Rachel Gunn, R.N., Fox, 1992.
The John Larroquette Show (also known as *Crossroads* and *Larroquette*), NBC, 1993.
"Blossom in Paris: Part 1," *Blossom,* NBC, 1993.
"Eggs," *The John Larroquette Show* (also known as *Crossroads* and *Larroquette*), NBC, 1994.
Someone Like Me, NBC, 1994.
The Cosby Mysteries, NBC, 1994.
The Martin Short Show, 1994.
Hardball, 1994.
Pig Sty, UPN, 1995.
Pearl, CBS, 1996.
Cosby, CBS, 1996–2000.
Men Behaving Badly, 1997–98.
Damon, Fox, 1998.
Costello, Fox, 1998.
Odd Man Out, ABC, 1998–99.
"If Memory Serves," *Providence,* NBC, 1999.
It's Like, You Know ..., ABC, 1999.
Grown Ups, ABC, 1999.
Action, Fox, 1999.
Jack & Jill, The WB, 1999.
D.C., The WB, 2000.
"Action Mountain High," *Grounded for Life,* 2001.
Raising Dad, 2001.
Men, Women & Dogs, 2001.
So Downtown, 2003.
(Segment) *JKX: The Jamie Kennedy Experiment,* The WB, 2003–2004.
"Quest for Fire," *Listen Up,* CBS, 2004.
Rodney, ABC, 2004.

WILLIAMS, Chris
(Christopher J. Williams, Christopher James Williams)

PERSONAL

Full name, Christopher James Williams; born in Westchester, NY; brother of Vanessa Williams (an actress).

Addresses: *Agent*—Agency for the Performing Arts, 405 South Beverly Dr., Beverly Hills, CA 90212. *Manager*—Artist Management, 1118 15th St., Suite 1, Santa Monica, CA 90403.

Career: Actor. Also works as a stand–up comedian; performed with the Groundlings.

Awards, Honors: MTV Movie Award nomination (with others), best on–screen team, 2005, for *Dodgeball: A True Underdog Story.*

CREDITS

Film Appearances:
Production manager, *Blankman,* Columbia, 1994.
Marksman, *Major Payne,* Universal, 1995.
Television testimonial number two, *Nice Guys Sleep Alone,* The Asylum, 1999.
Blue eyed man, *Personals* (also known as *Hook'd Up*), Unapix Entertainment Productions, 1999.
Payton and X–Ray, *Octopus 2: River of Fear* (also known as *Octopus II*), Nu Image Films, 2001.
Broadway Bill, *Friday After Next,* New Line Cinema, 2002.
Shawn, *Final Draft,* Shoreline Entertainment, 2003.
Nigel, *Max Payne: Hero* (short), 2003.
Boyfriend number three, *Mean Jadine* (short), 2004.
Dwight, *Dodgeball: A True Underdog Story* (also known as *Dodgeball* and *Voll auf die nusse*), 2004.
Tina, *The World's Fastest Indian,* Magnolia Pictures, 2005.
Malik, *Bam Bam and Celeste,* 2005.
(Uncredited) Marcus, *Scary Movie 4,* Weinstein Company, 2006.
Bobby, *Swedish Auto,* 2006.
Himself, *A Really Intimate Portrait … of a Complete Unknown* (short), 2006.
George Higgins, *Look,* 2007.
2–Much, *Urban Decay,* Arsenal Pictures, 2007.
Sammy, *The Mayor's Limo,* 2008.

Television Appearances; Series:
Professor Chris Williams, *One Saturday Morning* (also known as *Disney's "One Saturday Morning"*), ABC, 1997.

Various, *Hype,* The WB, 2000.
Ralph Snow, *The Wedding Bells,* Fox, 2007.

Also appeared as voice, *A Kitty Bobo Show,* Cartoon Network.

Television Appearances; Miniseries:
(Uncredited) Brother at funeral, *Nothing Lasts Forever,* CBS, 1995.

Television Appearances; Movies:
Master of ceremonies, *The Courage to Love,* Lifetime, 2000.
Daryl Fibbs, *Pixel Perfect,* Disney Channel, 2004.

Television Appearances; Specials:
Assistant director, *Tracy Ullman in the Trailer Tales,* HBO, 2003.
I Love the '90s: Part Deux, VH1, 2005.

Television Appearances; Episodic:
Paramedic number one, "A Funny Thing Happened on the Way Home from the Forum," *The Fresh Prince of Bel–Air,* NBC, 1992.
Young men, *Where I Live,* ABC, 1992.
Waiter, "Loveless in San Francisco," *All–American Girl,* ABC, 1994.
Helmsman, "Shadow," *JAG,* NBC, 1995.
Piano bar waiter, "Nice Work If You Can Get It," *Cybill,* CBS, 1995.
Donnie, "The Bodyguard," *Martin,* Fox, 1996.
(As Christopher James Williams) Derek Kobey, "Ranger Jarod," *The Pretender,* NBC, 1997.
(As Christopher James Williams) Attendant, "Shadow of Angels: Parts 1 & 2," *Profiler,* NBC, 1997.
Krazee–Eyez Killa, "Krazee–Eyez Killa," *Curb Your Enthusiasm,* HBO, 2002.
Toronto leather daddy, *Queer as Folk,* Showtime, 2003.
Agent Quigley, "Playing Tight," *The Shield,* FX Channel, 2004.
Blind man, "Security for Kenny Rogers," *Reno 911!,* Comedy Central, 2004.
Willie, "Cool Jerk," *Listen Up,* CBS, 2004.
Lieutenant Reed Owens, "Committed," *CSI: Crime Scene Investigation* (also known as *C.S.I.* and *Les Experts*), CBS, 2005.
Krazee–Eyez Killa, "The End," *Curb Your Enthusiasm,* HBO, 2005.
Tyrell, "Cooking with Jesus," *Weeds,* Showtime, 2006.
Agent Thorpe, "Mr. Monk and the Really, Really Dead Guy," *Monk,* USA Network, 2007.

Also appeared as Eddie, "John, I've Been Thinking," *Buddies,* ABC; Todd Carr, *Californication.*

RECORDINGS

Video Games:

Voice of Ben Moseley and additional voices, *Minority Report,* Activision, 2002.

Assistant coach and various, *NBA '06,* Sony Computer Entertainment America, 2005.

Voice of Crunch, *Crash Tag Team Racing,* Vivendi Universal Games, 2005.

(As Christopher J. Williams) Voice of Sergeant Cross, *Need for Speed: Most Wanted,* EA Games, 2005.

Voice of Boog, *Open Season,* 2006.

Voice of Cop and various, *Saints Row,* THQ, 2006.

Various, *Pimp My Ride,* Activision, 2006.

Additional voices, *Spider-Man 3,* Activision, 2007.

WINNING, David 1961–

PERSONAL

Born May 8, 1961, in Calgary, Alberta, Canada.

Addresses: *Agent*—Agency for the Performing Arts, 405 South Beverly Dr., Beverly Hills, CA 90212.

Career: Director, producer, and writer. University of Calgary, Calgary, Alberta, Canada, instructor, 1985–86.

Awards, Honors: AMPIA Awards, best feature drama and best of festival, Alberta Motion Picture Industries Association, 1986, both for *Storm;* Special Jury Award, Alberta Motion Picture Industries Association, 1989, three Gemini Award nominations, best direction in a dramatic or comedy series, Academy of Canadian Cinema and Television, 1989, 1990, two Awards of Merit, International Television Movie Festival, 1989, Silver Plaques, best director and best television drama, Chicago International Film Festival, 1992, all for *Friday the 13th;* Certificate of Merit, best direction—dramatic series, Chicago International Film Festival, 1993, for *Street Justice;* Special Award, direction—television drama, Columbus International Film and Video Festival, 1994, for *Matrix;* Bronze Award, 1994, and Gold Award, 1995, television series direction, Worldfest Houston, Gold Hugo Awards, best direction—children's television, Chicago International Film Festival, 1994, 1995, Bronze Plaque Award, direction—children's television, Columbus International Film and Video Festival, 1994, Gemini Award nomination, best direction in a dramatic or comedy series, 1997, all for *Are You Afraid of the Dark;* Gold Award, theatrical feature films—thriller, Worldfest Houston, 1997, for *Exception to the Rule;* Gold Award, theatrical feature films—thriller, Worldfest Charleston, 1997, for *One of Our Own;* Gold Plaque, best variety, Chicago International Television Festival, 2000, for *Match Made in Heaven;* Gold Plaque, best direction—variety or entertainment, Chicago International Film Festival, Honorable Mention, entertainment, Columbus International Film and Video Festival, Bronze Medal, television programming and promotion—craft: program—best direction, New York Festivals, 2000, Gold Award, Silver Award, and Bronze Award, television and cable production—television series—dramatic, WorldFest Houston, 2001, Directors Guild of Canada Craft Award nomination, outstanding achievement in design, Directors Guild of Canada Team Award(with others), outstanding achievement in a television series—drama, 2002, Gold Plaque Award, special achievement in direction, Chicago International Film Festival, Gold Medal, television programming and promotion—craft: program–best direction, New York Festivals, 2003, all for *Twice in a Lifetime;* Gold Award, television and cable production—television series—dramatic, WorldFest Houston, 2001, 2002, Platinum Award, television and cable production—directing—television, WorldFest Houston, Gold Plaques, special achievement in direction and best dramatic series, Chicago International Film Festival, 2004, Gold Award, WorldFest Houston, television and cable production—directing—television, Certificate of Merit, special achievement in direction, Chicago International Film Festival, 2005, all for *Andromeda;* Gold Plaque, special achievement in direction, Chicago International Film Festival, Gold Awards, television and cable production—Television series—dramatic, WorldFest Houston, 2001, 2002, for *Earth: Final Conflict;* Honorable Mention and Bronze Plaque Award, entertainment, Columbus International Film and Video Festival, Silver Award and Bronze Award, television and cable production—Television series—dramatic, WorldFest Houston, Bronze Medal, television programming and promotion—action/adventure, New York Festivals, Leo Award, dramatic series—best director, Motion Picture Arts and Sciences Foundation of British Columbia, 2003, all for *Dinotopia;* Gold Award, television and cable production—Television series—dramatic, WorldFest Houston, 2003, for *Body & Soul;* Silver Plaque, special achievement in direction, Chicago International Film Festival, Bronze Plaque Award, entertainment, Columbus International Film and Video Festival, Gold Award, television and cable production—feature made for television/cable, WorldFest Houston, 2003, both for *He Sees You When You're Sleeping;* Platinum Award, television and cable production—directing—television, WorldFest Houston, Silver Plaque, special achievement—direction, Chicago International Film Festival, 2005, both for *Stargate: Atlantis;* Gold Award and Platinum Award, television and cable production, WorldFest Houston, Leo Award nomination, best direction in a youth or children's program or series, Directors Guild of Canada Team Award nomination, outstanding television series—family, Silver Plaque, special achievement—direction, Chicago International Film Festival, 2006, all for *Naturally, Sadie;* Platinum Award, fantasy/horror, WorldFest

Houston, Silver Plaque, special achievement—direction, Chicago International Film Festival, 2007, both for *Something Beneath;* Platinum Award, best director, WorldFest Houston, Certificate of Merit, special achievement—direction, Chicago International Film Festival, 2007, both for *Past Sins;* Gold Award, television and cable production—directing—television, WorldFest Houston, Silver Plaque, special achievement: direction, Chicago International Film Festival, 2007, both for *Dinosapien.*

CREDITS

Film Work:

Director, producer, editor, and cinematographer, *The Visitors,* Groundstar Entertainment, 1977.

Director, producer, editor, and cinematographer, *Game Over,* Groundstar Entertainment, 1978.

Director and producer, *Sequence,* Groundstar Entertainment, 1980.

Director and music editor, *Storm* (also known as *Turbulence*), Warner Bros. Home Video, 1987.

Director, producer, supervising editor, and editor, *Killer Image* (also known as *Meurtre dans l'objectif*), Paramount Home Video, 1992.

Director, *Turbo: A Power Rangers Movie,* Twentieth Century–Fox, 1997.

Director, *Exception to the Rule* (also known as *Nach gefahrlichen regeln*), Artisan, 1997.

Director, *Profile for Murder,* Prism Entertainment, 1997.

Director, *One of Our Own* (also known as *Dener P.D.: One of Our Own*), 1998.

Film Appearances:

(Uncredited) Body in elevator and voice on tape machine, *Game Over,* Groundstar Entertainment, 1978.

(Uncredited) Commuter, *Superman III,* 1983.

(Uncredited) Young Jim, voice of radio announcer, and man in wilderness (dream), *Storm* (also known as *Turbulence*), Warner Bros. Home Video, 1987.

(Uncredited) Voice of boyfriend on answering machine, *Profile for Murder,* Prism Entertainment, 1997.

Television Creative Consultant; Series:

Twice in a Lifetime, PAX and CTV, 1999.

Television Director; Movies:

Don't Look Behind You (also known as *Du entkommst mir nicht*), 1999.

He Sees You When You're Sleeping (also known as *Mar Higgins Clark and Carol Higgins Clark's "He Sees You When You're Sleeping"*), PAX, 2002.

Past Sins, Lifetime, 2006.

Something Beneath, Sci–Fi Channel, 2007.

Black Swarm, 2008.

Television Director; Pilots:

Merlin (movie; also known as *Merlin: The Magic Begins* and *Merlin: The Quest Begins*), 1998.

Television Work; Specials:

Director and editor, *All Star Comedy,* 1982.

(Uncredited) Executive producer, *Cameras Rolling: 20 Days on Set,* 2000.

Television Director; Episodic:

Profile, 1982.

"The Sweetest Sting," *Friday the 13th* (also known as *Friday the 13th: The Series* and *Friday Curse*), syndicated, 1989.

"Scarlet Cinema," *Friday the 13th* (also known as *Friday the 13th: The Series* and *Friday Curse*), syndicated, 1989.

"Jack–in–the–Box," *Friday the 13th* (also known as *Friday the 13th: The Series* and *Friday Curse*), syndicated, 1989.

Street Justice, syndicated, 1992–93.

"Straight Home," *Neon Rider,* syndicated, 1992.

Are You Afraid of the Dark?, Nickelodeon, 1993–95.

"False Witness," *Matrix,* USA Network, 1993.

Sweet Valley High (also known as *California College: Les jumelles de Sweet Valley* and *Francine Pascal's "Sweet Valley High"*), Fox, 1995–97.

"It Came from Beneath the Sink," *Goosebumps,* Fox, 1996.

"Black Widow," *Dead Man's Gun,* Showtime, 1997.

Breaker High, UPN, 1997.

"Fear City," *Night Man* (also known as *Nightman*), syndicated, 1998.

"The People's Choice," *Night Man* (also known as *Nightman*), syndicated, 1998.

"Gore," *Night Man* (also known as *Nightman*), syndicated, 1999.

Twice in a Lifetime, PAX and CTV, 1999–2001.

"Molly Brown," *Call of the Wild* (also known as *Jack London's "Call of the Wild"*), Animal Planet, 2000.

Andromeda (also known as *Gene Roddenberry's "Andromeda"*), NBC, 2000–2005.

Earth: Final Conflict (also known as *EFC, Gene Roddenberry's "Battleground Earth," Gene Roddenberry's "Earth: Final Conflict," Invasion planete Terre,* and *Mission Erde: Sie sind unter uns*), syndicated, 2001–2002.

"Saviors," *Body & Soul,* 2002.

Dinotopia (also known as *Dinotopia: The Series*), ABC, 2002–2003.

"Childhood's End," *Stargate: Atlantis* (also known as *La porte d'Atlantis* and *Stargate: Atlantis*), Sci–Fi Channel, 2004.

"Year of the Dragon," *Naturally, Sadie* (also known as *The Complete Freaks of Nature*), Disney Channel, 2006.

"Double Jeopardy," *Naturally, Sadie* (also known as *The Complete Freaks of Nature*), Disney Channel, 2006.

"Smother's Day," *Naturally, Sadie* (also known as *The Complete Freaks of Nature*), Disney Channel, 2007.

"Poetic Justice," *Naturally, Sadie* (also known as *The Complete Freaks of Nature*), Disney Channel, 2007.

"We'll Meet Again," *Blood Ties,* Lifetime, 2007.

"Drawn & Quartered," *Blood Ties,* Lifetime, 2007.

"Post Partum," *Blood Ties,* Lifetime, 2007.

"5:55," *Blood Ties,* Lifetime, 2007.

"Without a Paddle," *Dinosapien,* Discovery Kids, 2007.

"Monster in the Woods," *Dinosapien,* Discovery Kids, 2007.

"Critters," *Dinosapien,* Discovery Kids, 2007.

"Dawn of the Dinosaur," *Dinosapien,* Discovery Kids, 2007.

Television Appearances; Movies:

(Uncredited) Voice, news announcer, informant, and reverend on telephone, *Past Sins,* 2006.

(Uncredited) Voice of beast in woods, angry Arab guest, and Television announcer, *Something Beneath,* Sci–Fi Channel, 2007.

Television Appearances; Specials:

Phil Donahue, Rod Serling, Primitive man, and others, *All Star Comedy,* 1982.

Storm: In the Making, 1983.

Cameras Rolling: 20 Days on Set, 2000.

WRITINGS

Screenplays:

The Visitors, Groundstar Entertainment, 1977.

Game Over, Groundstar Entertainment, 1978.

Sequence, Groundstar Entertainment, 1980.

Storm (also known as *Turbulences*), Warner Bros. Home Video, 1987.

Killer Image (also known as *Meutre dans l'objectif*), Paramount, 1992.

Television Writer; Movies:

Additional writer: action scenes, *Don't Look Behind You* (also known as *Du entkommst mir nicht*), 1999.

(Uncredited) *Something Beneath,* Sci–Fi Channel, 2007.

OTHER SOURCES

Periodicals:

Calgary Herald Sunday Magazine, January 13, 1991.

Calgary Magazine, September, 1987.

Vancouver Sun, December 4, 1999.

WINSLOW, Michael 1958–
(Michael L. Winslow)

PERSONAL

Full name, Michael Leslie Winslow; born September 6, 1958, in Spokane, WA; son of Robert (served in the Air Force) and Verdie Winslow; married Belinda Church, May 11, 1985 (died, May 13, 1993); married Angel Baytops, May 3, 1997 (divorced, May 25, 2001); married Sharon, June 12, 2003; children: (first marriage) three. *Education:* Studied political science for a year at the University of Colorado at Denver.

Addresses: *Agent*—Cunningham, Escott, and Dipene Agency, 10635 Santa Monica Blvd., Suite 140, Los Angeles, CA 90025; Venture IAB, 2509 Wilshire Blvd., Los Angeles, CA. *Contact*—c/o 895 Bentley Circle, Winter Springs, FL 32708.

Career: Actor. Toured as a comedian; appeared in various television commercials including Gateway computers; served as spokesperson for Cancer Foundations, 2007.

Member: American Federation of Television and Radio Artists, Screen Actors Guild.

CREDITS

Film Appearances:

(Film debut) Welfare comedian, *Cheech and Chong's Next Movie* (also known as *High Encounters of the Ultimate Kind*), Universal, 1980.

Nate, *Underground Aces,* 1980.

Superman Nut, *Cheech and Chong's "Nice Dreams"* (also known as *Nice Dreams*), Columbia, 1981.

Gowdy, *T.A.G.: The Assassination Game* (also known as *Everybody Gets It in the End, Kiss Me, Kill Me,* and *Tag: The Assassination Game*), New World, 1982.

Voice of the Mountain, *Heidi's Song* (animated), Paramount, 1982.

Lippy, *Alphabet City,* Atlantic, 1984.

Spencer, *Grandview, U.S.A.,* Warner Bros., 1984.

Voice of Mogwai and Gremlins, *Gremlins,* 1984.

J. D., *Lovelines* (also known as *Suenos juveniles*), TriStar, 1984.

Cadet Larvell Jones, *Police Academy* (also known as *Police Academy: What an Institution!*), Warner Bros., 1984.

Voice, *Starchaser: The Legend of Orin* (animated; also known as *Gonggan jonsol Orin*), Atlantic, 1985.

Officer Larvell Jones, *Police Academy 2: Their First Assignment,* Warner Bros., 1985.

Sergeant Larvell Jones, *Police Academy 3: Back in Training,* Warner Bros., 1986.

Sergeant Larvell Jones, *Police Academy 4: Citizens on Patrol* (also known as *Citizens on Patrol: Police Academy 4*), Warner Bros., 1987.

Radar technician, *Spaceballs,* Metro–Goldwyn–Mayer/ United Artists, 1987.

Ronny Walker, *Zartliche chaoten* (also known as *Lovable Zanies* and *Three Crazy Jerks*), 1987.

Ronny Walker, *Zartliche chaoten 2* (also known as *Lovable Zanies II* and *Three Crazy Jerks II*), 1988.

Starke Zeiten, 1988.

Sergeant Larvell Jones, *Police Academy 5: Assignment Miami Beach,* Warner Bros., 1988.

Sly, *Buy and Cell,* Empire Films, 1989.

Sergeant Larvell Jones, *Police Academy 6: City Under Siege,* Warner Bros., 1989.

Hap, *Think Big,* 1990.

Airport cop, *Far Out Man* (also known as *Soul Man II*), CineTel, 1990.

Reporter, *Going Under,* 1990.

Sergeant Larvell Jones, *Police Academy 7: Mission to Moscow,* Warner Bros., 1994.

Lee Davis, *Lycanthrope* (also known as *Bloody Moon*), Spectrum Films, 1997.

Michael Winslow Live, 1999.

Horner's friend number two, *The Blur of Insanity,* 1999.

Jeremy, *He Outta Be Committed,* 2000.

Voice, *The Trumpet of the Swan,* 2001.

Officer number one, *The Biggest Fan,* Quick Feathers Pictures, Inc., 2002.

Michael Winslow: Comedy Sound Slapdown! (also known as *The Michael Winslow Experience*), Image Entertainment, 2002.

Officer John Wyndham, *Lenny the Wonder Dog,* North by Northwest Entertainment, 2004.

Himself, *Before They Were Kings: Vol. 1,* Xenon Entertainment Group, 2004.

Michael Winslow: Live at the Improv, Ryko Distribution, 2006.

Coach Al Jefferson, *Coming Attractions,* 2006.

Dr. Murphy, *RoboDoc,* 2007.

Film Work:

Special vocal effects, *Gremlins,* Warner Bros., 1984.

Assistance, *Back to the Future III,* Universal, 1990.

Executive producer, *Michael Winslow: Comedy Sound Slapdown!* (also known as *The Michael Winslow Experience*), Image Entertainment, 2002.

Executive producer, *Lenny the Wonder Dog,* North by Northwest Entertainment, 2004.

Television Appearances; Series:

Voice of Plutem/Glax, *The Space Stars,* NBC, 1981.

Sergeant Larvelle Jones, *Police Academy: The Series,* 1997–98.

Television Appearances; Movies:

Dumas, *Extralarge: Ninja Shadow* (also known as *Extralarge: L'ombra del guerriero*), 1993.

Dumas, *Extralarge: Lord of the Sun* (also known as *Extralarge: Il signore del sole*), 1993.

Dumas, *Extralarge: Indians,* 1993.

Dumas, *Extralarge: Gonzales' Revenge,* 1993.

Dumas, *Extralarge: Diamonds* (also known as *Extralarge: Pioggia di diamanti*), 1993.

Dumas, *Extralarge: Condor Mission* (also known as *Extralarge: Operazione Condor*), 1993.

Television Appearances; Specials:

Presenter, *The 58th Annual Academy Awards Presentation,* ABC, 1986.

The Second Annual Star–Spangled Celebration, 1988.

The 3rd Annual American Comedy Awards, ABC, 1989.

Miss Hollywood Talent Search, syndicated, 1989.

Television Appearances; Pilots:

Redlight, *Nightside,* ABC, 1980.

Michael, *Irene,* NBC, 1981.

Television Appearances; Episodic:

Student, "Psyched Out," *The White Shadow,* 1981.

"Space Case," *Reading Rainbow,* PBS, 1986.

"The Second Time Around/Hello, Spencer/Runaway, Go Home," *The Love Boat,* ABC, 1986.

"My Stepmother, Myself/Almost Roommates/ Cornerback Sneak," *The Love Boat,* ABC, 1986.

"Happily Ever After/Have I Got a Job for You/Mr. Smith Goes to Minikulu," *The Love Boat,* ABC, 1986.

Lewis Delgado, "The Wrong Man," *Shades of LA,* 1990.

Chuck the Great, "Pet Psychic," *Harry and the Hendersons,* 1991.

Chuck the Great, "Wild Things," *Harry and the Hendersons,* 1992.

"976 Ways to Say I Love You," *Baywatch Nights* (also known as *Detectives on the Beach*), 1995.

Jimi Hendrix look–a–like, "Drew Gets Married," *The Drew Carey Show,* ABC, 1997.

"'Family Guy' Viewer Mail #1," *Family Guy* (animated; also known as *Padre de familia*), Fox, 2002.

(As Michael L. Winslow) Himself, "The Movie," *Ed,* NBC, 2003.

The Daily Buzz, 2004.

Voice of Larvelle Jones, "Sausage Fest," *Robot Chicken* (animated), Cartoon Network, 2006.

Himself, "Glyne tabber og gylne oyeblikk," *Gylne tider,* 2007.

Also appeared in *The Gong Show,* syndicated.

Television Appearances; Specials:

The 58th Annual Academy Awards Presentation, ABC, 1986.

The Second Annual Star–Spangled Celebration, ABC, 1988.
Miss Hollywood Talent Search, syndicated, 1989.
The 3rd Annual American Comedy Awards, ABC, 1989.

RECORDINGS

Albums:
I Am My Own Walkman, 1985.
Citizens on Patrol, MCA Records, 1987.

Video Games:
Voice of pedestrian, *Grand Theft Auto: San Andreas* (also known as *GTA: San Andreas* and *San Andreas*), Rockstar Games, 2004.

WRITINGS

Film Writing:
Michael Winslow: Comedy Sound Slapdown! (also known as *The Michael Winslow Experience*), Image Entertainment, 2002.
Before They Were Kings: Vol. 1, Xenon Entertainment Group, 2004.
Michael Winslow: Live at the Improv, Ryko Distribution, 2006.

WINTERS, Jonathan 1925–

PERSONAL

Full name, Jonathan Harshman Winters III; born November 11, 1925, in Dayton, OH; son of Jonathan Harshman, Jr. (a banker) and Alice Kilgore (a radio personality; maiden name, Rodgers) Winters; married Eileen Ann Schauder, September 11, 1948; children: Jonathan IV, Lucinda Kelley. *Education:* Attended Kenyon College, 1946; Dayton Art Institute, B.F.A., art, 1950. *Avocational Interests:* Painting.

Addresses: *Agent*—Rebel Entertainment Partners, Inc., 5700 Wilshire Blvd., Suite 456, Los Angeles, CA 90036.

Career: Actor, comedian, writer, producer, and editor. WING, Dayton, OH, radio disc jockey, 1949; WBNS–TV, Columbus, OH, television announcer and comedian, 1950–53; appeared in nightclubs and cabarets, 1953–59, and in concert halls, 1961—; did radio voice work for commercials for Wish Bone salad dressings, c. 1970s; appeared in television commercials for Good Humor Ice Cream, c. 1970s, Hefty garbage bags, 1979, Tostitos tortilla chips, 1995, California, 1998, California

fresh eggs, 1999, and Tuesday Morning retail stores, 2004. Previously worked as a painter and a disc jockey. *Military service:* United States Marine Corps, 1943–46, Pacific Theater of Operations.

Member: American Federation of Television and Radio Artists, American Guild of Variety Artists, Screen Actors Guild, Writers Guild of America.

Awards, Honors: Grammy Award nomination, best comedy album, 1960, for *The Wonderful World of Jonathan Winters;* Grammy Award nomination, best comedy performance, 1961, for *Here's Jonathan;* Grammy Award nomination, best comedy performance, 1962, for *Another Day, Another World;* Golden Globe Award nomination, best motion picture actor—musical/comedy, 1964, for *It's a Mad Mad Mad Mad World;* Grammy Award, best recording for children, 1975, for *The Little Prince;* Lifetime Achievement Award in Comedy, American Comedy Awards, 1987; Emmy Award, best supporting actor in a comedy series, 1991, for *Davis Rules;* American Comedy Award, funniest male performer in a television special (leading or supporting), network, cable, or syndication, 1991, for *And His Traveling Road Show;* inducted in the United States Comedy Hall of Fame, 1993; inducted in the Canadian Comedy Hall of Fame, 1994; Grammy Award, best spoken comedy album, 1996, for *Crank(y) Calls;* Mark Twain Prize in Humor, 1999; Lifetime Achievement Award, Ojai Film Festival, 2000; Lifetime Achievement Tribute, Orinda Film Festival, 2003; Emmy Award nomination, outstanding guest actor in a comedy series, 2003, for *Life with Bonnie;* DVDX Award, best supporting actor in a DVD premiere movie, DVD Exclusive Awards, 2005, for *Comic Book: The Movie;* Star on the Hollywood Walk of Fame—Television; seven other Grammy Award nominations.

CREDITS

Film Appearances:
Voice of Sir Quigley Broken Bottom, *Saiyu–ki* (also known as *Alakazam the Great, The Magic land of Alakazam,* and *The Enchanted Monkey*), 1960.
Lennie Pike, *It's a Mad Mad Mad Mad World* (also known as *It's a Mad, Mad, Mad, Mad World*), United Artists, 1963.
Henry/Wilbur Glenworthy, *The Loved One,* Metro–Goldwyn–Mayer, 1965.
Officer Norman Jones, *The Russians Are Coming! The Russians Are Coming!,* United Artists, 1966.
Professor Klobb, *Penelope,* Metro–Goldwyn–Mayer, 1966.
Jasper Lynch, *Eight on the Lam* (also known as *Eight on the Run*), United Artists, 1967.
The Midnight Oil, 1967.
Dad and narrator, *Oh Dad, Poor Dad, Mama's Hung You in the Closet and I'm Feeling So Sad,* Paramount, 1967.

General Billy Joe Hallson, *Viva Max!,* Commonwealth United, 1969.

English tour guide, tourist number one, little boy tourist, and Texas tourist, *The Special London Bridge Special,* 1972.

Sonic Boom, 1974.

H. S. and Harvey Tilson, *The Fish That Saved Pittsburgh,* United Artists, 1979.

Tyler, *Long Shot,* 1981.

Voice of Molester, Porky Pine, and other characters, *Pogo for President: Go Pogo* (also known as *Go Pogo, I Go Pogo,* and *Pogo for President*), 1984.

Emerson Foosnagel III, *E. Nick: A Legend in His Own Mind,* 1984.

W. D. Westmoreland, *Say Yes,* 1986.

Himself, *The Wonderful World of Jonathan Winters,* 1986.

Tyler, *The Longshot,* 1986.

Ralph, *Moon over Parador,* Universal, 1988.

Storyteller, *Rabbit Ears: Paul Bunyan,* 1990.

Voice of Wade Pig, *Tiny Toon Adventures: How I Spent My Vacation* (animated; also known as *How I Spent My Vacation*), 1992.

Himself, Maude Frickert, and other characters, *Gone Fish'n,* 1993.

Wainwright Barth, *The Shadow,* Universal, 1993.

Voice of the thief, *The Princess and the Cobbler* (animated; also known as *Arabian Knight*), Miramax, 1993.

Grizzled man, *The Flintstones,* Universal, 1994.

Whoppa Chopper pilot, Ohio cop with bullhorn, and Jeb, *The Adventures of Rocky and Bullwinkle* (also known as *Die Abenteuer von Rocky und Bullwinkle*), Universal, 2000.

Edwurd Fudwupper Fibbed Big, 2000.

Himself, *Squatching,* 2002.

Voice of Santa, *Santa vs. the Snowman 3D* (short), 2002.

Uncle Bill, *Swing,* Crazy Dreams Entertainment, 2003.

Himself, *Tell Them Who You Are* (documentary), THINKFilm, 2004.

Wally (army buddy number two), *Comic Book: The Movie,* Miramax Home Entertainment, 2004.

Thomas, *Cattle Call* (also known as *National Lampoon's "Cattle Call"*), Lions Gate Films, 2006.

Himself, *Certifiably Jonathan,* 2007.

Film Editor:
Gone Fish'n, 1993.

Television Appearances; Series:
The Garry Moore Show, CBS, 1954–63.

The Steve Allen Show (also known as *The Steve Allen Plymouth Show*), NBC, 1954–61.

Host, *And Here's the Show,* NBC, 1955.

NBC Comedy Hour, NBC, 1956.

The Jonathan Winters Show, NBC, 1956–57.

Masquerade Party, CBS, 1958.

The Jack Paar Program, NBC, 1962–63.

Voice of the Giant, *Linus the Lionhearted* (animated), CBS, 1964–66, then ABC, 1966–1969.

The Andy Williams Show, NBC, 1965–71.

The Dean Martin Show, 1966–73.

The Jonathan Winters Show, CBS, 1967–69.

Hot Dog, 1970.

Host, *The Wacky World of Jonathan Winters,* syndicated, 1972–74.

Humorist, *Good Morning, America,* ABC, 1975–76.

Mearth, *Mork and Mindy,* ABC, 1981–82.

Voice of Papa Smurf, Grandpa Smurf, and additional voices, *The Smurfs* (animated; also known as *Smurfs Adventures*), NBC, 1981–1990.

Hee Haw, CBS, 1983–84.

Additional voice, *Yogi's Treasure Hunt* (animated), syndicated, 1985.

Voice of Wishing Well, *Star Fairies* (animated), 1986.

Voice of Roger Gustav, Mr. Freebus, and additional voices, *The Completely Mental Misadventures of Ed Grimley* (animated), NBC, 1988.

Voice of Coach Cadaver, *Rick Moranis in Gravedale High* (animated; also known as *Gravedale High*), NBC, 1990.

Voice of Igor and Granny, *Little Dracula* (animated), 1991.

Gunny Davis, *Davis Rules,* ABC, 1991, then CBS, 1991–92.

Voice of Mayor Cod, *Fish Police* (animated), CBS, 1992.

Host, *Jonathan Winters: Spaced Out,* Showtime, 1993.

Bloopy's Buddies, 1996.

Television Appearances; Miniseries:
Professor Albert Paradine II, *More Wild, Wild West,* CBS, 1980.

Voice of Humpty Dumpty, *Alice in Wonderland* (animated; also known as *Alice through the Looking Glass*), CBS, 1985.

Television Appearances; Movies:
Jeremiah "Jerry" Klay, *Now You See It, Now You Don't,* NBC, 1986.

Additional voice, *The Little Troll Prince* (animated), syndicated, 1987.

Television Appearances; Pilots:
Take One, NBC, 1981.

Faith, CBS, 1994.

Television Appearances; Specials:
Atlantic City Holiday, 1956.

Jonathan Winters Presents a Wild Winters Night, NBC, 1964.

The Jonathan Winters Special, NBC, 1964.

The Jonathan Winters Show, NBC, February, 1965.

The Jonathan Winters Show, NBC, May, 1965.

With Love, Sophia, 1967.

The Wonderful World of Jonathan Winters, NBC, 1970.

Movin', 1970.

Plimpton! Did You Hear the One About ...?, 1971.

Disney World: A Gala Opening (also known as *The Grand Opening of Walt Disney World*), 1971.

Special London Bridge Special, 1972.

The Engelbert Humperdinck Special, 1973.

The Fricker Fracus (animated), CBS, 1973.

Jonathan Winters Presents Two Hundred Years of American Humor, NBC, 1976.

Freedom Is, syndicated, 1976.

Dean Martin's Red Hot Scandals of 1926, 1976.

Dean Martin's Red Hot Scandals Part 2, 1977.

Dean Martin's Christmas in California, 1977.

Uncle Tim Wants You!, 1977.

Bob Hope Special: Bob Hope for President, 1980.

Take One Starring Jonathan Winters, 1981.

Bob Hope Special: Bob Hope in "Who Makes the World Laugh"—Part One, 1983.

The Suzanne Somers Special, 1983.

The Great Standups (also known as *The Great Stand-ups: Sixty Years of Laughter*), 1984.

The World's Funniest Commercial Goofs, ABC, 1985.

NBC's 60th Anniversary Celebration, NBC, 1986.

Host, *King Kong: The Living Legend,* syndicated, 1986.

David Letterman's 2nd Annual Holiday Film Festival, NBC, 1986.

Bob Hope's High-Flying Birthday, NBC, 1986.

Bob Hope's Tropical Comedy Special from Tahiti, NBC, 1987.

Voice of Grandpa, *'Tis the Season to Be Smurfy* (animated), NBC, 1987.

Jonathan Winters: On the Ledge, 1987.

Happy Birthday, Bob—50 Stars Salute Your 50 Years with NBC, NBC, 1988.

Jonathan Winters Show, Showtime, 1988.

Host, *Showtime Presents: Jonathan Winters and Friends,* Showtime, 1989.

Hanna-Barbera's 50th: A Yabba Dabba Doo Celebration (animated), TNT, 1989.

Jonathan Winters and His Traveling Roadshow (also known as *And His Traveling Road Show*), Showtime, 1990.

Narrator, *Paul Bunyan,* Showtime, 1990.

Voice of Harry, *Wake, Rattle and Roll* (animated), syndicated, 1990.

The 5th Annual American Comedy Awards, ABC, 1991.

Voice of Abracadabra and the owl, *The Wish That Changed Christmas* (animated), CBS, 1991.

Himself and Pike the van driver, *Something a Little Less Serious: A Tribute to "It's a Mad Mad Mad Mad World,"* 1991.

The 5th Annual American Comedy Awards, 1991.

Himself, *Spaced Out!,* 1992.

Voice of narrator, *Frosty Returns* (animated), 1993.

Jonathan Winters: Spaced Out, Showtime, 1993.

Presenter, *The 8th Annual American Comedy Awards,* ABC, 1994.

Bob Hope's Birthday Memories, 1994.

The Second Annual Comedy Hall of Fame, 1994.

Voice of Pocket watch, *The Bears Who Saved Christmas* (animated), 1994.

Montreal International Comedy Festival '94, 1994.

Who Makes You Laugh?, 1995.

Voice, *Daisy-Head Mayzie* (animated), 1995.

Who Makes You Laugh?, 1997.

Phil Silvers: Top Banana, 1997.

Voice of Santa, *Santa vs. the Snowman,* ABC, 1997.

Norman Jewison on Comedy in the 20th Century: Funny Is Money, Showtime, 1999.

Uncomfortably Close with Michael McKean: Jonathan Winters, Comedy Central, 2000.

Jonathan Winters: On the Loose, PBS, 2000.

Comedy Central Presents the Second Annual Kennedy Center Mark Twain Prize Celebrating the Humor of Jonathan Winters, Comedy Central, 2000.

The Joke's on Thee, 2001.

The 1st 13th Annual Fancy Anvil Awards Show Program Special ... Live! ... in Stereo, Cartoon Network, 2002.

The Three Stooges 75th Anniversary Special, NBC, 2003.

Honoree, *100 Greatest Stand-Ups of All Time,* Comedy Central, 2004.

Television Appearances; Episodic:

"The House," *Omnibus,* CBS, 1954.

Comedian, *The Colgate Comedy Hour* (also known as *Michael Todd Revue, Colgate Variety Hour,* and *Colgate Summer Comedy Hour*), 1955.

Tonight! (also known as *Knickerbocker Beer Show, The Knickerbocker Beer Presents "The Steven Allen Show," The Steve Allen Show,* and *Tonight*), 1957.

The Jackie Gleason Show, 1957.

The Arlene Francis Show, 1957, 1958.

Person to Person, 1958.

The Jack Paar Tonight Show (also known as *The Jack Paar Show*), 1958, 1962.

What's My Line?, 1958, 1960, 1964.

Lord Nikidik, "The Land of Oz," *Shirley Temple Theatre* (also known as *Shirley Temple's Storybook*), NBC, 1960.

Barnaby, "Babes in Toyland," *Shirley Temple Theater,* NBC, 1960.

"The Jack Paar Variety Show," *Startime* (also known as *Ford Startime* and *Lincoln-Mercury Startime*), 1960.

Fats Brown, "A Game of Pool," *The Twilight Zone* (also known as *Twilight Zone*), CBS, 1961.

I've Got a Secret, 1962.

The Jerry Lewis Show, 1963.

NBC Monitor Show, NBC, 1963.

Voice, "Mocking Bird," *Linus! The Lion Hearted,* 1964.

Voice, "Adrift on the Rapids," *Linus! The Lion Hearted,* 1964.

The London Palladium, NBC, 1966.

"Murder at N.B.C.," *Bob Hope Presents the Chrysler Theatre* (also known as *The Chrysler Theater* and *Universal Star Time*), 1966.

Dateline: Hollywood, 1967.

The Carol Burnett Show (also known as *Carol Burnett and Friends*), 1967–68.

The Smothers Brothers Comedy Hour, 1967, 1969.

Rowan & Martin's Laugh–In, 1970.

The Mike Douglas Show, 1970, 1974.

"Jonathan Winters," *This Is Your Life,* 1971.

Voice of himself and Maude Frickert, *The New Scooby–Doo Movies* (animated; also known as *Scooby–Doo Meets the Harlem Globetrotters* and *Scooby–Doo's New Comedy Movie Pictures*), 1972.

The Mouse Factory, syndicated, 1972.

The Tonight Show Starring Johnny Carson, NBC, 1972, 1973, 1974, 1988.

Voice, "Maude Loves Papa," *Wait Till Your Father Gets Home* (animated), syndicated, 1974.

Hollywood Squares, NBC, 1976.

Night watchman and talking pumpkin, "Halloween Hall o' Fame," *Disneyland* (also known as *Disney's Wonderful World, The Disney Sunday Movie, The Magical World of Disney, The Wonderful World of Disney, Walt Disney, Walt Disney Presents,* and *Walt Disney's Wonderful World of Color*), 1977.

"Mickey's 50," *Disneyland* (also known as *Disney's Wonderful World, The Disney Sunday Movie, The Magical World of Disney, The Wonderful World of Disney, Walt Disney, Walt Disney Presents,* and *Walt Disney's Wonderful World of Color*), 1978.

The Muppet Show, 1980.

Dave McConnell, "Mork and the Family Reunion," *Mork and Mindy,* 1981.

"Turn Me On/Treasure Hunt/A Child Will Become Father," *Aloha Paradise,* ABC, 1981.

Mearth, "The Mork Report," *Mork and Mindy,* 1982.

World of Disney, CBS, 1982.

Late Night with David Letterman, NBC, 1986.

Voice of Stanley, "Who Bopped Bugs Bunny?," *Tiny Toon Adventures* (animated), 1990.

Voice of Stinkbomb, "Smell Ya Later," *Animaniacs* (animated; also known as *Steven Spielberg Presents "Animaniacs"*), The WB, 1994.

Voice, *Johnny Bravo* (animated), 1997.

Bloopy's Buddies, syndicated, 1998.

"Phyllis Diller: First Lady of Laughter," *Biography,* Arts and Entertainment, 2000.

Q. T. Marlens, "Money Plus Marlens Makes Four," *Life with Bonnie,* ABC, 2002.

"Andy Williams," *Biography,* Arts and Entertainment, 2003.

Jimmy Kimmel Live, ABC, 2005, 2006.

Also appeared as additional voice, *Captain Planet and the Planeteers* (animated); additional voices, "One Sweet and Sour Chinese Adventure to Go," *Bill & Ted's Excellent Adventures* (animated); in *Talent Scouts.*

Television Executive Producer; Specials:

Jonathan Winters: Spaced Out (also known as *Spaced Out!*), Showtime, 1993.

Stage Appearances:

John Murray Anderson's Almanac (revue), Imperial Theatre, New York City, 1954.

RECORDINGS

Albums:

The Mad, Mad, Mad World of Jonathan Winters, 1965.

The Little Prince, c. 1975.

Crank(y) Calls, Audio Select, 1995.

Recorded comedy albums for Verve/Metro–Goldwyn–Mayer, 1960–64, including *Another Day, Another World, The Wonderful World of Jonathan Winters, Down to Earth with Jonathan Winters, Here's Jonathan, Humor Seen through the Eyes of Jonathan Winters,* and *Whistle–Stopping with Jonathan Winters;* also recorded an album with Columbia Records.

Music Videos:

Appeared in Genesis's "I Can't Dance."

WRITINGS

Television Specials:

The Wonderful World of Jonathan Winters, NBC, 1970.

Jonathan Winters Presents Two Hundred Years of American Humor, NBC, 1976.

Uncle Tim Wants You!, 1977.

Jonathan Winters: Spaced Out (also known as *Spaced Out!*), Showtime, 1993.

The Unknown Jonathan Winters: On the Loose, Fox Lorber, 2000.

Books:

(With Philip Cammarata) *Did Anyone Bring an Opener?,* Harper, 1959.

Mouse Breath, Conformity and Other Social Ills, Bobbs–Merrill, 1965.

Winter's Tales: Stories and Observations for the Unusual, Random House, 1987, expanded edition, Silver Springs Books, 2001.

Hangings, Random House, 1988.

Jonathan Winters: After the Beep, Putnam, 1989.

Hang–Ups, 1990.

OTHER SOURCES

Periodicals:

Time, November 8, 1999, p. 153.

U.S. News & World Report, November 1, 1999, p. 23.

Variety, October 25, 1999, p. 60.

WISEMAN, Frederick 1930–

PERSONAL

Born January 1, 1930, in Boston, MA; son of Jacob Leo and Gertrude Leah (maiden name, Kotzen) Wiseman; married Zipporah Batshaw, May 29, 1955; children: David B, Eric T. *Education:* Williams College, B.A., 1951; Yale University School of Law, LL.B., 1954; also attended University of Paris.

Addresses: *Office*—Zipporah Films, 1 Richdale Ave., Unit Four, Cambridge, MA 02140–2610. *Agent*—Patrick Herold, International Creative Management, 10250 Constellation Way, 9th Floor, Los Angeles, CA 90067.

Career: Director, producer, film editor, and sound editor. Zipporah Films, Cambridge, MA, founder, general manager, and documentary filmmaker, 1970—. American Museum of Natural History, member of advisory committee for Margaret Mead Film Festival, 1992—; Human Rights Watch International Film Festival, member of festival committee, 1994—; New York Documentary Festival, member of advisory board, 1997—. John F. Kennedy Center for the Performing Arts, member of artistic board for American National Theatre, 1985; Harvard University, member of honorary advisory committee for American Repertory Theatre, 1986—; Theatre for a New Audience, member of artistic council and board of directors, 1998—. Worked as a lawyer in Paris, 1956–58; Boston University, Boston, MA, lecturer in law, 1958–61; Brandeis University, Waltham, MA, research associate in sociology, 1962–66; visiting lecturer at other universities. *Military service:* U.S. Army, 1955–56.

Member: International Documentary Association (member of board of directors, 1986—), Academy of Television Arts and Sciences (fellow), American Academy of Arts and Sciences (fellow), American Academy of Arts and Letters (honorary member), Organization for Social and Technological Innovation, Les Amis du Cinema du Reel Association (honorary member), Massachusetts Bar Association.

Awards, Honors: Mannheim Film Ducat, best feature, International Filmfest Mannheim–Heidelberg, 1967, for *Titicut Follies;* Emmy Award, outstanding achievement in news documentary programming, 1969, for *Law and Order;* Emmy Awards, best director and outstanding achievement in news documentary programming, 1970, and Columbia Dupont Award, excellence in broadcast journalism, all for *Hospital;* Gabriel Award for Personal Achievement, Catholic Broadcasters' As-

sociation, 1975; Guggenheim fellowship, 1980–81; John D. and Catherine T. MacArthur Foundation grant, 1982–87; Columbia Dupont Award, excellence in broadcast journalism, 1975, for *Juvenile Court;* decorated chevalier de l'Ordre des Arts et des Lettres, 1987, decorated commander, 2000; nomination for Grand Jury Prize, documentary category, Sundance Film Festival, 1988, for *Missile;* Career Achievement Award, International Documentary Association, 1990; FIPRESCI Award, Berlin International Film Festival, 1990, for *Near Death;* Peabody Personal Award, 1991; Grand Prix, Marseille Festival of Documentary Film, 1998, and Golden Satellite Award nomination, best documentary film, International Press Academy, 1999, both for *Public Housing;* Rosenberger Medal, University of Chicago, 1999; Lifetime Achievement Award, Human Rights Watch International Film Festival, 2000; Silver Hugo Award, best documentary, Chicago International Film Festival, 2001, for *Domestic Violence;* Career Achievement Award, DoubleTake Documentary Film Festival, 2002; Award of Merit, Yale Law Association, 2002; Dan David Prize Laureate, 2003; Special Achievement Award, American Society of Cinematographers, 2006; George Polk Memorial Award for career achievement, Department of Journalism, Long Island University, 2006; Lifetime Achievement Award, Chicago International Documentary Festival, 2007; honorary degrees include L.H.D. from University of Cincinnati, 1973, Williams College, 1976, and John Jay College of Criminal Justice of the City University of New York, 1994, and D.F.A. from Lake Forest College, 1991, Princeton University, 1994, and Bowdoin College, 2005.

CREDITS

Film Producer, Director, and Film Editor:
Titicut Follies, 1967.
High School, 1968.
Law and Order (also known as *The Greater Good*), Zipporah Films, 1969.
Hospital, Zipporah Films, 1970.
Basic Training, Zipporah Films, 1971.
Essene, Zipporah Films, 1972.
Juvenile Court, Zipporah Films, 1973.
Primate, Zipporah Films, 1974.
Welfare, Zipporah Films, 1975.
Meat, Zipporah Films, 1976.
Canal Zone, Zipporah Films, 1977.
Sinai Field Mission, Zipporah Films, 1978.
Manoeuvre (also known as *Maneuver*), Zipporah Films, 1979.
Model, Zipporah Films, 1980.
Seraphita's Diary, Zipporah Films, 1982.
The Store, Zipporah Films, 1983.
High School II, Zipporah Films, 1993.
Ballet, Zipporah Films, 1995.
Public Housing, Zipporah Films, 1997.

Domestic Violence 2, Zipporah Films, 2002.

La derniere lettre (also known as *The Last Letter*), Ad Vitam, 2002, subtitled version, Zipporah Films, 2003.

Most of these documentary films were eventually broadcast as television specials by PBS.

Documentary Film Producer, Director, Film Editor, and Sound Editor:

Racetrack, Zipporah Films, 1985.

Multi–Handicapped, Zipporah Films, 1986.

Deaf, Zipporah Films, 1986.

Blind, Zipporah Films, 1986.

Adjustment and Work, Zipporah Films, 1986.

Missile, Zipporah Films, 1987.

Near Death, Zipporah Films, 1989.

Central Park, Zipporah Films, 1989.

Aspen, Zipporah Films, 1991.

Zoo, Zipporah Films, 1993.

La Comedie–Francaise ou L'amour joue, Zipporah Films, 1996.

Belfast, Maine, Zipporah Films, 1999.

Domestic Violence, Zipporah Films, 2002.

The Garden, Zipporah Films, 2002.

State Legislature, Zipporah Films, 2007.

Most of these documentary films were eventually broadcast as television specials by PBS.

Film Work; Other:

Producer (with Shirley Clarke), *The Cool World,* Cinema V, 1963.

Film Appearances:

To Render a Life, 1992.

Cinema Verite: Defining the Moment (documentary; also known as *Cinema verite–Le moment decisif*), National Film Board of Canada, 1999.

There Is No Direction (documentary short film), Temps Noir/Muse Films/Central Films, 2005.

Stage Director:

(And producer) *Tonight We Improvise* (video sequences), American Repertory Theatre, Cambridge, MA, 1986–87.

Life and Fate, American Repertory Theatre, 1988.

The Last Letter (one–woman show), American Repertory Theatre, 1988, then La Comedie Francaise, Paris, 2000, later Theatre for a New Audience, Lucille Lortel Theatre, New York City, 2003–2004.

Hate, American Repertory Theatre, 1991.

Welfare: The Opera, American Music Theatre Festival, Philadelphia, PA, 1992.

Oh les beaux jours, La Comedie Francaise, Paris, 2006.

Stage Appearances:

The filmmaker, *Tonight We Improvise* (video sequences), American Repertory Theatre, Cambridge, MA, 1986–87.

Oh les beaux jours, La Comedie Francaise, Paris, 2007.

Major Tours:

The Last Letter, North American cities, 2001.

WRITINGS

Documentary Film Scripts:

Basic Training, Zipporah Films, 1971.

Welfare, Zipporah Films, 1975.

Canal Zone, Zipporah Films, 1977.

Model, Zipporah Films, 1980.

Seraphita's Diary, Zipporah Films, 1982.

Racetrack, Zipporah Films, 1985.

Missile, Zipporah Films, 1987.

Central Park, Zipporah Films, 1989.

La derniere lettre (also known as *The Last Letter*), Ad Vitam, 2002, subtitled version, Zipporah Films, 2003.

Stage Scripts:

(With David Slavitt) *Welfare: The Opera,* libretto by Slavitt, music by Lenny Pickett, American Music Theatre Festival, Philadelphia, PA, 1992, then Theatre at St. Anne's Center for Restoration and the Arts, New York City, 1997.

The Last Letter (one–woman show; based on the novel *Life and Fate* by Vasily Grossman), La Comedie Francaise, Paris, 2000, then Theatre for a New Audience, Lucille Lortel Theatre, New York City, 2003–2004.

Other:

Contributor to periodicals, including *Film Library Quarterly, New Yorker, Sight and Sound,* and *Threepenny Review.*

OTHER SOURCES

Books:

Atkins, Thomas R., *Frederick Wiseman,* Monarch Press, 1976.

Contemporary Literary Criticism, Volume 20, Gale, 1982.

Encyclopedia of World Biography, 2nd edition, Gale, 1998.

International Directory of Films and Filmmakers, Volume 2: *Directors,* 2nd edition, St. James Press, 1991.

Electronic:
Zipporah Films Web site, http://www.zipporah.com, August 15, 2007.

WOLSKI, Dariusz 1956–
　　(Darek Wolski, Dariusz A. Wolski, Darrick Wolski)

PERSONAL

Full name, Dariusz Adam Wolski; born in 1956, in Warsaw, Poland. *Education:* Attended Poland's national film school.

Addresses: *Agent*—The Mack Agency, 4705 Laurel Canyon Blvd., Suite 204, Valley Village, CA 91607.

Career: Cinematographer. Began career working on student films at Columbia University, New York City; worked as a production assistant and assistant cameraman in New York City; worked as an assistant on documentaries for the BBC; worked on more than 100 music videos; also worked as a cinematographer on commercials, including Acura TV, 2002, Canon electronics, Levi's clothing, Honda automobiles; directed commercials for Nike.

Member: Academy of Motion Picture Arts and Sciences (Cinematographers Branch), 2004.

Awards, Honors: MTV Video Music Award nomination, best cinematography, 1990, for "Janie's Got a Gun"; American Society of Cinematographers Award nomination, outstanding achievement in cinematography in theatrical releases, 1996, for *Crimson Tide;* MTV Video Music Award nomination, best cinematography, 2001, for "Stan."

CREDITS

Film Cinematographer:
Droga z pierwszenstwem przejazdu (short), 1979.
Kregoslup, 1979.
W starym piecu, 1979.
Nightfall, Metro–Goldwyn–Mayer, 1988.
Fifteenth Phase of the Moon, 1990.
Romeo Is Bleeding, Gramercy Pictures, 1993.
The Crow, Miramax, 1994.
Crimson Tide, Buena Vista, 1995.
The Fan, Columbia TriStar, 1996.
Dark City, New Line Cinema, 1998.
A Perfect Murder, Warner Bros., 1998.

(As Darek Wolski) *Coyote Ugly,* Buena Vista, 2000.
The Mexican (also known as *La Mexicana*), Dream-Works, 2001.
(As Dariusz A. Wolski) *Bad Company* (also known as *Ceska spojka*), Buena Vista, 2002.
Pirates of the Caribbean: The Curse of the Black Pearl (also known as *P.O.T.C.*), Buena Vista, 2003.
Hide and Seek, Twentieth Century–Fox, 2005.
Pirates of the Caribbean: Dead Man's Chest (also known as *P.O.T.C. 2, Pirates 2,* and *Rummty II*), Buena Vista, 2006.
Pirates of the Caribbean: At World's End (also known as *P.O.T.C. 3* and *Pirates 3*), Buena Vista, 2007.
Sweeney Todd: The Demon Barber of Fleet Street (also known as *Sweeney Todd*), DreamWorks, 2007.

Film Work; Other:
Camera assistant, *Callneczka,* 1978.
Gaffer, *Death of a Prophet,* 1981.
Camera assistant, *Almonds and Raisins: A History of Yiddish Cinema,* 1983.
Camera operator, *Almost You,* Twentieth Century–Fox, 1985.
Additional photographer, *Heart,* 1986.
(As Darek Wolski) Assistant camera, *Parting Glances,* Cinecom Pictures, 1986.
First assistant camera: third unit, *Cherry 2000,* Orion, 1987.
(As Derek Wolski) First assistant camera, *Hail! Hail! Rock 'n' Roll!,* Universal, 1987.
(As Darek Wolski) Second unit director, *Coyote Ugly,* Buena Vista, 2000.

Film Appearances:
Callneczka, 1978.

Television Work; Movies:
(As Darek Wolski) Gaffer, *Death of a Profit,* 1981.
(As Darrick Wolski) Assistant camera, *The Brass Ring,* 1983.
Second assistant camera, *Murder: By Reason of Insanity,* 1985.
Cinematographer, *American Playhouse: "Land of Little Rain"* (also known as *The Land of Little Rain*), 1989.
Cinematographer, *Chains of Gold,* Showtime, 1991.

RECORDINGS

Music Videos (as Cinematographer):
Loudness' "This Lonely Heart," 1987.
Neil Young's "This Note's For You," 1988.
Stevie Winwood's "Holding On," 1988.
Neil Young's "Hey Hey," 1988.
Hall and Oates' "Downtown Life," 1988.
Four Tops' "Indestructible," 1988.
Bobby Brown's "Roni," 1989.
Aerosmith's "Janie's Got a Gun," 1989.

Paula Abdul's "Forever Your Girl," 1989.
Vanessa Williams' "Darlin' I," 1989.
Gladys Knight's "License to Kill," 1989.
Crosby, Stills and Nash's "American Dream," 1989.
Quincy Jones, Ray Charles and Chaka Kahn's "Ill Be Good to You," 1989.
Debby Harry's "Sweet & Low," 1990.
Tom Petty's "Yer So Bad," 1990.
"Eternal Flame," *Bangles Greatest Hits,* CBS Music Video, 1990.
Cathy Dennis's "Touch Me (All Night Long)," 1991.
Natalie Cole's "Unforgettable," 1991.
ZZ Top's "Give It Up," 1991.
"When It's Love," *Van Halen: Video Hits, Vol. 1,* Warner Reprise, 1996.
The Dandy Warhols', "Not If You Were the Last Junkie on Earth," 1997.
Eminem's "Stan," 2000.
"If It Isn't Love," *20th Century Masters: The Best of New Edition—The DVD Collection,* Universal Music Group, 2004.
"Forever Your Girl," *Video Hits: Paula Abdul,* 2005.

Also worked on music videos for David Bowie, Elton John, and Sting.

ZEDIKER, Kara

PERSONAL

Born in Kankakee, IL.

Addresses: *Agent*—Mitchell K. Stubbs and Associates, 8675 West Washington Blvd., Suite 203, Culver City, CA 90232.

Career: Actress.

CREDITS

Film Appearances:
Redhead, *The Babe,* Universal, 1992.
Ellen, *The Sex Monster,* Trimark Pictures, 1999.
Molly, *Standing By,* 2000.

Marci, *Rock Star,* Warner Bros., 2001.
Stacy, *Hip! Edgy! Quirky!,* Digital Evolution, 2002.
Claire, *Random Shooting in L.A.,* Collaboration Filmworks, 2002.

Television Appearances; Episodic:
Teen girl, *Angel Street,* CBS, 1992.
Gina Pagano, "Pagano's Folly," *The Untouchables,* syndicated, 1993.
Ivy, "Curious Jarod," *The Pretender,* NBC, 1996.
Serena, "The End of the Beginning," *Hercules: The Legendary Journeys,* syndicated, 1997.
Ivy, "Mr. Lee," *The Pretender,* NBC, 1999.
Calla, "The Long Goodbye," *It's Like, You Know …,* ABC, 1999.
Lynn, "Meet By–Product," *The King of Queens,* CBS, 2000.
Debbie, "Old Yeller," *Becker,* CBS, 2000.
Elizabeth Nash, "1:00 p.m.–2:00 p.m.," *24,* Fox, 2002.
Elizabeth Nash, "2:00 p.m.–3:00 p.m.," *24,* Fox, 2002.
Elizabeth Nash, "3:00 p.m.–4:00 p.m.," *24,* Fox, 2002.
Elizabeth Nash, "4:00 p.m.–5:00 p.m.," *24,* Fox, 2002.
Mimi, "Flesh and Blood," *Strong Medicine,* Lifetime, 2002.
Sara Bonner, "Just Say No," *Joan of Arcadia,* CBS, 2003.
Penny Halliwell, "Witchstock," *Charmed,* The WB, 2004.
Emily Runyon, "Love Don't Love Nobody," *10–8: Officers on Duty* (also known as *10–8* and *10–8: Police Patrol*), ABC, 2004.
T'Pau, "Awakening," *Enterprise* (also known as *Star Trek: Enterprise*), UPN, 2004.
T'Pau, "Kir'Shara," *Enterprise* (also known as *Star Trek: Enterprise*), UPN, 2004.
Amber Durgee, "Bodies in Motion," *CSI: Crime Scene Investigation* (also known as *C.S.I., CSI: Las Vegas,* and *Les experts*), CBS, 2005.
Stacy Russell, "Watch over Me," *Without a Trace* (also known as *W.A.T.*), CBS, 2006.

Television Appearances; Other:
Nicky Quade, *Chameleon II: Death Match* (movie), UPN, 1999.
Herself and Nicky Quade, *The Making of "Chameleon II: Death Match"* (special), UPN, 1999.

Cumulative Index

To provide continuity with *Who's Who in the Theatre*, this index interfiles references to *Who's Who in the Theatre*, 1st–17th Editions, and *Who Was Who in the Theatre* (Gale, 1978) with references to *Contemporary Theatre, Film and Television*, Volumes 1–83.

References in the index are identified as follows:

CTFT and volume number—*Contemporary Theatre, Film and Television*, Volumes 1–83
WWT and edition number—*Who's Who in the Theatre*, 1st–17th Editions
WWasWT—*Who Was Who in the Theatre*

D

H

I

L

M

W

X

Y

Z